Information Quality and Governance for Business Intelligence

William Yeoh
Deakin University, Australia

John Talburt
University of Arkansas - Little Rock, USA

Yinle Zhou
IBM Corporation, USA

A volume in the Advances in Business Strategy and Competitive Advantage (ABSCA) Book Series

BUSINESS SCIENCE Reference
An Imprint of IGI Global

Managing Director: Lindsay Johnston
Production Manager: Jennifer Yoder
Development Editor: Allyson Gard
Acquisitions Editor: Kayla Wolfe
Typesetter: Ian Leister
Cover Design: Jason Mull

Published in the United States of America by
Business Science Reference (an imprint of IGI Global)
701 E. Chocolate Avenue
Hershey PA 17033
Tel: 717-533-8845
Fax: 717-533-8661
E-mail: cust@igi-global.com
Web site: http://www.igi-global.com

Library of Congress Cataloging-in-Publication Data

Information quality and governance for business intelligence / William Yeoh, John Talburt, and Yinle Zhou, editors.
pages cm
Includes bibliographical references and index. Summary: "This book presents the latest exchange of academic research on all aspects of practicing and managing information using a multidisciplinary approach that examines its quality for organizational growth"-- Provided by publisher. ISBN 978-1-4666-4892-0 (hardcover) -- ISBN 978-1-4666-4893-7 (ebook) -- ISBN 978-1-4666-4894-4 (print & perpetual access) 1. Business intelligence. 2. Knowledge management. 3. Information technology--Management. I. Yeoh, William, 1979- II. Talburt, John, 1945- III. Zhou, Yinle, 1986-

HD38.7.I534 2014
658.4'72--dc23

2013033229

This book is published in the IGI Global book series Advances in Business Strategy and Competitive Advantage (ABSCA) (ISSN: 2327-3429; eISSN: 2327-3437)

British Cataloguing in Publication Data
A Cataloguing in Publication record for this book is available from the British Library.

Advances in Business Strategy and Competitive Advantage (ABSCA) Book Series

ISSN: 2327-3429
EISSN: 2327-3437

Mission

Business entities are constantly seeking new ways through which to gain advantage over their competitors and strengthen their position within the business environment. With competition at an all-time high due to technological advancements allowing for competition on a global scale, firms continue to seek new ways through which to improve and strengthen their business processes, procedures, and profitability.

The **Advances in Business Strategy and Competitive Advantage (ABSCA) Book Series** is a timely series responding to the high demand for state-of-the-art research on how business strategies are created, implemented and re-designed to meet the demands of globalized competitive markets. With a focus on local and global challenges, business opportunities and the needs of society, the **ABSCA** encourages scientific discourse on doing business and managing information technologies for the creation of sustainable competitive advantage.

Coverage

- Adaptive Enterprise
- Balanced Scorecard
- Business Models
- Entrepreneurship & Innovation
- Ethics and Business Strategy
- Globalization
- Outsourcing
- Small & Medium Enterprises
- Strategic Alliances
- Strategic Management
- Value Creation

IGI Global is currently accepting manuscripts for publication within this series. To submit a proposal for a volume in this series, please contact our Acquisition Editors at Acquisitions@igi-global.com or visit: http://www.igi-global.com/publish/.

The Advances in Business Strategy and Competitive Advantage (ABSCA) Book Series (ISSN 2327-3429) is published by IGI Global, 701 E. Chocolate Avenue, Hershey, PA 17033-1240, USA, www.igi-global.com. This series is composed of titles available for purchase individually; each title is edited to be contextually exclusive from any other title within the series. For pricing and ordering information please visit http://www.igi-global.com/book-series/advances-business-strategy-competitive-advantage/73672. Postmaster: Send all address changes to above address.

Titles in this Series

For a list of additional titles in this series, please visit: www.igi-global.com

Information Quality and Governance for Business Intelligence
William Yeoh (Deakin University, Australia) John R. Talburt (University of Arkansas at Little Rock, USA) and Yinle Zhou (IBM Corporation, USA)
Business Science Reference • copyright 2014 • 297pp • H/C (ISBN: 9781466648920) • US $185.00 (our price)

International Business Strategy and Entrepreneurship An Information Technology Perspective
Patricia Ordóñez de Pablos (Universidad de Oviedo, Spain)
Business Science Reference • copyright 2014 • 306pp • H/C (ISBN: 9781466647534) • US $185.00 (our price)

Implementing IT Business Strategy in the Construction Industry
Goh Bee Hua (National University of Singapore, Singapore)
Business Science Reference • copyright 2013 • 354pp • H/C (ISBN: 9781466641853) • US $185.00 (our price)

Chaos and Complexity Theory for Management Nonlinear Dynamics
Santo Banerjee (Politecnico di Torino, Italy)
Business Science Reference • copyright 2013 • 449pp • H/C (ISBN: 9781466625099) • US $185.00 (our price)

Integrated Operations in the Oil and Gas Industry Sustainability and Capability Development
Tom Rosendahl (BI Norwegian Business School, Norway) and Vidar Hepsø (Norwegian University of Science and Technology, Norway)
Business Science Reference • copyright 2013 • 457pp • H/C (ISBN: 9781466620025) • US $185.00 (our price)

Cultural Variations and Business Performance Contemporary Globalism
Bryan Christiansen (PryMarke, LLC, USA)
Business Science Reference • copyright 2012 • 418pp • H/C (ISBN: 9781466603066) • US $185.00 (our price)

Management Information Systems for Enterprise Applications Business Issues, Research and Solutions
Adamantios Koumpis (ALTEC Software S.A., Greece)
Business Science Reference • copyright 2012 • 324pp • H/C (ISBN: 9781466601642) • US $185.00 (our price)

Leadership in the Digital Enterprise Issues and Challenges
Pak Yoong (Victoria University of Wellington, New Zealand)
Business Science Reference • copyright 2010 • 340pp • H/C (ISBN: 9781605669588) • US $180.00 (our price)

IGI GLOBAL
DISSEMINATOR OF KNOWLEDGE
www.igi-global.com

701 E. Chocolate Ave., Hershey, PA 17033
Order online at www.igi-global.com or call 717-533-8845 x100
To place a standing order for titles released in this series, contact: cust@igi-global.com
Mon-Fri 8:00 am - 5:00 pm (est) or fax 24 hours a day 717-533-8661

Editorial Advisory Board

List of Reviewers

Table of Contents

Detailed Table of Contents

Organizations are currently investing more in information technology to store and process a vast amount of information. Generally, this information does not comply with any standard, which hinders the decision-making process. The cause of the difficulties can be attributed to Information Quality (IQ), which has technical characteristics related to the architecture used in Data Warehouse (DW) and Business Intelligence (BI) environments. On the basis of the relevant literature in IQ, DW, and BI, a research model was created to identify the relations between components of DW/BI architecture and IQ dimensions. This research model was applied in a real case study (Big Financial Company in Brazil). This case study involved semi-structured interviews with managers and analysts. This chapter attempts to provide a better understanding of the relations between IT architecture and IQ in DW and BI environments. The authors hope to motivate the discussion around the development of IQ-oriented architectures for BI and the relationship between these concepts.

Information quality is critical for any business. It is particularly important for mission critical information systems that manage the lifecycle of an engineering asset. Quality of information or lack thereof in these systems can be traced to technical, organisation, as well as human sources. It is, therefore, extremely important to ascertain the causes that contribute to lack of information quality in asset lifecycle management systems. Depending upon the business area, organisations take proactive or reactive approach to establishing, maintaining, and enhancing their information quality. Among proactive approaches, the ability of the organisation to measure information quality dimensions forms the foundation of a solid information quality management initiative. Such a measurement, however, is an intricate task because these dimensions are subjective, can be context dependent as well as independent, and are interdependent, since each dimension impacts other dimensions. This research employs productive perspective to information and applies Six-Sigma methodology to assess its quality in information systems utilised to manage engineering asset lifecycle. It utilises analytical hierarchy process and quality function deployment to convert subjective information quality dimension into objective metrics, assesses the relationship between various information quality dimensions, and ascertains critical to quality factors. The results thus obtained form the basis for monitoring of information quality aimed at its continuous improvement. This study contributes to literature and practice by providing a method for assessing correlation of information quality dimensions, applying six sigma to information, and controlling quality of information.

Wiki is a typical representative of the User-Generated Content. Its appearance greatly promotes the creation, organization, management, and sharing of knowledge on the Internet. As articles grow rapidly in Wikis, the quality of the articles has aroused many people's concerns. The topics on how to assess and control the quality of articles have attracted many researchers. However, few studies have been conducted to investigate the status of this research topic. This chapter explores the current research status and trends of wikis' quality and governance. The authors selected papers from the databases of ISI, EI, IEEE, and other widely used databases. They reported the trends and research of wikis' quality and governance using bibliometric analysis and content analysis of a total of 99 relevant papers. The results show that although the research topics in the field have experienced a very rapid development, they are still at an early age that lacks theories to support them. The discipline of Library and Information Science was found to play a very active role in this new area. Future research agenda and directions are also discussed.

Chapter 9
Social Media Tools for Quality Business Information 167
Sérgio Maravilhas, CETAC.MEDIA - Porto University, Portugal & Aveiro University, Portugal

Information, as a tool to reduce uncertainty and to develop knowledge in organizations, is an important aid in the decision-making process and must be of quality to improve its value. We are living in an information society where organizational and personal life are mediated by information and knowledge, with the help of technologies that gather, disseminate, and deliver that raw material to support our decisions. There are several characteristics that describe the quality of information that will allow the analysis of the value of the information used. In the globalized world we are living in, quality information warrants best results when competing with other organizations. Its value is related to the results that it will allow to be obtained and the dependability on its context. Marketing trends and competitive information is needed for clear decision making about what products to develop, for what customers, at what cost, through which distribution channels, reducing the uncertainty that a new product/service development always brings with it. Social Media tools allow the knowledge of competitor's moves and the analysis of trends from the communications exchanged in the networks of individual consumers, making it easy for companies to develop solutions according to their clients and prospects desires. Learning how to extract quality information, unbiased, valuable for business, from these social tools is the aim of this work, sharing with the interested parties some ways of using it for their profit and competitive sustainability.

Chapter 10
Improving Spatial Data Quality through Spatial ETL Processes 194
Elzbieta Malinowski, University of Costa Rica, Costa Rica
Sehyris Campos, University of Costa Rica, Costa Rica

The growing availability of spatial data related to different aspects makes managers at different levels of administration aware of the possibilities to enhance decision making processes through map visualization. Currently, the so-called location intelligence is identified as an important trend for the next-generation business intelligence solutions. However, before considering spatial data as "first-class citizens," users that are not experts in geo-fields (e.g., cartography, surveying) should learn about possible problems that may arise while using and producing spatial data. These problems must be solved to improve spatial data quality and to increase the benefits that this data can deliver. Unfortunately, there is still a poor connection in applying scientific solutions, international standards, or technological advances for improving spatial data quality in everyday usage of this data. In this chapter, the authors refer to different problems that may exist in handling spatial data and show several examples of how these problems can be detected and solved using spatial ETL tools. Problem detection is based on a set of control parameters derived from the international standard.

such as where profiling can be best be applied to get appropriate benefit and value, the techniques of establishing profiling, and the types of actions that may be taken once the results of profiling are available. The chapter describes components able to be drawn together to provide a system of control that can be applied around a business intelligence system to enhance the quality of organisational decision making through monitoring the characteristics of arriving data and taking action when values are materially different than those expected.

Research has shown that IT project failure rates increase in line with project size, and by the time you reach projects over $10M, the failure rate hits 100%. Hughes and Stodder go on to show that at an average cost of $12.8M, large data warehousing projects were failing 65% of the time for internally built apps and 86% of the time for purchased packages. The outtake here is that small projects are by far more successful. How can this be achieved on large projects? It is possible to be successful at the enterprise level, but it requires a fresh approach to project execution, an ability to deliver projects in small, incremental chunks while maintaining business involvement and support, and setting clear, achievable objectives throughout the program.

Organizational knowledge management resources are a combination of articles, guidelines, and process documents. The content in these resources typically ranges from about a few words to a few hundred words. These pieces of content are called medium-sized content. While most organizations do not pose a limit on how long or short each content piece should be, most content sizes default to this limit due to various reasons. Assigning a metadata and taxonomy to the medium-sized content pieces are challenging because of a limited number of repetition of keywords, the limited size of the content, and the existence of other content without which this content is not conceptually complete. This results in challenges for knowledge managers in organizing and structuring this content as well as making it intelligent enough for search engines and business intelligence tools. This chapter presents an approach to creating metadata for these content pieces by proposing a three structure metadata consisting of a static part, a dynamic part, and a conceptual part that links to other pieces of related information.

All financial services companies use external sources of consumer income data to assess credit risk, develop risk mitigation strategies, and create pre-approved marketing offers. International credit card issuers spend more than a billion dollars in marketing and invest hundreds of millions in product development based on data from third party vendors. The accuracy of income data is the foundation for their business decisions. The purpose of this engagement was to evaluate the accuracy of third party data providers by measuring the data across six dimensions – Accuracy, Relevancy, Completeness, Coverage, Effectiveness, and Cost. The data provided by the three vendors for this project was incorrect by more than 20% on 75% of the records. The goal of the project was to demonstrate the ability to improve the accuracy of multi-source income data used in credit card marketing applications.

Foreword

When deciding whether to invest time and effort in reading any text, readers are facing an essential dilemma: Will I get more out of this than I invest reading it? In the data quality world, readers are faced with essentially three types of reference materials. First, there is some pretty vacuous practitioner guidance. This follows the form: Five Easy Steps to Achieve Data Quality. The fundamental problem is that almost nothing about data quality/governance is easy, and readers would be well advised to consider the cost of such advice before basing courses of action upon it. The second set of reference materials come from the academic literature, and while (in my humble opinion) more useful than the first, it is just not accessible to folks who are attempting to make a difference. Examples of these might include titles such as: "Improving data quality and data mining using multiple, noisy labelers." Essentially the guidance requires an advanced degree to even determine whether it might be applicable. In addition, there is a pretty large gap with many academic practitioners solving problems in theory that have no basis in the real world.

Now there is a third option: *Information Quality and Governance for Business Intelligence.* This book is a combination of useful guidance and case studies that will help both practitioners find solutions to their immediate challenges and researchers find focus for their academic efforts. The editors have done a terrific job of selecting a number of specific foci at the intersection of practice and research and obtained some very articulate contributors to produce a highly readable yet rigorous contribution at the interaction of data quality and governance. However, let us not forget that all the work in these important areas would be for naught if we were not able to achieve some desired outcome. Whether you call it Business Intelligence, Advanced Analytics, or just useful organizational outcomes, the purpose of governing good quality data has got to be something tangible or one can ask the question: What was it all for? And while it is often said that the most useful outcome of a BI effort is another deeper question, readers can rest assured that taking the time to read *Information Quality and Governance for Business Intelligence* will lead them towards that next insight at a cost that will be well worth their time!

Peter Aiken
The Data Management Association International, USA

Peter Aiken, *PhD, is acknowledged to be a top data management authority. As a practicing data manager, consultant, author, and researcher, he has been actively attempting to improve this area for more than twenty-five years. His expertise has been sought by some of the world's most important organizations, and his achievements have been recognized internationally. In addition to examining more than 500 data management practices, he has spent multi-year immersions with organizations as diverse as the US DoD, Deutsche Bank, Nokia, Wells Fargo, and the Commonwealth of Virginia. As President of DAMA International (dama.org), his practice leadership is unquestioned. He has been a member of the Information Systems Department at Virginia Commonwealth University's Business School since 1993 and jointly owns, with the University, Data Blueprint (.com) an award winning, data management/IT consulting firm. His latest book is The Case for the Chief Data Officer: Recasting the C-Suite to Leverage your most Valuable Asset.*

Preface

Although Business Intelligence (BI) applications have been dominating the technology priority list of many organizations, these efforts often fail to accomplish their objectives. In many cases, the reason for the failure is directly attributable to the poor quality of the underlying information. Achieving and sustaining high-levels of information and data quality draws on knowledge and skills across a number of disciplines such as quality management, information technology, project management, and change management. At the same time, a typical business intelligence endeavor has to address a growing number of data and information quality conundrums including cross-functional information integration of data from disparate source, the emergence of "big data" with its increasing volume, velocity, and the lack of effective information quality and governance strategies and policies.

Information (IQ) is a body of knowledge and practice around realizing the maximum value from an organization's information assets by assuring that the information products produced from that information will meet the expectations of ("are fit for use by") the people and system using them. Of these information products, perhaps none are more critical than business intelligence applications. BI application must deliver the right information, in the right form, to the right people at the right time for more informed decision-making. The quality of BI output is directly related to the quality of the input data. Successful information quality and governance programs are fundamental to the success of any business intelligence initiative, especially those at the enterprise level. Unfortunately, the information quality and governance capabilities in many organizations are not up to the levels needed to support their BI applications. Therefore, the mission of this book is to advance research and practice in the field of information quality and business intelligence. The book is a peer-reviewed publication dedicated to the exchange of the latest research on all aspects of practicing and managing information quality and governance for business intelligence in organizations. This book contains 21 chapters and is organized as follows.

The 1st chapter by Foshay, Taylor, and Mukherjee, "A Conceptual Model of Metadata's Role in BI Success," describes how organizations can increase the levels of use of their BI systems by providing the right metadata to users. A conceptual model is proposed to describe how metadata contributes the level of BI system use by creating positive attitudes toward the information available.

In "Understanding the Influence of Business Intelligence Systems on Information Quality: The Importance of Business Knowledge," Popovic and Jaklic show how Business Intelligence System (BIS) maturity affects IQ dimensions, as well as the role that business knowledge may exert in mobilizing this link. The hypotheses are tested across 181 medium and large organizations.

The 3rd chapter, "Subjective Information Quality in Data Integration: Evaluation and Principles," authored by AbuHalimeh and Tudoreanu, focuses on the science of human perception of information quality, and describes a subset of information quality dimensions, which are termed Subjective Information Quality (SIQ). The chapter explores SIQ while considering information obtained from multiple sources.

Authored by Decker, Liu, Talburt, Wang, and Wu, the 4th chapter, "A Case Study on Data Quality, Privacy, and Entity Resolution," presents ongoing research conducted through collaboration between the University of Arkansas at Little Rock (UALR) and the Arkansas Department of Education to develop an entity resolution and identity management system for a business intelligence system. The research is the first known of its kind to evaluate privacy-enhancing entity resolution rule sets in a state education agency.

Chapter 5 is titled "Business Intelligence for Healthcare: A Perscription for Better Managing Costs and Medical Outcomes." Cook and Neely use an interpretive case study approach to describe data quality problems in the healthcare supply chain and their integration with a business intelligence system in two companies.

Authored by Schmidt and Prado, the 6th chapter, "IT Architecture and Information Quality in Business Intelligence Environments," presents a research model to identify the relations between components of data warehouse/business intelligence architecture and information quality dimensions. The model has been applied in a case study.

Chapter 7, "Information Quality Assessment for Asset Management Systems," authored by Lee and Haider, presents the research which employs productive perspective to information, provides a method for assessing correlation of information quality dimensions, and applies Six-Sigma methodology to assess its quality in information systems utilized to manage engineering asset lifecycle and control quality of information.

In "Trends and Research of Wikis' Quality and Governance Based on Bibliometric and Content Analyses," Zhu, Huang, Liu, and Du explore the current research status and trends of wikis' quality and governance by using bibliometric analysis and content analysis.

The 9th chapter is titled "Social Media Tools for Quality Business Information." Maravilhas presents the work of how to extract quality information, unbiased, valuable for business, from social media tools, and sharing with the interested parties some ways of using it for their profit and competitive sustainability.

Chapter 10, "Improving Spatial Data Quality through Spatial ETL Processes," authored by Molinowski and Campos, studies different problems that may exist in handling spatial data and shows several examples of how these problems can be detected and solved using spatial ETL tools.

Chapter 11 is titled "Principled Reference Data Management for Business Intelligence." Milman, Oberhofer, Pandit, and Zhou discuss a principled approach towards management, stewardship, and governance of reference data to ensure quality and operational excellence across BI systems in the domain of typical reference data management concepts and features, leading to a comprehensive solution architecture.

Authored by Sundararaman, the 12th chapter, "Effective Measurement of DQ/IQ for BI," provides an overview of the existing frameworks for measurement of DQ for BI, analyzes the gaps therein, and reviews proposed solutions and provide a direction for future research and practice in this area.

The 13th chapter, "Data Profiling and Data Quality Metric Measurement as a Proactive Input into the Operation of Business Intelligence Systems," authored by Delaney proposes the use of data profiling techniques as a means of early discovery of issues and changes within the source system data and examines how this knowledge can be applied to guard against reductions in the decision-making capability and effectiveness of an organization.

Chapter 14 is titled "Agile Information Management Governance: Can You Scale it to the Enterprise?" Bates researches the possibility of scaling success of small projects to enterprise level projects by delivering projects in small, incremental chunks while maintaining business involvement and support, and setting clear, achievable objectives throughout the program.

In "Challenges of Structure and Organization in Medium-Sized Content," Chakrabarty presents an approach to create metadata for content pieces by proposing a three structure metadata consisting of a static part, a dynamic part, and a conceptual part that links to other pieces of related information.

Chapter 16, "A Case Study to Improve Data Vendor Selection," authored by McGraw presents a project of improving the accuracy of multi-source income data used in credit card marketing applications. The project evaluates the accuracy of third-party data providers by measuring the data across six dimensions.

The 17th chapter by Zhou and Talburt, "Strategies for Large-Scale Entity Resolution Based on Inverted Index Data Partitioning," presents a data partitioning strategy to perform entity resolution on large datasets and discusses the importance of index-to-rule alignment, pre-resolution index closure, post-resolution link closure, etc. in a distributed processing environment.

The 18th chapter, "A Dual-Database Trusted Broker System for Resolving, Protecting, and Utilizing Multi-Sourced Data," authored by Gibson and Holland, presents a system to allow for the sharing of data between government agencies while upholding the strictest interpretations of rules and regulations protecting individual privacy and confidentiality.

Chapter 19 is titled "Business Intelligence Architecture in Support of Data Quality." Breur suggests an innovation to data warehouse architecture to improve data integration in BI projects. Two suggestions are made to deliver information products in the smallest possible chunks and BI teams need to provide better stewardship when they facilitate discussions between departments.

The 20th chapter is titled "The Value of Data Quality." Hillard introduces a trading approach to information that changes the mindset of the managers of information who become motivated to maximise the value of the content they are responsible for. The approach also creates the opportunity to move the focus of data governance away from what is often perceived to be compliance activities to helping to establish pricing and the market as a whole.

The last chapter in this book deals with "Data Protection and BI: A Quality Perspective." The author, O'Brien, examines the relationship between Data Protection (DP), Information Quality (IQ), and Data Governance (DG). This chapter provides an overview of how techniques and practices from IQ and DG can ensure that BI projects are grounded on appropriate privacy controls.

We hope that this book will stimulate further studies in information quality and governance for business intelligence.

William Yeoh
Deakin University, Australia

John Talburt
University of Arkansas – Little Rock, USA

Yinle Zhou
IBM Corporation, USA

Acknowledgment

This book would not have been possible without the support and assistance of many special people. First, we would like to express our deepest gratitude to the reviewers for their timely and constructive comments on the papers that greatly improved the quality of the final versions. Of course, we thank the authors for providing excellent chapters and timely extended revisions. Finally, we are grateful to the IGI Global staff for their support, guidance, and patience during the production of this book.

William Yeoh
Deakin University, Australia

John Talburt
University of Arkansas – Little Rock, USA

Yinle Zhou
IBM Corporation, USA

Chapter 1
A Conceptual Model of Metadata's Role in BI Success

Neil Foshay
St. Francis Xavier University, Canada

Andrew Taylor
Bradford University, UK

Avinandan Mukherjee
Montclair State University, USA

ABSTRACT

Modern organizations rely on Business Intelligence (BI) systems to provide the information needed to support a wide array of decisions, many of which have significant financial and strategic consequences. As such, information quality is critically important but is also highly contextual, meaning that information that is of sufficient quality for one purpose may not be so for others. The implication of this fact is that users must have the ability to assess information for its fitness to specific purposes. The authors submit that metadata provides this capability. Metadata is information that serves to provide insight into the meaning, quality, location, and lineage of information resources (for example, data elements, queries, and reports) provided by BI systems. In this chapter, they describe how organizations can increase the levels of use of their BI systems by providing the right metadata to users. The authors propose a conceptual model that describes how metadata contributes to the level of BI system use by creating positive attitudes toward the information available. They validate the model through consultation with experts in the fields of BI, information quality, and metadata management as well as through a survey of over 250 BI practitioners.

DOI: 10.4018/978-1-4666-4892-0.ch001

INTRODUCTION

Information is a strategic asset for organizations in today's highly competitive business environment. This information, when leveraged effectively, can be used to strategic advantage (Huang, Liu, & Chang, 2012). Consequently, many organizations today construct business intelligence (BI) systems to support organizational decision making (Kiron, Shockley, Kruschwitz, Finch, & Haydock, 2012). BI systems are a collection of tools and processes that serve to acquire and integrate data in order to provide information that can be used to drive smart business decisions. Effectively leveraging BI capabilities provides the potential for significant organizational benefits (Jourdan, Rainer, & Marshall, 2008; Crable, Brodzinski, & Frolick, 2008). For this reason, BI has been recognized as a top IT priority in recent years (Grajek & Pirani, 2012).

Notable success stories notwithstanding, many BI implementations have been deemed failures by their organizations (Inmon, Strauss & Neushloss, 2008). BI systems are significantly underutilized in many organizations, especially when compared with standalone applications such as spreadsheets and personal databases (Burns 2005; Morse 2007). This phenomenon has significant implications: first, underutilization of expensive BI systems implies a poor return on investment on these systems and second, the overuse of personal databases and spreadsheet software for decision support opens the door to significant risks, including poor decision quality (Lawson, Baker, Powell & Foster-Johnson, 2009; Panko & Aurigemma 2010).

The goal of BI is to provide knowledge workers with the information needed to formulate their decisions which are often strategic in nature and have significant organizational impacts in terms of investment, resource allocation, etc. As such, information quality is critically important to the overall success of BI systems (Popovic, Hackney, Coelho & Jaklic, 2012), and the consequences of poor quality can be dire (Watts, Shankaranarayanan & Even, 2009). Information quality is a multifaceted concept that is measured by dimensions such as accuracy, completeness and consistency (Wixom & Watson, 2001). However, it is also highly contextual – it is the user who determines if the information is of sufficient quality to be used for a specific purpose (Wang & Strong, 1996).

A basic question that must be asked is: how do BI users know if specific information is fit for the purpose they intend to use it for? We believe that users must understand the meaning of the information as well as its quality in order to assess its fitness for purpose. To facilitate this understanding, we propose that users must have access to high-quality metadata. Metadata is itself a type of information that serves to provide users with knowledge about information resources without having "full advance knowledge of their existence or characteristics" (Dempsey & Heery, 1998, p. 145). Metadata can be viewed as a fundamental component of information quality. Shanks and Darke (1998) claim that there are two basic elements of information quality: the content (the information itself) and the structure (the metadata that describes the information).

In this chapter we explore how organizations can increase the levels of use of their BI systems, focusing on the influence of one element of information quality: metadata, thus addressing a gap in the existing literature. We address the following fundamental questions:

1. What types of metadata are required to assist users gain an appropriate level of knowledge about their information?
2. Why is this knowledge useful and valuable?
3. What is metadata's role in the success of BI systems?

In order to address these questions we propose a conceptual model, informed by both information systems and marketing research literature, which explains the contribution of metadata to BI system success, as measured by level of use. We validate our model through consultation with a panel of BI, information quality and metadata experts and through a survey targeting BI practitioners – those who design, build and support BI systems.

BACKGROUND AND CONCEPTUAL MODEL

Numerous studies have examined factors that contribute to BI system success. Wixom and Watson (2001) propose that management support, a strong business champion, appropriate resources, user participation, BI team skills and factors related to source systems influence organizational, project and technical implementation success which in turn positively impact data and system quality. These contribute to higher decision-oriented net benefits to individuals, groups and the overall organization. Yeoh and Koronios (2010) offer a similar framework, proposing seven success factors grouped in three categories: organizational, process and technology. Ramamurthy, Sen & Sinha (2008) view BI as a major IT infrastructure innovation and propose that implementation success is dependent upon organizational factors such as management commitment and absorptive capacity as well as characteristics of the innovation (the BI system). Isik, Jones & Sidorova (2011) argue that BI system success requires specific BI capabilities, including effective user access to information and effective integration with other systems. Popovic, Hackney, Coelho & Jaklic (2012) highlight 'BI maturity' combined with an effective analytical decision-making culture, as important success factors. Sen, Ramamurthy & Sinha (2012) state that BI 'process maturity' is critically important and propose a five stage model covering both the development and on-going operation of BI systems to measure this maturity. It is important to note that most of the studies cited above have acknowledged that data or information quality is a key BI system success factor. We view metadata as a major component of information quality.

Figure 1 presents our proposed conceptual model. We submit that successful BI systems are those that are used extensively and propose that an important factor in determining the level of use is user attitudes toward the information provided. We measure three dimensions of attitudes toward information: cognition, affect and conation. We

Figure 1. Conceptual model

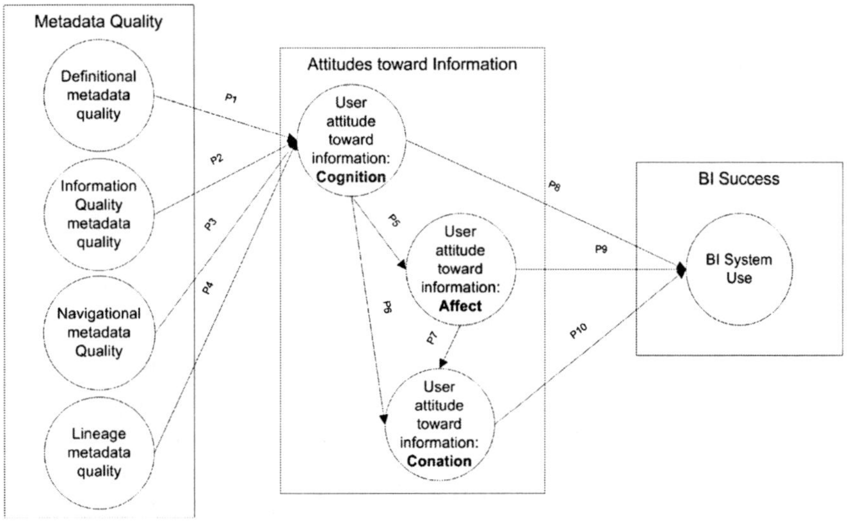

contend that providing end-users with the right metadata (i.e., regarding meaning, quality, location and lineage) is a key factor in influencing end-user attitudes toward information. While we propose that metadata is a key factor in BI system success, it is important to acknowledge that there are numerous other factors at play as described later in this section. The remainder of this section outlines the theoretical foundation for our model as well as our research propositions.

Metadata Quality

We argue that user knowledge of the information they use for analysis and decision support is critically important to BI success and that this knowledge is facilitated by access to the right metadata. The concept of metadata has existed for a very long time. For example, libraries have been creating metadata for centuries, in the form of book indexes and catalogs. To illustrate this concept, consider an academic journal article. The associated metadata might include an abstract, a list of authors, the volume and issue, publication date and a set of keywords that identify the major themes in the article.

Metadata is a broad concept, and its definition varies by context. In general terms, metadata can be thought of as a means to describe, locate and manage information-based resources within an organization. Tannenbaum (2002) states that metadata serves to answer a number of important questions regarding information resources which allows these resources to be located, understood and placed into their proper context. This, in turn, allows the resources to be used (and reused) appropriately for a diverse set of purposes.

Metadata has been present in information systems since the 1960s (in, for example, database data dictionaries) but has gained the attention of information systems professionals in recent years as organizations have grasped the value of information as a strategic corporate asset and have constructed BI systems to unlock its value (Sen 2004). In a BI context, metadata has been observed to improve both decision process efficiency and the quality of decision outcomes (Even, Shankaranarayanan & Watts, 2006; Fisher, Smith & Ballou, 2003). In its absence, users may need to invest excessive effort to gain an understanding of available data, or may avoid using a BI system entirely (Haley and Watson, 1998).

Even within the confines of business intelligence, metadata is a broad concept. To illustrate, Table 1 presents a non-exhaustive list of BI-related information resources that need to be described by metadata.

For the purposes of this study, we focus on the information resources that are of most interest to BI end users: data elements, reports and documents. The question we must answer is: what specific types of metadata must be provided to end users to effectively describe these resources? A review of the available literature makes it clear that there is no consensus regarding a) the types of metadata required by BI end-users and b) how metadata, holistically, contributes to the success of BI systems. Shankaranarayan and Even (2006) state that BI metadata is an 'enigma' that is inherently complex and is not well understood by IT professionals who are unclear of its "role and value" (p. 88). Synthesizing the available research literature indicates that BI metadata has four basic purposes i.e. to:

- Provide users with clear, standardized definitions of the 'business' meaning of information;
- Explain information quality;
- Allow users to locate information resources; and
- Define the 'lineage' of information.

Explaining the business meaning of information to users is the most fundamental purpose of metadata as users need this understanding in order to use this information effectively (Gabriel, Hoppe & Pastwa, 2010). This need goes far beyond

Table 1. BI-related information resources and associated metadata

Information Resource	Metadata
Data elements	The most atomic information resources associated with a BI system are the data elements stored the underlying data warehouse / data mart and presented on reports and documents. Metadata associated with data elements include: • Business definition (meaning/interpretation); • Domain (allowable values); • Technical description (length, type, default values); • Business rules; • Calculations; • Quality information; • Source and lineage; • Data governance information: ownership and stewardship.
Data Models (ERDs)	Data model-related metadata includes descriptions of fact and dimension entities, subject areas, star-schemas, OLAP cubes and other model related information.
Reports	Pre-built reports are an important output from BI systems. Definitions of reports would include statement of report purpose, intended audience, frequency of publication, last publication date, author and other information that would allow the report to be located and understood.
Semi-structured and unstructured documents	It is common to create semi-structured (e.g., Excel spreadsheets) and unstructured (e.g., Word and PowerPoint) documents based on information sourced from a BI system. The metadata for these documents is similar to that of reports.
SQL queries and stored procedures	SQL queries are often used (and reused) to generate reports and other metrics
Extract, Transform and Load (ETL) rules and logic	This class of metadata includes: • Relationships/lineage between data element sources and targets. Critical metadata for functions such as impact analysis; • The rules and logic used to clean transform and aggregate data in the data warehouse.
ETL Process statistics	The ETL process includes all of the steps required to obtain/extract data from source systems, transform and clean the data and load data into the target data warehouse tables. Metadata associated with the ETL process includes error rate statistics, cycle times, load times, and other statistics important to managing the data warehouse operational environment and for capacity planning.

what would typically exist in a database 'data dictionary' and must include business-oriented definitions, business rules that explain the data's context and calculations and logic used to create derived data in order to fully understand its meaning (Shankaranarayanan & Even, 2004). The information provided by BI systems is often complex and is often obtained from multiple heterogeneous sources where information that is conceptually similar is defined in different ways (Wells and Hess, 2002). As such, metadata must provide standardized definitions of the meaning of the information in terms users are able to understand (Sen and Jacob, 1998). Shanks and Darke (1998) define the characteristics of metadata that provide the meaning of information. They claim that metadata should be syntactically consistent, valid and complete, provide a definition of the meaning of information that is useful to all users of the information and facilitate a consensus regarding this meaning.

Information quality is a key BI success factor (Wixom and Watson 2001; Isik, Jones & Sidorova, 2011). The most commonly cited purpose for metadata in a BI context is to provide insight into information quality. Shankaranarayan and Even (2004) propose that quality metadata can help users assess the quality of information used in the context of decision making processes. Fisher, Smith and Ballou (2003) claim that the information supplied through BI systems should be of good quality, but often it is not. Experienced

BI users develop, over time, an understanding of the nuances and eccentricities of the information that has quality issues and develop strategies to compensate. This deep understanding of data is not possible for all users (e.g., inexperienced or casual users) and quality metadata can thus be of great worth to them. Quality information should be communicated to users through 'tags' stored along with the actual information. The purpose of these tags is to advise users regarding the accuracy, completeness and consistency of the information (Watts, Shankaranarayanan & Even, 2009).

Information quality metadata can be seen to be a means by which end-users can determine the *appropriate* use of information. In many cases, the information available from a BI system is not perfect. With access to information quality metadata, end-users have the ability to understand the specific issues with the information and can thus judge whether or not it can be used for a specific purpose.

The third purpose for BI metadata is to allow users to locate the information they need. Shin (2003) proposes that the ability to locate required information highly correlates with user satisfaction. As such, users must be provided with a mechanism (i.e., metadata) that explains the structure (the way that data is organized) and content of the data warehouse supporting BI systems. Shankaranarayan and Even (2004) state that metadata is extremely important from a data management perspective, as it can be used to organize and categorize data in a manner that allows for "more efficient searching, on-going maintenance, integrity preservation and control over data redundancy (p. 8).

Finally, metadata can be used to explain the lineage, or provenance of information. Given that the information provided by BI systems is often obtained from a variety of sources, users' understanding of this information can be enhanced through an explanation of the original source of the information, in addition to any operations performed on the data - for example, standardization, cleansing or aggregation (Even, Shankaranarayanan and Watts, 2006).

Based on our synthesis of the literature, we propose that there are four types of metadata that should be provided to users to facilitate their understanding of information and information quality: definitional, information quality, navigational and lineage. Table 2 presents a summary of each type as originally proposed by Foshay, Mukherjee & Taylor (2007), along with a simple example. We provide metadata for a notional measure called "net revenue - goods" and propose the following sample scenario:

An inexperienced end-user performs a search against her organization's financial BI system in order to find all revenue reports available. Using the system's search function (driven by navigational metadata keywords) she types the terms 'revenue' and 'reports'. The search facility returns a list of five reports. The end-user selects one of the reports which then appears online on her computer monitor. One of the columns in the report is titled 'net revenue - goods'. The end-user notices that the 'net revenue - goods' column heading is hyperlinked. She hovers her cursor over the column heading and left clicks. A new window pops up and the information in the 'sample metadata' column appears.

Our model proposes that it is the quality of metadata, not simply its presence, which positively influences attitudes toward information. One could argue that poor quality metadata is actually worse than no metadata at all. For definitional, information quality and lineage metadata, the model focuses on assessing the overall information quality of these types of metadata - how effectively they inform end users about the information in a BI system. Leveraging the work of Wang and Strong (1996) and Nelson, Todd and Wixom (2005) we propose that the information quality of these three categories of metadata should be measured by accuracy, completeness, consistency

Table 2. Metadata types and sample metadata

<table>
<tr><th>Definition</th><th colspan="3">Sample Metadata for "Net Revenue - Goods"</th></tr>
<tr><th colspan="4">Definitional</th></tr>
<tr><td>Definitional metadata is any information that conveys the meaning of data in the BI system (or, for example, on reports) to end users. Included in this category are business definitions, calculations, business rules and allowable values. Definitional metadata answers the question: what does this data mean, from a business perspective?</td><td colspan="3">Business meaning: Calculated data element that aggregates income, in USD, from sales of goods, minus the cost associated with returned or undeliverable merchandise, discounts and allowances for all products except bulk products. Also called "Net Sales - goods" or "Net Income - goods". Note that Net Revenue refers specifically to income from goods sold. A distinct Net Revenue data element is used to store services net revenue (Net Revenue – Service) as the calculations are different.
Calculation: Gross Revenue Dollars – (Total Cost of Returns Dollars + Total Cost of Undeliverable Product Dollars + Discount Dollars + Allowance Dollars).
Business rules: Net revenue figures for goods sold must never be aggregated with services net revenue. For all internal reporting Net Revenue - goods figures must be rounded to the nearest dollar. Net Revenue figures must always be reported in USD.
Data Type: Decimal, 0 decimal places
Steward: Janice McKnight (Dept. of Finance)
Owner: VP Finance</td></tr>
<tr><th colspan="4">Information Quality</th></tr>
<tr><td>Information quality metadata advises users about the currency (freshness), accuracy, validity or completeness of the data elements in the BI system (or on reports, queries or OLAP cubes). Data quality metadata answers the business user's question: does this data possess sufficient quality for me to use it for a specific purpose?</td><td colspan="3">Quality profile as of May 1, 2013
Last updated: April 30, 2013
Completeness: 97%
Quality profile:
Net Revenue – goods figures in the data warehouse are certified to be 100% accurate for all transactions occurring after Oct 1, 1999 for all product groups except bulk products.
Known integrity issues:
Prior to Oct 1, 1999, return transactions are missing so Net Revenue - Goods may be overstated.
Revenue figures for bulk products are entered manually into the SAP GL system. For a three week period (Oct 1 – 21, 2004) no entries were made and source documents were never found.</td></tr>
<tr><th colspan="4">Navigational</th></tr>
<tr><td>Navigational metadata provides users with a means to search for data (or other resource, such as a report). In other words, navigational metadata lets users 'Google' their data warehouse / BI system to search for what they need and to get an understanding of relationships between data objects of various types. Navigational metadata answers the question: where can I find the data I need?</td><td colspan="3">Keywords: Sales, Revenue, Income Statement Item
Aliases: Net Sales - goods, Net Income - goods
Metric Group: Net Revenue
Related to metric groups: Gross Revenue, Net Revenue – services
Where Used:
• Daily Revenue Report;
• Monthly Revenue Report;
• Finance Dashboard.</td></tr>
<tr><th colspan="4">Lineage</th></tr>
<tr><td rowspan="3">Lineage information tells users about the original source of data in a BI system (or, for example, on a report) and describes what has been done to the data (for example, cleansing, transformation or aggregation) prior to being loaded into the BI system. Lineage information answers the user's questions: where did this data originate, and what's been done to it?</td><td>Source System</td><td>Table</td><td>Element</td></tr>
<tr><td>SAP GL</td><td>GLT007</td><td>REV_GROSS
RET_VAL
DISC_VAL
UNDEL_VAL</td></tr>
<tr><td colspan="3">Transformations:
See 'calculations' in the definitional metadata section.</td></tr>
</table>

and format. Additionally, currency is an important consideration for quality and lineage metadata as this information can change over time. The fourth category, Navigational metadata, provides a means to allow end-users to search for data and other information objects in a data warehouse. As such, the Navigational meta-data quality should be assessed based on its effectiveness in locating required information rather than describing the characteristics of the information. Navigational metadata relates to the concept of 'locatability of data' associated with the Task-Technology Fit (TTF) model of technology acceptance developed by Goodhue and Thompson (1995). Table 3 presents the items that can be used to measure metadata quality.

Table 3. Metadata quality items

Type	Item
Definitional	The business definitions provided are quite accurate.
	The business definitions provide all I need in order understand the meaning of information.
	Generally, I find the quality of business definitions to be consistent.
	Business definitions are presented in a format that is clear and understandable.
Information Quality	Generally, I find the quality information provided to be accurate.
	I get all the quality data I need to determine if information is fit for specific purposes.
	The quality information provided is dependable.
	Quality information is presented in a format that is clear and understandable.
	The quality information provided is generally up to date
Lineage	The lineage information provided is accurate.
	I have access to all of the lineage information I need.
	The lineage information provided is dependable.
	Lineage information is presented in an appropriate format
	The lineage information is usually up to date.
Navigational	I know that if I need to find certain information, the search facility will help me do so.
	The search facility provided is effective in helping me locate data.
	Generally, it is easy for me to find the information I need, even if I've never accessed it before.

Attitudes toward Information

We propose that metadata, while clearly only one factor, plays a significant role in facilitating BI system success. Metadata, when of sufficient quality, positively influences user attitudes toward the information available through BI systems. These positive attitudes, in turn, impact the level of use of these systems. In many cases and unlike other types of operational IS (e.g., Enterprise Resource Planning, Supply Chain Management, etc.) users are not compelled to use BI systems to carry out core job functions. As such, BI systems are highly volitional; end-users generally have a choice regarding whether or not they use them to support their day to day analysis and decision making activities (Popovic, Hackney, Coelho & Jaklic, 2012; Shin 2003). Given the volitional nature of BI, it is conceptually meaningful to view BI end-users as being analogous to consumers, in a marketing context, who must be convinced that BI systems will provide some benefit to them. A major goal of IT teams building and supporting BI systems should be to actively 'market' BI to end-users in order to make them 'loyal consumers' (consistent, frequent users of BI). We propose that a key part of this marketing effort must be to work to ensure that the information provided by BI systems is viewed positively by users.

An individual's attitude represents a "summary evaluation of a psychological object captured in dimensions like: good/bad, pleasant/unpleasant, likeable/dislikable" (Ajzen, 2001 p. 28). The importance of user attitudes in information system success is well documented. In particular, user attitudes play a central role in the Davis (1989) technology acceptance model (TAM), where user attitudes toward an information system are seen to directly impact the intention to use the system, and ultimately the use of the system. Attitude-related research is extremely important in the marketing field particularly as it relates to consumer behavior. Researchers in marketing seek to understand the factors that influence buying behavior and ultimately, customer loyalty. Given the parallels between consumers in a marketing context and BI end-users, we believe that it is appropriate to leverage the marketing perspective on attitudes and loyalty in this study to model how metadata contributes to successful BI implementations.

The marketing literature defines loyalty as "a deeply held commitment to re-buy or re-patronize a preferred product/service consistently in the future, thereby causing repetitive same-brand or same brand-set purchasing" (Oliver 1999 p. 34). There are three stages, or dimensions, of consumer attitudes that are antecedents of loyalty: cognition, affect and conation (Dick and Basu 1994; Oliver 1999; Chiou, Droge and Hanvanich 2002). Oliver (1999) describes the three dimensions as 'phases'. The first phase is cognition, the second is affect and the third, conation. These phases can be seen as 'building blocks', with the earlier phases supporting the later. Specifically, phase one (cognition), is an antecedent of phases two and three (affect and conation) and phase two (affect) is an antecedent of conation. For the purposes of this study, it is assumed that high quality metadata serves to positively influence cognition – a BI user's understanding of available information resources.

Cognition is "knowledge and perceptions that are acquired by a combination of direct experience with the attitude object and related information from various sources" (Schiffman and Kanuk 2000 p. 202). In a customer loyalty context, cognition is related to a consumer's awareness of the attributes of a brand relative to its competitors and whether or not one brand is preferable to others (Oliver 1999). Cognition (understanding) of information is an important concept for this study. We argue that metadata is an important resource for BI end-users to use to learn about the information that is available to them. Further, as described in section 2.1, we believe that users must understand the meaning, quality, location and lineage of the information they use. We offer the following propositions:

P_1: High quality definitional metadata will positively influence end-users' cognition of information;

P_2: High quality information quality metadata will positively influence end-users' cognition of information;

P_3: High quality navigational metadata will positively influence end-users' cognition of information;

P_4: High quality lineage metadata will positively influence end-users' cognition of information.

Affect is the second antecedent of loyalty and describes an individual's emotions or feelings toward an object and reflects the degree of pleasure/displeasure that an individual associates with the object (Schiffman and Kanuk, 2000). As such, affect towards an object is seen as being evaluative in nature. The affective dimension of attitude is thought to be stronger than the cognitive dimension in influencing loyalty (Oliver 1999). For the purposes of this research, affect refers to an end-user's positive or negative emotions and feelings toward the information available through BI systems.

Agarwal and Karahanna (2000) support the notion that affect is an important factor in the acceptance of technology. They introduce a concept called "cognitive absorption" as a determinant of technology acceptance that is composed of five dimensions: temporal dissociation, focused immersion, heightened enjoyment, control, and curiosity. They state that "Prior work in individual psychology, however, suggests that holistic experiences with technology as captured in constructs such as enjoyment and flow are potentially important explanatory variables in technology acceptance theories" (p. 665). Heightened enjoyment, and to an extent curiosity, can be considered affective in nature. Hackbarth, Grover and Yi (2003) propose that 'playfulness' and 'computer anxiety' play an important role in shaping user perception of the ease of use of an information system. Of these two factors, the negative impacts of computer anxiety had a far stronger influence on perceived ease of use relative to the impact of playfulness. Igbaria (1994) also found computer anxiety to be a factor in the adoption of microcomputer technology. These studies demonstrate that affect regarding technology can have a powerful influence on beliefs regarding the use of that technology. For the purposes of this study, we propose that higher levels of understanding (cognition) will be correlated with greater affect toward information. In other words, understanding information removes some of the stress and anxiety associated with using it. This is an important notion as often this information is intended to be used to make important decisions that can have significant financial implications (Watson, Fuller & Ariyachandra, 2004). We offer the following proposition:

P_5: The greater the end-user cognition of information, the more positive will be their affect toward that information.

Conation is concerned with the likelihood or tendency that an individual will undertake an action or act in a particular way. For example, conation might reflect an individual's intent to purchase or re-purchase a product or, in the context of this study, to use information to support analysis and decision making activities (Dick and Basu, 1994; Schiffman and Kanuk, 2000). Conation is also referred to as behavioral intention and implies a deep commitment on the part of an individual to purchase (or repurchase) a brand. In IS research, behavioral intention is viewed as an antecedent to system use, most prominently in the Davis (1989) technology acceptance model. Conation is influenced by both cognition of and affect for, an object (Oliver 1999). Conation has three distinct dimensions: switching costs, sunk costs and expectations (Dick and Basu 1994).

Switching costs refers to costs related to moving from one supplier of a product or service to another (Porter 1980). In the context of BI, switching costs refer to the cost to an end-user of selecting alternatives (e.g., creating Excel spreadsheets, etc.) to obtain required information. Sunk costs refer to investments (time, effort, money) that have been made and cannot be recovered. In a BI environment, sunk costs might refer to factors such as the time and effort expended by an end-user to become educated regarding information provided by a BI system. The final dimension is expectation which reflects the perceived fit between an individual's needs and the ability of an attitude object to meet those needs (Dick and Basu 1994). We propose that expectation, in the context of this study, relates to a BI user's perception that available information will be useful for analysis or decision-related activities. We propose that both cognition of and affect for information are antecedents of conation and offer the following propositions:

P_6: The greater the end-user cognition of information, the greater will be the intent to use that information to support decision-related activities;

P_7: The more positive that end-user affect toward information is, the greater will be the intent to use that information to support decision-related activities.

Table 4 presents the items that operationalize the 'Attitudes toward Information' component of our research model.

Table 4. Attitudes toward information items

Category	Item Text
Cognition	I feel that I have a solid understanding of the information from the BI system I've used in the past.
	When using information for the first time, I feel that I will be able gain sufficient understanding to use it appropriately.
	I understand the information well enough to use it appropriately for analysis and decision making.
	I can explain the meaning of the information from the BI system that I use to others when asked.
Affect	In general, I have a positive impression of the information available from the BI system.
	I feel I will get a positive outcome by using the information that's available from the BI system.
	I like using available information for analysis and decision making.
Conation	I intend to use the information available from the BI system as much as possible.
	I often try to identify new ways to use available information.
	I encourage others to use the information available from the BI system to support their analysis and decision making activities.

BI Success

A good deal of research has been done to assess IS success. The two most influential models are the DeLone & McLean (D&M) (1992, 2003) information systems success model and the Technology Acceptance Model (Davis, 1989). TAM views system use as its success measure, while the D&M model proposes that 'net benefits' to individuals and ultimately the organization are the final success variables. However, the D&M model recognizes that in order to achieve these benefits, extensive use of the system in question is necessary. Further, associating specific benefits to the use of an IS like a BI system has proven to be problematic (Popovic, Hackney, Coelho & Jaklic, 2012). For this reason, we selected BI system use as our measure of success. System use is assessed by the frequency, duration and intensity of usage. We propose that positive attitudes toward information are an important factor in assuring the level of use of a BI application, which lead to the following propositions:

P_8: The greater the end-user cognition of information, the greater will be the use of the BI system;

P_9: The more positive the end-user affect toward information, the greater will be the use of the BI system;

P_{10}: The greater the intent to use information, the greater will be the level of use of the BI system.

Table 5 presents the items that operationalize the 'BI Success' component of our research model.

MODEL VALIDATION

In order to assess the usefulness and validity of the conceptual research model, we engaged thought-leaders from the business intelligence, metadata management and information quality fields and conducted a survey targeting BI practitioners. First, we consulted with a total of eight highly-regarded thought leaders. These individuals had one or more of the following characteristics: they were noted speakers (at events such as Data Warehouse Institute (TDWI) conferences), authors of books, contributors to leading practitioner publications (such as the Business Intelligence Journal) and/or highly sought after consultants.

Our panelists were posed a standard set of open ended questions during a series of telephone interviews, each of which lasted 30 to 60 minutes. The questions focused on the nature and operation

Table 5. BI success items

Category	Item Text
BI System Use	I use the BI system frequently to support decision making activities
	I consider myself to be a heavy user of the BI system.
	Using the BI system to assist me with decision-related tasks fully absorbs my attention.
	I usually spend a significant amount of time using the BI system each time I access it.

of end-user metadata in a BI context and allowed the experts wide latitude in their responses. The feedback received was instructive, and validated the core components of our model. Panelists were unanimous in the view that metadata is a key success factor for most BI systems, as illustrated by their following comments:

- "Yes metadata is critical – it is 'part and parcel' of an overall BI solution. Without metadata, the system is like a person without a leg; it can limp along but its activities are constrained;"
- "It not possible to maintain and grow the BI system without formal metadata management. The basic reason for this is that it is too expensive to train people to use the system without it;"
- "End user metadata is absolutely vital; it is as important as the data itself."

Panelists agreed that in would be rare for BI systems to be successful, in terms of overall levels of use, without metadata:

- "…only if the BI system is simple and users can easily find and understand the data;"
- "There is a scenario where a BI system can function without metadata. This would be where data is universally understood by all users. Typically, this would be when there are a small number of expert users who are intimately familiar with the data."

Panelists generally agreed that an important measure of BI success is the extent to which the system is used. As illustrated by the following comments, panelists also confirmed our hypotheses regarding how metadata fosters use:

- "…Metadata allows knowledge workers to understand the quality characteristics (how accurate, how complete) and lineage (where does the data come from) – which allows users to trust the information;"
- "The concept as to why metadata is important is pretty simple: it allows users to find, understand and trust the data they need in the data warehouse;"
- "…when they look at information (e.g., on a report) in the absence of metadata they are just looking at values having no intrinsic meaning. Metadata provides context. Content without the context is meaningless;"
- "Metadata is important because in its absence, users will draw their own conclusions regarding, for example, the meaning and source of the information. This means that information may be misinterpreted and that there is potential that different users will draw different conclusions."

To summarize, our interviews confirmed that metadata allows users to comprehend and develop a comfort level with the information provided by a BI system, thus making them more willing to use it for more and more varied purposes. This comfort level was characterized as 'understanding and trust' which aligns with our attitude constructs cognition and affect. The concept of 'willingness to use' information is closely aligned with the concept of conation.

Our second step to validate our conceptual model was to engage BI practitioners – individuals who design, build and manage BI systems - through an online survey. The goals of the survey were to confirm that we had identified the correct types of metadata to support BI end-users, the types of metadata currently provided and to assess end-user perceptions of currently available metadata. Overall, responses were received from BI practitioners from 266 organizations in the US and Canada. Table 6 presents a breakdown by industry.

Regarding the types of metadata required by end-users, BI practitioners were in general agree-

Table 6. Industry breakdown

Banking / Finance	13.9%
Manufacturing	13.9%
Insurance	10.8%
Healthcare / Medical	8.8%
Retailer / Wholesaler / Distributor	7.2%
Other	6.8%
Government	6.4%
Education	5.2%
Professional Services / Consulting	4.8%
Telco	4.4%
Transportation / Shipping / Travel Services	4.4%
Computer Hardware / Software / Data Processing	4.0%
Utilities	3.6%
Publishing / Media / Advertising	2.8%
Mining / Oil / Gas	2.0%
Agriculture / Forestry	0.8%
Professional Assn. or Non-Profit	0.4%

ment with the four categories proposed. Two additional categories were suggested: audit and ETL operational metadata. Audit metadata was seen to be required to support US-based legislative/regulatory requirements such as the Sarbanes-Oxley Act. We view this as a specialized requirement that would not be beneficial (or even available to) the vast majority of end-users. The second proposal was for ETL operational metadata – statistics regarding data warehouse load times, number of errors encountered during load cycles, etc. We believe that this type of metadata would have little relevance for business end-users and would likely be required only by the technical team that supports a BI system.

In terms of the types of metadata that are currently provided to end-users, approximately 87% of the organizations studied provide one or more types – only 13% indicated none is provided. Not surprisingly, the most commonly provided type of metadata is definitional – (78%). Approximately half (51%) of the responding organizations in the study provide information quality metadata. Lineage (36%) and navigational (32%) are the least commonly provided. The most common combination of categories is definitional and quality (43%). 14% of organizations provide all four categories of metadata.

Respondents were also asked to speculate regarding user perceptions of the usefulness of and satisfaction with the various categories of metadata provided. The results are presented in Table 7. Definitional metadata is seen to be the most useful to users and lineage the least useful. While metadata is deemed useful, practitioners feel that end-users are ambivalent regarding the quality of the metadata available to them (overall average satisfaction score – 5.4 on a 9 point scale). The results indicate that end-users are looking for 'better' metadata and that BI practitioners understand this.

One reason for this inadequate user satisfaction with available metadata may be attributable to the methods by which metadata is delivered. As presented in Figure 2, the most common delivery method (64%) is via static documentation (e.g., Word, Excel or PDF documents), which is far

Table 7. Metadata usefulness and satisfaction

Usefulness*				Satisfaction**			
Definitional	Quality	Navigational	Lineage	Definitional	Quality	Navigational	Lineage
8.0	7.5	6.9	6.6	5.9	5.5	5.1	5.1

*1 = not useful at all…5 = neutral …9 = very useful

**1 = very unsatisfied...5 = Neutral…9 = very satisfied

Figure 2. Metadata delivery methods

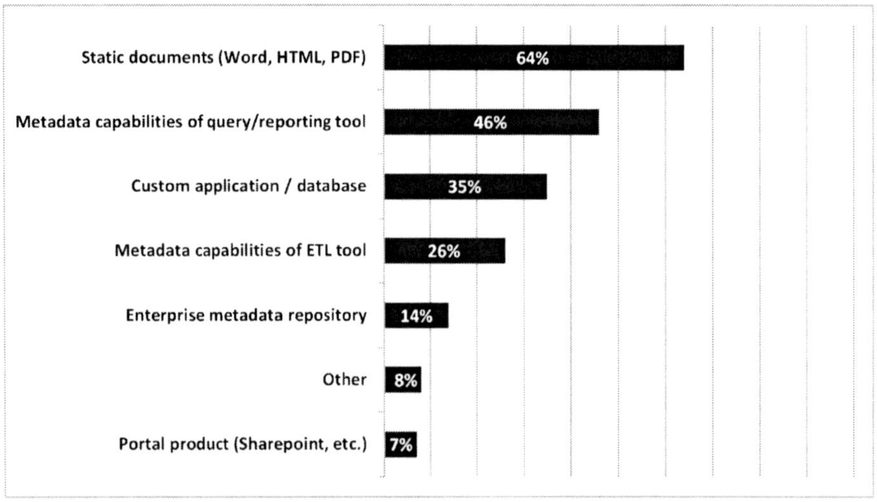

from ideal from an access perspective. Less than half of responding organizations leverage the metadata capabilities of BI tools (46%) or ETL tools (26%).

DISCUSSION AND CONCLUSION

In this study, we addressed three questions:

1. What types of metadata are required to assist users gain an appropriate level of knowledge about their information?
2. Why is this knowledge useful and valuable?
3. What is metadata's role in the success of BI systems?

Regarding question 1, based on the results of our survey, the four types of metadata we hypothesized to be useful to end-users were validated by participating BI practitioners. As previously stated, metadata is a concept that is not well defined or understood in a BI system context. The metadata types defined in this study (definitional, information quality, navigational and lineage) offer clarity and a holistic framework that can be leveraged by researchers working in the BI area. From a practical perspective, the categories offer a useful framework which can be used for a variety of purposes. First, this framework can be used by BI practitioners to develop and articulate a metadata implementation roadmap and to prioritize specific metadata projects. Additionally, this framework can be used to facilitate more effective communications regarding metadata within BI project teams and with BI end-users, as illustrated by this comment from one of our participants:

On our side we gained a better appreciation of metadata overall. Just clarifying the 4 different types was good for our team. It turns out that each team member of my BI team had slightly different definition of metadata from the different roles they play. For example I was mostly concerned with Navigation, whereas my Sr. DW Architect would be thinking from an information quality point of view. Now we can have a common language and appreciate each other's views.

Based on BI practitioners' perception of user satisfaction with available metadata, it seems that there is significant room for improvement. On a positive note, the vast majority of practitioners who participated in the study seem to be aware that the metadata they provide today is not adequate; perhaps due to its static nature and because the real metadata needs of end-users are currently not well understood. Practitioner awareness of issues with existing metadata is important – they know they need to make improvements. As presented in section 2, we have developed a set of survey items to assess the quality of the four categories of metadata. These items could provide value to BI practitioners in surveying their end-user communities to identify the specific metadata-related issues that exist in their organizations.

Regarding questions 2 and 3, our interviews with BI, information quality and metadata expert practitioners served to validate our conceptual model. Metadata was stated to be critically important to success in all but the smallest and simplest BI systems. Further, our panelists clearly supported our view that attitudes toward information are an important factor in BI system use. Users must understand and trust data in order to feel willing to use it. Given this feedback, we feel confident that our conceptual model has validity and offers both academic and practical contributions.

From an academic perspective, our model serves to extend the information system success research area. First of all, our model offers an alternative view of the factors that contribute to the success of information systems, specifically BI systems, as measured by the level of use. The D&M model (1992, 2003) proposes that information and system quality, in addition to user satisfaction are the primary antecedents of system use. Davis' TAM (1989) views the primary antecedents to be the perceived usefulness and ease of use of a system, in addition to the behavioral intent to use the system. The sole product of a BI system is information. We propose that attitudes toward the information produced by a BI system are important determinants of use. We hypothesize that high degrees of cognition of and affect for information (i.e., understanding and trust) positively influence conation (user willingness to use the information for important purposes), which in turn, influences use.

We further propose that metadata plays a significant role in influencing attitudes toward information. Other studies have investigated metadata (most often, quality metadata) in a BI context. However, none has looked at metadata in a holistic way and examined its role in BI success. This study offers a clear and concise framework for examining metadata's impact on BI system success. 'Good' metadata helps users understand their information, thus starting the process of forming positive attitudes. Metadata in this context is seen as an information resource (a 'help' feature) that assists end-users in gaining insight regarding the information resources available through BI systems (for example, data elements that can be used to develop queries, pre-built reports or BI-sourced documents such as spreadsheets).

From a practical perspective, the implications of our conceptual model are significant. Our conceptual model strongly suggests that BI practitioners can reap large rewards by focusing their efforts on shaping user attitudes toward information – helping them understand and form positive impressions toward it. It is useful for BI practitioners to think about the end-users that they support as their consumers. They need to think of ways to market the information available from BI systems to these end-users in the same way as marketers encourage consumers to consider buying their product or service. This might be done, for example, by compiling testimonials and case studies that demonstrate the value provided by this information.

We believe that our conceptual model offers a significant contribution to BI research. In the future, the proposed model needs to be empirically tested in a variety of different contexts. For example, the model should be deployed in different industry sectors, in organizations of various sizes, in different geographies and in varying BI system contexts. From an industry perspective, future research should test the model in different organizational contexts to determine if the factors that encourage or inhibit use are common across industries. For example, does the proposed model apply equally well to organizations in the High Tech versus Pharmaceutical industries? Similarly, future studies should apply the model to organizations of differing sizes and operational complexity. Organizational size may be measured in terms of employees or revenues. Operational complexity can be examined in terms of management structure, geographic dispersion or by number and complexity of products or services offered. The research model should be tested in different geographies to determine if it is effective in different cultural contexts – i.e., does the research model have the same degree of applicability in North America and Asia? Finally, future research should also determine if the research model is applicable in different BI system contexts, including varying size and complexity (data volume, number of subject areas and number / sophistication of users).

ACKNOWLEDGMENT

Portions of this chapter originally appeared in the article "Does data warehouse end-user metadata add value?" in the journal *Communications of the ACM*, Volume 50, Issue 11.

REFERENCES

Agarwal, R., & Karahanna, E. (2000). Time flies when you're having fun: Cognitive absorption and beliefs about information technology usage. *Management Information Systems Quarterly*, *24*(1), 665–694. doi:10.2307/3250951

Ajzen, I. (2001). Nature and operation of attitudes. *Annual Review of Psychology*, *52*, 27–58. doi:10.1146/annurev.psych.52.1.27 PMID:11148298

Burns, M. (2005). Business intelligence survey. *CA Magazine*, *138*(5), 18.

Chiou, J. S., Droge, C., & Hanvanich, S. (2002). Does customer knowledge affect how loyalty is formed? *Journal of Service Research*, *5*(2), 113–124. doi:10.1177/109467002237494

Crable, E., Brodzinski, J., & Frolick, M. (2008). The intelligent new business electronic application and automated underwriting solution at the western-southern life insurance company. *Information Systems Management*, *25*(2), 155–158. doi:10.1080/10580530801941231

Davis, F. D. (1989). Perceived usefulness, perceived ease of use, and user acceptance of information technology. *Management Information Systems Quarterly*, *13*(3), 319–331. doi:10.2307/249008

Delone, W. H., & McLean, E. R. (1992). Information systems success: The quest for the dependent variable. *Information Systems Research*, *3*(1), 60–95. doi:10.1287/isre.3.1.60

DeLone, W. H., & McLean, E. R. (2003). The DeLone and McLean model of information systems success: A ten-year update. *Journal of Management Information Systems*, *19*(4), 9–30.

Dempsey, L., & Heery, R. (1998). Metadata: A current view of practice and issues. *The Journal of Documentation*, *54*(2), 145–172. doi:10.1108/EUM0000000007164

Dick, A. S., & Basu, K. (1994). Customer loyalty: Toward an integrated conceptual framework. *Academy of Marketing Science Journal*, *22*(2), 99–113. doi:10.1177/0092070394222001

Even, A., Shankaranarayanan, G., & Watts, S. (2006). Enhancing decision making with process metadata: Theoretical framework, research tool, and exploratory examination. In *Proceedings of the 39th Hawaii International Conference on System Sciences* (HICSS-39). Kauai, HI: IEEE Press.

Fisher, C. W., Smith, I. C., & Ballou, D. P. (2003). The impact of experience and time on the use of data quality information in decision making. *Information Systems Research, 14*(2), 170–188. doi:10.1287/isre.14.2.170.16017

Foshay, N., Mukherjee, A., & Taylor, A. (2007). Does data warehouse end-user metadata add value? *Communications of the ACM, 50*(11), 70–79. doi:10.1145/1297797.1297800

Gabriel, R., Hoppe, T., & Pastwa, A. (2010). Classification of metadata categories in data warehousing - A generic approach. In *Proceedings of AMCIS 2010*. AMCIS.

Goodhue, D. L., & Thompson, R. L. (1995). Task-technology fit and individual performance. *Management Information Systems Quarterly, 19*(2), 213–236. doi:10.2307/249689

Grajek, S., & Pirani, J. A. (2012). Top-ten IT issues, 2012. *EDUCAUSE Review, 47*(3), 36.

Hackbarth, G., Grover, V., & Yi, M. Y. (2003). Computer playfulness and anxiety: Positive and negative mediators of the system experience effect on perceived ease of use. *Information & Management, 40*(3), 221–232. doi:10.1016/S0378-7206(02)00006-X

Haley, B., & Watson, H. (1998). Managerial considerations. *Communications of the ACM, 41*(9), 32–37. doi:10.1145/285070.285077

Huang, T. C., Liu, C., & Chang, D. (2012). An empirical investigation of factors influencing the adoption of data mining tools. *International Journal of Information Management, 32*(3), 257–270. doi:10.1016/j.ijinfomgt.2011.11.006

Igbaria, M. (1994). An examination of the factors contributing to microcomputer technology acceptance. *Accounting. Management and Information Technologies, 4*(4), 185–201. doi:10.1016/0959-8022(94)90023-X

Inmon, W., Strauss, D., & Neushloss, G. (2008). A brief history of data warehousing and first-generation data warehouses. In *DW2.0* (pp. 1–22). Burlington, UK: Morgan Kaufmann. doi:10.1016/B978-0-12-374319-0.00001-4

Isik, O., Jones, M. C., & Sidorova, A. (2011). Business intelligence (BI) success and the role of BI capabilities. *Intelligent Systems in Accounting. Financial Management, 18*(4), 161–176.

Jourdan, Z., Rainer, R. K., & Marshall, T. E. (2008). Business intelligence: An analysis of the literature. *Information Systems Management, 25*(2), 121–131. doi:10.1080/10580530801941512

Kiron, D., Shockley, R., Kruschwitz, N., Finch, G., & Haydock, M. (2012). Analytics: The widening divide. *MIT Sloan Management Review, 53*(2), 1–22.

Lawson, B. R., Baker, K. R., Powell, S. G., & Foster-Johnson, L. (2009). A comparison of spreadsheet users with different levels of experience. *Omega, 37*(3), 579–590. doi:10.1016/j.omega.2007.12.004

Morse, J. N. (2007). Beyond spreadsheets and silos: enriching financial planning using hyperion strategic finance. *Journal of Global Business Issues, 1*(2), 115.

Nelson, R. R., Todd, P. A., & Wixom, B. H. (2005). Antecedents of information and system quality: An empirical examination within the context of data warehousing. *Journal of Management Information Systems, 21*(4), 199–235.

Oliver, R. L. (1999). Whence customer loyalty? *Journal of Marketing, 63*, 3–44. doi:10.2307/1252099

Panko, R. R., & Aurigemma, S. (2010). Revising the Panko-Halverson taxonomy of spreadsheet errors. *Decision Support Systems, 49*(2), 235–244. doi:10.1016/j.dss.2010.02.009

Popovic, A., Hackney, R., Coelho, S., & Jaklic, J. (2012). Towards business intelligence systems success: Effects of maturity and culture on analytical decision making. *Decision Support Systems*, *54*(1), 729–739. doi:10.1016/j.dss.2012.08.017

Porter, M. (1980). *Competitive strategies: Techniques for analyzing industries and competitors*. New York: MacMillan.

Ramamurthy, K., Sen, A., & Sinha, A. P. (2008). An empirical investigation of the key determinants of data warehouse adoption. *Decision Support Systems*, *44*(4), 817–841. doi:10.1016/j.dss.2007.10.006

Schiffman, L., & Kanuk, L. (2000). *Consumer behavior*. Upper Saddle River, NJ: Prentice Hall.

Sen, A. (2004). Metadata management: Past, present and future. *Decision Support Systems*, *37*(1), 151–173. doi:10.1016/S0167-9236(02)00208-7

Sen, A., & Jacob, V. S. (1998). Industrial-strength data warehousing. *Communications of the ACM*, *41*(9), 28–31. doi:10.1145/285070.285076

Sen, A., Ramamurthy, K., & Sinha, A. P. (2012). A model of data warehousing process maturity. *IEEE Transactions on Software Engineering*, *38*(2), 336–353. doi:10.1109/TSE.2011.2

Shankaranarayanan, G., & Even, A. (2004). Managing metadata in data warehouses: Pitfalls and possibilities. *Communications of the Association for Information Systems*, 14.

Shankaranarayanan, G., & Even, A. (2006). The metadata enigma. *Communications of the ACM*, *49*(2), 88–97. doi:10.1145/1113034.1113035

Shanks, G., & Darke, P. (1998). Understanding data quality in a data warehouse. *The Australian Computer Journal*, *30*(4), 122–128.

Shin, A. (2003). An exploratory investigation of system success factors in data warehousing. *Journal of the Association for Information Systems*, *4*(1), 141–170.

Tannenbaum, A. (2002). *Metadata solutions: Using metamodels, repositories, XML, and enterprise portals to generate information on demand*. Boston: Addison-Wesley.

Wang, R., & Strong, D. M. (1996). Beyond accuracy: What data quality means to data consumers. *Journal of Management Information Systems*, *12*(4), 5–33.

Watson, H. J., Fuller, C., & Ariyachandra, T. (2004). Data warehouse governance: Best practices at blue cross and blue shield of North Carolina. *Decision Support Systems*, *38*(3), 435–450. doi:10.1016/j.dss.2003.06.001

Watts, S., Shankaranarayanan, G., & Even, A. (2009). Data quality assessment in context: A cognitive perspective. *Decision Support Systems*, *48*(1), 202–211. doi:10.1016/j.dss.2009.07.012

Wells, J. D., & Hess, T. J. (2002). Understanding decision-making in data warehousing and related decision support systems: An explanatory study of a customer relationship management application. *Information Resources Management Journal*, *15*(4), 16–32. doi:10.4018/irmj.2002100102

Wixom, B. H., & Watson, H. J. (2001). An empirical investigation of the factors affecting data warehousing success. *Management Information Systems Quarterly*, *25*(1), 17–41. doi:10.2307/3250957

Yeoh, W., & Koronios, A. (2010). Critical success factors for business intelligence systems. *Journal of Computer Information Systems*, *50*(3), 23–32.

KEY TERMS AND DEFINITIONS

Affect: Reflects an individual's feelings toward some object. In this chapter, the object is the information supplied by a BI system.

Attitude: An individual's overall positive or negative evaluation of some object, as described by what they know about it, how they feel about it and how they intend to behave toward it. In this chapter, the object is the information supplied by BI systems.

Business Intelligence (BI) System: A collection of technologies, tools and processes that convert data into information that is useful for organizational decision making.

Cognition: Refers to an individual's awareness and understanding of an object. In this chapter, the object is information found in a BI system.

Conation: Indicates the likelihood or tendency that an individual will act in a certain way. In this chapter, it refers to an individual's disposition toward using information supplied by a BI system.

Information Quality: A measure of how 'fit for purpose' is the information provided by an information system. It is often measured by dimensions such as accuracy, completeness, currency, relevance and format.

Information Systems Success: A measure of the extent to which an information system provides value to individuals, groups and organizations. In the context of BI systems, success is measured by the degree to which it improves organizational decision processes and decision quality.

Metadata: A form of information that describes an 'information object' (like a data element in a table or information presented on a report) so that it can be understood by someone who has not previously encountered or used the information object. In this chapter, we propose that there are four types of metadata that foster this understanding (cognition): definitional, quality, lineage and navigational.

Chapter 2
Understanding the Influence of Business Intelligence Systems on Information Quality:
The Importance of Business Knowledge

Aleš Popovič
Faculty of Economics, University of Ljubljana, Slovenia & ISEGI, Universidade Nova de Lisboa, Portugal

Jurij Jaklič
Faculty of Economics, University of Ljubljana, Slovenia & ISEGI, Universidade Nova de Lisboa, Portugal

ABSTRACT

The IS literature has long highlighted the positive impact of information provided by Business Intelligence Systems (BIS) on decision-making, particularly when organizations operate in highly competitive environments. The primary purpose of implementing BIS is to utilize diverse mechanisms to increase the levels of the two Information Quality (IQ) dimensions, namely information access quality and information content quality. While researchers have traditionally focused on assessing IQ criteria, they have largely ignored the mechanisms to boost IQ dimensions. Drawing on extant literature of BIS and IQ, the research sought to understand how, at its present level of development, BIS maturity affects IQ dimensions, as well as the role that business knowledge may exert in mobilizing this link. The authors test the hypotheses across 181 medium and large organizations. Interestingly, the data describe a more complex picture than might have been anticipated.

DOI: 10.4018/978-1-4666-4892-0.ch002

INTRODUCTION

In a decision-support context, business intelligence systems (BIS) emerged as a promising technological solution with a wide range of analytical capabilities to provide stakeholders at various organizational levels with valuable information for their decision-making. When properly used, BIS assist management in developing a data-based decision-making environment that provides more consistent results compared to non-business intelligence (BI) methods. Although business value of BIS can only result from changes and innovations in ways of working (Peppard, Ward, & Daniel, 2007), it can be achieved indirectly through the utilization of improved (quality of) information. Hence, it is crucial to understand the means by which BIS improve information quality (IQ) and the factors that affect the ability to increase the success of BIS initiatives in terms of IQ improvement.

While implying that the biggest problems of providing quality information for knowledge-intensive activities relate to information content quality rather than information access quality (Davenport, Jarvenpaa, & Beers, 1996; Strong, Lee, & Wang, 1997), it was previously suggested that at the current level of development BIS implementation projects do not adequately address the information content quality problems (Popovič, Coelho, & Jaklič, 2009). Thus, there still exists a gap between the quality information provided by BIS and the IQ expectations of knowledge workers when using information. Clearly, in order to improve the information content quality organizations need to primarily identify as accurately as possible knowledge workers' needs. This is a difficult task due to the non-routine and creative nature of knowledge workers' activities and requires an in-depth understanding of managerial business processes, knowledge of contemporary managerial concepts, and capabilities of BI technologies to improve the managerial an operational business processes.

Our research aims to address the question of how can business knowledge for BI initiatives contribute to narrow the previously mentioned IQ gap. The purpose of this work is therefore to explore the role that business knowledge may play in mobilizing the link between BIS maturity and resulting IQ dimensions.

The outline of the paper is as follows: In the next Section we introduce the fields of BIS maturity, IQ, and the role of business knowledge in development of BIS. Next, we develop the hypotheses and present the methodological framework for the study. The proposed research model and hypotheses are then tested. Lastly, we conclude with a discussion of the main findings and future research directions.

Business Intelligence System Maturity, Information Quality, and the Role of Business Knowledge

While the significance of organizational performance is widely recognized in the literature (Richard, Devinney, Yip, & Johnson, 2009), empirical studies suggest business strategies are an important determinant of organizational performance (McAdam & Bailie, 2002; Singh, Darwish, Costa, & Anderson, 2012). Successful business strategies are inherently dependent on the skills of the "company management team's ability to implement the strategies" (Herring, 1992, p. 54). However, the strategy can be no better than the information from which it is derived. The more complete and farsighted the information, the more likely the strategy is to be successful. According to Herring (1992), two basic categories of information are required for formulating the strategy: 1) information and data about the organization's resources and capabilities; and 2) relevant information about the organization's business environment, including customers, competitors, the industry structure, and other competitive forces that shape the markets in which the organization competes. Nevertheless, literature warns against the considerably varying quality of the two presented sets of information. As Herring has already suggested, organizations possess relatively complete "information about their own capabilities and resources", but "only a few firms allocate sufficient resources to collect and analyze the information" (1992, p. 54) about their business environment.

Business Intelligence

To service knowledge workers' complex information needs, BIS emerged as a technological solution offering organizations the required data analysis and reporting capabilities. The roots and range of the concept of the value of BIS stretch back much further and are also embedded in different schools of thought, including information theory and system dynamics, systems theory, organizational development, and management science (De Voe & Neal, 2005; Smith & Crossland, 2008). According to prior research, the literature lacks systematic attention to the benefits organizations that use BIS have actually achieved (Dodson, Arnott, & Pervan, 2008), consequently Elbashir, Collier, & Davern (2008) highlight the need for further research into the realization of such benefits. Findings from Jourdan, Rainer, & Marshall (2008) suggest the benefits of BIS have not been adequately researched and thus need further attention.

Value in the form of quality information is a matter of great interest in today's business environment. Organizations are recognizing that making quality decisions depends upon the quality of information available to support these decisions (Ge & Helfert, 2007), thus making the provision of quality information the key to gaining a competitive advantage (Gorla, Somers, & Wong, 2010; Salaun & Flores, 2001). In the view of Souchon & Diamantopoulos (1996), simply acquiring or possessing information is not directly related to organization's performance, but it is rather the utilization of information (as reflected in the decision-making process) that is the key link between information acquisition and the organization's performance. Thus, if organizations want the available quality information to contribute to their performance it must be used within processes (Raghunathan, 1999; Salaun & Flores, 2001). To contribute to organizational performance information must support decisions in those organizational processes whose results add value to organizations. Organizations which have learned to react to information have a better understanding of their internal operations (Berente, Vandenbosch, & Aubert, 2009) and their markets (Sinkula, 1994), all of which can help them in the creation of a sustainable competitive advantage (Gorla, et al., 2010) and potentially leading to an enhanced organizational performance (Jaworski & Kohli, 1993).

If we think of BIS as providing (quality) business information and business analysis in support of fact-based decisions in the context of business processes, it becomes clear that BIS are closely linked to business processes when delivering business value (Williams & Williams, 2007). According to Kovačič & Bosilj-Vukšić (2005), IQ is a key element in business process management by enabling the follow up of results, online process analysis and control, and consecutively the dynamic adjustment of the organization.

In making enterprise-wide decisions there are basically two approaches for organizations to follow, namely analytical decision-making and intuitive decision-making. Most knowledge workers make their decisions generally using easy and intuitive methodologies which take specific elements into account such as experience, knowledge and the available information. Such an approach leads to a stagnant decision-making style unsuitable for the unstable conditions determined by frequent and rapid changes in the business environment (Vercellis, 2009). In fact, decision-making processes within today's organizations are often too complex and dynamic to be effectively dealt with through an intuitive approach, and instead require a more rigorous analytical approach.

BIS above all support analytical decision processes on different organizational levels. Consequently, Marchand & Raymond (2008) suggest that BIS hold some of the greatest potential for achieving information asymmetry compared to competitors and thus attaining a comparative advantage via the implementation of IT.

Business Intelligence System Maturity

To do that organizations are in need of a clear roadmap to maximize their IT investment performance (Leem, Kim, Yu, & Paek, 2008). Accordingly, the assessment of an IT investment must be based upon a *maturity model*, also known as stages theory, not only to determine the current stage of implemented technology but also to show its next step (Benbasat, Dexter, & Mantha, 1980). In the field of BIS a maturity model illustrates how BIS evolve from low-value, cost-center tools to high-value, strategic utilities that drive performance (Dinter, 2012; TDWI, 2005).

Thus, it is important for organizations to strive after a mature BIS in order to capture the true benefits of BI initiatives (Chamoni & Gluchowski, 2004; Popovič, et al., 2009). However, organizations do not develop a mature BIS overnight; rather, it is the result of a progression through a series of earlier stages. Each stage builds on a previous stage and provides a greater set of capabilities. A 'mature' BI is one that has evolved to the point that it is integral to the functioning of the organization.

In the current business environment, there is no lack of BI or BIS maturity models (Dinter, 2012; Hribar Rajterič, 2010), yet they are relatively few compared to maturity models from other disciplines. What is more, not many attempts have been made to scientifically define the maturity of BIS (Lahrmann, et al., 2011), although many models can be found in the professional field. BIS maturity models describe the evolution of an organization's BIS capabilities. TDWI (2005), for example, proposes analyzing the technological part of BIS maturity through a system's architecture, scope, type of system, and analytics. Claraview's (2005) BIS maturity model suggests categories such as data sources, data integration, data stores and analytical applications to show different BIS maturity stages. Chamoni & Gluchowski (2004) emphasize technology as one of the three categories in their five-stage BIS maturity model with analytics and system design as the top priorities. Besides dealing with BI and BIS, these models also address other fields such as performance management or information management, or derive from other fields and have been adapted for use within the BI field. Maturity models in the field of BI are above all developed either by software companies (the providers of BI solutions) or consulting firms which are often sponsored by BI solution providers.

Business Intelligence Systems and Information Quality

There is no unanimous agreement on how BIS provide value for organizations (Petter, et al., 2008). According to De Voe & Neal (2005), the business value of BIS means getting the right information to the right user at the right time. As far back as the 1980s Porter & Millar recognized that "organizations are increasingly aware of the potential of information in providing competitive advantage and sustaining their success" (Kirk, 1999). Similarly, Al-Hakim (2007) believes that the capability and maturity of an organization to gather, manage the quality and use its information can mean the difference between success and failure. For more and more organizations, information has increasingly become a critical resource and an asset in their business processes (Citroen, 2011). According to Stvilia, Gasser, Twidale, & Smith (2007, p. 1720), for organizations' "processes that depend on information, the quality of information is one of the key determinants of the quality of their decisions and actions". In the view of Thierauf (2001), organizations that have successfully implemented BIS have better and timelier access to customer activities, marketplace trends, supply chain issues and other key performance indicators that cannot be easily measured in a non-BI environment. Consequently, Petrini & Pozzebon (2009) suggest the role of BIS is to create an informational environment in which gathered operational data can be analyzed to provide quality information relevant to the decision-making process.

Although this is a relatively limited view of the potential value that the implementation of these systems brings to organizations (Popovič, Turk, & Jaklič, 2010), improved IQ is certainly the most tangible benefit (Watson, Goodhue, & Wixom, 2002) and thus the most appropriate to be analyzed. All other outcomes, such as better decisions, improved processes, and increased market share are based on improved IQ. Therefore, the foremost purpose of implementing BIS is to increase the level of IQ provided to knowledge workers at various levels of an organization.

Awareness of IQ as an issue emerged slowly during the early years of computers when researchers slowly developed an awareness of the need to measure data quality. However, more recent IQ researches show the topic in question is also of current concern to organizations, for example: Forslund (2007) studies the measurement of IQ in the order fulfillment process, Rossin (2007) investigates the impact of IQ on the performance characteristics of supply chains, Vanden (2008) focuses on the role of IQ in determining option prices, whereas Koivumaki, Ristola, & Kesti (2008) research the effects of IQ of mobile information services on user satisfaction and service acceptance. In today's business environment quality information is a matter of primary interest. Making a high quality decision depends upon the quality of the information used to support the decision (Ge & Helfert, 2007). Organizations are nowadays recognizing that the provision of quality information is the key to gaining a competitive advantage (Popovič & Habjan, 2012).

In the IS literature, IQ is one of the major dimensions for evaluating the success of IS (DeLone & McLean, 1992). The existing literature suggests IQ is a vaguely defined concept (Eppler, 2006; Lillrank, 2003) and there is no single established definition for it (Ruževičius & Gedminaitė, 2007). Some of the proposed definitions view IQ as the characteristic of information to be of high value to its users (Wang, 1998), as "information that is fit for use by information consumers" (Huang, Lee, & Wang, 1999), as "the characteristic of information to meet or exceed customer expectations" and/or "information that meets specifications or requirements" (Kahn, Strong, & Wang, 2002, p. 188), or as "the degree to which the information is represented and to which the information can be perceived and accessed" (Hu & Feng, 2005, p. 38).

In this work we adopt the definition offered by Ruževičius & Gedminaitė (2007), which is based on some of the above definitions:

IQ refers to information characteristics and dimensions to meet or exceed expectations, requirements or needs of the information consumer/knowledge worker.

The field of IQ evaluation has been extensively researched and several criteria for assessing IQ have been presented (Eppler, 2006; Raghunathan, 1999). The term *IQ* encompasses traditional indicators of data quality, factors affecting the use of information, and features related to information access. To understand and analyze the benefits of BIS it is necessary to understand IQ as a broad concept which embraces all of the abovementioned aspects. The Eppler's IQ framework (Eppler, 2006) provides one of the broadest and most complete analyses of IQ criteria. His review of 20 selected IQ frameworks suggests that most frameworks are often domain-specific and rarely analyze interdependencies between the IQ criteria. Next, these frameworks do not take specifics of information in knowledge-intensive processes into account. BIS, by definition, support analytical decision-making and thus knowledge-intensive decision processes.

The outcome of Eppler's research is a framework of 16 criteria providing four views on IQ (relevant information, sound information, optimized process, and reliable infrastructure). The first two views, relevance and soundness, relate to actual information itself and hence the term content quality. The remaining views, process and infrastructure, relate to whether the delivery process and infrastructure are of adequate quality and hence the term media quality, which stresses the channel by which information is accessed (Eppler, 2006). In this work we use the terms *information content quality* and *information access quality*.

The contribution of high-quality information to organizations is that it makes it easier to convert available information into knowledge, by helping to interpret and evaluate the information, by assisting the connection with prior knowledge, and by facilitating the application of the information to new contexts (Eppler & Wittig, 2000). Eppler (2006) postulates that such an application of knowledge can be described from the point of view of who is applying it (e.g., the knowledge worker) or how it is applied (e.g., in a knowledge-intensive process).

The Role of Business Knowledge in Business Intelligence Systems Success

In the literature many meanings are associated with the term knowledge work. Eppler (2006, p. 24), citing different authors, exemplifies knowledge work as "the production and transmission of knowledge", "human mental work performed to generate useful information", "skillful collection, analysis, synthesis, and application of information", work that involves "analyzing and applying specialized expertise to solve problems, to generate ideas, or to create new goods and services" or as "white collar work which uses and produces information, is creative and often non-routine."

Eppler suggests that all of the presented definitions have in common "the fact that knowledge work focuses on information that has to be made useful; hence, the connection between knowledge work and information quality" (2006, p. 25). Even though knowledge work is often non-routine and creative, it can nonetheless be sequenced and broken down into specific steps. This can be referred to as knowledge-intensive processes. In this work we adopt Eppler's (2006, p. 25) definition of a knowledge-intensive process:

A productive series of activities that involves information transformation and requires specialized professional knowledge. Knowledge-intensive processes can be characterized by their often non-routine nature (unclear problem space, many decision options), the high requirements in terms of continuous learning and innovation, and the crucial importance of interpersonal communication on one side and the documentation of (high quality) information on the other.

Knowledge work can thus be organized into knowledge-intensive processes. Examples from the literature of activities which are described as knowledge-intensive processes are, for instance, product design, product development, market research, planning, analytical decision-making etc.

Moreover, organizations also need appropriate professional business knowledge and specialized information knowledge to successfully use BI initiatives (Moss & Atre, 2003; Thierauf, 2001).

The implementation of BIS can improve IQ in many ways, such as: faster access to information, easier querying and analysis, a higher level of interactivity, improved data consistency due to data integration processes and other related data management activities (e.g. data cleansing, unification of definitions of key business terms, master data management). It is no surprise then that IQ is considered one of the most important

BIS implementation success measures (Petter, DeLone, & McLean, 2008).

Notwithstanding the contribution of implemented BI technology to improved IQ, such benefit is usually limited and doesn't sufficiently add to BIS benefits. In the context of BIS implementation initiatives accurately identifying knowledge workers' information needs serves as a proxy for providing relevant information through BIS so as to increase information utilization as main success mechanism. Thus, the use of BIS is affected by the available *knowledge* from business and technical users of these systems. It has been shown that user characteristics, namely user skills, knowledge, and innovativeness, impact the use of decision-support systems (Basole & Chao, 2004; Dishaw & Strong, 1999). For BIS, Williams & Williams (2007) believe systems usage will improve if organizations ensure appropriate professional business knowledge and specialized information knowledge for BI initiatives.

For organizations, an important related determinant of IQ is the *alignment of business and IT goals*, which can be only attained when adequate business knowledge is available. Specifically, such alignment is then reflected in the information content quality provided by BIS. According to Saunders & Jones (1992), to promote the achievement of organizational goals the planning of IS must be tied to organizational planning. Ang, Davies, & Finlay (2001) investigated the impact of organizational and other factors on information systems usage in the Malaysian public sector and found that goal alignment was the second strongest predictor of IT usage.

CONCEPTUAL RESEARCH MODEL

Hypotheses Development

For developing long-term, efficient and scalable BIS' architecture, Moss & Atre (2003) point out the importance of data integration, choosing the right data sources and providing analytics to suit the user's information needs. In the same context, Gangadharan & Swami (2004) propose an effective data integration process, integrated enterprise portal infrastructure, and the delivery of answers to all key business questions as criteria for evaluating the completeness and adequacy of BIS' infrastructure.

Based on the reviewed BIS maturity models we found no evidence of an agreement on the BIS maturity concept. A deeper study of these models (Popovič, et al., 2009) suggests that none of them addresses maturity in a holistic way, but is more focused on the aspects it covers. In line with the purpose of this research we can derive two main emphasizes from the reviewed models. First, there is an awareness of the importance of integrating large amounts of data from disparate sources (Elbashir, et al., 2008; Jhingran, Mattos, & Pirahesh, 2002) and an awareness of the need to cleanse the data extracted from the sources (Bouzeghoub & Lenzerini, 2001) within the field of BIS. Second, organizations are focusing on technologies (e.g. querying, online analytical processing, reporting, data mining) for the analysis of business data integrated from heterogeneous source systems (Davenport & Harris, 2007; Turban, Sharda, Aronson, & King, 2008). On this basis, we propose the first hypothesis:

H1: Business intelligence system maturity consists of data integration and analytics.

Organizations, however, are still faced with the question of how they can evaluate the quality of the information acquired. Although the field of IQ evaluation has already been extensively researched, most of the proposed IQ frameworks do not address the issue of IQ evaluation comprehensively enough. To evaluate IQ we adopt Eppler's (2006) IQ framework since it provides one of the broadest and most thorough analyses of the IQ evaluation criteria. The framework in essence divides its criteria into two segments: a) criteria dealing with information content quality (relevance and soundness), which relates to actual information itself; and b) criteria addressing information media quality (referenced herein as information access quality), which relates to whether delivery process and infrastructure are adequate in quality. For knowledge workers, both segments, media and content quality may be perceived as one final product – information and its various characteristics – however, since they fall into separate areas of responsibility (Eppler, 2006) it is useful to address them separately.

As previously established, the foremost purpose of implementing BIS is to increase the level of IQ provided to knowledge workers at various levels of an organization. Koronios & Lin (2007) identified some BI technologies and activities, namely data cleansing, data integration, data tools and data storage architecture, as key factors influencing IQ. For example, considering Eppler's framework, data warehousing can imply an increase in content quality from the comprehensiveness and consistency criteria points of view with data integration and cleansing, but it can also improve media quality since users do not have to search for data within different data sources and combine it in information. In the data integration segment, the implementation of BIS therefore contributes to both information content quality (e.g. consistency and correctness) and information media quality (e.g. timeliness and convenience). Data management activities should result above all in content quality (e.g. comprehensiveness, consistency and applicability). Moreover, BIS maturity can influence content quality through a feedback loop: through a better insight into data it allows the perception of errors in data collection, and it consecutively improves data quality control in data collection. In the analytics segment, the greater maturity of analytical technologies (e.g. interactive reports, OLAP, data mining, and dashboards) is expected to impact on both media quality (e.g. through interactivity and convenience) and somewhat on content quality (e.g. comprehensiveness and clarity). For example, through improved interactivity (media quality indicator) users do not receive information just delivered but are able to explore it and gain more relevant information (an indicator of content quality) for appropriate decisions. Nevertheless, Eppler (2006) argues that technology mainly influences media quality and has limited possibilities of influencing content quality, and Gurbaxani & Whang (1991, p. 60) similarly affirm that "modern information technology can reduce the costs of communicating information by improving the quality and speed of information processing". The limited influence of technology on information content quality can be attributed to the fact that for information content the most important activity is to adequately specify knowledge workers' needs and requirements, which is a business issue rather than technological one. We can thus presume the maturity of BIS affects both dimensions of IQ, each in its own way.

We propose the concept of IQ as involving two dimensions that are both positively, yet with different strengths affected by the maturity of BIS. In this context, hypotheses 2a, 2b and 2c are put forward:

H2a: Business intelligence system maturity has a positive impact on content quality;

H2b: Business intelligence system maturity has a positive impact on information access quality;

H2c: Business intelligence system maturity has a different positive impact on content quality and information access quality.

To understand how the implementation of BIS actually contributes to solving issues of IQ in knowledge-intensive activities it is important to be familiar with the problems that may arise. Lesca & Lesca (1995), for example, emphasize the limited usefulness of information due to an overload of information, ambiguity due to a lack of precision or accuracy leading to differing or wrong interpretations, incompleteness, inconsistency, information that is not reliable or trustworthy, inadequate presentation and inaccessible information. Similarly, Strong et al. (1997) note problems such as too much information, subjective production and changing task needs.

The limited influence of technology on information content quality can be attributed to the fact that for information content the most important activity is to adequately specify knowledge workers' needs and requirements, which is a business issue rather than technological one. A clearer definition of their needs would ensure the comprehensiveness and conciseness of information. This emphasizes the need for the simultaneous implementation of contemporary managerial concepts that better define information needs in managerial processes by connecting business strategies with business process management. The latter includes setting organizational goals, measuring them, monitoring and taking corrective actions, and goes further to cascade organizational goals and monitoring performance down to levels of individual business activities. For example, a more extensive examination of critical success factors and related information needs might provide a better understanding of the information needs (Huotari & Wilson, 2001).

Tesch, Sobol, Klein, & Jiang (2009) recognize IS development as a knowledge intensive process requiring integration across disciplines with domain knowledge as essential for successful systems design and implementation. However, data analysis as a BIS development phase is different from a system analysis phase in a traditional IS development methodology (Moss & Atre, 2003). It is a business-focused activity, not a system focused activity. In the context of BIS development it is therefore reasonable to assume that appropriate business knowledge will increase the chance of success in terms of improved information (mostly content) quality.

In IS development two areas of knowledge are needed: knowledge on business processes and knowledge on IT, which is to support the processes (Milovanović, 2006). While Milovanović (2006) asserts that users possess the former type of knowledge and information specialists possess the later one, it is worth to note that in the case of BIS development a knowledge gap often occurs.

On one side, business processes supported by BIS are usually less structured, less defined and even not clearly understood by the users due to non-routine nature of managerial activities. Contemporary managerial concepts, such as business performance management, put in place more structured approaches for managerial processes, which in consequence enable better understanding of information needs. Similarly, Brohman, Parent, Pearce, & Wade (2000) recognize the importance of a better understanding of the data analysis process.

On the other side, it is important that business users possess knowledge on IT used in BIS, at least to some extent. This type of knowledge enables them to understand the possibilities for changing the current managerial practices. This knowledge therefore becomes the base for new spiral of knowledge creation in IS development context (Milovanović, 2006).

Therefore, we expect that employing business knowledge for BI initiatives will improve the impact of BIS maturity on IQ, mostly on the content dimension of it. We thus upgrade previously studied conceptual model (Popovič, et al., 2009) by putting forward the following two hypotheses:

H3a: The relationship between business intelligence system maturity and information content quality is stronger the higher the level of business knowledge for business intelligence initiatives;

H3b: The relationship between business intelligence system maturity and information access quality is stronger the higher the level of business knowledge for business intelligence initiatives.

Methodology

The hypotheses were tested by analyzing the data collected through a survey in medium and large organizations. The questionnaire was developed by building on the previous theoretical basis in order to ensure content validity. Measurement items for the survey were developed based on the literature review and expert opinions. All constructs in the proposed model are based on reflective multi-item scales. Pre-testing was conducted using a focus group involving 3 academics interested in the field and 7 semi-structured interviews with selected CIOs who were not interviewed later. This was also used to assure face validity. We used a structured questionnaire with a combination of 7-point Likert scales and 7-point semantic differentials.

Besides pre-testing a pilot study was conducted. Pilot tests are recommended for all fixed design research studies as a way to estimate the appropriateness of the overall study design and instrument design (Cooper & Schindler, 2003). In particular, Moore & Benbasat (1991) recommend that participants in a pilot study be asked to comment on the length, wording and instructions for using the instrument. For this research, a pilot study was conducted by administering the questionnaire to a small subset of the study's population and then by asking those participants to comment on those aspects of the instrument suggested by Moore & Benbasat (1991). The pilot study sampling frame included participants personally known by the researcher. Qualitative data collected in response to the request for feedback were assessed to determine whether adjustments to the instrument design or to its administration were warranted prior to proceeding with the full study. The only adjustments made at this time were to the set of measurement items which was expanded to include additionally identified items.

Based on the reviewed business intelligence and business intelligence systems' maturity models we modeled the business intelligence system maturity concept as a second-order construct formed by two first-order factors: data integration and analytics. Through the data integration construct we seek to measure the level of data integration for analytical decisions within organizations through two indicators: i) how the available data is integrated; and ii) whether data in data sources is mutually consistent. Here it is appropriate to note that data might be scattered over a multitude of data sources and yet be logically integrated (Bell & Grimson, 1992), which we took into account when setting up the data integration indicators (see Table 1). The data integration construct is also supported by the findings of Lenzerini (2002) who argues that for organizations: a) the problem of designing data integration systems is important in current real world applications; b) data integration aims at combining data residing in different sources, and providing the user with a unified view of these data; and c) since sources are generally autonomous in many real-world applications the problem arises of mutually inconsistent data sources.

Within the analytics construct we look at the different analyses the BIS enables. Although many kinds of analytics are provided by the BIS literature, we selected those indicators most used in previous works: paper reports (TDWI, 2005; Williams & Williams, 2007), ad-hoc reports (Claraview, 2005), OLAP (Davenport & Harris, 2007; TDWI, 2005), data mining (TDWI, 2005), dashboards, key performance indicators ('KPIs') and alerts (Davenport & Harris, 2007; Williams & Williams, 2007).

To measure IQ we adopted previously researched and validated indicators provided by Eppler (2006). We included 11 of the 16 IQ criteria from Eppler's framework in the research instrument. Since we are interested in the quality of available information for decision-making itself, we left out those media quality criteria measuring the infrastructure through which the information is actually provided since they relate to technological characteristics of BIS that we examine through the BIS maturity construct. According to this framework, the infrastructure level

Table 1. Indicators for the constructs

Construct	Label	Indicator (Description)
		(1 = Statement A best represents the current situation 7 = Statement B best represents the current situation)
Data integration	DI1	Data are scattered everywhere – on the mainframe, in databases, in spreadsheets, in flat files, in Enterprise Resource Planning ('ERP') applications. – Statement A Data are completely integrated, enabling real-time reporting and analysis. – Statement B
	DI2	Data in the sources are mutually inconsistent. – Statement A Data in the sources are mutually consistent. – Statement B
		(1 = Not Existent … 7 = Very much present)
Analytics	A1	Paper Reports
	A2	Interactive Reports (Ad-hoc)
	A3	On-Line Analytical Processing ('OLAP')
	A4	Analytical Applications, including Trend analysis, 'What-if' scenarios
	A5	Data Mining
	A6	Dashboards, including Metrics, Key Performance Indicators ('KPIs'), Alerts
		(1 = Strongly Disagree … 7 = Strongly Agree)
Information Content Quality	CQ1	The scope of information is adequate (neither too much nor too little).
	CQ2	The information is not precise enough and not close enough to reality.
	CQ3	The information is easily understandable by the target group.
	CQ4	The information is to the point, without unnecessary elements.
	CQ5	The information is contradictory.
	CQ6	The information is free of distortion, bias or error.
	CQ7	The information is up-to-date and not obsolete.
Information Access Quality	MQ1	The information provision corresponds to the user's needs and habits.
	MQ2	The information is processed and delivered rapidly without delay.
	MQ3	The background of the information is not visible (author, date etc.).
	MQ4	Information consumers cannot interactively access the information.
Business Knowledge	BK1	We possess appropriate professional business knowledge for business intelligence initiatives

contains criteria which relate to the infrastructure on which the content management process runs and through which information is provided. These criteria refer to a system's easy and continuous accessibility, its security, its maintainability over time and at a reasonable cost, and its high speed or performance.

In order to assess the impact of business knowledge on the relationship between BIS maturity and information content quality we included a question about the availability of such knowledge for BI initiatives. The importance of business knowledge for BI initiatives has been established in previous works (Moss & Atre, 2003; Williams & Williams, 2007). The moderating nature of business knowledge over the BIS maturity-information quality relationships was modeled through the use of an interaction term. This term was implemented creating a new construct, having as indicators the products of the standardized indicators relative to the underlying constructs involved in the interaction, following the approach of (Chin, Marcolin, & Newsted, 2003).

The target population for this study was all Slovenian medium- and large-sized organizations listed in the database published by the Agency of the Republic of Slovenia for Public Legal Records and Related Services (AJPES). At the time of data gathering for this study 1,329 Slovenian organizations met the criteria and were eligible for inclusion in the study.

Questionnaires were sent to all addresses on the AJPES file and addressed to CIOs estimated as having adequate knowledge of business intelligence systems and the quality of available information for decision-making. All participants received the paper questionnaire, an introductory letter explaining the purpose and goals of the research, and a return envelope with postage paid for submitting the answers. Upon completion of the survey, participants either submitted their responses to the server, where they were collected and stored until retrieved by the researcher, or returned their answers with business reply mail, where they were collected and stored by the researcher in the same database as responses from the Web. The Web survey was hosted on a server operated by the researcher's home institution and completely mirrored the paper survey.

A total of 149 managers responded while, at the same time, 27 questionnaires were returned to the researchers with 'return to sender' messages, indicating that the addresses were no longer valid or the companies had ceased to exist. Follow-up surveys were sent out two weeks after the initial call and resulted in an additional 32 responses. We followed the approach of Prajogo & McDermott (2005) and discounted the number of 'return to sender' mails so the final response rate was 13.6%.

Given that non-profit organizations were excluded from the study, the sample is an adequate representation of the population of Slovenian medium- and large-sized organizations by industry. Data collected were examined and analyzed using SPSS 18.0 for Windows and SmartPLS 2.0.

RESULTS

Data analysis was carried out using a form of structural equation modeling ('SEM'). For the estimation of the model we employed SEM-PLS (Structural Equation Models by Partial Least Squares) (Ringle, Wende, & Will, 2007), also known as PLS Path Modelling ('PLS').

We first examined the reliability and validity measures for the model constructs. In the initial model not all reliability and convergent validity measures were satisfactory. Once all the items that did not load satisfactorily had been removed, the model was rerun. Figure 1 shows the results of testing the measurement model in the final run. In the final model all Cronbach's Alphas exceed the 0.70 threshold and were very marginal to 0.80. Without exception, latent variable composite reliabilities are higher than 0.80, and in general near 0.90, showing a high internal consistency of indicators measuring each construct and thus confirming construct reliability. The average variance extracted ('AVE') is higher than 0.50 (mostly around or higher than 0.60), except for Business intelligence system maturity construct (marginal to 0.50), indicating that the variance captured by each latent variable is significantly larger than variance due to measurement error, and thus demonstrating a convergent validity of the constructs. Reliability and convergent validity of the measurement model was also confirmed by computing standardized loadings for indicators and bootstrap *t*-statistics for their significance. All standardized loadings exceed (or were very marginal to) the 0.70 threshold and they were found, without exception, significant at 0.1% significance level, thus confirming a high convergent validity of the measurement model.

To assess discriminant validity, the following two procedures were used: 1) a comparison of item cross loadings to construct correlations, and 2) determining whether each latent variable shares

Figure 1. Final model of BIS maturity impact on IQ with the interaction effect of business knowledge

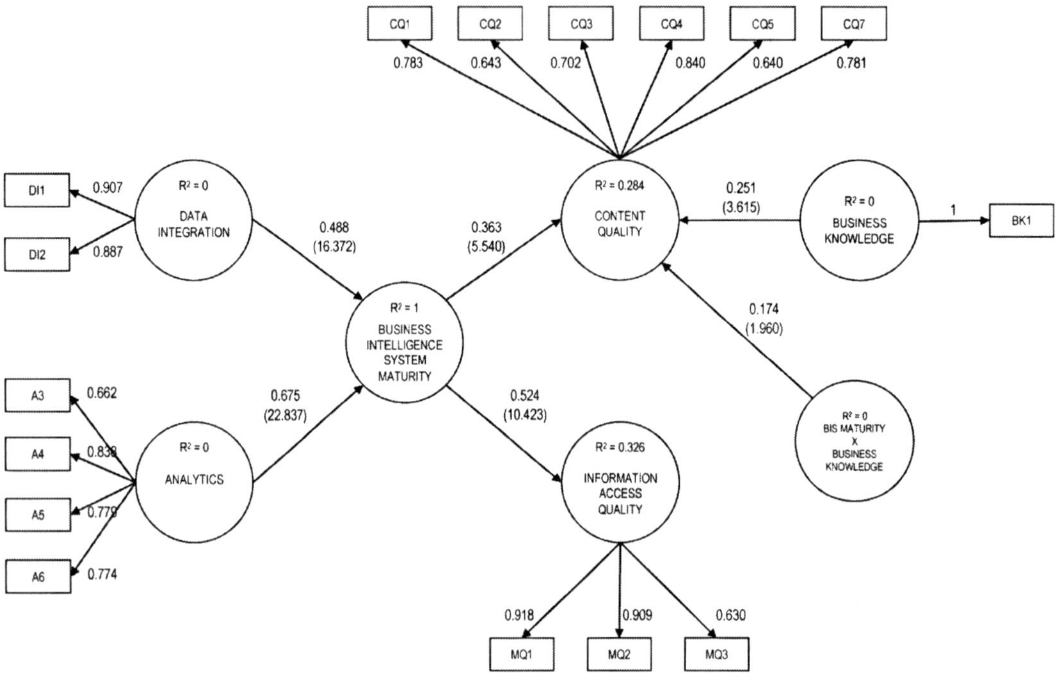

more variance with its own measurement variables or with other constructs. The first procedure for testing discriminant validity was to assess the indicator loadings on their corresponding construct. All the item loadings met the requirements of the first procedure in the assessment of discriminant validity. For the second procedure we compared the square root of the AVE for each construct with the correlations with all other constructs in the model. All the constructs show evidence for acceptable validity.

A bootstrapping with 500 samples has been conducted to test the hypothesized relationships between the constructs. As shown in Figure 1, the standardized path coefficients range from 0.251 to 0.675 while the R^2 is moderate, i.e. between 0.284 and 0.326, for all endogenous constructs. We can see that about 33% of the variance in information access quality is explained by the influence of BIS maturity, while about 28% of the variance in content quality is explained by the influence of BIS maturity and business knowledge.

As indicated by the path loadings, BIS maturity has significant direct and different positive influences on content quality ($\hat{\beta}$ = 0.363, $p < 0.001$) and information access quality ($\hat{\beta}$ = 0.524, $p < 0.001$). The *t*-statistic for the difference of the two impacts is 2.9 with $p = 0.004$ hence confirming that the two hypothesized impacts are indeed different. These results thus confirm our theoretical expectation and provide support for *H2a*, *H2b*, and *H2c*. To derive additional relevant information, sub-dimensions of the second-order construct (BIS maturity) were also examined. As evident from the path loadings of data integration and analytics, each of these two dimensions of BIS maturity is significant ($p < 0.001$) and of moderate to high magnitude ($\hat{\beta}$ = 0.488 and $\hat{\beta}$ = 0.675), supporting *H1* as conceptualization of the dependent construct as a second-order structure.

Moreover, the impact of business knowledge on information content quality is found to be significant and positive ($\hat{\beta}$ = .251, p<.001) while the impact of business knowledge on information access quality is positive ($\hat{\beta}$ =.066) but not significant. The interaction effect of business knowledge on the relationship between BIS maturity and content quality is found to be significant and positive ($\hat{\beta}$ =.174, p<.01) thus supporting hypothesis *H3a*. On the other hand, the interaction effect of business knowledge on the relationship between BIS maturity and information access quality is positive ($\hat{\beta}$ =.141) but not significant and thus not supporting hypothesis *H3b*.

FINDINGS

Our analysis confirms the conceptualization and operationalization of business intelligence systems maturity as a second-order construct. Through a comprehensive literature review and quantitative study of medium- and large-sized organizations, this research reveals two dimensions of BIS' maturity: data integration and analytical capabilities. Data integration reflects data consistency in sources and the level of data integration in organizations, whereas analytics reflects the level of analytical capabilities organizations posses. To achieve higher levels of data integration organizations need to have their data highly integrated, enabling real-time reporting and analysis, and their data sources mutually consistent. When implementing data integration within BIS, just employing technologies such as extract-transform-load tools or data warehouses is not enough. Implementing data integration also includes the execution of mandatory activities regarding data management, such as the identification of users' needs, data unification, data cleansing, and improvement of data quality control in data collection. Data integration thus consists of implementing the right technologies as well as activities for data management. Achieving higher levels of analytical capabilities, on the other hand, depends upon implementing advanced analytical tools such as interactive reports, OLAP, data mining and dashboards. Further, the results also suggest that basic analytical capabilities, such as paper and interactive reports, do not have any noticeable impact on the maturity of BIS.

The results also indicate the relative importance of the data integration and analytics dimensions regarding BIS maturity. Results suggest both dimensions are important yet analytics is considerably more important for achieving higher BIS maturity than data integration. This can be explained by data integration being a starting point for implementing BIS. For organizations to reach a higher level of BIS maturity it is thus important to solve data integration issues (e.g. data quality and security issues, metadata management issues, lack of IT data integration skills, and data transformation and aggregation) first. BIS have frequently been unable to get results to users in a timely manner because of data-integration problems. On the other hand, higher levels of BIS' maturity require the introduction of advanced analytical technologies, such as OLAP, data mining and dashboards. Since analytics are highly dependent on an organization's ability to integrate data from its various sources, data integration can be viewed as a prerequisite for successful use of analytical capabilities. Nevertheless, employing advanced analytical tools falls short if organizations do not provide knowledge workers who understand their business processes in detail with the knowledge and skills for carrying out complex analysis.

Next, this study suggests BIS maturity positively impacts IQ. More precisely, the results reveal that a higher level of BIS maturity has a significant positive impact on both segments of IQ, namely information content quality and information access quality, as they were conceptualized in our model. Higher levels of information content quality are achieved in organizations through comprehensive, accurate, clear, concise, consistent and current information. Achieving higher levels of information access quality, on the other hand, depends upon the provision of convenient, timely and traceable access to information. The findings show that the implementation of BIS explains about 33% of the access quality variation and, coupled with adequate business knowledge, it explains about 28% of the variation in content quality.

Even if both IQ segments are evidently well addressed with the implementation of BIS, one may expect that projects dealing with implementation of BIS are focused more on issues related to the main IQ issues in knowledge-intensive activities, i.e. content quality issues. This means that the implementation of such systems should contribute more to content quality than to information access quality. The results show that the implementation of BIS indeed differently impacts the two dimensions of IQ: higher levels of BIS maturity affect information access quality more than content quality. It appears as organizations implementing BIS give less emphasis to the quality of information content and rather call attention to the information access quality.

There are a few possible reasons for this. First, organizations can incur relatively high costs in seeking out quality information content that is not readily available. As information in organizations is often incomplete and vague, organizations need to introduce controls and measurements in business processes. Moreover, due to common functional organizations' structures, relevant and accurate information is often unavailable or so expensive to extract and combine that it is not done. Another, perhaps even bigger problem is multiple definitions of the same concepts among different organizational functions where organizations need to put in even greater efforts to make these definitions consistent between them. Functional structures often lead to information silos that organizations tackle through the implementation of new technologies, such as data warehousing.

Second, taking Eppler's (2006) arguments into account which assert that technology mainly influences information access quality and has limited possibilities of influencing content quality, another possible explanation for the observed result is that implementation projects, even those resulting in highly mature BIS, are still mostly technologically-oriented. More or less only those data management activities that are required for implementing data warehouses are subsumed. It seems that organizations avoid more demanding data management approaches that would lead to the higher content quality of the information provided by their BIS. The unsuitability of content quality affects future uses of information and can easily lead to a less suitable business decision: analyzing poor content does not provide the right understanding of business issues which, in turn, affects decisions and actions. Therefore, such approaches and focuses of BI projects result in dissatisfaction with BIS and ultimately in non-use of these systems, bringing a lower success rate of BIS projects. Another possible explanation for the observed results would be that most BIS implementation projects are still often managed and run by technical users who rarely, if at all, include business users into the design of BIS. Thus the focus of these systems easily turns from knowledge workers' actual needs (i.e. providing content quality) to addressing technical issues of providing rapid processing and delivery of information (i.e. access quality). Last but not least, another reason could be that organizations lack appropriate managerial methods for addressing information content quality issues.

Thus, to better address content quality issues through the implementation of BIS it is crucial to accurately define knowledge workers' needs – an usually difficult task considering the nature of knowledge workers' activities. While the development of BIS is supposed to be mainly a business-focused activity, we could expect that appropriate business knowledge will increase the odds of success in terms of improved information (content) quality. The results show that the impact of business knowledge on the relationship between BIS maturity and information content quality is positive; it reinforces the direct impact of BIS maturity on content quality. Note that the impact of BIS maturity on content quality can exceed the impact over information access quality for companies with business knowledge significantly higher than average. On the other hand for companies with very low business knowledge, the effect of BIS maturity on content quality can be almost nonexistent. This implies that higher levels of BIS maturity will have a stronger effect on information content quality in organizations with better business knowledge related to BI initiatives.

These findings have important implications for management: achieving higher levels of business knowledge for BI initiatives results in a stronger impact of BI maturity on information content quality. The targeted business knowledge includes the ability to understand and define as accurately as possible knowledge workers' needs which would improve the comprehensiveness and conciseness of information. Such business knowledge would ideally include knowledge about contemporary managerial concepts and proper metadata management that could improve the clarity of information. This further indicates that BI implementation projects need to be business-focused and business-led, since this would result in improved potential value of BIS and easier justification of investments into these systems.

FUTURE RESEARCH DIRECTIONS

It seems plausible that the present study has uncovered just a locus, the role of business knowledge as a moderating organizational variable acting to influence the impact of BIS on IQ. We propose that it is time to deepen our understanding about the types of business knowledge mobilizing the BIS – IQ bond. To the list of organizational variables influencing the BIS – IQ link may be added, however tentatively, the impact of existing organizational culture, as a power-related moderator acting to influence the strength of the studied link. An understanding of culture is important to the study of IS effectiveness in that a) culture can influence the successful implementation and use of IS, and b) it is often somewhat blamed when organizations experience failure (Leidner & Kayworth, 2006). We also propose that including additional external variables (such as economic adversity) may offer useful traction to researchers wishing to investigate this intriguing research area, as well as considering the influence from the stance of volitional environment (Ajzen & Madden, 1986).

CONCLUSION

Drawing on extant literature our investigation sought to learn from organizations that have implemented a BIS, where we examined the role that business knowledge exerts in mobilizing the link between BIS maturity and IQ dimensions, as conceptualized in our model. The results clearly suggest that appropriate professional business knowledge for BI initiatives significantly contributes to a higher level of content quality of information provided by BIS. Having in mind that historically and still today the major quality problems that managers are faced with when using information are related to the relevance of information (e.g. information overload) they receive, the results of the study give a clear direction for BIS project managers and sponsors. Just implementing state-of-the-art BI technologies without providing project team members with adequate business knowledge in terms of contemporary managerial methods, such as business performance management, will most probably fall short in adequate use of BIS and consequently in lower pay-off of BI investments. Thus, this study may be of value to both the academic and practitioner communities.

ACKNOWLEDGMENT

Portions of this chapter originally appeared in the article "The impact of business intelligence system maturity on information quality" in the journal *Information Research*, Vol. 14, No 4 and article "Towards business intelligence systems success: Effects of maturity and culture on analytical decision making" in the journal *Decision Support Systems*, Vol. 54, No. 1.

REFERENCES

Ajzen, I., & Madden, T. J. (1986). Prediction of goal-directed behavior: Attitudes, intentions, and perceived behavioral control. *Journal of Experimental Social Psychology*, *22*(5), 453–474. doi:10.1016/0022-1031(86)90045-4

Al-Hakim, L. (2007). *Information quality management: Theory and applications*. Hershey, PA: Idea Group Pub.

Ang, C.-L., Davies, M., & Finlay, P. N. (2001). An empirical model of IT usage in the Malaysian public sector. *The Journal of Strategic Information Systems*, *10*(2), 159–174. doi:10.1016/S0963-8687(01)00047-6

Basole, R., & Chao, R. (2004). *Location-based mobile decision support systems and their effect on user performance.* Paper presented at the Americas Conference on Information Systems (AMCIS) 2004. New York, NY.

Bell, D., & Grimson, J. (1992). *Distributed database systems*. Reading, MA: Addison Wesley.

Benbasat, I., Dexter, A. S., & Mantha, R. W. (1980). Impact of organizational maturity on information system skill needs. *Management Information Systems Quarterly*, *4*(1), 21–34. doi:10.2307/248865

Berente, N., Vandenbosch, B., & Aubert, B. (2009). Information flows and business process integration. *Business Process Management Journal*, *15*(1), 191–141. doi:10.1108/14637150910931505

Bouzeghoub, M., & Lenzerini, M. (2001). Introduction to data extraction, cleaning, and reconciliation. *Information Systems*, *26*(8), 535–536. doi:10.1016/S0306-4379(01)00038-2

Brohman, M. K., Parent, M., Pearce, M. R., & Wade, M. (2000). *The business intelligence value chain: Data-driven decision support in a data warehouse environment: An exploratory study.* Paper presented at the 33rd Hawaii International Conference on System Sciences. Hawaii, HI.

Chamoni, P., & Gluchowski, P. (2004). Integration trends in business intelligence systems - An empirical study based on the business intelligence maturity model. *Wirtschaftsinformatik*, *46*(2), 119–128. doi:10.1007/BF03250931

Chin, W. W., Marcolin, B. L., & Newsted, P. R. (2003). A partial least squares latent variable modeling approach for measuring interaction effects: Results from a Monte Carlo simulation study and an electronic-mail emotion/adoption study. *Information Systems Research*, *14*(2), 189–217. doi:10.1287/isre.14.2.189.16018

Citroen, C. L. (2011). The role of information in strategic decision-making. *International Journal of Information Management*, *31*(6), 493–501. doi:10.1016/j.ijinfomgt.2011.02.005

Claraview. (2005). *Business intelligence maturity model*. Retrieved January 20, 2007, from http://www.claraview.com

Cooper, D. R., & Schindler, P. S. (2003). *Business research methods* (8th ed.). Boston: McGraw-Hill/Irwin.

Davenport, T. H., & Harris, J. G. (2007). *Competing on analytics: The new science of winning*. Cambridge, MA: Harvard Business School Press.

Davenport, T. H., Jarvenpaa, S. L., & Beers, M. C. (1996). Improving knowledge work processes. *Sloan Management Review*, *37*, 53–66.

De Voe, L., & Neal, K. (2005). When business intelligence equals business value. *Business Intelligence Journal*, *10*(3), 57–63.

DeLone, W. H., & McLean, E. R. (1992). Information systems success: The quest for the dependent variable. *Information Systems Research*, *3*(1), 60–95. doi:10.1287/isre.3.1.60

Dinter, B. (2012). *The maturing of a business intelligence maturity model*. Paper presented at the AMCIS 2012. Seattle, WA.

Dishaw, M. T., & Strong, D. M. (1999). Extending the technology acceptance model with task-technology fit constructs. *Information & Management*, *36*(1), 9–21. doi:10.1016/S0378-7206(98)00101-3

Dodson, G., Arnott, D., & Pervan, G. (2008). *The use of business intelligence systems in Australia*. Paper presented at the ACIS 2008: 19th Australasian Conference on Information Systems. Christchurch, New Zealand.

Elbashir, M. Z., Collier, P. A., & Davern, M. J. (2008). Measuring the effects of business intelligence systems: The relationship between business process and organizational performance. *International Journal of Accounting Information Systems*, *9*(3), 135–153. doi:10.1016/j.accinf.2008.03.001

Eppler, M. J. (2006). *Managing information quality: Increasing the value of information in knowledge-intensive products and processes* (2nd ed.). Berlin: Springer.

Eppler, M. J., & Wittig, D. (2000). *Conceptualizing information quality: A review of information quality frameworks from the last ten years*. Paper presented at the Fifth Conference on Information Quality. St. Gallen, Switzerland.

Forslund, H. (2007). Measuring information quality in the order fulfilment process. *International Journal of Quality & Reliability Management*, *24*(5), 515–524. doi:10.1108/02656710710748376

Gangadharan, G. R., & Swami, S. N. (2004). Business intelligence systems: Design and implementation strategies. In V. Lužar-Stiffler (Ed.), *Proceedings of 26th International Conference on Information Technology Interfaces (ITI 2004)* (Vol. 1, pp. 139-144). Cavtat, Croatia: ITI.

Ge, M., & Helfert, M. (2007). *A theoretical model to explain effects of information quality awareness on decision making*. Funchal.

Gorla, N., Somers, T. M., & Wong, B. (2010). Organizational impact of system quality, information quality, and service quality. *The Journal of Strategic Information Systems*, *19*(3), 207–228. doi:10.1016/j.jsis.2010.05.001

Gurbaxani, V., & Whang, S. (1991). The impact of information systems on organizations and markets. *Communications of the ACM*, *34*(1), 59–73. http://doi.acm.org/10.1145/99977.99990 doi:10.1145/99977.99990

Herring, J. P. (1992). The role of intelligence in formulating strategy. *The Journal of Business Strategy*, *13*(5), 54–60. doi:10.1108/eb039518 PMID:10121463

Hribar Rajterič, I. (2010). Overview of business intelligence maturity models. *Management*, *15*(1), 47–67.

Hu, W., & Feng, J. (2005). Data and information quality: An information-theoretic perspective. *Computing and Information Systems*, *9*(3), 32–47.

Huang, K. T., Lee, J. Y., & Wang, R. Y. (1999). *Quality information and knowledge*. Upper Saddle River, NJ: Prentice Hall.

Huotari, M.-L., & Wilson, T. D. (2001). Determining organizational information needs: The critical success factors approach. *Information Research, 6*(3).

Jaworski, B. J., & Kohli, A. K. (1993). Market orientation: Antecedents and consequences. *Journal of Marketing*, *57*(3), 53–70. doi:10.2307/1251854

Jhingran, A. D., Mattos, N., & Pirahesh, H. (2002). Information integration: A research agenda. *IBM Systems Journal*, *41*(4), 555–562. doi:10.1147/sj.414.0555

Jourdan, Z., Rainer, R. K., & Marshall, T. E. (2008). Business intelligence: An analysis of the literature. *Information Systems Management*, *25*(2), 121–131. doi:10.1080/10580530801941512

Kahn, B. K., Strong, D. M., & Wang, R. Y. (2002). Information quality benchmarks: Product and service performance. *Communications of the ACM*, *45*(4), 184–192. doi:10.1145/505248.506007

Kirk, J. (1999). Information in organisations: directions for information management. *Information Research, 4*(3).

Koivumaki, T., Ristola, A., & Kesti, M. (2008). The effects of information quality of mobile information services on user satisfaction and service acceptance-empirical evidence from Finland. *Behaviour & Information Technology*, *27*(5), 375–385. doi:10.1080/01449290601177003

Koronios, A., & Lin, S. (2007). Information quality in engineering asset management. In *Information quality management: Theory and applications*. Hershey, PA: Idea Group Pub.

Kovai, A., & Bosilj-Vukšić, V. (2005). *Management poslovnih procesov: Prenova in informatizacija poslovanja s praktičnimi primeri*. Ljubljana: GV Založba.

Lahrmann, G., Marx, F., Winter, R., & Wortmann, F. (2011). *Business intelligence maturity: Development and evaluation of a theoretical model*. Paper presented at the 44th Hawaii International Conference on System Sciences (HICSS). Hawaii, HI.

Leem, C. S., Kim, B. W., Yu, E. J., & Paek, M. H. (2008). Information technology maturity stages and enterprise benchmarking: An empirical study. *Industrial Management & Data Systems*, *108*(9), 1200–1218. doi:10.1108/02635570810914892

Leidner, D., & Kayworth, T. (2006). Review: A review of culture in information systems research: Toward a theory of information technology culture conflict. *Management Information Systems Quarterly*, *30*(2), 357–399.

Lenzerini, M. (2002). Data integration: A theoretical perspective. In L. Popa, S. Abiteboul, & P. G. Kolaitis (Eds.), *Proceedings of the 21st ACM SIGMOD-SIGACT-SIGART Symposium on Principles of Database Systems* (pp. 233-246). New York, NY: ACM.

Lesca, H., & Lesca, E. (1995). *Gestion de l'information, qualité de l'information et performances de l'entreprise*. Paris: Litec.

Lillrank, P. (2003). The quality of information. *International Journal of Quality & Reliability Management*, *20*(6), 691–703. doi:10.1108/02656710310482131

Marchand, M., & Raymond, L. (2008). Researching performance measurement systems: An information systems perspective. *International Journal of Operations & Production Management*, *28*(7), 663–686. doi:10.1108/01443570810881802

McAdam, R., & Bailie, B. (2002). Business performance measures and alignment impact on strategy. *International Journal of Operations & Production Management, 22*(9), 972–996. doi:10.1108/01443570210440492

Milovanovi. (2006). Knowledge sharing between users and information specialists: Role of trust. *Facta Universitatis, Series: Economics and Organization, 3*(1), 51-58.

Moore, G. C., & Benbasat, I. (1991). Development of an instrument to measure the perceptions of adopting an information technology innovation. *Information Systems Research, 2*(3), 192–222. doi:10.1287/isre.2.3.192

Moss, L. T., & Atre, S. (2003). *Business intelligence roadmap: The complete project lifecycle for decision-support applications*. Reading, MA: Addison-Wesley Professional.

Peppard, J., Ward, J., & Daniel, E. (2007). Managing the realization of business benefits from IT investments. *MIS Quarterly Executive, 6*(1), 1–11.

Petrini, M., & Pozzebon, M. (2009). Managing sustainability with the support of business intelligence: Integrating socio-environmental indicators and organisational context. *The Journal of Strategic Information Systems, 18*(4), 178–191. doi:10.1016/j.jsis.2009.06.001

Petter, S., DeLone, W. H., & McLean, E. R. (2008). Measuring information systems success: Models, dimensions, measures, and interrelationships. *European Journal of Information Systems, 17*(3), 236–263. doi:10.1057/ejis.2008.15

Popovi, A., Coelho, P. S., & Jaklič, J. (2009). The impact of business intelligence system maturity on information quality. *Information Research, 14*(4).

Popovi, A., & Habjan, A. (2012). Exploring the effects of information quality change in road transport operations. *Industrial Management & Data Systems, 112*(9), 1307–1325. doi:10.1108/02635571211278947

Popovi, A., Turk, T., & Jaklič, J. (2010). Conceptual model of business value of business intelligence systems. *Management, 15*(1), 5–30.

Prajogo, D. I., & McDermott, C. M. (2005). The relationship between total quality management practices and organizational culture. *International Journal of Operations & Production Management, 25*(11), 1101–1122. doi:10.1108/01443570510626916

Raghunathan, S. (1999). Impact of information quality and decision-maker quality on decision quality: A theoretical model and simulation analysis. *Decision Support Systems, 26*(4), 275–286. doi:10.1016/S0167-9236(99)00060-3

Richard, P. J., Devinney, T. M., Yip, G. S., & Johnson, G. (2009). Measuring organizational performance: Towards methodological best practice. *Journal of Management, 35*(3), 718–804. doi:10.1177/0149206308330560

Ringle, C. M., Wende, S., & Will, A. (2007). *SmartPLS 2.0 M3*. Hamburg, Germany: University of Hamburg.

Rossin, D. F. (2007). An exploratory analysis of information quality in supply chains: Efficient and responsive models. *Journal of Global Business Issues, 1*(2), 151–158.

Rueviius, J., & Gedminait, A. (2007). Business information quality and its assessment. *The Engineering Economist, 52*(2), 18–25.

Salaun, Y., & Flores, K. (2001). Information quality: Meeting the needs of the consumer. *International Journal of Information Management, 21*(1), 21-37.

Saunders, C. S., & Jones, J. W. (1992). Measuring performance of the information systems function. *Journal of Management Information Systems, 8*(4), 63–82.

Singh, S., Darwish, T. K., Costa, A. C., & Anderson, N. (2012). Measuring HRM and organisational performance: Concepts, issues, and framework. *Management Decision*, *50*(4), 651–667. doi:10.1108/00251741211220282

Sinkula, J. M. (1994). Market information processing and organizational learning. *Journal of Marketing*, *58*(1), 35–45. doi:10.2307/1252249

Smith, D., & Crossland, M. (2008). Realizing the value of business intelligence. In D. Avison, G. M. Kasper, B. Pernici, I. Ramos, & D. Roode (Eds.), *Advances in information systems research, education and practice* (Vol. 274, pp. 163–174). Berlin: Springer. doi:10.1007/978-0-387-09682-7-9_14

Souchon, A. L., & Diamantopoulos, A. (1996). A conceptual framework of export marketing information use: Key issues and research propositions. *Journal of International Marketing*, *4*(3), 49–71.

Strong, D. M., Lee, Y. W., & Wang, R. Y. (1997). Data quality in context. *Communications of the ACM*, *40*(5), 103–110. doi:10.1145/253769.253804

Stvilia, B., Gasser, L., Twidale, M. B., & Smith, L. C. (2007). A framework for information quality assessment. *Journal of the American Society for Information Science and Technology*, *58*(12), 1720–1733. doi:10.1002/asi.20652

TDWI. (2005). *2005 TDWI poster: Business intelligence maturity model*. Retrieved November 10, 2009, from http://tdwi.org/Publications/display.aspx?ID=7288

Tesch, D., Sobol, M. G., Klein, G., & Jiang, J. J. (2009). User and developer common knowledge: Effect on the success of information system development projects. *International Journal of Project Management*, *27*, 657–664. doi:10.1016/j.ijproman.2009.01.002

Thierauf, R. J. (2001). *Effective business intelligence systems*. New York: Quorum Books.

Turban, E., Sharda, R., Aronson, J. E., & King, D. (2008). *Business intelligence: A managerial approach*. Upper Saddle River, NJ: Prentice Hall.

Vanden, J. M. (2008). Information quality and options. *Review of Financial Studies*, *21*(6), 2635–2676. doi:10.1093/rfs/hhl040

Vercellis, C. (2009). *Business intelligence: Data mining and optimization for decision making*. Chichester, UK: John Wiley & Sons.

Wang, R. Y. (1998). A product perspective on total data quality management. *Communications of the ACM*, *41*(2), 58–65. doi:10.1145/269012.269022

Watson, H. J., Goodhue, D. L., & Wixom, B. H. (2002). The benefits of data warehousing: Why some organizations realize exceptional payoffs. *Information & Management*, *39*, 491–502. doi:10.1016/S0378-7206(01)00120-3

Williams, S., & Williams, N. (2007). *The profit impact of business intelligence*. San Francisco, CA: Morgan Kaufmann.

ADDITIONAL READINGS

Cavalcanti, E. P. (2005). The Relationship between Business Intelligence and Business Success. *Journal of Competitive Intelligence and Management*, *3*(1), 6–15.

Choo, C. W. (1996). The knowing organization: How organizations use information to construct meaning, create knowledge and make decisions. *International Journal of Information Management*, *16*(5), 329–340. doi:10.1016/0268-4012(96)00020-5

Cottrill, K. (1998). Turning competitive intelligence into business knowledge. *The Journal of Business Strategy*, *19*(4), 27–30. doi:10.1108/eb039948

Culnan, M. J. (1985). The dimensions of perceived accessibility to information: Implications for the delivery of information systems and services. *Journal of the American Society for Information Science American Society for Information Science*, *36*(5), 302–308. doi:10.1002/asi.4630360504

Davenport, T. H., & Beers, M. C. (1995). Managing information about processes. *Journal of Management Information Systems*, *12*(1), 57.

Davenport, T. H., Harris, J. G., & Morison, R. (2010). *Analytics at Work: Smarter Decisions, Better Results*. Boston, Massachusetts: Harvard Business School Publishing.

Dinter, B., & Goul, M. (2010). *The impact of national culture on business intelligence maturity models*. Paper presented at the ICIS 2010.

Elam, J. J., & Leidner, D. G. (1995). EIS adoption, use, and impact: the executive perspective. *Decision Support Systems*, *14*(2), 89–103. doi:10.1016/0167-9236(94)00004-C

Elbashir, M. Z., Collier, P. A., & Sutton, S. G. (2011). The Role of Organizational Absorptive Capacity in Strategic Use of Business Intelligence to Support Integrated Management Control Systems. *Accounting Review*, *86*(1), 155–184. doi:10.2308/accr.00000010

Frishammar, J. (2003). Information use in strategic decision making. *Management Decision*, *41*(4), 318–326. doi:10.1108/00251740310468090

Gallagher, C. A. (1974). Perceptions of the Value of a Management Information System. *Academy of Management Journal*, *17*(1), 46–55. doi:10.2307/254770

Glazer, R. (1993). Measuring the value of information: the information-intensive organization. *IBM Systems Journal*, *32*(1), 99–110. doi:10.1147/sj.321.0099

Goodhue, D. L., & Thompson, R. L. (1995). Task-Technology Fit and Individual Performance. *Management Information Systems Quarterly*, *19*(2), 213–236. doi:10.2307/249689

Jukic, B., Jukic, N., & Velasco, M. (2009). Enterprise Information Systems Change, Adaptation and Adoption:A Qualitative Study and Conceptualization Framework. *Information Resources Management Journal*, *22*(1), 63–87. doi:10.4018/irmj.2009010104

Kahn, B. K., Strong, D. M., & Wang, R. Y. (2002). Information Quality Benchmarks: Product and Service Performance. *Communications of the ACM*, *45*(4), 184–192. doi:10.1145/505248.506007

Leonard-Barton, D., & Deschamps, I. (1988). Managerial Influence in the Implementation of New Technology. *Management Science*, *34*(10), 1252–1265. doi:10.1287/mnsc.34.10.1252

Marchand, D. A., Kettinger, W. J., & Rollins, J. D. (2000). Information orientation: People, technology and the bottom line. *Sloan Management Review*, *41*(4), 69–80.

McFarlan, F. W. (1984). Information technology changes the way you compete. *Harvard Business Review*, *62*(3), 98–103.

Melville, N., Kraemer, K., & Gurbaxani, V. (2004). Information Technology and Organizational Performance: An Integrative Model of IT Business Value. *Management Information Systems Quarterly*, *28*(2), 283–322.

Nelson, R. R., Todd, P. A., & Wixom, B. H. (2005). Antecedents of Information and System Quality: An Empirical Examination Within the Context of Data Warehousing [), M.E. Sharpe Inc.]. *Journal of Management Information Systems*, *21*, 199–235.

Owens, I., Wilson, T. D., & Abell, A. (1995). Information and business performance: a study of information systems and services in high-performing companies. *Information Research, 1*(1). Retrieved from http://informationr.net/ir/1-2/paper5.html

Redman, T. C. (1998). The Impact of Poor Data Quality on the Typical Enterprise. *Communications of the ACM, 41*(2), 79–82. doi:10.1145/269012.269025

Seah, M., Hsieh, M. H., & Weng, P.-D. (2010). A case analysis of Savecom: The role of indigenous leadership in implementing a business intelligence system. *International Journal of Information Management, 30*(4), 368–373. doi:10.1016/j.ijinfomgt.2010.04.002

Seddon, P. B., Calvert, C., & Yang, S. (2010). A Multi-Project Model of Key Factors Affecting Organizational Benefits from Enterprise Systems. *Management Information Systems Quarterly, 34*(2), 305–328.

Thomas, J. H. (2001). Business Intelligence - Why? *eAI Journal*, 47-49.

Trkman, P., McCormack, K., de Oliveira, M. P. V., & Ladeira, M. B. (2010). The impact of business analytics on supply chain performance. *Decision Support Systems, 49*(3), 318–327. doi:10.1016/j.dss.2010.03.007

Wixom, B. H., & Watson, H. J. (2001). An empirical investigation of the factors affecting data warehousing success. *Management Information Systems Quarterly, 25*(1), 17–41. doi:10.2307/3250957

Yeoh, W., Koronios, A., & Gao, J. (2008). Managing the Implementation of Business Intelligence Systems: A Critical Success Factors Framework. *International Journal of Enterprise Information Systems, 4*(3), 79–94. doi:10.4018/jeis.2008070106

KEY TERMS AND DEFINITIONS

Business Intelligence: The ability of an organization to plan, predict, solve problems, comprehend, innovate and learn in ways that increase organizational performance, organizational knowledge, improve decision activities, managerial processes and operational business processes, enable effective actions, and help to establish and achieve business goals.

Business Intelligence System: Technological solution holding quality information in well-designed data stores with a wide range of capabilities to provide users with timely access, effective analysis and insightful presentation of the valuable information for their analytical fact-based decision-making.

Business Intelligence System Maturity: Characterizes the capability and level of advancement of a business intelligence system. It guides evaluation, improvement and development of an approach to increase a system's capability.

Business Knowledge: In the business intelligence system context it represents professional knowledge that project team members possess regarding the contemporary managerial concepts for better defining information needs in managerial processes that are of non-routine and creative nature. By connecting business strategies with business process management it thus changes the current managerial practices using business intelligence systems.

Information Access Quality: Refers to connecting customer expectations and requirements for information from the access to information point of view. In the Eppler's framework it comprises the optimized process and the reliable infrastructure levels with the following dimensions: convenience, timeliness, traceability, interactivity, accessibility, security, maintainability, and fastness.

Information Content Quality: Refers to meeting customer expectations and requirements for information from the content point of view. In the Eppler's framework it comprises the relevance and the soundness levels with the following dimensions: comprehensiveness, accuracy, clearness, applicability, conciseness, consistency, correctness, and currency.

Information Quality: Meeting both customer expectations (subjective information quality) and customer requirements (objective information quality) for information while minimizing or eliminating defects, deficiencies and/or nonconformance in the information product or process.

Chapter 3
Subjective Information Quality in Data Integration:
Evaluation and Principles

Ahmed AbuHalimeh
University of Arkansas – Little Rock, USA

M. Eduard Tudoreanu
University of Arkansas – Little Rock, USA

ABSTRACT

This chapter focuses on the science of human perception of information quality and describes a subset of Information Quality (IQ) dimensions, which are termed Subjective Information Quality (SIQ). These dimensions typically require a user's opinion and do not have a clear mathematical technique for finding their value. Note that most dimensions can be measured through multiple techniques, but the SIQ ones are most useful when the user's experience, opinion, or performance is accounted for. This chapter explores SIQ while considering information obtained from multiple sources, which is a common occurrence when employing visualizations to perform business or intelligence analytics. Thus, the issues addressed here are the assessment of subjective perception of quality of data shown through visual means and principles on how to estimate the subjective quality of combined information sources.

INTRODUCTION

Modern analytics tools employed in business, intelligence, and even science, rely increasingly on rapid exploration of multiple information spaces and on a combination of various information dimensions and sources performed by an analyst. Integrating information quality involves providing users with a unified view of this data quality. This process becomes significant in a variety of situations both commercial and scientific, particularly with the widespread use of information visualization to allow end-users prompt access to large amounts of data. Integrating information appears with increasing frequency as the volume and the need to share existing information grows.

DOI: 10.4018/978-1-4666-4892-0.ch003

Information quality (IQ) is not a simple scalar measure, but can be defined on multiple dimensions, with each dimension yielding different meanings to different information consumers and processes. Each dimension can be measured and assessed differently. Information Quality assessment implies providing a value for each dimension about how much of the dimension or quality feature is achieved in order to enable adequate understanding and management.

This chapter focuses on a subset of IQ dimensions, which we term subjective information quality (SIQ). These dimensions typically require a user's opinion and do not have a clear mathematical technique for finding their value. Note that most dimensions can be measured through multiple techniques, but the SIQ ones are most useful when the user's experience, opinion, or performance, are accounted for. The objective dimensions are the dimensions that can be largely and commonly assessed via mathematical or functional forms. It is possible for the same dimension to be measured by both subjective and objective means, depending on the context. For example, accuracy can be objectively computed when one checks the contents of a warehouse against an electronic inventory record. However, accuracy can also be subjectively employed, as for example, the estimation of the amount of shade in a specific area. Table 1 shows all IQ dimensions and the relative importance or usefulness of objective metrics versus subjective ones (Pipino, Lee, & Wang, 2002).

Table 1. IQ dimensions and the relative usefulness of objective metrics versus subjective ones

Dimension	Objective Assessment (width of gray area proportional to relevance of objective metrics)	Subjective Assessment (width of white area shows relevance for subjective)
Believability	Apply a formula (integration only)	User's opinion and experience determines whether they trust the data
Ease of Manipulation	Time to perform a computation	User's experience or performance with the data
Interpretability	Whether some computation is successful	User can understand the data correctly
Relevancy	Can produce a valid result	Helps the user in their task
Reputation	Apply a formula (integration only)	The user can judge or assume the accuracy based on the result of the objective assessment
Value-Added	Can increase the value of data	The user can judge or assess the value added to the data
Objectivity	Formulas applied	User opinion
Timeliness	Can reflect how up-to-date the data is with respect to the task	User judges based on previous experience
Understandability	Can provide clear and simple data	User can understand the data easily
Concise Representation	The shortest representation is known	User judges based on previous experience
Appropriate Amount of Data	The needed amount is known	User expertise is required
Security	Against a standard metric	Users experience or performance with the data
Accessibility	Against a standard metric	Based on user's experiences
Consistent Representation	Count different representations	User's opinion
Accuracy	Formula based on known, exact value	Expert estimation when exact value not available
Completeness	Count missing values in structured sources	User's opinion for unstructured text

The purpose of this chapter is to distill a set of rules/principles to enable users to estimate or determine the quality of the visual information. The rules can subsequently be used to estimate these quality dimensions, which can be presented to the users in near real time to help them perceive the subjective quality of the combined information and the major components of that data.

The chapter also highlights two scientific studies that provide insight into SIQ and provide the basis for the principles described here. Information quality has been traditionally driven by practitioners in the field, but enough momentum and research has been developed to allow the growth of a more scientific body of knowledge. This studies aim at furthering the science of subjective information quality, and at providing guidance to IQ practitioners.

Information Quality Framework

In the current information quality framework, data is being captured from various sources and stored in a database. An information quality specialist performs regular IQ assessment of the quality of each data source using questioners and sample data and users. Theses are then attached to each information source, which in a typical scenario would be database tables. When a user retrieves information combined from different sources, our techniques are applied and overall SIQ estimation is provided. The problem addressed in this chapter is that there are no known methods, especially for SIQ, to assess the quality of information that needs to integrate data from multiple databases.

This chapter proposes a revised framework that can support integration of multiple data sources and SIQ assessment (Figure 1). The solution is to investigate rules and principles that would enable an IQ specialist to derive formulas to estimate the value of SIQ for integrated data sources. These formulas will be customized by the IQ specialist to their particular data source, and could be derived by sampling a small number of integration cases. The end-users will benefit from the SIQ estimation in near real time to help them perceive the subjective quality of the combined information and the major components of that data.

PROBLEM

Modern analytics techniques rely on fast, continuous, and interactive user exploration that employs graphical representations, in what is being termed visual analytics. Such techniques

Figure 1. Proposed IQ framework with the specialist deriving SIQ integration formula

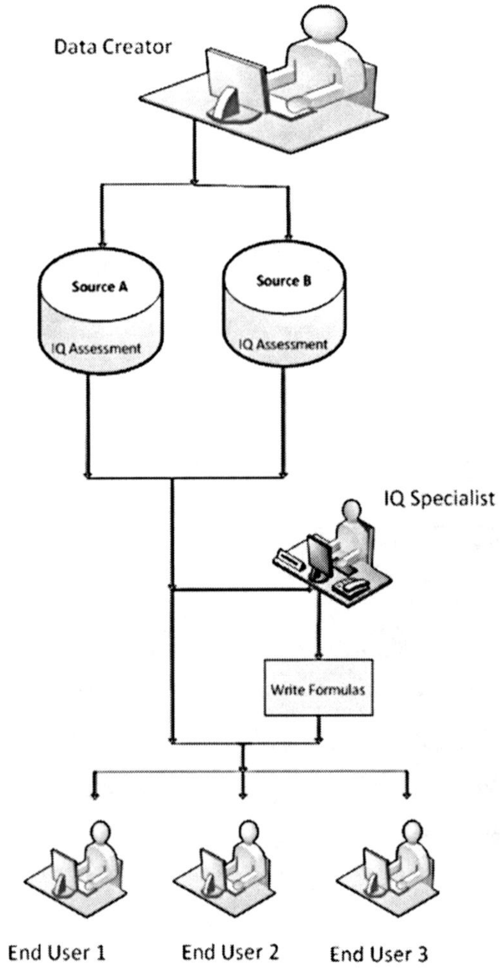

result in multiple changes the information being studied, but current IQ methods cannot convey SIQ because no methods exist for continuously updating the quality of the current information in a short period of time. Combining information from different information sets using a mixture of several different operations is crucial for data analytics, but may also lead to several information quality problems, such as duplication, inconsistency and missing values. Other subjective Information Quality issues such as believability, value-added, and trust measurements are also difficult and slow to estimate. The propagation of the quality is not a simple additive model; it is entirely possible for two pieces of information with high-quality ratings to result in low quality information, if, for example, the two contradict each other. The opposite is also true, in that two pieces of low quality data can complement each other with a net boost in quality.

Current information quality integration techniques treat all IQ dimensions as mathematical entities and combine them through statistical methods (Pipino, Lee, &Wang, 2002; Lin & Hua, 2008; Caballero, Verbo, Calero, & Piattini, 2007; Peralta, Ruggia, Kedad, & Bouzeghoub, 2004; Motro & Rakov, 1996; Ballou, InduShobha, Chengalur-Smit, & Wang 2006). However, most people do not treat information in a statistical manner and may find value in seemingly low quality information or fault in information that is statistically of high quality. This becomes more important for the SIQ dimensions, in which the user's opinion is the most important measure. There are no methods for determining/estimating SIQ from multiple sources that have been verified or derived from actual human observations. As such, data quality of subjective dimensions is not appropriately conveyed for information obtained through a combination of multiple information sources. This holds true even if the quality of the individual sources is known.

Current techniques for determining subjective information quality (SIQ) are time consuming and effort-intensive because they require surveys, sampling, and statistical analysis. Analyzing and assessing the quality takes a long time in the order of days, if not weeks. Such methods are not appropriate for real-time analytics, where data combination and refinement must take place in a short period of time.

Another problem resides in a lack of visualization tools that present the quality of the information together with the information itself, and thus the full fitness of the information for any particular user is not realized. Some properties of the information may become apparent through visual examination, without the need to perform extensive computations in the background. Using visualizations would be the best technique to display the growth of the information along with its quality, and also show how the different SIQ dimensions would affect each other through the information propagation process.

BACKGROUND

Data and Information Quality Assessment

- **Data quality assessment:** Pipino, Lee, and Wang's article (2002) describes the subjective and objective assessments of data quality, and presents three functional forms for developing objective data quality metrics. The article presents approaches that combine the subjective and objective assessments of data quality, and illustrate how it has been used in practice. Data and information are often used synonymously. In practice, managers differentiate information from data intuitively, and describe information as data that has been processed. Their research does not provide visual techniques to present the subjective quality, and it takes time to determine the quality of data. Also, their approach is not based on observations of the end-users. Their work focuses on the data coming from one data source;

- **Examining fitness for use:** Tyi and Ballou's (2008) research discusses the term data quality, or "fitness for use," which implies the concept of data quality is relative. Thus, data with quality considered appropriate for one use may not possess sufficient quality for another use. The trend toward multiple uses of data, exemplified by the popularity of data warehouses, has highlighted the need to address data quality concerns. Furthermore, fitness for use implies that one needs to look beyond traditional concerns with the accuracy of the data. Data found in accounting-type systems may be accurate but unfit for use if that data is not sufficiently timely. Also, personnel databases situated in different divisions of a company may be correct but unfit for use if the desire is to combine the two and they have incompatible formats. A related problem with multiple users of data is that of semantics. The data gatherer and initial user may be fully aware of the nuances regarding the meaning of the various data items, but that will not be true for all of the other users. Thus, although the value may be correct, it can easily be misinterpreted. Also, the capability of judging the reasonableness of the data is lost when users have no responsibility for the data's integrity and when they are removed from the data creators. Such problems are becoming increasingly critical as organizations implement data warehouses;
- **Anchoring data quality dimensions ontological foundations:** Wand and Wang's project (1996) addresses the impacts of poor data quality on the overall effectiveness of organizations. In a world where people are moving to total quality management, one of the critical areas is data. The quality of a product depends on the process by which the product is designed and produced. Likewise, the quality of data depends on the design and production processes involved in generating the data. To design for better quality, it is necessary first to understand what quality means and how it is measured. Data quality, as presented in their work, is a multidimensional concept. Frequently mentioned dimensions are accuracy, completeness, consistency, and timeliness. The choice of these dimensions is primarily based on intuitive understanding, industrial experience, or literature review. However, a literature review shows that there is no general agreement on data quality dimensions;
- **A homogeneous framework to measure data quality:** Bobrowski, Marre, and Yankelevich (1999) presented a methodology to measure data quality within organizations. First, a list of IQ criteria must be set up. These IQ criteria are divided into directly and indirectly assessed criteria. Scores for the indirectly assessed IQ criteria are computed from the directly assessed IQ criteria. In order to assess the direct criteria, traditional software metrics techniques were applied. These techniques measured data quality following the goal-question-metric methodology: For each directly assessed criterion, a question is set up that characterizes the criterion, and then a metric is derived to answer that question, giving a precise evaluation of the quality. From these metrics a user questionnaire is set up, which is based on samples of the database.

Subjective Quality and User Opinion

- **Measuring data believability - a provenance approach:** Prat and Madnick (2008) presented the main concepts of a model for representing and storing data provenance, which included ontology of the sub-dimensions of data believability. They used aggregation operators to compute believability across the sub-dimensions of data believability. Our work focuses on subjective evaluation of believability for visual presentation and aims to help in developing a method that will enable users to better estimate the quality of the data coming from different sources. Our results may be better at determining SIQ measures than the statistical methods employed for their data provenance model;
- **The credibility of online information:** The research of Huerta, Esperanza, and Ryan (2003) examines the factors affecting the credibility of online information. It uses the Elaboration Likelihood Model (Petty & Cacioppo, 1986) as a theoretical framework, proposing a comprehensive model that includes factors from traditional means of communication and the Web. A field experiment was conducted that manipulated quality of content, reputation of the web site owner, attractiveness, modality of exposure, and simulation. Out of these factors, quality of content and reputation of the Web site owner show statistical significance in the expected direction;
- **A methodology for information quality assessment:** Lee, Strong, Kahn, and Wang (2002) developed a methodology, called AIM quality (AIMQ), to form a basis for IQ assessment and benchmarking. The methodology was illustrated through its application to five major organizations. The methodology encompasses a model of IQ, a questionnaire to measure IQ, and analysis techniques for interpreting the IQ measures. They developed and validated the questionnaire and used it to collect data on the status of organizational IQ. These pieces of data were used to assess and benchmark IQ for four quadrants of the model, which rely on questionnaires to find IQ scores. Our work uses different data from multiple sources, and we aim to help in developing a method that will enable users and organizations to better estimate the SIQ dimensions of the data coming from different sources;
- **A method for measuring believability in data integration:** Lin and Hue research (2008) reports a method for measuring data quality in data integration. The article focuses on believability, a major aspect of quality. The authors present an approach for computing believability based on metadata. In their method, they make explicit use of lineage-based measurements and develop a precise approach to measuring data quality. Believability is itself divided into sub-dimensions: believability of source, believability compared to internal common-sense standard, and believability based on temporality of data. They present metrics for assessing the believability of data resulting from one process run; the believability of a data value is computed based on the lineage of this value. The next steps of their research will concentrate on the refinement of the proposed metrics in conjunction with further testing on real case studies, and the development of a tool to capture metadata. Their research only focuses on the believability, and does not include the human interactions with quality. Believability is one of the subjective data quality dimensions that we discussed in this chapter;

- **Beyond accuracy; what data quality means to data consumers:** Wang and Strong (1996) developed a framework that captures the aspects of data quality that are important to data consumers. A two-stage survey and a two-phase sorting study were conducted to develop a hierarchical framework for organizing data quality dimensions. Their framework captures dimensions of data quality that are important to data consumers. Intrinsic DQ denotes that data have quality in their own right. Contextual DQ highlights the requirement that data quality must be considered within the context of the task at hand. Representational DQ and accessibility DQ emphasize the importance of the role of systems. These findings are consistent with our understanding that high-quality data should be intrinsically good, contextually appropriate for the task, clearly represented, and accessible to the data consumer;
- **Internet data quality: perceptions of graduate and undergraduate business students:** Klein (2002) examines user perceptions of the quality of information found on the Internet using surveys of graduate and undergraduate students taking specific courses. The Wang and Strong (1996), framework was applied in the study as a tool for measuring data quality. The objective of the study is to further improve the understanding of users' evaluations of internet information quality by comparing perceptions of graduate and undergraduate students. The study was built on prior research aimed at understanding the dimensions of data quality. The findings of this study suggest that additional research in this area would be beneficial. Future research should focus on surveying a larger, less narrowly focused user population and on surveying users about their perceptions of the data quality of specific web sites;
- **User perceptions of data quality - internet and traditional text sources:** Klein' (2001) work also studies users' perceptions of the quality of information found on the Internet and in traditional text sources .As the previous study, this uses a survey based on the Wang and Strong (1996) framework. Her focus, as ours, was on the consumers (users) of data and information. Several differences between our work and Klein's study are noted. First, the sample size was relatively small. Second, all of the surveyed users were students taking an MBA courses. Third, respondents were asked questions about the quality of Internet and traditional text sources in general rather than being asked questions about specific Internet sites and text sources. Forth, our work examines how users perceived data stemming from multiple sources. We propose a set of principles of estimating data quality. The principles can subsequently be used to estimate these quality dimensions and present them to a user. Our studies researches various types data sources, and focus on how people perceive subjective dimensions such as believability, accuracy, and value-added. Our work assumes the data source is already assessed and the quality is known for the subjective IQ dimensions;
- **The market for lemons: quality uncertainty and the market mechanism:** George Akerlof's (1970) studies the relationship between quality and uncertainty. His work includes interesting and important problems for the theory of markets. On the one hand, the interaction of quality differences and uncertainty may explain important institutions of the labor market. Our research will help to answer some of the introductory questions of the signaling theory. Our research will provide set of principles help filling the gaps in the prob-

lem of adverse selection (Polborn, Hoy, & Sadanand. (2006); Dionne, Gouriéroux,, & Vanasse (2001), presented by George Akerlof's "The Market for Lemons" (Akerlof, 1970), which brought informational issues at the forefront of economic theory. There are other various psychology concepts that can help in the development of effective principles to better the awareness and estimation of subjective information quality. The principles mentioned in this chapter may help the signaling theory, that is work similar to the market for lemons, to better understand the quality of the signal veracity. Cognitive bias in all its forms, anchoring, subjective validation, and so on, have a heavy effect on most SIQ metrics. The most affected may be believability, where people tend to be biased toward certain information. Others such as subjective accuracy and value-added may not be as heavily influenced by biases, but an IQ specialist still needs to understand the effect of these biases. Samples of measurements can be taken to various data types and sources to identify the most common biases.

Automated Database and Data Integration Quality Assessment

- **Stanford entity resolution framework:** The goal of the SERF project (Stanford Entity Resolution Framework, 2010) is to develop a generic infrastructure for Entity Resolution (ER). ER (also known as reduplication or record linkage) is an important information integration problem. For instance, two records on the same person may provide different name spellings, and addresses may differ. The goal of ER is to "resolve" entities, by identifying the records that represent the same entity and reconciling them to obtain one record per entity. Our work focuses on a full view of the IQ dimensions including the subjective dimensions;
- **Stanford trio project:** Trio (Stanford Trio Project, 2010), is a new kind of database management system (DBMS), one in which data dimensions, uncertainty of the data, and data lineage are all first-class citizens. Combining data, uncertainty, and lineage yields a data management platform that is useful for data integration, data cleaning, and information extraction systems. They also look at data combination through regular SQL operations, and are more interested in objective IQ, not SIQ;
- **A data quality measurement information model:** Caballero, Verbo, Calero and Piattini (2007) propose a Data Quality Measurement Information Model (DQMIM), which provides a standardization of the referred terms by following ISO/IEC 15939 as a basis. They deal with the concepts implied in the measurement process, and not with the measures themselves. In order to make operative the DQMIM, the researchers have also introduced an XML schema, which can be employed to outline Data Quality Measurement Plans;
- **A framework for data quality evaluation in a data integration system:** Peralta, Ruggia, Kedad, and Bouzeghoub project (2004), addresses the problem of data quality evaluation in data integration systems. They present a framework, which is a first attempt to formalize the evaluation of data quality. It is based on a graph model of the data integration system, which allows them to define evaluation methods as graph properties. In their project they only focus on data freshness and currency dimension;

- **Estimating the quality of data in relational databases:** Motro and Rakov (1996) propose a standard for rating information sources with respect to their quality. An important consideration is that the quality of information sources often varies considerably when specific areas within these sources are considered. They describe an approach that uses dual quality measures to gauge the distance of the information in a database from the truth, and propose to combine manual verification with statistical methods to arrive at useful estimates of the quality of databases. Motro and Rakov show how to derive quality estimates for individual queries from such quality specifications. In their project they focus only on two dimensions: accuracy and completeness;
- **Sample-based quality estimation of query results in relational database environments:** The approach in Ballou, Chengalur-Smith, and Wang (2006) provides a basis for the systematic analysis of the quality of information products (IPs). Their research uses the relational algebra framework to develop estimates for the quality of query results based on the quality estimates of samples taken from the base tables. Their procedure requires an initial sample from the base tables; these samples are then used for all possible information IPs. Each specific query governs the quality assessment of the relevant samples. By using the same sample repeatedly, their approach is relatively cost effective. They examine various, relevant statistical issues, including how to deal with the impact on quality of missing rows in base tables. They do not discuss any data quality dimensions; instead they measure the quality based on a specified condition, whether acceptable or not acceptable. Their work assumes the quality of the data is not known.

APPROACH

The problems of unclear and slow estimation and evaluation of subjective information quality measures will be addresses in two parts: 1) rules and principles derived from SIQ studies and best practices, and 2) user-centered evaluation of Subjective Information Quality. The chapter also has a part describing how subjective information quality can be adapted to the study of research similar to signaling theory and the market for lemons.

Our work included extensive studies of three quality dimensions: accuracy, believability, and value-added. Accuracy is defined as the extent to which information is correct and reliable (Pipino, Lee, & Wang, 2002). Believability is defined as the extent to which information is regarded as true and credible and the value-added dimension is defined as the extent to which information is beneficial and provides advantages for its use. The reason for focusing on these three dimensions is that each has a different blend of assessment methods. Accuracy can be measured through objective methods, in addition to subjective methods. Believability is mainly a subjective dimension, although there are potential mathematical models for belief, which may or may not be applicable to believability. Value-added tends to be mostly a SIQ dimension with little mathematical background in computing a metric. This will provide a wide range of different dimension options to help develop an understanding of how the SIQ dimensions interact with each other. These three dimensions are interrelated due to the nature of subjective information quality, which resides at the intersection between human and computers.

To determine how people perceive the SIQ dimension and their characteristics, different information sets from multiple information sources are assessed through empirical evaluations of how SIQ is regarded by users. We rely on information sets with already known quality, such as average temperatures in the United States, lab data on gold nanoparticles infused in bone cells, and economics information such as budget data. The information used is available and easily estimated by an average person living in the US for at least one SIQ dimension. The information sets are modified in different percentages and scenarios and presented to the user to determine how people can perceive small information quality variations. Also, the idea of how human actors discover different characteristics of the SIQ dimensions will be evaluated. The experimental work will help in understanding the characteristics of the SIQ, the sensitivity of people's perception of information quality, and possible subjective information quality thresholds.

Limitation and Methods

This chapter is limited on information integration operations that can be easily understood by a human and delimits those computer functions such as SQL queries that are too complex to be understood and interactively manipulated by people. The operations considered in our work are intended for use with visual representations, and as such, the complexity of these operations is limited by what people can perceive. Very complex operations, such as those that can only be handled by a machine, are beyond the scope of this work, primarily because the quality of the information integration may be highly nondeterministic and difficult to interpret and estimate by a human.

SUBJECTIVE INFORMATION QUALITY ASSESSMENT PRINCIPLES

The first set of principles presented here are a direct result of the experimental work in SIQ, while the second one is based on best practices. Following similar fields of science that depend on human behavior, such as psychology or human-computer interface, we distill our findings into a set of principles. For each task, an IQ professional would need to determine how these principles can be incorporated into the SIQ assessment particular to the data types and end-users:

People rely on a limited number of heuristic principles which reduce the complex tasks of assessing probabilities and predicting values to simpler judgmental operations. (Kahneman & Tversky, 1972; Tversky & Kahneman, 1973)

1. Information integration does not necessarily improve the perceived accuracy:
   a. Adding high quality information to existing data does not help people estimate the overall accuracy better;
   b. Low-quality information integrated with target data helps people better estimate accuracy.

Our findings show that, for a temperature map integration, visualizations with single maps perform better than other types of visualizations, although no significant difference was found, on any of the dependent variables, between single-map and double maps in which one of the panels has poor accuracy. Moreover, users seem to perform better with additional inaccurate information than with completely accurate one:

2. Believability can suffer from an intrinsic bias.

The results show that when presented with a choice of two tasks, users prefer (or are biased) for one of them, and consequently, seem to be biased against the other task. Most people, under most conditions, and without being to check accuracy believed in the same task.

Cognitive psychology and cognitive bias in psychology will help with the assessment of SIQ. Consider the answer to the following questions:

Why people think that almost accurate visualizations are worse than the ones that have 12% errors?

Why most people are confident in their answers?

Why the image seems to inspire more confidence then text?

Cognitive bias is a general concept that covers many distortions created in the human mind that are not easy to eliminate, which can lead to illogical reasoning, flawed judgment, or skewed perceptions. Many of these biases are studied for how they affect belief formation, business decisions, and scientific research. The main biases types that are related and apply to our results are: anchoring, attentional bias, confirmation bias, selective perception, and subjective validation.

Anchoring is one of the cognitive bias types that describes the common human tendency to rely too much on one point of view or piece of information when making decisions. During normal decision-making, anchoring occurs when individuals overly rely on a specific piece of information to govern their thought-process.

Attentional bias (Bar-Haim, Lamy, Pergamin, Bakermans-Kranenburg, & van IJzendoorn, 2007; Schoth & Liossi, 2010) is another type of cognitive bias, occurs due to a lack of focus. One example is when a person does not examine all possible outcomes when making a judgment about a correlation or association. They may focus on one or two possibilities, while ignoring the rest.

Confirmation bias is the cognitive bias type that shows the people's tendency to favor information that confirms their preconceptions or hypotheses regardless of whether the information is true. Selective perception encompasses a number of cognitive biases related to the way expectations affect perception. It is possible for people to feel drunk, for example, just because they thought they were consuming an alcoholic beverage. The result is also seen in the medical field in the form of the placebo effect:

3. Accuracy, believability, and value-added are not always interrelated dimensions.

It is entirely possible for some pieces of information to be believable but not necessary to be accurate or add value to a specific task. When the information is accurate and adds value to the targeted task, then the information becomes trusted and believed and the interrelationship between these dimensions is achieved and become significant:

4. Subjective Information quality is task and data dependent.

This principle stems from the nature of the human and problem factor, and it suggests that an IQ professional will have to sample some typical data integration tasks that are common with their data consumers. Based on the findings regarding bias and perception of accuracy, the IQ professional can develop a simple linear and threshold- based formula to estimate SIQ. This formula can then be automatically computed when users demand data to be integrated from various sources.

Other Useful Principles for Improving IQ

5. It's better to be approximately right than exactly wrong;
6. Know your task and goals;
7. Do not judge data based on your personal beliefs.

Many decisions are based on beliefs (Kahneman & Tversky, 1972; Tversky & Kahneman, 1973). It is not always true that the believable information to be accurate or add value to a specific task.

8. The accurate information for the right task increases the value of the information and increases the believability specific task;
9. Use your logic effectively.

If the analysis is overcomplicated, it may lead to an overload. The best approach to simplify is to understand and estimate the quality of what is presented:

- Start with the known points and proceed to the unknown ones in logical order;
- Look at the data as whole then at parts of it and back to the whole, linking a particular point to the general points available logically;
- Always starts with the simple points and proceed to the more complex points to help gradually build assumption.

We then move on to the last few principles:

10. Divide task.

To make better estimate the data quality, one should specify each individual dimension to be assessed:

11. Look at the combined data.

Look at the combined data and check the following variables or ask the following questions:

- Is the amount of information sufficient for the specified task?
- If the answer is no, then add more data, and look again;
- Is the data is relevant to the specified task?
- Is the data meaningful?
- Is the data logically accepted?
- Is the data true and reliable for the specified task?
- Is the data true and credible for the specified task?
- Is the data beneficial for the specified task?

Finally:

12. Revise assessment and refine results as you combine data.

EVALUTION OF SUBJECTIVE INFORMATION QUALITY

This section provides a scientific foundation for the principles presented in the previous section. Highlights from three experiments are described below to provide the reader with a broad picture of how the scientific method can be applied to determine people's perception of SIQ. The section does not explore all the minutiae of the experiments, as they are detailed in other scholarly articles listed in the Additional Reading section.

Perception of Accuracy

An experiment to determine how end-users perceive accuracy is outlined below. Accuracy is an interesting IQ dimension in that it can be assessed both via exact, algorithmic methods and through subjective judgment. Exact accuracy, for example, can be achieved when one checks the accuracy of transaction data against the balance of a bank account, and subjective accuracy is employed in the estimation of the amount of oil being spilled into the ocean from a deep-water oil rig.

The experiment sought to uncover how subjective rating varies with actual data quality, and how additional information supports better assessment. An orthogonal issue is data integration. Decision makers, experts, and regular users often have to combine information from different sources to get a unified view of the information, or to help guide decisions on larger amounts of information from various sources. This process has become significant in a variety of situations both commercial and scientific. Combining data has become increasingly important as organizations strive to integrate an increasing quantity of internal and external information. Users must combine data for a variety of reasons. Some of those reasons are:

- To have more attributes;
- To get more detailed information for an attribute or item for different purposes and cases; or
- Users cannot find an answer or a solution from a single dataset or data source.

Our results are based on a study on the perceived accuracy of weather data in the United States. The study employed data that can be easily judged by an average person living in the US. The data was obtained from the National Oceanic and Atmospheric Administration's (NOAA) website, and presented that data through well-established visual representations. The investigators introduced a controlled amount of error in each visualization. Participants did not know the exact percentage of error introduced and were asked to estimate the visualization's overall accuracy. The study also examined the effect of data integration by including visualizations with two panels, each conveying complementary weather data for winter and summer. The same amount of controlled error was thus presented to participants both as a single-panel and as double-panel visualizations. The additional panel itself also had the accuracy controlled and varied from completely accurate to fifty percent errors.

The study results showed that estimated accuracy is non-linear as a function of the actual accuracy, and that data integration may not always help users. Participants did not make constant estimation errors, nor did their estimation error increased or decreased with the actual accuracy. Multiple peaks and valleys are apparent in Figure 2, which suggests that people may not be able to distinguish between certain levels of accuracy, and that certain thresholds make accuracy estimation easier for a given number of actual error levels. The actual accuracy was found to be a statistically significant factor that determine the level of errors made by the user ($p = 0.0192$).

With regard to data integration, the study found that introducing additional, error-free data, such as temperatures for summer in addition to those for winter, resulted in worse accuracy assessment than additional data with error. For this weather data set, we found the counterintuitive result that single datasets (for example winter only) are bet-

Figure 2. Average of the percent of user error as a function of the actual accuracy level of the data

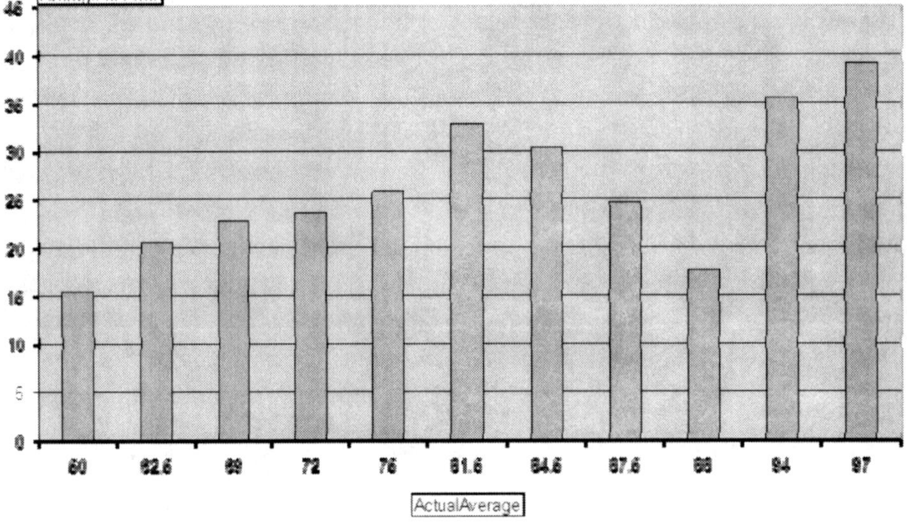

ter estimated than datasets with double the amount of information (winter and summer) as shown in Figure 3. This additional information was found to be a statistically significant factor that determined the level of errors the users make ($p = 0.0004$).

No significant difference was found, on any of the dependent variables, between single-map and double maps in which one of the panels is 50% accurate. It appears that, for this task, users perform better with additional inaccurate information than with completely accurate one. This behavior would be difficult to incorporate in a statistical model for data integration. It may be that various thresholds may exist for when users are able to best use additional information.

Perception of Believability

Believability, defined as the extent to which information is true and credible (Pipino, Lee, & Wang, 2002), is one of the major information quality dimensions that play a role in the operational fitness and sound decision making. We discuss an empirical evaluation of how people perceive data shown through visual and textual representations. The experiment covered the variation of the subjective rating of believability as a function of the different pieces of information displayed and the role of additional information in the assessment of believability.

Our results are based on a study that has the concentration of gold particles added to the bone cells as a substrate. The study employed data that can be easily read by an average person. The data was obtained from the Nanotechnology Center at University of Arkansas at Little Rock. The investigators introduced two types of data: lab notes (textual) and microscopy (image). The study assessed the believability of each type of data as well as the believability of the integration of text and image.

Believability was assessed with regard to two different concentrations of gold particles. Participants were asked to express their belief that the presented data was of a given concentration. The design of the study surreptitiously forced participants to provide their opinion based solely on belief because scientists could not determine any difference in results between the two concentrations. Thus, believability was measured alone without interference from other IQ dimensions, more importantly accuracy, which can skew the results for believability when people tend to not

Figure 3. The percentage of error made by the user in estimating the accuracy of single and double map visualizations

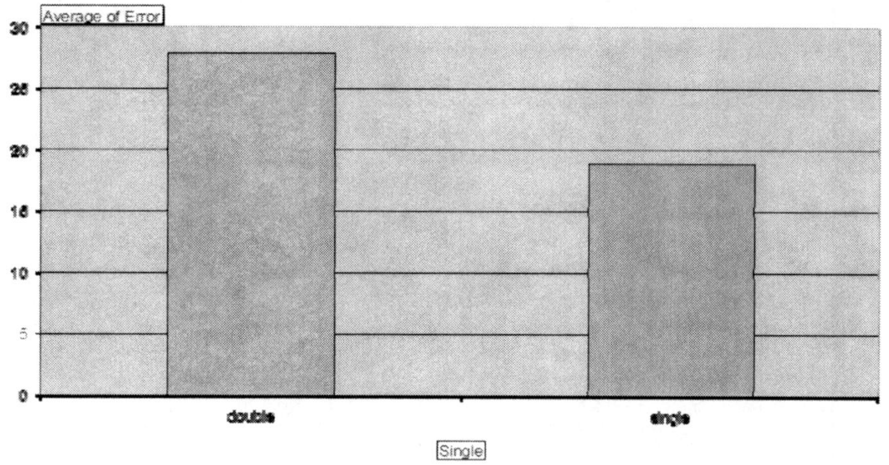

believe data that appears inaccurate. Note that choosing experts for the study would result in them validating accuracy rather than believability because experts already use and trust these visual tools and lab notes.

The study revealed that believability varies with the type of data source (image, text, or both), and that it behaves differently for each task as shown in Figure 4. An ANOVA revealed that source, image, text, or both, is a significant factor for believed concentration ($p = 0.0516$).A Tukey pairwise comparison found significant differences between image and both ($p = 0.0398$). As expected, actual concentration is not a statistically significant factor.

The results show a user preference (or bias) for one of the tasks, specifically a gold particle concentration of 160 μg/ml task, and consequently a bias against the 10 μg/ml task. Figure 4 show that most people and under most conditions believed the concentration to be 160 μg/ml. Believability was task dependent in our experiment, which may make automated estimation of this dimension a complicated endeavor. A different behavior of believability assessment is observed for the two tasks, none of them being simple averaging. The combination of the two datasets seems to affect slightly negatively the combination of text and images for the preferred task (160 μg/ml), while for the biased-against task (10 μg/ml) the combination improves the level of believability when compared to either image or text.

Most people are confident in their answers, which translates into them being confident in their belief. Image seems to inspire more confidence then text. For confidence, the combination of image and text produces a result that is about the average of the individual confidence levels. Figure 5 illustrates the collected data.

Estimating Value-Added

Value added refers to "extra" feature(s) of an item of interest (product, service, person, etc.) that go beyond the standard expectations and provide something "more" while adding little or nothing to its cost. Each industry has its own definition of value-added. The definition of value-added varies in accounting, economics, marketing or educa-

Figure 4. User believability in the two gold particle concentrations. The information is broken down by data source type and believed concentration (10 μg/ml or 160 μg/ml). The y-axis shows the number of answers who believed in a given concentration.

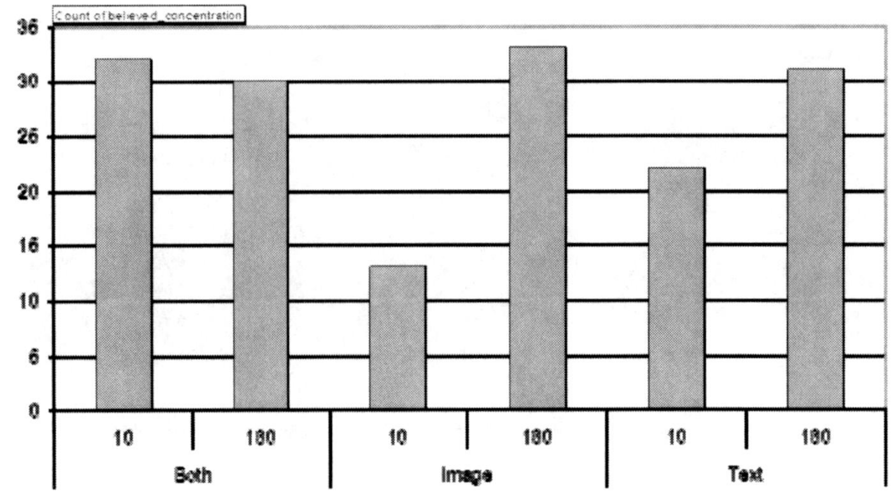

Figure 5. Average rating of users' confidence in their answers broken down by source type and believed concentration (10 µg/ml or 160 µg/ml). Note than 1 for user rating means "Not confident at all", 2 means "Somewhat not confident", 3 "Neutral", 4 represents "Confident", and 5 represents "Very Confident".

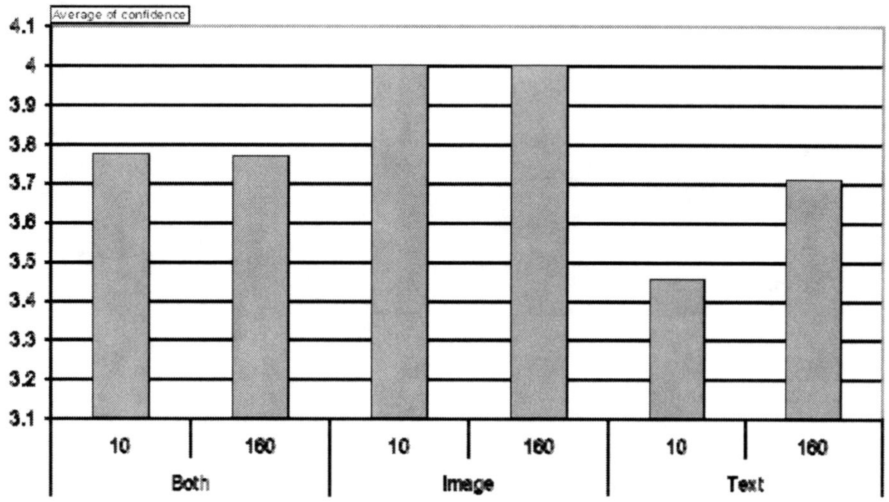

tion. The value-added of information is defined as the extent to which information is beneficial and provides advantage from its use (Pipino, Lee, & Wang, 2002) and it is one of the information quality (IQ) dimensions that can be best assessed through subjective, empirical means rather than through algorithmic means.

The experiment described next is an empirical evaluation of how people perceive the value-added of data shown through visual representations. Single and composite visualizations are shown to users and they are asked to provide value-added for a given task. The aspects of SIQ covered in this experiment include how subjective rating varies with different data categories displayed, and how additional information influences the assessment of value-added. Our approach was to divide two sets of data in two components, and to keep two parts anonymous as Budgets A and B, then ask the participants to recreate the two data sets. The visualizations represent competing U.S. budgets, with party affiliation replaced by two neutral names: John and Mary. The study employed data that can be easily judged by an average person. The data was obtained from the Office of Management and Budget (OMB, 2011), and one political candidate's web proposal (Genuine, 2011). The study assessed the value-added of each visualization part as well as the value-added of the integration of the different parts. The value-added is determined by amount of dollars the participants would pay for one of the selected visualization parts. The participants did not have to actually spend the selected sum money, only to indicate which amount seems appropriate.

The study revealed that value-added varies with the information parts displayed, and that it behaves differently for each task. Users assessed themselves as being neutral to confident in their results, with the combined data scoring the lowest, and single data (John's budget) scoring the highest.

As shown in Figures 6 and 7, the value-added of Budget A is the lowest when participants were presented with combined visualizations. More answers selected Budget B for Mary's budget condition than for John's budget or combined. The value-added of Budget B is high in the combined and John's budget condition, while the value-added of Budget B is the lowest in Mary's budget condition, and thus showing combined information

Figure 6. Average value-added of Budget A broken down by budget originator

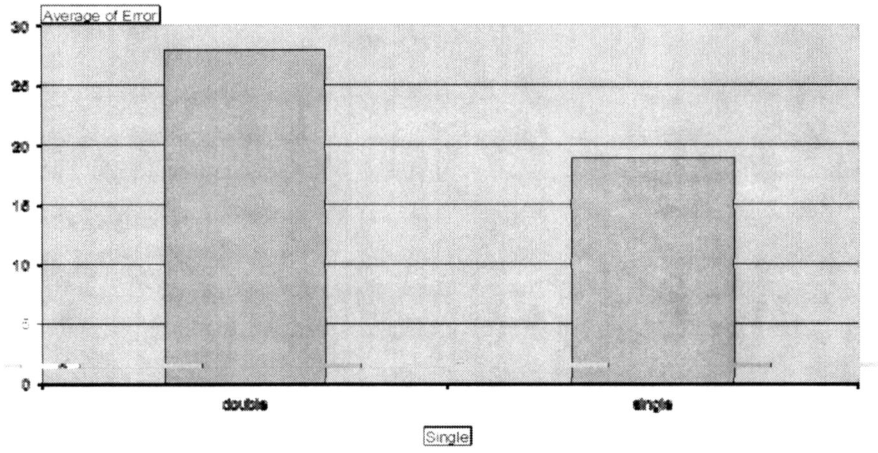

Figure 7. Average value-added of Budget B broken down by budget originator

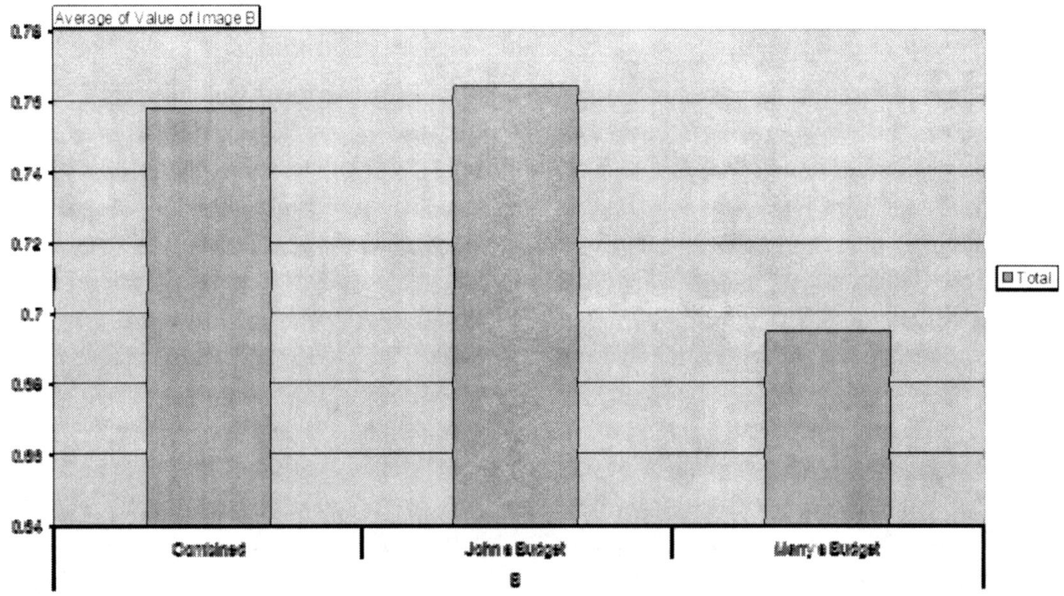

does not necessarily improve the overall subjective assessment of value-added.

The results show the, when users were asked to match Budget A or B to either John or Mary, a preference (or bias) for Budget A was recorded in the combined condition. The bias with Budget B is for Mary's budget. Further research is needed to better explain the existence of this kind of biases.

Value-added was task dependent in our experiment, which may make automated estimation of this dimension a complicated endeavor. A different behavior of value-added assessment is observed for all tasks, though none of them is simple averaging. The combination of the two datasets/images seems to affect slightly negatively the combination of data/images for the preferred Budget B; while for Budget A the combination negatively affect the level of value-added when compared to either John's budget or Mary's budget.

POTENTIAL APPLICATION OF SUBJECTIVE IQ

The research into subjective information quality would help answer some of the introductory questions of the signaling theory by Michael Spence (1973, 2002). The signaling theory has been presented as a solution to the problem of adverse selection (Polborn, Hoy, & Sadanand, 2006; Dionne, Gouriéroux, & Vanasse, 2001) presented by George Akerlof's "The Market for Lemons" chapter (Akerlof, 1970), which brought informational issues at the vanguard of economic theory.

Lemon Market effects have also been noted in other markets. The Information Market is among those markets where Information Asymmetry is present, and data provenance can be from different sources with possibly unknown quality:

Studies of signaling theory often examine the quality of the signaler (source of information). Future research would benefit from examining in more depth the various qualities signaled and more carefully linking the signals used to measure these qualities. At its essence, the link between a signal and the underlying quality represents a measurement issue that we call signal fit. (Connelly, Certo, Ireland, & Reutzel, 2011)

Signaling theory examines the quality based on the reputation of the information source, so the quality is assumed to be known based on the signal, which is similar with this chapter because various aspects of information's quality are studied:

The usefulness of a signal to the receiver depends on the extent to which the signal corresponds with the sought-after quality of the signaler (i.e., referred to as signal fit) and the extent to which signalers attempt to deceive (i.e., average honesty). Since both are required, some scholars define this combination as signal reliability, other scholars use the term credibility to describe the same notion, the extent to which the signaler is honest and the signal corresponds with signaler quality. (Davila, Foster, & Gupta, 2003)

There is common confusion between signal fit, honesty, reliability, and related terms, often using them interchangeably, but research into SIQ may help clarify their distinct underlying concepts of the signal fit as the three dimensions of SIQ that were studied here: believability, accuracy, and value-added. Our research could be linked to the signaling theory, especially if the signal are sent and received visually. The information provided through visualizations and the visualization itself will be the signal to a specific goal/task. The principles provided in this dissertation will help the receiver of the information visually to discover the quality of the signal veracity. Our work will help in understanding the characteristics of the SIQ of the signal (information), the sensitivity of people's perception of (Signal) Information Quality, and possible Subjective Information Quality thresholds. If the signals (information) provided are implausible or far from reality the signaling equilibrium will break down.

The research into subjective information quality would also help and support the Technology Acceptance Model (Davis 1989; Chuttur 2009). The Technology Acceptance Model (TAM) is a theory originating from the area of information systems, which analyzes and models the acceptance of technology by end-users. According to TAM, end-users decide how and when to use new technology based on two gate factors:

- **Perceived usefulness (PU):** This was defined by Davis (1989) as "the degree to which a person believes that using a particular system would enhance his or her job performance;"

- **Perceived ease-of-use (PEOU):** "The degree to which a person believes that using a particular system would be free from effort."

These factors could significantly be attributed to subjective information quality (SIQ) as well, and may help and support SIQ assessment. The research outcomes (techniques, rules) can be also used to expand the TAM to adopt new factors such as perceived accuracy, perceived believability, and perceived value added, which will support and interact with two the other existing factors (perceived usefulness, perceived ease of use).

CONCLUSION

Our work on subjective information quality resulted in experimental results about how people perceive IQ and combinations of information with various levels of quality. The chapter also presented a set of principles to facilitate more precise estimation of SIQ. The principles can be employed to derive rules, which are subsequently used to estimate these quality dimensions and present them to a user. Our data substrate for the end-user was visualizations that convey information. The computed SIQ measure could be represented through visual representations in order to allow a better, more intuitive, means of communicating the information quality to users.

FUTURE WORK

Assessing information quality is not an easy task and requires knowledge and awareness of the subjective and objective information quality metrics. Further studies may focus on additional tasks to better understand the existence of preferences for and biases against tasks. Such investigations may also need to be determined for other data types and data presentation methods.

Subjective assessment is not limited to accuracy, believability and value added, and our plans are to consider other SIQ dimensions and verify whether their behavior is similar to the subjective accuracy. Other dimensions that are inherently subjective, such as reputation, may lead to the development of a more complete theory of SIQ.

Any theory of SIQ may need to also consider the effect of data integration, an important topic in information and data quality. This chapter also showed that combining information or adding extra information is not always beneficial. Furthermore, for the cases when additional data is included, lower quality data may provide better support for subjective evaluation than higher quality data.

REFERENCES

Akerlof, G. A. (1970). The market for lemons: Quality uncertainty and the market mechanism. *The Quarterly Journal of Economics*, *84*(3), 488–500. doi:10.2307/1879431

Ballou, D. P., Chengalur-Smith, I. N., & Wang, R. Y. (2006). Sample-based quality estimation of query results in relational database environments. *IEEE Transactions on Knowledge and Data Engineering*, *18*(5), 639–650. doi:10.1109/TKDE.2006.83

Bar-Haim, Y., Lamy, D., Pergamin, L., Bakermans-Kranenburg, M. J., & van IJzendoorn, M. H. (2007). Threat-related attentional bias in anxious and nonanxious individuals: A meta-analytic study. *Psychological Bulletin*, *133*(1), 1–24. doi:10.1037/0033-2909.133.1.1 PMID:17201568

Bobrowski, M., Marre, M., & Yankelevich, D. (1999). A homogeneous framework to measure data quality. In *Proceedings of the 4th International Conference on Information Quality*, (pp. 115-124). IEEE.

Caballero, I., Verbo, E., Calero, C., & Piattini, M. (2007). A data quality measurement information model based on iso/iec 15939. In *Proceedings of the 12th International Conference on Information Quality* (pp. 393-408). IEEE.

Chuttur, M. Y. (2009). Overview of the technology acceptance model: Origins, developments and future directions, Indiana University, USA. *Sprouts: Working Papers on Information Systems, 9*(37).

Cohen, B. D., & Dean, T. J. (2005). Information asymmetry and investor valuation of IPOs: Top management team legitimacy as a capital market signal. *Strategic Management Journal, 26*(7), 683–690. doi:10.1002/smj.463

Connelly, B. L., Certo, S. T., Ireland, R. D., & Reutzel, C. R. (2011). Signaling theory: A review and assessment. *Journal of Management, 37*(1), 39–67. doi:10.1177/0149206310388419

Davis, F. (1989). Perceived usefulness, perceived ease of use, and user acceptance of information technology. *Management Information Systems Quarterly, 13*(3), 319–340. doi:10.2307/249008

Genuine, M. (2011). *Miller's genuine draft*. Retrieved April 20,2011, from http://millergd.blogspot.com/2011/04/interactive-chart-on-ryan-budget-vs.html

Hoffer, G. E., & Pratt, M. D. (1987). Used vehicles, lemons markets, and used car rules: Some empirical evidence. *Journal of Consumer Policy, 10*(4), 409–414. doi:10.1007/BF00411482

Huerta, E., & Ryan, T. (2003). *The credibility of online information*. (Doctoral dissertation). Claremont Graduate University.

Kahneman, D., & Tversky, A. (1972). Subjective probability: A judgment of representativeness. *Cognitive Psychology, 3*(3), 430–454. doi:10.1016/0010-0285(72)90016-3

Klein, B. D. (2001). User perception of data quality: Internet and traditional text sources. *Journal of Computer Information Systems, 41*(4), 9–15.

Klein, B. D. (2002). Internet data quality: Perceptions of graduate and undergraduate business student. *Journal of Business and Management, 8*(4), 425–432.

Lee, Y. W., Strong, D. M., Kahn, B. K., & Wang, R. Y. (2002). AIMQ: A methodology for information quality assessment. *Information & Management, 40*(2), 133–146. doi:10.1016/S0378-7206(02)00043-5

Lin, M. O., & Hua, Z. (2008). A method for measuring data quality in data integration. In *Proceedings of International Seminar on Future Information Technology and Management Engineering*. FITME.

Motro, A., & Rakov, I. (1996). Estimating the quality of data in relational databases. In *Proceedings of the 1st International Conference on Information Quality*. Retrieved from http://mitiq.mit.edu/ICIQ/Documents/IQ%20Conference%201996/Papers/EstimatingtheQualityofDatainRelationalDb.pdf

OMB. (2011). Retrieved June 10, 2011, from http://www.whitehouse.gov/omb/

Peralta, V., Ruggia, R., Kedad, Z., & Bouzeghoub, M. (2004). A framework for data quality evaluation in a data integration system. In *Proceedings of the 19th Brazilian Symposium on Databases*. SBBD.

Petty, R. E., & Cacioppo, J. T. (1986). The elaboration likelihood model of persuasion. *Advances in Experimental Social Psychology, 19*, 123–205. doi:10.1016/S0065-2601(08)60214-2

Pipino, L. L., Lee, Y. W., & Wang, R. Y. (2002). Data quality assessment. *Communications of the ACM,45*(4),211–218.doi:10.1145/505248.506010

Polborn, M. K., Hoy, M., & Sadanand, A. (2006). Advantageous effects of regulatory adverse selection in the life insurance market. *The Economic Journal*, *116*(508), 327–354. doi:10.1111/j.1468-0297.2006.01059.x

Prat, N., & Madnick, S. (2008). Measuring data believability: A provenance approach. In *Proceedings of the 41st Annual Hawaii International Conference on System Sciences*, (pp. 393-402). IEEE.

Schoth, D. E., & Liossi, C. (2010). Attentional bias toward pictorial representations of pain in individuals with chronic headache. *The Clinical Journal of Pain*, *26*(3), 244. doi:10.1097/AJP.0b013e3181bed0f9 PMID:20173439

Spence, M. (1973). Job market signaling. *The Quarterly Journal of Economics*, *87*(3), 355–374. doi:10.2307/1882010

Spence, M. (2002). Signaling in retrospect and the informational structure of markets. *The American Economic Review*, 434–459. doi:10.1257/00028280260136200

Stanford Entity Resolution Framework. (2010). Retrieved May 15, 2010, from http://infolab.stanford.edu/serf/

Stanford Trio Project. (2010). Retrieved May 15, 2010, from http://infolab.stanford.edu/Trio

Tayi, G. K., & Ballou, D. P. (1998). Examining data quality. *Communications of the ACM*, *41*(2), 54–57. doi:10.1145/269012.269021

Tversky, A., & Kahneman, D. (1973). Availability: A heuristic for judging frequency and probability. *Cognitive Psychology*, *5*(2), 207–232. doi:10.1016/0010-0285(73)90033-9

Wand, Y., & Wang, R. Y. (1996). Anchoring data quality dimensions in ontological foundations. *Communications of the ACM*, *39*(11), 86–95. doi:10.1145/240455.240479

Wang, R. Y., & Strong, D. M. (1996). Beyond accuracy: What data quality means to data consumers. *Journal of Management Information Systems*, *12*(4), 5–34.

ADDITIONAL READING

Abuhalimeh, A., & Tudoreanu, M. E. (2011). Subjective Evaluation of Value-Added in Visualization of Data. SigIQ workshop in Shanghai, China.

Abuhalimeh, A., Tudoreanu, M. E., & Mustafa, E. (2011). Subjective Evaluation of Beliebvability in Visualization of Data. In Proceedings ICIQ Conference (Adelaide, Australia). (pp. 112-123). Proceedings ICIQ Conference (Adelaide, Australia). pp. 267-276.

Abuhalimeh, A., Tudoreanu, M. E., & Peterson, E. (2010). Subjective Evaluation of Perception of Accuracy in Visualization of Data. In Proceedings ICIQ Conference (Little Rock, AR) (pp. 112-123). Proceedings ICIQ Conference (Little Rock, AR), pp. 112-123.

KEY TERMS AND DEFINITIONS

Accuracy: The extent to which data is correct and reliable. One of the three IQ dimensions which was analyzed both from an absolute and SIQ perspective.

Believability: The extent to which data is regarded as true and credible. One of the studied SIQ dimensions.

Information Quality (IQ): The fitness for use of the information provided.

Information Quality Integration: Determining the quality of information that is obtained from performing various operations on data stemming from multiple sources. The assumption is that individual sources have a known quality.

Subjective IQ (SIQ): The quality that typically requires a user's opinion and do not have a clear mathematical technique for finding their value.

Value Added: The extent to which data is beneficial and provides advantages from its use. One of SIQ dimension analyzed in this chapter.

Visual Analytics: is the integration of interactive visualization with analysis techniques to answer a growing range of questions in science, business, and intelligence.

Visualization: The translation of information into a visible form that highlights important features, including commonalities and anomalies.

Chapter 4
A Case Study on Data Quality, Privacy, and Entity Resolution

William Decker
University of Arkansas – Little Rock, USA

John Talburt
University of Arkansas – Little Rock, USA

Fan Liu
University of Arkansas – Little Rock, USA

Pei Wang
University of Arkansas – Little Rock, USA

Ningning Wu
University of Arkansas – Little Rock, USA

ABSTRACT

This chapter presents ongoing research conducted through collaboration between the University of Arkansas at Little Rock and the Arkansas Department of Education to develop an entity resolution and identity management system. The process includes a multi-phase approach consisting of data-quality analysis, selection of entity-identity attributes for entity resolution, development of a truth-set, and implementation and benchmarking of an entity-resolution rule set using the open source entity-resolution system named OYSTER. The research is the first known of its kind to evaluate privacy-enhancing, entity-resolution rule sets in a state education agency.

INTRODUCTION

Pending regulation and recent funding opportunities present a unique opportunity to evaluate data housed in academic organizations and to improve processes and frameworks through which data systems may be improved. Research yields a number of instances where student academic data has been breached: one institution had records for 40,000 students compromised in 2010 (University of Hawaii, 2010); another institution reported Social Security numbers (SSNs), along with confidential student academic records, were breached for 21,000 students (Miami University, 2005).

Research for an entity resolution (ER) framework, which relies less on confidential student data, is described in this case study. This approach is characterized as context-sensitive, as it utilizes data elements considered "directory information." In this approach, we define directory information as data attributes about a student that can be

DOI: 10.4018/978-1-4666-4892-0.ch004

made legally public. In the United States (U.S.) education system, this is regulated by the Family Educational Rights and Privacy Act (FERPA) under the U.S. Department of Education. FERPA-based identity attributes can utilize information commonly published in telephone directories and might include attributes such as student name, address, telephone, date of birth, field of study, and grade-level, among other low-risk identifiers.

Motivated by these challenges, research is described in this case study to accomplish three primary research objectives: 1) data quality analysis of educational data; 2) development of a truth set and a privacy-preserving entity resolution (ER) framework; and 3) a quantitative evaluation of the ER framework's value. The work is motivated by both ongoing challenges inherit in academic databases and the requirement to correctly resolve student records while preserving the privacy of student data.

BACKGROUND

Public elementary and secondary schools had 49.4 million students enrolled in the 2009-10 school year (Institute of Education Sciences, 2011). In the same year, approximately 21.5 million students were enrolled in public post-secondary schools. Institutions receiving public funds from the U.S. Department of Education (USDOE) are subject to the FERPA (20 U.S.C. § 1232g; 34 CFR Part 99). FERPA is administered by the Family Policy Compliance Office of the U.S. Department of Education.

Under the precept of better decisions require better information, significant resources were provided to develop databases that house educational data and empower educators with data-driven decision-making capabilities. This is evidenced through the USDOE's award of four rounds of statewide longitudinal data system (SLDS) grants to U.S. states in 2006, 2007 and 2009 (two rounds were issued in 2009). Forty-one states and the District of Columbia received at least one grant to build a statewide longitudinal data system (Institute of Education Sciences, 2011). These systems were built in order to "efficiently and accurately manage, analyze, and use education data, including individual student records" (Institute of Education Sciences, 2011).

One need not extensively search to find evidence of student privacy breaches. In 2005, a former University of Texas at Austin student was found guilty of hacking the university system and "illegally possessing almost 40,000 Social Security numbers" (Associated Press, 2005). In October 2010, the University of Hawaii-West Oahu released a statement notifying approximately 40,000 individuals that their personal information may have been compromised (University of Hawaii, 2010). In September 2012, Miami University reported, "a grade report from the fall 2002 semester had been unwittingly placed by a now-retired faculty member into a file that was accessible via the Internet. The report included the Social Security numbers and grade information on the more than 21,000 students" (Miami University, 2005). In a 2006 issue of EDUCAUSE Review, it was reported that colleges and universities accounted for more than one-third of the publicly reported information security breaches in 2005 and the first half of 2006, yet colleges and universities provide insufficient training in privacy and security issues (Cate, 2006).

In an effort to help address these challenges, the Arkansas Department of Education (ADE) started collaborations with the Center for Advanced Research in Entity Resolution and Information Quality (ERIQ) at the University of Arkansas at Little Rock (UALR) in 2010. The OYSTER Open Source Project, which was first used as a tool for teaching entity resolution at UALR, was initially supported by much of this work with the ADE. OYSTER has since developed into a platform capable of supporting record linking, entity identity information management and master data management processes in small to medium-sized organizations (OYSTER Entity Resolution, 2013).

Related Research

A review of related research demonstrated ER tools often rely upon high-risk personal information to determine whether multiple references to an individual refer to the same individual or to different individuals. The rampant growth in the collection of personal identity information (PII) by educational agencies in the U.S. has increased the reliance on self-submitted reference data from educational institutions, namely the Social Security number (SSN). It can be demonstrated that user-submitted SSNs are often erroneous and, in some cases, may be a poor quality entity identity reference attribute for correctly resolving student records. This poses information quality concerns for institutions and their stakeholders. Furthermore, the prevalence of SSNs in educational datasets has been documented as susceptible to misuse. Proposed changes in law, FERPA, and public concern over privacy suggests educational institutions must implement information quality approaches that mitigate privacy concerns while ensuring a high degree of information quality. This is the primary focus of this case study: an entity resolution framework that increases quality of data reporting for the ADE while simultaneously exploring ways to safeguard student privacy through use of directory data attributes.

This work builds upon the body of knowledge with regard to both information quality and entity resolution, particularly as applied in the context of privacy in educational records, and is applicable in other domains where "low-risk" data is desired in ER rule sets.

Information quality is a survival issue for both public and private sectors (MIT Information Quality Program, 2011). The discipline has matured over the last two decades, primarily from the data quality concepts of Total Data Quality Management (TDQM) and the Deming Cycle (Lee, Pierce, Talburt, & Wang, 2007). The International Conference on Information Quality, held at the Massachusetts Institute of Technology, has advanced this field of research. Information quality is generally used to describe the quality of content in information systems and, more specifically, as the "fitness for use of the information provided" (Information Quality, 2012). Wang and Strong identified dimensions used in assessing quality and categorized them into four areas of information quality:

- **Intrinsic Information Quality:** Intrinsic IQ includes the elements of *believability* and *reputation*. These elements encompass more than the traditional dimensions of accuracy and objectivity;
- **Contextual Information Quality:** Contextual IQ refers to the concept that data quality must be considered within the environment in which the information is used. The dimensions of *completeness* and *timeliness* are examples of data quality dimensions within this area;
- **Representational Information Quality:** Representational IQ includes the aspects of data quality related to the *format* and the *meaning* of the data;
- **Accessibility Information Quality:** Wang and Strong found that information system professionals understand accessibility IQ well. Accessibility general describes the *access* and *security* measures. Particularly with the transition from traditional paper-based reports to online data, accessibility is thought to be a critical component of information quality.

A core concept in information quality practice is to manage information as a product (Wang, Lee, Pipino, & Strong, 1998). This approach can be compared to treating information as a by-product (Lee, Pipino, Funk, & Wang, 2006). Lee and others define an information product (IP) as "a collection of data element instances that meets the specified requirements of a data consumer." The authors envelop this concept into four principles: (1) understand the consumer's data needs; (2) manage information as the product of a formal production process; (3) manage information as a product within a life cycle; and (4) designate an information product manager (Lee, Pipino, Funk, & Wang, 2006).

ER, a closely related field to information quality, is defined as "the process of determining whether two references to real-world objects are referring to the same object or to different objects" (Talburt, 2011). Early research on ER began in the 1960s (Newcombe & Kennedy, 1962; Fellegi & Sunter, 1969; Tepping, 1968). Recent research on ER can be found at the Stanford University InfoLab, with specific regard to the Stanford Entity Resolution Framework (Stanford University, 2011), as well as the Center for Advanced Research in Entity Resolution and Information Quality (ERIQ) at the University of Arkansas at Little Rock (University of Arkansas at Little Rock, 2011). ER is a task shared by many disciplines but known by different names. Deduplication, data integration, heterogeneous database join, computer vision and record linkage are commonly used in the computer science domain. Common entity-resolution methods include "exact matching, merging, edit distance, Soundex, similarity matching, common string frequencies, and clustering" (Herzog et al, 2007), (Christen, 2013) (as cited in Holland, 2010, pg 8). A review demonstrates varying terminology used to describe the process and processes of ER. In *Entity Resolution and Information Quality*, ER is described in a larger context as encompassing five major activities (Talburt, 2011):

1. **Extraction:** This process involves locating and collecting entity-identity references from unstructured information;
2. **Preparation:** Preparation encompasses many subtasks, but commonly includes using profiling, standardizing, cleansing, and related data quality processes in order to prepare the data for entity resolution;
3. **Resolution:** The entity resolution step includes the process by which it is decided if two references are belong to the same set of attributes or to different attributes;
4. **Identity Management:** Identity management encompasses the processes necessary for building and maintaining a persistent record of entity-identity data throughout the ER life-cycle;
5. **Relationship Analysis:** Entity relationship analysis involves exploring the various associations among different, but related, entities. A common relationship explored is that of the *household*—an attempt to understand the individuals living at the same address. In this research, relationship analysis will be important when performing ER on students who have a twin enrolled in the public school system.

Organizations are often tasked with preserving data privacy while simultaneously ensuring utility of data. These can be daunting objectives, often at conflict. Therefore, the objective has to be "maximizing the utility of a data set while minimizing the risk of privacy loss due to the use of the data set" (Jagannatha, 2010). Jagannatha describes two categories of privacy models, perturbation and differenterial privacy. Pertubration models attempt to achieve data privacy through masking of data either upon input of data into a database or at data ouput through the addition of noise. Differential privacy models attempt to achieve privacy by masking data through the use of aggregate queries. Both privacy models relate to this case study but data is neither masked on input nor ouput, nor is noise added to anonomiyze the results. Rather, this aproach opts for data attributes based on critera sensitive to the context in which the data will be used, often at the direction of applicable govermental laws or policies.

Specifically, selection of data attributes permissiable as "directory information" under FERPA is utilized. Notably, this represents the omission of attributes such as SSN, student identification number, transcript records or grades and the use of directory information, such as name, address, phone number and email address, dates of attendance, degrees, enrollment status and other non-sensitive, low-risk entity identity attributes.

Privacy is considered an intrinsic dimension of information quality (Lee, Pipino, Funk, & Wang, 2006), as well as a fundamental right afforded to students in public educational institutions under FERPA (U.S. Department of Education, 2011). Privacy is an important element of any information system, particularly those containing PII. A study by the Fordham School of Law found that there was a "growing trend among state departments of education to establish statewide longitudinal databases of personally identifiable information for all K-12 children, within a state in order to track progress and change over time" (Reidenber & Debelak, 2009).

Outside of federal privacy laws, literature regarding privacy in academic databases is limited. A 2011 paper by David J. Meske used a theoretical framework to explore the current state of protecting information assets in the California public university systems. Meske found a discrepancy in privacy efforts between two- and four-year institutions and recommended a full-time person responsible for protecting PII (Meske, 2011).

Yinle Zhou described and defined entity identity information management (EIIM) and its relation to the Stanford Entity Resolution Framework (SERF). (Zhou, 2012) This case study utilizes the areas explored by Zhou, with regard to data structures and rule mapping strategies, to resolve longitudinal records that span multiple years. It builds on the research conducted by Zhou and Talburt by incorporating asserted resolution, the "use of a trusted information source which asserts or declare that references or identity structures are equivalent (or not equivalent)" (Zhou & Talburt, 2011). Nelson, et al. designed and constructed an ER system that supports EIIM and asserted resolution (Nelson, 2011). OYSTER is used as the primary software program to evaluated the ER rule set in this case study.

MAIN ISSUES

There are two center challenges presented with this work: 1) data quality, as it relates to identity reference attributes fit for ER; and 2) preserving privacy while ensuring sufficient identity data for accurate ER. A simple description of the problem is to be able to identify whether or not two different student identities relate to the same real-world student or to two different students. Consider, for example, the following scenarios. Note that these and all other examples of student data shown in this chapter are based on the content of real student records that have been altered to assure anonymity.

Scenario 1

Arman Jones, a ninth grader at Mariana East-Side High School, withdraws from school on October 1, 2010. He has a birthdate of September 15, 1995. He is home schooled for two years. On August 15, 2012, student records indicate a student named Armando Jones enrolled as an eleventh grader at Mariana West-Side High School. The student records also indicate that Armando Jones, also a male, has a birthdate of September 15, 1995. Is Arman Jones the same real-world student as Armando Jones?

Scenario 2

Student records indicate a student named Peirce Tyler, a male sixth grader, attends Prime Middle School, and has a birth date of April 15, 2002. Similarly, student records indicate that Pierce Tyler, a male sixth grader, also attends Prime Middle

School and has a birth date of April 15, 2002. Records for both Peirce Tyler and Pierce Tyler show similar academic performance, attendance and the guardian names. Is Peirce Tyler the same real-world person as Pierce Tyler?

Scenario 3

Student records indicate a student named Chris Jones, a male ninth grader, attends East-Side High School, and has a birth date of October 15, 1999. The mailing address for Chris Jones is listed as 101 East Capitol St., Wichita, Arkansas. Similarly, student records indicate that Chris Jones, a male ninth grader, also attends East-Side High School and has a birth date of October 5, 1999 and has a mailing address of 101 East Capitol St., Wichita, Arkansas. Is Chris Jones the same real-world student as Chris Jones?

Depending upon the entity identity-reference data quality, each of these scenarios can be difficult to resolve by computer. Our case study demonstrates the ability to solve these types of questions through use of ER algorithms. The research is particularly unique to the use of algorithms which rely on directory, or "low-risk" identity-reference data. These challenges will be explored more in the following sections.

Data Quality

Preliminary research is relevant and demonstrative of the challenge. It is a comprehensive data-quality assessment to understand the fitness of use of commonly used record identifiers, including student ID, SSN, first name, middle name, last name, date of birth and related entity-identity attributes. The data- quality analysis is described in detail in subsequent sections but an opportunity is made here to illustrate the data quality of user-submitted SSNs.

Following institutional review board approval (IRB), research was conducted to identify the extent of data-quality issues in a sample educational database at the ADE. An application (see Figure 1) was developed using Structured Query Language (SQL).

The SQL-based application, although an early prototype, showed significant utility. The application allowed validation of SSNs. Under guidance of an approved ADE Memorandum of Understanding (MOU), as well as IRB approval, 512,668 distinct SSNs were analyzed. In total, 21,330 (4%) of SSNs were found to be potentially erroneous.

The application was expanded to operate off a stored procedure that allowed three methods by which SSN validation could occur:

1. **Distinct SSN Input:** Allowed validation of single SSN based upon user's entry into web interface;
2. **File Input:** Accommodated bulk validation of SSNs from a file. File could be uploaded as a comma separated value (CSV) into web interface;
3. **Table Input:** Designed to capture SSN, date of birth, and optional state of issuance

Figure 1. SSN validation tool

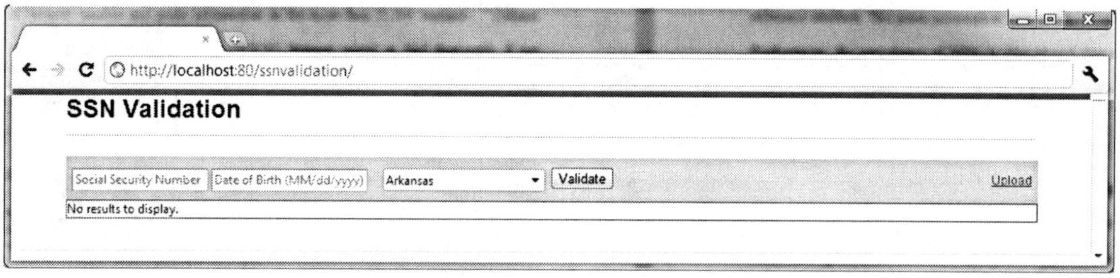

from a given database table and perform intra-database SSN validation.

Twelve SSN validation rules, each analyzing part of the SSN, were implemented as part of the SSN Validation application. The nine-digit SSN is composed of three components. The first three digits is the area number, the second set of two digits the group number and the final set of four digits the serial number. The rules used in the SSN validation prototype are provided below:

1. SSN cannot equal 000000000;
2. All characters must be valid numbers between one and nine;
3. SSN State Area Number cannot equal 000;
4. SSN High Code cannot equal 00 and must be between 01 and 99;
5. SSN Serial Number cannot equal 0000 and must be between 0001 and 9999;
6. SSN State Area Number cannot equal 666;
7. SSN State Area Number cannot be between 900 and 999;
8. SSN State Area Number cannot be larger than 772, as this was the last State Area Number that had been assigned at the time of the analysis;
9. Based upon the SSN's Group Number (odd group numbers 01 through 09, odd numbers 11-99, even numbers 02-08 and even numbers 10-98), the fourth and fifth digits must be less than or equal to the last number issued for that Group Number;
10. The SSN must have a Group Number lower than the last Group Number issued, or else it is invalid;
11. Based upon the individual's date of birth (more accurately, year of issue), the SSN must contain a valid Area Number and Group Number combination. This rule check has not been fully implemented;
12. The SSN must not belong to a deceased individual, as recorded by the Social Security Administration's Death Master File. The *Death Master File* was purchased from the U.S. Department of Commerce and contained approximately 90 million Social Security numbers for individuals who have been recorded as deceased from 1936 through 2011.

The analysis results based of the preceding rule set is provided in Table 1. An SSN is distinct in any one rule, but one SSN may invalidate more than one rule.

PRIVACY-ENHANCING ENTITY RESOLUTION AND IDENTITY MANAGEMENT

Data Set Used in this Case Study

The data set used in this case study was drawn from K-12 student records of fiscal year 2010 in the database at the ADE, which contained all the

Table 1. SSN validation analysis

Error Description	Non-Distinct Count*	Percent of Total
SSN cannot equal 000000000.	18	0.004%
SSN State Area cannot be greater than 772	19,149	3.735%
Digits 4 and 5 cannot equal 00.	390	0.076%
SSN Group Number is out of range of valid numbers.	1,410	0.275%
Last 4 digits cannot equal 0000.	20	0.004%
SSN cannot start with 666	1	0.000%
SSN belongs to a deceased individual	1,043	0.203%
SSN cannot be between 900 and 999	18,962	3.699%

records of students enrolled in K-12 public schools in the state of Arkansas in the year of 2010. The records were collected and reported by each school to the ADE through the Arkansas Enterprise Data System. Figure 2 shows the information system architect used to collect student data from school districts.

Each public school submits and certifies its data nine times per school year though the Arkansas Enterprise Data System. Each data collection is known as a cycle. Student records are collected in six of the nine cycles from each school district. Thus, normally in a school year, each individual student has six records in the database at the ADE. However, due to some other reasons, such as transferring out of state, and transferring into the state, some students may not have exactly six records per school year.

Therefore, in order to establish an effective and functional identity management system, an ER must be developed to first link all the student records referring to the same real-world entity together. Exploring a preliminary entity-resolution framework became one of the objectives of this research.

Reference Data Assessment

The first step of ER begins with an assessment of the reference data. Once the assessment is completed, a general idea of the quality of the data can be obtained.

The process of assessing the data quality is known as data profiling. Data profiling provides useful descriptive statistics of the data such as minimum, maximum, mean, mode, and also metadata information of the data, such as pattern, data type, length, occurrence of null values, blank value, and entropy.

In ER, the accuracy, completeness and entropy of the data are important metrics in designing an effective ER strategy. Each record in the data set consists of many attributes. In this research, there are 39 attributes. Twenty-five of the 39 attributes

Figure 2. Arkansas Enterprise data system

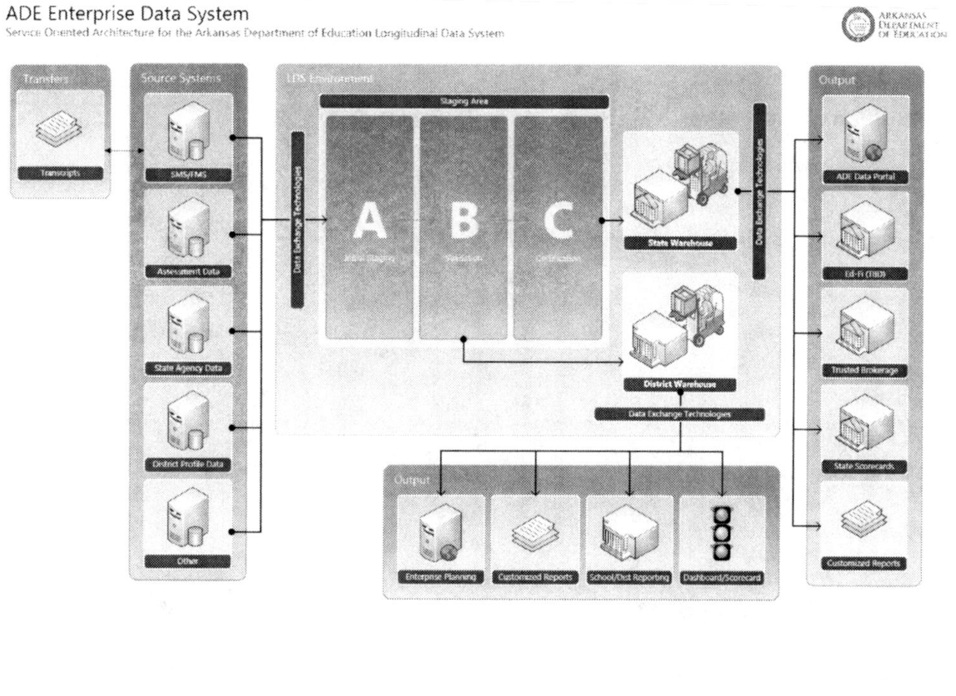

are displayed in Figure 3. Each attribute can hold different values. It is not efficient to include all the attributes in the ER strategy due to storage and processing limitations. The attributes with the best distinguishing and matching ability should be selected to build the ER strategy.

The following guidelines were used to identifying candidate entity-identity attributes:

1. The attribute must be of high completeness;
2. The attribute must be of neither too high nor too low entropy;
3. The attribute must be of high accuracy.

An experiment was not conducted to study the trade-off between completeness and entropy because intuitively low completeness provides little information for supporting an ER process. We associated high completeness to high entropy and we also took incomplete values into the computing of entropy. Therefore, low completeness yielded low entropy.

Completeness was calculated by counting the number of null values and blank values of an attribute:

$$completeness = 1 - \frac{number\ of\ nulls + blanks}{total\ number\ of\ records}$$

Entropy in this context refers to the amount of information contained in an attribute. For example, the attributes gender and gifted status both have two different possible values. Knowing a student's gifted status contains less information than knowing the student's gender, because over 95 percent of gifted statuses are NO, while the ratios of two genders are almost half-to-half. Thus, gender provides more information in identifying a student in this research. Entropy is able to quantify the expected value of information of an attributes. It was calculated by the formula below:

$$entropy = H\left(X\right) = -\sum_{i=1}^{n} p\left(x_i\right)\log_b p\left(x_i\right)$$

x_i denotes the different values of attribute X, $p\left(x_i\right)$ stands for the probability of the attribute X has the value of x_i. b is the base of the logarithm used. The common value of b is 2.

Accuracy was calculated by verifying the record value against some business rules, provided there are business rules defined for the values of the attribute:

$$accuracy = 1 - \frac{number\ of\ erroneous\ records}{total\ number\ of\ records}$$

Figure 3. Completeness analysis of entity-identity reference data

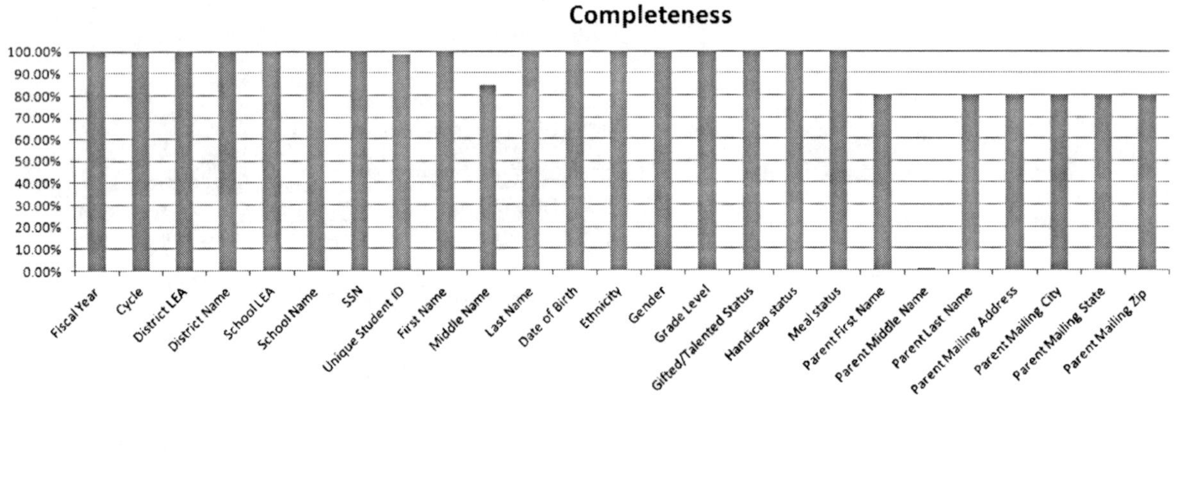

Accuracy is not easy to calculate in the data set of this research. Since the business rules used to constrain the attributes are not well defined, only data type and value length were used in this research. No rules were used to check erroneous values, such as misspelling and incomplete information. The erroneous values can often become one of the most challenging problems in ER. This research yielded approaches to solve this problem, which will be discussed later in this section.

To profile the data, queries were developed in Structured Query Language (SQL). There are 3,234,292 records in the table of the test data.

As identified in Figure 3, except for the entity-identity attribute of a parent's middle name, all of the attributes have a completeness score of more than 80 percent.

Next, the data was profiled to determine if it could provide sufficient distinguishing and identifying ability. In other words, can the candidate entity identity attributes be used to establish the rules in the ER process? The entropy of each attribute can be one of the indicators for its ability to distinguish and identify entities in the data set. The higher the entropy is, the more information the attribute contains, which means the attribute is more capable of identifying a reference to a real-world entity. Thus, an attribute with high entropy is an ideal candidate attribute for constructing ER rules. In Figure 4, SSNs and unique student IDs have the highest entropies. However, one of the primary objectives of the research is to develop an ER strategy that does not use SSN as an identity attribute. While the unique student ID was a student identifier being applied in the ADE student database provided by a third party provider, the research showed it yielded an error rate greater than 3 percent. A secondary objective of this research is to achieve high-accuracy ER without reliance on a proprietary identifier provided by a third party. Therefore, both of the attributes with the best entropies were removed from consideration for constructing the ER strategy. The attributes with the entropies less than 10, such as District LEA, Parent Mailing State, and Retention status are of low distinguishing and identifying abilities. They were not considered in the earlier stages of ER rules development. Although attributes such as first name, last name and date of birth are not as high as student SSN in entropy when considered alone, when combined they yield acceptable entropy. In other words, the

Figure 4. Entropy analysis of entity-identity reference data

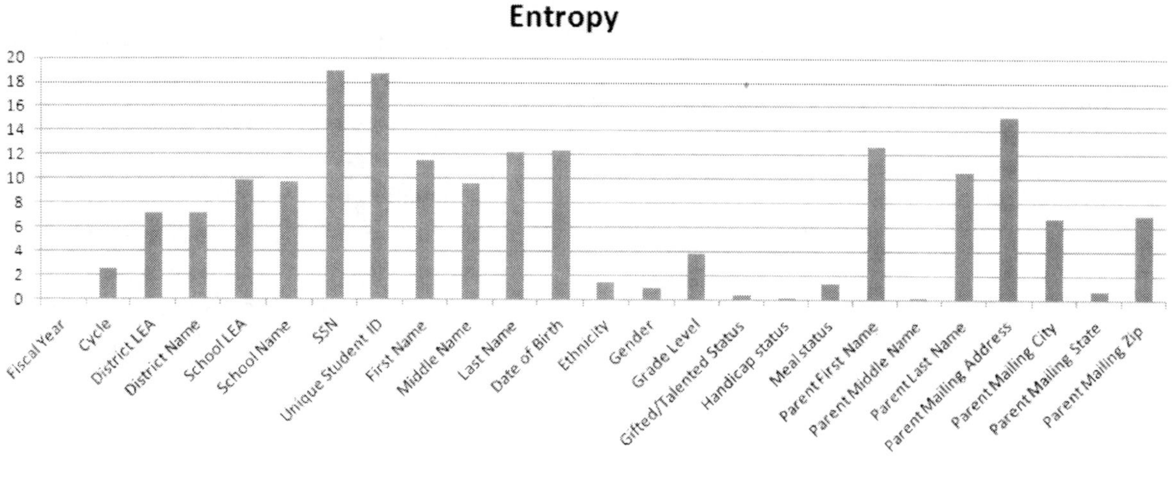

degree of entropy increases once the combined attributes are considered.

Table 2 shows the entropies of some combinations of attributes first selected to build ER rules.

Entity Resolution Rules Development Framework

The ER rules development is an iterative process of benchmark making/refinement, rules developing/refinement, and analysis of matching results. After a successive iteration, the benchmark is closer to the truth, and the rules are more accurate in matching records to the real-world entities (Figure 5).

Table 2. Uniqueness of selected common combinations of attributes

Combinations	Entropy
First Name + Last Name	18.49
First Name + Last Name + Date of Birth	18.96
First Name + Middle Name + Last Name	18.98
First Name + Last Name + Parent First Name	19.16

Figure 5. Entity resolution rule development framework

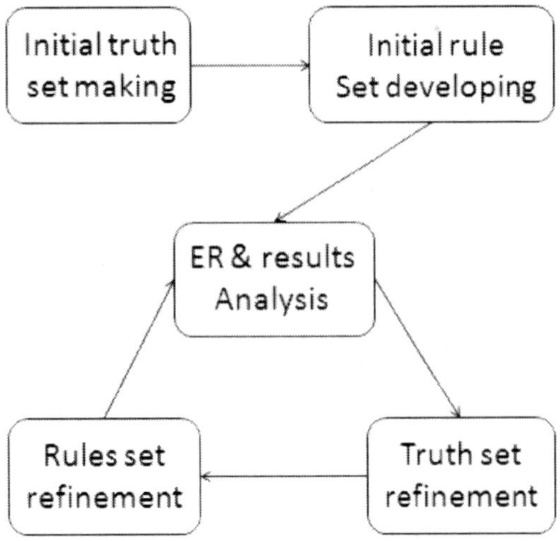

Benchmarking

In many practical applications that require ER, there is no benchmark that can be used to estimate the accuracy of a set of entity-resolution rules. Thus, it is important to derive a benchmark from the original data set, which is manually manageable and also representative for the whole data set. In this research, a truth set was used to serve as a benchmark.

The first step in developing a benchmark is to obtain a random sample and ensure every record in this sample refers a distinct real-world entity. In other words, no two records in the sample refer to the same real-world entity. The random sample is called the seed of this entire process. The size of the seed is very important. It can be neither too large to be within a manually manageable level nor too small to represent the entire population of the original data set. It depends on the resources available to the research team and the statistical characteristics of the data set. In this study, a seed size of 500 was produced, because 500 records are manageable by a single researcher and the Unique Student ID has an error rate of at least 3 percent. Five hundred records are large to cover some records with erroneous values.

The method of producing a seed is discussed below:

1. Randomly select 500 records from the data set using the best method that fits the data. In this research, a SQL random selection function was applied;
2. Manually check the 500 records to ensure they are unique. If there is more than one record referring to the same real-world entity, keep only one record and remove the remaining records, which refer to the same real-world identity. Next, add the same number of records randomly selected from the data set, which ensures the seed size of 500 again contains 500 records.

A technique was used in this research to help manually check the uniqueness of the records in the seed. OYSTER, the open-source entity resolution and identity management system, is used to match the 500 records based on SSN, unique student ID, first name, last name, and date of birth, respectively. Although the goal is an ER algorithm which doesn't utilize SSN or the proprietary unique student ID, this technique allowed for expedited confirmation of the seed. The clusters of the size greater than one were examined manually to determine whether they refer to the same real-world entity or to different real-world entities. It reduced the workload significantly from comparing the 500 records pair-wise.

After obtaining the seed, the second step is to grow the seed into a truth set, which contains all the records from the original data set, which correspond to the real-world entities represented by the records in the seed.

Although SSNs and unique student IDs cannot be applied in ER rules, they can greatly expedite development of the truth set. Here are the details of how the truth set was established in this research:

1. Assign a truth ID to each record from one to 500;
2. Use OYSTER to process the seed in Identity Capture mode based on exact match on the truth ID. OYSTER appended a unique ID consisting of 16 characters to each record, and generated an *identify* file which saved the 500 records, containing their attributes values, and OYSTER IDs in Extensible Markup Language (XML) format;
3. Use OYSTER to process the identity file generated in *Step 2* as one input and the original data set as another input in *Identity Resolution* mode based on exact match on SSN. Import the result to a database table named LinkSSN for further analysis. This process allowed the researcher to discover all records with the same SSN as the ones in the identity file and to assign the same OYSTER ID to the records;
4. Use OYSTER to process the identity file generated in *Step 2* as one input and the original data set as another input in Identity Resolution mode based on exact match on the proprietary Unique Student ID. Import the result to a database table named LinkUSI for further analysis. This process allows the researcher to discover records with the same proprietary Unique Student ID as the ones in the identity files and to assign the same OYSTER ID to records;
5. Perform a database full join to LinkSSN and LinkUSI where the LinkSSN.recordID equals LinkUSI. recordID. The recordID of the records in the tables were carried from the original data set. Therefore, if two records were joined into one tuple, they are the same one from the original data set;
6. Examine the tuples in the joined table by comparing the OYSTER ID from LinkSSN and LinkUSI. Build the truth set.

This process yielded four comparison results, which are described below:

1. OYSTER IDs from LinkSSN and LinkUSI are the same. This indicated the records were clustered correctly with a high confidence level, even if not 100 percent, in both tables;
2. OYSTER ID from LinkSSN is different from the one from LinkUSI. This indicated the records were matched into different clusters. The records in these two clusters are distinguished and separated by OYSTER IDs and were manually examined to determine which one, or if both, of the records were incorrect. The incorrect record is removed;
3. OYSTER ID from LinkSSN is NULL. This indicated the record was only matched into one cluster in the seed by the proprietary Unique Student ID, but not SSN. Two pos-

sible explanations were discovered: 1) SSN failed in matching the record (false negative); 2) the proprietary unique student ID incorrectly matched the record to a cluster (false positive). The other records in the cluster were examined, and then it was manually determined whether the record should be included in the cluster;

4. OYSTER ID from LinkUSI is NULL. This result is similar to the previous scenario, except the SSN and the Unique Student ID are switched.

For example, several records in the joined table are displayed in Table 5.

Recall the records with ID 2543255, 2540886, 2536239 and 2538546 in the original data set together with 2535713 and 2532793. They are shown in Table 3. They had different SSNs, but the same proprietary unique student ID. After manually examining the other information such as first name, middle name, last name and date of birth, it could be concluded that the six records referred to the same real-world entity. Therefore, records with ID 2543255, 2540886, 2536239 and 2538546 were added to the truth set.

Table 4 displays another student record example.

Another example is demonstrated in Table 5.

The records from the original data set are shown in the Table 6. It was determined manually that the records with ID2951848 should be removed from the truth set.

After adding in false negatives and removing false positives, the truth table is near complete. In this case study, a truth set of size of 3279 was derived after this stage. It was then imported to a database table named Truth. It may still contain a few false positives and several false negatives, but the results demonstrated that the clustering is more accurate than SSNs and unique student IDs. Furthermore, it can be refined in the ER rules development stage.

Table 3. More records clustered by proprietary student ID than SSN

LinkSSN.recID	LinkSSN.OysterID	LinkUSI.recID	LinkUSI.OysterID
2535713	1LCIJMOINQTHN2CW	2535713	1LCIJMOINQTHN2CW
2532793	1LCIJMOINQTHN2CW	2532793	1LCIJMOINQTHN2CW
null	null	2543255	1LCIJMOINQTHN2CW
null	null	2540886	1LCIJMOINQTHN2CW
null	null	2536239	1LCIJMOINQTHN2CW
null	null	2538546	1LCIJMOINQTHN2CW

Table 4. More records were clustered by SSN than the proprietary unique student ID

LinkSSN.recID	LinkSSN.OysterID	LinkUSI.recID	LinkUSI.OysterID
416489	TYBD5PCQ19U85G78	416489	TYBD5PCQ19U85G78
415013	TYBD5PCQ19U85G78	415013	TYBD5PCQ19U85G78
415518	TYBD5PCQ19U85G78	415518	TYBD5PCQ19U85G78
416000	TYBD5PCQ19U85G78	416000	TYBD5PCQ19U85G78
2951848	TYBD5PCQ19U85G78	null	null

Table 5. Multiple records of the same SSN referring to different students

ID	SSN	Unique Student ID	First Name	Middle Name	Last Name	Date of Birth	...
416489	123456702	1112223333	BRANDY	RAY	CURRY	1992-12-04	...
415013	123456702	1112223333	BRANDY	RAY	CURRY	1992-12-04	...
415518	123456702	1112223333	BRANDY	RAY	CURRY	1992-12-04	...
416000	123456702	1112223333	BRANDY	RAY	CURRY	1992-12-04	...
2951848	123456702	1116666333	ALICE	EDDIE	WILLIAMS	1992-12-04	...

Table 6. Multiple records of different SSNs referring to the same student

ID	SSN	Unique Student ID	First Name	Middle Name	Last Name	Date of Birth	...
2535713	123456786	1222223333	MCKENEAL	ELLEN	Henry	1995-07-10 00:00:00	...
2532793	123456786	1222223333	MCKENEAL	ELLEN	Henry	1995-07-10 00:00:00	...
2543255	765432151	1222223333	MCKENEAL	ELLEN	Henry	1995-07-10 00:00:00	...
2540886	765432151	1222223333	MCKENEAL	ELLEN	Henry	1995-07-10 00:00:00	...
2536239	765432151	1222223333	MCKENEAL	ELLEN	Henry	1995-07-10 00:00:00	...
2538546	765432151	1222223333	MCKENEAL	ELLEN	Henry	1995-07-10 00:00:00	...

Entity Resolution Rules Development

The development of ER rules is not a one-stop process. It starts with an initial rule set and continues with an iterative process including clustering results analysis, truth set refinement, and rules set refinement.

The initial rule set has to be simple, but general. It could provide a foundation for further analysis and refinement. Based on the profiling results, the initial rule set was designed to contain only one rule. That was clustering the records based on first name exact match, last name exact match and date of birth exact match. Use OYSTER process the *identity* file generated in the previous section as one input and the original data set as another input in identity resolution mode based on this rule set. Import the result to a database table, named InitialClustering, for further analysis.

Clustering Result Analysis

Perform a database full join on table Truth obtained in last section and table InitialClustering where the Truth.recordID equals InitialClustering.recordID. Next, examine the tuples in the joined table by comparing the OYSTER ID from table Truth and table InitialClustering. Apply the same method described in the previous section to determine the correct and incorrect clustered records in both table Truth and table InitialClustering.

Truth Set Refinement

Modify the truth set based on the analysis result. Ensure that when comparing with table InitialClustering, there is no false positive or false negative being found in the truth set.

In this case study, 54 records were added to the truth set in this stage, which yielded a refined truth set in the size of 3333. For example, the table shows record 2999643 and 2911540 are different in both SSNs and proprietary unique student IDs, thus the record 2911540 was not in the initial truth set. But it was clustered by the initial rule set due to exact match on first name, last name and date of birth. After manually examination, it was included in the truth set.

Table 7, displays the two student records discussed.

Rule Refinement

Taking the clustering analysis result, investigate the reason why the current rules produced the false positives and missed the false negatives. Adjust the existing rules to reduce false positives, and introduce new rules to resolve false negatives.

It is usually because the some rules are too loose, allowing the records sharing a few common attributes are clustered incorrectly. For example, Table 8 shows two clusters obtained by a rule exact match on first name, date of birth and a fuzzy match on last name with a qTR value greater than 0.25. A qTR is a metric that measures the similarity between two strings proposed in *q-Gram Tetrahedral Ratio (qTR) for Approximate Pattern Matching* (Holland & Talburt, 2010). This rule was able to link records, which are slightly off in last names. Thus records 160157 and 162453 were linked correctly, though their last names were not exactly the same. However, records 859869 and 1055012 were linked incorrectly. Because the qTR value between "MILLER" and "MILLSAP" was 0.29.

Thus, these rules should be modified to be stricter. For example, add more attribute matching conditions to the rules. The parents' mailing address of records 160157 and 162453 were the same, while those of records 859869 and 1055012 were different. Thus the rule could be modified to exact match on first name, parents mailing address, date of birth and a fuzzy match on last name with a qTR value greater than 0.25. An alternative

Table 7. Two records were matched by an ER rule that were not included in the initial truth set

ID	SSN	Unique Student ID	First Name	Middle Name	Last Name	Date of Birth	...
2999643	111177444	7412589635	ALLYSON	MARY	GRAIG	1995-02-01	...
2911540	111127444	7539512483	ALLYSON	MARY	GRAIG	1995-02-01	...

Table 8. Records incorrectly linked because of loose ER rules

ID	SSN	Unique Student ID	First Name	Middle Name	Last Name	Date of Birth	Parent Mailing Address	...
160157	122365492	4445556662	SARAH	Lyn	STEAKLEY (BURNS)	1999-07-07	101 East Capitol St	
162453	122365492	4445556662	SARAH	Lyn	STEAKLEY	1999-07-07	101 East Capitol St	
859869	789654246	3366885522	MARK	TY	MILLER	1994-08-08	369 East Capitol St	...
1055012	685239441	7755884429	MARK	DON	MILLSAP	1994-08-08	P O BOX 546	...

Table 9. Missing letter presented in one of the records prevent exact match ER

ID	SSN	Unique Student ID	First Name	Middle Name	Last Name	Date of Birth	...
647093	555666803	null	GRACEYBELLE	CAROL	JOHNSON	1999-09-09	...
648627	555666803	null	GRACYBELLE	CAROL	JOHNSON	1999-09-09	...

way is to increase the qTR threshold to 0.3, because the qTR value between" STEAKLEY (BURNS)" and "STEAKLEY" is 0.46.

False negatives are usually caused by the absence of rules to cluster the records. By investigate the similarities of the records, new rules which could bring them together can be discovered. For example, the two records in Table 9 could not be clustered because there was a letter "E" missing in the first name of the second record. To solve this problem, a rule linking the records based on Levenshtein distance similarity of 0.8 on first name, exact match on middle name, last name and date of birth could be added to the rules set. An example of this is demonstrated in Table 9.

When the new rules set is defined, use OYSTER to process the *identity* file and the original data set in Identity Resolution mode based on it. Another iteration of clustering results analysis, truth set refinement and rules set refinement starts again. This iterative process stops when the truth set remains stable (no false positive or false negative be found), and there is no way to improve the rules set by only reducing false positives and negatives without introducing new ones. The remaining false positives and negatives are considered to be caused by the nature of the data quality issue.

In this case study, the final truth set consisted of 3333 records. The rule set was defined in Table 10.

Table 11 shows a few examples of false negatives. Because of the absence of other supportive attributes such as parents' mailing addresses and

Table 10. Entity resolution rules set

	First Name	Last Name	Date of Birth	Parent Mailing Address
Rule 1	LED(0.8)	Exact	Exact	
Rule 2	Exact	QTR(0.3)	Exact	
Rule 3	Exact	Exact		Exact
Rule 4	reorder letters according alphabetic value	Exact	Exact	
Rule 5	First 5 letters exact match	Exact	Exact	

Table 11. Records that could not be clustered by ER rules due to lacking or support attributes

ID	SSN	Unique Student ID	First Name	Middle Name	Last Name	Date of Birth	...
22125	266611150	8884449995	AMY	DANIE	JACKSON	1993-02-17	
1584592	266611150	8884449995	AMY	DANIE	PARSONS	1993-02-17	
632693	333666953	1115556662	DEVON		FRANKLIN (CYS)	1993-05-16	...
572435	333666953	1115556662	G.	DEVON	FRANKLIN	1993-05-16	...

change of names information, they could not be clustered correctly.

RESULTS

We use this section to demonstrate application of the ER rule set on the four sample scenarios described in the beginning of this chapter.

Scenario 1

Scenario 1 describes two different student records that share the same last name and date of birth. However, one record listed the student first name as Arman and the second record lists the first name as Armando. Neither parent name nor address is listed for either record. In this scenario, Rule 5 will successfully resolve the two records since the student records share the same last name and date of birth and the first five letters of the first name (Arman and Armando) are the same.

Scenario 2

Scenario 2 describes two different student records that share the same last name and date of birth. First name values for the two records differ: one has a first name Peirce and the other has a first name of Pierce. Although the first names differ, they share the same letters of the alphabet. Rule 4 will combine the records because the last name and date of birth are the same and an alpha reorder of the first name characters will produce the same string.

Scenario 3

In Scenario 3, student records share the same first name, last name and mailing address. However, one record shows a date of birth of October 15, 1999 and the other student record has a date of birth of October 5, 1999. Although the dates of births differ, Rule 3 will resolve the two records to the same identity since the first name, last name and mailing address is the same for each student record.

After application of the ER rule set to the sample scenarios, we quantity the results when applied to the sample data set. These entity resolution results were obtained by applying the rules set defined in Table 10 to the student data. The performance of the rules set measured against the truth set is shown in Table 12.

The results indicate 0 false positives and a false negative rate of only 0.57% for the truth set used in this case study. The results demonstrate the effectiveness and efficacy of the research applied to a real-world data set.

CONCLUSION AND FUTURE WORK

This research specifically addresses significant concerns within academic institutions (data quality and privacy), but also provides an approach in which academic institutions could develop a comprehensive identity management strategy on which student privacy and data quality serve as a central implementation driver. This work builds on existing ER knowledge with a privacy-preserving framework; however, its application focuses on educational data sets and data elements, which are considered confidential information under FERPA. Future work might explore additional attributes and their reference value in ER as well as governance structures and security frameworks which further protect the privacy of student re-

Table 12. Performance of the rules set measured against the truth set

	False Positive	False Negative
Number of	0	19
Rate of	0%	0.57%

cords. There are two research areas this work is starting to explore and these will be discussed below.

Probabilistic Matching

The ER engine used in our framework relies on the exact match scheme, in which a pair of records is considered to be a match if they agree exactly on each element of a rule, and a mismatch otherwise. For example, when comparing two records "Mary Doe, 10/25/1980, 123 Main Street" and "Mary Doe, 10/28/1980, 123 Main Street," on first name, last name, birthday, and street address, the pair of records is not considered a match due to the mismatch on the element birthday, even though they are likely referring to the same person. One limitation of the exact match is that it assumes each attribute is equally important when deciding a match.

Probabilistic matching, first proposed by Fellegi and Sunter (Fellegi and Sunter, 1969), provides a probabilistic model for record matching. It classifies a pair of records as a match, a possible match, or non-match based on the matching score of the records. It differs from the exact match in the way that it assigns an individual agreement weight to each element based on their ability to identify a true match and uses these weights to calculate the matching score. A decision rule is used to classify a pair of records as a match, a possible match, or non-match based the matching score. Since possible matches will be the primary focus of further analysis and review, probabilistic matching can potentially identify some true matches that might be otherwise missed if using exact match. Several challenges exist for probabilistic matching. Our future work will focus on two issues: 1) design a good decision rule that produces low false positives and low false negatives; and 2) extend the concept of element based individual agreement weight to the element value based weight to distinguish a rare element value from a popular value. This can further enhance the performance of probabilistic matching.

Identity Management

Identity management covers broad aspects, including data quality, data management, data privacy and security, data policies, and risk management surrounding the handling of identity records. With ER being used to resolve student records and produce identity references, it becomes very important to maintain and manage a large and ever growing number of identity records and references over time. As contents of identity records may change over time, such as a student changes address, parent's address, or transfers to a different school, appropriate identity governance structures are needed for efficient management of changes in data. In addition, to ensure the quality as well as privacy and security of data, proper policies should be in place for controlling the data access and updates. Our future work in this area will focus on designing proper procedures, policies, and strategies for identity management and governance.

REFERENCES

Arkansas Department of Education. (2009, May 28). Average Daily Membership. Little Rock, Arkansas, United States of America.

Arkansas Department of Education. (2011, August 01). Unpublished - Four Year Adjusted Cohort Graduation Rate FAQs. Little Rock, Arkansas, United States of America.

Arkansas Department of Education. (2012). *Annual Statistical Report*. Little Rock.

Arkansas Department of Education. (n.d.). *Statewide Information System Reports - Enrollment by Grade*. Retrieved March 3, 2012, from ADE Data Center: http://adedata.arkansas.gov/statewide/State/EnrollmentByGrade.aspx

Arkansas Legislature. (2005). *Chapter 86 General Provisions*. Retrieved July 24, 2012, from http://www.arkleg.state.ar.us/assembly/ArkansasCodeLargeFiles/Title%204%20Business%20and%20Commercial%20Law-Chapter%2086%20General%20Provisions.htm

Arveson, P. (n.d.). *The Deming Cycle*. Retrieved January 3, 2012, from The Balanced Scorecard Institute: http://www.balancedscorecard.org/thedemingcycle/tabid/112/default.aspx

Associated Press. (2005, September 7). *Ex-student sentenced for computer hacking*. Retrieved July 4, 2011, from Security on MSNBC.COM: http://www.msnbc.msn.com/id/9239576/

Cate, F. H. (2006). The Privacy and Security Policy Vacuum in Higher Education. *EDUCAUSE Review*, *41*(5), 18–29.

Christen, P. (2008). Abstract Febrl – A Freely Available Record Linkage System with a Graphical User Interface. *Proceeding of the 14th ACM SIGKDD international conference on Knowledge discovery and data mining*, (pp. 1065-1068).

Fellegi, I. P., & Sunter, A. B. (1969). A Theory for Record Linkage. *Journal of the American Statistical Association*, *64*(328), 1183–1210. doi:10.1080/01621459.1969.10501049

Gibson, N., & Talburt, J. (2010). HIVE: Crowdsourcing Education Data. *Journal of Computing Sciences in Colleges*, *25*(5), 71–78.

Hashemi, R., Talburt, J. R., & Wang, R. (2006). Significance test for the talburt-wang similarity index. In J. R. Talburt, E. Pierce, N. Wu, & T. Campbell (Ed.), *9th International Conference on Information Quality* (pp. 125-132). Cambridge: MIT IQ Publishing.

Holland, G. (2010). *Knowledge-Driven Identity Resolution For Longitudional Education Data.*

Holland, G., & Talburt, J. R. (2010). q-Gram Tetrahedral Ratio (qTR) for Approximate Pattern Matching. *2010 Annual Acxiom Laboratory for Applied Research Conference*. Conway.

How are school districts in Arkansas funded? (n.d.). Retrieved July 4, 2012, from Lamar Warriors: http://www.lamarwarriors.org/board/funding%20information/how_are_schools_funded.pdf

Human Inference. (2011). *DataCleaner*. Retrieved July 4, 2012, from DataCleaner: http://datacleaner.eobjects.org/

Information Quality. (2012, May 3). Retrieved May 12, 2012, from Wikipedia: http://en.wikipedia.org/wiki/Information_quality

Institute of Education Sciences. (2011). *Public Elementary and Secondary School Student Enrollment and Staff Counts From the Common Core of Data: School Year 2009-10*. National Center of Education Statistics.

Institute of Education Sciences. (2011). *Statewide Longitudional Data Systems Grant Program*. Retrieved January 5, 2012, from National Center for Education Statistics: http://nces.ed.gov/programs/slds/stateinfo.asp

Jagannatha, G. (2010, May). Data Privacy in Knowledge Discovery. 5-10.

Janert, P. K. (2011). *Data Analysts with Open Source Tools*. Sebastopol: O'Reilly Media, Inc.

Kimball, R., & Caserta, J. (2004). *The data warehouse ETL toolkit: Practical techniques for extracting, cleaning, conforming, and delivering data*. John Wiley & Sons.

Lee, Y. W., Pierce, E., Talburt, J., & Wang, R. Y. (2007). A Curriculum for a Master of Science in Information Quality. *Journal of Information Systems Education*.

Lee, Y. W., Pipino, L. L., Funk, J. D., & Wang, R. Y. (2006). *Journey to Data Quality*. Cambridge: The MIT Press.

Luenberger, D. G. (2006). *Information Science*. Princeton: Princeton University Press.

Meske, D. J. (2011, August). Data Loss: Protecting Personally Identifying Information (PII) at Public Higher . La Verne, California.

Miami University. (2005, September 15). *Privacy Help*. Retrieved July 4, 2011, from Miami University: http://www.miami.muohio.edu/documents_and_policies/privacyhelp.cfm

MIT Information Quality Program. (2011). *MIT Information Quality Program*. Retrieved April 20, 2012, from MIT Information Quality: http://mitiq.mit.edu/

Nelson, E. (2011). *Design and Construction of An Entity Resolution System that Supports Entity Identity Information Management and Asserted Resolution*.

Newcombe, H. B. (1988). *Handbook of Record Linkage*. Oxford University Press.

Newcombe, H. B., & Kennedy, J. M. (1962). Record linkage: making maximum use of the discriminating power of identifying information. *Communications of the ACM*, *5*(11), 563–566. doi:10.1145/368996.369026

Oracle Corporation. (2011). *MySQL*. Retrieved July 4, 2012, from MySQL: http://www.mysql.com/

OYSTER Entity Resolution. (2012, June 13). Retrieved July 4, 2012, from SourceForge.NET: http://sourceforge.net/projects/oysterer/

Pushkarev, V., Neumann, H., Varol, C., & Talburt, J. (2010). An overview of open source data quality tools. *Information and Knowledge Engineering Conference*. Las Vegas.

Reidenber, J. R., & Debelak, J. (2009). *Children's Educational Records and Privacy*. Fordham Center on Law and Information Policy.

Standard University. (2011). *Stanford Entity Resolution Framework*. Retrieved March 6, 2012, from The Standard University InfoLab: http://infolab.stanford.edu/serf/

Summers, D. C. (2006). *Quality* (4th ed.). Upper Saddle River: Pearson Prentice Hall.

Talburt, J. R. (2011). *Entity Resolution and Information Quality*. Burlington: Morgan Kaufmann.

Tepping, B. J. (1968). A Model for Optimum Linkage of Records. *Journal of the American Statistical Association*, *63*(324), 1321–1332. doi:10.1080/01621459.1968.10480930

The Right of Privacy. (2004). Retrieved February 4, 2012, from Exploring Constitutional Conflicts: http://law2.umkc.edu/faculty/projects/ftrials/conlaw/rightofprivacy.html

University of Arkansas at Little Rock. (2011). *Center for Entity Resolution and Information Quality*. Retrieved November 14, 2011, from University of Arkansas at Little Rock: http://ualr.edu/eriq/

University of Hawaii. (2010, October 28). *Inadvertent data exposure by UH West O'ahu affects Mānoa students*. Retrieved July 4, 2011, from The University of Hawaii System: http://www.hawaii.edu/news/article.php?aId=3990

U.S. Department of Education. (2004, February 10). *Executive Summary of the No Child Left Behind Act of 2001*. Retrieved July 4, 2011, from ED.gov: http://www2.ed.gov/nclb/overview/intro/execsumm.html

U.S. Department of Education. (2008, October). *Elementary & Secondary Education: A Uniform, Comparable Graduation Rate*. Retrieved from ED.gov: http://www2.ed.gov/policy/elsec/reg/proposal/uniform-grad-rate.pdf

U.S. Department of Education. (2008). *High School Graduation Rate Non-Regulatory Guidance.*

U.S. Department of Education. (2011, April 8). *Family Educational Rights and Privacy Act*. Retrieved January 17, 2012, from ED.gov: http://www2.ed.gov/policy/gen/guid/fpco/ferpa/index.html

Verizon. (2012). *2012 Data Breach Investigations Report*. Retrieved May 14, 2012, from Verizon Business: http://www.verizonbusiness.com/resources/reports/rp_data-breach-investigations-report-2012_en_xg.pdf

Wang, R., & Strong, D. (1996). Beyond Accuracy: What Data Quality Means to Data Consumers. *Journal of Management Information Systems*, 5–34.

Wang, R. Y., Lee, Y. W., Pipino, L. L., & Strong, D. M. (1998, July 15). *MIT Sloan Management Review*. Retrieved May 15, 2012, from Manage Your Information as a Product: http://sloanreview.mit.edu/the-magazine/1998-summer/3947/manage-your-information-as-a-product/

Weill, P., & Ross, J. W. (2004). *IT Governance*. Boston: Harvard Business School Publishing.

Wu, N., Pierce, E., Talburt, J., & Wang, R. (2006). An Information Theoretic Approach to Information Quality Metrics. *International Conference on Information Quality*, (pp. 13-25).

Xu, X., Yuruk, N., Feng, Z., & Schweiger, T. (2007). SCAN: A Structural Clustering Algorithm for Networks. *The Thirteenth ACM SIGKDD International Conference on Knowledge Discovery and Data Mining.*

Zhou, Y. (2012). *Modeling and Design of Entity Identity Information in Entity Resolution Systems.*

Zhou, Y., & Talburt, J. R. (2011). The Role of Asserted Resolution in Entity Identity Information Management. *The 2011 International Conference on Bioinformatics and Computational Biology.*

ADDITIONAL READING

Daggett, L. M. (2008). FERPA in the Twenty-First Century: Failure to Effectively Regulate Privacy for All Students. *Cath. UL Rev.*, *58*, 59.

English, L. P. (1999). Improving data warehouse and business information quality: methods for reducing costs and increasing profits.

Fisher, C., Lauría, E., Chengalur-Smith, S., & Wang, R. (2012). *Introduction to information quality*. AuthorHouse.

Glenn, D. (2008). Huge databases offer a research gold mine—and privacy worries. *The Chronicle of Higher Education*, A10.

Janert, P. (2010). *Data Analysis with Open Source Tools: A hands-on guide for programmers and data scientists*. O'Reilly Media, Incorporated.

Lee, Y. W., Strong, D. M., Kahn, B. K., & Wang, R. Y. (2002). AIMQ: a methodology for information quality assessment. *Information & Management*, *40*(2), 133–146. doi:10.1016/S0378-7206(02)00043-5

Nelson, E., & Talburt, J. (2011). Entity Resolution for Longitudinal Studies in Education using OYSTER. In Proceedings: The 2011 International Conference on Information and Knowledge Engineering (IKE'11).

Pipino, L. L., Lee, Y. W., & Wang, R. Y. (2002). Data quality assessment. *Communications of the ACM*, *45*(4), 211–218. doi:10.1145/505248.506010

Steinberg, M. B. (2003). A Comparative Study of the Policies, Procedures, Training and Enforcement of the Family Educational Rights and Privacy Act (FERPA) at Public and Private Colleges and Universities in Four Carnegie Classifications of Institutions of Higher Education in the United States (Doctoral dissertation, University of Louisville).

Talburt, J. R. (2010). *Entity resolution and information quality*. Morgan Kaufmann Pub.

Torgo, L. (2003). *Data mining with R*. CRC Press.

Wang, R. Y. (1998). A product perspective on total data quality management. *Communications of the ACM*, *41*(2), 58–65. doi:10.1145/269012.269022

Weeks, K. M. (2001). Family-Friendly FERPA Policies: Affirming Parental Partnerships. *New Directions for Student Services*, (94): 39–50. doi:10.1002/ss.10

Witten, I. H., & Frank, E. (2005). Data Mining: Practical machine learning tools and techniques. Morgan Kaufmann. Zhou, Y., & Talburt, J. R. The Role of Asserted Resolution in Entity Identity Information Management.

Yau, N. (2011). *Visualize this: the flowing data guide to design, visualization, and statistics*. Wiley.

Zhou, Y., & Talburt, J. R. (2011, November). Entity Identity Information Management (EIIM). In International Conference on Information Quality (ICIQ-11), Adelaide, Australia (pp. 327-341).

Zhou, Y., Talburt, J. R., Su, Y., & Yin, L. (2010, November). OYSTER: A Tool for Entity Resolution in Health Information Exchange. In Conference Name Proceedings of the 5th International Conference on Cooperation and Promotion of Information Resources in Science and Technology (COINFO 2010 E-BOOK) (pp. 358-364). Scientific Research Publishing.

KEY TERMS AND DEFINITIONS

Entity Resolution: Entity Resolution is the process of deciding whether two references to real-world objects in an information system are references to the same object or to different objects.

Fuzzy Match: Fuzzy Match is the technique of finding objects that match a pattern approximately. It works with matches that may be less than 100% perfect when finding correspondences between objects in a database of previous translations.

Levenshtein Distance: Levenshtein Distance is a string metric for measuring the difference between two sequences. Informally, the Levenshtein distance between two words is the minimum number of single-letter edits (insertion, deletion, substitution) required to change one word into the other.

OYSTER: OYSTER (Open sYSTem Entity Resolution) is an entity resolution system developed by University of Arkansas at Little Rock (UALR) that supports probabilistic direct matching, transitive linking, and asserted linking. OYSTER is unique among other ER systems in that it is built to incorporate Entity Identity Information Management (EIIM).

QTR: QTR is a simply yet systematic approach to approximate pattern matching and test comparison utilizing tetrahedral numbers and a comprehensive q-gram algorithm.

Truth Set: A set of labeled data used presenting the ground true labeling results, which is used to evaluate the performance of the other labeling algorithms.

Chapter 5
Business Intelligence for Healthcare:
A Prescription for Better Managing Costs and Medical Outcomes

Jack S. Cook
SUNY Brockport, USA

Pamela A. Neely
SUNY Brockport, USA

ABSTRACT

Using an interpretive case study approach, this chapter describes the data quality problems in two companies: (1) a Multi-Facility Healthcare Medical Group (MHMG), and (2) a Regional Health Insurance Company (RHIS). These two interpretive cases examine two different processes of the healthcare supply chain and their integration with a business intelligence system. Specifically, the issues examined are MHMG's revenue cycle management and RHIS's provider enrollment and credentialing process. A Data and Information Quality (DIQ) assessment of the revenue cycle management process demonstrates how a framework, referred to as PGOT, can identify improvement opportunities within any information-intensive environment. Based on the assessment of the revenue cycle management process, data quality problems associated with the key processes and their implications for the healthcare organization are described. This chapter provides recommendations for DIQ best practices and illustrates these best practices within this real world context of healthcare.

DOI: 10.4018/978-1-4666-4892-0.ch005

INTRODUCTION

Organizations rely on data for a multitude of applications: customer service and relationship management, decision making, business intelligence (BI), and regulatory compliance. One of these, BI has the potential for improving the quality of information in any industry, although there is currently a push specifically in healthcare to be smarter about its management of key performance outcomes. One contributing factor motivating industry leaders is that healthcare organizations tend to be rich in data, but information poor. Although, healthcare organizations have been slow to embrace BI, these organizations are beginning to search for methods to deliver information to decision makers in more intelligent ways. The two main drivers for developing BI within healthcare are a desire to lower costs and improve patient outcomes. Therefore, one option is for BI to form the heart of any system that delivers organizationally sustaining data to providers and healthcare managers so they can make decisions that positively impact patient and service outcomes, while better managing the revenue cycle.

The challenge is to convince administrators, clerical staff, clinicians and physicians to buy-in to the importance of integrating previously disparate data to create a real-time view of the relationship between a patient, the provider, and the payer or payers. This chapter focuses on business intelligence (BI) systems that support healthcare, and the data and information quality (DIQ) issues that are inherent in any environment that is information intensive. BI has tremendous potential to impact healthcare, from multiple perspectives – patients, providers and payers. From a patient's perspective, BI can provide clinicians treatment and immunization recommendations that are preventative in nature, improving both diagnostic accuracy and better implemented care plans. Billing is critical in today's healthcare environment; providers transmit claims to multiple payers, and payment denials are common. BI dramatically improves data and information quality. Therefore, from the provider's perspective, IT professionals can streamline the complex billing process using BI. From a payer's perspective, a better connection to providers and a more intelligent way to enroll and credential them will reduce claims adjustments and disputes.

This chapter provides a brief literature review of healthcare, business intelligence (BI), as well as data and information quality (DIQ). Then the chapter discusses the healthcare industry as a whole with a particular emphasis on stakeholders and their interrelationships. After the literature and industry review, the chapter examines two cases that make the point that BI is a reasonable approach to manage key healthcare performance outcomes. The first case examines the process of adult immunization, specifically with respect to the Zoster vaccine. This case focuses on four key outcomes: medical outcomes, financial performance, compliance and overall customer satisfaction. The second case details the process that a payer performs to enroll and credential a healthcare provider. This second case looks at the key outcomes of compliance, customer satisfaction and financial performance. Next, we examine background information pertaining to healthcare, business intelligence and data and information quality.

BACKGROUND

Healthcare: As defined by the U.S. Department of Health and Human Services, a healthcare provider is "a provider of services as defined in §1861(u) of the Act (Social Security Act), a provider of medical or health services as defined in §1861(s) of the Act, and any other person or organization who furnishes, bills, or is paid for healthcare services or supplies in the normal course of business." (U.S. Department of Health and Human Services, 2001) Until recently, healthcare providers were paid when sick people sought treatment. Quality and outcomes were not rewarded, but rather providers were paid based on how much was done to treat the patient. In the future, healthcare providers will be given financial incentives to keep people well, and quality, not treatment, will matter a great deal. This shift from volume to value will require a rethinking of treatment plans and a shift towards preventative care.

Ensuring the health of its citizens continues to be at the forefront of politics in the United States, as well as on many corporate and personal agendas. Healthcare systems are judged based on three criteria: access, cost and quality (Shortell, 2004). With respect to access, the United States has been for some time the only industrialized country that does not guarantee health coverage to all of its citizens. Access to healthcare grew to a national crisis. In 2005, 46.6 million Americans were uninsured (ABC News, 2006). With the passage of the Patient Protection and Affordable Care Act (PPACA) in 2010, commonly referred to as Obamacare or the Affordable Care Act, together with the Health Care and Education Reconciliation Act, the U.S. healthcare system received its most significant government expansion and regulatory overhaul since the passage of Medicare and Medicaid in 1965 (Vicini & Stempel, 2012). The goal of Obamacare is to provide affordable health insurance for all U.S. citizens, and to reduce the growth in healthcare spending. Largely due to health reform and other federal policies, the number of uninsured Americans fell for the first time in four years according to the 2011 Census (Broaddus & Park, 2012).

From a cost perspective, the U.S. also has the costliest healthcare system. It is expected that the federal government will foot the bill for approximately 93% ($931 billion) of the Medicaid expansion costs over the period 2014 – 2022, while states will fund the remaining $73 billion (Angeles, 2012). Even for individuals covered by health insurance, the cost of healthcare can be prohibitive. Some predict that Obamacare should reduce the growth in healthcare spending in the long run. The current $2.8 trillion U.S. healthcare system costs almost $9,000 a year for every man, woman, and child in the U.S (ObamaCare Facts, 2013). Websites such as healthcarebluebook.com can give customary and reasonable charges for many procedures, but the actual charges vary widely.

Business Intelligence (BI): BI supports human intelligence with "technologies, applications and processes for gathering, storing, accessing and analyzing data to help users make better decisions" (Wixom & Watson, 2010, p. 14). BI is used in many industries, including healthcare (Olinsky & Schumacher, 2010; Sillup, Klimberg, & McSweeney, 2010). As indicated in the previous section, a number of healthcare systems, such as EHRs, CDS and RCM systems contain elements that qualify them as BI systems.

Wixom and Watson (2010) contend that BI is about getting the data in (via a data warehouse or data mart) and getting the data out (using organizational specific tools to meet decision making purposes). They provide a model of a BI-based organization that includes the traditional data warehouse elements and data integration coupled with analytical tools that have historically been of the online analytical processing (OLAP) and decision support type. These historical tools are now under the umbrella of BI technologies and applications, and are not listed separately. Additionally, and equally as important, the model includes processes related to metadata, data quality and governance. The recognition of these processes as important to the BI environment reinforces the need for practitioners to evaluate BI as a system, not simply a technology.

Two distinct types of BI have evolved: strategic and operational (Imhoff, 2005). Operational business intelligence (OBI) is relevant to both healthcare cases discussed in this chapter. OBI supports more agile decision making at all organizational levels (Marjanovic, 2010). OBI is a flexible, transparent and cost effective way of tightly integrating BI with an organization's constantly evolving business processes (Indart, 2006).

An important aspect of BI is the ability to analyze data and return information that can be used in decision making. Related to BI is the field of big data analytics. As data has become more abundant there is a need for new technologies and techniques to analyze this data effectively (Chen, Chiang, & Storey, 2012). Another challenge in healthcare is the abundance of free text that is not easily analyzed. Doctors' notes, prescription information and notes attached to test results can all be found in the typical healthcare system. New technologies in text analytics are necessary to adequately mine the data to affect decision making (Chen et al., 2012).

New government incentives, specifically the Health Information Technology for Economic and Clinical Health (HITECH) Act, which is part of the American Reinvestment and Recovery Act of 2009 and administered by the Centers for Medicare & Medicaid Services (CMS), stipulates that, beginning in 2011, healthcare providers will be offered financial incentives for demonstrating meaningful use of electronic health records (EHR). Incentives will be offered until 2015, after which time penalties may be levied for failing to demonstrate such use. The Act also establishes grants for training centers for the personnel required to support a health IT infrastructure.

With the HITECH Act providing funding and incentives for new technologies like patient sensors, new methods will be required to analyze data streamed from such mobile devices. Wactler et al (2011) envision that these new technologies must be part of an interoperable, digital infrastructure that is part of a universal system of health data and knowledge. Data in these systems must be diverse and allow for decision support. Furthermore, they contend that patients must be an integral part of the process, taking a major role in their own health and treatment. Data mining approaches, with their associated visualization techniques, could be one way to facilitate the analysis of this enormous amount of data (Hanauer, Zheng, Ramakrishnan, & Keller, 2011). BI systems can include components of scenario-based association mining, allowing healthcare providers new information on leading indicators of specific diseases (Lin, Brown, Yang, Li, & Lu, 2011). Overall BI can lead to greater improvements in patient care and payment flow, but the challenge will be developing new technologies, along with new policies and procedures to ensure that the information in these systems is of the highest quality.

Data Quality Management (DQM): Weber, Otto and Osterle, (2009) define DQM as quality-oriented management of data as an asset, that is, the planning, provisioning, organization, usage, and disposal of data that supports both decision-making and operational business processes, as well as the design of the appropriate context, with the aim to improve data quality on a sustained basis. The management of DIQ is also referred to as data governance.

DQM needs to integrate business and IT functions in order to address both organizational and technical perspectives (Abate, Diegert, & Allen, 1998). Although business and IT departments collaborate to a certain extent, the responsibility of improving data quality (DQ) and managing corporate data is often left to the latter (Friedman, 2008). Holding IT accountable for DIQ, even though data collectors are often outside the scope of control of IT, makes no sense. The analogy would be if management held manufacturing responsible for quality when ninety plus percent of the raw materials and components are supplied by outside vendors and what operators do is assemble components of questionable quality into a product. Obviously, if what is purchased is defective, no amount of proper assembly will make a quality product. The same is true for DIQ. If data collectors input garbage, no amount of work on the part of IT will make system output satisfactory to data consumers. Holding IT responsible for DIQ ignores the critical organizational factors, outside of the control of IT, that are necessary to ensure quality data and information is provided to decision makers. In fact, the quality of data and information is dependent on how it is used, also known as fitness-for-use (Neely & Cook, 2011). And decision makers should specify to data collectors what data is needed and how that data should look; in other words, decision makers need to specify the dimensions of data quality that are important to them.

Data quality is more than accuracy. In fact, Wang & Strong (1996) surveyed end-users and identified fifteen dimensions of quality, grouped into four categories: (1) intrinsic, (2) contextual, (3) representational and (4) accessibility. Intrinsic data quality refers to the dimensions inherent to the data itself, and includes believability, accuracy, reputation, and objectivity. Contextual data quality relates to perceptions of quality: timeliness, appropriate amount of data, value-added, relevancy, and completeness. The dimensions of representational data quality affect how the end user perceives the receipt of the data and includes ease of understanding, representational consistency, concise representation and interpretability. The final category, accessibility, has two dimensions: accessibility and access security.

It is difficult to trust your business intelligence system when DIQ is poor, and processes are ill conceived. Within healthcare, a reduced number of denials for claim payment and increased patient care (Leape et al., 1993) can result from improved DIQ because the system can notify providers of immunization and care plans automatically. This should result in better patient satisfaction. Fewer adjustments to the claims processing system (Romano Mj, 2011), decreased time to enroll providers, and reduced labor with respect to enrolling providers will result in better provider satisfaction and an increase in revenues in general (Rauscher & Wheeler, 2008).

DIQ in healthcare will continue to be of the utmost importance, for patient safety and satisfaction as well as the financial health of the system. Given the unique nature of the payment system in healthcare, it is critical that systems facilitate providers being paid. Getting paid from sometimes multiple payers, when payers have the ability to deny payment for a multitude of reasons, is much more challenging than in almost any other industry.

Interplay between DIQ and BI: Quality can be dramatically improved; for example, medical errors account for the deaths of at least 200,000 people in the U.S. even though the US healthcare system has traditionally been known for high quality (Harmon, 2009). As many as one in seven patients experience an adverse event, at an estimated cost to Medicare of $324 million in just October 2008 (Levinson, 2010) and as many as one in three patients experience a medical error (Classen et al., 2011). Medical errors are of four types: diagnostic, treatment, preventative and other (Leape, Lawthers, Brennan, & Johnson, 1993). Business intelligence (BI) systems could help to alleviate many of these errors. For example, diagnostic errors could be mitigated with BI by utilizing data mining techniques to look for cause and effect of lifestyle factors. These lifestyle factors could guide the diagnostician towards additional testing, ultimately resulting in a correct diagnosis. With respect to treatment errors, BI can be used as a longitudinal resource, ensuring that treatment protocols do not conflict with past history. Preventative errors also utilize the analytical capabilities of BI systems to determine what diseases a patient may be susceptible to and guide caregivers to provide prophylactic treatment.

Each of the previous types of medical errors is person-related. The final category, "Other", is system related. These errors include failure of communication, equipment failure and other system failures. Increasingly, healthcare systems are incorporating aspects of business intelligence, providing analysis of collected patient and financial data, as indicated in the previous paragraph. Intrinsic to systems is the quality of the data held in those systems. The issue of quality is exacerbated as data moves from primary to secondary sources. Thus, if we could improve the data and information quality (DIQ), we may be able to reduce the incidence of patient death and ultimately improve the quality of healthcare in general.

In addressing some of the concerns with quality, the U.S. government has allocated approximately $19 billion a year to be used by healthcare providers to implement electronic health record systems (EHRs) (Keehan et al., 2011). By using decision-support tools or BI, these systems can increase the adherence to protocol-based systems. Additionally, there should be a reduction in adverse drug events and medication errors (Wu et al., 2006). However, these systems can be costly and there is a need to study the return on investment. Bardhan and Thouin (2012) show that the use of EHRs can positively impact the treatment for heart attacks, heart failures and pneumonia. Furthermore, using financial management systems can result in lower operating expenses. On the other hand, Romano (2011) studied clinical decision making systems (CDS) and did not find a correlation between visits with and without a CDS on the quality of care. Linder et al. (2007) had a similar finding. Their study examined EHR use and ambulatory care quality and found no significant association. According to Giannangelo and Fenton (2008), in order for the EHRs to be effective, there must be a standard of codification and it must be used consistently to ensure that data is correct and reliable. This codification, particularly within the financial portion of the system, can lead to more effective revenue cycle management (RCM).

RCM is the collection of methods used to manage claims processing payment and revenue generation. Unlike the standard business-to-business or business-to-consumer model, whereby an invoice or request for payment is generated and the payment is made, a significant proportion of the revenue in healthcare is derived from non-patient payment (e.g., a third party), resulting in multiple streams of payments that must be managed. RCM is a frequent component of BI, allowing managers to increase the speed and amount of patient revenue collection (Rauscher & Wheeler, 2008). A potential consequence of the Patient Protection and Affordable Care Act is that serving publicly insured patients may have a negative impact on revenue cycle management (Rauscher & Wheeler, 2010). However, to the contrary, findings from their research indicate that hospitals with a higher Medicare and Medicaid payer mix actually collect revenues in higher percentages and quicker than hospitals with more privately insured or self-pay patients.

A properly implemented business intelligence system can play a vital role in ensuring quality throughout the data and information lifecycle. Thus, this chapter examines the connections between these two very important and mutually dependent areas of practice, BI and DIQ, in such a data-rich environment as healthcare. The PGOT framework, discussed next, provides an excellent mechanism for evaluating opportunities for improving quality.

Data and Information Quality Framework – PGOT

As evidenced by frameworks such as COBIT (Boritz, 2005), IT governance has been at the forefront of management concerns for a number of years. Increasingly, the challenge is to govern not only the systems, but also the data residing in the systems (Maguire, 2008). As indicated earlier, DIQ is dependent on how the data is used. Thus, acceptable quality in one instance may be unacceptable in another. For example, prescription information may be entered into a system for a patient. The data is accurate, but incomplete. The system has not captured the fact that the patient is seeing a specialist who has prescribed other medications that negatively interact with what the primary care physician has prescribed. Proper data governance, across all care providers, could help to alleviate this problem.

Compared with the extensive research literature on IT governance, academic interest and research on data governance and its relationship to business intelligence is still in its infancy. As introduced in Neely and Cook (2011), the PGOT (**P**eople, **G**overnance, **O**perations, and **T**echnology) framework provides a foundation for evaluating the quality of data and information. Figure 1 presents an enhanced version of the PGOT with an increased emphasis on the people within the system. The governance plans, operational efficiency and technical competency of the systems continue to be a driving force in the overall quality of the data and information. Based on contingency theory of organizational design, the underlying assumption of the PGOT framework is that there is no universal design applicable to all organizations for data and information quality, and healthcare is no exception. It is the contextual factors in healthcare that impact the contribution of data governance in enhancing IT governance and organizational performance. This framework focuses on long-term data and information quality improvement and error prevention, rather than correction. In the two cases discussed later, business intelligence systems are the mechanism by which DIQ is improved. The usefulness of a BI system is directly correlated to the quality of the data that it contains and the information it produces.

It is impossible to ensure "perfect" data quality on all dimensions given that the quality of data and information is dependent on its use; that is, decision making in context. The role of the data governance council, and by extension the chief data steward, business data steward and technical data steward, is to ensure the data and information is of sufficient quality to best meet the demands of most decision makers. The business data steward must define the business requirements and expectations, and trust the technical data steward to work with developers to build a system that meets data and information quality-related business requirements. In addition, the chief data steward must design and implement plans, policies and procedures that comply with legal and ethical requirements and meets the needs of data consumers.

Although perfect data is impossible, there are multiple feedback loops illustrated throughout the framework, many of them resulting from data quality audits, to help in the identification of opportunities to continuously improve DIQ. Therefore, the ability to audit the data and information quality from an operational, technical, and compliance perspective is vital to DQM. As a result, the BI system should have embedded continuous auditing controls, and metrics from such audits should be frequently analyzed for system usability and reliability.

The roles of the people who influence, manage and use the BI system with an emphasis on the data governance system are illustrated in Figure 2. The PGOT framework will be used to focus attention on DIQ within the BI system, specifically in the healthcare industry. The next section describes the healthcare environment and this is followed by a description of two case studies, illustrating how a methodical approach to examining DIQ can help to improve the quality and usefulness of the BI system, and ultimately impact the satisfaction of the patients and providers.

BETTER MANAGING COSTS AND MEDICAL OUTCOMES USING DIQ AND BI

Medicare and Medicaid continue to ratchet down provider payments, and will continue to do so. Fee for service is becoming less prevalent, while value-added and bundled services, referred to within the industry as episodic payments, will increase. Many payers already pay a lump sum for maternity. Physician procedural income will decline while their employment and integration with healthcare facilities will increase. As a result, hospitals, physicians and other healthcare providers will either find a way to deliver healthcare for less money or go out of business. The fundamental challenge of healthcare reform is to simultane-

Figure 1. DIQ in context: PGOT research framework

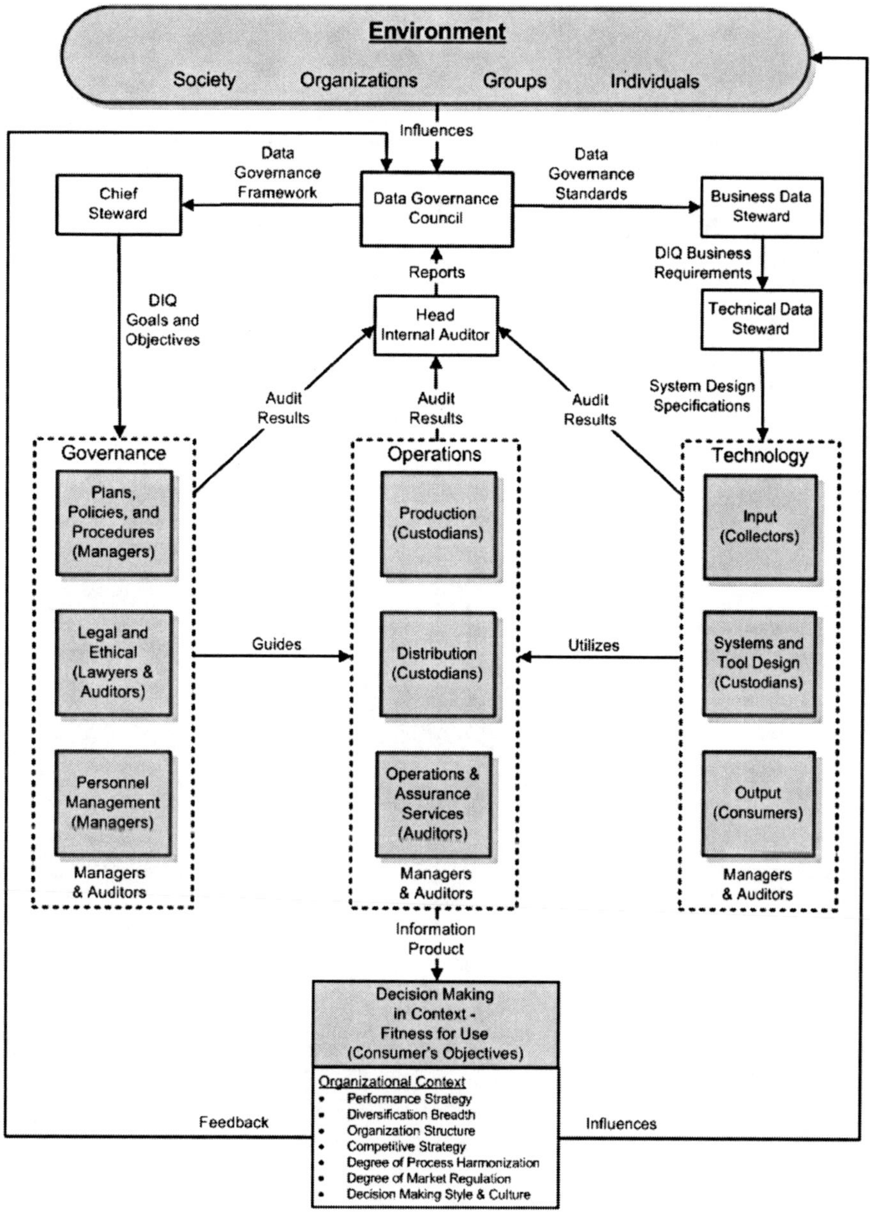

ously improve the quality of care while lowering its costs. Although profitability is a dirty word in healthcare, without it, healthcare will not have the funds needed to provide better care for patients, whether it is acquiring the latest technology or hiring adequate staff to treat patients.

To improve quality, many healthcare organizations turn to the National Committee for Quality Assurance (NCQA), an independent 501(c) non-profit organization in the United States designed to improve healthcare quality. It manages voluntary accreditation programs and certifies physician organizations, and accredits managed care organizations and preferred provider organizations. NCQA's accreditation program represents the most rigorous standards of their kind. The NCQA seal

Figure 2. Roles within data governance

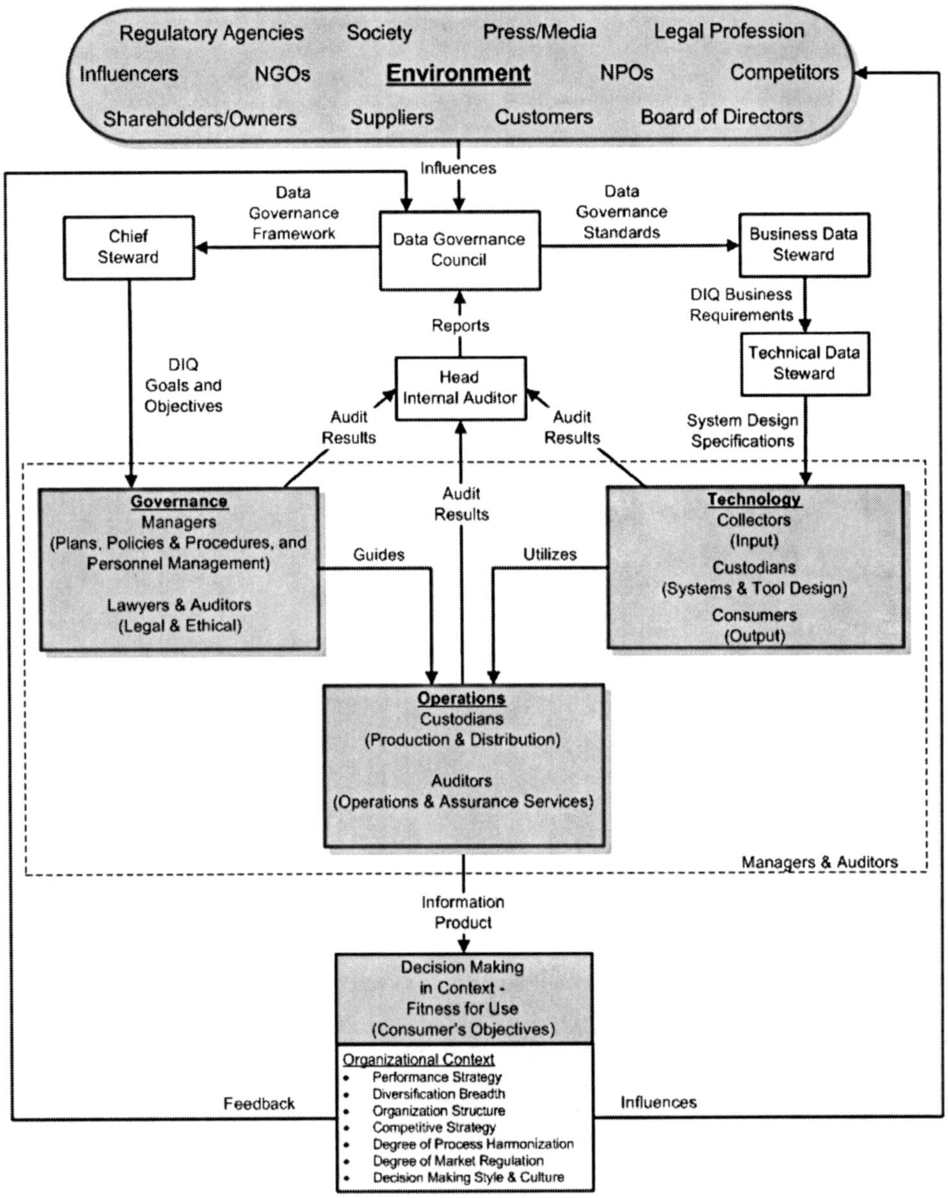

is a widely recognized symbol of quality. Health plans today face a rigorous set of more than 60 standards and must report on their performance in more than 40 areas in order to earn NCQA's seal of approval.

The NCQA's Patient Centered Medical Homes (PCMH) is an innovative program for improving primary care that describes clear and specific criteria for organizing care around patients, working in teams, and coordinating and tracking care over time. The use of the word home in this context does not imply a physical place, rather PCMH is an organization model for providing comprehensive, coordinated high quality primary care that is patient-centered, safe and accessible (Agency for Healthcare Research and Qulaity, 2012). NCQA facilitates a partnership between a patient, and their personal primary care physician, and when appropriate, the patient's family. The primary care clinician leads a team that takes collective responsibility for patient care, providing for the patient's healthcare needs and arranging for appropriate care with other qualified clinicians, when needed. The medical home is intended to result in more personalized, coordinated, effective and efficient care (Agency for Healthcare Research and Qulaity, 2012).

Figure three shows stakeholders of the healthcare supply chain, including NCQA. At the far left, pharmaceutical companies, medical device manufacturers, and biotech companies sell products to distributors and wholesalers for redistribution to the rest of the supply chain. Even though patients are the ultimate consumer of healthcare, they are but one of many groups that pay for healthcare. Payers refer to all those entities that pay the healthcare providers and include employer groups, Medicaid, Medicare, State Children's Health Insurance Programs (SCHIP), commercial insurers and self-pay. Just as there are a multitude of payers, there are many providers. Home health agencies, long-term care facilities, hospitals, outpatient treatment, specialty care and physicians all provide care for patients. To the far right, of the figure, we see the most fundamental relationship in the healthcare supply chain – physician/patient relationship. It is this relationship that is the focus of the PCMH mentioned in the previous paragraph. As if that was not enough complexity in the supply chain, there are a number of accrediting agencies and regulatory agencies that interact with the healthcare industry. Lastly, the press, legal profession, competitors and board of directors of the healthcare facilities themselves all influence the supply chain. Within this complex environment, we are going to focus on two case studies. The first one involves the processes needed to get paid for vaccinating adults against shingles in a multi-facility medical group. The second case involves the processes required for an insurance company to enroll and credential providers from a large medical provider.

Case 1: Multi-Facility Healthcare Medical Group (MHMG)

This case examines a primary care healthcare group that operates in ten locations. The multi-facility healthcare medical group (MHMG) offers services to patients that include family and internal medicine, pediatrics, pharmacy, eye care, urgent care and other specialties. From this point forward, the organization will be referred to as MHMG. Although MHMG, in general, manages acute illnesses, provides preventive care, and treats chronic conditions, this particular case focuses exclusively on preventive care management and in particular, immunizations. As with most healthcare organizations, MHMG increasingly focuses on two important aspects of healthcare, namely cost and quality. From a quality perspective, the National Committee for Quality Assurance (NCQA) has awarded all ten practices of MHMG with its highest designation – level 3 Patient Centered Medical Home (PCMH).

Before we begin detailing the challenges faced by MHMG, let's examine two out of three processes that are interconnected: provider onboarding, and the revenue management cycle (see Figure 4). Let's begin by examining the provider onboarding cycle. First, MHMG must recruit healthcare providers. Generically a provider is a professional engaged in the delivery of health services and includes physicians, dentists, nurses, pediatricians, optometrists, and psychologists. In the medical field, hospitals and long-term care facilities are also called providers. Once a provider is recruited, an employment offer must be extended and accepted. Then MHMG credentials the provider. Credentialing is the process of reviewing a healthcare provider's qualifications. Academic background, training, and clinical experience are examined to determine if criteria for clinical privileges are met. Privileging defines a provider's scope of practice and the clinical services he or she may provide. Last, the provider must be enrolled with payers so that when claims are submitted, they are paid correctly. Once the provider has completed the onboarding process they will be scheduled to treat patients. This is the touch point between provider onboarding and the revenue management cycle.

The revenue management cycle has many more steps than the provider onboarding cycle, and requires the participation of numerous individuals such as patients, patient service representatives (PSRs), business service representatives (BSRs), providers, coders, billers and collections. Most patients would be surprised at the large percentage of times healthcare facilities are denied payment from insurance companies, Medicaid, and Medicare.

This particular case examines the revenue management cycle for vaccines. The immune system tends to weaken over time, putting older adults at risk for infectious diseases. The Advisory Committee on Immunization Practices (ACIP) at the Center for Disease Control (CDC) suggests that adults 60 years or older receive the following vaccinations: influenza vaccine, Tdap vaccine, Pneumococcal vaccine and Zoster vaccine. MHMG follows the CDC recommendations.

What precipitated the initiation of this business intelligence project was the large number of denials for the Zoster vaccine. The Zoster vaccine is designed to prevent shingles. Anyone who has had chicken pox is at risk for shingles. Shingles (herpes zoster) is a painful, blistering skin rash that occurs when the virus that caused chicken pox becomes active in the nerves of older adults. Why the virus becomes active in older adults is unclear and typically only one attack occurs.

The challenge from a business perspective is that insurance coverage varies by contract and even patient group; sometimes coverage is under pharmacy benefits, other times medical benefits, or not covered at all. Some payers set the age at 55 rather than 60. To further complicate matters, each of the ten facilities has different processes for verifying coverage, administering the vaccine, and billing. Inconsistent coverage and a nonstandard vaccination process have resulted in many payment denials. The Zoster vaccine is expensive, costing over $200 per shot. However, the total cost was much higher. Patients receive bills that they were not expecting, resulting in vigorous complaints. Clinical and business staff was confused about how to verify insurance coverage and frustrated from all the patient complaints. As a result, some providers stopped giving the immunization and when they did give it, the coders spent an inordinate amount of time verifying every encounter form, calling both pharmacy and medical staff. Something needed to be done.

Most of these denials were the result of poor quality data resulting from an ill-defined vaccination process. The data in the system was incorrect concerning whether the benefits were covered by medical or pharmacy. Often, the amount of the copay was incorrect. When the provider accessed the patient's electronic health record, the data concerning vaccination was often missing or inaccurate.

Even in healthcare, it is not economically or practically feasible to ensure DIQ on all dimensions of quality. Thus, some element of satisficing is necessary. As providers and business managers of healthcare facilities go about the business of managing their operations and reporting financial results, they must be aware of the inherent tradeoffs in DIQ. In healthcare, relevancy is a critical dimension, as well as access security due to the privacy and security rules associated with the Health Insurance Portability and Accountability Act of 1996 (HIPAA). Relevancy occurs when data provides benefit to a decision maker who uses it and finds it helpful for the task at hand. Other important dimensions that should be part of the design of any healthcare BI system include objectivity, completeness and interpretability. Objectivity refers to the extent to which data are unbiased, unprejudiced and impartial. Completeness specifies that data are of sufficient breadth, depth and scope for the task at hand. Interpretability refers to the extent to which data are in an appropriate language and their definitions are clear. Interpretability is always of concern in the medical field, where entire courses exist that focus exclusively on medical terminology.

DIQ impacts all types of transactional systems, and healthcare is heavily transactional in nature. Within the healthcare industry, Kerr, Norris and Stockdale (2008) describe the development and implementation of programs to improve data quality, thus making the strategic management of data quality a part of day-to-day business. Ge and Helfert (2008) examine the four categories of DIQ described earlier and show that improving representational DIQ may intensify the positive effects of contextual DIQ in inventory management. Can this lesson be extrapolated to healthcare systems? Probably so. Authors are in agreement that data quality is a critical success factor (Wixom & Watson, 2001), and that the choice of attributes is a non-trivial decision (Pighin & Ieronutti, 2008).

As can be seen in Figure 5, the PGOT framework can easily be adapted to healthcare. The focus continues to be on people and their interactions with the system. As indicated earlier, IT does not bear the full brunt of responsibility for DIQ in the system. Instead, it is a shared responsibility, with all members along the DIQ information product operations chain (e.g., auditors, data collectors, data custodians, data consumers and managers) accountable for the quality of the data and information. The primary job of many of these stakeholders is not technology (e.g. patient service representatives, nurses, physicians, payers, providers and patients) and it is important that they understand the importance of DIQ.

From a collector's perspective, a busy nurse or physician must appreciate the importance of accurate data entry for downstream use in the billing process. The nurse in the room with the patient will be able to see that he or she is reacting poorly to a drug. This adverse effect must be entered, accurately, into the system so that the physician who uses the BI system two years later will not prescribe a similar drug. Healthcare BI systems in particular must also meet many legal regulations and ethical considerations, and it is vital that policies, plans and procedures be in place for compliance purposes. The focus of the MHMG case is on the revenue management cycle and the next case on the provider enrollment cycle. Operationally, in another healthcare study, we could also have other cycles such patient-physician, physician-pharmacy, and patient-health insurance provider. The focus of the technology piece will be to ensure that the previous issues can be adequately implemented in the BI system.

The process improvement team first mapped out the current state. The clinical and business staff at each of the 10 facilities were interviewed to determine what the current process was for administering the Zoster vaccine. What resulted was not a single process map but rather 10 distinctly different processes. Figure 6 shows the process maps for three out of the ten sites. At this point, three things became clear. MHMG needed to determine how big the problem was, what was critical for a newly designed process if a new process was warranted and third, create this new standardized process for administering vaccines.

Since every facility was doing things differently, data had to be tracked and trended by site. The metrics vary greatly by site. For example one site administered the vaccine to over 50% of their patients who were 65 and older that visited MHMG in the first nine months of 2012 whereas another site administered the vaccine to less than 1% of those patients who were over 65. Note that MGMH used 65 as the cutoff for their analysis rather than 60. Claims denials ran slightly higher than 54% for the entire organization. That means over half of the vaccines that were administered in the first nine months of 2012 MHMG was not paid for them, resulting in a write-off of approximately $100,000. So clearly the problem impacts patients and MHMG in a significant way. Keep in mind, the numbers cited here are only for the Zoster vaccine. Even though the organization focused on this particular vaccine, the lessons learned were leveraged across all vaccines.

Now that the organization had verified this was a problem worthy of pursuit, the next step was to determine what was critical to stakeholders. For patients, it was critical for them to know up front what their coverage was and if a copay or self-pay was needed, and that it was paid at the time the vaccine was administered. For providers, they also needed to know coverage at the time of the encounter. For coders, they needed a seamless billing system that did not require them to call the pharmacy and medical staff every time they encountered a chart that indicated the vaccine has been administered.

The process improvement team, using their definition of what was critical-to-care (CTC), developed a much more straightforward standardized process with far fewer steps (see Figure 7). The new process consists of three major phases: business intelligence system, patient care, and billing. Now before a patient arrives, the business intelligence system identifies coverage and copay amount for each patient who meets the criteria for the vaccine. In order to test the effectiveness of the new process, two pilot sites were chosen. As often is the case, the two sites that volunteered were sites that had performed much better than the other sites using the old process. In fact, their claims denial percentage was much lower than the organization as a whole (32.6% in the first nine months of 2012 compared to 54%). To proceed with the pilot, standard operating procedures for collecting and posting copays were developed as well as new pharmacy and billing procedures. Furthermore, in order to verify results of the pilot, new reconciliation and control reports were created.

The pilot ran for the last three months of 2012 and the results were significant (see Figure 8). With the new BI system, denials went from 32.59% to 5.65%, providers increased the number of shots they were giving patients, and feedback from staff and providers was positive. The staff commented they could now concentrate on patient care rather than insurance issues concerning this vaccine. The organization rolled out the new process to all 10 facilities starting January of 2013 and expects to have a financial impact on the organization amounting to approximately $600,000 gross revenues and $200,000 in net profit in 2013. This estimated impact is based on a single vaccine and when the principles learned from this project are rolled out to other vaccines, the impact on the organization will be in the millions.

Prior to the creation of the business intelligence system, there was no easy way for staff to determine which patients that were visiting over the next couple days met the criteria for vaccination. Clinicians often missed opportunities to provide preventive care as recommended by clinical guidelines, forgoing the associated revenue stream. With the creation of a business intelligence component to their electronic health records system, MHMG can identify patients that qualify for vaccines, lab work, and exams covered by their particular insurance company. Alerts in the system can remind clinicians of interventions and screening tests while the patient is in the examination room.

For the Zoster vaccine, the new system generates a list of patients with appointments two business days from now that meet vaccine criteria. For each of these patients, their payment type is examined: commercial insurance, self-pay, or government program such as Medicare or Medicaid. Government programs cover this vaccine under pharmacy benefits and the pharmacy system verifies coverage and copay and notes in the patient's electronic health record whether the vaccine is covered and if so, what the copay amount is. For commercial insurance, the insurance verification unit (IVU) verifies coverage and copay, noting whether the vaccine is covered and if so, what the copay amount is.

As the results show, the implementation of the business intelligence system had a large impact on the medical outcomes, financial performance, compliance (with CDC recommended care), and overall customer satisfaction. The lessons learned from this project are now being replicated with other vaccines. Next, we examine another part of the healthcare supply chain – provider credentialing and enrollment.

Case 2: Regional Health Insurance Company (RHIS)

This case involves a regional health insurance company and a provider group. This regional health insurance company, referred to here as RHIS, is located in the United States and is a nonprofit health insurer. It has provided health insurance for over 8 decades and currently serves approximately 2 million members. The provider group represents almost 1,000 specialists and primary care providers in negotiating payment rates with third party and credentialing providers. The specialist and primary care provider (SPCP) group will be referred to here as the SPCP group for short. The SPCP group is certified by the National Committee for Quality Assurance (NCQA).

SPCP group has many providers, in many different locations, with differing rates depending on the service(s) rendered. Keeping provider data current in RHIS is challenging. SPCP requests monthly additions and updates to provider information. The SPCP group submits these changes to RHIS in three ways: (1) carve-out list, (2) all employee list and (3) modifications based on a printed copy of the provider database. A carve out list is a list of medical services that are separated from a contract and paid under a different arrangement. Reports have overlaps in information and many people touch these reports before the department ultimately responsible for handling provider file maintenance receives them. For example, sometimes, the duplicate requests found on these three reports are inconsistent. Properly maintaining the provider file is important since the provider record drives the reimbursement the provider will receive.

As a result of a poor process, the following impacts were felt by both RHIS and the SPCP group: (1) system updates lagged well behind requests for updates due to the many "touches", (2) reimbursements to the providers were not timely nor accurate due to lag time mentioned in the first point, (3) inaccurate and untimely reimbursements result in almost 10,000 adjustments per year, (4) credentialing had to perform duplicative tasks in order to complete their new provider process in a timely manner and (5) the SPCP group was very dissatisfied. This dissatisfaction led to the group withholding repayment of over $1 million in overpayments to induce RHIS to reduce the time it took to make updates and to increase the accuracy of the provider file database itself.

The provider file data management (PFDM) department loads and maintains the provider information in all RHIS systems. As mentioned before, the provider record drives provider reimbursement. PFDM processes service requests from SPCP, resulting in three main activities: the creation of new provider recorders, punching through the carve-out list, and making demographic updates. The analysis of the service request process requires all three activities are examined.

The primary objective of this process improvement project was to reduce the time it takes to react to requests for changes from SPCP. Specifically, it addressed reducing the times associated with three activities: the creation of new provider recorders, punching through the carve-out list and making demographic updates. The primary objective of the new provider creation process was to reduce the time it takes to create a new provider record from its current baseline of 55 calendar days to seven calendar days. The primary objective for punching through the carve-list was to reduce the time it takes from its current baseline of 40 calendar days to seven calendar days. Lastly, the primary objective for updating provider demographics was to reduce the time it takes from its current baseline of 50 calendar days to ten calendar days. Secondary, but important, benefits included reduced time to research the provider record requests and reduce the number of claim payment adjustment and the resulting increase in satisfaction from SPCP as a result.

By implementing a business intelligence system, the data was cleansed, multiple handoffs eliminated, cycle time targets met, and greater customer satisfaction achieved. These two examples illustrate why it is important for healthcare to embrace BI.

Solutions and Recommendations

BI systems have the potential to move the healthcare industry forward. They provide information that will enable better patient care and can help healthcare as a business survive with expedited payments. However, these benefits will only accrue if the data that drives the information is of high quality and is appropriate for the decisions being made.

The PGOT framework, with its focus on the systemic effects of DIQ, can provide structure to the development and use of a BI system in healthcare. Thoughtful consideration of the implications of policies and procedures with respect to DIQ, appointing appropriate people in key roles such as Chief Data Steward and a Governance Council, and ensuring that systems are operationally and technically aligned with the DIQ goals, can help ensure that the BI systems can provide the information needed by providers to make good patient and business decisions.

As seen in the MHMG case, one of the difficulties facing healthcare, is the lack of consistency across multiple locations. Given the size and scope of current healthcare organizations, it is common to find each unit operating independently, particularly with respect to the systems that are in place. Figure 5 illustrates how the PGOT can be applied to healthcare, specifically with respect to revenue cycle management, a key driver of the success of the healthcare business. By examining the BI system with respect to DIQ systemically, we can help ensure that the organization as a whole is running at optimal efficiency. For example, DIQ governance in healthcare can center on claims processing. As indicated earlier, the healthcare industry does not deal with one payer and one payee, but rather multiple payers and payees. As seen in Figure 4, the revenue cycle management can only be enabled if the providers are successfully enrolled in the system with the right credentials and privileges. Without providers, there would be nothing to bill for. Without billing, the healthcare business would not be able to support itself.

Thus, our recommendation is that a multi-step approach be followed:

1. Create a high-level context diagram that shows the system connections to the environment and closely examine the roles of people as they apply to the process (Figures 3 and 4);
2. Create a process flow chart that shows the stakeholders, activities and system data flows in question (Figure 6);
3. Align the PGOT framework (Figure 1) to the process flow chart to identify areas of concern (Figure 5);
4. Implement interventions to close the gap between the "as is" and the "to be" (Figure 7);
5. Track performance and continue to make adjustments as needed (Figure 8).

With this methodical approach to examining the problem and solution, with a careful examination of the DIQ issues along the way, the BI system can be implemented to take full advantage of the power that it holds.

Figure 3. Healthcare stakeholders and supply chain

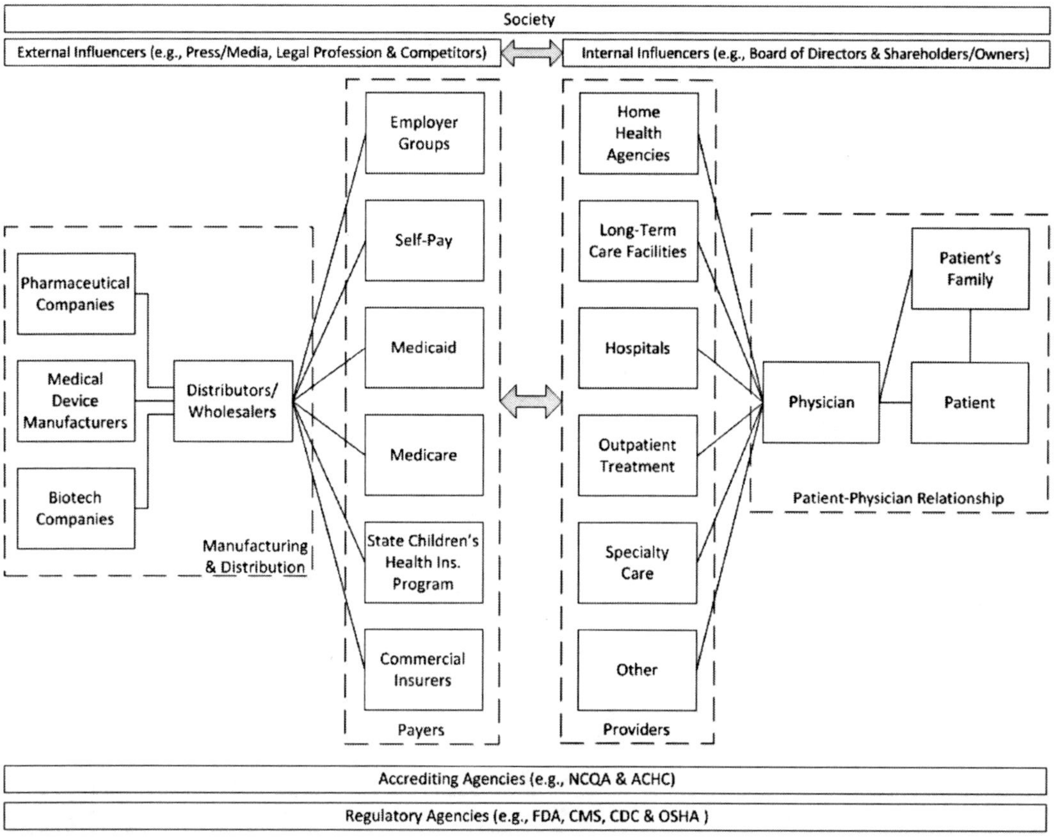

Figure 4. Revenue management and provider enrollment cycles

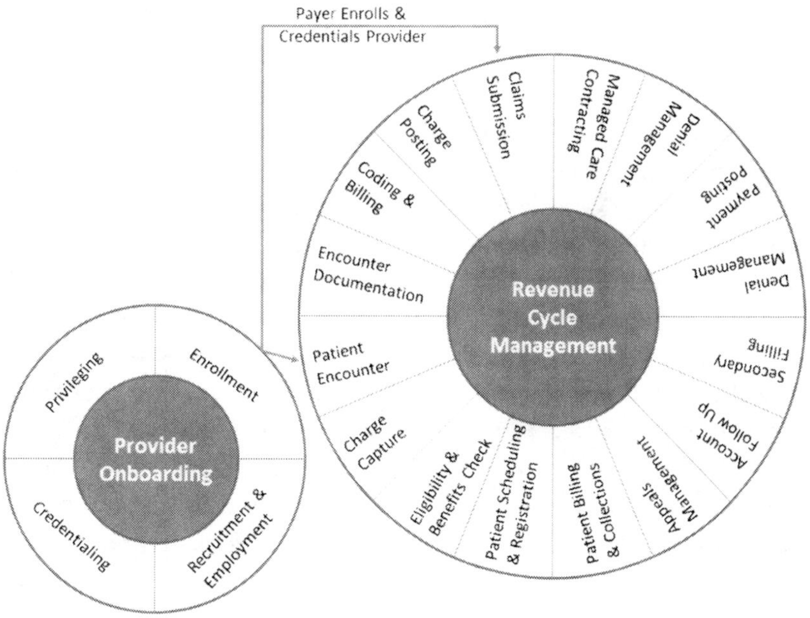

Figure 5. PGOT applied to healthcare: Case 1

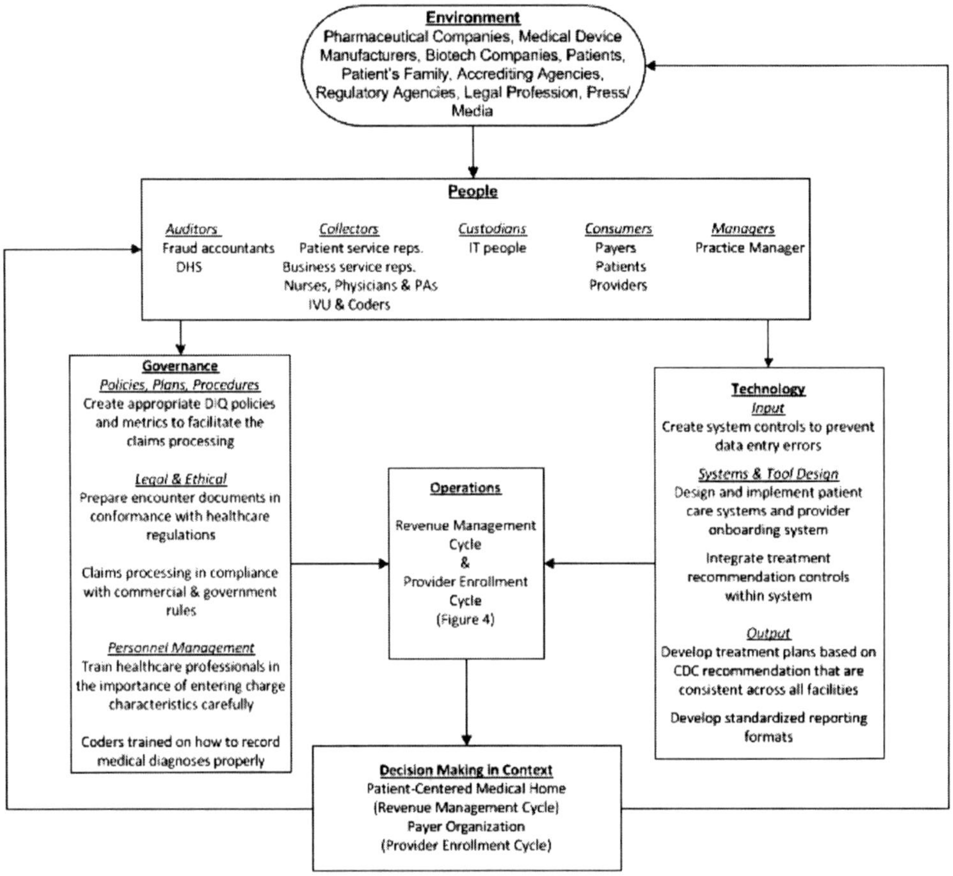

FUTURE RESEARCH DIRECTIONS

DIQ is a critical aspect of any system. The PGOT encompasses DIQ in all types of systems, including BI. It is this area where the two intersect that is interesting to analyze in terms of similarities and differences. There is potential for collaboration between the BI and DIQ research communities. Clearly, DIQ is a critical success factor in BI. As indicated earlier, data quality processes are an explicit part of the BI model. Some elements of the PGOT model exist elsewhere in the BI model, such as people, technologies, governance and metadata. As we begin to develop a roadmap for BI and DIQ integration, there are questions to be answered. Can PGOT simply be embedded in the data quality processes of BI development? How, if at all, are BI systems different with respect to DIQ than TPS or ERP systems? For example as we look at the 15 dimensions of quality raised earlier, how would users of a BI system prioritize the dimensions compared to users of an accounting information system (AIS), which is fundamentally a TPS? Would healthcare BI users value different data quality dimensions than AIS users? Should the people aspects of DIQ be tightly coupled with the people aspects of BI or are they completely different stakeholders? These and other questions should be addressed as we move towards interdisciplinary research between the two fields.

Figure 6. Immunization flowchart: Before implementing business intelligence

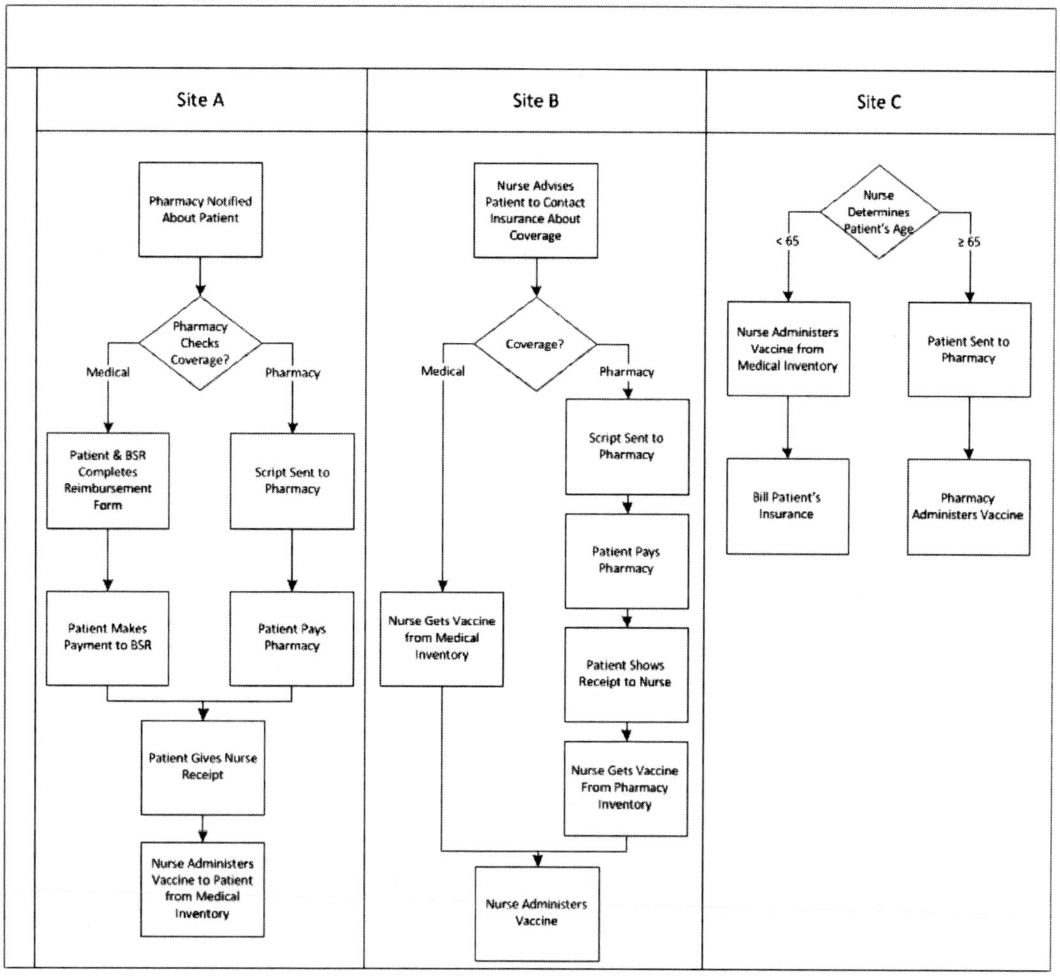

The focus of the preceding paragraph was on the people that interact with the healthcare BI system, and research questions that have not yet been addressed. However, the PGOT also addresses technical considerations and there is a great opportunity for collaborative work between the Computer Science (CS) community and DIQ researchers. For example, data profiling and enrichment are critical factors as we move forward towards more managed care of the healthy individual. In addition, as discussed earlier, there is a great deal of unstructured data in a healthcare BI system. The CS and information science communities are doing research on word mining and automatic classification of terms. Semantic knowledge bases can allow for better coding of physician notes and other free text. In addition, privacy and security issues are critical in a healthcare environment. These are all areas where DIQ researchers can collaborate with their technical colleagues.

Another fruitful collaboration in this arena would be the cross-business disciplinary research. Accountants understand the numbers and MIS researchers understand the technical aspects of metadata. The metadata of a system can be a strong indicator of the potential success of the BI system, as this information flows with the data

Figure 7. Immunization flowchart: After implementing business intelligence

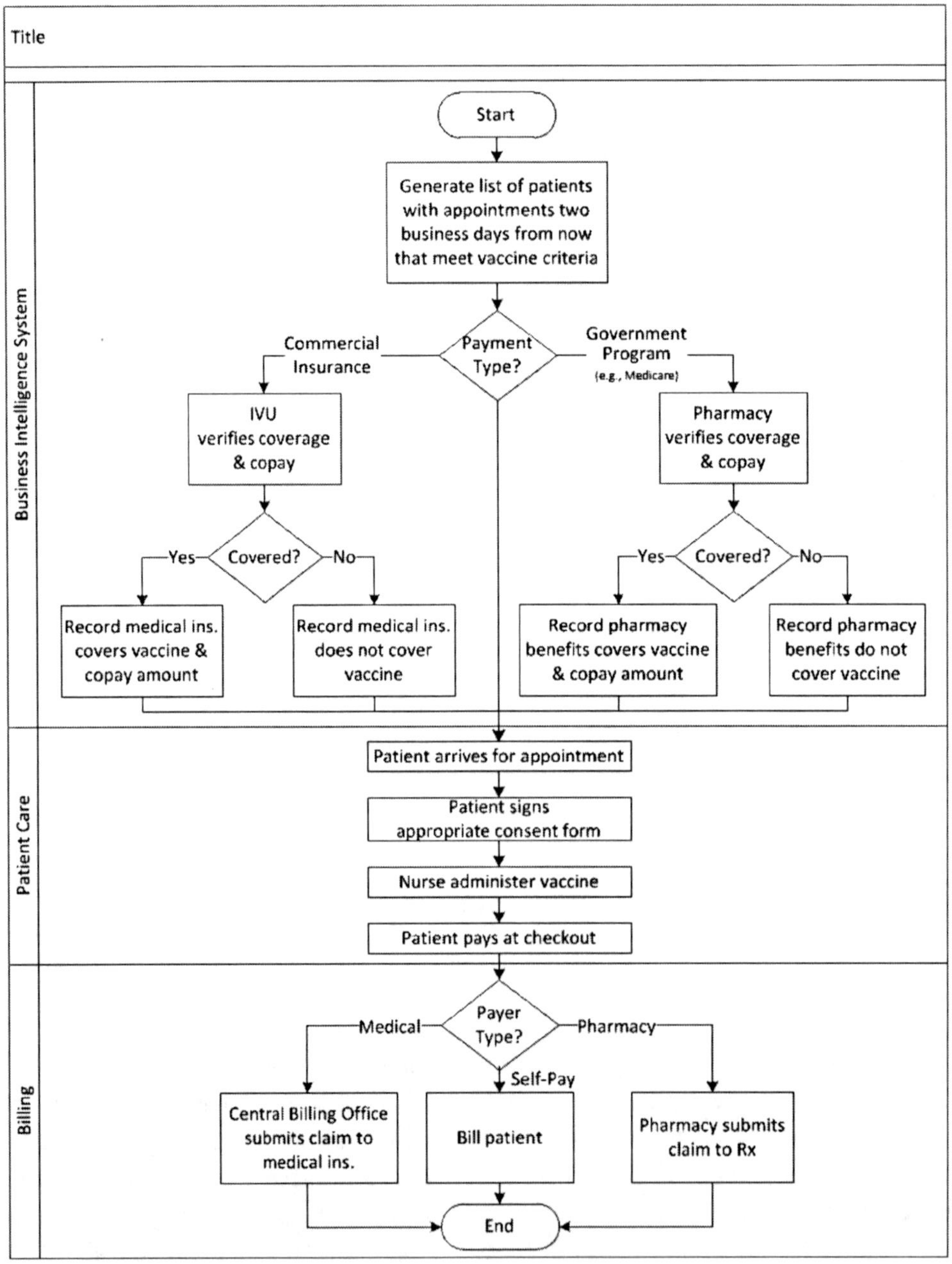

from primary systems into secondary systems, such as BI. As the accountants determine what metadata is important (data collected, alternative definitions, etc.) the MIS researcher can implement technical controls for capturing this metadata.

CONCLUSION

This paper describes two case studies in the healthcare industry. By weaving the elements of the PGOT framework throughout the narrative,

Figure 8. Percentage of denials before and after BI system rollout

	2012	Total Claims	Total Denials	% Denials
Before Improvements	Jan.	30	10	33.33%
	Feb.	22	8	36.36%
	Mar	22	8	36.36%
	Apr	50	8	16.00%
	May	36	10	27.78%
	Jun	50	16	32.00%
	Jul	34	14	41.18%
	Aug	52	14	26.92%
	Sep	60	26	43.33%
	Averages	39.56	12.67	32.59%
After	Oct	112	8	7.14%
	Nov	164	14	8.54%
	Dec	156	2	1.28%
	Averages	144.00	8.00	5.65%

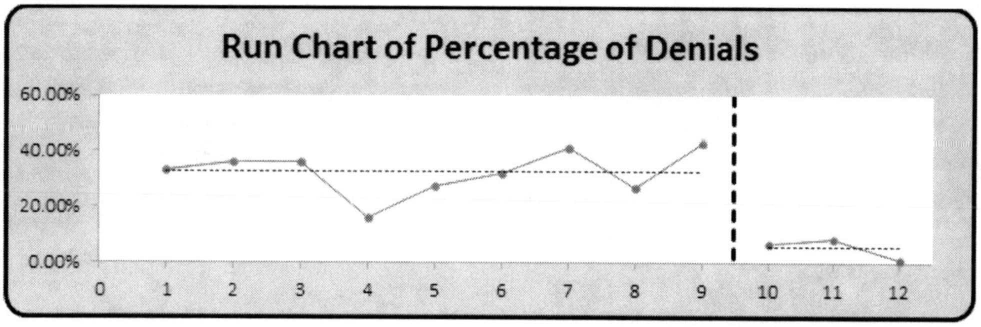

several opportunities for improvement were suggested and discussed. This led to recommendations for best practices. This paper adds to the theoretical literature by operationalizing a theoretical model and showing the interconnections within an overall DIQ system. It adds to the practical literature by offering specific recommendations for practice. DIQ is obviously an important issue in healthcare. It affects the ability of providers and business managers at all levels to make decisions. Within the healthcare industry there are many opportunities for improved decision making, which can directly impact medical outcomes and the bottom line.

There are many organizational systems including transaction processing systems (TPS), management information systems (MIS), enterprise resource planning systems (ERP) and business intelligence (BI) systems. As discussed in the literature review, BI is not just a technology. It is the system which collects, stores, and analyzes business data to support decision making. Key components of this system include source systems, the data warehouse and associated metadata, and the analytical tools such as data mining and general statistical analysis. Moving data from the sources to the data warehouse requires data integration which is both a technology and a process. Metadata, data quality and data governance processes ensure that data moves through the system efficiently and effectively (Wixom & Watson, 2010). Integrating DIQ methodologies into the BI system will help to ensure that the system addresses the end user needs. The descriptions of the cases in this chapter show how this can be accomplished.

REFERENCES

Abate, M. L., Diegert, K. V., & Allen, H. W. (1998). A hierarchical approach to improving data quality. *Data Quality*, *4*(1), 10.

Agency for Healthcare Research and Qulaity. (2012). *Patient centered medical home*. Retrieved 1/16/2013, from http://pcmh.ahrq.gov/portal/server.pt/community/pcmh__home/1483/PCMH_Defining%20the%20PCMH_v2

Angeles. (2012). *How health reform's medicaid expansion will impact state budgets federal government will pick up nearly all costs, even as expansion provides coverage to millions of low-income uninsured Americans*. Retrieved March 5, 2013 http://www.cbpp.org/cms/index.cfm?fa=view&id=3801.

Bardhan, I. R., & Thouin, M. F. (2012). Health information technology and its impact on the quality and cost of healthcare delivery. *Decision Support Systems*, *55*(2),438-449. doi: http://dx.doi.org/10.1016/j.dss.2012.10.003

Bitterer, A., Schlegel, K., Hostmann, B., Gassman, B., Beyer, M. A., Herschel, G., & Andrews, W. (2007). *Hype cycle for business intelligence and performance management, 2007*. Stamford, CT: Gartner Research.

Boritz, J. E. (2005). IS practitioners' views on core concepts of information integrity. *International Journal of Accounting Information Systems*, *6*, 20. doi:10.1016/j.accinf.2005.07.001

Broaddus, M., & Park, E. (2012). *Number of uninsured fell in 2011, largely due to health reform and public programs*. Washington, DC: Dept of Health and Human Services.

Byrd, L. W., & Byrd, T. A. (2012). The impact of clinical information technology on information quality in US hospitals. *International Journal of Healthcare Technology and Management*, *13*(1), 71–87. doi:10.1504/IJHTM.2012.048948

Chen, H., Chiang, R. H. L., & Storey, V. C. (2012). Business intelligence and analytics: From big data to big impact. *Management Information Systems Quarterly*, *36*(4), 1165–1188.

Classen, D. C., Resar, R., Griffin, F., Federico, F., Frankel, T., Kimmel, N., & James, B. C. (2011). Global trigger tool shows that adverse events in hospitals may be ten times greater than previously measured. *Health Affairs*, *30*(4), 581–589. doi:10.1377/hlthaff.2011.0190 PMID:21471476

Davenport, T. H. (2010). Business intelligence and organizational decisions. *International Journal of Business Intelligence Research*, *1*(1), 1–12. doi:10.4018/jbir.2010071701

Friedman, T. (2008). *Gartner study on data quality shows that IT still bears the burden*. Stamford, CT: Gartner Group.

Ge, M., & Helfert, M. (2008). Effects of information quality on inventory management. *International Journal of Information Quality*, *2*(2), 15. doi:10.1504/IJIQ.2008.022962

Giannangelo, K., & Fenton, S. (2008). EHR's effect on the revenue cycle management coding function. *Journal of Healthcare Information Management*, *22*(1), 26–29. PMID:19267004

Hanauer, D. A., Zheng, K., Ramakrishnan, N., & Keller, B. J. (2011). Opportunities and challenges in association and episode discovery from electronic health records. *IEEE Intelligent Systems*, *26*(5), 83–87.

Harmon, K. (2009). *Deaths from avoidable medical error more than double in past decade, investigation shows*. Scientific American Blog.

Imhoff, C. (2005). Streaming processes for front-line workers: Adding business intelligence for operations. *Operational Business Intelligence White Paper, Intelligent Solutions Inc.* Retrieved from http://www.tdwi.com

Indart, B. (2006). Operationalizing business intelligence – Turning insight into actions. *Business Intelligence Journal, 11*(2), 35.

Keehan, S. P., Sisko, A. M., Truffer, C. J., Poisal, J. A., Cuckler, G. A., Madison, A. J., & Smith, S. D. (2011). National health spending projections through 2020: Economic recovery and reform drive faster spending growth. *Health Affairs, 30*(8), 1594–1605. doi:10.1377/hlthaff.2011.0662 PMID:21798885

Kerr, K. A., Norris, T., & Stockdale, R. (2008). The strategic management of data quality in healthcare. *Health Informatics Journal, 14*(4), 259–266. doi:10.1177/1460458208096555 PMID:19008276

Leape, L. L., Lawthers, A. G., Brennan, T. A., & Johnson, W. G. (1993). Preventing medical injury. *QRB. Quality Review Bulletin, 19*(5), 144. PMID:8332330

Levinson, D. R. (2010). *Adverse effects in hospitals: National incidence among medicare beneficiaries*. Washington, DC: Center on Budget and Policy Priorities.

Lin, Y.-K., Brown, R. A., Yang, H. J., Li, S.-H., & Lu, H.-M. (2011). Data mining large-scale electronic health records for clinical support. *IEEE Intelligent Systems, 26*(5), 87–90.

Linder, J. A., Ma, J., Bates, D. W., Middleton, B., & Stafford, R. S. (2007). Electronic health record use and the quality of ambulatory care in the United States. *Archives of Internal Medicine, 167*(13), 1400–1405. doi:10.1001/archinte.167.13.1400 PMID:17620534

Maguire, H. (2008). Extending the boundaries of IQ: Can collaboration with information management improve corporate governance? *International Journal of Information Quality, 2*(1), 23. doi:10.1504/IJIQ.2008.019561

Marjanovic, O. (2010). The importance of process thinking in business intelligence. *International Journal of Business Intelligence Research, 1*(4), 29–46. doi:10.4018/jbir.2010100102

Neely, M. P., & Cook, J. S. (2011). Fifteen years of data and information quality literature: Developing a research agenda for accounting. *Journal of Information Systems, 25*(1), 79–108. doi:10.2308/jis.2011.25.1.79

News, A. B. C. (2006). *Fast facts on the U.S. health care crisis*. Retrieved 01/15/2013, from http://abcnews.go.com/WNT/PrescriptionForChange/story?id=2563381

ObamaCare Facts. (2013). *ObamaCare facts: Dispelling the myths*. Retrieved 03/06/2013, from http://obamacarefacts.com/obamacare-facts.php

Olinsky, A., & Schumacher, P. A. (2010). Data mining for health care professionals: MBA course projects resulting in hospital improvements. *International Journal of Business Intelligence Research, 1*(2), 30–41. doi:10.4018/jbir.2010040104

Pighin, M., & Ieronutti, L. (2008). A methodology supporting the design and evaluating the final quality of data warehouses. *International Journal of Data Warehousing and Mining, 4*(3), 20. doi:10.4018/jdwm.2008070102

Rauscher, S., & Wheeler, J. R. (2008). Effective hospital revenue cycle management: Is there a trade-off between the amount of patient revenue and the speed of revenue collection? *Journal of Healthcare Management*, *53*(6), 392. PMID:19070334

Rauscher, S., & Wheeler, J. R. C. (2010). Hospital revenue cycle management and payer mix: Do Medicare and medicaid undermine hospitals' ability to generate and collect patient care revenue? *Editorial Board*, *37*(2), 90–104.

Romano, M. J., & Stafford, R. S. (2011). Electronic health records and clinical decision support systems: Impact on national ambulatory care quality. *Archives of Internal Medicine*, *171*(10), 897–903. doi:10.1001/archinternmed.2010.527 PMID:21263077

Shortell, S. M. (2004). Increasing value: a research agenda for addressing the managerial and organizational challenges facing health care delivery in the United States. *Medical Care Research and Review*, *61*(3suppl), 12S–30S. doi:10.1177/1077558704266768 PMID:15375281

Sillup, G. P., Klimberg, R. K., & McSweeney, D. P. (2010). Data-driven decision making for new drugs: A collaborative learning experience. *International Journal of Business Intelligence Research*, *1*(2), 42–59. doi:10.4018/jbir.2010040105

Sunyaev, A., & Chornyi, D. (2012). Supporting chronic disease care quality: Design and implementation of a health service and its integration with electronic health records. *Journal of Data and Information Quality*, *3*(2). doi:10.1145/2184442.2184443

U.S. Department of Health and Human Services. (2001). *Final rules for administrative simplification*. Retrieved 1/15/2013, from http://aspe.hhs.gov/admnsimp/final/PvcPre02.htm

Vicini, J., & Stempel, J. (2012). *US top court upholds healthcare law in Obama triumph*. Retrieved from http://www.reuters.com/article/2012/06/28/usa-healthcare-court-idUSL2E8HS4WG20120628

Wactler, H., Pavel, M., & Barkis, W. (2011). Can computer science save healthcare? *IEEE Intelligent Systems*, *26*(5), 79–83.

Wang, R. Y., & Strong, D. M. (1996). Beyond accuracy: What data quality means to data consumers. *Journal of Management Information Systems*, *12*(4), 5–34.

Weber, K., Otto, B., & Österle, H. (2009). One size does not fit all---A contingency approach to data governance. *Journal of Data and Information Quality*, *1*(1), 4. doi:10.1145/1515693.1515696

Wickramasinghe, N., & Schaffer, J. L. (2006). Creating knowledge-driven healthcare processes with the intelligence continuum. *International Journal of Electronic Healthcare*, *2*(2), 164–174. PMID:18048242

Wixom, B. H., & Watson, H. J. (2010). The BI-based organisation. *International Journal of Business Intelligence Research*, *1*(1), 13–28. doi:10.4018/jbir.2010071702

Wu, S., Chaudhry, B., Wang, J., Maglione, M., Mojica, W., Roth, E., & Shekelle, P. G. (2006). Systematic review: Impact of health information technology on quality, efficiency, and costs of medical care. *Annals of Internal Medicine*, *144*(10), 742–752. doi:10.7326/0003-4819-144-10-200605160-00125 PMID:16702590

KEY TERMS AND DEFINITIONS

Carve Out: Accessing coverage for a specific type of service through a contract separate from that established with the primary providers.

Co-Payment: A cost-sharing arrangement that requires the person insured to pay a specified flat dollar amount, usually on a per-unit-of-service basis, with the third-party payer reimbursing a portion of the remaining charges.

Provider: Generically, a professional engaged in the delivery of health services, including physicians, dentists, nurses, podiatrists, optometrists, and clinical psychologists. Hospitals and long term care facilities are also providers.

Provider Credentialing: The process of reviewing a healthcare provider's qualifications (e.g., academic, training and clinical experience) to determine if criteria for clinical privileges are met.

Medicare: A U.S. federal government-sponsored healthcare insurance program primarily for people over 65, independent of their income; as well as younger disabled people and dialysis patients.

Medicaid: A U.S. health assistance program for certain people and families with low incomes and resources.

PGOT: A framework used to evaluate data and information quality; it partitions an information system into People, Governance, Operations, and Technology.

Chapter 6
IT Architecture and Information Quality in Data Warehouse and Business Intelligence Environments

Samuel Otero Schmidt
University of Sao Paulo, Brazil

Edmir Parada Vasques Prado
University of Sao Paulo, Brazil

ABSTRACT

Organizations are currently investing more in information technology to store and process a vast amount of information. Generally, this information does not comply with any standard, which hinders the decision-making process. The cause of the difficulties can be attributed to Information Quality (IQ), which has technical characteristics related to the architecture used in Data Warehouse (DW) and Business Intelligence (BI) environments. On the basis of the relevant literature in IQ, DW, and BI, a research model was created to identify the relations between components of DW/BI architecture and IQ dimensions. This research model was applied in a real case study (Big Financial Company in Brazil). This case study involved semi-structured interviews with managers and analysts. This chapter attempts to provide a better understanding of the relations between IT architecture and IQ in DW and BI environments. The authors hope to motivate the discussion around the development of IQ-oriented architectures for BI and the relationship between these concepts.

DOI: 10.4018/978-1-4666-4892-0.ch006

INTRODUCTION

Organizations are increasing their investment in information technology (IT) so that they can collect, store and process a vast amount of information. The purpose of this investment is to employ information in making improvements, better decision-making and providing companies with a competitive advantage. However, there is a problem faced by many organizations which is how to handle such a large volume of information. Generally this information does not comply with any standard or repeat data, which hinders the decision making process, especially at a strategic level. One of the causes of this difficulty is Information Quality (IQ) which has both technical features, such as information integration and data warehouse, and non-technical features, such as the lack of strategic cohesion across the organization, to allow stakeholders to have the right information in the right format at the right time (Madnick *et al.*, 2009). The technical characteristics of IQ are essentially based on the architecture used in the Data Warehouse (DW) and Business Intelligence (BI) environments (Jarke & Vassiliou, 1997). The environment of DW/BI is characterized by its analytical objective, i.e. it is aimed at providing IQ for decision makers (senior management, analysts and experts).

There are several studies in the academic literature about the concept of DW and BI, but few of them address the question of the choice of the DW/BI architecture. Some of the first and best-known studies on these topics were conducted by Inmon (1996) and Kimball (1996) in the 1990s, when a number of companies began building DW/BI environments (Wixom & Watson, 2001). Both authors helped formulate the concept of the analytic environment and to differentiate between this type of environment and the Transaction System (TS) environment.

In the opinion of Inmon (2005), DW is a more efficient model to store corporate information. This is because, a centralized database makes it possible to share all the information needed for different business areas, and allows the DW to be integrated with historical information - usually within a time span of five years or more, and with non-volatile information. Kimball and Ross (2002) present a different architecture with a proposal to quickly meet users' needs through a distributed database, known as Data Marts (DM), and the use of specific information for each business area.

These two authors opened up a discussion about the importance of IT architecture in providing information for businesses, and enabling a proper infrastructure, database, model and IT team to be obtained in an analytical environment. In this context, it is worth highlighting the importance of IQ for an analytical environment. Wixom and Watson (2001) argue that the IQ can provide several benefits to users: a better understanding of the context of the decision, improved decision making and changes in the way people work. From a DW/BI perspective, by employing appropriate tools of access and searching for information, users are able to make faster and more wide-ranging decisions. In general, DW/BI can make data accessible to the final users and reduce the required time and effort needed to provide access to the information (Graham, Coburn & Oleson, 1996).

According to Ariyachandra and Watson (2010), the choice of the architecture is an important decision. A project, called DWQ – Foundations of Data Warehouse Quality (Jarke & Vassiliou, 1997; Jarke *et al.*, 1999), carried out by a research group from some European universities at the end of the 1990s, tried to establish a framework, with the intention of analyzing the DW/BI architecture and IQ factors involved in this approach. Despite these efforts, there is still a gap in the literature about the ways to detect the relationships between the components of DW/BI architecture and their links with IQ dimensions.

The overall goal of this chapter is to analyze the components of IT architecture and IQ dimensions in a DW/BI environment. Three specific aims have been defined to achieve this: (1) To describe the components of the DW/BI architecture; (2) to describe the most relevant IQ dimensions in this context; (3) to identify the relationships between the components of DW/BI architecture and IQ dimensions.

BACKGROUND

Information Quality

Although there is no consensus about the distinction between Data Quality (DQ) and IQ, there is a tendency to apply DQ to refer to technical problems and IQ for non-technical issues. DQ is the syntax of the data, i.e. the structure and form. IQ is about semantics, i.e. the meaning of this data in time, space and context, i.e. to transform information into any component that affects the interpretation and transformation of data into information (Madnick *et al.*, 2009). In this chapter, this distinction is not applied and we adopt the term IQ.

According to Kahn and Strong (1998), IQ is the information characteristic and is also the indicator to measure if the users' expectations were met. Bailey and Person (1983) identified the complexity of measuring IQ from the users' point of view, so in order to enable this measurement, they developed a tool to evaluate the satisfaction of IT systems users through the use of IQ dimensions, for example: precision, reliability, currency, relevance.

Other important aspects are which tools are used to evaluate how the IQ dimensions are influenced by Information Systems (IS) contexts inside the companies (Ong & Lai, 2007; Ge & Helfert, 2007; Wu & Wang, 2006) and the fact that an evaluation tool dedicated to BI context was not identified on the literature.

On the basis of the literature, particularly on studies regarding IQ, 12 dimensions were selected to be part of this research and can be considered to have relations with the DW/BI context (Table 1).

Components of the Data Warehouse and Business Intelligence Architecture

According to Ariyachandra and Watson (2010), given the fact that companies spend millions of dollars on DW/BI architectures, the lack of academic research on this subject is surprising. Studies conducted by Jarke and Vassiliou (1997) highlight the importance of the choice of IT architecture for the success of DW/BI solutions. In the research studies of Ariyachandra and Watson (2005), Sen and Sinha (2007), Sen and Sinha (2005) and Simoes (2010), seven types of architecture were cited for DW/BI: Independent DMs; DM Bus Architecture; Enterprise DW; DW with Operational Data Store (ODS); Hub and Spoke; Federated; and Distributed DW Architecture. All these architectures have their respective components and when connected, they establish the architecture. Figure 1 presents a general overview of components of DW/BI architecture. The aim of this chapter is to evaluate how each component may, positively or negatively affect IQ in the DW/BI environment, since the architecture and its components might limit or add to the IQ that is already known by the final users. The nine components of DW/BI architecture considered in this study are listed below:

- **Transactional System (TS):** Legacy systems or actual TSs execute daily transactions inside the organization, and provide a data source for the DW/BI, e.g.: Enterprise Resource Planning Systems and Online Transaction Processing (OLTP) (Simoes, 2010; Inmon, 2005);
- **Staging Area (SA):** This is a database or storage area that provides the connection between TS and DW, ODS or DM. The decision about whether this area should exist or not and how it will be structured, basically depends on two goals: obtaining data from TS to the last destination in the short-

Table 1. Information quality dimensions in DW/BI environments

Authors	Dimensions	Definition
Wand and Wang, 1996; Jarke and Vassiliou, 1997; Pipino, Lee and Wang, 2002; Michnik et al., 2009	Accessibility	The extent to which data is available, or easily and quickly retrievable
Wang, Kon and Reddy, 1995; Jarke and Vassiliou, 1997; Wixom and Watson, 2001; Michnik et al., 2009	Accuracy	The recorded value corresponds to the actual value
Wang, Kon and Reddy, 1995; Jarke and Vassiliou, 1997	Availability	The data exists in some form that can be accessed
Wand and Wang, 1996; Jarke and Vassiliou, 1997;Wixom and Watson, 2001; Pipino, Lee and Wang, 2002	Completeness	The extent to which data is not missing and is of sufficient breadth and depth for the task at hand
Delone and Mclean, 1992; Pipino, Lee and Wang, 2002	Conciseness	The extent to which the data is represented in a compact form
Jarke and Vassiliou, 1997; Wixom and Watson, 2001; Pipino, Lee and Wang, 2002	Consistency	The extent to which data is presented in the same format
Wang, Kon and Reddy, 1995; Wand and Wang, 1996; Jarke and Vassiliou, 1997; Pipino, Lee and Wang, 2002	Interpretability	The extent to which the data is expressed in appropriate languages, symbols and units, and the definitions are clear
Pipino Lee and Wang, 2002	Quantity	The extent to which the volume of data is appropriate for the task at hand
Wang, Kon and Reddy, 1995; Wand and Wang, 1996; Pipino, Lee and Wang, 2002	Reliability	The extent to which data is correct and reliable
Pipino, Lee and Wang, 2002	Reputation	The extent to which data is highly regarded in terms of its source or content
Wand and Wang, 1996; Pipino, Lee and Wang, 2002, Michnik et al., 2009	Security	The extent to which access to data is restricted appropriately to maintain its security
Delone and Mclean, 1992; Wand and Wang, 1996; Jarke and Vassiliou, 1997; Pipino, Lee and Wang, 2002	Timeliness	The extent to which the data is sufficiently up-to-date for the task at hand

Figure 1. General overview of the nine components of DW/BI architecture

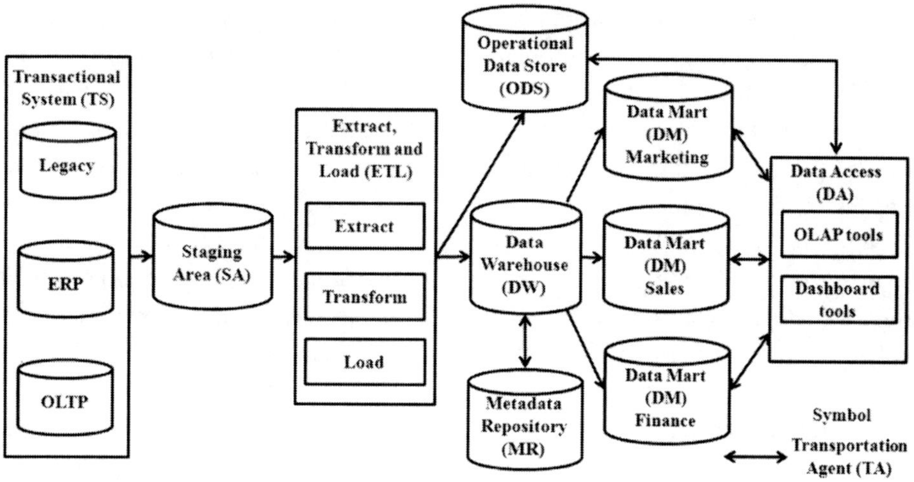

est time possible; being able to carry out data extraction and recovery without having to restart the process (Simoes, 2010; Inmon, 2005);

- **Metadata Repository (MR):** MR shows how data has to be interpreted by the user, its source, security privilege, quality metrics (i.e.: how many times the data was accessed). MR can be locally distributed or centralized with DW (Inmon, 2005; Kimball & Ross, 2002);
- **Extract, Transform and Load (ETL):** ETL is made to extract data from TS for other components of the analytical environment. After the extraction, there is transformation and integration for data handling, to load the information in DW, DM, ODS or MR;
- **Data Warehouse (DW):** DW is a database that is generally relational and normalized; its aim is to be integrated, time-variant, non-volatile and to share information between all the departments of an organization, in a scalable way (Kimball & Ross, 2002). In general, it is in DW, that data exists at the lowest level of atomicity (Inmon, 2005);
- **Data Mart (DM):** DM is a database, which contains specific information from various departmental areas (e.g: Marketing, Sales, HR, Finance) (Silvers, 2008). In general, DM has aggregated data, based on dimensional modeling. However, if DM architecture is used in bus, there might be an integration of available data through conformed dimensions, which would transform DM to DW (Kimball & Ross, 2002). As regards this study, the most general definition for DM will be adopted;
- **Operational Data Store (ODS):** ODS provides operational data extracted from TSs in real time, since its objective is to generate management reports (Silvers, 2008; Sen & Sinha, 2005; Kimball & Ross, 2002);
- **Data Access (DA):** DA is the last layer to explore and analyze data and On-line Analytical Processing (OLAP) and dashboard tools are used to offer a view of the dimensions and facts (Kimball & Ross, 2002);
- **Transportation Agent (TA):** TAs are schedules/controls of transferences and network infrastructure, that allow communication between all the components. It is an important component, since DW/BI uses a large volume of data and TA capacities/velocity may be factors that limit the success of the architecture.

RESEARCH MODEL

For this research, the following conceptual assumptions are presumed:

- The tools to evaluate IQ and the use of information are influenced by the context of the IS (Ong & Lai, 2007; Ge & Hekfert, 2007; Wu & Wang, 2006). On this research one tries to develop tools to evaluate the IQ on the context of BI systems;
- Based on the perceptions of the companies' employees, it is possible to evaluate the IQ that comes from the IT systems of the organizations (Ge & Hekfert, 2007);
- IQ is frequently discussed in data warehousing literature, mainly regarding the aspects in which the high IQ level is the fundamental reason to the decision makers to build a DW (Wixom & Watson, 2001; Watson & Haley, 1997). The most significant benefit provided by a DW is the IQ;

- More studies are needed to explore the IQ dimensions related to DW, mainly, concerning BI architecture (Ariyachandra & Watson, 2010; Wixom & Watson, 2001).

Considering these assumptions was possible to analyze the relationship between IQ and DW/BI. The relationship between the 9 components of DW/BI and the 12 IQ dimensions is set out in Figure 2. The impacts of the components on the IQ dimensions were defined in a four-point scale: high positive impact, some positive impact, some negative impact and high negative impact. The blank spaces appear when no positive or negative relations were identified or when it is possible to have positive and negative impact. The impacts were interpreted in qualitative terms through the information searched for in the literature and perceptions of the author. This chapter endeavored to examine the main relations that were found and did not involve an exhaustive attempt to cover all possible relationships.

There are 63 relations that could be positive or negative (see Figure 2). The details about the relations are given for each IQ dimension:

- **Reliability:** Four relations were identified for this dimension: ETL has an important role to play in evaluating reliability, because business rules in the transformation process can be employed to check how much data is reliable. In addition, it is possible to load a reliability data metric inside MR. MR can serve as a repository of quality metrics, so that the user is able to evaluate the quality of the decision regarding the IQ obtained. The DA is where the reliability is confirmed, since users are very often interested in validating information and through the analysis they will be able to check whether the data is reliable or not;
- **Interpretability:** Five relations were identified for this dimension: MR has a high positive impact on this dimension, by con-

Figure 2. Relationships between the components of the DW/BI architecture and IQ dimensions

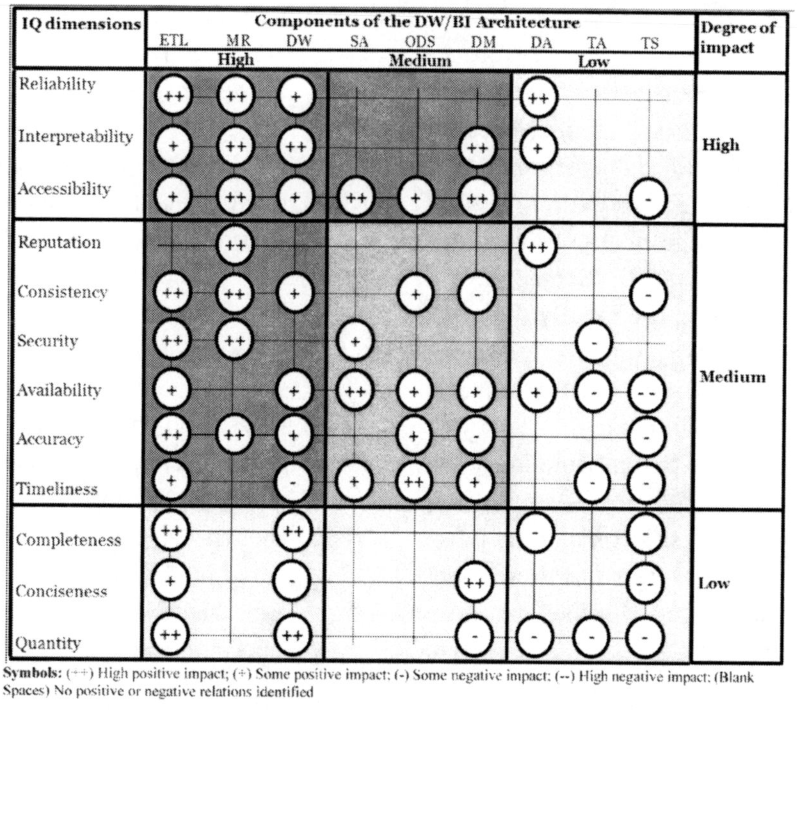

Symbols: (++) High positive impact; (+) Some positive impact; (-) Some negative impact; (--) High negative impact; (Blank Spaces) No positive or negative relations identified

veying the meaning of the information introduced, showing how it should be used and also making clear what the context is with regard to the current situation. MR has to be closely integrated with DA, to make the significance of the information understandable to users. ETL influences interpretability, because it lays down the business rules for handling information. DW may be able to enhance interpretability, because this component contains the lowest level of granularity in which it is possible to understand the information in a detailed way and make an accurate interpretation of it. DM provides data that are closer to the subjects of interest to the users;

- **Accessibility:** Seven relations were identified for this dimension: ETL is made to load data in ODS, DW and DM with right of access being granted to users and it also enables data to be accessed in the different types of components. MR can also obtain access to information and control this in its repository; in this way it is likely to keep a history of the information that has been accessed. SA, ODS and DW positively influence this dimension, since it can recover data without the need to access it again in TS. DM improves Accessibility, because there is specific information from each department, which makes the information more available to the final user, and thus improves access control. TS may have a negative impact because usually the users are not allowed to access it directly in order to avoid security issues and performance problems in TS environment;
- **Reputation:** Two relations were identified for this dimension: When the data is underutilized by the users, MR may keep information about the metrics that were used, which will show users whether the information in question has a good reputation or not. In this case, DA has the same impact as what was found for reliability;
- **Consistency:** Six relations were identified for this dimension: TS could have negative impact on data consistency. A negative impact occurs when data is included twice. In this case, this information has to be handled by ETL which plays a crucial role in ensuring consistency, since DW must not be loaded twice with the same information; in this way, one can attempt to obtain a single version of the information. Both DW and ODS have a positive impact on this dimension, because they seek to receive integrated data and as a result, enhance the consistency. DM might have a negative impact, since the same data might be loaded in different DMs, and often there is not a single version of the information. Most of the time MR might have a positive impact if there is a single and centralized MR and through these components, it is feasible to carry out an analysis to determine how often that information was loaded in DW, DM or ODS. Nevertheless, if there are many local MRs for each DM, there might be a high negative impact on this dimension;
- **Security:** Four relations were identified for this dimension: SA has a high positive impact on this dimension, because with this layer it is possible to restrict the access of other components. In general, only ETL has access to SA. ETL plays a key role in this dimension, because it can load data with a degree of safety and privileges and in addition, it may also conceal the data so that users are able to analyze it without having access to confidential information. The privilege access control is generally stored in MR. TA may have a negative impact, due to the existence of safety risks in this component;

- **Availability:** Eight relations were identified for this dimension: TA may have a negative impact on access to the information, if the network is not available. In the case of TS, there is a high negative impact, because priority with regard to TS availability is given to its operational needs and not to information that may be available in the analytical environment. In general, there are specific outlets for the availability of data and many TSs have to be offline, so that ETL Extraction can be carried out through batch routines (Strong, Lee & Wang, 1997). If it is decided to directly access TS, there may be competition with the operational processing and access provided by this component. SA seeks to reduce the impact of TS, since its availability is found in the analytical environment and this allows information to be recovered without accessing TS again. ODS, DW, DM and DA can also have positive impacts, because they are made available to the users of the analytical environment as well;
- **Accuracy:** Six relations were identified for this dimension: TS is one of the components that has the greatest effect on data precision, since data that is included in this layer will permanently influence all the other stages, and once the fact has occurred it is not possible to repeat it. Both ODS and DW have a positive impact on this dimension, because in general, information stored in the database has already been handled by ETL, which avoids syntax errors and redundancy, and thus improves the accuracy. DM may have a negative impact due to the fact that information might be spread over various DMs and also be extracted from different sources. ETL aims to handle and clean data while MR provides the real meaning of data and its standard, and hence avoids conformation mistakes;
- **Timeliness:** Seven relations were identified for this dimension: TS has a negative impact on this dimension, since it may take some time for the transaction to be extracted. On the other hand, SA has a positive impact, because if there are any problems arising from the ETL processing or it is necessary to restart the process, this component avoids searching for the data again in the TS. ODS is supplied with the information in a more immediate way when compared to DW or DM; that is why it has a high positive impact on this dimension (Silvers, 2008). DM can be directly updated without an integration process, so it is time saving, because, if there is a DW component the information should be consolidated in a single DW which will consume more time than DM. TA may have a negative impact on the length of time required for transferring a large volume of data;
- **Completeness:** Four relations were identified for this dimension which is adversely affected by TS, where in-depth information is modeled. ETL may help provide completeness through data extraction from different sources and integrate this information in DW, where it is possible to allocate a large volume of data at the lowest level of granularity. Later on, DA may have a negative impact, depending on the query or cube created and executed by the user;
- **Conciseness:** Four relations were identified for this dimension: It should be noted that DM has a high positive impact on this dimension, because in this component there is aggregated and summarized data, which compacts the information. Moreover, DW has a large volume of data

with low levels of granularity, which can have a negative impact on this dimension. ETL aims to compact data through cleaning. In TS there is no compacted data, so it may have a negative impact;

- **Quantity:** Six relations were identified for this dimension: TS has a negative impact on data quantity, because generally, there is no scope for the extraction of data through batch routines over a long period of time. ETL and DW aims to enhance the quality of the analytical environment and has a large volume of data that may be accessed so long as there is compliance with the requirements of information from users and also with regulatory mandates such as SOX (Sabherwal & Becerra-Fernandez, 2010); however DM is limited in terms of data quantity. DA and TA may have a negative impact on these dimensions, since if DA is employed, users may have to search for an unnecessary amount of data or obtain a large volume of data that may impair the TA capacity.

RESEARCH METHOD

This research is exploratory and qualitative and the methodology employed in only based on a single case study. This strategy investigates contemporary phenomena in their real context, where the boundaries between a phenomenon and the context itself are not clearly defined (Yin, 2010). Moreover, it is especially useful in the generation and theory building where little data or theory exist (Eisenhardt, 1989).

Object of the Study

The case study was conducted at a large Financial Company (FC) in Brazil. FC has more than 30.000 employees of which over 2.000 work in the area of IT. The main activities of this company are accounting, transactions, issuing credit cards, internet banking and insurance. There are offices and agencies spread throughout all of the states in Brazil and other countries. The revenue is more than $15 billion dollars per year and the annual expenditure on DW/BI projects and maintenance is more than $500 million dollars. There are more than 3.000 users of the DW/BI systems who use the following: Data Stage and PowerCenter (ETL tools), Statistical Analysis System (SAS), such as the ODS database, DB2 and Oracle (such as DW and DM), MicroStrategy and Cognos (for OLAP tools). The main part of the information source comes from the Mainframe (the TS). The type of architecture currently used is a Distributed DW. The organization has distributed ETL processing, running for the legacy DMs, and is currently implementing new architecture based on Hub and Spoke.

Data Collection

A questionnaire was prepared and given to each one of the interviewees. The interviews were conducted between the second half of 2011 and first half of 2012 with five employees who work at IT department and had experience in DW/BI environment.

It is possible to verify at the Table 2 that most of the respondents have a lot of years of experience in DW/BI environments, so it was easy to interview them about the architecture and components of DW/BI.

Data Analysis

At the beginning, it was possible with FC to understand how the IT DW/BI team sees the importance of IQ dimensions. Table 3 shows how the IQ dimensions are ranked in importance and the results show that Accuracy and Reliability were more important than the others, which corresponds with the findings of Sen & Sinha, 2007; Ariyachandra & Watson, 2005; Jarke & Vassiliou,

Table 2. Interviewees profiles

IT Area	Position	Year of Experience in DW/BI Environments	Years Working for FC	Sex
ETL	Coordinator	8	26	Male
ETL	Senior Analyst	7	1	Male
ETL	Senior Analyst	12	2	Male
Support Infrastructure	Senior Analyst	6	23	Male
Data Access Tools	Analyst	3	1	Male

Table 3. Dimensions in the DW/BI environment ranked in order of importance

Dimensions	Ranking of Importance
Accuracy, Reliability	1
Consistency, Security	2
Availability	3
Completeness, Reputation	4
Accessibility	5
Timeliness, Interpretability, Quantity	6
Conciseness	7

1997. Accuracy applies to the activities of the daily users when they need accurate information to send to the Government, or to investors and stakeholders. Consistency is concerned with the need to have a single version of the truth, and Security is really important for FC, because there is a high risk of violation of data by employees, hackers with criminal intentions. Availability is the main objective of the framework responsible for supporting the infrastructure. The importance of Reputation is in understanding where the source of the data (e.g.: TS) is and how IQ can be found at this source. In the case of FC, the new ETL seeks to provide a better MR and integration and thus be able to show what is the source of all the information at DW/BI. Completeness is improved by the integration at the ETL level, but it remains unclear how the user sees this dimension, so there is a lack of a perception of the high importance that it has. Accessibility is important, because the daily operations are so critical that they run in the TS (or Mainframe), and cannot be accessed at any time during the day, as in the batch window. This is important to avoid a high concurrence in the TS processes which risk having an impact on the operations. Timeliness is not so critical, which means the users have a one- day delayed view. The need for quantity is common for DW/BI systems, especially those using a DW component. Interpretability is also important and is an intrinsic part of BI applications, e.g.: MR components. Conciseness is also common, although in fact the user is only concerned about the need for information and not about conciseness.

In Table 4 it is possible to identify the most important components in the DW/BI environment. On the basis of the interviewees' perceptions within the ETL, DW and DM are the most important components for the new framework. This is consistent with the research model (See Figure 2).

The ODS is also really important of great significance, but it is not as structured. For the new architecture, FC seeks to create a new ODS for SAS users with high standards of timeliness,

Table 4. Components in the DW/BI environment ranked in order of importance

Components	Importance Ranking
ETL, DW, DM	1
ODS, MR, DA, TA	2
SA	3
TS	4

consistency, and security. Currently, each department has its own SAS data set, and in the case of the new framework, it is important to integrate all the data sets in a single ODS component. In fact, the importance of MR is understood, and there is a desire to improve the use of this component by centralizing it in a single MR. DA is really important to provide different views of the information and good interpretability by means of cubes and graphics. TA is necessary to transport a huge volume of data, and maintain security. However TS which is in the last place is not viewed as an important component, since it is only required to extract the data. This finding is also consistent with the research model, because usually the TS is not implemented for DW/BI purposes, but to serve operational requirements instead.

FUTURE RESEARCH DIRECTIONS

To conclude, although there are some limitations in this research, it should be noted that this is only a preliminary study and it was not possible to cover all the potential relationships between components of the DW/BI and IQ dimensions that might exist in the IS literature. When a case study is used, it is not possible to generalize the results. However, it is recommended that on the basis of the considerations outlined in this chapter, further studies should be undertaken in this field. These might involve the following:

- Replicating the interviews with BI users to understand better how the components could be related to IQ;
- Carrying out further research to identify which IQ dimensions are important for the BI context;
- Conducting new studies to analyze their impact on the different types of DW/BI architecture in IQ;
- It is hoped that this study will stimulate a theoretical discussion around the development of DQ/IQ-oriented architectures for BI.

CONCLUSION

This chapter has made two contributions to this field of study:

1. **There are IQ dimensions which are more important in DW/BI environments:** The case study at FC showed that there is perceived to be a ranking level of importance concerning some IQ dimensions in DW/BI environments. These findings are important for organizations, since they identify and prioritize some IQ dimensions as a means of guiding and enhancing the success of DW/BI architecture;
2. **The components of DW/BI architecture are associated with IQ dimensions:** On the basis of the literature review, a research model was created with the relationships between the components of the DW/BI architecture and IQ dimensions (see Table 1). By means of the case study it was possible to determine that some relations are true in the reality of FC. The ETL, DW and DM were the components that had most positive impacts within the dimensions. The reason for this was that all three components were specifically formed to supply the information requested by users and enable them to make better decisions (Inmon, 2005; Silvers, 2008; Kimball & Ross, 2002). According to Silvers (2008), and the case of study of FC, the three components are of extreme importance in DW/BI. On the other hand, it is worth analyzing the large number of negative impacts on TS and TA. The negative impacts on TS can be interpreted as implying that

this component was not usually implemented for analytical purposes, and hence its main objective was to support operational requirements. This study can serve as a valuable contribution, because if companies wish to be more competitive, they must implement TS for an analytical as well as an operational environment. The TA usually has negative impacts, because users want to obtain a huge volume of data in the least time possible and, very often, the TA has a limited amount of throughput to transport it. It is hoped that this study will stimulate a theoretical discussion around the development of DQ/IQ-oriented architectures for BI.

REFERENCES

Ariyachandra, T., & Watson, H. (2005). Key factors in selecting a data warehouse architecture. *Business Intelligence Journal*, *10*(2), 19–26.

Ariyachandra, T., & Watson, H. (2010). Key organizational factors in data warehouse architecture selection. *Decision Support Systems*, *49*(2), 200–212. doi:10.1016/j.dss.2010.02.006

Bailey, J. E., & Pearson, S. W. (1983). Development of a tool for measuring and analyzing computer user satisfaction. *Management Science*, *29*(5), 530–545. doi:10.1287/mnsc.29.5.530

DeLone, W. H., & McLean, E. R. (1992). Information systems success: The quest for the dependent variable. *Information Systems Research*, *3*(1), 60–95. doi:10.1287/isre.3.1.60

Eisenhardt, K. M. (1989). Building theories from case study research. *Academy of Management Review*, *14*(4), 532–550.

Ge, M., & Helfert, M. (2007, November). A review of information quality research - Develop a research agenda. In *Proceedings of the 12th International Conference on Information Quality*. Cambridge, MA: MIT.

Graham, S., Coburn, D., & Oleson, C. (1996). *The foundations of wisdom: A study of the financial impact of data warehousing*. Toronto, Canada: International Data Corporation.

Inmon, W. H. (1996). *Building the data warehouse*. New York: John Wiley & Sons Inc.

Inmon, W. H. (2005). *Building the data warehouse*. New York: Wiley Publishers.

Jarke, M., Jeusfeld, M. A., Quix, C., & Vassiliadis, P. (1999). Architecture and quality in data warehouse: An extended repository approach. *Information Systems*, *24*(3), 229–253. doi:10.1016/S0306-4379(99)00017-4

Jarke, M., & Vassiliou, Y. (1997). Foundations of data warehouse quality - A review of the DWQ Project. In *Proceedings of the 2nd International Conference on Information Quality*. Cambridge, MA: MIT.

Kahn, B. K., & Strong, D. M. (1998). Product and service performance model for information quality: An update. In *Proceedings of the 1998 Conference on Information Quality*. Cambridge, MA: MIT.

Kimball, R. (1996). *The data warehouse toolkit: Practical techniques for building dimensional data warehouses*. New York: John Wiley & Sons Inc.

Kimball, R., & Ross, M. (2002). *The data warehouse toolkit: The complete guide to dimensional modeling*. New York: Wiley.

Madnick, S. E., Wang, Y. W., Lee, H., & Zhu, H. (2009). Overview and framework for data and information quality research. *Journal of Data and Information Quality*, *1*(1), 1–22. doi:10.1145/1515693.1516680

Ong, C. S., & Lai, J. Y. (2007). Measuring user satisfaction with knowledge management systems: Scale development, purification, and initial test. *Computers in Human Behavior*, *23*(3), 1329–1346. doi:10.1016/j.chb.2004.12.012

Pipino, L., Lee, Y. W., & Wang, R. Y. (2002). Data quality assessment. *Communications of the ACM*, *45*(4), 211–218. doi:10.1145/505248.506010

Sabherwal, R., & Becerra-Fernandez, I. (2010). *Business intelligence: Practices, technologies, and management*. Hoboken, NJ: John Wiley & Sons Inc.

Sen, A., & Sinha, A. P. (2005). A comparison of data warehousing methodologies. *Communications of the ACM*, *48*(3), 79–84. doi:10.1145/1047671.1047673

Sen, A., & Sinha, A. P. (2007). Toward developing data warehousing process standards: An ontology-base. *IEEE Transactions on Systems, Man and Cybernetics. Part C, Applications and Reviews*, *37*(1), 17–31. doi:10.1109/TSMCC.2006.886966

Silvers, F. (2008). *Building and maintaining a data warehouse*. Boston: Auerbach. doi:10.1201/9781420064636

Simoes, D. (2010). *Conceptual framework for the construction and evaluation of data warehouses*. Paper presented at the Iberian Conference on Information Systems and Technologies. Santiago de Compostela, Spain.

Strong, D. M., Lee, Y. W., & Wang, R. Y. (1997). Data quality in context. *Communications of the ACM*, *40*(5), 103–110. doi:10.1145/253769.253804

Wand, Y., & Wang, R. Y. (1996). Anchoring data quality dimensions in ontological foundations. *Communications of the ACM*, *39*(11), 86–95. doi:10.1145/240455.240479

Wang, R. Y., Kon, H. B., & Reddy, M. P. (1995). Toward data quality: An attribute-based approach. *Decision Support Systems*, (13): 349–372. doi:10.1016/0167-9236(93)E0050-N

Watson, H., & Haley, B. (1997). Data warehousing: A framework and survey of current practices. *Journal of Data Warehousing*, *2*(1), 10–17.

Wixom, B. B. H., & Watson, H. J. (2001). An empirical investigation of the factors affecting data warehousing success. *Management Information Systems Quarterly*, *25*(1), 17–41. doi:10.2307/3250957

Wu, J. H., & Wang, Y. M. (2006). Measuring KMS success: A respecification of the DeLone and McLean's model. *Information & Management*, *43*(6), 728–739. doi:10.1016/j.im.2006.05.002

Yin, R. K. (2010). *Case study research: Design and methods* (4th ed.). London: Sage.

ADDITIONAL READING

AbuAli, A. N., & Abu-Addose, H. Y. (2010). Data Warehouse Critical Success Factors. *European Journal of Scientific Research*, *42*(2), 326–335.

Ariyachandra, T., & Watson, H. J. (2006). Which data warehouse architecture is most successful? *Business Intelligence Journal*, *11*(1), 4–6.

Arnott, D., & Pervan, G. (2008). Eight key issues for the decision support systems discipline. *Decision Support Systems*, *44*(3), 657–672. doi:10.1016/j.dss.2007.09.003

Ballou, D. P., & Pazer, H. L. (2003). Modeling completeness versus consistency tradeoffs in information decision contexts. *IEEE Transactions on Knowledge and Data Engineering*, *15*(1), 240–243. doi:10.1109/TKDE.2003.1161595

Bharati, P., & Chaudhury, A. (2004). An empirical investigation of decision-making satisfaction in web-based. *Decision Support Systems*, *37*(2), 187–197. doi:10.1016/S0167-9236(03)00006-X

Breslin, M. (2004). Data warehousing battle of giants: comparing the basics of the Kimball and Inmon models. *Business Intelligence Journal*, *9*(1), 6–20.

Chen, L., Soliman, K. S., Mao, E., & Frolick, M. N. (2000). Measuring user satisfaction with data warehouses: an exploratory study. *Information & Management*, *37*(3), 103–110. doi:10.1016/S0378-7206(99)00042-7

Delone, W. H. (2003). The DeLone and McLean model of information systems success: a ten-year update. *Journal of Management Information Systems*, *19*(4), 9–30.

DeLone, W. H., & McLean, E. R. (2002, January). Information systems success revisited. In System Sciences, 2002. In *Proceedings of the 35th Annual Hawaii International Conference on System Sciences* (HICSS), pp. 2966-2976.

Eppler, M. J. (2006). *Managing information quality: increasing the value of information in knowledge-intensive products and processes*. Springer.

Foley, É., & Guillemette, M. G. (2010). What is Business Intelligence? [IJBIR]. *International Journal of Business Intelligence Research*, *1*(4), 1–28. doi:10.4018/jbir.2010100101

Gardner, S. R. (1998). Building the data warehouse. *Communications of the ACM*, *41*(9), 52–60. doi:10.1145/285070.285080

Gorla, N., Somers, T. M., & Wong, B. (2010). Organizational impact of system quality, information quality, and service quality. *The Journal of Strategic Information Systems*, *19*(3), 207–228. doi:10.1016/j.jsis.2010.05.001

Hayen, R. L., Rutashobya, C. D., & Vetter, D. E. (2007). An Investigation of the Factors Affecting Data Warehousing Success. *Issues in Information Systems*, *8*(2), 547–553.

Hou, C. K. (2012). Examining the effect of user satisfaction on system usage and individual performance with business intelligence systems: An empirical study of Taiwan's electronics industry. *International Journal of Information Management*, *32*(6), 560–573. doi:10.1016/j.ijinfomgt.2012.03.001

Hwang, H. G., Ku, C. Y., Yen, D. C., & Cheng, C. C. (2004). Critical factors influencing the adoption of data warehouse technology: a study of the banking industry in Taiwan. *Decision Support Systems*, *37*(1), 1–21. doi:10.1016/S0167-9236(02)00191-4

Hwang, M. I., & Xu, H. (2005). A Survey of Data Warehousing Success Issues. *Business Intelligence Journal*, *10*(4), 7–13.

Jaklič, J., Popovič, A., & Coelho, P. S. (2011). The Impact of Quality Information Provided by Business Intelligence Systems on the Use of Information in Business Processes. In *ENTERprise Information Systems* (pp. 158–167). Springer Berlin Heidelberg. doi:10.1007/978-3-642-24358-5_16

Knight, S. A., & Bum, J. (2005). Developing a framework for assessing information quality on the World Wide Web. *Informing Science. International Journal of an Emerging Transdiscipline*, *8*(5), 159–172.

Lawyer, J., & Chowdhury, S. (2004, January). Best practices in data warehousing to support business initiatives and needs. In *System Sciences, 2004. Proceedings of the 37th Annual Hawaii International Conference on* (pp. 9-pp). IEEE.

Lee, Y. W., Strong, D. M., Kahn, B. K., & Wang, R. Y. (2002). AIMQ: a methodology for information quality assessment. *Information & Management*, *40*(2), 133–146. doi:10.1016/S0378-7206(02)00043-5

Madnick, S. E., Wang, R. Y., Lee, Y. W., & Zhu, H. (2009). Overview and framework for data and information quality research. [JDIQ]. *Journal of Data and Information Quality*, *1*(1), 2–22. doi:10.1145/1515693.1516680

Mannino, M., Walter & Walter, Z. (2006). A framework for data warehouse refresh policies. *Decision Support Systems, 42(1)*, 121-143.

Mannino, M., Hong, S. N., & Choi, I. J. (2008). Efficiency evaluation of data warehouse operations. *Decision Support Systems*, *44*(4), 883–898. doi:10.1016/j.dss.2007.10.011

Nelson, R. R., Todd, P. A., & Wixom, B. H. (2005). Antecedents of information and system quality: an empirical examination within the context of data warehousing. *Journal of Management Information Systems*, *21*(4), 199–235.

Nemati, H. R., Steiger, D. M., Iyer, L. S., & Herschel, R. T. (2002). Knowledge warehouse: an architectural integration of knowledge management, decision support, artificial intelligence and data warehousing. *Decision Support Systems*, *33*(2), 143–161. doi:10.1016/S0167-9236(01)00141-5

Popovic, A., & Jaklic, J. (2010). Benefits of business intelligence system implementation: an empirical analysis of the impact of business intelligence system maturity on information quality. In *European, Mediterranean & Middle Eastern Conference on Information Systems, Abu Dhabi, UAE.*

Popovič, A., Turk, T., & Jaklič, J. (2010). Conceptual model of business value of business intelligence systems. *Management: Journal of Contemporary Management Issues*, *15*(1), 5–30.

Ramakrishnan, T., Jones, M. C., & Sidorova, A. (2012). Factors influencing business intelligence (BI) data collection strategies: An empirical investigation. *Decision Support Systems*, *52*(2), 486–496. doi:10.1016/j.dss.2011.10.009

Ramamurthy, K. R., Sen, A., & Sinha, A. P. (2004). An empirical investigation of the key determinants of data warehouse adoption. *Decision Support Systems*, *44*(4), 817–841. doi:10.1016/j.dss.2007.10.006

Seddon, P. B. (1997). A respecification and extension of the DeLone and McLean model of IS success. *Information Systems Research*, *8*(3), 240–253. doi:10.1287/isre.8.3.240

Turban, E., Sharda, R., & Delen, D. (2010). *Decision Support and Business Intelligence Systems* (9th ed.). New Jersey: Prentice Hall.

Verbitskiy, Y., & Yeoh, W. (2011). Data quality management in a business intelligence environment: from the lens of metadata. In *Proceedings of 16th International Conference on Information Quality* (pp.435-447), University of South Australia.

Wang, Y. M., & Wang, Y. S. (2009). Examining the dimensionality and measurement of user-perceived knowledge and information quality in the KMS context. *Journal of Information Science*, *35*(1), 94–109. doi:10.1177/0165551508092260

Watson, H. J. (2009). Tutorial: Business Intelligence – Past, Present, and Future. *Communications of the Association for Information Systems*, *25*(39), 487–510.

Wixom, B., Ariyachandra, T., Goul, M., Gray, P., Kulkarni, U., & Phillips-Wren, G. (2011). The Current State of Business Intelligence in Academia. *Communications of the Association for Information Systems*, *29*, 16.

Yeoh, W., & Koronios, A. (2010). Critical success factors for business intelligence systems. *Journal of Computer Information Systems*, *50*(3), 23–32.

KEY TERMS AND DEFINITIONS

BI Architecture: A group of IT components (DW, DM, ODS and others) that establish the architecture.

Business Intelligence (BI): BI does not have a single definition. It is umbrella term that combines tools, architecture, methodology, databases (DW or DM) and applications.

Data Mart (DM): A departmental database that contains specific relevant information.

Data Warehouse (DW): A database that should be integrated, time-variant, non-volatile and to share information between all the departments of an organization.

Extract, Transform and Load (ETL): A data warehousing process which has three main steps: Extract – reading data from source systems; Transform – to make the data useful for analysis and reporting and Load – put the data into a DW, DM, ODS or MR.

Information Quality (IQ): The holistic quality of information, including their dimensions (Accessibility, Accuracy, Completeness and others).

IQ-Oriented Architectures for BI: Developing BI architectures to improve the IQ dimensions. In other words, BI architectures should be created based on IQ dimensions priorities.

Chapter 7
Information Quality Assessment for Asset Management Systems

Sang Hyun Lee
University of South Australia, Australia

Abrar Haider
University of South Australia, Australia

ABSTRACT

Information quality is critical for any business. It is particularly important for mission critical information systems that manage the lifecycle of an engineering asset. Quality of information or lack thereof in these systems can be traced to technical, organisation, as well as human sources. It is, therefore, extremely important to ascertain the causes that contribute to lack of information quality in asset lifecycle management systems. Depending upon the business area, organisations take proactive or reactive approach to establishing, maintaining, and enhancing their information quality. Among proactive approaches, the ability of the organisation to measure information quality dimensions forms the foundation of a solid information quality management initiative. Such a measurement, however, is an intricate task because these dimensions are subjective, can be context dependent as well as independent, and are interdependent, since each dimension impacts other dimensions. This research employs productive perspective to information and applies Six-Sigma methodology to assess its quality in information systems utilised to manage engineering asset lifecycle. It utilises analytical hierarchy process and quality function deployment to convert subjective information quality dimension into objective metrics, assesses the relationship between various information quality dimensions, and ascertains critical to quality factors. The results thus obtained form the basis for monitoring of information quality aimed at its continuous improvement. This study contributes to literature and practice by providing a method for assessing correlation of information quality dimensions, applying six sigma to information, and controlling quality of information.

DOI: 10.4018/978-1-4666-4892-0.ch007

INTRODUCTION

Contemporary businesses are capturing, processing, and storing more than information than ever before. However, enormity of information is not of much use, if it does not conform to high standards of quality. Businesses are information driven and their competitiveness and profitability depends upon the quality of information available to their decision makers and knowledge workers. Engineering Asset managing organisations are no exception, and are dependent upon the information and its quality to institute effective planning, control, and management of their Asset base. However, a fundamental issue with ensuring information quality (IQ) is that it is hard to determine the quality of information while it is being captured and processed. It is only when it is being acted upon that an informed judgment can be made about its quality. The degree of quality of information is further subjected to the bias of its stakeholders. It is due to the same complexity that research and practice is replete with IQ assessment frameworks; whereas each of them serves specific industries, contexts, and objectives.

IQ has many dimensions and each dimension has a positive or negative correlation with other dimensions. These dimensions form the basic building block of IQ. IQ dimensions are a set of IQ attributes that reflect a single aspect or combined aspects of IQ (Stvilia, Gasser, Twidale, & Smith, 2007). Therefore, IQ dimensions can be used to interpret the degree of quality of information in quantitative terms as well as qualitative descriptors. Nevertheless, understating how each IQ dimension works and how it affects other IQ dimension is critical for IQ assessment and management. This paper proposes a methodology to assess how IQ can be measured by tracing the root cause of poor information in IQ dimensions as well as their correlation.

This paper begins with an analysis of information in Asset management paradigm. The paper then explains a Six-Sigma based IQ measurement and management framework based on productive perspective of information. The next section applies the framework in an Asset managing organisation and explains the process of converting information stakeholders' responses to objective measurements relating to IQ dimensions; using analytical hierarchy process (AHP) to establish the degree of relationship; and using quality function deployment (QFD) to extract the critical to quality (CTQ) factors precisely and logically. The paper concludes with a discussion of this research's potential value.

ASSET MANAGEMENT

The term Asset in engineering organisations is taken as the physical component of a manufacturing, production or service facility, which has value, enables services to be provided, and has an economic life greater than twelve months (Haider, 2011), such as manufacturing plants, roads, bridges, railway carriages, aircrafts, water pumps, and oil and gas rigs. The scope of Asset management activities extends from establishment of an Asset management policy and identification of service level targets according to the expectation of stakeholder and regulatory/legal requirements, to the daily operation of Assets aimed at meeting the defined levels of service. Asset managing organisations, therefore, are required to cope with the wide range of changes in the business environment; continuously reconfigure manufacturing resources so as to perform at accepted levels of service; and be able to adjust themselves to change with modest consequences on time, effort, cost, and performance.

Asset management can be classified into three levels, i.e. strategic, tactical, and operational (Figure 1). Strategic level is concerned with understanding the needs of stakeholders and market trends, and linking of the requirements thus generated to the optimum tactical and operational activities. Operational and tactical levels

Figure 1. Scope of asset management (Haider, 2011)

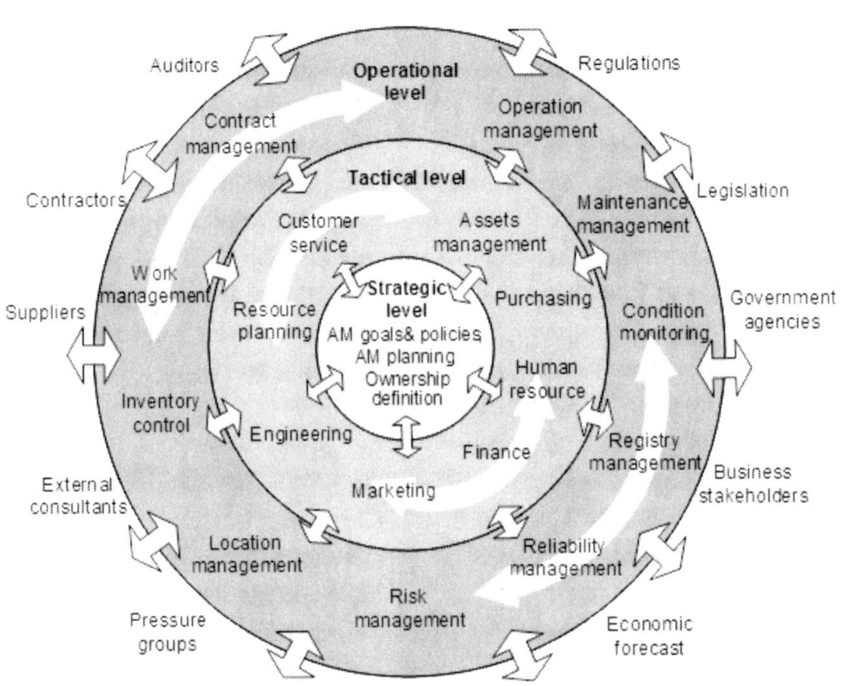

are underpinned by planning, decision support, monitoring, and review of each lifecycle stage to ensure availability, quality, and longevity of Asset's service provision. The identification, assessment, and control of risk is a key focus at all levels of planning, with the results from this process providing inputs into the Asset management strategy, policies, objectives, processes, plans, controls, and resource management.

SCOPE OF INFORMATION IN ASSET MANAGEMENT

In theory IT in Asset management have three major roles; firstly, IT is utilised in collection, storage, and analysis of information spanning Asset lifecycle processes; secondly, IT provides decision support capabilities through the analytic conclusions arrived at from analysis of data; and thirdly, IT provides an integrated view of Asset management through processing and communication of information and thereby allow for the basis of Asset management functional integration. IT for Asset management seeks to enhance the outputs of Asset management processes through a bottom up approach. This approach gathers and processes operational data for individual Assets at the base level, and on a higher level provides a consolidated view of entire Asset base (Figure 2).

At the operational and tactical levels, IT systems are required to provide necessary support for planning and execution of core Asset lifecycle processes. For example, at the design stage designers need to capture and process information such as, Asset configuration; Asset and/or site layout design and schematic diagrams/drawings; Asset bill of materials; analysis of maintainability and reliability design requirements; and failure modes, effects and criticality identification for each Asset. Planning choices at this stage drive future Asset behaviour, therefore the minimum requirement

Figure 2. IT concerns in asset management (IIMM, 2011)

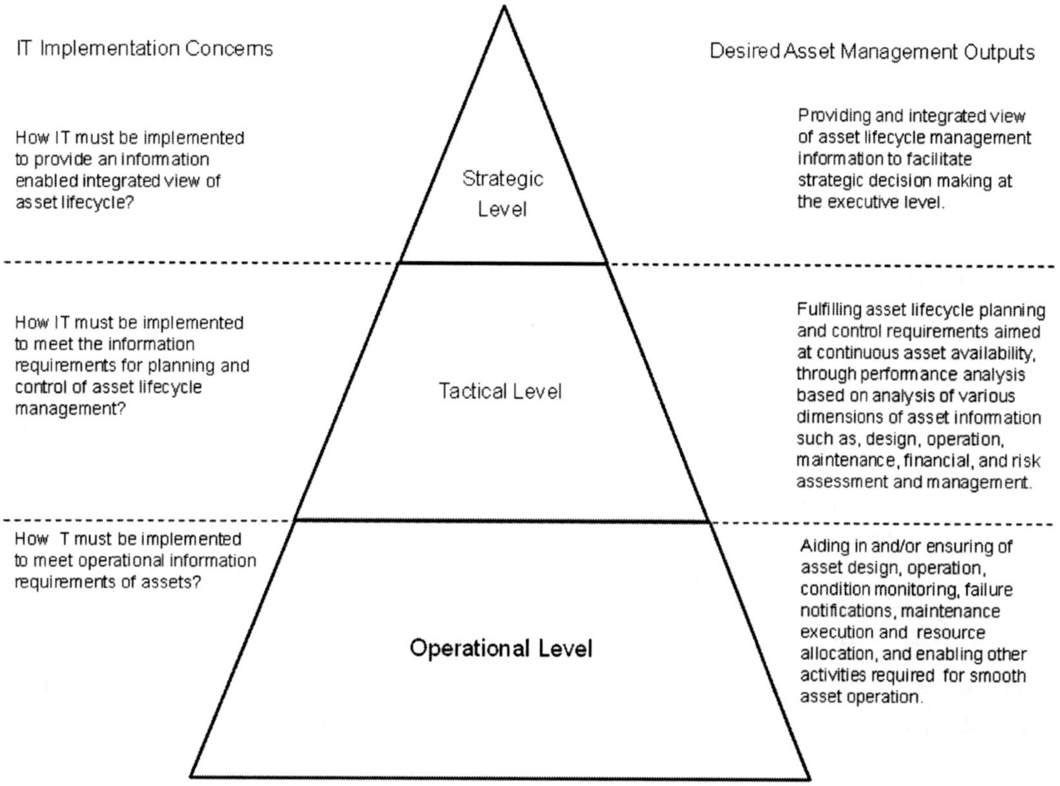

laid on IT at this stage is to provide right and timely information, such that informed choices could be made to ensure availability, reliability and quality of Asset operation. An important aspect of Asset design stage is the supportability design that governs most of the later Asset lifecycle stages. The crucial factor in carrying out these analyses is the availability and integration of quality information, such that analysis of supportability of all facets of Asset design and development, operation, maintenance, and retirement are fully recognised and defined. Nevertheless, effective Asset management requires the lifecycle decision makers to identify the financial and non-financial risks posed to Asset operation, their impact, and ways to mitigate those risks. This can only be achieved if credible, timely, accurate, interoperable, and integrated operational, control, financial, and administrative information is available, so that deviations from the normal operational pattern could be identified and analysed in a holistic manner. However, this complicates the task of ensuing information quality, since each quality dimension is dependent upon the other in more than one ways. For example, timeliness of failure information is dependent on completeness and/or accessibility of condition information; accessibility is dependent on availability of information; and availability is dependent upon security, credibility, and integrity of information, and so on. On the other hand, even if all the permutations described above work perfectly (which is only theoretically possible), interoperability of condition information to generate alarms and alerts for follow maintenance tasks still depends on a number of other quality dimensions. There are three major issues here, i.e. how can IQ be assessed within multiple IQ dimensions? what factors are critical to IQ? and how can correlations of IQ dimensions be analysed?

The following sections present a case study of how these issues have been addressed in a Korean Asset managing organisation. In order to resolve these issues, this research takes product perspective (Wang, Lee, Pipino, & Strong, 1998) of information and applies six-sigma methodology to information. Six-sigma has attracted little attention in IQ area despite the fact that it has been making remarkable success in manufacturing quality area. It enables organisations to structurally manage quality for high quality of products (Hekmatpanah, Sadroddin, Shahbaz, Mokhtari, & Fadavinia, 2008). This research utilises QFD to translate subjective information quality measurements into objective criteria that can be quantified and measured. This research, thus, ensures that customer requirements are precisely translated into relevant technical descriptors (Aboelmaged, 2010) through the use of AHP. AHP is a structured technique that has been used a tool of decision making (Saaty, 2008). AHP facilitates logical decision making processes and provides numerical priorities as a relative importance. Applying AHP to IQ dimensions in this research allows for numerical prioritization of IQ dimensions. These priorities serve as a weighted scale in QFD to address customers' requirements more accurately and logically. This makes the process of finding CTQ factors though a QFD more credible. CTQ represent the characteristics that are vital to information stakeholders' satisfaction (Linderman, Schroeder, Zaheer, & Choo, 2003). Six-Sigma methodology, thus, allows for the root causes of poor quality and CTQ factors.

BASIS OF IQ ASSESSMENT FRAMEWORK

Treating information as a product is to provide a well-defined product process and produce high quality information product rather than treating information solely as the by-product of business process execution (Wang, 1998). This concept is fundamental to IQ assessment. Table 1 shows the analogy between product manufacturing and information manufacturing to manage information as a product.

This product perspective is based on continuous improvement of information through the extension of well-known PDCA (Plan-Do-Check-Act) cycle. PDCA cycle in information paradigm could be interpreted as EIIA (Establishing–Identifying–Implementing–Assessing) cycle. The establishing phase establishes IQ objectives and requirements from information stakeholders (users, designers, producers, maintainers, managers, owners, custodians) to asses IQ related issues. This stage establishes the anomalies in data conventions as well as business rules. The identifying phase deals with assessment of the root cause of IQ issues. For example, the non-availability of information could be due to lack of access to information or lack of completeness of information. An important aspect at this stage is to ascertain the correlation between various IQ dimensions that contribute to or are affected by the IQ issues identified by information stakeholders. The implementing phase measures and analyzes IQ by revealing critical to quality factors, and takes steps to remove IQ issues. Lastly, the assessing phase compares IQ after improvements undertaken at

Table 1. Products vs. information manufacturing (Wang, 1998)

	Product Manufacturing	Information Manufacturing
Input	Raw Material	Raw data
Process	Assembly Line	Information System
Output	Physical Products	Information Product

step three to ensure compliance to base line quality standards (customer requirements).

Using the product perspective and EIIA cycle the authors developed the IQ assessment framework, shown in Figure 3.

THE CASE STUDY

The case study was undertaken at one of the largest Asset managing organisations located in Seoul, South Korea. As per university of South Australia ethics committee instructions case study and any of its participants must not be identified. Therefore, the case study organisation is being referee to as company ABC. The company itself restricted the authors to not to disclose the implementation and findings of the whole IQ assessment framework due to sensitivity of the business as well as the information involved. Therefore, we present the findings from phase 2 and 3 and remaining parts are explained in a generalized way.

This research follows a qualitative interpretive approach with survey as the primary data collection method. However, in addition to survey, data in this research has been triangulated from other sources, such as face to face interviews, content analysis, and direct observation. This survey instrument consists of three sections, i.e. general information regarding IQ initiatives, relative importance of IQ dimensions, and the relationship of IQ dimension with each other. The general information section focuses on job descriptions and field experience so that results could be classified according to job descriptions as well as experience of knowledge workers with IQ. In the relative importance of IQ dimensions section, questions are asked about IQ dimensions and their relative importance to other dimensions so that pairwise comparison of IQ dimensions is carried out. Lastly, in the relationship of IQ dimension section, questions are asked about mutual relationship of IQ dimensions to disclose the impact strength of an IQ dimension to other IQ dimensions.

The survey questionnaire was distributed among 68 IQ stakeholders (i.e. information users, information producers, information managers, and information custodians) in company ABC, and 57 responses were selected as acceptable survey responses. As the survey questionnaire contains the pairwise comparison questions, we used consistency index (CI) for selection criterion. CI indicates logical consistency among pairwise comparison judgments in a perfect pairwise

Figure 3. EIIA cycle based IQ assessment framework (Lee & Haider, 2012)

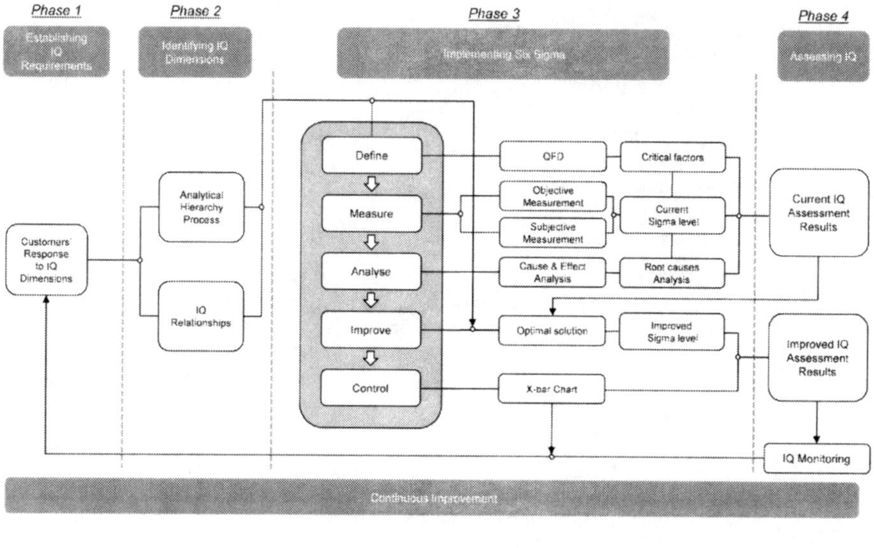

comparison case. For example, if CI value is 0.0, it means there is no logical inconsistency among the pairwise comparison answers from the participants. As the value of CI grows, the degree of logical inconsistency among the pairwise comparison answers is also considered to grow. In the survey we conduced, CI threshold value is set to 0.1 and the responses that CI value exceeds 0.1 were not accepted.

Establishing IQ Requirements (Phase 1)

The first phase of the 'establish IQ requirement' seeks information stakeholders' requirements with regards to IQ. An Asset managing organisation acquires, processes, and stores enormous amount of information on a daily basis. Company ABC is no different, though, it also has another dimension since it is public organisation. This means that they have to comply with government regulations regarding information exchange, processing, security, and management. Frequently amended regulations by government results in not only the frequent re-engineering of business processes but information structures and flows are also revised according to the amended policies of government. This undermines company ABC's quality of information because they need to revise information schema and address information migration or modification on a continuous basis. Therefore, information stakeholders such as information producers, processors, custodians, and managers were chosen as the participants of the survey exercise.

As IQ dimensions can be context dependent as well as context independent, and can be interpreted in different ways according to different types of information usages and business rules. Fifteen IQ dimensions were chosen for this research, which include accuracy, conciseness, completeness, consistency, timeliness, security, appropriateness, relevancy, ease of understanding, interpretability, objectivity, believability, accessibility, ease of operation, and reputation. The table consists of four quadrants that illustrate context independent data perspective (CIDP), context independent user perspective (CIUP), context dependent data

Table 2. Classification of IQ issues/problems (Ge & Helfert, 2007)

	Data Perspective	User Perspective
Context-independent	Spelling error Missing data Duplicate data Incorrect value Inconsistent data format Out-dated data Incomplete data format Syntax violation UnIQue value violation Violation of integrity constraints Text formatting	The information is inaccessible The information is insecure The information is hardly retrievable The information is difficult to aggregate Errors in the information transformation
Context-dependent	Violation of domain constraint Violation of organisation's business rules Violation of company and government regulations Violation of constraints provided by the database administrator	The information is not based on fact The information is of doubtful credibility The information presents an impartial view The information is irrelevant to the work The information consists of inconsistent meanings The information is incomplete The information is compactly represented The information is hard to manipulate The information is hard to understand

perspective (CDDP), and context dependent user perspective (CDUP) IQ problems (Table 2).

In the first part of the survey the set of IQ issues and IQ dimensions (Table 3) were given and respondents were asked to rate each of the IQ issues on the basis of their importance on an ordinal scale of 1-5, and their possible impact on IQ dimensions.

This research categorizes IQ dimensions by the 'Conformance to Specifications' (CTS) i.e. the dimensions that are product quality oriented and measureable objectively; 'Meets or Exceeds

Table 3. Weight of importance of IQ issues and their impact on IQ dimensions

IQ Issues	Weight of Importance	Dimensions Impacted by the IQ Issues														
		A	**B**	**C**	**D**	**E**	**F**	**G**	**H**	**I**	**J**	**K**	**L**	**M**	**N**	**O**
Spelling error	3	X											X	X	X	
Missing data	4								X				X			
Duplicate data	4		X		X					X					X	
Incorrect value	5	X											X			X
Inconsistent data format	5			X	X					X	X			X		
Out-dated data	5					X							X			
Incomplete data format	5				X				X	X						
Syntax violation	4	X							X							
UnIQue value violation	5										X					
Violation of integrity constraints	3				X						X					
Text formatting	4				X				X	X				X	X	
Violation of domain constraint	5				X				X							
Violation of organisation's business rules	5								X							
Violation of regulations	5								X							
Violation of constraints	5									X	X					
Information is inaccessible	2								X					X		
Information is insecure	3						X									
Information is hardly retrievable	2													X	X	
Information is difficult to aggregate	3														X	X
Errors in Information transformation	4	X	X	X	X	X	X	X			X			X	X	
Information is not based on fact	5															X
Information is of doubtful credibility	3												X			X
Information presents an impartial view	5											X				
Information is irrelevant to the work	3															
Inconsistent meanings	5				X											
Information is incomplete	4			X												
Information is compactly represented	2		X													
Information is hard to manipulate	3														X	
Information is hard to understand	2									X						

Accuracy(A), conciseness (B), completeness (C), consistency (D), timeliness (E), security (F), appropriateness (G), relevancy(H), ease of understanding (I), interpretability (J), objectivity (K), believability (L), accessibility (M), ease of operation (N), and reputation (O).

Customers' Expectation' (MECE), i.e. the dimensions that are more service quality oriented and capture the essence of 'fitness for use'; 'Information Product Quality' (IPQ) i.e. the dimensions that are associated with the features of information as product; and the 'Information Service Quality' (ISQ) i.e. the IQ dimensions that are related to the process of delivering right information at right time to right stakeholders. The hierarchy of IQ dimensions within each category is based on PSP/IQ Model (Kahn & Strong, 1998).

Identifying IQ Dimensions (Phase 2)

At the second stage, survey respondents were asked to rate IQ dimensions against other dimensions within the categories described above. Table 4 shows the results of the IQ dimension and their relative importance. The results indicate that the MECE weights higher (0.603) than the CTS's (0.397). It is not unreasonable to postulate that company ABC gives much more weight to 'fitness for use' perspective of information than product perspectives of information. However the reason why C-ISQ weight is less than C-IPQ's can be explained that IQ dimensions included in C-IPQ are the most objective aspects of IQ. As to the M-IPQ and M-ISQ in MECE, M-ISQ weight is significantly higher (0.755) than M-IPQ's (0.245).

It is not surprising that as M-ISQ contains subjective aspects of IQ and more service related attributes to information customers, this is much more emphasized to a public sector organisation. A closer look at IQ dimensions reveals that the dimensions in CTS have similar weights in C-IPQ and C-ISQ respectively. This means that all the IQ dimensions listed in the CTS should be treated with almost equal importance. In contrast, the IQ dimensions listed in the MECE have uneven distribution. This means that certain IQ in the MECE should be treated more intensively due to the difference in the level of importance. Interestingly, the 'believability' dimension is significantly regarded as important one compared to other dimensions even though it is a highly subjective dimension. Judging from the definition of

Table 4. Summary of AHP results applied to company ABC

Categories			Weight	IQ Dimensions	Weight
Conformance to Specifications (CTS)	0.397	Information Product Quality (C-IPQ)	0.684	Accuracy	0.297
				Conciseness	0.235
				Completeness	0.216
				Consistency	0.252
		Information Service Quality (C-ISQ)	0.316	Timeliness	0.460
				Security	0.540
Meets or Exceeds Customer's Expectations (MECE)	0.603	Information Product Quality (M-IPQ)	0.245	Appropriateness	0.059
				Relevancy	0.259
				Ease of Understanding	0.176
				Interpretability	0.175
				Objectivity	0.332
		Information Service Quality (M-ISQ)	0.755	Believability	0.487
				Accessibility	0.108
				Ease of Operation	0.069
				Reputation	0.336

the 'believability' that information is accepted or regarded as true, real, and credible (Wang & Strong, 1996), the level of importance respondents have given to this dimension is easily understood. With regard to the result of the relationship of each IQ dimension in M-ISP, the most related IQ dimensions against each four dimension were determined by survey participants to discover how much they affect each other.

The survey asked the respondents to rate each IQ dimension according to its relationships with other IQ dimensions. For this paper the authors presents results of four IQ dimensions, i.e. believability, accessibility, ease of operation, and reputation. The 'Believability' dimension embraces the information attribute that are related to credibility from IQ customers. This attribute represents IQ customers' satisfaction while using it. Therefore, the set of IQ dimensions, i.e. 'objectivity', 'ease of operation', 'reputation', 'relevancy', and 'accuracy' were chosen as the list of most related IQ dimensions for respondents to rate the degree of relationship of 'believability'. Figure 4 shows the relationship results of 'believability'. From all respondents' point of view, 'reputation' is the most related dimension (41%).

'Reputation' means the information that is trusted or highly regarded in terms of their source or contents (Wang & Strong, 1996). In other words, 'reputation' represents the raw information sources that are used to create the information product. The quality of 'believability', therefore, interacts strongly with the 'reputation' compared to the rest of dimensions. Interestingly, while the 'ease of operation' is rated by 15% from information users, no one in the information producers choose the dimension. This means that information producers believe 'ease of operation' is not related to 'believability' but for information users, it is somehow related to 'believability'. This is pretty obvious result because the aspects of 'ease of operation' contain information users' conveniences and we could find out that 'ease of operation' affects the quality of 'believability' to information users.

The 'accessibility' dimension represents the information attribute that is available or easily and quickly retrievable (Wang & Strong, 1996). Based on the definition of 'accessibility', the set of IQ dimensions which are regarded as the most related dimensions, 'objectivity', 'ease of operation', 'relevancy', 'timeliness', and 'believ-

Figure 4. Relationship of 'believability' IQ dimension

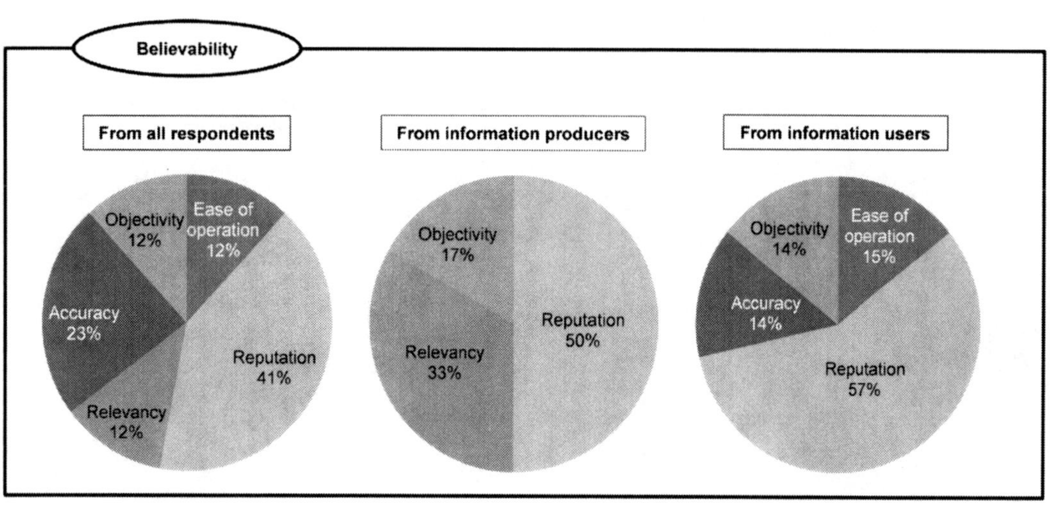

ability' were chosen from the respondents. Figure. 5 shows the relationship of 'accessibility' with other dimensions. From all respondents' view, 'consistency' is outlined as the most related dimension (35%). Given the attribute of 'consistency, it should not surprise us that the dimension marks the highest relationship percentage. The attributes of 'consistency' relate to the information that is always presented in the same format and is compatible with previous information (Wang & Strong, 1996). This is because a query is a key for information access from information system and it is highly related to information retrieval. As to the dimension of 'timeliness', while it rates the second related dimension from information producers, no one from information users answers that 'timeliness' is related to 'accessibility'. As the 'timeliness' concerns how long the information remains valid, it could be related to information producers rather than information users when they retrieve information form information system.

The 'ease of operation' dimension embodies the information attribute that is easily managed and manipulated (i.e. updated, moved, aggregated, reproduced, and customized) (Wang & Strong, 1996). The set of IQ dimensions related to this dimension include, 'interpretability', 'consistency', and 'reputation' were chosen. Figure 6 shows the relationship of 'ease of operation' with these dimensions as deemed by the survey respondents. From all respondents' point of view, 'interpretability' has the highest score (47%) whereas 'reputation' is second (29%) and 'consistency' (24%) respectively. Even though 'interpretability' ranked as the most related IQ dimension from all respondents, the degree of 'reputation' has a different relative rate between the two groups toward the relationship with 'ease of operation'. As we have seen the relationship between 'believability' and 'reputation', 'reputation' also has higher percentage relationship with 'ease of operation' from information users. It appears likely to us that the information users prefer to use information from reliable sources for correctness rather than 'consistency'.

The definition of 'reputation' is highly related to the source of information. After providing the definition of 'reputation' to participant, the set of IQ dimensions related to this dimension including 'consistency', 'relevancy', 'completeness', and 'ease of operation' were chosen from the respondents. Figure 7 shows the relationship of 'reputa-

Figure 5. Relationship of 'accessibility' IQ dimension

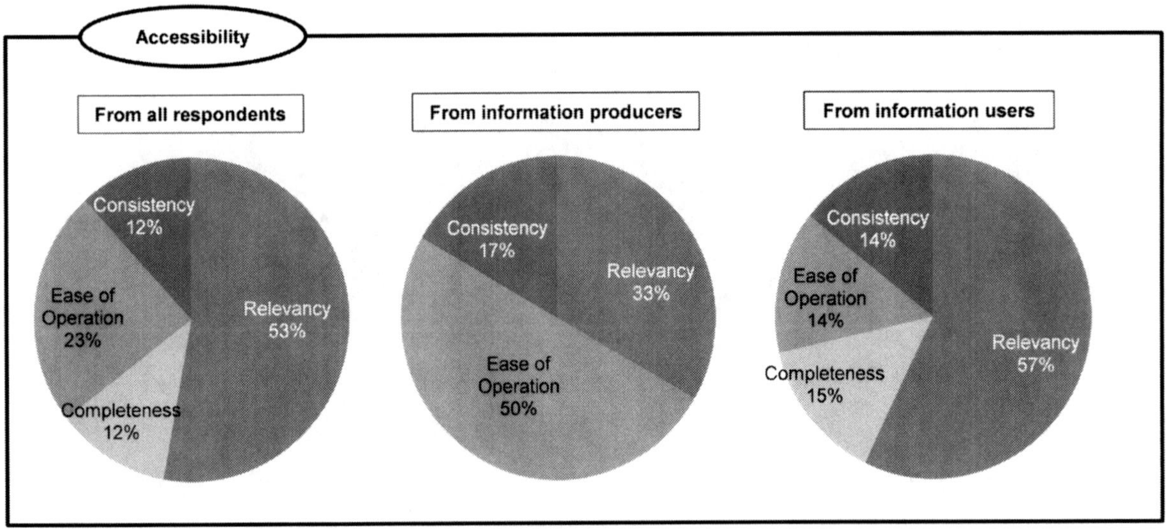

Figure 6. Relationship of 'ease of operation' IQ dimension

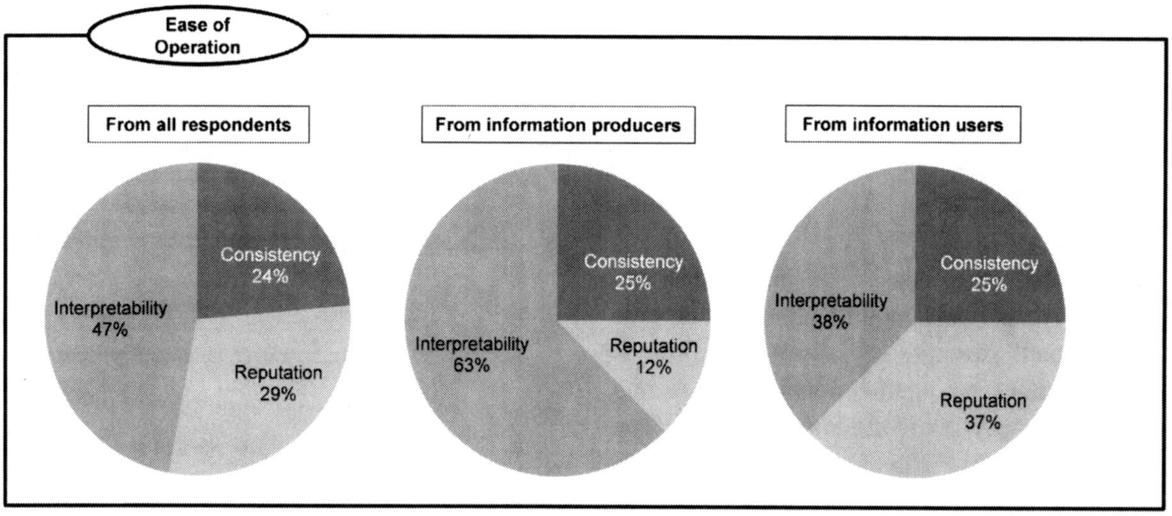

Figure 7. Relationship of 'reputation' IQ dimension

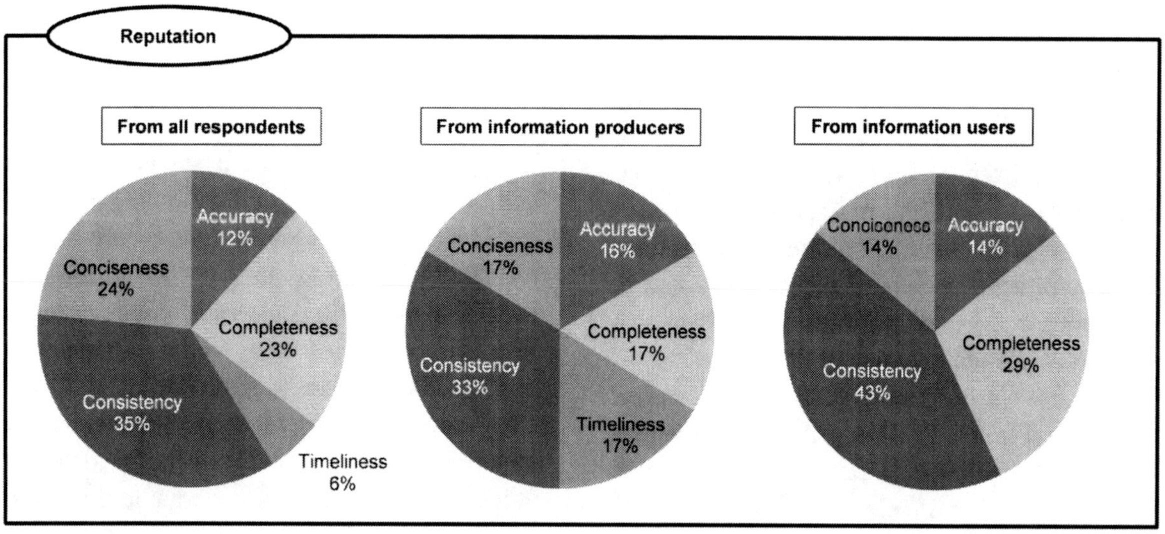

tion' with other dimensions. From all respondents' point of view, the 'relevancy' dimension has the highest relationship with the 'reputation'. Since 'reputation' concerns trustable sources and contents of information, it is highly reasonable that the 'relevancy' has the strongest relationship with the 'reputation'. As the 'relevancy' dimension is mostly related to supporting a given process, helping decision making, adapting to other application and linkage, there is a striking connection between 'reputation' and 'relevancy'. In terms of 'relevancy' dimension from different groups, there is a relative difference. The significant disparity seems to be explained by the different task roles of the two groups. In general, information producers are supposed to generate information based on their task. As the 'ease of operation' is directly linked with the task at hand, information producers may believe that easily operating information enables information to improve its reputation.

Implementing Six-Sigma (Phase 3)

Stage 1: Define

The 'define' stage consists of three steps, i.e. process, scope, and requirements. At process step, overall structure of information flow is drawn to provide a top down view of IQ from a business perspective. In the scope step, the scope of IQ from an information system perspective is defined to profile IQ dimensions and to identify problems related to IQ. In the requirements step, the specifications of each IQ dimension and IQ rules are defined to meet the customers' requirements utilising the results of the phases above by creating the QFD to identify the correlation of each IQ dimension. Customized IQ specifications based on IQ dimensions as assessment criteria must be established in this stage. Simultaneously, determining of potential CTQs must be conducted at the beginning of this phase. CTQs must be interpreted from qualitative customers' requirements and be measured in the measure stage of Six-Sigma. A QFD is important outcome of this stage.

The House of Quality (HOQ) is the kernel of QFD (Figure 8). Here, customer requirements (block number 1) matrix is replaced with customer responses collected from the phase 1 of IQ assessment framework. Technical requirements, which are related to business rules (block number 2) matrix is represented in the hierarchy of IQ dimensions according to phase 2 of IQ assessment framework. Inter-relationships matrix (block number 3) is calculated according to the results of AHP in the phase 2 of IQ assessment framework. Correlation of IQ dimensions (block number 4) matrix is filled by the results of IQ relationship in the phase 2 of IQ assessment framework and its directions (i.e. positive or negative combination) of improvement (block number 5)

Figure 8. Quality function deployment (House of Quality)

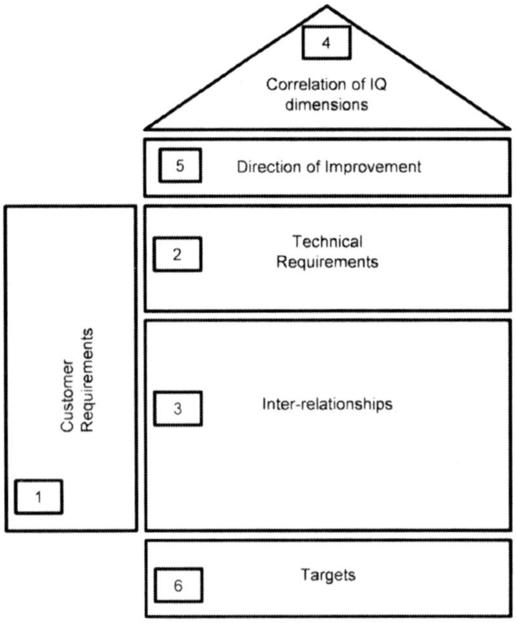

are defined accordingly. Finally, in targets matrix (block number 6), objective or subjective measure and Six-Sigma level specification are defined to each IQ dimension respectively. Figure 9 shows the QFD result from company ABC. Based on the house of quality, customer requirements are listed on the block 1 area. As the four quadrants of IQ problems' classification (i.e. CIDP, CDDP, CIUP, and CDUP) covers comprehensive customer requirements to IQ, all the lists in the four quadrants are described on the block 1 area having individual weights of importance which are worked out from the survey. Even though this research utilises the four quadrants for customers' requirements, it can be modified according to organisations' special circumstances.

As to the technical requirements, IQ dimensions are listed with their relative importance which is worked out from AHP results. The IQ dimension lists also can be modified according to organisations' special circumstances or demands. From the 'establishing IQ requirement phase', the mapping between IQ problems and IQ

Figure 9. QFD results from company ABC

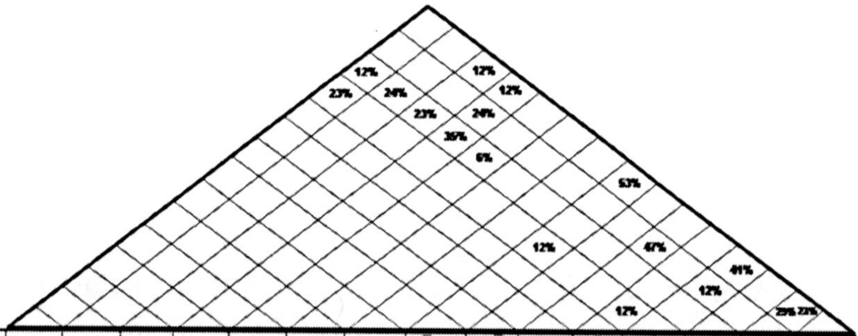

WHATS \ HOWS	Weights of Importance	Accuracy	Conciseness	Completeness	Consistence	Timeliness	Security	Appropriateness	Relevancy	Ease of Understand	Interpretability	Objectivity	Believability	Accessibility	Easy of Operation	Reputation
Direction of improvement									↓	↓		↑	↑			↑↓
		Conformance to Specification						Meets or Exceeds Customer's Expectations								
		Information Product Quality				Information Service Quality		Information Product Quality					Inforamtion Service Quality			
Weights of importance		0.297	0.235	0.216	0.252	0.460	0.540	0.059	0.259	0.176	0.175	0.332	0.487	0.108	0.069	0.336
Spelling error	3	0.891											1.461	0.324	0.207	
Missing data	4								1.036				1.948			
Duplicate data	4		0.940		1.008					0.704					0.276	
Incorrect value	5	1.485											2.435			1.680
Inconsistent data format	5				1.260					0.880	0.875			0.540		
Out-dated data	5					2.300							2.435			
Incomplete data format	5			1.080	1.260				1.295	0.880						
Syntax violation	4	1.188							1.036							
Unique value violation	5										0.875					
Violation of integrity constraints	3				0.756						0.525					
Text formatting	4				1.008				1.036	0.704				0.432	0.276	
Violation of domain constraint	5				1.260				1.295							
Violation of organization's business rules	5								1.295			1.660				
Violation of company and government regulations	5								1.295			1.660				
Violation of constraints provided by the database administrator	5									0.880	0.875					
The information is inaccessible	2								0.518					0.216		
The information is insecure	3						1.620									
The information is hardly retrievable	2													0.216	0.138	
The information is difficult to aggregate	3														0.207	1.008
Errors in the information transformation	4	1.188	0.940	0.864	1.008	1.840	2.160	0.236			0.700			0.432	0.276	
The information is not based on fact	5															1.680
The information is of doubtful credibility	3												1.461			1.008
The information presents an impartial view	5											1.660				
The information is irrelevant to the work	3								0.777							
The information consists of inconsistent meanings	5				1.260											
The information is incomplete	4			0.864												
The information is compactly represented	2		0.470													
The information is hard to manipulate	3														0.207	
The information is hard to understand	2									0.352						
Assessment methodology		O	O,S	S	S	O,S	O	O,S	S	S	S	S	S	O,S	S	S
Six sigma specification																
Absolute importance		4.752	2.350	2.808	8.820	4.140	3.780	0.236	9.583	4.048	3.850	4.980	9.740	2.160	1.587	5.376
CTQ selection		6	12	11	3	7	10	15	2	8	9	5	1	13	14	4

dimensions is referenced to fill out the inter-relationships on the block 3 area. Based on the IQ dimensions' relationship survey results, correlation of IQ dimension area is supposed to be filled out. In this case study, four IQ dimension in M-SIQ were conducted and its results are shown on the block 4 area. The direction of improvement on the block 5 area is dependent upon IQ responsible persons and it can be optional. Lastly, target block contains assessment methodology, Six-Sigma specification, the aggregate of importance, and CTQs selection order. Six-Sigma speciation represents each IQ dimension's tolerances. Since each IQ dimension has difference tolerance toward six sigma level, it can be various according to different types of organisations. Aggregate of importance shows the summation of each IQ dimension's importance respectively and its results are used for CTQ selection.

Stage 2: Measure

The 'measure' stage consists of two stages, i.e. information collection and information measurement. In the information collecting stage, identifying criteria, measurement systems, scales and sampling methods are considered. Once the information collecting stage is complete, the information measurement calculates current sigma level with the specification of each IQ dimension and IQ rules. In the information measurement stage, the method of IQ measurement can be categorized to objective and subjective measurement. And then, individual participants' AHP results were utilised to discover mutual IQ dimensions' relationship calculating correlation coefficient (r) of IQ dimensions. Given a set of observations (x1, y1), (x2,y2),...(xn,yn), the formula with sample mean and standard deviation for computing the correlation coefficient is given by (1):

$$r = \frac{1}{n-1} \Sigma \left(\frac{x - \overline{x}}{Sx} \right) \left(\frac{y - \overline{y}}{Sy} \right) \quad (1)$$

Correlation coefficient (r) using MinTab software and its results are shown in Table 5 and its matrix plot is illustrated in Figure 10.

Matrix plot represents the relationship of two different variables. In the matrix plot, different IQ dimensions are placed in X-Y axis and their relationship, obtained from Table 4 is placed in it. From the matrix plot and IQ dimensions' correlation coefficient table, we found out that 'believability' and 'reputation' dimensions have relatively high negative correlation.

The 'believability' dimension is mainly concerned with its credibility by those who use, manipulate, and manage the information. The 'reputation' dimension mainly concerns with the sources of information which is used to generate the information. In general, the correlation between 'believability' and 'reputation' is likely to have strong positive correlation because reliable source of information guarantee credible information by information customers.

Therefore, the IQ dimensions' correlations cannot be generalized. In other words, particular positive correlations of IQ dimensions are circumstantial and can be negative or positive correlations for each business.

Stage 3: Analyze

'Analyze' stage consists of quality evaluation and defects analysis based on 'define' and 'measure' stages. CTQs determined at 'define' step are listed, and finding the influencing factors to CTQs and root causes are the goals of 'analyze' stage. Ac-

Table 5. IQ dimensions' correlation coefficient

	Believability	Accessibility	Ease of Operation
Accessibility	-0.687		
Ease of Operation	-0.421	0.085	
Reputation	-0.143	-0.394	-0.372

Figure 10. Matrix plot of IQ dimensions

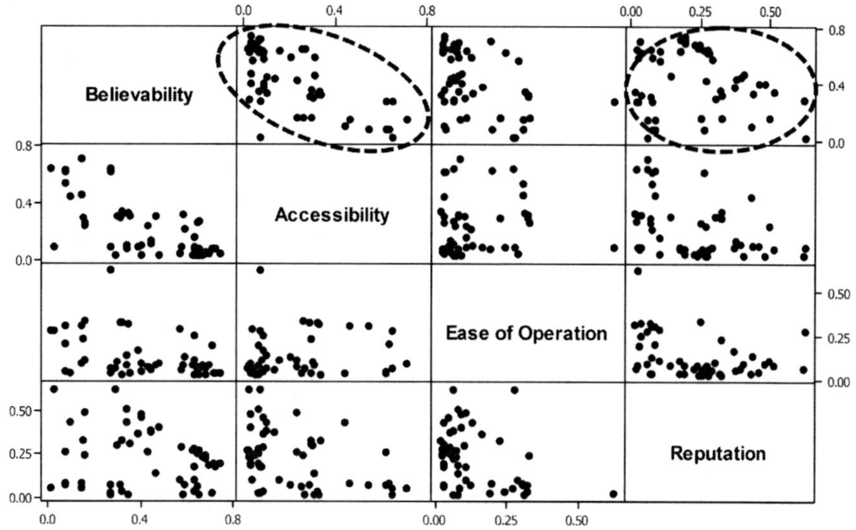

cording to information types, graphical analysis, statistical inference including interval estimation and hypotheses testing, and regression analysis can be utilised. Discovering vital few from trivial many in the process helps to capture critical reasons of CTQs because the controllable factors which affect output always presence. As shown in Figure 11, trivial many and vital few are contained while process or system is processed from input to output. Here, X is the independent variable and Y is the dependent variable. Therefore, Y depends on X. By adjusting X, Y can be improved. In other words, finding X's trivial many and vital few and adjusting X is the goal of 'analyze' stage. Various possible reasons that affect output are extracted through brainstorming, fishbone or logic tree diagram and those selected reasons are analyzed to address the relationship with output Y.

In order to extract vital few from trivial many and possible X, interview responses were utilised to drive a cause & effect analysis. The cause and effect diagram helps certain problems to visually display the many potential causes for a problem or effect. When utilising a team approach to

Figure 11. Vital few and trivial many in the system (Choi, Lee, Kim, & Kim, 2005)

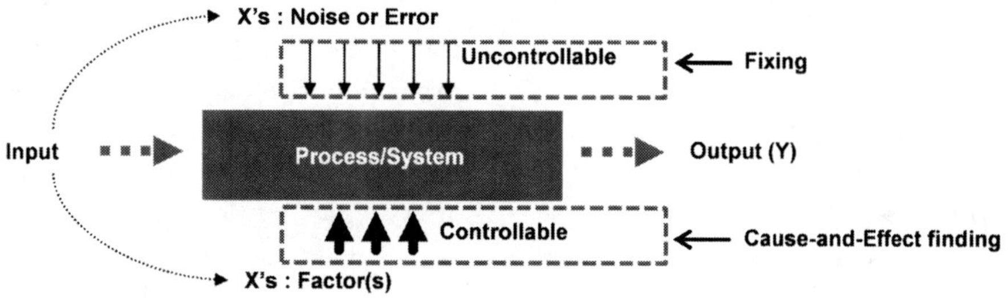

problem solving, there are often many opinions as to the problem's root cause. One way to capture these different ideas and stimulate the team's brainstorming on root causes is the cause and effect diagram, commonly called a fishbone. The fishbone helps to visually display the many potential causes for a specific problem or effect. Listing of trivial many, vital-few, and fishbone diagram are the major outcomes of this stage.

Stage 4: Improve

Six-Sigma results come from actual changes to business processes are applied at 'improve' stage. This stage makes the process changes. However, the process improvements are critical in measuring and validating the impact of improvements. The objective of improve stage is to identify improvement breakthroughs, identify high gain alternatives, select preferred approach, design the future state, determine the new sigma level, and create a preliminary implementation plan. As there are many factors that affect output Y they need to be categorized into uncontrollable and controllable factors. If the factors are not controllable, they can be fixed and alternative factors for instance, controllable factors should be managed to improve process or system. In the case of company ABC, the authors found that the generation of poor information is related to often changed polices or amending of regulations. Unfortunately, as it is impossible to control government regulations, it should be regarded as uncontrollable factors and fixed. For understanding of quality system and maintaining improved quality of information continually, standardization is essential. The improved process from the 'improve' stage is standardized in the 'control' stage monitoring the process performance. If the standardization is not successful, the variance of the process has high possibility of increasing and process improvement is vulnerable to be discontinued. In addition, performance measuring time also increased that leads customers' dissatisfaction.

Stage 5: Control

The 'control' stage consists of two steps: controlling and monitoring. The main objective of this stage is to maintain high quality of information products. In controlling step, representing IQ assessment results for information system, standardizing the IQ assessment framework, and generating documents are conducted. In the monitoring step, X-bar char representing each IQ dimensions with upper and lower control level and inspection lists are designed. An X-bar chart is a control chart used for monitoring information by collecting sample at regular intervals (Hsieh, Lin, & Manduca, 2007). Accordingly, each IQ dimension of sampled information in information system is monitored by using the X-bar chart at regular intervals to prevent production of poor information and to ensure the high quality of information.

By using the X-bar chart, if a certain dimension exceeds the specified limits, then the X-bar chart would raise alarm about that dimension. Figure 12 shows an example of IQ dimensions' monitoring. In this figure, the subjective or objective method can be applied. According to the different tolerance level of each IQ dimension in an organisation, the sigma value can be converted based on the upper or lower control (specification level). This is because quality is defined differently at different levels and different view-points. Hence, the tolerance of sigma level needs to be carefully calculated while identifying IQ dimensions. Basically having control limits and specification limits would not suffice. When organisations maintain these limits, the usages of the control limits are very low because the actual information users or managers regard information that does not exceed the specification limits as valid information. Therefore, having limits is not suitable for information system. It is rather beneficial to have specification level and corresponding alarming level.

Figure 12. X-bar chart for IQ dimension monitoring

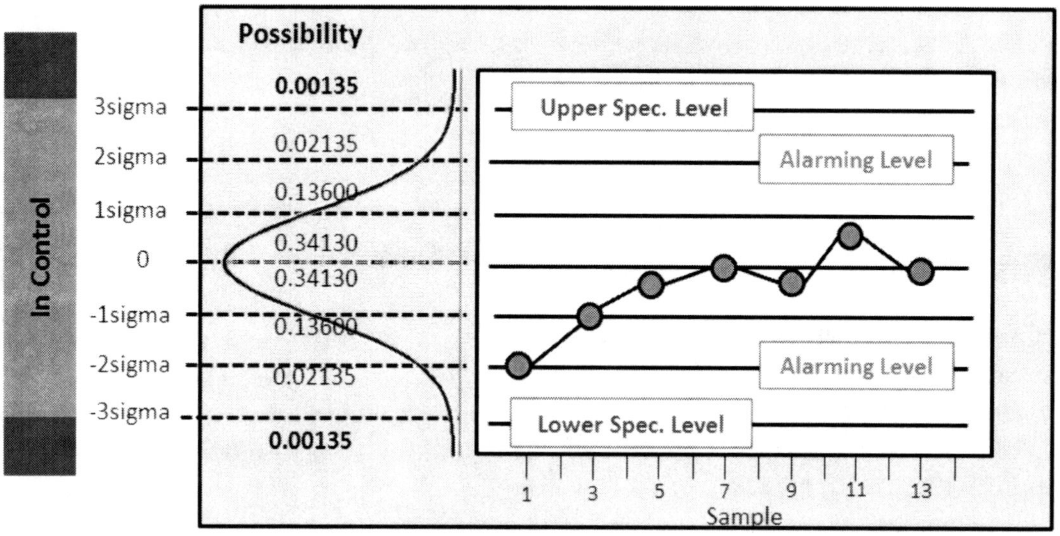

Assessing IQ (Phase 4)

It is difficult to maintain high quality of information without continuous IQ improvement activities by those who are responsible for information. Therefore, embedding IQ culture into business process is mandatory. Continually collecting IQ issues, quality target setting and monitoring quality status are recommended for continuous improvement by assessment results. In addition, regular comparison between current sigma level and improved sigma level is also required. This is most emphasized in this phase. Finally, all the outcomes from implementing Six-Sigma should be managed to be shared with all employees. As to system maintenance and operations, focusing on information flow as an assessment framework can be more efficient. Information flow management which includes data format change, code transformation, and mapping history is critical factor of high quality of information.

CONCLUSION

This study addressed three research questions: First, how can IQ be assessed within multiple IQ dimensions? Second, what factors are critical to IQ? And third, how can correlations of IQ dimensions be analyzed? By taking into account the product perspective of information, we can conclude that, firstly, regardless of organisations' size or type, precise IQ assessment can be achieved systematically according to customers' requirements. As we have seen the IT concerns in Asset management according to the different levels (i.e. operational, tactical, and strategic). Each level has different IQ demands, therefore, applying a solid IQ assessment framework yields more efficient results. Secondly, as extracting critical factors to IQ without considering their relationship with other factors is likely to lead to improper assessment outcomes. Thirdly, we could find IQ dimensions have their positive or negative relationship with other dimensions using both AHP method and matrix plot calculating IQ dimensions correlation coefficient. However, the point that the authors would like to highlight is that correlation of IQ dimensions cannot be generalized because they are not static but dynamic according to their usages.

REFERENCES

Aboelmaged, M. G. (2010). Six sigma quality: A structured review and implications for future research. *International Journal of Quality & Reliability Management*, *27*(3), 268–317. doi:10.1108/02656711011023294

Choi, S. K., Lee, J. S., Kim, T. K., & Kim, W. H. (2005). *LG global standard six sigma training* (Vol. 1). LG Electronics.

Ge, M., & Helfert, M. (2007). *A review of information quality research-develop a research agenda*. Paper presented at the 12th International Conference on Information Quality. New York, NY.

Haider, A. (2011). *Information technologies implementation and organisational behavior: An asset management perspective*. Paper presented at the Technology Management in the Energy Smart World (PICMET). New York, NY.

Hekmatpanah, M., Sadroddin, M., Shahbaz, S., Mokhtari, F., & Fadavinia, F. (2008). Six sigma process and its impact on the organisational productivity. *World Academy of Science. Engineering and Technology*, *43*, 365–369.

Hsieh, C., Lin, B., & Manduca, B. (2007). Information technology and six sigma implementation. *Journal of Computer Information Systems*, *47*(4), 1.

IIMM. (2011). International infrastructure management manual (4th ed.). Wellington, NZ: National Asset Management Steering (NAMS) Group.

Kahn, B. K., & Strong, D. M. (1998). *Product and service performance model for information quality: an update*. Paper presented at the 1998 Conference on Information Quality. Cambridge, MA.

Lee, S. H., & Haider, A. (2012). *Assessing information quality by six sigma method* (Vol. 7240, pp. 323–334). Berlin, Germany: Springer Berlin Heidelberg. doi:10.1007/978-3-642-29023-7_32

Linderman, K., Schroeder, R. G., Zaheer, S., & Choo, A. S. (2003). Six sigma: A goal-theoretic perspective. *Journal of Operations Management*, *21*(2), 193–203. doi:10.1016/S0272-6963(02)00087-6

Saaty, T. L. (2008). Decision making with the analytic hierarchy process. *International Journal of Services Sciences*, *1*(1), 83–98. doi:10.1504/IJSSCI.2008.017590

Stvilia, B., Gasser, L., Twidale, M. B., & Smith, L. C. (2007). A framework for information quality assessment. *Journal of the American Society for Information Science and Technology*, *58*(12), 1720–1733. doi:10.1002/asi.20652

Wang, R. Y. (1998). A product perspective on total data quality management. *Communications of the ACM*, *41*(2), 58–65. doi:10.1145/269012.269022

Wang, R. Y., Lee, Y. W., Pipino, L. L., & Strong, D. M. (1998). Manage your information as a product. *Sloan Management Review*, *39*(4), 95–105.

Wang, R. Y., & Strong, D. M. (1996). Beyond accuracy: What data quality means to data consumers. *Journal of Management Information Systems*, 5–33.

KEY TERMS AND DEFINITIONS

AHP (Analytic Hierarchy Process): The analytic hierarchy process is a structured decision making technique utilising pairwise comparison survey.

Asset Management: Asset management is the combination of management, financial, engineering, and other practices applied to physical Assets in pursuit of economic life-cycle costs.

Critical to Quality (CTQ): CTQ is a process characteristic or component which has a direct effect on the overall process quality.

Information Quality: Information quality is conformance to specifications to meet or exceed information users' expectations.

Information Quality Assessment: Information Quality Assessment is the process of assigning numerical or categorical values to information quality dimensions in a given setting.

Information Quality Dimension: Information Quality Dimension is a quality attribute that represents a single aspect or construct of information quality.

Six Sigma: Six Sigma is a set of tools and strategies to improve process by reducing variation within D (Define)-M(Measure)-A(analyse)-I(Improve)-C(Control) process.

QFD (Quality Function Deployment): QFD is a methodology to define the customer's desires prioritizing and translating them into engineering requirement to meet intended requirements.

Chapter 8
Trends and Research of Wikis' Quality and Governance Based on Bibliometric and Content Analysis

Qinghua Zhu
Nanjing University, China

Linghe Huang
Nanjing University, China

Jia Tina Du
University of South Australia, Australia

Hua Liu
Nanjing University, China

ABSTRACT

Wiki is a typical representative of the User-Generated Content. Its appearance greatly promotes the creation, organization, management, and sharing of knowledge on the Internet. As articles grow rapidly in Wikis, the quality of the articles has aroused many people's concerns. The topics on how to assess and control the quality of articles have attracted many researchers. However, few studies have been conducted to investigate the status of this research topic. This chapter explores the current research status and trends of wikis' quality and governance. The authors selected papers from the databases of ISI, EI, IEEE, and other widely used databases. They reported the trends and research of wikis' quality and governance using bibliometric analysis and content analysis of a total of 99 relevant papers. The results show that although the research topics in the field have experienced a very rapid development, they are still at an early age that lacks theories to support them. The discipline of Library and Information Science was found to play a very active role in this new area. Future research agenda and directions are also discussed.

DOI: 10.4018/978-1-4666-4892-0.ch008

INTRODUCTION

Wiki is a new form of information production and organization, which is also known as Collective Intelligence, Peer Production, and User Innovation community (Bonabeau, 2009; Viégas, Wattenberg, & Mckeon, 2007; West & Lakhani, 2008). Wiki breaks thoroughly the traditional mode of information production and organization, and adopts the incentive mechanism instead of the contracting mechanism, which fully makes use of the activity and creativity of the public (Greengard, 2011). Using modern computer network technologies, wiki allows anyone to generate information almost anywhere at any time in a collaborative way. Meanwhile, anyone can access the information on wikis without any restrictions.

Wikipedia is a representative of wikis, which has become one of the most popular online communities and sources for online information. In January 2013, there were 285 registered languages and 38 million registered users on the Wikipedia. All of the language versions had more than 24 million articles and the number of the articles that users edited was more than 1.5 billion (Wikipedia, 2013). Whether we admit it or not, Wiki has become one of the most important knowledge resources and has been used in domains ranging from science, education, to enterprise. According to Alexa, which provides traffic data, global rankings, and other information on 30 million websites, Wikipedia is one of the top 10 websites on the Web (Alexa, 2013). However, the information quality of wikis has been controversial, largely because of lacking of experts' participation in and quality control mechanisms of information production. In order to better utilize online information resources and promote wikis' development, it is thus significant to evaluate and govern wikis' quality.

As a research topic, information quality (IQ) has a long history, especially for the traditional information systems. Quite a few researchers have undertaken a lot of research on the definition of IQ, evaluation model, and quality governance (Lee, Strong, Kahn, & Wang, 2002; Strong, Lee, & Wang, 1997). There has been a deep understanding of the evaluation and governance of the information quality both in academia and practice. However, the methods being employed to evaluate the wikis' quality remain confusing and the results of such research are contradictory. For instance, *Nature* reported that Wikipedia had come close to Britannica in terms of the accuracy of its science (Giles, 2005). In contrast, Anderka and Stein (2012) found that more than one fourth of English Wikipedia articles contains at least one quality flaw, 70% of which concern article verifiability entries. Under these circumstances, the governance of wikis' quality becomes very difficult. It is necessary to make a systematic review on the current research about the evaluation and governance of wikis' quality. However, few studies have been able to offer us answers to the questions such as what are the disciplines and journals focusing on this field; what are the important institutes and authors; which sub-topics are the most frequently studied, and which theories and methodologies are often used to explore the related studies. These questions will be addressed in this book chapter using both bibliometric and content analyses. Furthermore, based on our analysis, future research agenda and directions will also be put forward at the end of the chapter.

RESEARCH AIMS AND QUESTIONS

This paper aims to investigate the current research status of wikis' quality and governance and put forward future directions on this topic. Table 1 lists the research questions to be addressed in the study.

Table 1. Research questions

Q1	What are the changes on the article numbers from 2000 to 2012?
Q2	What are the most productive journals publishing related papers?
Q3	Who are the most prolific authors and institutes publishing related papers?
Q4	What are the hotspots?
Q5	What are the changes on the research topics over the years?
Q6	What are the core authors and co-authorship on this filed?
Q7	What are the most frequently used theories?
Q8	Which research methods are often used in related studies?
Q9	What are the future directions of the topic?

METHODOLOGY

Approaches

There are generally three approaches to assess the status and development of a discipline or a research subject. The first approach is to use bibliometric analysis to discover the research progress and frontiers (Culnan, 1987; Hawkins, Larson, & Caton, 2003). The second one is to use classifications to code interesting elements such as research topics, methods, levels of analysis, and reference discipline of published articles in the field (Romano & Fjermestad, 2002; Vessey, Ramesh, & Glass, 2002). And the third method is to use surveys or interviews to collect researchers' perceptions (Vogel, Lee, & Limayem, 2003; Watson, Taylor, Higgins, Kadlec, & Meeks, 1999). In this study, we considered a combination of the first and second approaches, namely, the bibliometric analysis and classification-based coding. Bibliometric analysis will help us to gain a general bird view on the topic and its related research situations, while the classification-based approach is able to allow us to capture the diversity in the research, thus leading to a deep understanding about the research field.

The bibliometric analysis is useful to investigate the development and situation of research, which are widely used by scholars when conducting reviews (Costas, van Leeuwen, & Bordons, 2010). In this paper, we undertook the bibliometric analysis with mature methods including basic descriptive statistics, co-word analysis, and social network analysis. Table 2 presents the bibliometric approaches.

At the descriptive statistics stage, we intended to answer the first three research questions (i.e. Q1-Q3) listed in Table 1. The questions are to be addressed by calculating a series of statistics about the amounts of papers, journals, authors, and their institutes to demonstrate the annual situation and the change of related items. In the second stage, we used keyword frequency analysis and co-word analysis to find out the hotspots and sub-topics in this field (Q4-Q5). At the third stage, the social network analysis was employed to identify the co-authorship (Q6).

After the bibliometric analysis, classifications were used to code methods and theories in this research field via content analysis and to answer the questions Q7-Q8. In the coding process, three student-coders evaluated and coded the papers separately in order to decide which methods and

Table 2. The stages of bibliometric analysis

Methods	Items	Purposes
Descriptive statistics	Years, Authors, Institutes, Journals	To answer Q1-Q3
Keyword frequency analysis and Co-word analysis	Keywords	To answer Q4-Q5
Social network analysis	Authors, Institutes	To answer Q6

theories applied in these papers. After several iterations, the fourth author resolved the disagreements among three coders. The coding results and disagreements as well as the resolutions for any disputes were carefully checked. Before future analyses, we discussed all disagreements and achieved a consensus. In addition, the reliability of the coding results was evaluated by Cohen's Kappa Coefficient, and the results show that the kappa coefficients across all categories are highly significant. The kappa values for the three categories ranged from 0.75 to 0.84, all exceeding the 0.70 standard recommended.

Data Collection

The databases we chose for the research data collection included ISI Web of Knowledge, Engineering Village, ACM Digital Library, IEEE Xplore Digital Library, and Wiley Online Library. We searched the databases on the following fileds: title, keywords, and abstract. And two search terms were used: "wiki* AND quality/governance" and "wikipedi* AND quality//governance". The span of searched time was from 2000 to 2012. A total of 320 papers were retrieved from these databases. The selection of the sample papers is as follows: we first excluded 113 papers which are book reviews, editorials, meeting abstracts, news, letters, and notes. Secondly, another 108 papers were excluded, which do not focus on the quality of wikis but simply applied wikis to improve the quality of nature language processing, search engine, and other fields. Finally, a total of 99 articles were included for the analysis.

THE FINDINGS OF BIBLIOMETRIC ANALYSIS

In this section, we presented the bibliometric analysis of these papers, with the aim to answer the research questions Q1-Q6 in Table 1.

The Changes on the Article Numbers

Figure 1 depicts the changing frequency of the articles from 2005 to 2012.

The figure reveals a growth in the number of related articles about wikis' quality and governance. The first article on this field was published in 2005, four years later after the foundation of the Wikipedia. This field has maintained steady growth during the period from 2005 to 2009 and stayed at a low output level in 2010. After 2010, the research of this topic has experienced a significant growth. It is worth mentioning that the decline in 2012 is caused by the research period. We therefore believe that that research about wikis' quality and governance is an emerging area.

The Most Productive Journals

There are 41 journals that published a total number of 55 articles and eight of them (19.5%) published more than two articles, which account for 40% of total articles published in journals ($n = 55$). This suggests that there is a discrete contribution and tendency, namely, a few journals contributed about half of the journal articles.

Figure 1. The changes on the article numbers

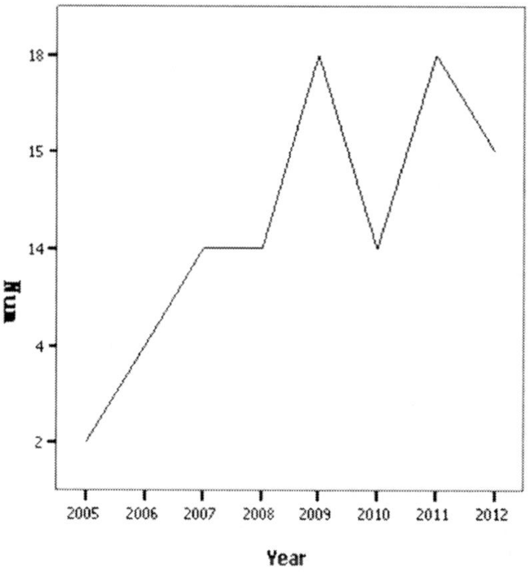

Table 3 shows the top eight journals, which were ranked by the frequency.

As shown in Table 3, *First Monday*, which is one of the first open access, peer–reviewed journals on the Internet, solely devoted to the Internet has published the most related articles. This is followed by *Journal of the American Society for Information Science & Technology,* which publishes research and development in a wide range of subjects and applications in information science and technology, was the second prolific journal. An interesting finding is that among the top eight journals that published related articles, six of them were information studies related journals, which indicates that the discipline of Library and Information Science played a very active role in this new area.

Besides 55 articles which were published in 41 journals, there were 44 conference papers. Table 4 shows the top three conferences which published more than two articles.

The conference that published the most articles on this field was the *5th International Symposium on Wikis and Open Collaboration*, which took place in Orlando on Oct 25-27, 2009, followed by the *Proceedings of the 6th International Workshop of the Initiative for the Evaluation of XML Retrieval*, which was held in Dagstuhl Castle on December 17-19, 2007, and the *2010 ACM Conference on Computer Supported Cooperative Work* in Savannah, Georgia, USA, on February 6-10 in 2010. One notable feature of the conference papers is that their content is usually novel and they often report latest research results. According to the statistics, about half of papers related to wiki quality and governance were conference papers. It demonstrates that the research area was developed rapidly in the recent years.

Table 3. The prolific journals

Journal	Number	Percentage (%)
First Monday	6	6.06
Journal of the American Society for Information Science & Technology	4	4.04
Journal of Management Information Systems	2	2.02
International Journal of Information Management	2	2.02
Journal of Information Science	2	2.02
Reference Services Review	2	2.02
ACM Transactions on Management Information Systems	2	2.02
Journal of the American Medical Informatics Association	2	2.02
Sum	22	22.22

Table 4. The prolific conferences

Conference	Number	Percentage (%)
The proceedings of 5th International Symposium on Wikis and Open Collaboration	3	6.82
The Proceedings of the 6th International Workshop of the Initiative for the Evaluation of XML Retrieval	2	4.55
2010 ACM Conference on Computer Supported Cooperative Work	2	4.55
Sum	7	15.92

The Most Prolific Authors and Institutions

During the observation period, there were 306 authors (including second authors, third authors, etc.) from 127 institutions contributed to the total of the 99 articles. Table 5 presents the top 10 prolific authors and their institutions.

According to the Price's law, the core authors contribute the half of the total articles in a research topic (Egghe, 1987). The minimum quantity of articles which are published by a core author is m, $m = 0.749 * \sqrt{n_{max}}$, where n_{max} is the num-

Table 5. The top 10 prolific authors and their institutions

Article Number	Author	Institution
4	Aniket Kittur	Carnegie Mellon University
3	Aixin Sun	Nanyang Technological University
3	Ba-Quy Vuong	Nanyang Technological University
3	Ee-Peng Lim	Nanyang Technological University
2	Aaron Halfaker	University of Minnesota
2	Benno Stein	Bauhaus-University Weimar
2	Besiki Stvilia	Florida State University
2	Christian Wagner	City University of Hong Kong
2	Daniel H. Dalip	Federal University of Minas Gerais
2	Hady W. Lauw	Nanyang Technological University

ber of the articles which are published by the most prolific author (Dafermos & Rodnianski, 2005). In this paper, $m = 1.498$, after rounding, $m = 2$. There were 27 authors publishing more than two articles, about 9.85% of the total number of authors. The total number of articles contributed by these authors was 59, 59.60% of the total authors. These data indicate that although the research topic is very new, there have already been core authors.

The Gini coefficient is one of the most widely used indicators in economics and sociology to describe the inequality of a distribution. The Gini coefficient is bounded between 0 and 1,with smaller values representing higher equality (Dorfman, 1979). In this paper, we employed the Gini coefficient to represent the degree of distribution of authors' output. The formula of computing the Gini coefficient is $g = p_5 - p_1$, where g is the Gini coefficient, p_5 denotes the percentage of the output of the authors whose contribution is the most according to "five-group" method, and p_1 denotes the percentage of the output of the authors whose contribution is the smallest.

After the calculation, the number of the top 20% of authors was 55 and the number of their contribution was 87, accounting for 87.88% of the total. The number of the final 20% of authors was also 55 and their contribution number was 55, accounting for 55.58% of the total. Therefore, the Gini coefficient of the output of authors was $g = 0.8788 - 0.5558 = 0.323$. This reflects that the contribution of the authors in this research topic is equally distributed even though there have been core authors.

Table 6 shows the institutions which had more than two publications.

As one of the most famous university of computer science and information science, Carnegie Mellon University was the most prolific institution. Further statistical analysis reveals that the average number of articles which were published by the institutions was 0.78. More specifically, most of the institutions (83.46%) published only one article.

Co-Authors Analysis

Identified by Derek J. de Solla Price in his seminal work Little Science, Big Science (de Solla Price, 1986), the trends of team work in scientific research would be largely increased that "by 1980 the single author paper will be extinct". The scientific research collaboration, also known as co-authorship, which implies strong social bonds

Table 6. Prolific institutions

Institution	Article Number
Carnegie Mellon University	4
University of Alberta	3
Nanyang Technological University	3
University of Leipzig	3
Technical University of Denmark	3

within and between scholar communities, has since then become a great interest of researchers.

In this study, we adopted weighted undirected co-authorship networks. The scholars were abstracted as nodes, and the nodes will be connected by an edge if two of them published a paper collaboratively. The weight of the edges between nodes was determined by the frequency of paper that the authors collaboratively produced. The more papers the authors published together, the more powerful their bonds were defined in this model. Here, we ignored the differences between conference papers and journal papers. The direction in network study reveals a hierarchy between the relationships. However, the cooperation between scholars is difficult to be determined simply by catalogue information or paper content. Thus, for the purpose of this study, relationships between authors were defined undirected. Data were cleaned in Excel, and then imported into network analysis software Ucinet.

We adopted three common centrality metrics including degree centrality, closeness centrality, and betweenness centrality (Wasserman & Faust, 1994), for their use on binary, undirected co-authorship networks. In analysis, normalized values were used for better comparisons. The distribution of the normalized values sorted descended of the three metrics is shown in Figure 2.

Degree centrality is a metric of node defined as the total number of edges that are adjacent to this node (Borgatti, 2005). It represents local centrality by calculating the number of immediate neighbors. In this paper, we did not consider in-centrality or out-centrality because the model was undirected. However, the weight of edge would contribute to the degree centrality of the nodes it connects.

From the results, the degrees of nearly 22.89% of the nodes were below two, among them 6.82% were isolated. Michael F Martone was ranked top as the degree of him was 2.016, followed by Daniel Hasan Dalip and Marcos Andre Goncalves whose degrees were 1.882, respectively. Sharp decrease was identified at the degree value of 1.21, which illustrates the higher 2.81% of scholars were locally centralized. According to the descriptive report of degree centrality, network centralization was 1.53% and heterogeneity was 0.66%. The low centralization shows the looseness of the entire network.

Figure 2. Distribution of three centralities

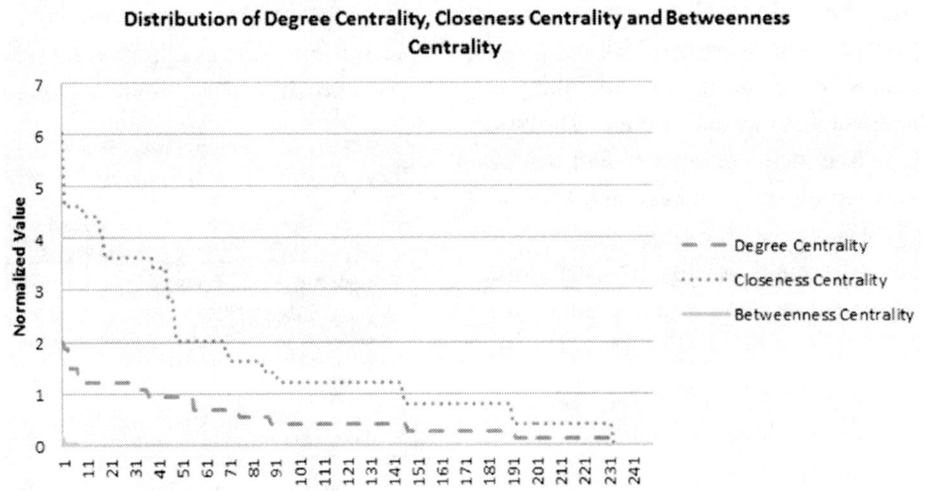

Closeness centrality, put forth by Freeman, expands the definition of degree centrality by focusing on how close an author is to all the other authors. It is calculated by adding up the weight of shortest paths (or geodesic distance) from a specific node to all the other ones. Therefore, the closeness centrality implies the global centrality of each node (Freeman, 1979). In this study, we applied the sum of reciprocal distances as the metric of closeness centrality, which works well for disconnected graph though it is not original Freeman's work. The result shows the similar distribution of degree centrality. Michael F Martone was still ranked first under this metric. The leading group was identified before the first sharp decrease at the value of 4.435, 6.43% of the authors. The second dramatic decrease happened at the value of 3.427, and 11.24% of all the authors belonged to this group. The network centralization was 9.09%, implying that from the global perspective, the whole graph was centralized at slight level.

Betweenness centrality represents a different operationalization of centrality (Freeman, 1977). It is based on determining how often a particular node is found on the shortest path between any pair of nodes in the network. Therefore it represents the flow control of a particular node. The results surprisingly reveals that only Michael F Martone, Daniel Hasan Dalip, Marcos Andre Goncalves, Robert Kraut, Besiki Stvilia, Aniket Kittur and Christian Wagner had meaningful values while others had values of 0. Among the seven authors, the betweenness degree of Michael F Martone was 0.183, far exceeding the rest of others whose degrees ranged from 0.01 to 0.029.

To comprehensively understand the network structure, we calculated the density of graph, and then classified the cohesive subgroups within the graph. The density is an indicator for the general level of connectedness of the graph. If every node is directly connected to every other node, we will have a complete graph. The density of a graph is defined as the number of links divided by the number of vertices in a complete graph with the same number of nodes (Otte & Rousseau, 2002). In this study, the overall density of the network was 0.015 and the standard deviation was 0.134. The value shows the collaboration between scholars in this field is in the starting phase.

A component of a graph is a subset with the characteristic that there is a path between any node and any other node of this subset. A co-authorship network usually consists of several disconnected components because of isolated research groups. Figure 3 is the co-authorship network.

Around 78 weak components were found and 40 of them consisted of three or more members. Particularly, four large groups were comprised of ten or more members, and the largest one contained sixteen members. The data demonstrates cooperation in small-scale groups.

A clique in a graph is a subgraph in which any node is directly connected to any other node of the subgraph (Otte & Rousseau, 2002). Namely, a clique must be a complete graph, which is quite strict. By setting the minimum number of clique size as 3, 44 cliques were found. But based on the undirected co-authorship model, one co-author paper published will simply make the set of authors a clique, casting doubt on the significance of the conclusion. After looking into the data piece by piece, all the cliques were constructed due to only one paper. Since the strictness of concept clique, we further looked for n-clique in the network. N-clique is a subgraph in which the geodesic distance between each node is no longer than N, a less stingy concept than the original clique requiring complete graph. However no meaningful 3 or 4 clique was found, either.

Core-periphery analysis aims to classify the nodes into two categories according to their locations in the network: core and periphery; and to calculate the correlation between them (Ocholla, Onyancha, & Britz, 2010). Setting density of core-to-periphery ties zero, we had the result with both starting fitness and final fitness 0.228.

The result shows that 60 of the authors were in the position of core, while other 189 were in the

Figure 3. The co-authorship network

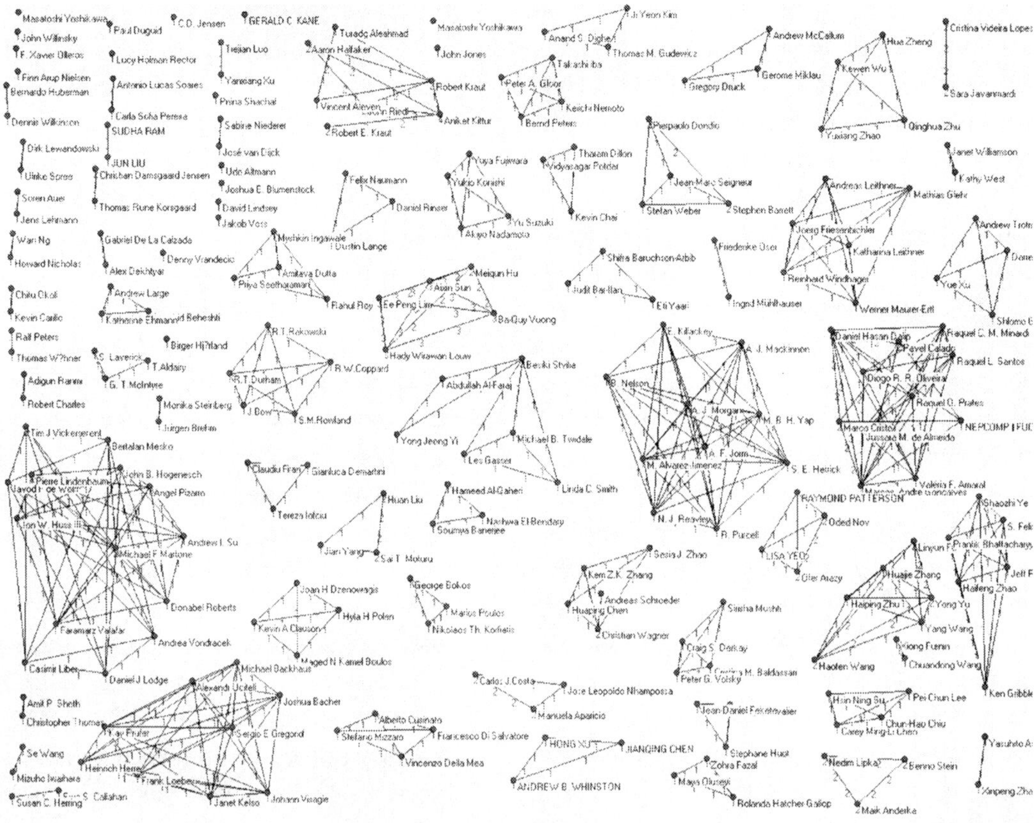

periphery. The density matrix tells that the density of core authors was 0.138, and that of periphery authors was 0.012.

In this study, we investigated the co-authorship network of research on quality control and governance of Wiki. Our graph indicates the network consists of 4 large subnets and 36 small ones. Isolated fractions are comparatively small, but the connectivity of the graph is low.

Centrality metrics reveal the attributes of individual scholars in the co-authorship network. Degree centrality and closeness centrality determine the local and graphic central position of the nodes respectfully. As a result, Michael F Martone, Tim J Vickers, and Daniel Hasan Dalip were ranked in the top group under both metrics. Their positions in the network are of vital importance both locally and graphically. Considering the result of betweenness centrality, Michael F Martone was dominant in flow control, and Daniel Hasan Dalip was also in a significant position. Both of the two authors played in a role of "bridge" in the network, whose behaviors will exert influential impact on the network structure.

Cohesive subgroup analysis demonstrates the attributes of network as a whole. The low density means the loose cooperation between scholars or scholar communities probably due to this specific field of study remains in the early stage. As scholars draw more focus on the topic, the density may increase. As mentioned at the beginning of this part, there are large four subnets and the connectivity of the network is low. Most of the components in the network are constructed by one study, and few interactions exist in the subnets. As such, at present, scholars prefer to cooperate with particular set of partners. From the core-periphery analysis, 60 authors, namely 24.10% were in the core area. The huge difference in matrix density between core and periphery fortifies, the conclusion that broad and strong cooperation has emerged.

The Research Topics and Hotspots

Keyword Frequency Analysis

The word frequency analysis method is an approach to efficiently determine the research hotspots or sub-topic by using the keywords or descriptors of articles in a research field (He, 1999). In this paper, the statistical analysis of keyword frequency and the dynamical analysis of keyword frequency were implemented in order to identify the hotspots and sub-topics in wikis' quality and governance.

A pool of keywords was acquired by means of the keywords modification process, which contained 183 keywords with 286 frequencies. The average number of keywords per article was 2.89. Table 7 presents the 26 keywords that were frequently used (used at least two times).

As shown in Table 7:

1. "Wikipedia" was the most frequently used keyword. Largely, this is because Wikipedia is the biggest website of Wikis. Thus, the research that used the data from Wikipedia is representative. Another potential reason might be that the databases of articles and authors of Wikipedia can be freely downloaded;
2. "Quality", "Information quality", and "Article quality" are the more frequently used keywords. These keywords indicate that most articles in this field concentrated on the information quality of wikis;
3. Some keywords were used to describe the ultimate goal of the research in the field. For instance, 'Quality assessment", "Reputation", and "Trust". We may infer that lots of research aims to answer such questions as how to assess the article quality of wikis? What about the quality of one

Table 7. The frequently used keywords

No.	Keywords	Frequency	No.	Keywords	Frequency
K1	Wikipedia	44	K14	Reference services	3
K2	Wiki	10	K15	Collaborative authoring	2
K3	Quality	8	K16	Collaborative knowledge	2
K4	Information quality	7	K17	Edit History	2
K5	Article quality	4	K18	Experience	2
K6	Collaboration	4	K19	lexical clue	2
K7	Internet	4	K20	Open Content	2
K8	Quality Assessment	4	K21	Social computing	2
K9	Reputation	4	K22	Social media	2
K10	Web 2.0	4	K23	Trust	2
K11	Coordination	3	K24	Virtual teams	2
K12	Encyclopedias	3	K25	Wikis	2
K13	Peer Review	3	K26	WikiWork	2

article in wikis? and How to governance the quality?

4. In wikis, each article is edited through collaboration among many participants. Thus, the article quality has a lot to do with the behavioral characteristics. In Table 7, "Coordination", "Collaborative authoring" and "Collaborative knowledge" reflect the collaboration essence;

In order to draw an evolution of this research topic, we conducted the dynamical analysis of keyword frequency. We expanded the range of keywords from the popular keywords listed in Table 7 to the annual popular words. In addition, attention was paid to the keywords first appeared and consistently used in recent years.

In order to facilitate the analysis of the dynamic characteristics of the research topic, we considered the period from 2005 to 2007 as one single year unit. There are two reasons: First, the annual publication in this period was low (20 for 3 years) compared to other years. Second, the first wikis' quality related paper was published in 2005, but only two papers in that year. Thus, the period from 2005 to 2007 could be considered as the start period of this research topic.

Table 8 presents the evolution of popular keywords, with the percentage of each keyword.

Through the analysis of the changes and consistency of the annual keywords and percentage, the trends of topic changes over years have emerged:

1. "Quality of Wikipedia" was always the core topic in the period from 2005 to 2007. It seems that there was no other websites of wikis which can replace Wikipedia in the research field;
2. The first paper tagging "Assessment" was published in 2008 and the percentage was increased in 2009, but decreased during the following three years. It demonstrates that the sub-topic 'assessment of information quality of wikis' had been a hotspot. For instance, Druck, Miklau, and McCallum (2008) used the discriminative probabilistic models to predict the quality of a article. Hasan Dalip, André Gonçalves, Cristo, and Calado (2009) explored a significant number of information quality indicators to assess the quality of Wikipedia articles. The research tried to seek a good method to scientifically assess the quality of articles' quality of wikis;
3. In the period from 2010 to 2012, some keywords which described the behavioral characteristics of participants appeared. This marks that many scholars began to explore the wiki's quality form the origins i.e. the collaborative approach among thousands of participants in wikis. Some research found that the quality of articles in wikis

Table 8. The annual popular keywords from 2005 to 2012

2005-2007 (20 Papers)	2008 (14 Papers)	2009 (18 Papers)
Wikipedia (22.22%) Article quality (7.40%) Collaborative authoring (7.40%) Content-quality (3.70%) Wikis (3.70%)	Wikipedia (17.65%) Wiki (8.82%) Encyclopedias (5.88%) Assessment (2.94%) Information quality (2.94%)	Wikipedia (11.32%) Quality (5.66%) Assessment (3.77%) Reputation (3.77%) Social media (3.77%)
2010(14 Papers)	**2011(18 Papers)**	**2012(15 Papers)**
Wikipedia (16.33%) Wiki (8.16%) Collaborative knowledge (4.08%) Coordination (4.08%) Information quality (4.08%)	Wikipedia (17.07%) Information Quality (3.66%) Wiki (3.66%) Article quality (2.44%) Collaboration (2.44%)	Wikipedia (10.00%) Quality (7.50%) Edit History (5.00%) Reputation (2.50%) Contributor type (2.50%)

has a great relation with the amount of the participants, the types of the participants, and the interactions between participants (Kittur & Kraut, 2008; Ransbotham, Kane, & Lurie, 2012). Moreover, the research of behavioral characteristics of participants can help administrators and designers to optimize the wiki system so as to improve the quality of articles or reduce the vandalisms in the process of editing the articles.

Co-Word Analysis

Co-word analysis is an important method in the field of information science. Based on co-existence frequency of pairs of words or phrases, co-word analysis is used to discover linkages among subjects in a research field and thus to trace the development of science (Bhattacharya & Basu, 1998; He, 1999). In this paper, we used the co-word analysis to expand our work on searching for key sub-topics in this research field. We developed the co-occurrence matrix of the 26 keywords presented in Table 7, then transformed it into correlation matrix by using Ochiia coefficient (Shi, Yang, Yang, & Liu, 2012). The formula of Ochiia coefficient is:

$$O(k_1, k_2) = \frac{Num(k_1, k_2)}{\sqrt{N(k_1) * N(k_2)}}$$

where $O(k_1, k_2)$ represents the Ochiia coefficient between the keywords k_1 and k_2, $Num(k_1, k_2)$ is the number of co-occurrence of k_1 and k_2, $N(k_1)$ and $N(k_2)$ respectively represent the frequency of k_1 and k_2. Part of the correlation matrix is shown as Table 9.

Then we imported the correlation matrix into SPSS to conduct the clustering analysis. The results of clustering are shown in Figure 4. At the same time, we used the Ucinet to draw the graph of network of co-occurrence, as shown in Figure 5. According to the results of clustering, we divided the research topic into 4 sub-topics: (1) the research of collaborative mode of participants in wikis; (2) the research of trust and reputation in wiki system; (3) the research of assessment of article quality in wikis; and (4) the research of governance of the wikis' quality. We discussed these sub-topics in the light of related literature in the following sections:

1. The research of trust and reputation. As a new social media, wiki has gained more and more attention. The important reason for the success of wiki might be that it has successfully encouraged thousands of people to contribute to editing articles. Meanwhile, it has also caused the problem of trust. Because ordinary people generally lack of professional knowledge. Thus, there were some

Table 9. Part of the correlation matrix

	Article Quality	Collaboration	Coordination	Information Quality
Article quality	1	0	0	0
Collaboration	0	1	0.5773502691	0.5669467095
Coordination	0	0.5773502691	1	0
Information quality	0	0.5669467095	0	1

Figure 4. The results of clustering of popular keywords

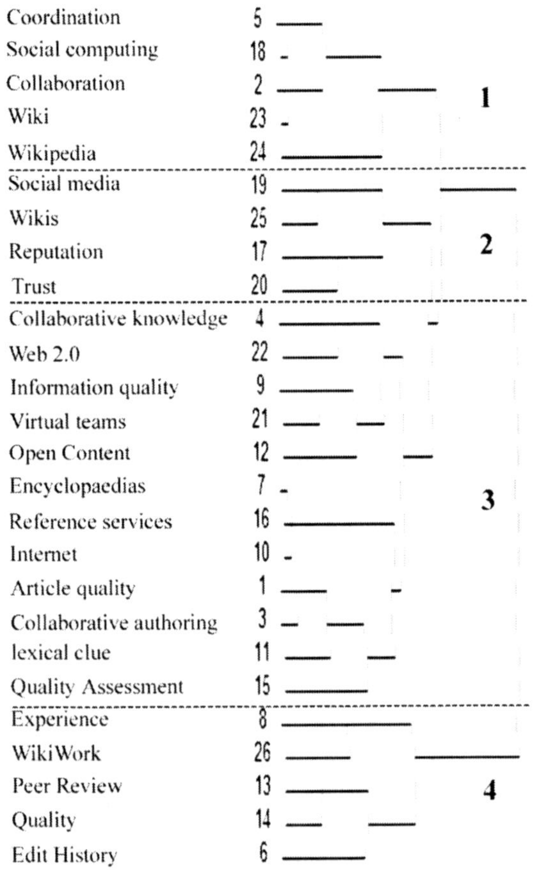

papers which expressed people's worry about wikis' quality in the early stage of this research field. For instance, Duguid (2006) thought that it was impossible to guarantee the article quality because of self-organization in Wikipedia. Barrett et al (2006) thought that trust in Wikipedia content quality had been seriously questioned. Spoerri (2007) admitted that Wikipedia was very popular, whereas some investigations suggested that Wikipedia was discouraged in academic area;

2. The research of collaborative mode of participants in wikis. Thousands of articles in wikis are the results of effective collaboration among participants. Thus, the collaborative mode affects the quality of articles. For example, Ransbotham and Kane (2011) found that participant retention does not have a strictly positive effect on article quality. Kittur and Kraut (2008) found that it is impossible to improve article quality simply by increasing the number of participants. Understanding the behaviors of participants

Figure 5. The graph of network of co-occurrence

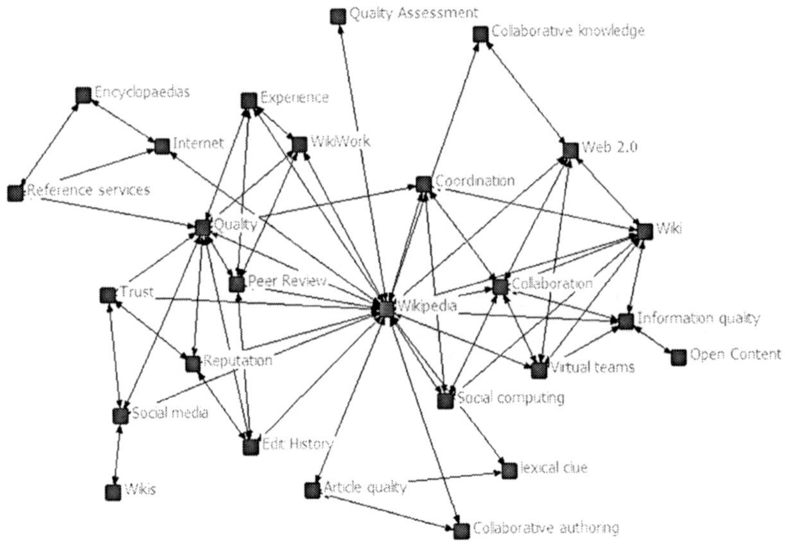

in wikis can help designers to optimize the wiki system;

3. The research of assessment of article quality in wikis. This sub-topic is the most important topic in this research field and has the largest number of papers. The topics of these papers are mainly focusing on three aspects: the indicators of article quality, the methods to assess article quality, and assessing the article quality in Wikipedia. For instance, Thomas and Ralf (2009) offered new metrics for an efficient quality assessment. The metrics are based on the life-cycles of articles. Hasan Dalip et al (2009) employed the machine learning techniques to assess the quality of content in Wikipedia;
4. The research of governance of the wikis' quality. Along with the rapid development of wikis, the question of article quality has aroused more and more attention. In addition to the assessment of article quality, the governance of the wikis' quality may have more realistic significance. Stvilia et al (2008) claimed that wikis' quality is determined by the organization model of information. Thus, they believed that wiki system should accept the advantage of the organization model of information of the traditional information systems. Liu and Ram (2011) suggested that the quality of wikis' articles is not only dependent on the different types of participants but also on how they collaborate. At the moment, the research of governance of the wikis' quality proceeds from the both side: modifying the process of creating and editing articles and the organization model of information, and editing rules according to the behavior characteristics of participants.

THE FINDINGS OF CONTENT ANALYSIS

Theories in Wikis' Quality and Governance

Theories are very important for a research project. Thus, we aimed to find out what theories have been used in this research field. Theories were identified by carefully reading the abstract, keywords, the sections of theory, and even full-text of papers. It is found that not all the papers used theories. Only 21 of 99 papers were written using one or more specific theories. Table 10 presents five frequently employed theories.

There are some observations we could draw from the statistical data:

1. Wiki is a complex system and participants and articles are two important elements. There are three relational network in the system: the network of participants, the network of articles and the network of particles

Table 10. The frequently used theories

Theory	Frequency (Percentage)	Usage
Link analysis	4 (19.05%)	Often used as a tool to explore the relationship among articles
Peer review model	4 (19.05%)	Often used to explain the model of information production of wikis
Social network theory	4 (19.05%)	Often used to explore the relationship of participants in wikis
Small world Theory	1 (4.76%)	Often used to the explain the characteristics of the network of participants or articles
The long tail	1 (4.76%)	Often used to explain the characteristics of the contribution of participants

and articles. This might be the reason why the theories of network are widely applied;
2. The relatively low usage of theories reflects that the research field is still in the start-up period.

Methodologies in Wikis' Quality and Governance

The frequently used research methods were divided into two main types: empirical methods and non-empirical methods. We found that empirical methods were the predominant over the period from 2005 to 2012. About 87.88% papers employed empirical methods. Among these empirical methods, mathematical statistics was the most widely used method. Table 11 shows six frequently used methods.

As shown in Table 11, the mathematical method played a very important role in this field. Particularly, mathematical methods were important in three study areas: model specification, statistical analysis, and factor analysis.

Future Research Directions

In this paper, we investigated the current research status of wikis' quality and governance based on the bibliometric and content analysis by addressing the research questions Q1 to Q8. The results show that it is a new research field and has been experiencing a rapid growth since 2005. Some future directions of this research topic have emerged based on our analysis:

Table 11. The six frequently used empirical methods

Rank	The Name of the Empirical Methods
1	Mathematical statistics
2	Regression analysis
3	Survey method
4	Correlation analysis
5	Coding
6	Decision tree

1. Improving the definition of IQ and making more operational processes involved in the assessment of the quality of articles. Although there have been many definitions of IQ, it is essential to rethink this problem in the environment of wikis. Compared to assessing the quality of websites, the process of assessing the articles in wikis may be more complex due to the facts that each article is created and edited cooperatively and the wiki system is more open than other websites. Thus, the indicators of quality should incorporate the features of cooperation behaviors of participants and develop more comprehensive models and operational processes to assess the articles of wikis;
2. Studying the influence of the collaboration modes of participants on the quality of articles. Understanding the correlation between the mode of collaboration of participants and the quality of articles would be able to help managers and designers to set appropriate rules or to optimize the wiki system in order to control the process of knowledge production;
3. Deepening the theoretical research. Currently, there are many empirical studies on this topic, whilst a few focus on theory research. In wikis, there are a lot of phenomena need to be explored. Such as, the motivation for participants, the conflicts in the process of knowledge production, and the dynamic characteristics of participants' behavior.

CONCLUSION

In this paper, relying on the analysis of a comprehensive coverage of papers in wikis' quality and governance over a period from 2000 to 2012, we uncovered the current research status and trends in this research field. The trends of the research were investigated from various angles and answered nine research questions in this paper.

Our findings indicate that the research of wikis' quality and governance is still in the start-up period, but with a rapid development. An important finding is that the discipline of Library and Information Science plays a very active role in this new area. 35% of journals which have published related papers are information studies related journals. Although the research topic is relatively new, the core authors have emerged.

At the moment, there are four sub-topics in the field: the research of collaborative mode of participants in wikis; the research of trust and reputation in wiki system; the research of assessment of article quality in wikis; and the research of governance of the wikis' quality. Among these sub-topics, the research of assessment of article quality in wikis has the largest number of papers. There have been many studies focusing on the indicators of article quality and the automatic methods to assess the quality of the articles. Yet it is essential to incorporate the features of cooperation behaviors of participants and to develop more comprehensive models and operational processes to assess the quality of articles. So far, the number of the papers about governance of the wikis' quality is still very low. This is an important area for further research. In addition, the studies in wikis' quality and governance lack of theoretical foundation. In future, researchers should strengthen the research toward theoretical construction.

There are some limitations in the paper: (1) The collection of papers was from certain databases. As such, other papers about this topic may be ignored. The small amount of data influenced the reliability of results to some extent; (2) The study only focused the academic papers while overlooking the dissertations and books; and (3) The main method used to analyze the topic was the bibliometric analysis. Further in-depth content analysis is needed in order to know more details in this field.

ACKNOWLEDGMENT

The authors would like to thank Chenju ZHU, Kaiyue WANG, and Ying WU from the School of Information Management at Nanjing University for their excellent contributions during the coding stage. The authors also acknowledge the National Social Science Foundation of China for the full financial support (10ATQ004) to this study. Finally, the authors thank the reviewers, editors and publishers for their support to this chapter.

REFERENCES

Alexa. (2013). *The top 500 sites on the web.* Retrieved January 10, 2013, from http://www.alexa.com/topsites

Anderka, M., & Stein, B. (2012). *A breakdown of quality flaws in wikipedia.* Paper presented at the 2nd Joint WICOW/AIRWeb Workshop on Web Quality. Lyon, France.

Bhattacharya, S., & Basu, P. K. (1998). Mapping a research area at the micro level using co-word analysis. *Scientometrics*, *43*(3), 359–372. doi:10.1007/BF02457404

Bonabeau, E. (2009). Decisions 2.0: The power of collective intelligence. *MIT Sloan Management Review*, *50*(2), 45–52.

Borgatti, S. P. (2005). Centrality and network flow. *Social Networks*, *27*(1), 55–71. doi:10.1016/j.socnet.2004.11.008

Costas, R., van Leeuwen, T. N., & Bordons, M. (2010). A bibliometric classificatory approach for the study and assessment of research performance at the individual level: The effects of age on productivity and impact. *Journal of the American Society for Information Science and Technology, 61*(8), 1564–1581.

Culnan, M. J. (1987). Mapping the intellectual structure of MIS, 1980-1985: A co-citation analysis. *Management Information Systems Quarterly, 11*(3), 341–353. doi:10.2307/248680

Dafermos, M., & Rodnianski, I. (2005). A proof of Price's law for the collapse of a self-gravitating scalar field. *Inventiones Mathematicae, 162*(2), 381–457. doi:10.1007/s00222-005-0450-3

de Solla Price, D. J. (1986). *Little science, big science..., & beyond*. New York: Columbia Unviersity Press.

Dondio, P., Barrett, S., Weber, S., & Seigneur, J. (2006). Extracting trust from domain analysis: A case study on the wikipedia project. In *Proceedings of the IEEE ATC 06*. IEEE.

Dorfman, R. (1979). A formula for the Gini coefficient. *The Review of Economics and Statistics, 61*(1), 146–149. doi:10.2307/1924845

Druck, G., Miklau, G., & McCallum, A. (2008). *Learning to predict the quality of contributions to wikipedia*. Paper presented at the AAAI Workshop on Wikipedia and Artificial Intelligence. Chicago, IL.

Egghe, L. (1987). An exact calculation of Price's law for the law of Lotka. *Scientometrics, 11*(1), 81–97. doi:10.1007/BF02016632

Freeman, L. C. (1977). A set of measures of centrality based on betweenness. *Sociometry, 40*(1), 35–41. doi:10.2307/3033543

Freeman, L. C. (1979). Centrality in social networks conceptual clarification. *Social Networks, 1*(3), 215–239. doi:10.1016/0378-8733(78)90021-7

Giles, J. (2005). Internet encyclopaedias go head to head. *Nature, 438*(7070), 900–901. doi:10.1038/438900a PMID:16355180

Greengard, S. (2011). Following the crowd. *Communications of the ACM, 54*(2), 20–22. doi:10.1145/1897816.1897824

Hasan Dalip, D., André Gonçalves, M., Cristo, M., & Calado, P. (2009). *Automatic quality assessment of content created collaboratively by web communities: A case study of wikipedia.* Paper presented at the 9th ACM/IEEE-CS Joint Conference on Digital Libraries. Austin, TX.

Hawkins, D. T., Larson, S. E., & Caton, B. Q. (2003). Information science abstracts: Tracking the literature of information science: Part 2: A new taxonomy for information science. *Journal of the American Society for Information Science and Technology, 54*(8), 771–781. doi:10.1002/asi.10275

He, Q. (1999). Knowledge discovery through co-word analysis. *Library Trends, 48*(1), 133–159.

Kittur, A., & Kraut, R. E. (2008). *Harnessing the wisdom of crowds in wikipedia: Quality through coordination.* Paper presented at the 2008 ACM Conference on Computer Supported Cooperative Work. San Diego, CA.

Lee, Y. W., Strong, D. M., Kahn, B. K., & Wang, R. Y. (2002). AIMQ: A methodology for information quality assessment. *Information & Management, 40*(2), 133–146. doi:10.1016/S0378-7206(02)00043-5

Liu, J., & Ram, S. (2011). Who does what: Collaboration patterns in the wikipedia and their impact on article quality. *ACM Transactions on Manage. Information Systems, 2*(2), 1–23.

Ocholla, D. N., Onyancha, O. B., & Britz, J. (2010). Can information ethics be conceptualized by using the core/periphery model? *Journal of Informetrics*, *4*(4), 492–502. doi:10.1016/j.joi.2010.05.001

Otte, E., & Rousseau, R. (2002). Social network analysis: A powerful strategy, also for the information sciences. *Journal of Information Science*, *28*(6), 441–453. doi:10.1177/016555150202800601

Ransbotham, S., & Kane, G. C. (2011). Membership turnover and collaboration success in online communities: Explaining rises and falls from grace in Wikipedia. *MIS Quarterly-Management Information Systems*, *35*(3), 613–627.

Ransbotham, S., Kane, G. C., & Lurie, N. H. (2012). Network characteristics and the value of collaborative user-generated content. *Marketing Science*, *31*(3), 387–405. doi:10.1287/mksc.1110.0684

Romano, N. C., & Fjermestad, J. (2002). Electronic commerce customer relationship management: An assessment of research. *International Journal of Electronic Commerce*, *6*, 61–114.

Shi, Y. H., Yang, Z. K., Yang, H. H., & Liu, S. Y. (2012). *Study on the research hotspots of interactive whiteboards in education.* Paper presented at the 4th International Conference on Internet Multimedia Computing and Service. New York, NY.

Spoerri, A. (2007). What is popular on wikipedia and why. *First Monday*, *12*(4). doi:10.5210/fm.v12i4.1765

Strong, D. M., Lee, Y. W., & Wang, R. Y. (1997). Data quality in context. *Communications of the ACM*, *40*(5), 103–110. doi:10.1145/253769.253804

Stvilia, B., Twidale, M. B., Smith, L. C., & Gasser, L. (2008). Information quality work organization in wikipedia. *Journal of the American Society for Information Science and Technology*, *59*(6), 983–1001. doi:10.1002/asi.20813

Thomas, W., & Ralf, P. (2009). *Assessing the quality of wikipedia articles with lifecycle based metrics*. Paper presented at the 5th International Symposium on Wikis and Open Collaboration. Orlando, FL.

Vessey, I., Ramesh, V., & Glass, R. L. (2002). Research in information systems: An empirical study of diversity in the discipline and its journals. *Journal of Management Information Systems*, *19*(2), 129–174.

Viégas, F., Wattenberg, M., & Mckeon, M. (2007). The hidden order of wikipedia. *Lecture Notes in Computer Science*, (4564): 445–454. doi:10.1007/978-3-540-73257-0_49

Vogel, D., Lee, F. S. L., & Limayem, M. (2003). Virtual community informatics: A review and research agenda. *Journal of Information Technology Theory and Application*, *5*(1), 47–61.

Wasserman, S., & Faust, K. (1994). *Social network analysis: Methods and applications*. Cambridge, UK: Cambridge University Press. doi:10.1017/CBO9780511815478

Watson, H. J., Taylor, K. P., Higgins, G., Kadlec, C., & Meeks, M. (1999). Leaders assess the current state of the IS academic discipline. *Communications of the AIS*, *2*(2), 2–27.

West, J., & Lakhani, K. R. (2008). Getting clear about communities in open innovation. *Industry and Innovation*, *15*(2), 223–231. doi:10.1080/13662710802033734

Wikipedia. (2013). *List of wikipedias*. Retrieved January 10, 2013, from http://s23.org/wikistats/wikipedias_html.php

KEY TERMS AND DEFINITIONS

Bibliometric Analysis: Bibliometirc Analysis is a set of methods to quantitatively analyze scientific and technological literature. It is useful to investigate the development and situation of research, which are widely used by scholars when conducting reviews.

Content Analysis: Content analysis is a methodology in the social sciences for studying the content of communication. It can be used to make inferences about the antecedents of a communication, describe and make inferences about characteristics of a communication and make inferences about the effects of a communication.

Future Directions: For a research topic, future direction means a field in which researchers can continue to explore.

Information Quality: A measure of how 'fit for purpose' is the information provided by an information system. It is often measured by dimensions such as accuracy, completeness, currency, relevance and format.

Quality Governance: Quality governance is the combination of structure and process at and below board level to lead on trust-wide quality performance including: ensuring required standards are achieved, investigating and taking action on sub-standard performance, planning and driving continuous improvement, identifying, sharing and ensuring delivery of best-practice, identifying and managing risks to quality of care.

Research Status: Also known as research state and it can reflect the current state of understanding on a topic. In order to summarize the current state, we addressed eight questions in this chapter.

Wiki: Wiki is a new form of information production and organization, which has become one of the most important knowledge resources. Wiki makes it possible for anyone with a web browser and access to the Internet to edit the content of an information object and to link it to other information objects in the collection with very low overhead. The encyclopedia project Wikipedia is the most famous wiki on the public web.

Chapter 9
Social Media Tools for Quality Business Information

Sérgio Maravilhas
Porto University, CETAC.MEDIA - Portugal & Aveiro University, Portugal

ABSTRACT

Information, as a tool to reduce uncertainty and to develop knowledge in organizations, is an important aid in the decision-making process and must be of quality to improve its value. We are living in an information society where organizational and personal life are mediated by information and knowledge, with the help of technologies that gather, disseminate, and deliver that raw material to support our decisions. There are several characteristics that describe the quality of information that will allow the analysis of the value of the information used. In the globalized world we are living in, quality information warrants best results when competing with other organizations. Its value is related to the results that it will allow to be obtained and the dependability on its context. Marketing trends and competitive information is needed for clear decision making about what products to develop, for what customers, at what cost, through which distribution channels, reducing the uncertainty that a new product/service development always brings with it. Social Media tools allow the knowledge of competitor's moves and the analysis of trends from the communications exchanged in the networks of individual consumers, making it easy for companies to develop solutions according to their clients and prospects desires. Learning how to extract quality information, unbiased, valuable for business, from these social tools is the aim of this work, sharing with the interested parties some ways of using it for their profit and competitive sustainability.

DOI: 10.4018/978-1-4666-4892-0.ch009

INTRODUCTION

We are living in an information society (IS) (Webster, 2000) where organizational and personal life are mediated by information and knowledge (Castells, 2000; Negroponte, 1995), with the help of technologies that gather, disseminate and deliver that raw material to support our decisions (McGee & Prusak, 1995; Penzias, 1995; Tapscott, 1995; Tapscott & Williams, 2008; Ward & Peppard, 2002).

After World War II, in 1948, Claude Shannon formulated "The Mathematical Theory of Communication", better known by "Theory of Information" (Gleick, 2011). At the same time two almost simultaneous inventions, the transistor and the digital computer came to reveal themselves with an enormous revolutionary potential when the social effects of their application, producing new goods and services were discovered, especially in the production and distribution of a new immaterial good and service: the information (Castells, 2000). Information, opposite to material goods, is infinitely expandable, doesn't waste itself (meaning that we can give an information without losing it, which may allow us to give it to several people, something we can't do with a material good), and once created difficult to vanish (although its economical value may decrease). It's easy to transport and distribute and the costs of keeping it in data warehouses is lesser every day. The speed and easiness in processing and transporting information electronically, it's almost instantaneous ability in feed itself, start to subvert the traditional ways of labour division, fragmentation, expertise and centralization of the human experience and its sociological configuration (Cleveland, 1983, 1985).

Some authors (Brown & Duguid, 2000; Castells, 2000, 2004; Webster, 2000) observed that a huge transformation is taking place; that we are moving towards a society that is no longer dependant in a massive industrialization or agriculture. They often talk about the knowledge and information based transformation of the world economy we are living in, with flux and flows of information gaining advantage to the exchange of goods. This notion is interconnected with the birth of the information technology, characterized by computers and electronic means of producing and transmitting information at the speed of light through a network of other technological apparatus (Godeluck, 2000).

Nowadays, we tend to call information society to the constraints we move in, sociologically interpreted. An IS, tend to describe a society no longer based in the production of materials, goods, production means, but in the production of knowledge.

Information, as a tool to reduce uncertainty and to develop knowledge in organizations (Best, 1996b; Kahaner, 1997; Porter & Millar, 1985), is an important aid in the decision making process and must be of quality to improve its value (Best, 1996b; Beuren, 1998; Choo, 2003; Davenport, Marchand, & Dickson, 2004; Marchand & Horton Jr., 1986; Tapscott, 1999; Wilson, 1985, 1987).

There are several characteristics that describe the quality of information that will allow the analysis of the value of the information used. In the globalized world we are living in, quality information warrants best results when competing with other organizations (Brophy & Coulling, 1996; Redman, 1996; Wormell, 1990). Its value is related to the results that it will allow obtaining and it's dependable on its context (Best, 1996b; Davenport, 1997; Lattès, 1992; Marchand & Horton Jr., 1986; Orna, 1999; Penzias, 1989; Tapscott, 1995; Tapscott, Ticoll, & Lowy, 2000).

Quality information is needed to clear decision-making about what products develop, for what customers, at what cost, through which distribution channels, reducing the uncertainty that a new product/service development always brings with it (Garber, 2001; Kotler, Armstrong, Saunders, & Wong, 1999; Mohr, Sengupta, & Slater, 2010; Scott, 2008; Trott, 2008).

Competitive Intelligence (CI) aims to monitor a firm's external environment for information relevant to its decision-making process (Choo, 2003).

Intelligence activities are based on the intelligence cycle. The intelligence cycle involves accurately identifying your information needs, collecting relevant information, analysing it, communicating the results to the people who need it, and taking rapid and appropriate action (Besson & Possin, 1996; Martinet & Marti, 1995; Taborda & Ferreira, 2002).

As an excellent information source, the Internet provides significant opportunities for CI (Sage, 2013).

Internet search engines have been widely used to facilitate information search on the Internet (Gomes & Braga, 2001; Taborda & Ferreira, 2002). However, many problems minimize their effective use in CI research (Bedell, 2011; Kahaner, 1997).

Many major companies, such as Ernst & Young, Motorola, Xerox, and almost all the pharmaceutical companies, have formal and well-organized CI units that enable managers to make informed decisions about critical business matters such as investment, marketing, and strategic planning (Prescott & Miller, 2002).

Traditionally, CI relied upon published company reports and other kinds of printed information. In recent years, Internet has rapidly become an extremely good source of information about the competitive environment of companies (Hawthorne & Cromity, 2012; Ojala, 2012; Revelli, 2000; Sage, 2013).

Although the Internet represents significant CI opportunities, it has also many technical, cognitive, and organizational challenges. The amount of information available on the Internet is gigantic, so, CI professionals are constantly facing the problem of information overload (Barbosa & O'Reilly, 2011; Dearlove, 1998). "Information overload is a real phenomenon, but progress is being made in tapping into social media to increase marketing intelligence" (Hawthorne & Cromity, 2012, p.38).

Much time and effort is required for CI professionals to search for relevant information on the Internet and then analyze the information collected in the correct context.

Internet search engines have been useful in helping people search for information on the Internet. Nevertheless, the exponential growth of information sources on the Internet and the unregulated and dynamic nature of many Web sites are making it increasingly difficult to locate useful information using these search engines (Scott, 2008).

Social Media tools allow the knowledge of competitor's moves and the analysis of trends from the communications exchanged in the networks of individual consumers (Russell, 2011; Tsvetovat & Kouznetsov, 2011), making it easy for companies to develop solutions according to their clients and prospects desires (Berthon, Pitt, Plangger, & Shapiro, 2012; Bramston, 2009; Burgelman, Christensen, & Wheelwright, 2009; Canhoto, 2013; Christensen, Anthony, & Roth, 2004; Kotze, 2013).

Web 2.0 and Social Media are more than tools where you can keep track of your old school and college friends (Bedell, 2011). Due to the amount of information exchanged in these platforms, companies can look at Web 2.0 tools like Wikis, Blogs, Social Networking sites and so forth, to check for some pieces of information that come in first hand to these communication tools (Berkman, 2008; Brown, 2012; Canhoto, 2013). We have to trust in the human nature that makes us want to be appreciated by our peers and wait to see if someone discloses his research results and applications to the world, in a medium faster than company reports and research articles (Kotze, 2013). If we have enough patience, it will pay off the time spent in this activity because it will be possible to identify micro-trends that have not yet gained momentum (Sage, 2013).

Companies can use this information, from these social tools, for competitor surveillance, consumer satisfaction monitoring, trend development and technology watch.

There are not, yet, many bibliographic resources dealing with this subject, because it's still a new medium that needs to be proved and tested, that is being currently used to perform competitive strategies so companies can excel in their areas of business (Berthon, Pitt, Plangger, & Shapiro, 2012).

Learning how to extract quality information, unbiased, valuable for business, from these social tools is the aim of this work, sharing with the interested parties some ways of using it for their profit and competitive sustainability.

If properly done, this monitoring activity even allows a company to measure the level of satisfaction of its own employees by the analysis of the content of what they post online about their employer (Ojala, 2012).

That gives you clues about improvements and changes to be made.

We will start with a brief explanation of the importance of information quality and its value for decision making and business governance, describing CI and Social Networking, identifying some tools that will ease monitoring requirements, and conclude with a few ideas for analyzing Blogs, Wikis and Tag Clouds to identify consumer signals and trends (Barbosa & O'Reilly, 2011; Canhoto, 2013; Higham, 2010; Kotze, 2013; Rasquilha, 2010; Scott, 2008).

We will survey the applications of Web 2.0 relative to CI and consumer trends, and explore approaches of gathering information for CI through Web 2.0. Some applications of Web 2.0 (Blog, Wiki, RSS and Tag Clouding) are discussed for CI and business intelligence use.

QUALITY INFORMATION FOR BUSINESS GOVERNANCE

Wagner asserts that "the term 'quality of information' is scarce in the literature" (1990, p. 69).

Quality is a difficult concept to define because what is quality for one person may be different for another.

Some managers state that they will recognize quality when they see it. That may be possible if we are evaluating a tangible product but applying this to immaterial and intangible goods, like data, information and knowledge makes it more difficult.

For Ginman there is no "generally accepted definition of quality information. (...) Both quality and information are in themselves difficult concepts to grasp and to evaluate, and the whole process is further coloured by the subjective views of the person making the evaluation" (1990, p. 18). For that reason, several different definitions of quality arise "however, they all accept the notion that quality is defined by the customer" (Cortada, 1996, p. 6) and Redman suggests the need to "understand what customers want in their terms" (1996, p. 141). Other authors state that "quality is achieved when customer needs are met; quality is central to all organizations, not an optional extra; quality is not dependent on high price or high levels of resourcing" (Brophy & Coulling, 1996, p. 7).

Companies "must define, measure, analyze, and improve the quality of information, treating information as a product" because "creating quality information and organizational knowledge is the prerequisite for any firm to gain competitive advantage" (Huang, Lee, & Wang, 1998, p. 5, 6).

Relating the subject of information quality with business management and the need of quality information for good decision making, Marchand describes the differences and common points that connect the information quality and the product quality. His information quality list comprises eight dimensions:

1. The actual value an information product or service may have for the information user;
2. The 'features' associated with an information product or service;

3. The reliability of the information product or service;
4. Its meaning over time;
5. Relevance;
6. Validity;
7. 'Aesthetics';
8. Perceived value (1990, pp. 11, 12).

He concludes that "understanding the interrelationships among the dimensions of information quality is what is critical to strategic information management" (1990, p. 10).

For most of the evolution of the business management function, information quality has not been a major strategic asset, but "has been perceived and thought about as simply one aspect of decision-making (…) only one of the many dimensions of decision-making and often not a very important one" (1990, p. 8). Thinking about the business value of information quality and its relation with profitability, some authors (Brophy & Coulling, 1996; Cortada, 1996; Garvin, 1988) mention that quality, in general, increases profits by gaining the consumers preference and obtaining a bigger market share. In information, the same occurs because quality lowers the costs of production and the adequacy of the information product or service to the user's needs makes it preferable to the ones who need and use it (Marchand, 1990, pp. 15, 16). Therefore cost plays a significant role to lower the price charged to the user of that information.

Criteria for Quality Information

To be considered of quality, information must meet several criteria such as: completeness, accessibility, accuracy, precision, objectivity, consistency, relevancy, timeliness, and understandability (Brünger-Weilandt, Geiß, Herlan, & Stuike-Prill, 2011).

Burk and Horton state that the quality of information itself includes attributes and examples, such as "Accuracy – Precision; Comprehensiveness – Relevance; Credibility – Reliability; Currency – Simplicity; Pertinence – Validity" (Burk Jr. & Horton Jr., 1988, p. 93).

Other authors mention that information, to have quality, must be:

1. **Precise:** Correct and true;
2. **Timely:** Available when and where needed;
3. **Complete:** Ensuring the presence of its several elements;
4. **Concise:** Easy to handle;
5. **Authoritative:** Quality depends on the provider (Brown & Duguid, 2000; Cleveland, 1985; Cooke, 2001; Davenport, 1997; Davenport et al., 2004; Hinton, 2006; Marchand & Horton Jr., 1986; McGee & Prusak, 1995; Penzias, 1989, 1995; Shapiro & Varian, 1999).

For Marchand the quality of information products depends on their attributes such as coverage, reliability and validity, which makes it highly measurable and quantifiable. Also, when looking at the production level, the quality of information is associated with "meeting requirements and with doing the job right the first time within budget, and on time" (1990, p. 9).

Huang, Lee and Wang divide information quality (IQ) in four categories, each one with several dimensions, as follows:

1. **Intrinsic IQ:** Accuracy, objectivity, believability, reputation;
2. **Contextual IQ:** Relevancy, value-added, timeliness, completeness, amount of information;
3. **Representational IQ:** Interpretability, ease of understanding, concise representation, consistent representation;
4. **Accessibility IQ:** Access, security.

These authors consider that, defined by the perspective of the consumer, information quality "can be used by researchers and practitioners to direct their efforts for information consumers instead of the IS professionals" (Huang, Lee, & Wang, 1998, p. 42, 43).

If information is not delivered with the right quality, proportion and measure it can originate "information overload" (Dearlove, 1998), which occurs when excess of information suffocates businesses and causes employees to suffer mental anguish and physical illness, exacerbated nowadays by the huge amount of information from Web 2.0 and Social Media (Tapscott & Williams, 2008).

Information overload causes high levels of stress that can result in illness and the breakdown of individuals' personal relationships.

The effects of the "information glut are procrastination and time wasting, leading to the delaying of important decisions, distraction from main job responsibilities, tension between colleagues and loss of job satisfaction" (Dearlove, 1998, p. 111).

Remember that "information is a bit like money: the more you've got, the more headaches it causes — but you still can't get enough" (Suhr, 2004, p. 41).

So, it's important to understand that customers will evaluate the quality of information according to its adequacy to the satisfaction of their needs. After all, that's the reason why information is stored and disseminated, to satisfy someone's information needs. That is why it has to be of high quality in order to be used and aggregate value to the users' tasks being performed.

THE VALUE OF ACCURATE INFORMATION FOR BUSINESSES

According to Best it's not easy to assign a value to information and there is no "commonly accepted and universally applicable way of valuing the information resource" (1996a, p. 14).

Burk and Horton define information value as "the value attributed to information produced or acquired by organizations, entities and persons, and delivered in the form of an information product or service". For them, this value can be perceived immediately but, sometimes, this valuation occurs only several years later like in the case of "the values attached to information created by scientific research" that "are often realized long after it is created" (Burk Jr. & Horton Jr., 1988, p. 79).

Orna also points out the fact that information has no implicit value in itself since it depends on its use, purpose and context (1996, p. 20).

Wagner states that the "terms value and quality share a common meaning: the degree of excellence, but the former also denotes an economic exchange worth" (1990, p. 69), being the value of information and not the quality of information the preferred concept.

For Orna, the functional part of valuing can be defined as "the process of determining and applying appropriate criteria for estimating the value of things" (1996, p. 19).

An indirect valuation occurs, and the measures used are the value of the investment in information technologies used to hold the information, the costs associated with staff that collects and maintains the information resources, or the value the information has when it's put to a specific use.

To explain why the process of valuing is so difficult, we must remember that "fixing a value is always an indirect process that involves finding appropriate equivalents and standards, not necessarily or always in money terms, and the estimation of those who use it has to be taken into account as well" (Orna, 1996, p. 19).

McPherson (1994, pp. 207, 208) proposes three models for information valuing. The first one is related with the cognition process, in which the value is dependent on the contribution of information to the achievement of organizational goals. The second relates to the value of information when it enhances the knowledge not only in the user's brain but also in external, operational and recognizable actions that are observable. The third deals with traditional accounting, highly cost oriented that does not recognize the value of information unless it can be sold externally as a good or product.

Orna, to make this clearer, says that "to have value, information has to be transformed by human minds into knowledge, without which no products of tangible value can be created or exchanged" (1999, p. 141). That occurs because the valuation has three parts, the value triangle:

1. Object;
2. Human judgement;
3. Use to which person judging puts the object.

It's a three way relationship, involving human judgment, based on the relationship between the object valued and the person that judges and evaluates, and the relationship between that object and the uses that the human will put the object into. It also involves criteria, which imply thinking and feeling (1999, pp. 143, 144).

What we can observe is that it's not easy to apply to information the traditional economic and accounting measures applied to tangible products, the cost benefit analysis. Nevertheless, it's important to do so in order to avoid "failure to spot potential threats in time because of lack of intelligence gathering and correlations; failure in attempts to innovate; (…) and failure to recognize opportunities for using information resources more productively" (Orna, 1996, p. 25).

Information is called the 'glue' that holds the organizational structure together, and there are four ways of using information to create value for a business:

1. Minimize risks;
2. Reduce costs;
3. Add value, orienting the output to the market and customers;
4. Innovation, through the creation of new realities (Davenport, 1997; Davenport et al., 2004).

Characteristics of Valuable Information

Information has some characteristics that differentiate it from tangible products, such as: "If information is exchanged and traded, the value from using it can increase for all parties to the transaction. The value of information is not diminished by being used; it can be (…) used many times by many users for adding value to many activities and outputs" (Orna, 1999, p. 141).

Cleveland (1985, pp. 29-33) highlights the value of information and its characteristics, saying that information is:

1. **Expandable:** The more we have, the more we use and more valuable it gets;
2. **Compressible:** Can be concentrated, integrated, summarized, miniaturized for easier handling;
3. **Substitutable:** Replaces land, labour and capital;
4. **Transportable:** At the speed of light, using e-mail or video-conference we can be anywhere like if we were there;
5. **Diffusive:** It tends to leak and the more it leaks the more we have and the more of us have it, making it available to a growing number of people;
6. **Shareable:** Allows exchange and sharing transactions because giving or selling a information lets the seller to keep it anyway, unlike physical goods.

For Grant (2002, pp. 242; 245, 246; 516), information is the medium through which an organization relates to its environment and allows the individuals to know how to react and adapt to external changes. For him, the value of information is related to what he designates "imperfect availability of information" and "imperfection of information". If, in a given market, not all the players have access to all the information available, or it's difficult to identify all the information needed to decide effectively in accordance to other competitor's moves, then the ones who possess or know the sources where the information needed exists, have a competitive advantage in that market.

This is going to be very important because even if all the players have access to the same information, again it will be the use that they make of it that is going to distinguish the success that they can obtain. It's only after the information gets inside someone's mind and is applied and put to use in something useful, like a product or a process that has the preference of the consumers in that market, that it becomes valuable and originates a big return on investment to his owner, the "value for money" valuation (Best, 1996a; Grant, 2002; Kotler et al., 1999; Mohr et al., 2010; Orna, 1996, 1999).

Even if everybody can access quality patent information, not everyone will innovate thanks to that. Furthermore, not everyone that does innovate will be successful because the results will be dependent on the output obtained and the accession of the consumers to the solution found, that is to say, it will depend on the product's characteristics, on its adequacy to the market and its consumers' needs, and on consumer satisfaction.

Again, a method to value information can be "through seeking indirect evidence of its value to businesses in promoting competitiveness, productivity, or innovation and successful marketing of the results" (Orna, 1996, p. 26), "and in avoiding risk and reducing uncertainty" (Orna, 1999, p. 142).

Although an information can be valuable for a long period of time, certain types of information are only valuable within a given time frame limit (Huang, Lee, & Wang, 1998). Information may lose its value because its timing has passed, like if you could knew the lottery numbers in advance for a certain week, after that week those numbers would be useless, or "a tip on the fourth race at Belmont might be valuable at lunchtime and valueless by dinnertime. Yesterday's weather forecast is of merely historical interest tomorrow" (Cleveland, 1985, p. 29). Nevertheless, some information retains its value and can be applied in the same field or in complementary fields, enhancing the final result obtained with this strategy.

COMPETITIVE INTELLIGENCE AND BUSINESS MANAGEMENT

CI is the use of public sources to develop information about the competition, consumers, and market environment (J. Miller & Business Intelligence Braintrust, 2002).

CI is different from espionage (Bergier, 1970; Fialka, 1997; Guisnel, 1997; Rustmann Jr., 2002; Winkler, 1997), which implies illegal means of information gathering. CI is restrained to the gathering of public information (Kahaner, 1997; Mordecai, 2013c).

One of the main differences between CI and general business information, such as business growth rate and operating ratios, is that CI is of strategic importance on the organization. It is not only the collection of information from a variety of sources, but also the analysis and synthesis of such information, which could help the company decide the course of action to improve its position (Choo, 2003).

Because of the broad reach and potential of CI, involvement in intelligence activities can provide first-class training for managers and marketers. In fact, an increasing number of leading companies insist that their best people spend some time in intelligence operations prior to promotion to the highest ranks (J. Miller & Business Intelligence Braintrust, 2002; Prescott & Miller, 2002; Taborda & Ferreira, 2002).

Intelligence must be passed to decision makers in a timely manner, and in a style and format that will encourage them to take appropriate measures and decisions. Intelligence reports and briefings should aim, above all, for clarity and brevity, and should provide the decision maker with suggestions or recommendations for action (Besson &

Possin, 1996; Choo, 2003; Garber, 2001; Martinet & Marti, 1995).

Executives have a major part to play in ensuring the success of your intelligence activities. Among other things, they must offer commitment, involvement, and support (Johnson, 2005; Prescott & Miller, 2002). Managers have a part to play in making intelligence activities successful because they already spend lots of time talking with others and that enables them to collect information. However, it is essential that they keep their intelligence manager informed of any significant change in the business environment (J. Miller & Business Intelligence Braintrust, 2002; Prescott & Miller, 2002).

A typical CI process consists of a series of business activities that involve identifying, gathering, developing, analyzing and disseminating information (Besson & Possin, 1996; Martinet & Marti, 1995; Taborda & Ferreira, 2002).

"Every competitor broadcasts a large amount of data to you in their advertising and their product itself. Every feature that they have in their products and every special technique that's part of their service is data you can use" (Mordecai, 2013c).

The following list shows a typical sequence in which these activities take place: i) identify competitors, markets, customers, suppliers, or other variables in the environment to be monitored. Identify what information is to be collected; ii) specifically identify possible sources of information and collect the information from these sources; iii) evaluate the validity, reliability, and usefulness of the information collected; iv) gather information collected from different sources and integrate them; v) interpret and analyze the information for strategic or tactical significance. Draw conclusions and recommend actions; vi) disseminate and present analyzed findings to management; vii) respond to ad hoc inquiries for decision support (Ribault, Martinet, & Lebidois, 1995).

Information gathering and information analysis are the key areas of the CI process.

Competitive Intelligence and the Internet

The Internet is currently the most popular medium for gathering information and it has enormous advantages for that function (Russell, 2011; Tsvetovat & Kouznetsov, 2011). At the same time, it calls for a minimum level of expertise if it is to be effective. For instance, you need to be able to find specific information (Berkman, 2008), and that calls for familiarity with search engines and sophisticated retrieval techniques (Prior, 2006, 2007).

Nevertheless, "search engines are severely lacking in the realm of exploratory search. (...) If you want to find new things with which you're unfamiliar, the online world has a market gap" (Hawthorne & Cromity, 2012, p. 36). Social Media can reduce that gap.

With very few exceptions, standards for citing and classifying information are poor, unenforceable or non-existent, and there is a distinct absence of identifying information (metadata) (Chen, Chau, & Zeng, 2002). "Content often lacks depth and substance, and it is almost impossible to distinguish between fact, editorial, advertising and news. But, many of these disadvantages will be overcome with time" (Prior, 2007).

Commercial online databases, such as Dialog (http://www.dialog.com) and Lexis-Nexis (http://www.lexisnexis.com), contain a large amount of well-organized information on a variety of subjects, storing information ranging from company annual reports to US patent documents, and from history journals to chemistry periodicals (Chen et al., 2002; Taborda & Ferreira, 2002). These commercial databases are among the major sources used by CI professionals (Herring, 2002).

"Recent years have seen the tremendous growth of the Internet. Many commercial online databases are now accessible through the Internet. The Internet also enables organizations to monitor and search the websites of their competitors, alliances, and possible collaborators" (Chen et al., 2002). Internet-based information sources are becoming increasingly important in the CI process (Guisnel, 1997). "In the old days, corporate intelligence gathering meant painstakingly gleaning information from experts and competitors' reports, subscribing to expensive online data aggregators such as Factiva or Dialog, and scanning unstructured documents from the media" (Kotze, 2013).

Corporate Web sites usually contain useful information, including company history, corporate overviews, business visions and missions, product overviews, financial data, sales figures, annual reports, press releases, biographies of top executives, locations of offices, hiring ads, among others (Godeluck, 2000; Weiss, 2008).

The data is "valuable in providing direct or indirect contextual information and enable the CI professionals to analyze corporate strategies. Another reason attracting CI professionals to use the Internet is that most of the contents available on the Internet are free of charge" (Chen et al., 2002). In fact, Internet is now one of the most important resources for CI information collection (Deng & Luo, 2007; Kirsch, Gregory, Brown, & Charley, 2006).

Corporate or employees Wikis and Blogs also contain a vast amount of useable information because everybody likes to tell in what they are working, what are they good at, the results that they were capable of reaching with their work, the goals and objectives they provided and so on.

As Kotze (2013) declares "none of the employee's actions were 'leaks' and taken alone they are all innocuous. But taken together they may reveal more than the company wants. For the competitive intelligence professional at the competitor they are a vital stream of information."

Managers tend to think that more information is better. In today's business environment, however, it is not necessarily true. CI professionals could be spending too much time and effort on data collection rather than data analysis. For CI professionals to manually access the Internet, extract and analyse the information on every single Web page at a company Web site to locate the useful information, and to synthesize information is very exhausting and time consuming.

"To address this information and cognitive overload problem, research has been conducted in developing techniques and tools to analyze, categorize, and visualize large collections of Web pages, among other text documents" (Chen et al., 2002).

In turn, a variety of tools have been developed to assist searching, gathering, monitoring and analyzing information on the internet (Guisnel, 1997; Prescott & Miller, 2002; Revelli, 2000)[1].

SOCIAL MEDIA NETWORKING

Social Networks, made possible by Web 2.0, are one of several next generation communications and collaboration tools that include Blogs, Wikis and Social Bookmarking.

Participants worldwide contribute to and collaborate in readily available online discussions, creating new knowledge bases that can become recognized as information sources.

"Web 2.0 technologies transform broadcast media monologues (one too many) into social media dialogues (many to many). Social media is the product of internet-based applications that build on the technological foundations of Web 2.0" (Berthon, Pitt, Plangger, & Shapiro, 2012, p. 263).

Social networks are free to join, to search for a vast amount of reference questions, and to find experts for all kinds of requirements and research projects (Qualman, 2010).

The concept of a social network, meaning a social structure made of nodes (which are generally individuals or organizations) that are tied by one or more specific types of interdependency, is as valuable as the number of nodes that constitute it (Castells, 2004; Tapscott & Williams, 2008).

This means that, the bigger the number of nodes, the more valuable that network becomes (Godeluck, 2000).

With this in mind, it's easy to perceive that this trend in modern communication and interaction among humans will be very important to achieve results that it will be very difficult with other non-interactive means (Tapscott, 1995, 1999; Tapscott et al., 2000; Tapscott & Williams, 2008).

The relation of confidence among each node will open a number of possibilities that a traditional media, like TV or Newspapers, couldn't impose simply because we don't know who those people are or, if we do, we know that they are trying to earn something at our expenses (Tapscott et al., 2000).

With this new possibility, either we know the person communicating with us, or we know someone who knows him. That condition gives us the confidence and trust that will induce the preference on a certain product or service and makes us discard others. That's basic consumer behaviour (Scott, 2008).

For companies, this new possibility can be the most important decision of all times. It will allow to transform our brand in a major player among the preferences of customers (Carrera, 2012b; Hortinha, 2002; Mohr et al., 2010).

With Social Media companies can gain a better knowledge of their business environment, using visual tools that can enhance the analysis of the huge amount of posts, comments, and shares (Mordecai, 2013b).

Also for employees, that can be a major source of information and knowledge, because we can now access the information we need among a network of thousands of specialists in a certain subject that can answer us almost immediately saving us precious time in the searching process (Libert & Spector, 2009; Surowiecki, 2007).

If someone thought that social networking was only for the youngsters, like with MySpace (http://www.myspace.com), or with Facebook (https://www.facebook.com), that is a huge mistake. Web 2.0 introduced many new types of applications for users to express their thoughts, concerns, needs, desires and level of satisfaction with what they buy (Berthon, Pitt, Plangger, & Shapiro, 2012; Hawthorne & Cromity, 2012).

This allows, in a very fast and inexpensive manner, to scan the trends of a market, understand consumer motivation and the actual preferences in the business area where companies act and compete (Rasquilha, 2010)[2].

New applications of Web 2.0 provide new opportunities for CI, such as Web Blogs (Blogs) which are created by thousands of individuals (Blood, 2004; Deng & Luo, 2007), Wikis (ex. Wikipedia) which allow public group creation, RSS (Rich Site Summary or Really Simple Syndication) using XML (Extensible Markup Language) to classify and organize the information (Tsvetovat & Kouznetsov, 2011) making it more transparent and open (Carrera, 2012b; Hortinha, 2002; Scott, 2008).

All of them bring convenience for CI especially in collecting information. "In the view of CI, Web 2.0 paved new ways and channels for gathering information" (Deng & Luo, 2007).

All these tools, like Blogs and Wikis, provide intelligence for consumer trend monitoring (Barbosa & O'Reilly, 2011; Higham, 2010; Rasquilha, 2010; Sage, 2013).

In conjunction with existing consumer intelligence and CI resources, Social Networks can highlight significant issues that affect your brands, identify competitor weaknesses, opportunities in the marketplace and those specific to a brand (Qualman, 2010).

Monitoring Blogs and Podcasts can help develop actionable solutions to fuel organizations (Carrera, 2009, 2012a, 2012b; Hortinha, 2002).

When looking at Blogs and Wikis, we must also look at some of the networking sites, like LinkedIn.com, Xing.com, Facebook.com, Myspace.com, and search tools for people such as Zoominfo.com for company and competitor employees. Sites like these will mention what people are doing, their interests and past achievements. This information is very valuable because contacts can be found easily. "Sites such as LinkedIn.com and Xing.com allow you to see where people used to work as well as where they are now. The networking sites can also be searched using tools such as yoname.com and wink.com" (Weiss, 2008).

Also, creative consumers help companies developing new and better products by their feedback on using them and what to improve for better results (Berthon, Pitt, Plangger, & Shapiro, 2012).

Although Social Media includes Blogs, Podcasts, Wikis and more, we will just explore some of them, and will demonstrate how monitoring and analyzing what consumers create on Blogs and Wikis can enrich our understanding of their needs and desires (Higham, 2010; Hortinha, 2002; Kotler et al., 1999; Rasquilha, 2010; Scott, 2008), and thus support our CI efforts.

Online Social Networking for Business Intelligence

Online Social Networking enables us to find people who may not be familiar with our organisation, becoming quality prospects and then effective clients, creating an opportunity to connect with them and sell them our products and services.

Social Networking offers a high level of integration, and focuses on the sharing elements of the various applications. Sharing resources can increase the possibility of finding relevant information, like sharing our favourite bookmarks or photos and in return having access to the favourite resources of others who share our interests. It can mean being able to read comments and chat with people on topics of shared interest and being able to tap into collective knowledge (Russell, 2011)[3].

If we already know someone in that network, we can feel more comfortable that they can become quality prospects. And, because of that mutual connection, we can overcome difficulties and begin a business relationship with more trust.

These "new tools, based on social networking and deployed on mobile devices, are enabling companies to streamline operations, enhance customer satisfaction and improve financial performance across their entire businesses" (Bedell, 2011), allowing to accurately perform a SWOT (Strengths, Weaknesses; Opportunities and Threats) analysis to scan the macro-environment where the company develops its activity (Mordecai, 2013a).

Some advantages are that you can contact people or companies in your network to:

1. Regenerate old connections;
2. Maximise value in your weak connections;
3. Build business relationships with clients or hiring managers;
4. Find and meet prospective jobseekers;
5. Grow a referral network;
6. Enlarge your corporate and personal brand;
7. Make new connections and grow your sphere of influence;
8. Open doors to future career opportunities, increased salary or promotions;
9. Increase visibility, which improves influence and effectiveness internally with your organisation as well as externally;
10. Educate yourself and ask questions about other organisations;
11. Conduct competitive intelligence on companies, industries or individuals;
12. Make fewer cold calls and better prepare for them;
13. Leverage contacts you already have (Steckerl, 2007).

Although a major opportunity for business, companies with brands in the luxury market are failing to take advantage of these tools (Dickins, 2013).

As some authors declare, "better social searching tools will enable information professionals to find reliable sources for sentiment or common knowledge for word-of-mouth coverage" (Hawthorne & Cromity, 2012, p. 36), what is already being performed by some companies that analyze attitudes, emotions, brand evangelism, and its sponsor correlation present in the Social Media conversation share (Focalytic, 2013).

Social Interactions and Communities of Practice

The advantage of Blogs is that they facilitate the growth of Social Networks into true communities of practice (Blood, 2004). Much of the value of these networks is in their advantage for the "social capital required for effective decision support to grow based on relationships between analytically opinionated minds" (Johnson, 2005).

This defies the control hierarchies that still define most businesses where top-down decision making is still the rule of the day (Scott, 2008). Here, the reputations of writers are built on the value of their ideas, their ability to convince others that their ideas are valid and therefore develop the most respect and authority (Curtis, 2006; Kassel, 2008; A. Miller, 2007).

Collaboration applications that build such communities of practice socialize critical business decisions in an open forum based on the social capital of merit.

CONCERNS WITH NETWORKING SITES

"There's a tension between the audience participation model of Web 2.0 and business need for confidentiality and verification" (A. Miller, 2007). Some questions must be addressed like:

1. If an employee is blogging, what are they saying about the firm?
2. In a world where Wikis or Social bookmarks and tags are popular research tools, who is responsible for the accuracy and quality of information?
3. If you create an online community, how will you moderate what should be an open and free forum?
4. If you let your employees access Facebook at work, how can you be sure that they will remain alert to whether it's a work or social conversation they're having? (Steckerl, 2007).

According to some authors (A. Miller, 2007; Steckerl, 2007), other issues that raise some questions are:

1. **Privacy:** The more we share the more we are exposed. But, we will increase our benefit from the network with more exposure. This concept involves a little trust. For the network to be most useful to us there needs to be a little reciprocity. People very secretive about their privacy may not get great results from using these tools;
2. **Barriers to entry:** Getting started means investing time to put your information into the application. This can take a few minutes or a few hours, it depends on how much we want to disclose to the network. The more we share about us the easier it will be to make new connections. If we only upload a few contacts we get little benefit since these systems only search for connections through people we already know;
3. **Maintenance:** If we have a large network we can get to a point where we are receiving lots of requests. We can turn off e-mails about our connections, and with some networks we can even change our settings to accept requests from specific levels. We may get requests from people we don't know or don't remember. We shouldn't add everyone because we are a reflection of our networks;
4. **Cost:** Many of these services may begin to charge membership fees.

Sage (2013) warns that the "speed and volume of information that is published on social media can cause significant damage. (...) *A misleading comment* can damage a company's reputation in seconds". He also points out to the problem of hackers and cyber security because Social Media can be used by hackers to acquire "personal information about employees, then use it to befriend them. Having built a relationship, the criminal may be able to deceive the employee into revealing how to access to their company's *systems, and so opening the door to cyber attacks*". [4]

Ojala warns that "in minding our own business, we need to know what information about our employer can be gathered from social media *and whether it is what should be publicly available*" (2012, p. 53).[5]

The weakness in this new Social Networking sites is that "if users do not trust the system to protect their relationships, then they will not use the application effectively and gain very little incremental advantage from their connections" (Steckerl, 2007)[6].

In the end, the quality and value of this information will be dependent on the user and related to the results that it will allow obtaining, always integrated on its context.

SOCIAL TOOLS FOR THE WORKPLACE

The high number of social tools indicates an enthusiastic acceptance of this new media by individuals and companies (Steckerl, 2007).

Organisations cannot afford to ignore Social tools. If they don't know how they can use these tools, maybe they have already lost opportunities to faster competitors. For example, a business can help its staff save time searching if it encourages them to bookmark useful sites and share them with their co-workers.

We must remember that participation drives traffic. "Wikipedia is far more popular than Encarta, and Flikr is used more than Kodak Gallery. If you want people to use a tool, letting them contribute to it will engage their interest" (A. Miller, 2007).

For individuals, the benefits of using social tools often feel obvious but difficult or even impossible to measure. But, for most organisations, there's a need to demonstrate return on investment. "Those responsible for proving value have a dilemma: on the one hand, hard targets such as page hits or number of posts are easier to collect but have relatively little meaning" (A. Miller, 2007). On the other hand, measurements such as the ability of an organisation to innovate are hard to measure or directly attribute but are of fundamental importance to its financial health[7].

The idea that social tools are of interest to companies is unquestionable. As long as collaborators have basic Internet knowledge, the problem is the time needed to be actively involved. The more you use these new tools the more obvious the advantages become. To ignore these new tools is to ignore the unique benefits that they can offer (Zarrella, 2013).

Those companies who have opened their organisation to social tools had more positive results than they expected. The strategy is to treat your networked individuals as intelligent adults and minimize the need to be in control. Open and honest support is more constructive and usually works. However, we must stay involved and assume that the community can't grow without some time and attention (Curtis, 2006; Kassel, 2008; Steckerl, 2007).

SOME OF THE BIGGEST TOOLS AND HOW THEY OPERATE

For most of the services, the initial sign up is free. Users begin by filling out a form with personal data and then inviting friends. Some networks allow uploading current contacts, but others ask users to invite contacts directly through the application's interface. The connections then invite their own contacts, and that's how the network grows (Steckerl, 2007).

There are several Social Networking sites. Most of the applications competing for your attention offer a combination of professional and personal networking. Some of them are seriously oriented to business. From the top 20 players, three of them stand out:

1. **LinkedIn.com** (http://www.linkedin.com)**:** Profiles look very much like a CV, excellent mix of people from different levels in the organisation, and many industries (Schaffer, 2011). Used mostly as a business research tool without the noise and redundant information that occurs in other social media platforms (Ojala, 2012). A fast growing business network with more than 200 million members worldwide. The most concrete application of LinkedIn is developing a network of associates, an excellent way to stay connected with current and past friends and clients (Kawasaki, 2007). Search for: industry experts, potential employees, hiring managers, deal-makers, people from specific geographies, or people with particular keywords in their profiles;
2. **Plaxo.com** (http://www.plaxo.com)**:** Keeps all of your current contacts' information updated automatically thus is extremely useful in repair old relationships and staying in touch. Not a tool to build your network yet, though it does have a very useful 'mini Blog' feature to help you keep friends informed. More than 40 million people use Plaxo;
3. **Spoke.com** (http://spoke.com)**:** Focused on providing sales prospects. Deeply integrated, extracts contact data from enterprise applications (Outlook, Notes, etc.) to establish and leverage connections. Provides more than 30 million contacts.

There are so many Social Networks that they are too numerous to list here. Most of them, like friendster.com, flickr.com, orkut.com, among hundreds of others tend to serve only social categories like dating, common interests, finding friends, photo sharing and others not directly related to business. Nevertheless they might contain important information about their users like brands they wear, satisfaction, or not, with the products they own, special needs and interest in solve their problems with new technologies, products or services, among others (Mordecai, 2013a).

Some web sites can also be networking sites, like MySpace.com, Windows Live Spaces, LiveJournal.com, and Blogger.com.

Other networks with a decidedly business or professional purpose, ranked by number of users, are:

1. **Hi5.com** (http://www.hi5.com/)**:** More than 330 million users. General social networking and business;
2. **Passado.com** (http://passado.com)**:** More than 4 million users (already had more than 7 million);
3. **Europe's largest business network, now called Wasabi** (http://www.wasabi.com/signup)**:** More than 13 million users, about 6 million of whom are based in German-speaking countries. Business networking;
4. **Ryze.com** (http://www.ryze.com/)**:** More than 500,000 users. Business networking;
5. **Ecademy.com** (http://www.sunzu.com/)**:** Became Sunzu in January 2013. More than 100,000 users before the name change. Business networking.

Two other networks reflect some specialty in social networking:

1. **BiomedExperts** (http://www.biomed-experts.com)**:** "The first literature-based

scientific social network - brings the right researchers together and allows them to collaborate online. Collexis provides the BiomedExperts social network free of charge to researchers worldwide in an effort to increase collaborative biomedical research for the common good." More than 434.000 experts;

2. **globalEDGE** (http://globaledge.msu.edu/)**:** "Sponsored and developed by the International Business Center at Michigan State University includes more than 350.000 registered users from across the globe and connects users to prospective collaboration partners and industry experts."

Social Networks for Business Use

Social Networks are one source, among many others, to consider in everyday reference and research work. There are tools like SlideShare (http://www.slideshare.net) that makes possible to share slide presentations, and includes the text of the slides in a format called a transcript. We can use the search box to find relevant topics, watch the presentation slides at the SlideShare site, or download them for future use. Some require registration based on the poster's preference before downloading is permitted, and Vidipedia (http://www.vidipedia.org) which is a selection of a multimedia picture social networking. Similarly to Wikipedia, Vidipedia is a free encyclopaedia that anyone can edit, search for key terms or browse by category. The results are encyclopaedic answers that link to relevant videos. When only one result is available, the video is automatically launched and all videos can be downloaded. Running a search on a given term produces an extensive description with definitions and videos.

A great advantage of Social Networking is connecting anyone who needs with those who have direct experience with companies, products, or services and are experts in some field (Kassel, 2008).

Businesses can use social tools to improve creativity, productivity, collaboration and visibility in certain markets, as well as engaging clients and partners in more fruitful collaboration (Berkman, 2008; Brown, 2012; Holloman, 2012).

There are a huge range of tools and sites (Russell, 2011; Tsvetovat & Kouznetsov, 2011), including:

1. Wikis;
2. Blogs;
3. Mash-ups[8];
4. Social Tagging;
5. Instant Messaging;
6. Video;
7. Social Bookmarking;
8. Podcasts; and
9. Services, like Facebook, Twitter, NetVibes, Flock and others (A. Miller, 2007).

There are practical examples of how geographically dispersed organisations could improve networking, knowledge sharing and collaboration using these tools (Tapscott & Williams, 2008).

The biggest benefit of such social tools for business is that this ongoing social contact with a colleague or client can mean that face-to-face meetings start with a deeper personal trust and understanding (Berkman, 2008; Brown, 2012; Zarrella, 2009).

If a person posts in his or her Social Networking community something like "I'm walking my dog to the dog park and his leash just broke. It was brand new. I'm so frustrated" (Leonard, 2013), we get to know several important things that can be used on the behalf of our company. This person has a need, the need to purchase a new leash for the dog. We also know that there is frustration with a new leash that just got broke leaving a bad evaluation and opinion about the manufacturer of that product. That person shows a real love and care for its animal friend so he must want the best for it. A dog needs food, toys, veterinarian care, among other things and we may know where that person lives, which dog park uses and the stores where he passes to reach the park[9].

For a company in the pet business this is gold because we have a behavioural segmentation (Kotler et al., 1999; Scott, 2008) that allows contacting the owner with a full range of services and products adapted to the animal, the climate where it lives and other specific needs. Perhaps the dog breed, name and birth date of the animal are posted also in the network and the offers can be personalized to target the prospect with some empathy.

Leonard (2013) calls this "the Anatomy of an Expression of Intent" and this can be used in a large sort of situations like animals, children, jobs, marriages and other businesses if we pay attention and learn how to read between the lines.

Blogs

According to Blog search engine Technorati (http://www.technorati.com), more than 180 million Blogs are being written in the public cyberspace known as the Blogosphere, up from just 100,000 in late 2002. Technorati's '2013 Digital Influence Report' shows that "consumers are turning to blogs when looking to make a purchase. In fact, blogs rank favorably with consumers for trust, popularity and even influence" (Leonard, 2013).

The report states that blogs are now the third-most influential digital resource (31%) when making overall purchases, behind retail sites (56%) and brand sites (34%), making it a useful resource to watch for consumer behavior and needs.

Ojala states that "blogs – or at least some blogs – gained the status of reputable sources for reporting and informed commentary. Curated blog content of interest to business researchers is part of online services such as ProQuest (in its Entrepreneurship product), LexisNexis, and Factiva." (2012, p.53).

Some Blogs with interest in CI like Traction (http://traction.tractionsoftware.com), MovableType (http://www.movabletype.org), and Manila (http://manila.userland.com) are used to streamline dissemination and collection[10] (Johnson, 2005). Now, enterprises in every industry are learning the power and risks of unleashing their employees' ideas on both their colleagues and the marketplace (Blood, 2004; Qualman, 2010).

Blogs have also taken on a greater role in CI practice within the enterprise, alongside Blogs in product, R&D, information technology, legal and financial teams, sales and marketing and even executive management (Johnson, 2005). Today, blogging is helping to create real communities of practice within organizations large and small (Curtis, 2006).

To obtain information about "which Blogs are reliable and worthy, the content aggregator and distributor Newstex (http://newstex.com/)" (Ojala, 2012, p.53) is the right place to start.

Wikis

The Wiki is a new collaboration tool in the corporate environment and is gaining significance in organizational information sharing. Borrowed from the Hawaiian word for quick, the first Wiki was originally developed by Ward Cunningham in 1995. Today they take the form of dozens of software applications that have Wiki-like capabilities (Johnson, 2005). Like Blogs, Wikis allow for very easy publishing and commenting on topics of collective interest to the community. Its unique social dynamics, allowing all contributors to change anything on any or all of the documents available, subjects the entire community to consensus-building (Carrera, 2012b).

Many of these tools are open-source and available free of charge, such as OpenWiki, Kwiki and Twiki. The best example of a Wiki is the Wikipedia. It begun in 2001 to build a free, multi-lingual encyclopaedia of knowledge on every subject in the human knowledge (Johnson, 2005). It has now more than 4.000.000 individual articles and serves as the laboratory for what Wikis can ultimately become given time and attention in the enterprise (Libert & Spector, 2009; Qualman, 2010; Surowiecki, 2007).

Wikis are just like Blogs. With Wikis, the same social interaction happens, but much faster and with far more intense collaboration (Tapscott & Williams, 2008). "They are based on the notion that the best results come from allowing decision-making to emerge from the bottom up with minimal editorial control from the top down (Johnson, 2005).

Wikis are great tools because of their editing and contribution characteristics. Wikis are made of hypertext documents linked together and edited collectively by the community in a web browser interface (Qualman, 2010). It is a very open medium where all authors can add to, change, or delete other people's work. "To prevent the damaging effects of creative destruction this can obviously lead to, Wikis have a means of comparing two states of a page, known as a *diff*, so that revisions can be viewed and rolled back and mistakes can be corrected" (Johnson, 2005).

The only way anyone can write something that will survive is if it's written with such quality that even its opponents can agree that it has value (Carrera, 2009, 2012a; Tapscott & Williams, 2008).

In CI, focus must be on the analysis of options available and the arguments that make one course stand apart from its alternatives as superior. This ascertains the quality of the information retrieved, allowing for a sustainable business decision making in organisations.

RSS

The technology that made all this possible is RSS (Rich Site Summary or Real Simple Syndication). It is an XML specification for distributing published media files to a web address that can be read by a RSS feed reader[11].

RSS has become the modern example for what XML can do for the user. It is also the most widespread form of XML in use today. RSS could very well become the principal mean by which all data, structured or unstructured, is broadcasted and applied (Johnson, 2005). This includes applications such as change-detection in Weblogs, retrieving spam-free email, or passing transactional data through a complex workflow environment (Carrera, 2009, 2012a).

"In addition to receiving posts from news sites and other Weblogs, RSS feeds can contain data from corporate systems: sales information, financial data, inventory or vendor information, data from partner or distribution systems, competitor events, and all manner of real-time data relevant to the enterprise" (Johnson, 2005).

The challenge now is to disseminate examples where collaborative social community applications have an impact on competitive intelligence efficiency or effectiveness (Carrera, 2012b; Hortinha, 2002).

Tag Clouding

Analysis of Blogs, Wikis and Web pages is an excellent way to gain an understanding of the individuals who use those particular tools of Social Media, and thus put the information into context.

Social Media search engines provide important data through Tag Clouds and through lists, such as the week's top ten tags and/or Blogs. Tags are words that content creators use to describe their works (http://en.wikipedia.org/wiki/Tag_cloud). In effect, they are keywords, guides that lead content users to the posts of content creators. Analyzing Tag Clouds, groups of tags within content, provides powerful insights into what Blog and other Social Media content creators and users are interested in (Curtis, 2006).

Tag Clouds can be used to build up a picture of the demographics of particular sites as a Wordle[12]. If we look at a Tag Cloud and we see a big number of technology-related words, such as: Ajax, Apple, CSS, Linux and Web 2.0, this helps us to analyze what type of consumer uses that site, segmenting them in psychographic means, and correlate it to the site's popular tags.

To begin monitoring, we must match keywords with the tags created by active consumers. Content creators are active consumers that rely on tags to help other consumers find them. Tags connect content creators with the readers, and are an important tool for monitoring consumer trends.

Over time, the use of tags results in a folksonomy, "a user-defined, keyword system in which tags are defined by users rather than by a provided vocabulary. Unfortunately, folksonomies often diverge from keywords that researchers might use" (Curtis, 2006).

Tag Clouds provide an excellent way to identify the most popular trends and can be used in reverse. "Rather than matching keywords you choose in advance, let them lead you to toward what seems popular" (Curtis, 2006).

Squidoo (http://www.squidoo.com/browse/top_lenses) allows users to set up a web page where they control the content. Squidoo has a number of tags that will help you. Each web page (Squidoo calls them lenses) has the tags prominently displayed. In addition, the site has a number of tags compiled based on popularity, and category. After some examination we will have a better understanding of tags and consumer interests and needs disclosed in Social Media.

By watching tags carefully you can monitor and correlate product category, brands, uses, interests and needs. Tag Clouds will show consumer interests integrated in the social media space (Kassel, 2008; A. Miller, 2007; Steckerl, 2007).

This way, consumer trends can be revealed.

CONCLUSION

In the globalized world quality information warrants best results when competing with other organizations, enabling a competitive advantage.

After describing what CI is and what is it good for, we have mentioned the advantages of being involved in CI projects. How to receive information for competitive decisions and the benefits of continually scan the business environment are some issues also analysed.

We have described several web tools available for information retrieval purposes and some features of each one, after showing the relations and benefits of the Internet for CI.

Social Networking is getting involved and getting your brand name being discussed every time you can. With the Internet we have the ability to reach more people and make more money in a highly personalized manner, knowing their needs and desires and the trends that are getting more attention (Kassel, 2008; A. Miller, 2007). Nevertheless, Ethics and good practice still play a major part.

Companies look at Social Media as a way of attracting and retaining customers (Brown, 2012; Ojala, 2012; Schaffer, 2011; Zarrella, 2009, 2013) but are not taking benefit (Dickins, 2013) of its major advantage in obtaining feedback from the market and be aware of competitors moves and market trends discussed by the clients (Berkman, 2008; Holloman, 2012). Customer and employee satisfaction is another invaluable information scanning that social tools allow to perform (Hawthorne & Cromity, 2012; Ojala, 2012; Sage, 2013).

Being connected is an incredible leverage, invaluable in your business development (Steckerl, 2007). Connections can have many unexpected positive results (Carrera, 2009; Kawasaki, 2007).

Also, creative consumers help companies developing new and better products by their feedback on using them and what to improve for better results (Berthon, Pitt, Plangger, & Shapiro, 2012).

We've concluded with a short description of some of the social network tools that can be adopted to gain current awareness about all the unexpected events in the macro environment of the companies, allowing the anticipation of what's going on with trends among specific market segments (Higham, 2010; Sage, 2013).

Web 2.0 tools are impacting the definition, collection and dissemination of CI but there is still much more untapped potential (Canhoto, 2013; Ojala, 2012).

CI professionals must redefine their roles in terms of strategic analysis (Kotze, 2013). Regardless of whether you show enthusiasm or scepticism in the face of this new Internet collaborative and communication tools, there is no excuse to be uninformed.

Consumers have always wanted to be heard, have always wanted their desires to be taken into account in the creation of new products and services. Consumer trends begin life through a series of small or big signals (Rasquilha, 2010). Through monitoring and analyzing the Social Media space, information professionals can provide a valuable analysis within consumer trend monitoring, knowing the consumer's interests and needs directly from the consumer posts and commentaries (Curtis, 2006), building the adequate solution to those clients' problems[13].

Like much of the web, corporate Blogs of Social Network web sites can be a good place to keep track of what the company is exploring for future products and services (Ojala, 2012). Blogs also provide excellent flags in response to consumer needs (Blood, 2004; Carrera, 2012a; Hortinha, 2002). BlogPulse point us toward the direction of trends we might otherwise let go (Curtis, 2006)[14].

In a fast moving business world, like the one we are living in, it should be a competitive edge having the chance of monitoring the market trends, the competition moves and still improve internal communication to flat the channels and downsize the hierarchy inside companies.

We must watch closely what the competitor employees are posting online and also keep an eye on what our employees are posting and check if they are, unconsciously, giving away valuable information to the competitors. We are not the only ones looking at the competition; they are doing the same thing with us and our company. Be aware.

Sage (2013) explains that social intelligence is better than traditional market research because it provides answers that companies consider critical to business strategy.

Only future research will tell if this is effectively true and the real value obtained by companies that perform this task accurately.

It's our expectation to contribute to take this relevant subject further in ulterior research to disseminate all the advantages in adopting Web 2.0 tools in companies.

Let's hope CEO's learn how to leverage all this advantages and know how to make a good use for them all.

ACKNOWLEDGMENT

I wish to thank the Portuguese Science and Technology Foundation (FCT) and the support from the following programs: POPH - Programa Operacional Potencial Humano, QREN - Quadro de Referência Estratégica Nacional, and UE-FSE – União Europeia-Fundo Social Europeu.

REFERENCES

Barbosa, P., & O'Reilly, A. (2011). *Harvard trends: Tendências de gestão*. Porto, Portugal: Vida Económica.

Bedell, D. (2011, March). Business intelligence. *Global Finance,* 46-47.

Bergier, J. (1970). *A espionagem industrial*. Porto, Portugal: Editorial Inova.

Berkman, R. (2008). *The art of strategic listening: Finding market intelligence in blogs and social media*. Paramount Market Pub.

Berthon, P., Pitt, L., Plangger, K., & Shapiro, D. (2012). Marketing meets web 2.0, social media, and creative consumers: Implications for international marketing strategy. *Business Horizons*, (55): 261–271. doi:10.1016/j.bushor.2012.01.007

Besson, B., & Possin, J. (1996). *Do serviço de informação à inteligência económica: Detectar as ameaças e oportunidades da empresa*. Instituto Piaget.

Best, D. (1996a). Business process and information management. In D. Best (Ed.), *The fourth resource: Information and its management*. Hampshire, UK: Aslib/Gower.

Best, D. (1996b). *The fourth resource: Information and its management*. Hampshire, UK: Aslib/Gower.

Beuren, I. M. (1998). *Gerenciamento da informação: Um recurso estratégico no processo de gestão empresarial*. São Paulo, Brazil: Atlas.

Blood, R. (2004). *O livro de bolso do weblogue: Conselhos práticos para criar e manter o seu blogue*. Porto, Portugal: Campo das Letras.

Bramston, D. (2009). *Basics product design: Idea searching*. Lausanne: Ava Publishing.

Brophy, P., & Coulling, K. (1996). *Quality management for information and library managers*. Guildford: Aslib/Gower.

Brown, E. (2012). Working the crowd: Social media marketing for business (2ª ed.). London: British Informatics Society.

Brown, J., & Duguid, P. (2000). *The social life of information*. Boston: Harvard Business School Press.

Brünger-Weilandt, S., Geiß, D., Herlan, G., & Stuike-Prill, R. (2011). Quality: Key factor for high value in professional patent, technical and scientific information. *World Patent Information*, *33*(3), 230–234. doi:10.1016/j.wpi.2011.04.007

Burgelman, R., Christensen, C., & Wheelwright, S. (2009). Strategic management of technology and innovation (5ª ed.). Singapore: McGraw-Hill.

Burk, C. Jr, & Horton, F. Jr. (1988). *InfoMap: A complete guide to discovering corporate information resources*. Hoboken, NJ: Prentice Hall.

Canhoto, A. (2013). *Social media as a source of competitive intelligence*. Retrieved 28-02-2013, from http://anacanhoto.com/2013/01/18/social-media-as-a-source-of-competitive-intelligence/

Carrera, F. (2009). *Networking: Guia de sobrevivência profissional*. Lisboa, Portugal: Sílabo.

Carrera, F. (2012a). *Comunicar 2.0: A arte de bem comunicar no século XXI*. Lisboa, Portugal: Sílabo.

Carrera, F. (2012b). Marketing digital na versão 2.0: O que não pode ignorar (2ª ed.). Lisboa, Portugal: Sílabo.

Castells, M. (2000). *The information age: The rise of the network society* (2nd ed.). London: Blackwell.

Castells, M. (2004). *A galáxia internet: Reflexões sobre internet, negócios e sociedade*. Lisboa, Portugal: Fundação Calouste Gulbenkian.

Chen, H., Chau, M., & Zeng, D. (2002). CI spider: A tool for competitive intelligence on the web. *Decision Support Systems*, (34): 1–17. doi:10.1016/S0167-9236(02)00002-7

Choo, C. W. (2003). *Gestão de informação para a organização inteligente: A arte de explorar o meio ambiente*. Lisboa, Portugal: Editorial Caminho.

Christensen, C., Anthony, S., & Roth, E. (2004). *Seeing what's next: Using the theories of innovation to predict industry change*. Cambridge, MA: Harvard Business School Press.

Cleveland, H. (1983). A informação como um recurso. *Diálogo*, (16), 7-11.

Cleveland, H. (1985). *The knowledge executive: Leadership in an information society*. New York: Dutton.

Cooke, A. (2001). A guide to finding quality information on the internet: Selection and evaluation strategies (2ª ed.). Cornwall, UK: Library Association Publishing.

Cortada, J. (1996). *TQM for information systems management: Quality practices for continuous improvement*. Singapore: McGraw-Hill.

Curtis, P. (2006). *Gleaning consumer intelligence from blogs and podcasts*. Retrieved 02-12-2012, from http://www.freepint.com/issues/040506.htm#tips

Davenport, T. (1997). *Information ecology: Mastering the information and knowledge environment*. New York: Oxford University Press.

Davenport, T., Marchand, D., & Dickson, T. (2004). *Dominando a gestão da informação*. Porto Alegre, Portugal: Bookmann.

Dearlove, D. (1998). *Key management decisions: Tools and techniques of the executive decision-maker*. Wiltshire, UK: Financial Times/Pitman.

Deng, Z., & Luo, L. (2007). An exploratory discuss of new ways for competitive intelligence on web 2.0. In Wang (Ed.), Integration and innovation orient to e-society (pp. 597-604). Boston: Springer.

Dickins, J. (2013). Social media is an underused opportunity for luxury brands. *Digital Marketing Hub: The Guardian*. Retrieved 14-06-2013, from http://www.guardian.co.uk/media-network/media-network-blog/2013/jun/14/social-media-opportunity-luxury-brands

Fialka, J. (1997). *War by other means: Economic espionage in America*. Norton.

Focalytic. (2013). Social media content analysis of the 2013 masters golf tournament. *Focal Point*. Retrieved 16-06-2013, from http://www.focalytic.com/Portals/182440/docs/themastersgolfebook.pdf

Garber, R. (2001). Inteligência competitiva de mercado: Como capturar, armazenar, analisar informações de marketing e tomar decisões num mercado competitivo. São Paulo, Brazil: Madras.

Garvin, D. (1988). *Managing quality*. New York: Free Press.

Ginman, M. (1990). Quality information, and information for quality. In Wormell (Ed.), Information quality: Definitions and dimensions. London: Taylor Graham.

Gleick, J. (2011). *The information: A history, a theory, a flood*. St. Ives: 4th Estate.

Godeluck, S. (2000). *A explosão da economia na internet*. Lisboa: Livros do Brasil.

Gomes, E., & Braga, F. (2001). *Inteligência competitiva: Como transformar informação em um negócio lucrativo*. Rio de Janeiro, Brazil: Campus.

Grant, R. M. (2002). *Contemporary strategy analysis: Concepts, techniques, applications*. Oxford, UK: Wiley-Blackwell.

Guisnel, J. (1997). *Espionagem na internet: As guerras no ciberespaço*. Lisboa: Difusão Cultural.

Guynn, J. (2013). Facebook releases information on NSA requests for user data. *Los Angeles Times*. Retrieved 14-06-2013, from http://www.latimes.com/business/technology/la-fi-tn-facebook-releases-first-information-on-fisa-requests-20130614,0,3315731.story

Hawthorne, K., & Cromity, J. (2012, March/April). Social search for market intelligence. *Exploring Technology & Resources for Information Professionals,* 36-38.

Herring, J. P. (2002). Tópicos fundamentais de inteligência: Processo para identificação e definição de necessidades de inteligência. In Prescott & Miller (Eds.), Inteligência competitiva na prática. Rio de Janeiro, Brazil: Campus.

Higham, W. (2010). *The next big thing: Spotting and forecasting consumer trends for profit*. Bodmin: Kogan Page.

Hinton, M. (2006). *Introducing information management: The business approach*. Burlington, UK: Elsevier Butterworth-Heinemann.

Holloman, C. (2012). *The social media MBA: Your competitive edge in social media strategy development and delivery*. Hoboken, NJ: John Wiley & Sons.

Hortinha, J. (2002). *X-marketing*. Lisboa: Sílabo.

Huang, K., Lee, Y., & Wang, R. (1998). *Quality information and knowledge*. Upper Saddle River, NJ: Prentice Hall.

Johnson, A. (2005). Blogs, wikis & RSS: Colaborative social communities and the value of distributed CI. *Competitive Intelligence Magazine*. Retrieved 10-02-2013, from http://www.aurorawdc.com/blogswikisrss_scipcimag_20050102.pdf

Kahaner, L. (1997). *Competitive intelligence: How to gather, analyze, and use information to move your business to the top*. New York: Simon & Schuster.

Kassel, A. (2008). *Social networking: A research tool*. Retrieved 15/12/2012, from http://web.fumsi.com/go/article/find/3196

Kawasaki, G. (2007). *Ten ways to use linkedin*. Retrieved 05-01-2007, from http://blog.guykawasaki.com

Kirsch, G., Brown, J., & Charley, F. (2006). Using patents in competitive intelligence. *Competitive Intelligence Magazine*, *9*(1), 17–21.

Kotler, P., Armstrong, G., Saunders, J., & Wong, V. (1999). Principles of marketing (2ª ed.). Cambridge, UK: Prentice Hall.

Kotze, L. (2013). *Social media increasingly important in competitive intelligence*. Retrieved 08-03-2013, from http://www.ibis.co.za/Competitive-Intelligence-Blog/social-media-increasingly-important-in-competitive-intelligence.html

Lattès, R. (1992). *O risco e a fortuna: A grande aventura da inovação*. Lisboa: Difusão Cultural.

Leonard, H. (2013). *Blogs outrank social networks in influence*. Retrieved 09-03-2013, from http://www.businessinsider.com/blog-influence-outranks-social-networks-2013-3

Libert, B., & Spector, J. (2009). *Muitas cabeças pensam melhor: Como mobilizar o poder das multidões para o seu negócio*. Porto: Lua de Papel.

Marchand, D. (1990). Managing information quality. In Wormell (Ed.), Information quality: Definitions and dimensions. London: Taylor Graham.

Marchand, D., & Horton, F. Jr. (1986). *Infotrends: Profiting from your information resources*. Hoboken, NJ: Wiley.

Martinet, B., & Marti, Y. (1995). *A inteligência económica: Os olhos e os ouvidos da empresa*. Instituto Piaget.

McGee, J. V., & Prusak, L. (1995). *Gerenciamento estratégico da informação: Aumente a competitividade e a eficiência de sua empresa utilizando a informação como uma ferramenta estratégica*. Rio de Janeiro, Brazil: Campus.

McPherson, P. (1994). Accounting for the value of information. *Aslib Proceedings*, *46*(9), 203–215. doi:10.1108/eb051366

Miller, A. (2007). *Social tools for business use: Messages from a web 2.0 conference*. Retrieved 12-12-2012, from http://web.fumsi.com/go/article/find/3916

Miller, J., & Business Intelligence Braintrust. (2002). *O milênio da inteligência competitiva*. Porto Alegre. *The Bookman*.

Mohr, J., Sengupta, S., & Slater, S. (2010). Marketing of high-technology products and innovations (3ª ed.). Upper Saddle River, NJ: Pearson.

Mordecai, V. (2013a). 4 things social media analysis can tell you about your business. *Focal Point: Focalytic*. Retrieved 23-05-2013, from http://www.focalytic.com/focal-point/bid/291330/4-Things-Social-Media-Analysis-Can-Tell-You-About-Your-Business

Mordecai, V. (2013b). What businesses can gain from a custom social media listening tool. *Focal Point: Focalytic*. Retrieved 20-05-2013, from http://www.focalytic.com/focal-point/bid/291331/What-Businesses-Can-Gain-from-a-Custom-Social-Media-Listening-Tool

Mordecai, V. (2013c). What is competitive intelligence? *Focal Point: Focalytic*. Retrieved 14-06-2013, from http://www.focalytic.com/focal-point/bid/297577/What-Is-Competitive-Intelligence

Negroponte, N. (1995). *Being digital*. New York: Knopf.

Ojala, M. (2012, July/August). Minding your own business: Social media invades business research. *Exploring Technology & Resources for Information Professionals,* 51-53.

Orna, E. (1996). Valuing information: Problems and opportunities. In D. Best (Ed.), *The fourth resource: Information and its management*. Hampshire, UK: Aslib/Gower.

Orna, E. (1999). Practical information policies (2ª ed.). Cambridge, UK: Gower.

Penzias, A. (1989). *Ideas and information: Managing in a high-tech world*. New York: W. W. Norton.

Penzias, A. (1995). *Harmony: Business, technology & life after paperwork*. New York: Harper Collins.

Porter, M. E., & Millar, V. E. (1985). How information gives you competitive advantage. *Harvard Business Review, 63*(4), 149–160.

Prescott, J. E., & Miller, S. H. (2002). *Inteligência competitiva na prática: Técnicas e práticas bem sucedidas para conquistar mercados*. Rio de Janeiro: Campus.

Prior, V. (2006). *Competitive intelligence: An introduction*. Retrieved 06-10-2008 from http://www.freepint.com/issues/050106.htm#feature

Prior, V. (2007). *DIY detection: Competitive intelligence for SMEs*. Retrieved from http://web.freepint.com/go/features/2483

Qualman, E. (2010). *Socialnomics: Como os media sociais estão a transformar o modo como vivemos e como fazemos negócios*. Lisboa: Presença.

Rasquilha, L. (2010). *Tendências e gestão da inovação: Como aplicar as tendências na estratégia de inovação empresarial*. Lousã: Verlag Dashöfer.

Redman, T. (1996). *Data quality for the information age*. Norwood, MA: Artech House.

Revelli, C. (2000). *Inteligência estratégica na Internet: Como desenvolver eficazmente actividades de monitorização e de pesquisa nas redes*. Instituto Piaget.

Ribault, J.-M., Martinet, B., & Lebidois, D. (1995). *A gestão das tecnologias*. Lisboa: D. Quixote.

Russell, M. (2011). *Mining the social web: Analyzing data from Facebook, Twitter, LinkedIn, and other social media sites*. Sebastopol, CA: O'Reilly Media.

Rustmann, F., Jr. (2002). *CIA, Inc.: Espionage and the craft of business intelligence*. Dulles: Brassey's.

Sage, N. (2013). *How to create business value from social intelligence*. Retrieved 30-05-2013, from http://www.computerweekly.com/opinion/How-to-create-business-value-from-social-intelligence

Schaffer, N. (2011). *Maximizing LinkedIn for sales and social media marketing: An unofficial, practical guide to selling & developing B2B business on LinkedIn*. CreateSpace Independent Publishing Platform.

Scott, D. (2008). *As novas regras de marketing e relações públicas: Como usar os blogues, o podcasting, os media online e as notas informativas para chegar directamente aos consumidores*. Porto: Ideias de Ler.

Shapiro, C., & Varian, H. (1999). *Information rules: A strategic guide to the network economy*. Boston: Harvard Business School Press.

Steckerl, S. (2007). *Survival guide: Online social networking*. Retrieved 12/12/2012, from http://web.fumsi.com/go/article/use/2346

Suhr, C. (2004). A change of paradigms: looking back to the pioneer years of patent information management (1960-1990). *World Patent Information*, *26*(1), 41–43. doi:10.1016/j.wpi.2003.10.017

Surowiecki, J. (2007). *A sabedoria das multidões: Como a inteligência colectiva transforma a economia e a sociedade*. Porto: Lua de Papel.

Taborda, J. P., & Ferreira, M. D. (2002). *Competitive intelligence: Conceitos, práticas e benefícios*. Pergaminho.

Tapscott, D. (1995). *The digital economy: Promise and peril in the age of networked intelligence*. New York: McGraw-Hill.

Tapscott, D. (1999). *Creating value in the network economy*. Boston: Harvard Business School Press.

Tapscott, D., Ticoll, D., & Lowy, A. (2000). *Digital capital: Harnessing the power of business webs*. Boston: Harvard Business School Press. doi:10.1145/341836.336231

Tapscott, D., & Williams, A. (2008). *Wikinomics: A nova economia das multidões inteligentes*. Matosinhos: Quidnovi.

Trott, P. (2008). *Innovation management and new product development* (4ª ed.). Essex, UK: Prentice Hall | Financial Times.

Tsvetovat, M., & Kouznetsov, A. (2011). *Social network analysis for startups: Finding connections on the social web*. Sebastopol, CA: O'Reilly Media.

Wagner, G. (1990). The value and the quality of information: The need for a theoretical synthesis. In Wormell (Ed.), Information quality: Definitions and dimensions. London: Taylor Graham.

Ward, J., & Peppard, J. (2002). Strategic planning for information systems (3ª ed.). Chichester, UK: Wiley.

Webster, F. (2000). *Theories of the information society*. Cornwall, UK: Routledge.

Weiss, A. (2008). *If they only knew: Finding competitive intelligence from the web sites of your competitors*. Retrieved 21/01/2013, from http://web.fumsi.com/go/article/find/3355

Wilson, T. (1985). Information management. *The Electronic Library*, *3*(1), 62–66. doi:10.1108/eb044644

Wilson, T. (1987). Information for business: The business of information. *Aslib Proceedings*, *39*, 275–279. doi:10.1108/eb051066

Winkler, I. (1997). *Corporate espionage: What it is, why it's happening in your company, what you must do about it*. Rocklin. Prima Publishing.

Wormell, I. (1990). *Information quality: Definitions and dimensions*. London: Taylor Graham.

Zarrella, D. (2009). *The social media marketing book*. Sebastopol, CA: O'Reilly Media.

Zarrella, D. (2013). *The science of marketing: When to Tweet, what to post, how to blog, and other proven strategies*. Hoboken, NJ: John Wiley & Sons.

KEY TERMS AND DEFINITIONS

Business Information: Information needed by all kinds of organizations about their competitive environment to allow sound decision making, such as business growth rate and operating ratios. Some tools to gather this information can be used, like PEST analysis (information about the Political, Economical, Sociological and Technological factors that can affect the organization), and SWOT analysis (information about the Strengths, Weaknesses, Opportunities and Threats), amongst others.

Business Management: The activity of conducting all the necessary operations in order to make the organization grow, benefiting all the shareholders and stakeholders and the society in general. It involves several specialized functions like Finance, Marketing, Operations, Human Resources, Production, etc.

Competitive Intelligence: CI is the use of public sources to develop information about the competition, consumers, and market environment. It aims to monitor a firm's external environment for information relevant to its decision-making process. It involves accurately identifying your information needs, collecting relevant information, analysing it, communicating the results to the people who need it, and taking rapid and appropriate action. Traditionally, CI relied upon published company reports and other kinds of printed information. In recent years, Internet has rapidly become an extremely good source of information about the competitive environment of companies.

Information Quality: Quality information is needed to clear decision-making about what products develop, for what customers, at what cost, through which distribution channels, reducing the uncertainty that a new product/service development always brings with it. It warrants best results when competing with other organizations. To be considered of quality, information must meet several criteria such as: completeness, accessibility, accuracy, precision, objectivity, consistency, relevancy, timeliness, and understandability.

Information Value: The value attributed to information produced or acquired by organizations, entities and persons, and delivered in the form of an information product or service. Information has no implicit value in itself since it depends on its use, purpose and context. Its value is related to the results that it will allow obtaining and it's dependable on its context.

Market Trends: Trends begin by knowing the consumer's interests and needs. What's new and differentiates who wears it. In a fast moving business world it should be a competitive edge having the chance of monitoring the market trends. Market trends inform organizations about what products develop, for what customers, at what cost, through which distribution channels, reducing the uncertainty that a new product/service development always brings with it. To scan the trends of a market, understand consumer motivation and the actual preferences in the business area where companies act and compete may induce a competitive advantage.

Social Media: Online Web 2.0 tools like Wikis, Blogs, and Social Networking with a two way communication channel, allowing receiving and sharing information. Also allow the knowledge of competitor's moves and the analysis of trends from the communications exchanged in the networks of individual consumers, making it easy for companies to develop solutions according to their clients and prospects desires.

ENDNOTES

1 For a list of CI software, Cf. (http://www.thecisource.com/resources/software).

2 Cf., also, (http://trendwatching.com/).

3 Cf. Flock (http://www.flock.com/) and StumbleUpon (http://www.stumbleupon.com/).

4 In **Bold** in the original text.

5 In **Bold** and *Italic* in the original text.

6 Facebook releases information on NSA requests for user data (Guynn, 2013).

7 For information in Marketing metrics and analytics, Cf. (http://blog.eloqua.com/marketing-analytics/?utm_source=feedburner&utm_medium=email&utm_campaign=Feed%3A+ItsAllAboutRevenue+%28It%27s+All+About+Revenue%29). For calculating Return on Investment, Cf. (http://businesscenter.eloqua.com/roi-calculator/).

8 For good examples of Mash-ups, Cf. (Tapscott & Williams, 2008).

9 "Julie Doe posts (…): "I love this particular brand of soda, though I really wish they had a diet option!" Social media analysis can then add this (…) to the group of opportunities that your business can pursue" (Mordecai, 2013a).

10 See, for example: IceRocket (http://www.icerocket.com), Technorati (http://www.technorati.com), Google (http://blogsearch.google.com/blogsearch), NM Incite (http://nmincite.com), Blogger (Google-owned) (http://www.blogger.com/start), Bloglines (http://www.Bloglines.com), Feedster (http://www.feedster.com), del.icio.us (http://del.icio.us/), and Podcast Alley (http://www.podcastalley.com).

11 For a list of several news readers for Mac and Windows, Cf. RSS Info (http://blogspace.com/rss/readers) . You can subscribe to an RSS feed for each individual term, simplifying your monitoring.

12 "Wordle is a toy for generating 'word clouds' from text that you provide. The clouds give greater prominence to words that appear more frequently in the source text. You can tweak your clouds with different fonts, layouts, and color schemes. The images you create with Wordle are yours to use however you like. You can print them out, or save them to the Wordle gallery to share with your friends". Retrieved 03-11-2008 from (http://www.dailyack.com/2008/06/worlde.html).

13 Retrieved 02-11-2012 from http://www.buzzlogic.com/press/news.html?postdate=1225203064 now Twelvefold Media (http://www.twelvefold.com/splash/?postdate=1225203064).

14 Cf. (http://blog.blogpulse.com/).

Chapter 10
Improving Spatial Data Quality through Spatial ETL Processes

Elzbieta Malinowski
University of Costa Rica, Costa Rica

Sehyris Campos
University of Costa Rica, Costa Rica

ABSTRACT

The growing availability of spatial data related to different aspects makes managers at different levels of administration aware of the possibilities to enhance decision making processes through map visualization. Currently, the so-called location intelligence is identified as an important trend for the next-generation business intelligence solutions. However, before considering spatial data as "first-class citizens," users that are not experts in geo-fields (e.g., cartography, surveying) should learn about possible problems that may arise while using and producing spatial data. These problems must be solved to improve spatial data quality and to increase the benefits that this data can deliver. Unfortunately, there is still a poor connection in applying scientific solutions, international standards, or technological advances for improving spatial data quality in everyday usage of this data. In this chapter, the authors refer to different problems that may exist in handling spatial data and show several examples of how these problems can be detected and solved using spatial ETL tools. Problem detection is based on a set of control parameters derived from the international standard.

INTRODUCTION

Current advances in technology and information systems and new initiatives, e.g., creating Spatial Data Infrastructures (SDIs), open the possibility to publish and share spatial (or geographic) and conventional data among interested parties. A SDI is defined as "the technology, policies, standards, human resources, and related activities necessary to acquire, process, distribute, use, maintain, and preserve spatial data" (OMB, 2010). These spatial data repositories distributed over the Internet at national or global levels mainly represent public sector agencies that could play both roles: data

DOI: 10.4018/978-1-4666-4892-0.ch010

providers and consumers (Granell, Gould, Manso, & Bernabé, 2009; Elwood, 2008). SDIs' purpose is to serve as a foundation for an Information Society willing to use and share spatial data over the Internet that "allow nations to better address social, economic, and environmental issues" (GSDI, 2012).

SDIs and other kinds of spatial data repositories over the Internet, e.g., Google Maps, Microsoft Bing Maps, make data available to different kinds of users. This data may form part of different Business Intelligence (BI) solutions (Bédard, 2005; Intelli3, 2010; Badard & Dubé, 2009; Bimonte, Wehrle, Tchounikine, & Miquel, 2006; Di Martino, Bimonte, Berttolotto, & Ferrucci, 2009) and the so-called location intelligence is mentioned as an important trend for the next-generation BI (Mathew, 2012). Spatially-enhanced BI solutions can help improve the decisions made at the personal, local, national, or global levels, due to the fact that, as it is widely acknowledged, the presentation of data within a space helps discover patterns that otherwise would be difficult to find. For example, on a personal level, a user could determine if the land that s/he wants to buy is not close to a garbage disposal or high tension towers, or whether the area is over-populated; on a local level, municipalities could rely on this data to prepare plans for cantonal human development in order to improve living conditions and strengthen territorial planning, or business managers could evaluate the distribution of customers that generate more profit; on a national level, authorities could make better decisions to create risk prevention plans for hazardous areas (e.g., flooding, erosion, earthquake) taking into consideration population, house distribution, or road availability, or business executives could analyze performance data related to a specific business field.

Nevertheless, several issues must be addressed before considering spatial data as "first-class citizens" in the decision-making processes at different levels of management. Traditionally, spatial data was stored in a central repository in a specific format provided by software tools developed for Geographic Information Systems (GISs). This software was perceived as a standalone technology until mid-1990s and was used mainly by experts in the field, i.e., geo-specialists, e.g., geographers, cartographers, surveyors (Yeung & Hall, 2007). This limitation was imposed due to the complexity of tools that manage spatial data and the necessary specialized knowledge (geo-knowledge) required to understand the concepts related to spatial data format, as well as functions and operations. These geo-specialists were mainly in charge of digitalizing spatial data and they understood very well the particularities of spatial data and problems that may affect its quality. Furthermore, they were aware that GISs will not help them improve spatial data quality since these systems work under the assumption that data is perfect and do not provide the capabilities to establish data quality control (Delavar & Devillers, 2010). Although, spatial DBMSs (called geo-databases by geo-specialists) currently provide some controls, e.g., declarative and dynamic (triggers), that may help improve spatial data quality, the transition from the traditional storage of spatial data to a new alternative requires geo-specialists to acquire new knowledge that is not always an easy and time-efficient endeavor.

On the other hand, the technology has changed and other kinds of users with a profile that is usually unrelated to GISs are in charge of either collecting data from existing repositories or creating it from aerial photographs and satellite images (Mäkelä, 2006). As a consequence, many users and producers of spatial data are not trained in geo-fields and may not be aware of the existence and number of problems that this kind of data may have (Delavar & Devillers, 2010; Boin & Hunter, 2005; Wang & Strong, 1996). Therefore, there is a need to increase this awareness among non-expert users and look for solutions to improve spatial data quality. However, although research on spatial data quality has a 30-year history, there is generally a weak connection between academic research and everyday use of spatial data by non-expert users (Devillers et al., 2010). Many of the proposed solutions are complex in terms of statistics and modeling, which makes it difficult for typical users to understand and apply them (Devillers et al., 2010).

Furthermore, in order to ensure data quality for publishing consistent spatial data, it is necessary to establish national standards (adopted and adapted from international standards, e.g., ISO19113); however, this task demands leadership and coordination of various government authorities with long-term financial support that is not always readily available. Meanwhile, to increase stakeholders' trust in spatial data quality for making informed decisions, different techniques and tools may be applied; they are usually not well known among geo-specialists that are typically spatial data providers.

With the advent of data warehouses (DWs), extraction-transformation-loading (ETL) tools have been playing an important role to ensure that the data used for the decision-making processes is good quality data. The functionalities of these kinds of tools are constantly improving and extending, (e.g., fuzzy lookup, fuzzy grouping) and, in many cases, without the necessity of incurring to a high programming effort. However, even though research related to spatial data warehouses (SDWs) is not new, this area is not widely spread especially among the geo-specialists. Fortunately, spatial ETL tools have emerged (e.g., Safe Software, 2013; Intergraph, 2013; ESRI, 2013b; Spatialytics, 2013) independently from SDWs as a way of helping geo-specialists to work with spatial data originated from several sources that are characterized by a diversity of systems, formats, data types, or data models (Burnell & Raghavendran, 2008). These spatial ETL tools can be used by data providers or consumers, depending on the users' needs to transform spatial and conventional data. One of the goals of these transformations could be to improve spatial data quality that should be guided by some criteria, e.g., the ones established by the ISO19113 (2002) standard.

In this chapter, after revising different works related to the spatial data quality issues, we refer to difficulties that arise among geo-specialists for adopting new technologies that could help improve spatial data quality and provide some alternatives for analyzing data by non-expert users. Next, we refer to the need of extending BI solutions by incorporating spatial data. Then, we specify control parameters for spatial data quality based on the international standard and provide some examples of the spatial data available in Costa Rica that violate these parameters. In the next section, based on the open ETL software, we demonstrate how different spatial data quality problems can be tackled or removed. Finally, we discuss possible future work in the field and present conclusions.

BACKGROUND

Traditional BI solutions were developed for supporting decision-making processes using different kinds of data representation (e.g., tabular, graphs) and analysis tools. However, these solutions seldom included maps or geographic data due to high cost in spatial data acquisition and lack of tools that did not require specialized knowledge related to GISs for manipulating and analyzing spatial data. Fortunately, the situation has changed and currently users are given the possibility to benefit from spatial data (e.g., Integeo, 2013; GeoMe, 2013; WebiGeo, 2013; Oracle, 2011; Bing Maps, 2013; Pentaho, 2013).

Spatial data can be represented in two complementary ways according to application needs (Worboys & Duckham, 2004; Malinowski & Zimányi, 2009): the object-based approach decomposes space into identifiable objects describing their shapes. For example, the line can be used to describe a river or surface to represent a district. Another approach, called field-based, is used to represent phenomena that vary over space, associating a value to each point on a relevant space. Typical examples include vegetation, temperature, or pollution levels. In this chapter, we refer to the object-based representation.

A spatial object consists of two components: the descriptive component and the spatial component. The former includes conventional attributes describing an object (e.g., the name of a district, its population, and number of dwellings). The latter represents the geometry, which can be of various spatial data types used for different purposes: points for representing specific places (e.g., clinics or stores), lines for indicating linear extensions of objects (e.g., rivers or roads), or surfaces for modeling two-dimensional objects (e.g., administrative division of a country or representation of school districts).The combination of these spatial data types can represent more complex spatial objects, e.g., a road network through a set of lines (Malinowski & Zimányi, 2009). In addition, spatial objects must be associated with a spatial reference system (SRS) that defines parameters necessary for the identification and description of any point in a space and its corresponding representation in a map. In many occasions, SRS is expressed as codes using, e.g., European Petroleum Survey Group (EPSG) specification (EPSG, 2013). Furthermore, a particular characteristic when using spatial objects is to refer to topological relationships (Clementini & Di Felice, 1996). They describe how spatial values relate to each other, e.g., to test whether a river crosses a state or whether the airport is within the city limits.

Traditionally, data stored in GISs uses hybrid architecture of separate repositories for spatial and conventional data. Although this approach delivers much functionality for spatial data analysis, it lacks basic features for data integrity and control to prevent users from having inconsistent data. In looking for solutions to improve spatial data quality different initiatives have been undertaken from scientific communities, as well as from government and industry (e.g., Dassonville, 1999; Devillers, Gervais, Bédard, & Jeansoulin, 2002; Devillers, Bédard, Jeansoulin, & Moulin, 2007; Vasseur, Devillers, & Jeansoulin, 2003; Veregin, 1999). Spatial data quality research has a 30-year long tradition (Devillers et al., 2010) and it went through different phases. From the early stage, it was considered a part of the Geographic Information Science, providing guidance and elements to evaluate data quality for different types of spatial data representation, mainly using the existing methods in geo-science, e.g., cartography, geodesy, surveying, hydrography, and photogrammetry (Devillers et al., 2010). Then, the establishment of international standards provided users some general criteria for assessing spatial data quality. The standardization process was accelerated with the new initiatives of building SDIs (Granell et al., 2009; Jakobsson & Tsoulos, 2007; Sanderson, Ramage, & Van Linden, 2009; Smits et al., 2002). The possibility to obtain spatial data from different data providers over the Internet increases awareness about the importance of spatial data quality (Mäkelä, 2006; Larrivée, Bédard, Gervais, & Roy, 2011) and international organizations feel compelled to develop more standards related to GISs and Geomatics in order to facilitate data discovery and interchange.

The ISO Technical Committee (TC) 211, an international standards organization, and the Open Geospatial Consortium (OGC, formerly known as Open GIS Consortium), an industry consortium, are the main players in the area of standardization and unification of concepts related to geographical data. TC211 standards are presented as the ISO19100 series and take into account a wide variety of aspects, e.g., reference model, conceptual schema language, metadata, positioning services, web servers and services, among others. Three of these standards apply to spatial data quality:

1. ISO19113 (2002) establishes a set of principles for describing and reporting the quality of geographic information;
2. ISO19114 (2003) specifies a set of procedures for evaluating and reporting the quality of geographic information; and

3. ISO19138 (2006) extends ISO19113 to define a set of data quality measures.

However, the establishment of standards cannot guarantee its correct application and the existing research achievements do not necessarily equate to improvements in spatial data quality, due to the following reasons (Devillers et al., 2010), among others:

1. Spatial data producers sometimes lack the necessary knowledge and practice to provide spatial data with good quality;
2. Research in spatial data quality introduces concepts and techniques that are complex and difficult to understand by typical users;
3. Lack of approaches for solving real problems.

Spatial data quality can also be seen as a relative concept depending on user expectations (Olsen, 2003; ISO19113, 2002), e.g., a detailed representation of district borders is required for analyzing its vicinity or rivers passing through, but may not be crucial to represent population. In particular, data accuracy must be considered carefully to ensure that the spatial data values for an object are correct and represented in an unambiguous form (Olsen, 2003). Different techniques can be applied to find inaccurate data: re-verification and analytical techniques. Re-verification means checking every value in the original source, i.e., checking errors in data recollections. This is not always possible since data may be found on the Internet, available in SDIs or other kinds of repositories. Also, stakeholders may not count on the necessary geo-knowledge to perform this re-verification process, which takes a long time to complete. Analytical techniques involve the use of software with the skills of data or business analysts (Olsen, 2003). One of the possibilities is to use spatially enabled DWs and ETL processes.

SDWs can be implemented using currently available DBMSs that provide spatial extensions to their object-relational engines, e.g., PostgreSQL/PostGIS, MySQL, Oracle, or SQL Server, among others. Since spatial data can be considered as other types of data, different declarative and dynamic (triggers) controls can be implemented to ensure that inserted data satisfies established data quality criteria; this could not be done in earlier GISs. Furthermore, to clean, transform, and integrate data before loading it into SDWs or other repositories, ETL tools may be applied. Currently, these ETL tools expand their functionalities through the inclusion of spatial data and operations (e.g., Safe Software, 2013; Intergraph, 2013; ESRI, 2013b; Spatialytics, 2013).

SPATIAL DATA QUALITY AND BUSINESS INTELLIGENCE

Systems that operate over data include three different roles (Wang, Ziad & Lee, 2002):

1. Data collectors that create, collect, or supply data;
2. Data custodians that design, develop, or maintain the data and system infrastructure;
3. Data consumers that use the data in their work, e.g., to make decisions.

If data collectors are not aware of data quality and data custodians are not familiar with the methods to improve quality, the last element of the chain, i.e., data consumers, obtain incorrect or deficient data that can be harmful for the company/organization whether this data is operational or decisional (Talhofer, Hofmann, Hošková – Mayerová, & Kubícek, 2011). In particular, spatial data usage grows faster than the knowledge generated about its features and quality-related issues. Spatial data is usually retrieved from external sources available on the Internet, including SDI repositories, where data governance initiatives that ensure its high quality may be absent. As a consequence, there is a need to increase awareness of non-expert users about possible problems that may arise while using spatial data, existing standards that can guide them to improve spatial data quality and that can form part of processes for spatial data governance, and to get informed about different technological solutions that may help enhance spatial data quality.

Divergence of Solutions from Geo-Specialists and Informatics

Traditional hybrid architecture with the separation of spatial and conventional data can be described using as an example the widely-spread format called shape file (ESRI, 1998). It represents a theme (e.g., distribution of districts, clinics, cities) and includes several files, one of which is a binary representation of geometry and another one is a Dbase II or Access format for storing conventional data. Most GIS software is capable of using this modality of storage and its representation in GIS software is called a layer. GISs allow users to overlay layers in order to understand the relationships that may exist among geographic phenomena (e.g., precipitation and vegetation), to manage better cantonal development (e.g., considering house and road distributions), improve health systems (e.g., taking into account population distribution and locations of clinics and hospitals), among others. For example, Figure 1 shows the overlay of four layers related to clinics and hotels (triangles), fire risk zones (polygons), as well as fire stations (points) in Costa Rica. The representation of the layers shows many clwinics and hotels located in the risk zones and sometimes not enough fire stations to attend possible emergencies.

Nevertheless, this hybrid architecture has several inconveniences. For example, since each shape file is created by the geo-specialist interested in the theme, its quality depends on the level of producer awareness about different concepts related to data quality. By using different shape files available in Costa Rica, we found problems with unique identifiers, null or incorrect values, among others (more details will be given in the next section). Furthermore, since shape files are created separately, there is no control over the same data included in different shape files, e.g., codes and names for provinces are present in many files. This is similar to the situation we have had in past times before we could apply normalization principles to database design and referential integrity constraints to control data consistency.

Fortunately, the situation has changed with the addition of spatial features to the relational (in fact, the object-relational) DBMSs. These sys-

Figure 1. An example of overlaying four layers (clinics, hospitals, fire risk zones, and fire stations)

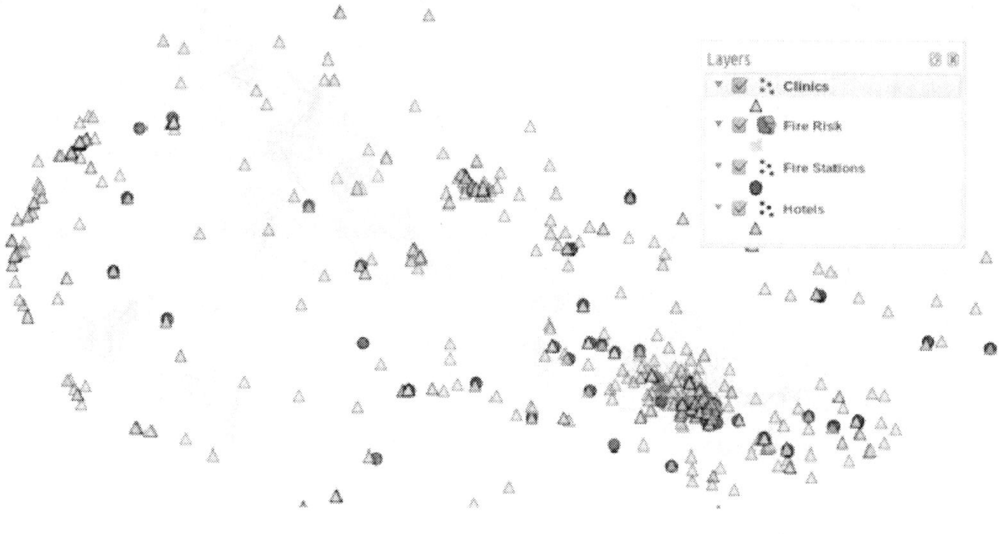

tems allow having a huge volume of conventional (e.g., string, numeric) and non-conventional (e.g., geometric, images) data in one repository. Moreover, they provide new features related to spatial data handling, e.g., spatial indexes, spatial functions and operations, and well-known elements, e.g., declarative integrity constraints, triggers. Therefore, they provide more functionality than traditional GISs for controlling spatial data quality. However, spatial DBMSs (SDBMSs) are not always considered as a storage alternative due to the lack of adequate training of geo-specialists in handling database concepts and the shortage of computer science specialists with knowledge of spatial data features. Furthermore, most of the projects related to spatial data require having knowledge of geo-specialists and they are usually more familiar with GISs than SDBMSs, choosing the former as a storage platform for applications. This situation is slowly changing, due to the fact that geo-specialists feel pressured to learn more about spatial database features and characteristics because of the increasing popularity of geo-databases (ESRI, 2012b) that use SDBMSs as storage.

The separation of geo- and informatics-specialists is also clear not only in a storage alternative, but also in other kinds of tools, e.g., spatial ETL, spatial OLAP, or spatial data mining. For example, spatial ETL facilitates the processes of data transformation and integration without making a significant programming effort and allowing automatic execution instead of manual revisions and corrections. Spatial OLAP replaces layers by hierarchies giving the possibility to aggregate data for a higher hierarchy level (e.g., provinces) using data from a lower hierarchy level (e.g., counties) that cannot be done in traditional GISs. Finally, spatial data mining allows users to discover patterns in large amounts of spatial and conventional data that may be difficult to find using traditional GIS techniques.

Necessity to Extend BI Solutions with Spatial Data

Geo-specialists in many occasions possess the tacit knowledge that allows them to automatically use spatial data, combine it, and explore it in a way that helps them find the necessary information for solving a problem. The effective transfer of this knowledge is not an easy task (Goffin & Koners, 2011) since it is based on a different mental model that perceives the spatial extension of objects and understands the layering principles when different aspects must be considered together (Goodchild, 2010). Usually this process is accompanied with GISs.

GISs offer a large variety of analysis tools (ESRI, 2012a); however, they usually are complex and suitable for specialists in a particular geo-field. For example, in Costa Rica a new system for land property rights registration and administration that will provide data to municipalities requires 165-hour training sessions for using it and only geo-specialists are taken into consideration (UE, 2012). This kind of systems raises concerns by non-expert users (mainly in charge of decision making) that spatial data requires a high level of expertise and many hours of training. Therefore, although GIS tools and applications meet the expectations of different types of geo-specialists, they represent a challenge for other specialists. This is clearly in contrast with the global tendency that the complexity of tools and systems should be hidden from non-expert users allowing them to be confident in looking for new data, convert it into new knowledge, and use it effectively for solving the issues or problems at hand. Additionally, GISs present information at a detailed level and, given the increasing amount of data, the task of analyzing large volumes of data to convert into information becomes difficult. Therefore, non-expert users require different possibilities of analysis.

The new tendency to include spatial data in BI solutions has been widely spread (Bédard, 2005; Intelli3, 2010; Badard & Dubé, 2009; Bimonte et al., 2006; Di Martino et al., 2009; Mathew, 2012). Spatial data can be incorporated in a dynamic spreadsheet-like environment that allows users to better visualize different indicators and look for some patterns that are easier to find in a space than trying to find them in a table or graph. However, even though companies or organizations have their own conventional data, acquisition of spatial data is a very costly and time-consuming effort. Therefore, in many cases publically available data is used. As we mentioned before, these decision makers may not be aware of spatial data quality and feel uncomfortable when they have to explain wrong decisions due to poor data quality (Devillers et al., 2010). Therefore, some mechanism and tools must be established and used to verify and correct (if any and if possible) spatial data quality.

Control Parameters for Spatial Data Quality and Issues with Shape Files

Spatial data quality can be seen from two points of view: internal quality (Aalders & Morrison, 1998; Aalders, 1999; Dassonville, 1999) measured considering its internal characteristics (e.g., data acquisition technologies, data model and storage) and external quality called the "fitness for use" (Jakobson & Tsoulos, 2007; Veregin, 1999; Chrisman, 1983) that reflects how well data meets users' needs. The information about internal data quality should be communicated in metadata files transmitted together with datasets by data producers (Devillers et al., 2007). However, this is not always the case since generating metadata is a time-consuming task and the producers not always take the responsibility to do it. Furthermore, it has been demonstrated that metadata has limited impact on a user's ability to understand the possible uses of data (Devillers et al., 2010; Boin & Hunter, 2005) due to its incompleteness or high level of complexity. On the other hand, internal data quality should be considered before the "fitness for use" is evaluated. Even though, several solutions can be provided to establish criteria and techniques for improving internal spatial data quality, in this section, we refer to the ISO19113 (2002) standard and also include some recommendations from other authors (Gervais, Bédard, Levesque, Bernier, & Devillers, 2010; Batini & Scannapieca, 2006; Delavar & Devillers, 2010). We simplify the explanation in order to facilitate the understanding by non-expert users of the principles established by the standard. We briefly show the evaluation criteria and some examples of poor spatial data quality provided by shape files in comparison to these criteria:

- **Completeness:** Refers to how well the available data is sufficient and necessary for a specific task. It is characterized by *commission* that specifies if the dataset includes unnecessary attributes or relationships and *omission* that specifies if some important attributes or relationships are missing:
    - Many times shape files do not fulfill the completeness criterion since they usually include the conventional data according to the particular interest of their creators and application domains. For example, the district shape file contains the attributes that refer to districts (name or code), but also includes the data related to codes and names for provinces (the commission principle). Furthermore, the district shape file also contains the numbers that show the population and dwellings in a specific district in a specific time. However, this data changes over time, and consequently should not be a part of a specific shape file (the commission principle). An additional relationship that indicates changes in

districts in different periods of time is missing (the omission principle). In addition, since the main purpose of shape files is to present the geometry of objects and their characteristics, some of the data that describes this geometry is missing (omission principle), e.g., area, number of islands, perimeter. Even though this data can be derived from the geometry, it may be unavailable for non-expert users that do not count on required geo-knowledge;

- **Logical Consistency:** Defines the degree of adherence to rules related to the data structure, attributes, and relationships. It takes into consideration several sub-elements referring to conceptual, domain, format, and topological consistencies:
  - **Conceptual Consistency:** Determines the accuracy of the conceptual schema. However, usually the datasets (in our case, the shape files) are implemented without following the principles established for the database design, leading to the data inconsistency problem. As an example, we use the shape file that represents Costa Rican districts. It includes 849 records for representing 475 districts, 45 of which are stored in more than one record (as many districts are formed by islands) and each district record includes only a part of the geometry. In these repeated records only the geometry is different, while conventional data, e.g., district population, number of dwellings, etc. are repeated. If the user wants to calculate the total population of Costa Rica considering the population of all districts as a starting point, s/he will obtain as a result 7 million in the year 2000, even though the real population was 3.8 million. Furthermore, other typical database controls are also missing, e.g., null values, referential integrity constraints, value range, among others. For example, the shape file representing rivers includes 31468 records and 15730 do not have names, which do not allow users to recognize them. The situation gets more complicated when several shape files contain data related to the same objects, as previously mentioned. This data repetition cannot be controlled as is usually the case for databases, since the changes in the same attribute in one shape file are not reflected in other shape files;
  - **Domain Consistency:** Can be defined as how well the values of the dataset represent the real values of the domain. For example, the name of a district should be within the expected values of district names. However, some shape files may not conform to this principle, e.g., including a name of an inexistent region or a value "No name" for rivers;
  - **Format Consistency:** Verifies if the data is represented according to the required physical structure. For example, the coordinates of some geometries specified in a shape file representing provinces are defined counterclockwise and others are expressed clockwise; therefore, some SDBMSs interpret counterclockwise orientation as holes, e.g., representing lakes within a land. This feature is known as ring orientation and if the geometries that represent spatial objects of interest (e.g., provinces) are defined with different orientations, some calculations and analysis can

generate incorrect results, e.g., the calculation of an area does not take holes into consideration. Also, provinces are defined by several linear segments that form a border; however, if some segments intersect, SDBMSs interpret the geometry as invalid;

- ◦ **Topological Consistency:** Determines correctness of topological characteristics of a dataset, e.g., how big should the "gaps" be between lines in order to consider them as separate lines. For example, when some lines represent rivers feeding other rivers, the touches topological relationship should be satisfied. However, the implementers can establish a tolerance degree so large that it affects the level of precision, and defines a feeding river as a river that is close enough to another river in terms of tolerance, but in reality these two rivers may not be related to each other directly. The topological consistency can be also enforced by establishing rules for spatial data representation, e.g., if the perimeter of a polygon is less than a specific value, the geometry can be stored as a point instead of a polygon;
- **Positional Accuracy:** Refers to the position of spatial objects and their closeness to the expected or true values, as well as an object's position relative to other spatial objects. The positional accuracy depends on the SRSs applied to represent objects on Earth. Therefore, this aspect is important to consider before other elements are revised. For example, computer science students taking a database course without knowledge related to spatial data and understanding of the effect of using different SRSs could not comprehend the reasons that explain why one layer representing the same country does not respect the positions of the same cities when overlapping with another layer. Evaluating the closeness of object coordinates to their real values is not an easy task; in many cases, it requires the presence of geo-specialists. On the other hand, the task of revising the relationships between different spatial objects can be checked through topological relationships. In many occasions, shape files may not fulfill this requirement since the topological relationships among spatial objects included in different shape files is not considered while creating these files. For example, in Costa Rica several districts were defined outside the boundaries of their corresponding counties or some clinics outside the Costa Rican territory;
- **Temporal Accuracy:** Also known as temporal consistency (Batini & Scannapieca, 2006), ensures the validity of the data with respect to time. This is closely related to the frequency of data changing in time and corresponding updates applied to older versions of spatial data. This element refers to spatial, as well as conventional data, and it is closely related to the next criterion of thematic accuracy. For example, the minimum level of administrative distribution in Costa Rica is represented by districts. However, when 10,000 inhabitants or more request the creation of a new district, a positive answer from the government changes the current administrative division. As a consequence, Costa Rica went from 467 districts in 2004 to 470 in 2008, and 475 districts in 2012. To ensure an adequate analysis, the temporal accuracy must be fulfilled, i.e., indicating the time frame when spatial data is valid or the sequences of time frames with their corresponding spatial representations;
- **Thematic Accuracy:** Refers to the validity of conventional data according to spatial data. It is closely related with the previous

criterion especially when the spatial objects change. For example, if a new district is formed, the corresponding shape file must include a new codification, as well as relate to updated populations and other kinds of conventional data. Furthermore, many shape files do not satisfy the requirement of thematic accuracy by inclusion of null values in object names (river names) or incorrect values (region names). Another example related to thematic accuracy is the population or number of dwellings of provinces and counties. The shape files representing these spatial objects include the mentioned numerical values. However, even though there is a strong hierarchical relationship with total inclusion of counties within its corresponding province, the sum of the population of the counties does not equal the population of the corresponding province.

Spatial Data Governance and BI Practice

Current problems with spatial data, especially represented as shape files, are due to the lack of spatial data governance initiatives in institutions responsible for generating and promoting the usage of spatial data. Many issues may influence this situation, among others:

1. The lack of knowledge about existing international standards does not allow responsible actors to establish a clear policy for data quality control;
2. The inability to assess profits adequately when using spatial data hampers the expansion of its usage;
3. The regulation of their accessibility and security defers its visibility to other users;
4. The limited knowledge of mechanisms for delivering spatial data over the Internet among geo-specialists delays its availability and makes the data outdated.

As a result, many public institutions generate their own spatial data, making the same or similar mistakes in spatial data representations and, therefore, unnecessarily wasting public money. The problem gets even more complex when SDIs are built without governmental leadership and clear directions about which aspects are important to consider for spatial data governance at the national level. For example, in Costa Rica many shape files generated by public institutions lack even an element as simple as metadata describing the origin and the producer of spatial data.

As a consequence, users at different administration levels may not consider spatial data as "first-class citizens" in their decision-making processes. These users, mainly from public sectors, do not have the resources and knowledge to overcome the sometimes complex problems of data integration and improvements in data quality. For example, in Costa Rica although many institutions produce spatial data that represents territory, this data is seldom used to support the decision processes because of a high level of distrust in terms of their quality, a lack of preparation to use it effectively, and a shortage in tools that do not require specialized geo-knowledge. These problems lead to a situation of total lack of, for example, urban planning where residential areas are merged with universities, restaurants, or shopping centers, because building permits or lending does not include the spatial analysis for types of objects exiting in the same area.

Solutions and Recommendations

Improvement in data quality can be achieved in different ways by using manual or automatic methods (ISO19114, 2003). The process of evaluating (and if possible improving) consists of a sequence of steps applied to static or dynamic (constantly changing) dataset (Pradinho et al., 2011). In this chapter, we describe a solution that uses the capability of the existing spatial ETL tools to develop processes that help improve quality in a static spatial dataset. We based our approach on the experience gained in implementing a prototype project that integrates a variety of shape files (and also conventional data) and loaded them into a SDW. This prototype was developed to show stakeholders at different levels of administration the possibility to incorporate spatial data into a BI platform to support decision-making processes. We guide our process of cleaning, transformation, and integration by complying with the criteria established in ISO1913 and explained in the previous section. Even though another standard (ISO19138, 2006) presents a set of data quality measures that can be used for quantitative evaluation of data quality based on the elements from ISO 19113, we do not include this evaluation due to its complexity and extension and because our goal is not a quantitative evaluation of a specific spatial dataset; instead, we focus on a qualitative evaluation and apply the indirect method (ISO19114, 2003) that allows us to estimate spatial data quality using information about the data.

Creation of a Spatial Data Warehouse

Before executing the spatial ETL processes, we need to create a repository for data storage. We implemented a SDW based on a multidimensional design principle (Malinowski & Zimányi, 2009) and used the snowflake schema as an implementation structure. We chose the multidimensional model since it always contains the time dimension facilitating the representation of changes in time that may occur to objects, e.g., when a new district is created. In this way, we were able to fulfill the temporal accuracy criterion (ISO19113, 2002) as explained before.

Furthermore, we also followed the common database principle of storing only one table that represents the object of interest with its corresponding attributes, e.g., storing districts and their characteristics in one table. This helps us improve a completeness criterion, eliminating the unnecessary attributes (the commission problem) and including others (the omission issue), as well as the conceptual consistency criterion (ISO19113, 2002). The last criterion was also enforced using the declarative control for defining different constraints, which was possible thanks to an object-relational DBMS with spatial extension (PostgreSQL/PostGIS) that we employed for implementation. For example, we defined *primary key constraint* to avoid inconsistencies, e.g., repeating the district code value and having rivers with no name, among others. In addition, we applied the *check constraint* for revising the geometry type (e.g., for point, line, or polygon) of the spatial objects before their insertions. The *referential integrity constraint* facilitates the control of data inconsistency, opening up the possibility of referencing objects instead of repeating them as was done for shape files.

The implemented tables with the above-mentioned constraints ensure that only data that fulfill them can be inserted, i.e., protect non-expert users from introducing errors as the ones in shape files. In order to insert data from available shape files that control the quality parameters described in previous sections, different ETL processes were developed.

Spatial ETL

The spatial ETL processes were implemented in GeoKettle (Spatialytics, 2013). It provides a graphical user interface allowing the specification of jobs and transformations. The jobs control the flow, i.e., execution order of the transformations (or failure management) during the execution process. The transformations are defined as a set of operations that need to be applied for the extracted data. Our ETL processes can be divided into four groups:

- **Data pre-processing:** Considers the semantic inconsistencies, as well as problems of individual records, such as missing values, null values, or outliers, among others. Several operations are used to achieve it. *Select Values* allows the implementer to select, rename, or discard attributes of working dataset, for example, to discard attributes representing the population or number of dwellings in the district shape file. Another operation, *Filter rows,* facilitates the creation of a subset of records based on some conditions; this operation can evaluate topological relationships, (e.g., intersects, contains, crosses) to determine, for example, whether a clinic is within the Costa Rican territory;
- **Data sorting:** Helps in the process of data grouping and can be performed with the *Sort rows* operation that sorts the records of a dataset based on a set of fields, specifying a sorting order (ascending or descending);
- **Data clustering or grouping:** Facilitates the formation of groups based on values of the indicated attribute(s). The *Group by* operation allows implementers to calculate aggregated values over a defined set of attributes, providing conventional aggregation functions, e.g., sum, average, minimum, maximum, as well as spatial aggregation functions, e.g., spatial union that transforms simple geometry (e.g., polygon representing a province) in a complex, aggregated geometry (e.g., multipolygon for representing a country);
- **Data transformation:** Considers data changes applied to both conventional and spatial data. For example, the *Set SRS* operation provides the ability to set a SRS on spatial attributes and allows the correct interpretation of geometry's definition. The user can select the SRS from a list of EPSG codes available or specify other SRS formats. The *Calculator* operation supports some basic operations that can be applied to spatial data (e.g., area, distance, or centroid), as well as functions for conventional data (e.g., upper/lower case, arithmetical or date operations). *Scripting* operations allow specifying codes, e.g., using the *JavaScript* component, for performing more specialized transformations based on available functions applied to different data types, including spatial data. However, some transformations on spatial data require geo-knowledge to use and write the appropriate code.

Examples of Controlling Spatial Data Quality through Spatial ETL Processes

To illustrate our approach, we show and describe some spatial ETL processes that we developed for improving spatial data quality.

The example of the ETL process shown in Figure 2 solves some problems related to positional accuracy, logical consistency, temporal accuracy, and completeness for the district shape file. The *"Set SRS"* component sets the SRS (in this case to the value WGS84, accepted worldwide and required by law in Costa Rica since 2007) on the geometry of a district to ensure the adequate interpretation of the coordinates that represent district borders (satisfying positional accuracy). The *filter* component ("District Code is valid?" in the figure) helps identify the records with an invalid district code (not satisfying the domain consistency criterion), which are stored in a temporary table for a later review with the help of a geo-specialist. The *select values* component ("Delete unused values" in Figure 2) facilitates the elimination of attributes (e.g., population or

Figure 2. ETL process applied to a district layer

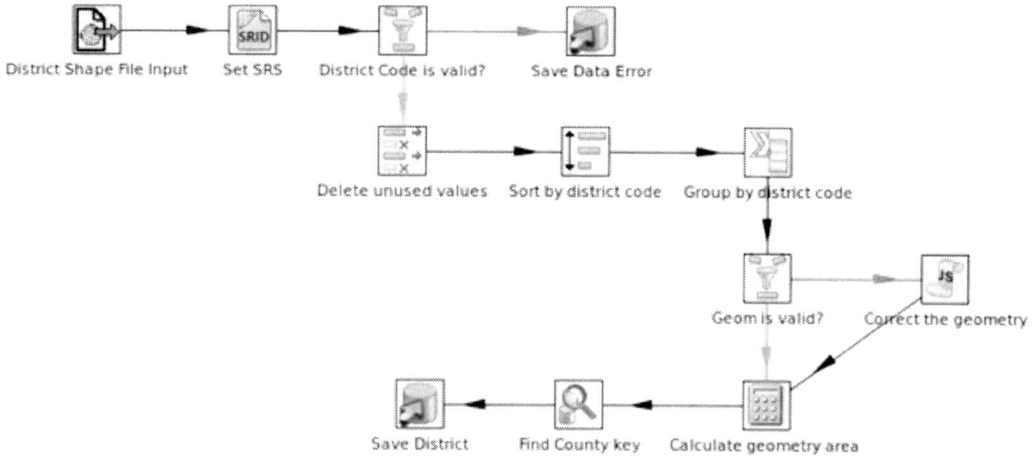

number of dwellings) that are time-dependent (considering the temporal accuracy and thematic accuracy) and unnecessary (fulfilling completeness with commission problem). If required, time-dependent attributes can later be used in the fact table as measures, e.g., thus helping us to represent changes in population in different periods of time for the same district. In this way, the temporal accuracy is satisfied since every time when the population or the number of dwellings change, a new record indicating these new values assigned to the corresponding district in specific time is inserted in the fact table.

The following step consists of improving conceptual consistency and eliminating the problem of record repetition without losing correct spatial representation of districts. To achieve this, the districts are sorted and grouped according to district code value ("Sort by district code" and "Group by district code" in Figure 2). The sort operation is required since the grouping operation only works on a sorted input. Then, the corresponding geometries are joined together by a spatial union operator; the result of this step is only one record per district with one attribute representing spatial extension of a district.

However, some geometries (identified through the "Geom is valid?" component in the figure) do not meet the criterion of format consistency because they represent non-simple geometries, having self-intersections in their definition. This problem can be solved (the "Correct the geometry" component in Figure 2) through the spatial operation known as *buffer.* The details of this step are shown in Figure 3, indicating that the *buffer* operation is applied twice with positive and negative values of a distance (0.00001 and -0.00001). This re-creates the geometry with a smaller amount of points and solves the previously mentioned problem.

Finally, before storing district data in the SDW, we perform other steps. First, we calculate the district's area (the "Calculate geometry area" component) to add more relevant data describing spatial property (the completeness criterion). Then, through the *lookup* component, we find the county key for each district (the "Find County key" component), ensuring the referential integrity constraints (conceptual consistency criterion).

An example of revising the positional accuracy through the ETL process is presented in Figure 4. We use two shape files: one to represent bank agencies and another one for districts that we already included as a table in a DBMS. As explained in the previous section, the coordinates of the bank agency are not always within spatial extension of

Figure 3. Details of buffer operation

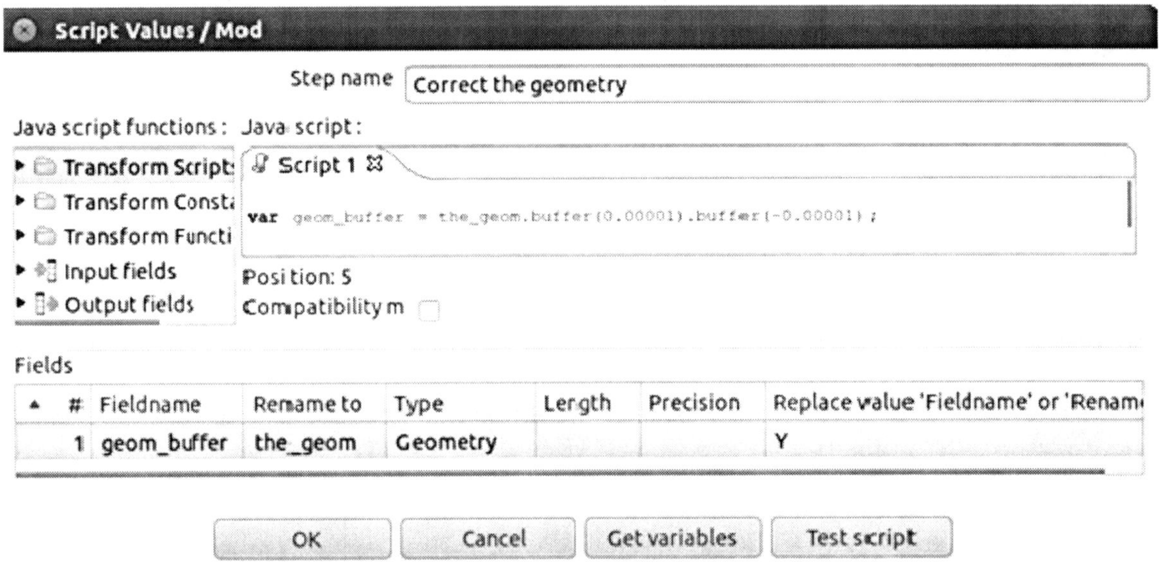

Figure 4. Verifications applied to the bank agencies layer

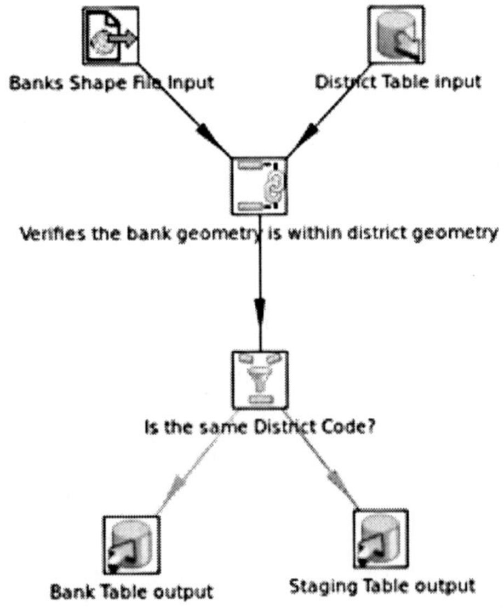

a district indicated by the name included in the corresponding attribute of the bank agency shape file. Therefore, before inserting data, the validation process is established. As shown in Figure 4, using the *within* topological relationship we retrieve the name of the district that contains the coordinate of the bank agencies. Then, through the *filter* component ("Is the same District Code?") the problematic records are separated and stored in a temporary table (the "Staging Table output" component) for later review with the help of a geo-specialist to decide whether to correct the coordinates of a bank agency or change the district name.

One interesting case refers to the shape file of rivers. Of 31468 records, 15730 have no name (null, empty, or "No Name" value). However, these rivers correspond to incoming flows into a main river and they should be recognizable. This situation violates the logical consistency, as well as thematic accuracy. In order to solve these problems and avoid the absence of names, we assigned a name for those rivers that interact (through *touches* topological relationship) with other river that has a valid name assigned. This process consists of two phases as shown in Figures 5a) and b).

The *trim* operation ("Trim the river name" in Figure 5a) removes the whitespace from the start and end of a river's name to facilitate the identification of null or empty strings in river names.

Figure 5. Cleaning of river layer: a) selection of valid name; and b) assigning valid name

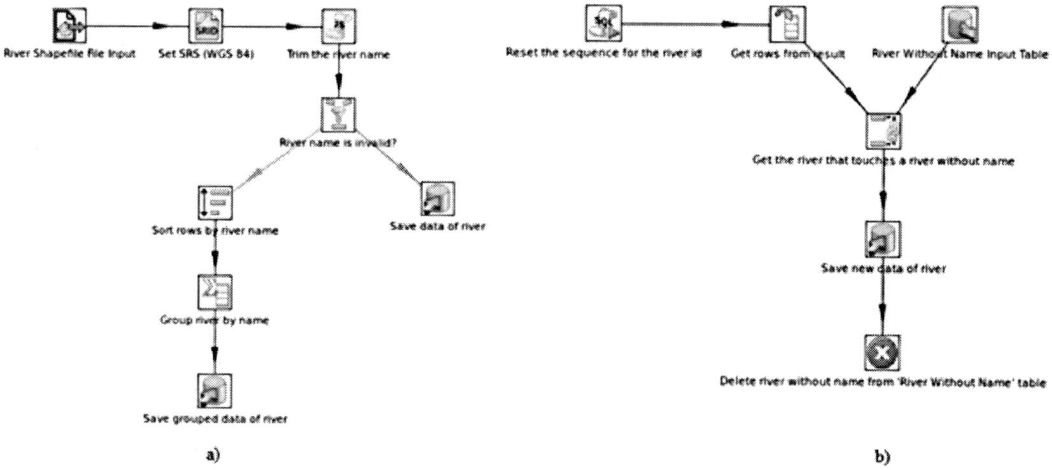

Then, through the *filter* component ("River name is invalid" in the figure) the rivers with no name are separated and stored into a temporal table ("Save data of river") to be processed later. In contrast, the rivers with a valid name are grouped by joining the corresponding geometries and are stored ("Group river by name" and "Save group data river" components, respectively).

Figure 5b) shows the processing tasks for rivers with no name. We identify the confluence points among rivers with and without names considering their adjacency through the *touches* topological relationship (the "Get the river that touches a river without name" component in the figure). Then, we create a new name as the concatenation of the known river name and a consecutive numeric attribute to identify the derived rivers. Finally, the rivers are stored in the SDW and deleted from the temporary table ("Save new data of river" and "Delete river without name" components, respectively). These transformations are repeated until all rivers have assigned names or there are no more rivers that fulfill the *touches* topological relationship. This process yields several benefits, including the improvement of the data quality (conceptual and domain consistency, thematic accuracy), as well as the establishment of the hierarchy among rivers, clearly showing feeding schema. Furthermore, another benefit is also achieved: improvement of the query performance for finding related rivers since there is no need to employ the expensive operation with a topological relationship; instead, the conventional join operation based on primary and foreign keys can be employed.

Spatial BI with Improved Data

The improvement in spatial data quality allows users to look for different solutions in analyzing spatial data, not only based on GISs. For example, spatial OLAP tools provide a spreadsheet like environment extended with maps that allow dynamic data manipulation and data aggregations. These kinds of applications are more suitable for non-expert users and may encourage them to undertake the decision-making process using spatial and conventional data.

FUTURE RESEARCH DIRECTIONS

Management of spatial data in BI solutions is a relatively new field. Therefore, many different research directions can be taken. For example, with respect to the ETL processes, considerations may be given to the aspects of optimization, parameterization, better adaption to existing SDBMSs, and extension of functionalities. Research related to optimization of conventional ETL processes can provide some insight (e.g., Simitsis, Vassiliadis, & Sellis, 2005; Albrecht & Naumann, 2008; Li, 2010). Parameterization could ensure the design and implementation of the ETL processes that consider the characteristics of different destination systems. For example, by using the same shape file, we found that SDBMSs differ in criteria to check the validity of a geometry. There are already existing solutions for transforming invalid geometry into a valid one and they can be included as a component of the ETL tool without forcing users to have knowledge about buffering, inverting the specification order for coordinates, or self-intersection lines as explained in the previous section (Oosterom, Quak, & Tijssen, 2005). In addition, existing tools for spatial ETL processes in general provide a graphical user interface and components that are easy to use. However, in some cases, it is necessary to include Java code to perform some tasks. To facilitate the use of these tools by users with no expertise in programming, more graphical components should be implemented. Furthermore, some additional components based on standardization criteria could form part of ETL solutions to increase users' awareness about spatial data quality and to contribute to its improvement, at least to some degree. It is also important to consider that spatial data transformations may introduce new data quality problems. This aspect should be carefully analyzed and some control mechanisms should be proposed.

Another area of research is related to the quality of spatial data. Data quality is one of the most important challenges that developing countries should overcome to ensure that decisions are made based on data that represents real situations (Malinowski, 2012). However, in Costa Rica and in other developing countries, procedures and formats for data publications and exchange are not well established. Publically available data needs extensive effort and specialized knowledge to improve its quality in order to support the decision-making processes at different levels of administration. In many occasions, the existing solutions are too complex (Devillers et al., 2010) for application by the users that are in charge of publishing data, some of the proposed solutions do not apply to the specificities of the country, and international standards need government support and leadership in order to be adopted and applied. Therefore, there is need, especially for developing countries, to propose and implement some standards considering particularities of that country and also ensuring the integration with international communities. These specifications should present in a clear and concise way the issues and solutions for improving spatial data quality. Gray (2010) indicates the 17 reasons for publishing spatial data online using OGC standard interfaces and ISO standard metadata. These reasons serve as a base for an extension of criteria about spatial data quality (Xia, 2012). However, more research and analysis should be done before accepting these criteria.

Many of the issues that require future research are described in Devillers et al. (2010) reflecting the results of 30 years of academic research in the field of spatial data quality. The failures and opportunities are the directions that should be taken to improve the existing situation. For example, the clear separation of academic community and practitioners must be solved by providing useful solutions and helping users from the non-academic world. Some practical, issue-oriented initiatives are needed to fulfill this gap and promote different alternatives among practitioners. In this way, user awareness about spatial data quality can be improved, especially among those who are unfamiliar with spatial data and need to incorporate it into BI solutions. Furthermore, there is a clear need for merging research related to spatial and conventional data quality (Batini & Scannapieca, 2006; Devillers et al., 2010). Data quality is a widely-known problem in different areas of human activities and spatial data is no longer the "microcosm" (Devillers et al., 2010) of geo-specialists. It now belongs to a wider community that also should be considered.

An important aspect in spatial data quality is to determine the criteria of data transformation to improve its quality. An interesting approach for improving conventional data quality is given by Low, Lee and Ling, (2001). They propose a knowledge-based framework for data cleaning that uses an expert system with rules applied to different categories and guide the cleaning process of elimination of duplicates. This approach could be extended to spatial data; however, a spatial expert system that incorporates international standards and users expertise should be developed first.

Another approach can be taken for evaluating spatial data quality based on overall opinion given by its users. The crowdsourcing initiatives are well known in different environments; they help users evaluate the quality of the products, make decisions about buying products or using services, among others. An interesting approach would be to propose tagging methods that allow users to vote about data quality and share their opinion with others. Even though quality requirements are both application and user-dependent (Wang et al., 2002), some common quality measures must be fulfilled in order to trust data. Different types of stakeholders could define various "fitness-for-use" groups and, based on that classification, evaluation criteria and tagging methods could be developed.

Furthermore, an awareness to build a new geomatics vision for sharing spatial data must be created (Bédard, 2008). This task is difficult to achieve among geo-specialists since they have many years of specialized training and they may limit their knowledge to their particular field of expertise (e.g., cartography, surveying) and do not consider nor promote data reusability by different stakeholders. The lack of a geomatics vision of data reuse among specialists from different fields forces institutions/organizations to create separate systems and to incur in high costs of digitalizing the same territory in different scales and geometries. For example, travel agencies in Costa Rica could not obtain the data related to beach sizes or the length of landing tracks in airports, because the shape files were created by separate institutions unrelated to tourism representing these spatial objects as points. Another example is the use of lines for spatial representation of risk zones that do not allow users to check whether other objects (schools, clinics, hospitals, etc.) are within these zones. Although the solution for using different spatial data types to represent the same object already exists in spatial databases, called multiple representations, e.g., Bédard and Bernier (2002), it is not widely known, particularly among geo-specialists.

The quality of conceptual and logical schemas is another aspect under study in research related to conventional data and that is also somehow being neglected for spatial data. A flawed conceptual schema design strongly impacts the development of systems and it must be detected as soon as possible in order to avoid inconsistencies at the logical and implementation levels (Batini & Scannapieca, 2006). However, even though the spatial database design is mentioned in several academic works (Bédard, 1999; Rigaux, Scholl, & Voisard, 2002; Shekhar & Chawla, 2003; Worboys & Duckham, 2004), it is not always used in real life. Common practice in developing different spatial applications is to use shape files, skipping conceptual and logical design phases. The culture of relying on the physical level design skipping conceptual and logical schemas has recently changed due to convergence of GISs and SDBMSs. However, even though many models for different kinds of applications have been proposed mainly using UML (ESRI, 2013a) and also some design steps have been specified (ESRI, 2013c), clear design principles are still lacking. The most common practice is to present tables or objects without relationships between them, i.e., in the same way as the shape files are created. As can be seen, this representation does not follow the basic database design rules and leads to well-known problems of data inconsistency.

CONCLUSION

Business Intelligence solutions are increasingly considering the inclusion of spatial data to enhance decision-making processes. Spatial data is widely available and can be used with different purposes and by different kinds of users. However, spatial data may represent risks if its quality is not a user concern. Poor data quality leads to poor decisions. Since current commercial GISs work under the assumption that data is perfect, users not trained in this field may not be aware of the presence of problems (Delavar & Devillers, 2010). As a consequence, growing usage of spatial data should increase the verification of its quality and apply corrections (if needed). On the one hand, consideration should be given to research related to spatial data quality. This research has a long tradition and is developed by a highly-skilled scientific community, as well as other centers and institutions from government or industry. However, the connections between academic research and the day-to-day use of spatial data by different types of users are generally not very strong (Devillers et al., 2010). On the other hand, many international standards can be adopted and adapted to national needs. These international standards are developed in response to the increasing initiatives of building SDIs that allow the sharing of spatial data over the Internet among different stakeholders.

Furthermore, even though new solutions for spatial data manipulation and control exist in the form of spatial DBMSs and spatial ETL tools, they are not always used to improve spatial data quality. These solutions require geomatics knowledge, i.e., joining geo and informatics knowledge. This is not easy to achieve since geo-specialists are more familiar with complex hybrid architectures of GISs and they not always have a strong informatics background; in contrast, informatics experts are not very skilled in applying their knowledge to spatial data handling, since spatial extension to current DBMSs is a relatively new technology.

In this chapter, we exemplified some problems that may occur when using traditional spatial data storage lacking control for data quality. We established a set of control parameters based on the ISO19113 standard and developed several spatial ETL processes to demonstrate how spatial data quality can be improved. We also showed that by using spatial DBMSs for data storage, additional controls can be applied in order to ensure the insertion of data fulfilling specified criteria. Even though some of the transformations presented in this chapter may be performed using only DBMSs, the ETL processes facilitate data integration, allow scheduling process execution, and decrease the programming effort due to graphical interface, among others.

We believe that there is still a need to fill the gap between the research related to spatial data quality and the usage of data by non-expert users, between the research community related to spatial and conventional data, as well as among geo and informatics specialists. Furthermore, expanding the existing tools for data transformation and analysis with spatial data will help in a better and practical way to provide spatial data to non-expert users in geo-concepts at different levels of management with the goal to better support the decision-making processes.

REFERENCES

Aalders, H. (1999). The registration of QUALITY in a GIS. In *Proceedings from the International Symposium on Spatial Data Quality* (pp. 23-32). IEEE.

Aalders, H., & Morrison, J. (1998). Spatial data quality for GIS. In *Geographic information research: Trans-Atlantic perspectives* (pp. 463–475). London: Taylor & Francis.

Albrecht, A., & Naumann, F. (2008). Managing ETL processes. In *Proceedings from the International Workshop on New Trends in Information Integration* (pp. 12 -15). IEEE.

Badard, T., & Dubé, E. (2009). Enabling geospatial business intelligence. *Technology Innovation Management Review*. Retrieved January 7, 2013, from http://timreview.ca/node/289

Batini, C., & Scannapieca, M. (2006). *Data quality: Concepts, methodologies and techniques*. Berlin: Springer.

Bédard, Y. (1999). Principles of spatial database analysis and design. In *Geographical information systems: Principles, techniques, application & management* (pp. 413–424). Hoboken, NJ: John Wiley & Sons.

Bédard, Y. (2005). Integrating GIS and OLAP: A new way to unlock geospatial data for decision-making. In *Proceedings from the Conference on Directions on Location Technology and Business Intelligence*. IEEE.

Bédard, Y. (2008). Geomatics. In *Encyclopedia of geographical information science* (pp. 195–197). Thousand Oaks, CA: SAGE Publications.

Bédard, Y., & Bernier, E. (2002). Supporting multiple representations with spatial databases view: Management and the concept of VUEL. In *Proceedings from the Joint Workshop on Multi-Scale Representations of Spatial Data*. IEEE.

Bimonte, S., Wehrle, P., Tchounikine, A., & Miquel, M. (2006). GeWOlap: A web based spatial OLAP proposal. In *Proceedings from the 2nd International Workshop on Semantic-Based Geographical Information Systems* (pp. 1596–1605). IEEE.

Bing Maps. (2011). *Business intelligence*. Retrieved January 10, 2013, from http://www.microsoft.com/maps/solutions/business-solutions/business-intelligence.aspx

Boin, A., & Hunter, G. (2005). Do spatial data consumers really understand data quality information? In *Proceedings from the 7th International Symposium on Spatial Accuracy Assessment in Natural Resources and Environmental Sciences* (pp. 215-224). IEEE.

Burnell, K., & Raghavendran, S. (2008). Spatial ETL tools: The bottom line of an enterprise GIS. In *Proceedings from the International Conference Map India*. IEEE.

Chrisman, N. (1983). The role of quality in the long term functioning of a geographical information system. In *Proceedings from the International Symposium on Automated Cartography* (pp. 79-87). IEEE.

Clementini, E., & Di Felice, P. (1996). Model for representing topological relationships between complex geometric features in spatial databases. *Information Sciences: an International Journal, 80*(1-4), 121–136. doi:10.1016/0020-0255(95)00289-8

Dassonville, L. (1999). Quality management, data quality and users, metadata for geographical information. In *Proceedings from the International Symposium on Spatial Data Quality* (pp. 133-143). IEEE.

Delavar, M., & Devillers, R. (2010). Spatial data quality: From process to decisions. *Transaction in GIS, 14*(4), 379–386. doi:10.1111/j.1467-9671.2010.01224.x

Devillers, R., Bédard, Y., Fisher, P., Stein, A., Chrisman, N., & Shi, W. (2010). Thirty years of research on spatial data quality: Achievements, failures, and opportunities. *Transaction in GIS, 14*(4), 387–400. doi:10.1111/j.1467-9671.2010.01212.x

Devillers, R., Bédard, Y., Jeansoulin, R., & Moulin, B. (2007). Towards spatial data quality information analysis tools for experts assessing the fitness for use of spatial data. *International Journal of Geographical Information Science*, *21*(3), 261–282. doi:10.1080/13658810600911879

Devillers, R., Gervais, M., Bédard, Y., & Jeansoulin, R. (2002). Spatial data quality: From metadata to quality indicators and contextual end-user manual. In *Proceedings from the OEEPE/ISPRS Joint Workshop on Spatial Data Quality Management* (pp. 45-55). IEEE.

Di Martino, S., Bimonte, S., Berttolotto, M., & Ferrucci, F. (2009). Integrating Google earth within OLAP tools for multidimensional exploration and analysis of spatial data. In *Proceedings from the International Conference on Enterprise Information Science* (pp. 940-951). IEEE.

Elwood, S. (2008). Grassroots groups as stakeholders in spatial data infrastructures: Challenges and opportunities local data development and sharing. *International Journal of Geographical Information Science*, *22*(2), 71–90. doi:10.1080/13658810701348971

EPSG. (2013). *Spatial reference list*. Retrieved January 3, 2013, from http://spatialreference.org/ref/epsg/

ESRI. (1998). *Shapefile technical description, an ESRI white paper*. Retrieved January 5, 2013, from http://www.esri.com/library/whitepapers/pdfs/shapefile.pdf

ESRI. (2012a). *ArcGIS for desktop extensions*. Retrieved January 5, 2013, from http://www.esri.com/software/arcgis/about/desktop-extensions

ESRI. (2012b). *Geodatabase: Overview*. Retrieved January 5, 2013, from http://www.esri.com/software/arcgis/geodatabase/index.html

ESRI. (2013a). *ArcGIS resource center: Data models*. Retrieved January 7, 2013, from http://resources.arcgis.com/content/data-models

ESRI. (2013b). *Data interoperability*. Retrieved January 7, 2013, from http://www.esri.com/software/arcgis/extensions/datainteroperability

ESRI. (2013c). *Geodatabase design steps*. Retrieved January 7, 2013, from http://webhelp.esri.com/arcgisdesktop/9.2/index.cfm?TopicName=Geodatabase_design_steps

GeoMe. (2013). *Visual business intelligence maps*. Retrieved January 10, 2013, from http://www.geo.me/visualbusinessintelligence

Gervais, M., Bédard, Y., Levesque, M., Bernier, E., & Devillers, R. (2010). Data quality issues and geographic knowledge discovery. In *Geographic data mining and knowledge discovery* (pp. 99–116). New York: Taylor & Francis.

Goffin, K., & Koners, U. (2011). Tacit knowledge, lessons learnt, and new product development. *Journal of Product Innovation Management*, *28*, 300–318. doi:10.1111/j.1540-5885.2010.00798.x

Goodchild, M. (2010). Geographic information systems. In *Research methods in geography: A critical introduction* (pp. 376–391). Oxford, UK: Wiley-Blackwell.

Granell, C., Gould, M., Manso, M., & Bernabé, M. (2009). Spatial data infrastructures. In *Handbook of research on geoinformatics* (pp. 36–41). Hershey, PA: IGI Global. doi:10.4018/978-1-59140-995-3.ch005

Gray, J. (2010). *Open geoprocessing standards and open geospatial data*. Retrieved February 4, 2013, from http://blog.okfn.org/2010/06/21/open-geoprocessing-standards-and-open-geospatial-data/

GSDI. (2012). *Global spatial data infrastructure*. Retrieved January 7, 2012, from http://www.gsdi.org/

Integeo. (2013). *Integrated geographics for business and government*. Retrieved January 10, 2013, from http://www.integeo.com/

Intelli3. (2010). *Map4Decision*. Retrieved 2013, from http://www.intelli3.com/map4decision

Intergraph. (2013). *GeoMedia fusion*. Retrieved January 10, 2013, from http://www.intergraph.com/literature/geomedia_fusion.pdf

ISO 19113. (2002). *Geographic information – Quality principles*. International Standard Organization.

ISO 19114. (2003). *Geographic information – Quality evaluation procedures*. International Standard Organization.

ISO 19138. (2006). *Geographic information – Data quality measures*. International Standard Organization.

Jakobsson, A., & Tsoulos, L. (2007). The role of quality spatial data infrastructure. In *Quality control handbook*. New York: McGraw-Hill.

Larrivée, S., Bédard, Y., Gervais, M., & Roy, T. (2011). New horizons for spatial data quality research. In *Proceedings from the 7th International Symposium on Spatial Data Quality*. IEEE.

Li, L. (2010). A framework study of ETL processes optimization base on metadata repository. In *Proceedings from the International Conference on Computer Engineering and Technology* (pp. 125-129). IEEE.

Low, W., Lee, M., & Ling, T. (2001). A knowledge-based approach for duplicate elimination in data cleaning. *Information Systems*, *26*(8), 585–606. doi:10.1016/S0306-4379(01)00041-2

Mäkelä, J. (2006). The impact of spatial data quality on company's decision making. *The International Archives of the Photogrammetry, Remote Sensing and Spatial Information Sciences, 34*.

Malinowski, E. (2012). Challenges for promoting decision-making processes based on spatial data analysis. In *Proceedings from the International Computer Symposium* (pp. 393-402). IEEE.

Malinowski, E., & Zimányi, E. (2009). *Advanced data warehouse design: From conventional to spatial and temporal applications*. Berlin: Springer.

Mathew, G. (2012). *5 macro trends shaping next-generation BI and analytics*. Retrieved January 8, 2013, from http://tdwi.org/articles/2012/02/07/5-macro-trends-bi-analytics.aspx

Olsen, J. (2003). *Data quality: The accuracy dimension*. New York: Morgan Kaufmann Publishers.

OMB. (2010). Office of management and budget. *Circular No.A-2*. Retrieved January 4, 2013, from: http://www.whitehouse.gov/omb/circulars_a016_rev/

Oosterom, P., Quak, W., & Tijssen, T. (2005). About invalid, valid and clean polygons. In *Proceedings from the 11th International Symposium on Spatial Data Handling* (pp. 1-16). IEEE.

Oracle. (2011). Putting business intelligence on the map. *Oracle Magazine*. Retrieved January 12, 2013, from http://www.oracle.com/technetwork/issue-archive/2011/11-may/o31bi-354140.html

Pentaho. (2013). *Pentaho Google maps dashboard*. Retrieved January 11, 2013, from http://community.pentaho.com/google_maps/

Pradinho, H., Alonso, J., Guerra, C., Pocas, I., Goncalves, J., & Marcos, B. (2011). *Report on pre-existing in situ and ancillary datasets for sites*. Retrieved January 15, 2013, from http://www.biosos.wur.nl/NR/rdonlyres/935FA85D-DC21-4FDC-ADE6-037FC172A312/156397/BIO_SOS_D41_Preexisting_data_sets.pdf

Rigaux, P., Scholl, M., & Voisard, A. (2002). *Spatial databases with application to GIS*. New York: Morgan Kaufmann.

Safe Software. (2013). *About FME spatial data transformation platform*. Retrieved January 5, 2013, from http://www.safe.com/fme/fme-technology/

Sanderson, M., Ramage, S., & Van Linden, L. (2009). SDI communities: Data quality and knowledge sharing. In *Proceedings of the 11th International Conference for Spatial Data Infrastructure*. Retrieved January 7, 2013, from http://www.gsdi.org/gsdiconf/gsdi11/papers/pdf/283.pdf

Shekhar, S., & Chawla, S. (2003). *Spatial databases: A tour*. Upper Saddle River, NJ: Prentice Hall.

Simitsis, A., Vassiliadis, P., & Sellis, T. (2005). Optimizing ETL processes in data warehouses. In *Proceeding from the International Conference on Data Engineering* (pp.564-575). IEEE.

Smits, P., Düren, U., Østensen, O., Murre, L., Gould, M., & Sandgren, U. … Konecny, M. (2002). INSPIRE: Infrastructure for spatial information in Europe, position paper. Brussels: European Commission, Joint Research Centre -Institute for Environment and Sustainability.

Spatialytics. (2013). *GeoKettle*. Retrieved January 5, 2013, from http://www.spatialytics/projects/geokettle

Talhofer, V., & Hofmann, A. Hošková–Mayerová, S., & Kubícek, P. (2011). Spatial analyses and spatial data quality. In *Proceedings from the 14th Agile International Conference on Geographic Information Science*. IEEE.

UE. (2012). *Unidad ejecutora catastro, Costa Rica*. Retrieved January 12, 2013, from http://www.uecatastro.org/

Vasseur, B., Devillers, R., & Jeansoulin, R. (2003). Ontological approach of the fitness of use of geospatial datasets. In *Proceedings from the 6th Agile Conference on Geographic Information Science* (pp. 498-504). IEEE.

Veregin, H. (1999). Data quality parameters. In *Geographical information systems* (pp. 177–189). Hoboken, NJ: John Wiley & Sons.

Wang, R., & Strong, D. (1996). Beyond accuracy: What data quality means to data consumers. *Journal of Management Information Systems, 12*(4), 5–33.

Wang, R., Ziad, M., & Lee, Y. (2002). Data quality. In *Spatial database systems: Design, implementation, and project management*. Berlin: Springer.

WebiGeo. (2013). *WebiGeo location intelligence*. Retrieved January 13, 2013, from http://www.galigeo.com/en/page/geospatial-solutions/products/webigeo.html

Worboys, M., & Duckham, M. (2004). *GIS: A computing perspective*. Boca Raton, FL: CRC Press.

Xia, J. (2012). Metrics to measure open geospatial data quality. *Issues in Science & Technology Librarianship, 68*.

Yeung, A., & Hall, G. (2007). *Spatial database systems: Design, implementation, and project management*. Berlin: Springer. doi:10.1007/1-4020-5392-4

ADDITIONAL READING

Anselin, L., & Getis, A. (2010). Spatial Statistical Analysis and Geographic Information Systems. In L. Anselin, & S. Rey (Eds.), *Perspective on Spatial Data Analysis* (pp. 35–47). Springer. doi:10.1007/978-3-642-01976-0_3

Bédard, Y. (2007). Geomatics: 26 Years of History Already! *Journal of Geospatial Information Sciences. Technology and Practice, 61*(3), 269–272.

Boin, A. (2008). *Exposing Uncertainty: Communicating Spatial Data Quality via the Internet*. VDM Publishing.

Bouzeghoub, M. (2004). A Framework for Analysis of Data Freshness. Proceedings from *the 2004 International Workshop on Information Quality in Information Systems* (pp. 59-67).

Crossland, M. (2009). Geografic Information Systems as Decision Tools. In M. Khosrow-Pour (Ed.), *Encyclopedia of Information Science and Technology* (pp. 1630–1633). Information Science Publishing.

Devillers, R., & Goodchild, H. (2009). *Spatial Data Quality: From Process to Decisions*. CRC Press.

Devillers, R., & Jeansoulin, R. (2006). *Fundamentals of Spatial Data Quality*. Wiley. doi:10.1002/9780470612156

Dong, X., Halevy, A., & Yu, C. (2009). Data Integration with uncertainty. *The International Journal on Very Large Data Bases, 18*(2), 469–500. doi:10.1007/s00778-008-0119-9

Droj, G., Suba, S., & Buda, A. (2010). Modern Techniques for Evaluation of Spatial Data Quality. *Journal of Geodesy and Cadaster*, 265-272.

Elwood, S. (2008). Grassroots Groups as Stakeholders in Spatial Data Infrastructures: Challenges and Opportunities Local Data Development and Sharing. *International Journal of Geographical Information Science, 22*(2), 71–90. doi:10.1080/13658810701348971

Frank, A. (2008). Analysis of Dependence of Decision Quality on Data Quality. *Journal of Geographical Analysis, 10*, 71–88. doi:10.1007/s10109-008-0059-3

Frank, A., Grum, E., & Vasseur, B. (2004). Procedures to Select the Best Dataset for a Task. Proceedings from *the 3rd International Conference on Geographic Information Science* (pp. 81-93).

Goodchild, M. (2008). Epilogue: Putting Research into Practice. In Stein, A., Shi, W., & Bijker, W. (Eds.), Quality Aspects in Spatial Data Mining (pp. 345–356). CRC Press.

Jakobsson, A. (2002). Data Quality and Quality Management – Examples of Quality Evaluation Procedures and Quality Management in European National Mapping Agencies. In Shi, W., Fisher, P., & Goolchild, M. (Eds.), Spatial Data Quality (pp. 216-229). Taylor & Francis.

Jakobsson, A. (2006). *On the Future of Topographic Base Information Management in Finland and Europe*. Unpublished doctoral dissertation, Helsinki University of Technology.

Jankowski, P. (2009). Towards Participatory Geographic Information Systems for Community-based Environmental Decision Making. *Journal of Environmental Management, 90*(6), 1966–1971. doi:10.1016/j.jenvman.2007.08.028 PMID:18550264

Kerski, J., & Clark, J. (2012). *The GIS Guide to Public Domain Data*. ESRI Press.

Kumi-Boateng, B., & Yakubu, I. (2010). Assessing the Quality of Spatial Data. *European Journal of Scientific Research, 43*(4), 507–515.

Miller, H., & Han, J. (Eds.). (2002). *Geographic Data Mining and Knowledge Discovery*. Taylor & Francis.

Redman, T. (1996). *Data Quality for the Information Age*. Artech House.

Sanderson, M., Ramage, S., & Van Linden, L. (2009). SDI Communities: Data Quality and Knowledge Sharing. Proceedings from *the 11th International Conference for Spatial Data Infrastructure*. Retrieved January 7, 2013, from http://www.gsdi.org/gsdiconf/gsdi11/papers/pdf/283.pdf.

Scannapieco, M., Pernici, B., & Pierce, E. (2002). IP-UML: Towards a Methodology for Quality Improvement Based on the IP-MAP Framework. Proceedings from *the 7th International Conference on Information Quality* (pp. 279-291).

Shankaranarayanan, G., & Wang, R. (2007). IPMAP: Current State and Perspectives. Proceedings from *the 12th International Conference on Information Quality* (pp. 500-517).

Shi, W., Fisher, P., & Goodchild, M. (2002). *Spatial Data Quality*. CRC Press. doi:10.4324/9780203303245

Vasseur, B., Devillers, R., & Jeansoulin, R. (2003). Ontological Approach of the Fitness of Use of Geospatial Datasets. Proceeding from *the 6th Agile Conference on Geographic Information Science* (pp. 498-504).

KEY TERMS AND DEFINITIONS

Geographic Information System: A system used for capturing, storing, manipulating and analyzing spatial data. Sometimes, this term refers to tools that facilitate interactive queries and editing data in maps.

Geomatics (Geo-Informatics): A term that combines different fields related to geo (Earth) (e.g., geodesy, land surveying, remote sensing, cartography, photogrammetry, and geography) and informatics.

Shape File: A data format used to store a geometry represented by points, lines, polygons, or a combination of them, as well as conventional data. It consists of, at least, two separate files and represents a theme.

Spatial Data: Data that describes the geographic location of features, their extensions, and shapes on Earth.

Spatial Data Infrastructure: A collection of technologies, policies, standards, human resources that facilitates the availability of and access to spatial data. It provides a basis for spatial data discovery and sharing among stakeholders from different sectors, e.g., governmental, commercial, non-profit, and academic, as well as by citizens in general.

Spatial Data Warehouses: Databases that integrate data (conventional and spatial) from different sources and are specially designed for supporting decision-making processes.

Spatial ETL: A process of *Extraction* to obtain spatial and conventional data from multiple and heterogeneous sources, *Transformation* to modify the data from source formats to a destination format that can be operational (transactional) databases, data warehouses, or other kinds of repositories.

Topological Relationships: A relationship existing between two spatial objects (the geometries) that describes how spatial values relate to each other, e.g., meets, overlaps, intersects, among others.

Chapter 11
Principled Reference Data Management for Business Intelligence

Ivan Milman
IBM Corporation, USA

Martin Oberhofer
IBM Corporation, USA

Sushain Pandit
IBM Corporation, USA

Yinle Zhou
IBM Corporation, USA

ABSTRACT

Most large enterprises requiring operational business processes (e.g., call center, human resources, order fulfillments, billing, etc.) utilize anywhere from a few hundred to several thousand instances of legacy, upgraded, cloud-based, and/or acquired information management applications. Due to this vastly heterogeneous information landscape, Business Intelligence (BI) systems (e.g., enterprise data warehouses) receive unconsolidated data from a wide-range of data sources with no overarching governance procedures to ensure quality, consistency, or appropriateness. Although different applications deal with their own flavor of data (e.g., master data, metadata, unstructured and structured data, etc.), reference data (residing in code tables) is found invariably in all of them. Given the critical role that BI plays in ensuring business success, the fact that BI relies heavily on the quality of data to ensure that the intelligence being provided is trustworthy and the prevalence of reference data in the information integration landscape, a principled approach towards management, stewardship, and governance of reference data becomes necessary to ensure quality and operational excellence across BI systems. In this chapter, the authors discuss this approach in the domain of typical reference data management concepts and features, leading to a comprehensive solution architecture for BI integration.

DOI: 10.4018/978-1-4666-4892-0.ch011

INTRODUCTION

An organization's approach to reference data management (RDM) can have a profound influence on the effectiveness of that organization's business intelligence processes, reference data are those data values that support consistent representation (coding) of key information within an organization or across groups of organizations. Reference data are usually sets of permissible values for an attribute (Xu, et al., 2012) or classification schemas that are referred to by system applications, data stores, processes, and reports, as well as by transactional and master records (McGilvray, 2008). These may be standard codes defined external to the organization such as currency codes and country codes (such as those defined by ISO – the International Organization for Standards), domain specific standards subscribed to by the organization such as the Logical Observation Identifiers Names and Codes (LOINC 1999, 2013) standard for coding medical laboratory observations, or internal standards such as internally developed product codes. Such reference data sets, comprising a range of permissible values for entity attributes, usually reside within specialized tables known as look-up, code, check, or domain tables (Xu, et al., 2012).

Although there are many classification schemes that address the various types of data, almost all recognize the categories of master data, metadata, reference data, and transactional data (Dreibelbis, et al., 2008) (McGilvray, 2008). Of these, reference data is most related to master data and metadata, but reference data is distinguished from them. Master data represents the common business objects (such as people, places, and things) that need to be agreed on and shared throughout an enterprise (Dreibelbis, et al., 2008). Reference data, while used to consistently author master data instances by governing the permissible set of values for a given master data attribute, is not the same as master data. Reference data is also different from metadata which literally means "data about data". Metadata labels, describes, and characterizes other data and make it easier to retrieve, interpret, or use information (McGilvray, 2008).

Figure 1 illustrates the concepts of master data, metadata and reference data by using an example. Assume international retailer ABC Inc. who sells luxury products around the world and whose customers tend to travel and shop across the countries. A global customer information integration project is conducted to improve customer information and relationship management. The master data table in Figure 1 has the customer records which are captured when customers are shopping around the world. For example, customer Carrie Lee is a Chinese citizen who lives in Beijing. She shops for ABC's products in Beijing, but due to her job, she often travels to United States and South Korea, and purchases ABC's products there, too. In different regions, ABC uses the local language for product information and customer information. Therefore, Carrie Lee's information in the integrated system is in three languages: Chinese, English, and Korean. To properly represent this information as master data entities, a well-defined set of reference data tables is required. The reference data table shown in Figure 1 gives the range of permissible values for the attribute *language* and follows the ISO 639-1 standard (ISO 639, 2013). The metadata table describes the data usage and data structure specifications for each attribute in the master data table and gives the requirement for the reference data table as well. For example, the definition of *language* in the metadata table links back to the *language* reference data table, which follows the ISO 639-1 standard.

Although reference data tends to change less frequently compared to master data or transactional data, it is not totally static. For example, in the United States, postal codes (zip codes) are generally classified as reference data, but are subject to change over time as older codes are divided and new codes added to reflect changes in the population. Master data tends to change more quickly by regularly updating and merging

Figure 1. An example of master data, metadata and reference data

Master Data (Customer Records)
record number, name, email, address, city, state/province, postal code, country, language
201341, Carrie Lee, xxx@xx.com, 123 Renmin Road, Beijing, Beijing, 999999, CN, en
302342, 李凯莉, xxx@xx.com, 人民路 123 号, 北京, 北京, 999999, 中国, zh
503234, ? ? ?, xxx@xx.com, 123 ? ? ? ?, ? ? ?, ? ?, 999999, ? ?, ko
...

Metadata
Attribute|Definition|Type|Length
record number|unique identifier for each customer record|numeric|20
name|customer full name|varchar|30
email|customer email and must contain symbol "@"|varchar|30
...
language|two letter ISO 639-1 code in which the record typed| char|2

Reference Data (Language Code)

Code	Language
en	English
zh	Chinese
ko	Korean
ar	Arabic
ja	Japanese
fr	French
es	Spanish
...	

records. Also, master data is highly shared within the enterprise, e.g. customer and product information is shared among different departments in a company. Reference data is not only shared within the enterprise but also across different enterprises. For example, the product type reference data is shared between NATO and the organizations that do business with it. From a data storage perspective, master data usually has more rows and columns per table but fewer tables per database. Semantically, reference data tends to have meaning at the row level, while master data has more meaning at the entity level.

Because of the importance of reference data in accurately characterizing attributes in master data and transactional data the use and proper management of reference data is critical in achieving high levels of data quality in an organization. Two representative examples illustrate the problems when reference data is not properly managed:

1. At DNB, BI systems incorrectly reported on customer status because one source system used the code 'A' to represent *Active* customers, while another source system used the code 'A' to represent *Inactive* customers (DNB ASA, 2012);
2. A hospital system in the UK incorrectly sent out letters notifying patients that they had a serious medical condition, because the hospital used one code to represent "no infections", while the health authority used the same code to represent "multiple infections" (BBC, 1999).

Mitigating these sorts of problems, enterprises need to deploy a system with a core set of reference data management capabilities. The first capability is to help accurately create reference data. Every reference data set created within a RDM system has a set of properties, such as code, name, description, sort order, review date, effective data, expiration data, version, lifecycle process, last update data, and so on (Xu, et al., 2012). Code versioning is a well-understood task in many development processes across many programming languages (Narayanan, et al., 2012). Versioning of reference data is an important feature of an RDM system to control versions of reference data entities. Because of its "agreed on" nature, especially for the reference data created by organizations to use internally and externally, any change of the reference data needs to be notified and approved by all stakeholders.

Reference data may reside in a hierarchy. For example, there is a hierarchical structure for country, state/province, city, etc. Each country has its own country code, such as the ones in ISO-3166-1 (ISO 3166-1, 2013). For each country, the state/province may have different representations, like abbreviation and full name. An RDM system offers the way to manage these hierarchical reference data structure efficiently by creating a linkage between the different levels of the hierarchy (e.g. city to state, state to county).

Reference data can support a data quality project by offering the permitted values for a domain when doing data attribute profiling. For example, the reference data table in Figure 1 can serve as a look-up table for the data profiling to check if all the values in the attribute *language* are within this table. Any value outside of the reference data range could be marked as an invalid value.

For a data integration project, which tries to integrate data from heterogeneous source systems, consolidation of reference data is required. This is known as semantic alignment or reference data translation (Pandit, et al., 2012). A well-defined RDM system can help data warehouse (DW) projects achieve data harmonization and consistent representation, which is one of the 16 dimensions of data quality called out in the Wang-Strong data quality framework (Wang & Strong, 1996). In addition, "coded data across disciplines" is listed among the top ten root condition of data quality problems by (Lee, et al., 2006).

Reference data plays an especially critical role in business intelligence (BI). BI is the collection and analysis of operational data that support the business planning and strategic decisions of an organization. Essentially, BI is an inferential process that looks at past operational performance to predict future trends and opportunities. Because BI plays such a critical role in business success, it is important that the users of the analysis understand that the quality of BI is only as good as the quality of the operational data upon which it is based.

This remainder of this chapter is structured as follows: The second section explains more about the need for principled reference data management for BI. The third section describes how to apply principled reference data management to BI, especially from a typical reference data management implementation and BI solution architecture perspective. The chapter concludes with a summary and a number of key takeaways.

THE NEED FOR PRINCIPLED REFERENCE DATA MANAGEMENT FOR BI

Medium to large-sized companies run several dozen to a few hundred, and in some instances, even a few thousand applications for operational business processes like call center, HR, opportunity to order management, order fulfillment, billing, etc. This IT environment is usually comprised of a heterogeneous mix of legacy applications, packaged applications and, with the rise of software as a service delivery models, cloud-service based applications. The very complexity and heterogeneous nature of this environment by necessity means that the interfaces to exchange data between systems are different.

Not surprisingly, given this context for the operational application environment, BI systems such as enterprise data warehouses (EDW) receive data from a myriad of different operational systems using a variety of techniques and interfaces. Moving data from the operational systems to the BI system is constrained by the following considerations:

- What interfaces do the source systems offer to the BI system for retrieving complete records as well as updates? For example, some legacy systems might only have batch interfaces or can provide only full records if a single attribute changed (instead of just the changed attributes);

- Since data extraction is I/O intensive – what time windows are permissible from a source system point of view to replicate data to a BI system?
- How current must the data in the BI system be for the reports executed in the BI system? Some reports might be ok with data updated only every week, while others (like operational reports) need the operational data available in near real-time or real-time.

Based on the above considerations, data is moved from source systems to the BI target system with one of the following techniques as shown in Figure 2:

- **Extract-Transform-Load (ETL):** This is still the most commonly used information integration technique in BI environments for moving large data volumes in periodically scheduled batches from source to the BI target system. Usually, the ETL process also applies data cleansing and harmonization. Data harmonization is a 2-step process. The first step is the mapping the various source data models to a common model used for data cleansing so that all ETL logic can operate on all records from all sources in a single model reducing ETL development cost. The second step is semantic data alignment which means to translate data values from the sources to their semantic counterparts understood by the target system. A key example for this second step is reference data alignment because many target systems reject records containing unknown reference data values from the sources. Today, the state of art is to rely on an enterprise information integration software solution for this integration. Nonetheless, custom-developed ETL solutions are still quite frequently used;
- **Data replication:** This approach usually uses a change data capture (Godinez, et al., 2010) technique on the source side, producing messages containing the changed records. These messages are then replicated with messaging infrastructure to the

Figure 2. Information integration for BI

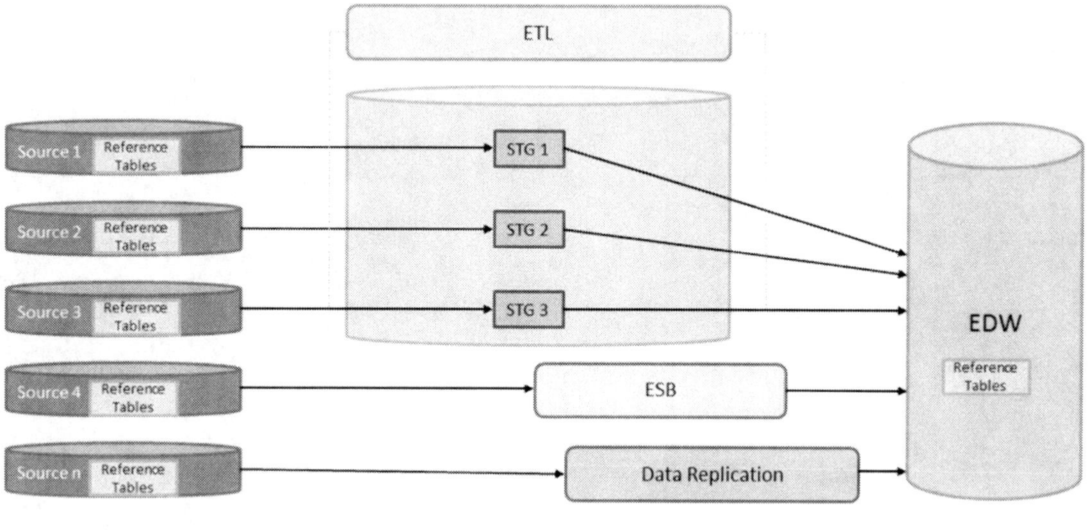

BI target system, where apply agents write the message content into the BI system. Usually this technique does not involve complex data cleansing and harmonization techniques. Large-scale deployments are able to replicate several hundred million messages per day using this approach. From a capture-perspective on the source side there are usually two choices available:

- Trigger-based implementations using SQL trigger statements on the source data tables to capture insert, update and delete operations;
- Transactional log file analysis.

The trigger-based approach has the advantage that the data replication technique does not need to know about the proprietary transactional log file formats by the vendors of database software, but has the disadvantage that insert, update and delete performance is degraded. The transactional log file analysis technique has the advantage that insert, update and delete performance is not affected – a particularly useful characteristic in systems with heavy OLTP workloads, but with the disadvantage that the provider of the transactional log file analysis technique must understand the transactional log file format by database vendors in order to extract the changed record information:

- **Enterprise Service Bus (ESB):** This approach is used for real-time integration but is rarely used for loading large amounts of data into BI target systems.

Given a typical architectural context (as outlined in Figure 2) that moves data from a heterogeneous set of sources to a BI target system, the problem of reference data alignment arises as illustrated with Figure 3 because the reference data tables in source and BI target systems usually differ because:

- The various packaged source applications like SAP, Siebel, Oracle, etc. or custom-built applications come with different reference data tables for the same reference data domains like country codes, marital status, product categories, etc.;
- Even if the source applications are just multiple instances of the same applications, reference data is typically customizable for each instance. We have seen in customer environments where multiple instances of the same application for the same approximately 200 countries on this planet had several thousand different country codes configured.

Figure 3. Need for reference data alignment

Source Table: Customer
Field: Country Code

Reference Value	Description
01	United States
02	Denmark
03	Germany
04	France

Target Table: Buyer
Field: Country Code

Reference Value	Description
DE	Denmark
US	United States
GE	Germany
FR	France

As a consequence we can have two different issues: First, the same reference value might have a different meaning between a source system and the BI target system. Second, it's possible that the same meaning (e.g. *Denmark* in Figure 3) has different reference data values between the source and the BI system. Without reference data alignment, as data is moved from sources to the BI target, the semantics of the data could be substantially changed. As a consequence, the quality and results of reports in the data warehouse are negatively affected – for example:

- Revenue by product category will not work well if the reference values defining the product categories are not harmonized;
- Revenue by country delivers unreliable results with inconsistent reference values for country codes;
- Revenue by customer segment is flawed if the reference values for customer segments are not aligned.

These problems are further complicated by the following factors:

- Reference values change over time, introducing inconsistencies when running reports on aggregated data over an extended period of time. To resolve this problem, you need to know the various versions of a reference value that refers to the same semantic concept. Therefore, you need to have historic and versioned reference data from sources and the BI target;
- If the reference values change over time, the transcoding tables need to be versioned as well. Furthermore, these updated transcoding tables must be distributed to the data movement infrastructures, and there may be different mechanisms required to provision and update the transcoding tables;
- As mentioned earlier in the paper, delivering a well-managed set of reference data hierarchies is also necessary for reporting and analysis. Many reports are interactive and hierarchical in nature. For example:
    - Sales by country;
    - Sales by state within a country;
    - Sales by city within a state within a country;
- Without governing who is changing reference values and transcoding tables with appropriate processes and approvals, it is impossible to assure appropriate and consistent semantics;
- You need to have the ability to centrally manage and distribute transcoding tables into different data movement infrastructures to control the alignment of reference data between source systems and BI systems.

For these reasons, BI systems require a principled approach to reference data management delivered through a dedicated reference data management system.

APPLYING PRINCIPLED REFERENCE DATA MANAGEMENT TO BI

As seen in the last section, a principled approach to reference data management is paramount for enabling a meaningful and efficient BI ecosystem. In line with the issues pointed out in the last section, a typical reference data management hub implementation (Chen et al, 2013) is comprised of a series of principled concepts exposed via a number of out-of-the-box features that allow enterprises and end-users to effectively address information integration challenges for a BI scenario. In this section, we describe these concepts and features, and demonstrate their efficacy in addressing the previously stated issues, eventually leading to effective solution architecture for BI.

As noted earlier, reports are typically organized around common classifications (sales by country, types of transactions, and so on). These common classifications would be represented as reference data dimensions in the data warehouse, shown in Figure 2. Thus, having the reference data defined in RDM hub, and then pushed into the warehouse, enables consistency and governance around reference data dimensions. To that extent, an RDM hub implementation provides mechanisms to author a consistent canonical definition of reference codes to be used in all tables in the warehouse. More advanced features of the RDM hub assist the user in the seamless definition of reference data hierarchies and maps. In addition, since reference data values can change over time, an RDM hub also provides a streamlined versioning model that allows stewards to seamlessly create new versions from existing ones. Having multiple versions of a set of related reference data values enables retaining key historic information that can be used to perform analysis on how the versions evolved and utilize that for reporting purposes.

Common mechanisms for defining reference data in an RDM hub include an authorship user interface (UI) that can be used to create a number of specialized *managed entities* for persisting reference data into the hub.

A managed entity is a blueprint of an abstract entity that contains enough information and properties that are necessary for managing the lifecycle of any entity that extends it. These properties include name and/or description, owner(s), version, lifecycle state, effective dating and type, among other things. Figure 4 shows a typical managed entity often utilized in a comprehensive implementation of an RDM hub. This abstract managed entity is extended to define several specific entities that, cumulatively, enable all the necessary features required to effectively manage reference data for the kind of business intelligence scenarios that we discussed in the last section. A reference

Figure 4. Reference data managed entity

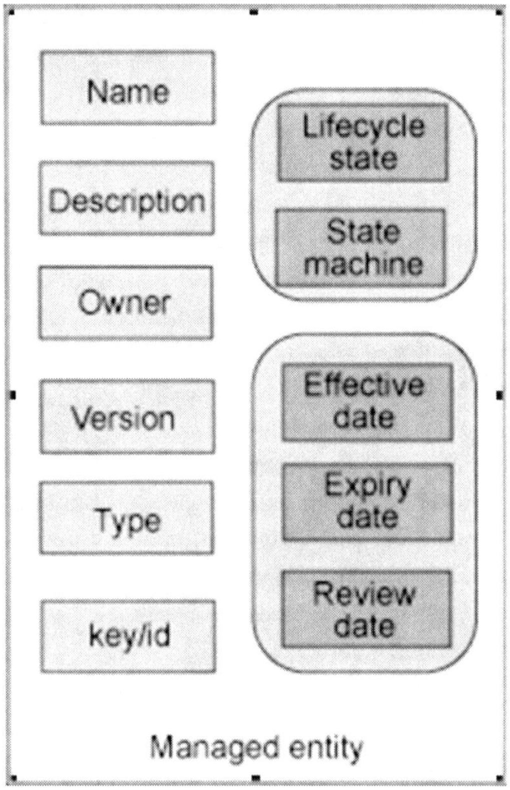

data logical model, comprising most typical RDM managed entities (reference data sets, maps and hierarchies) is illustrated in Figure 5.

Reference data sets are one of the first-class citizens in an RDM hub and are a kind of managed entity that can be used to store reference data values as shown in Figure 6.

Minimally, two specific properties (Code and Name) are required for each reference data value in a reference data set. *Code* represents the value used in dimensions, records, etc. to represent the concept described in text by the *Name* property. In such RDM implementations, they must be given an initial value at the time the reference data value is being created. Each reference data value usually tends to have a sequence number (to indicate position of this code within the set), and related audit information such as review date, effective date, and expiration date. Additional properties

Figure 5. Reference data logical model

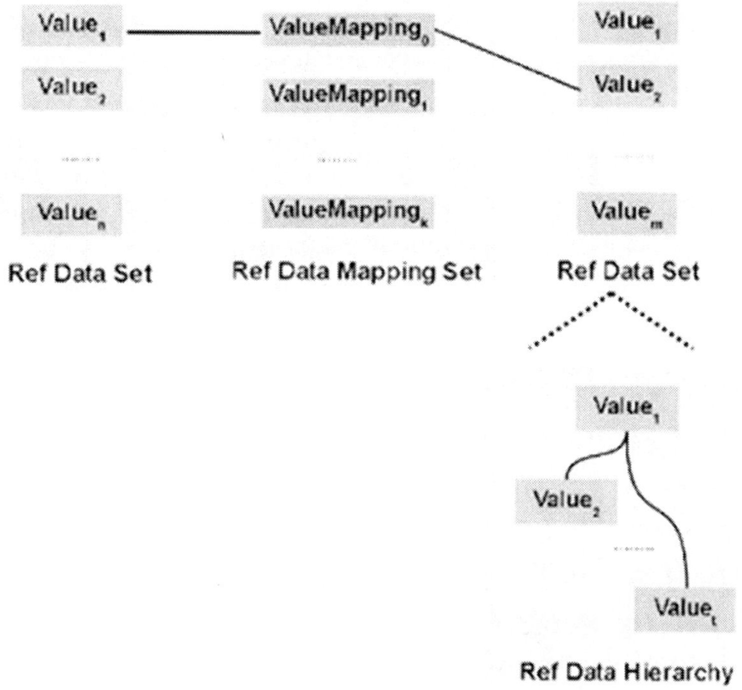

Figure 6. Reference data set

Code	Name
01	France
02	Denmark
03	Greece
04	France

can be added at the value level or at the set level (for example, a set may have a property pointing to the URL of the external standard defining that set.) Reference data sets can be organized using a grouping scheme into a folder hierarchy, for ease of use on the UI.

Since delivering a well-managed set of hierarchies is critical for reporting and analysis in BI systems, a typical RDM hub provides suitable functionality to define level-based hierarchies, where each level can take values from a specific reference data set. For example, in order to model a BI report having:

1. Sales by Country;
2. Sales by State within a Country; and
3. Sales by City within a State within a Country, sets of Countries, States and Cities would be represented as reference data.

The hierarchy can be modeled as custom relationships across these sets. Figure 7 shows a conceptual representation where Level 1 is defined by the Countries set, level 2 by States and level 3 by Cities. Similar to reference data sets, the RDM hub would be used to ensure the consistency, integrity and governance of these hierarchies before they are published to the warehouse.

In addition to governance and stewardship of reference data through a RDM specific user in-

Figure 7. A level-based hierarchy across reference data sets

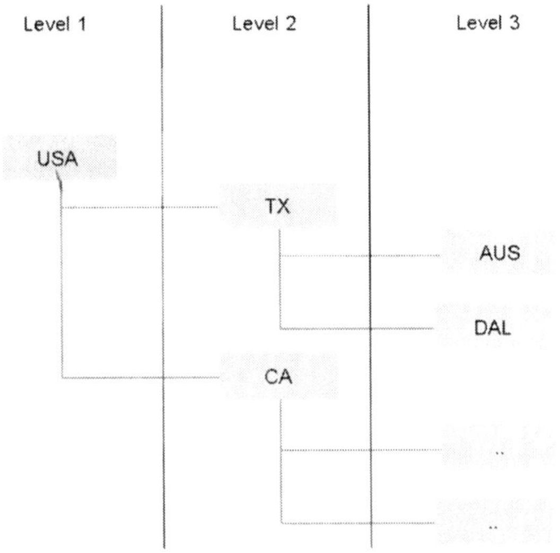

terface, another key part of the architecture is the ability to directly import and export reference data. Reference data is often stored in source repositories as databases, or may be extracted from repositories as CSV (comma-separated value) or XML files. A comprehensive RDM hub implementation provides several out-of-the-box mechanisms to import such reference data directly into a desired reference data set. Common options are UI-based import and a command-line reference data import tool. By linking the command line import tool to a recurring job defined on a fixed or variable time-window, the entire import process can be automated. Typically, application programming interfaces are also exposed to achieve fine-tuned control of the import process. Applying these import procedures to a BI scenario, we can pull in reference data sets and/or hierarchies from source and target BI systems into an RDM hub (as shown in Figure 8).

Once the data is imported into the RDM hub, different versions can be created – both to allow existing applications to use previous releases of the data, and to maintain a history of changes. Most typical RDM implementations provide intuitive ways to define new versions of a reference data set through the UI, whereby a context menu on an existing set gives options to optionally copy over all the existing data from the current version of the set.

Figure 8. Importing reference data (sets/hierarchies) from source/target BI systems

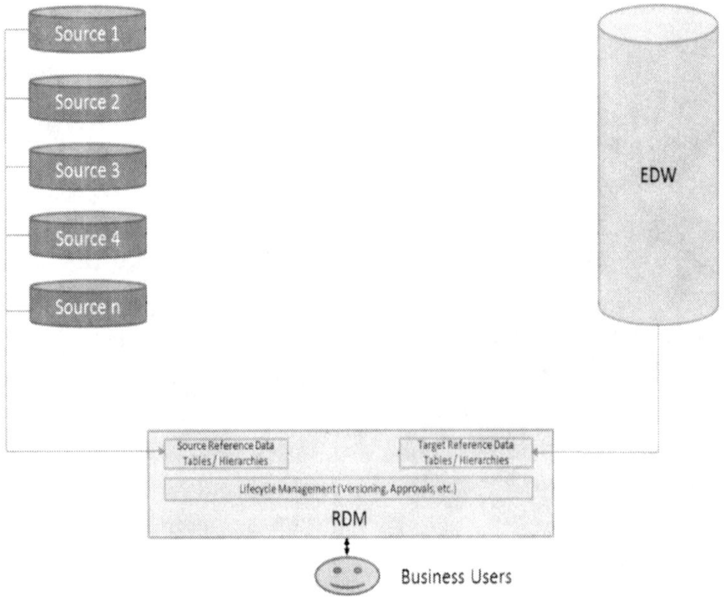

As illustrated in Figure 9, a new version may reflect only a delta correction from the previous version. In many cases though, the values in the new version may be entirely imported as part of a periodic batch import process. Most typical RDM hub implementations also provide means to compare across different versions for reporting purposes, whereby triggering a 'compare version' function after selecting 2 versions of the same set on the UI presents a detailed report on what changed in the reference data and what actions were performed to effect those changes. These reports can be exported in consumable formats for further transformation before consolidating in a final version for BI aggregation purposes. Versioning is used to understand data accumulated in BI systems over time where all different versions over time are visible. Therefore, you need complete reference data history. Also, mappings in ETL and ESB streams can "break" if new reference data sets are released without updating related mappings as well. Therefore – version control is not only required on the "basic" reference data sets, but also on "higher level" constructs built upon them like mappings and hierarchies.

Since multiple versions of a reference data set can co-exist in an RDM hub, lifecycle processes and/or state transition model play a key role in ensuring which version of a set gets distributed to a downstream system. Without imposing proper governance procedures like ensuring a set version has all necessary approvals before distribution, incorrect or non-aligned reference data might be chosen for distribution, which in turn, would result in inconsistent semantics down the chain in a BI target system. To address these issues, a typical RDM hub implementation contains a few out-of-the-box state-machine models that define the sequence of states a version of a set, mapping or hierarchy must go through before being finalized for distribution. Figure 10 shows one such state-machine, where a set version being worked upon in a *Draft* state must go through at least 2 state actions (Request Approval and Approve) before being ready for distribution (Approved state). Similarly, if a set version is rejected by a data steward upon inspection, it can be moved back to the *Draft* state via the *Re-work* state action. This state model may be customized to the specific BI scenario by adding/removing certain states.

Thus far, we have discussed how a typical reference data management hub implementation enables authoring, import, versioning and lifecycle management of reference data to ensure streamlined and well-governed data is pushed into data warehouses, enabling consistency and governance around reference data dimensions. Proceeding further, the next challenge is to ensure that the reference data from source systems is mapped to the common canonical reference data that is being used in the warehouse as part of the ETL process.

Figure 9. Delta changes to define a new reference data set version

Code	Name
01	France
02	Denmark
03	Greece
04	France

→

Code	Name
01	France
02	Denmark
03	Greece
04	China

Figure 10. Reference data state machine model

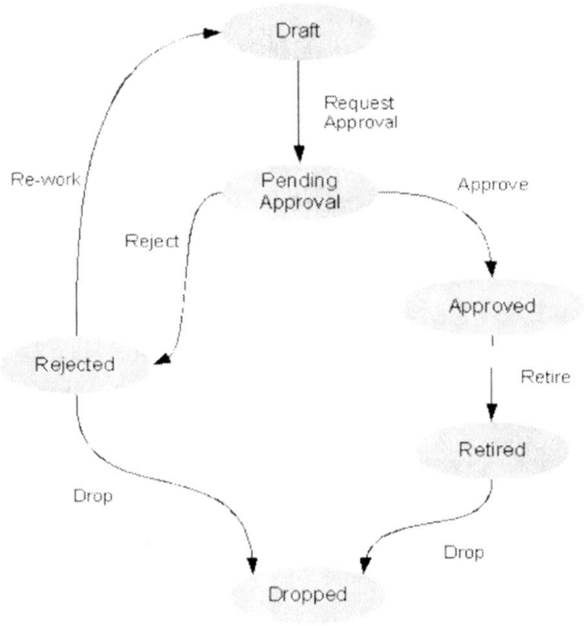

The standard pattern for moving transactional data (and other dimensions, like master data) into a warehouse is to use an ETL tool like InfoSphere DataStage (Alur, et al., 2008) to take updates from source systems and transform and load those into the dimensional tables in a warehouse. As discussed briefly in the previous section, the representation of the reference data in the different source systems invariably differs from the canonical representation in the warehouse. For example, a source system may represent countries using a numeric code like 91 (dialing code for India) or using the ISO-3166-1 two character standard (AF), while the warehouse might use the ISO-3166-2 3 character standard (AFG).

We already saw how a typical RDM hub implementation provides all the essential features that are ideal for managing the sets associated with the different source systems and the warehouse. Now, we shall discuss how an RDM hub can empower business data stewards to create the maps that can be used for translations and version them as necessary for the mappings between the sources and the warehouse. Let us revisit the transcoding scenario described in the last section. In Figure 3, fields representing country codes in source and target represent the set of country codes, which is a type of reference data. However, as observed, source and target reference values have different code representations for the same countries. Due to this reason, before performing data integration or distribution, there arises a need to transcode the source representation to one that can be understood by the target. In a typical RDM implementation, reference data transcoding is achieved through reference data mappings from a source reference data set to a target reference data set. Reference data mappings define relationships across reference data sets and values in those sets. Reference data mappings are also maintained as first-class citizens (like sets) and defined as managed mapping set entities within a typical reference data management hub implementation. Once a mapping set is created, individual value mappings can be created by selecting a source value and a target value from source and target sets respectively. Because these are managed entities, a reference data value mapping contains information like effective date, expiration date and so on, and may also contain any custom properties a data steward may create.

The transcoding defined through reference data map(s) can be simple (one-to-one) where a single source representation is mapped to a single target representation, or complex (one-to-many, many-to-one, or many-to-many), where one or more source representations are mapped to one or more target representations. An example of one-to-many scenario would be where a single canonical representation is mapped to multiple application specific representations in Figure 11.

Simple transcoding (Figure 12) would be applicable in scenarios where there is single source system or a set of source systems, all backed up by the same code table(s) and a single target system or a set of target systems, all backed up by the same code table(s). For performing the required mappings, reference data from source(s) and target(s) is imported into reference data management hub using one of the RDM hub import mechanisms. Once imported, a reference data mapping set can be defined using the UI with source and targets specified as the respective sets into which reference data was imported. Finally, the values mappings are created either using the UI or through import process. In order to perform import, a mapping file should be constructed with source and target specification and any desired properties for the mappings.

Complex transcoding is applicable in scenarios where there are either multiple source systems and/or multiple target systems all backed up by the different code table(s). For performing the required mappings, reference data from all sources and targets is imported into RDM hub using one of the mechanisms import mechanisms. Once imported, multiple mapping sets are defined using the UI with each pair of source and target specified as the respective sets into which reference data was imported. Finally, the values mappings are created and undergo change over time as part of lifecycle processes.

Let's consider this in more detail for BI. A key characteristic of BI systems is that they store transactional data like orders, invoices, etc. over extended periods of time. This transactional data is linked to master data like customer, product, etc. which usually references lots of reference data tables (e.g., units of measure, color codes, product categories, customer segments, country codes, etc.). In addition, several other reference data tables storing information like order types, invoice types, etc. are linked to the transactional data objects. As a consequence, reports like revenue by country, average order size by order category, revenue by product category, revenue by

Figure 11. Mapping across reference data set values

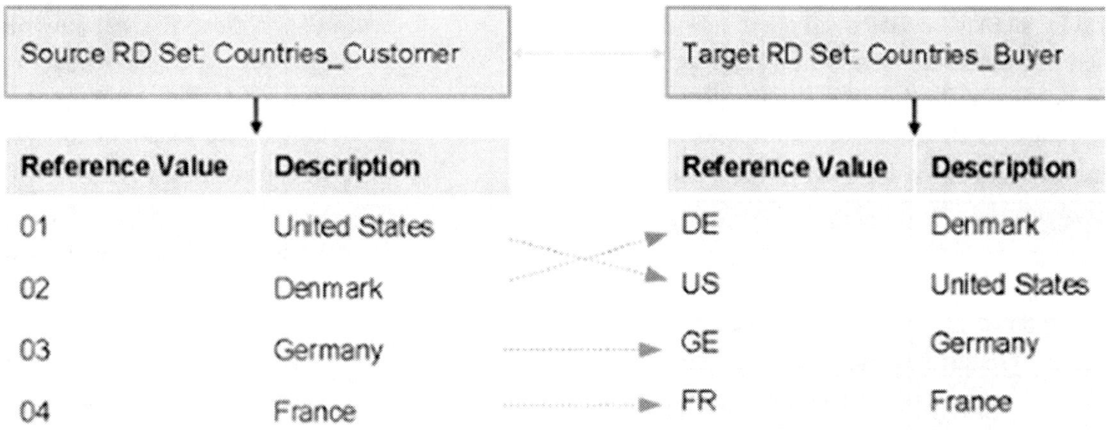

Figure 12. Overall solution architecture with a principled approach to RDM

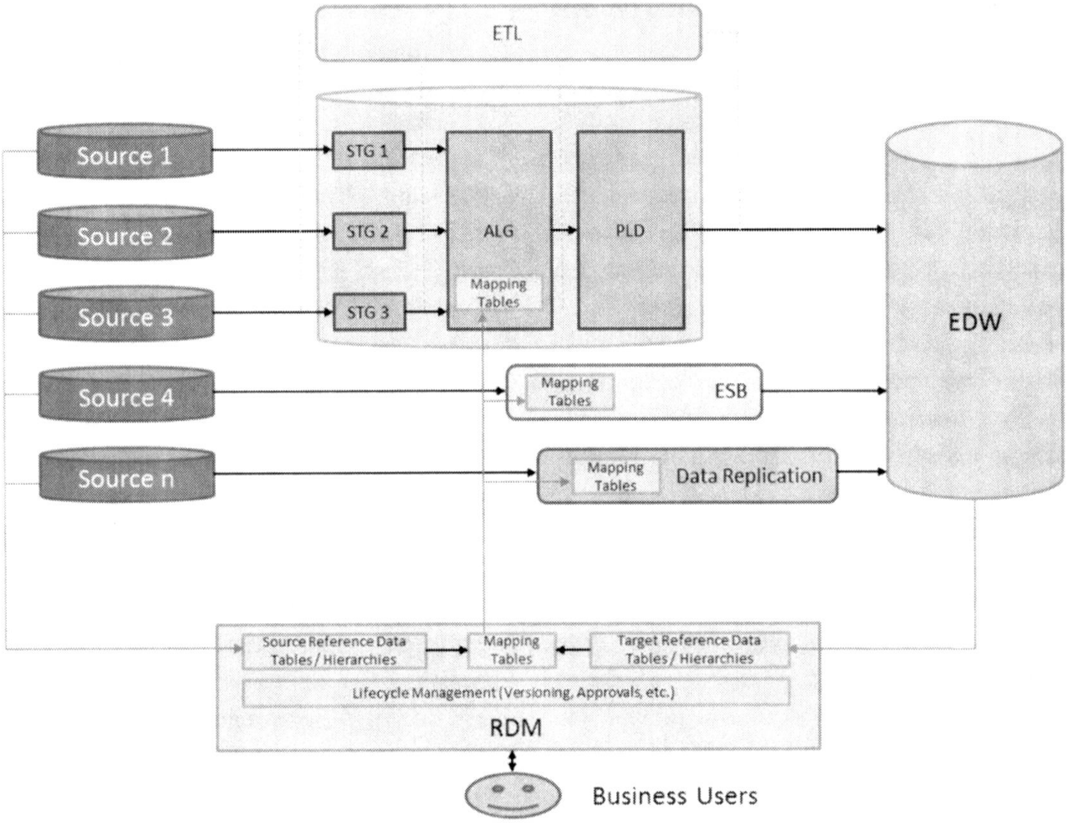

customer segment, etc. all aggregate information using attributes, where the permissible attribute values are reference data values in reference data tables. In order to run these reports with consistent and accurate results over time, the historic dimension of reference data over time needs to be dealt with. Each time reference data sets in an RDM system are updated, all mappings using the reference data sets must be updated as well. A consistent distribution of reference data sets and mappings needs to be done in a well-governed way. Consequently, for a BI system, one of the following choices could be considered:

1. Each time reference data set and mapping updates are delivered for the information integration layer that is feeding the BI system (as shown in Figure 14), a batch process must be executed on the data in the BI system as well updating the old reference data values to the latest version in all instances where the old value has been replaced by a new version. A new version of a mapping might be created due to the following reasons:
   a. The mapping must be changed so that the same source reference data value in a newer version of the mapping points to a different but existing target reference data value. This might be due to:
      i. Removal of a reference data value in the reference data set of the target;
      ii. An update on the previous target reference value making a different one more appropriate;
      iii. Discovering that the initial mapping contained a mistake which was later corrected;

  b. The mapping must be changed so that the same source reference data value in a newer version of the mapping points to a different and new target reference data value. In this case, the target reference data set was updated with a new reference data value;
2. Alternatively, the reference data sets for the BI target system are exported to the BI system not only with the scope of the current version, but also with the full history of each reference data value. If this approach is taken, report queries need to be written in a way that for attributes like country code, not only the current reference values (e.g. country code US for United States) are considered, but also all previous versions for the current value (e.g. country code US might have had the predecessors USA, 81, etc.). This ensures that for a revenue by country report, all items across the reference value US (current) and USA, 81, etc. (previous old versions) are considered to accurately summarize the revenue for the country United States.

As reference data goes through its lifecycle, stewards or business users perform changes (additions, deletions, updated) to these mappings as necessary. Eventually, these mappings can be exported and distributed to warehouses or for performing transcoding by an ETL system during the alignment stage.

A typical RDM hub implementation provides several out-of-the-box methods to export reference data sets and hierarchies, the most common being user interface based manual export, which requires no programming experience. Alternatives like batch export or utilizing RDM service interfaces and APIs require basic programming know-how. During data export, we may be faced with the issue of representational differences between the default out-of-the-box export format that a typical reference data management hub implementation provides, and one that is expected by target BI system(s). In some rare cases, the target systems can directly consume out-of-the-box exports, but in most scenarios, a transformation is required. In some cases, it may be desirable to get a delta export for the changes since last export for certain target systems rather than the entire set of reference data values or mappings. For enabling this, RDM hub programmatic APIs could be leveraged to compare the current version of the desired reference data set or mapping with the version that was last exported, and export only the changes. An output transformer could then just consume this delta file and transform it in a series of add/update jobs that could be directly executed on the target BI system(s). Figure 13 shows the overall solution architecture after applying the above described concepts and processes in a typical BI integration scenario. As shown, imported reference data sets undergo lifecycle transitions, versioning, hierarchy creation and so forth, all in a governed and managed environment. The mappings created between the values from reference data sets from source and target BI systems go thru a similar well-governed process, and are exported for transcoding in ETL, for alignment during data replication an even for real-time ESB processes.

CONCLUSION

In this chapter, we discussed how a principled approach to reference data management using a range of concepts and features provided by a typical Reference Data Management implementation, leads to a comprehensive solution architecture catering to an effective BI integration scenario. Such a typical RDM implementation directly addresses requirements like hierarchies, transcoding, etc that need to be fulfilled in a BI integration scenario. By imposing a standard governance and workflow procedure on authorship and editing of reference data sets, hierarchies and mappings, an RDM system ensures that the version of reference data distributed to target BI systems is governed (cleaned-up, well-aligned, gold version), in turn, maximizing the quality and trustworthy of the business insights being drawn upon using the BI system.

REFERENCES

Alur, N., Takahashi, C., Toratani, S., & Vasconcelos, D. (2008). *IBM InfoSphere DataStage data flow and job design*. IBM Redbooks Publication.

BBC. (1999). *Health hospital error blamed for smear scare*. Retrieved June 3, 2013, from http://news.bbc.co.uk/2/hi/health/394606.stm

Chen, W., Baldwin, J., Dunn, T., Grasselt, M., Hussain, S., & Mandelstein, D. et al. (n.d.). A practical guide to managing reference data with IBM InfoSphere master data management reference data management hub. *IBM Redbooks Publication*.

DNB ASA. (2012). *DNB ASA centralizes reference data management for more effective governance and reduced business risk*. Retrieved June 3, 2013, from http://www.ibm.com/common/ssi/cgi-bin/ssialias?subtype=AB&infotype=PM&appname=SWGE_IM_IP_USEN&htmlfid=IMC14762USEN&attachment=IMC14762USEN.PDF

Dreibelbis, A., Hechler, E., Milman, I., Oberhofer, M., Run, P. V., & Wolfson, D. (2008). *Enterprise master data management: An SOS approach to managing core information*. Boston, MA: Pearson PLC.

Godinez, M., Hechler, E., Koenig, K., & Lockwood, S. Oberhofer, & Michael, S. (2010). The art of enterprise information architecture: A systems-based approach for unlocking business insight. Boston, MA: Pearson PLC.

ISO 3166-1 Wiki Page. (n.d.). Retrieved Jan 27, 2013, http://en.wikipedia.org/wiki/ISO_3166-1

ISO 639 Web Page. (n.d.). Retrieved June 3, 2013. http://www.iso.org/iso/language_codes

Lee, Y. W., Pipino, L. L., Funk, J. D., & Wang, R. Y. (2006). *Journey to data quality*. Cambridge, MA: The MIT Press.

LOINC. (1999). *Logical observation identifiers names and codes (LOINC)*. Retrieved June 7, 2013, from http://loinc.org/faq/getting-started/loinc-and-other-standards/

McGilvray, D. (2008). *Executing data quality projects: Ten steps to quality data and trusted information*. Burlington, MA: Morgan Kaufmann.

Narayanan, R., Oberhofer, M., & Pandit, S. (2012). Metadata exploitation in large-scale data migration projects. In *Proceedings of AMCIS 2012*. AMCIS.

Pandit, S., Oberhofer, M., & Milman, I. (2012). Ontology-guided reference data alignment in information integration projects. In *Proceedings of AMCIS 2012*. AMCIS.

Wang, R. Y., & Strong, D. M. (1996). Beyond accuracy: What data quality means to data consumers. *Journal of Management Information Systems*, *12*(4), 5–33.

Xu, F., Pandit, S., & Mandelstein, D. (2012). *Introduction to IBM InfoSphere master data management reference data management hub v10*. Retrieved Jan 27, 2013, from http://www.ibm.com/developerworks/data/library/techarticle/dm-1210mdmhubv10/index.html

KEY TERMS AND DEFINITIONS

Data Quality: Data quality describes if the data is fit for the purpose it is supposedly used; well-known metrics include completeness and validity.

Managed Entity: The blueprint of an abstract entity that contains enough information and properties need to manage the lifecycle of any entity that extends it.

Master Data: Common business objects (such as customers, suppliers, vendors, products, employees, etc.) that need be agreed on and shared throughout an enterprise.

Metadata: Metadata is data describing and characterizing data assets to improve understanding of them, as well as enabling data provenance, impact analysis and the use of the data assets.

Reference Data: Data values that support consistent representation (coding) of key information used to categorize other data within an organization or across groups of organizations. Examples of reference data include gender, employee type, country codes and codes for medical diagnoses.

Reference Data Alignment: Reference data alignment is the process of mapping reference data from one or multiple source systems to their semantic equivalents in the target system.

Reference Data Management: A discipline to manage reference data with process-driven capabilities to create, maintain, version and approve all aspects of the reference data in a secure manner.

Chapter 12
Effective Measurement of DQ/IQ for BI

Arun Thotapalli Sundararaman
India/Birla Institute of Technology and Science, India

ABSTRACT

DQ/IQ measurement in general and in the specific context of BI has always been a topic of high interest for researchers. The topic of Data Quality (DQ) in the field of Information Management has been well researched, published, and studied. Despite such research advances, there has been very little understanding either from a theoretical or from a practical perspective of DQ/IQ measurement for BI. Assessing the quality of data for a BI System has been one of the major challenges for researchers as well as practitioners, leading to the need for frameworks to measure DQ for BI. The objective of this chapter is to provide an overview of the existing frameworks for measurement of DQ for BI, analyze the gaps therein, review proposed solutions, and provide a direction for future research and practice in this area.

INTRODUCTION

There has been a growing interest among researchers and industry practitioners in DQ, DQ assessment and improvement. However, the basic problem of DQ assessment and improvement still remains largely open. For example, Massachusetts Institute of Technology (MIT) has instituted Total Data Quality Management (TDQM) research effort which is grown from industry needs for high quality data. The objective of this program is to establish a solid theoretical foundation and devise practical methods for business and industry to improve DQ. The research scope of this program covers 3 areas i.e. 1) definition of DQ that addresses issues of data quality definition, measurement, and derivations; 2) Analysis of DQ Impact on Business that addresses the value chain relationship between DQ and business outcome

DOI: 10.4018/978-1-4666-4892-0.ch012

and 3) improvement of DQ that addresses various methods for improving DQ.

Thus research interest in DQ remains an enduring subject, which is reiterated even by very recent literature. For example, Fehrenbacher et al., 2012 state that the importance of DQ is ever increasing and that research in this field focuses mainly on *2 aspects i.e. criteria and assessment.* This recent work observes that while researchers have developed a number of frameworks, criteria lists and approaches for assessing and measuring DQ, still research in this discipline indicates that assessing DQ remains to be challenging. This work argues that although DQ is subjective, most of the existing frameworks and assessment methodologies do not often consider the context in which the assessment is performed. Through empirical data research this cited work suggests that the perceived importance of DQ criteria has changed over the last decade.

Heinrich et. al., 2009 observe that many DQ metrics are designed on an ad hoc basis and that they are often highly subjective and propose six normative requirements in order to enable a scientific approach and an evaluation of the metrics.

Direct references to DQ in BI Systems in published literature are limited. The same may be explored through references to related types of Information Systems such as DW, DSS, EIS or data mining. Similarly, the terms DQ and IQ have been used interchangeably in literature. There has been no consensus about the distinction between DQ and IQ – DQ may be referred to technical issues or quality in sources or 'raw data' and IQ may be referred to non-technical issues or quality in processed data stores or insights presented from data for decision making.

The objectives of this chapter are as follows:

- Identify gaps that exist in measuring DQ for BI based on published frameworks;
- Analyze existing DQ/IQ measurement frameworks in light of their applicability for BI;
- Examine DQ requirements (normative requirements) applicable to DQ for BI;
- Discuss at length a proposed framework and how it seeks to address the gaps;
- Consolidate findings and directions for future work in the study of measurement of DQ for BI.

In summary, past literature shows that poor quality of data in a warehouse adversely impacts the usability of the warehouse and managing DQ in a warehouse is very important (Shankaranarayanan, 2005). The needs of DQ definition and approach for DW and/or Decision Support Systems are unique and different. However, most of the research work focused on this specialized type of information system, have approached with metadata model (integrating / extending existing metadata in a warehouse with quality-related metadata, which has associated practical problems in implementation) and have not focused on implementation aspects of the framework.

BACKGROUND

There has been no consensus about the distinction between data quality and information quality. In this chapter, no distinction has been made and term data quality has been used to refer to the full range of issues.

Given the limited research advances in definition of DQ metrics or DQ measurement for BI, it will be valuable to focus on research based on DQ metrics requirements framework. As it applies to any other measurement, it is important to identify and summarize the requirements for DQ measurement. This view is supported in the works of Heinrich et. al., 2009. Such a focus is expected to guide the principles of DQ metrics definition and/or measurement – either for individual DQ dimensions or comprehensive (i.e. covering all DQ dimensions) DQ metrics such as overall DQ score (Sundararaman, 2012).

Heinrich et. al., 2009 observe that many DQ metrics are designed on an ad hoc basis to solve specific, practical problems and that they are often highly subjective. To enable a scientific foundation and an evaluation of the metrics, Heinrich et. al., 2009 propose six normative requirements for DQ metrics. These requirements are listed below:

- **Normalization:** An adequate normalization is necessary to assure that the values of the metric are comparable (for instance, to compare different levels of DQ over time (Pipino et al., 2002);
- **Interval Scale:** To support both the monitoring of the DQ level over time and the economic evaluation of measures the metrics should be interval scaled. This means that the difference between two levels of DQ must be meaningful;
- **Interpretability:** The metrics should be "easy to interpret by business users" and the values of the DQ metrics have to be comprehensible;
- **Aggregation:** The metrics must allow aggregation of the quantified values on a given level to the next higher level;
- **Adaptivity:** To quantify DQ in a goal-oriented way, the metrics need to be adaptable to the context of a particular application;
- **Feasibility:** To ensure practicality, the metrics should be based on input parameters that are determinable. When defining metrics, methods to determine the input parameters shall be defined.

DQ measurement in BI should be done to enable and support effective decision making. Traditional methods for evaluating DQ dimensions do so objectively without considering contextual factors such as the decision-task and the decision-maker's preferences. DQ Measurement is dependent on the purpose (task). The perceived quality of the data is influenced by the decision-task and that the same data may be viewed through two or more different quality lenses depending on the decision-maker and the decision-task it is used for. In their paper Shankaranarayanan and Cai, 2006 have justified the need for incorporating contextual considerations in DQ measurement. This important issue has not been explicitly addressed by previous DQ research. Shankaranarayanan and Cai underline the need for further research in the direction of implementation, while introducing a theoretical framework.

Woodall et. al., 2010 are of the view that no individual existing technique for measuring DQ is wholly suitable to assess DQ for all types of requirements due to the varying nature of requirements over time and organizational needs. The requirements may be different for every organization and even the same organization over time. They further observe that while some of the DQ assessment techniques are geared towards specific application areas and are often not suitable in different applications, other techniques are more general and therefore do not always meet specific requirements.

The key limitation of existing research is that it focuses merely on technical / architectural aspects of DQ. Addressing this limitation, Gustafsson et. al., 2006 present a framework for assessing DQ focusing on how data supports the business. In their work, the authors had customized the framework for an insurance company by weighting the dimensions of DQ and by relating DQ to the effect it impact on the enterprise's business. Research of DQ measurement has so far been focused on identifying a set of DQ factors or analyzing select set of DQ factors (e.g. timeliness or correctness). Even a recent study, Helfert et. al., 2009 reiterates this statement and emphasizes the need for comprehensive DQ measure considering all relevant DQ factors:

Several algorithms have been developed for a subset of dimensions, such as accuracy, completeness, consistency, and timeliness. The definition of an aggregate quality measure is still a much debated issue and existing contributions should be further analyzed and extended.... the most common approach used to obtain a data quality index is to consider all the measures associated with the different quality dimensions and combine them by using a weighed sum.

Thus, the study of a comprehensive assessment framework, covering all appropriate DQ factors remains an open area of research in the study of DQ, Alkharboush et. al., 2010. Batini et. al., 2006 emphasize the need for defining a comprehensive set of DQ measurement allowing objective assessment of the underlying DQ and appropriate assessment methods, while dealing with the problems associated with defining a reference set of data, quality dimensions and metrics. Table 1 shows how different works have focused only on select set of DQ factors and not in a comprehensive manner.

In summary, past literature confirms that poor quality of data in BI adversely impacts the usability of the System and managing DQ in BI is very important (Shankaranarayanan, 2005). The needs of DQ definition and measurement approach for BI Systems are unique and different. However, most of the research work have approached with metadata model (integrating / extending existing metadata with quality-related metadata), which has associated practical problems in implementation and have not focused on implementation aspects of the framework. Important directions in the study of DQ measurement for BI are as below:

1. DQ measurement framework focused on practical implementation aspects (Gustafsson et. al., 2006);
2. Measure DQ with specific business context (Even et. al., 2007).

METHODOLOGIES AND FRAMEWORKS

Issues – Gaps in Literature Related to DQ Measurement for BI

Based on the discussions in the previous section, gaps in published literature related to DQ measurement for BI are presented below:

Gap 1: DQ Factor relevant for BI: Most of the past research work lead to a set of DQ factors that are largely related to transaction processing

Table 1. Study of selected DQ factors

Name of the Work	DQ Factor(s)	Year	Reference
A Procedure to Develop Metrics for Currency and its Application in CRM	Currency	2009	Heinrich et. al., 2009
A novel data quality metric for timeliness Considering supplemental data	Timeliness	2009	Heinrich et. al., 2009
A conceptional approach to unify completeness, Consistency, and accuracy as quality dimensions of data values	Completeness, Consistency, and accuracy	2010	Kaiser, 2010
How to measure Data Quality – A Metrics based approach	Correctness and timeliness	2007	Heinrich et. al., 2007
Does the EU insurance mediation directive help to improve data quality? – A metric-based analysis	Correctness and completeness	2008	Heinrich et. al., 2008
Improving Data Quality: Consistency and Accuracy	Consistency and accuracy	2007	Cong et. al., 2007
Measuring Data Believability: a Provenance Approach.	Believability	2008	Prat et. al., 2008

systems. However, the DQ requirements for BI are different from transactional systems because data for BI are primarily used for decision making. A large number of quality issues relevant for BI cannot be expressed with traditional models, Alkharboush et. al., 2010;

Gap 2: Lack of context for use: Past research has not captured the context (i.e. how the data is used and its related outcome) while studying DQ measurement. Data is intended to be used for different business decisions and as such any measure of DQ should be sensitive to this context of business decisions for which the data is being used and the quality of business outcomes based on such decisions;

Gap 3: Relative importance of DQ factor: In a set of different DQ factors not every factor impacts the overall DQ equally. The degree of impact varies again based on the decision task for which the data is consumed – e.g. the impact of the DQ factor of timeliness on tactical decisions is different than that on credit decisions. Past research on DQ does not recognize this varying degree of impact;

Gap 4: Measurement of DQ should reflect the confidence of the users in the quality of data based on their experience with usage of the data.

Published literature materials call out some/all of these gaps specifically and provide a direction for further research. For example, Knight, 2011 opines that systems information quality (DQ) investigative frameworks, thus far, lack a widely accepted model with which researchers can conceptualize the context of their study, and identify the important DQ characteristics to be examined and empirically tested. The result is a widely varied body of literature lacking a coherent and consistent approach to identifying and measuring systems DQ. Similarly, Gibson, 2010 observes that DQ research to date has approached the subject independent from actual users although the interdependency between the two is obvious.

To summarize, these approaches have resulted in 4 major gaps that form the focus areas for the current research work. These major gaps identified are:

- DQ factors relevant to BI are not studied in detail;
- Lack of context (domain / industry/ function) in measurement of DQ;
- Relative influence of DQ factor not considered ("how" a factor impacts DQ and "extent" to which it impacts are not considered);
- Confidence level of users in quality of data and decisions are not captured.

Solutions: Existing Methodologies

The solution to the above gaps (or problems) in measurement of DQ for BI lies in developing a context based, comprehensive DQ measurement framework. Such a solution which is proposed in this section and elaborated in the next sections, involves approaching the problem of DQ definition based on the specific context of the measurement and covers a complete set of DQ factors. Such a framework is expected to provide information that helps organizations to take decisions in order to improve and assure the quality of information systems. IT Practitioners can look forward to deriving an objective measure of DQ with the use of such a framework. Such a framework may be evolved by adopting appropriate DQ measurement methodology from published literature. Table 2 provides a summary view of DQ assessment methodologies published in literature.

QAFD methodology combines quantitative objective, and qualitative subjective assessments to identify quality issues and select the appropriate quality improvement actions. Context-dependent indices, data quality rules, measurements,

Table 2. Existing DQ assessment methodologies

S No	Acronym	Name of the Methodology	Author	Reference
1	TDQM	Total Data Quality Management	Wang	Wang et. al. 1998
2	DWQ	The Datawarehouse Quality Methodology	Jeusfeld	Jeusfeld et. al.,, 1998
3	TIQM	Total Information Quality Management	English	English, L., 1999
4	AIMQ	A Methodology for Information Quality Assessment	Lee	Lee et. al., 2002
5	CIHI	Canadian Institute for Health Information Methodology	Long and Seko	Long. J et. al., 2005
6	DQA	Data Quality Assessment	Pipino.L, Lee.Y and Wang.R. Y.	Pipino, L. et. al., 2002
7	IQM	Information Quality Management	Eppler	Eppler, M., 2002
8	ITSAT	ITSAT Methodology	Falorsi, P., Pallara, S., Pavone, A., Alessandroni, A., Massella, E., and Scannapieco, M.	Falorsi et. al., 2003
9	AMEQ	Activity-based Measuring and Evaluating of product information Quality (AMEQ) methodology	Su and Jin	Su, Y and Jin, Z 2004
10	COLDQ	Loshin Methodology (Cost-effect Of Low Data Quality	Loshin	Loshin, 2004
11	DaQuinCIS	Data Quality in Cooperative Information Systems	Scannapieco, M., Pernici, B., and Pierce, E	Scannapieco et. al., 2005
12	QAFD	Methodology for the Quality Assessment of Financial Data	Amicis, De F. and Batini, C.	Amicis and Batini, 2004
13	CDQ	Comprehensive methodology for Data Quality Management	Batini, C., Cabitza,F., Cappiello,C. and Francalanci, C.	Batini et. al., 2008

and strategies for quantitative and qualitative assessments are defined. Therefore, of the different methodologies listed in Table 2, QAFD methodology appears to be most suited for a framework for measurement of DQ in BI. The phases and steps involved in QAFD are depicted in Figure 1.

Recommendations: DQ Dimensions for BI

In this Section we discuss the need for extending the DQ dimensions list to meet measurement requirements specific to BI. Of the different DQ methodologies listed in TABLE I., TIQM (Total Information Quality Management) needs specific mention in this context. The TIQM methodology has been designed to support data warehouse projects (English, 1999). DQ dimensions considered by TIQM methodology include "precision", "contextual clarity" and "rightness", besides a few other dimensions. The dimensions in Figure 1 need special attention in the context of their relevance to DQ for BI. It is recommended to include 4 DQ dimensions listed below in the study of DQ measurement for BI:

- Relevance of dimensions (contextual clarity);
- Relevance of measures (rightness);
- Granularity (precision);
- Aggregation (precision).

Figure 1. Phases of QAFD

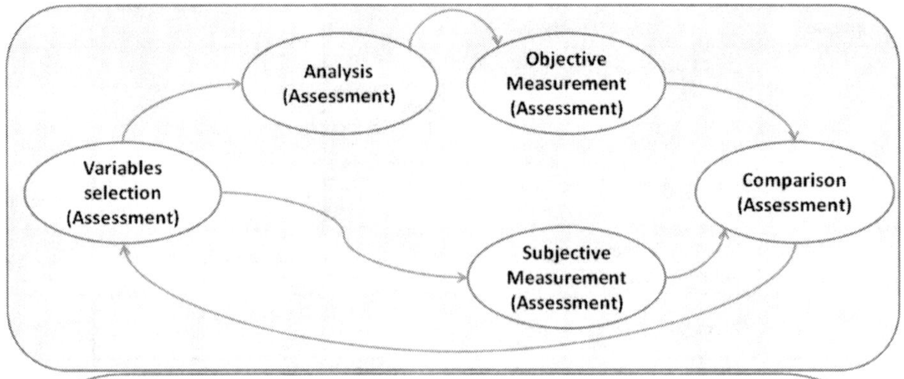

Phase 1 : **Variables selection**

Input → Financial variables and financial context

Data Analysis: identification and description of the most relevant financial registry variables, classification of the variables along 3 classes: qualitative / categorical, quantitative / numerical and dates

Output → Classification and groups of primary variables

Phase 2 : **Analysis**

Input → Classification and groups of primary variables, data quality analysis techniques, business rules, process analysis

DQ Requirements Analysis: Analysis of DQ dimensions, syntactic and semantic accuracy, internal and external consistency, completeness, currency, timeliness and uniqueness

Output → Identification of errors

Phase 3 : **Objective measurement**

Input → Identification of errors

Measurement of quality : Definition of indices for the evaluation and quantification of the global data quality level

Output → Quantitative objective assessment

Phase 4 : **Qualitative subjective assessment**

Input → Business and data quality expertise, measurement and classification and groups of primary variables

Measurement of quality: Business expert assessment, financial operator assessment, data quality expert assessment, comparison of subjective assessments

Output → Qualitative subjective assessment

Phase 5 : **Comparison**

Input → Qualitative objective dimensions, qualitative subjective dimensions

Measurement of quality: Calculation of discrepancies

Output → Assessment and improvement

Granularity of data in BI infers the level of details that it carries and thus refers to the depth of data available. High granularity refers to data that is at or near the transaction level. Data that is at the transaction level is usually referred to as atomic level data. Low granularity refers to data that is summarized or aggregated, usually from the atomic level data. Aggregation refers to summarization of data across different hierarchies of dimensions. Data may be lightly summarized as in daily or weekly summaries or highly summarized data such as yearly averages and totals. The BI System has to be designed at a right balance i.e. very high granularity may impact query performance or very low granularity may impact ability to conduct intended analysis. Thus, granularity and aggregation are very critical factors influencing the quality of decisions and thus DQ of a BI System:

- **Relevance of dimensions:** Presentation of appropriate and adequate attributes, with relevant hierarchies and dimensional attributes is essential for successful implementation of BI. For effective decision making, the users of BI slice and dice the business facts by different dimensions and at different levels (or hierarchies) within the selected dimension. Therefore, it is imperative to study relevance of dimensions as a DQ factor in the measurement of DQ for BI;

- **Relevance of measures:** On the same lines as above, inclusion of adequate business measures also assumes significance for successful implementation of BI. For effective decision making, the users of BI compare various measures or business facts for their decision making. Such an analysis is intended to provide insights to the users of BI and help them identify the root cause of problems that they like to fix. Therefore, it is imperative to study relevance of measures as a DQ factor for studying quality of outcomes from decision making process.

Recommendations: Framework

In this section a framework, which is derived from QAFD methodology referred earlier, is proposed for study of DQ measurement for BI. The steps proposed in QAFD methodology and the manner in which they have been adopted in this framework is outlined in Table 3.

The Figure 2 depicts a comprehensive view of the recommended framework for measurement of DQ for BI.

Recommended Steps for Implementation of the Framework

The proposed framework is context sensitive in that it differentiates different business domains and within a selected domain it recognizes the specific context associated with different functions and their decision making requirements.

Table 3. Adoption of QAFD for DQ measurement in BI

Step as Described in QAFD	Adoption in Recommended Framework
First, the methodology selects the most relevant DQ dimensions which are grouped in categories of "related issues" that are characterized by the same risk, business, and descriptive factors.	Business decisions were logically grouped based on "related issues" into "decision categories"
The most relevant DQ dimensions are identified.	Additional DQ dimensions appropriate for BI added, as discussed in previous section.
An objective assessment is performed based on quantitative indexes.	Step introduced for calibration, capturing "weightage" for the selected DQ dimensions, serving as a variable in computation of DQ score.
Subjective assessment is performed from three different perspectives; business experts, customers, and data quality experts. Each interviewee has to assess the quality level along each quality dimension. An overall assessment is obtained as the mean value of the subjective assessment of each class of experts.	Step introduced to capture "confidence factor" of experts in BI, serving as 2nd critical variable in computation of DQ score. A composite DQ score is computed based on both "weightage" and "confidence factor"
Finally, objective and subjective assessments are compared.	Independent assessment of DQ is conducted from BI users and is compared with DQ score computed by the framework.

The proposed framework may be implemented by following steps described in this section:

Step 1: Conduct research within the business function for which the framework is to be implemented and identify list of possible answers that users of BI expect to get from the System. This step is critical as it sets the foundation for multiple business decisions that the users of BI are likely to arrive at using the data that resides in the system. Decisions do not exist without questions and thus implementing this framework starts

Figure 2. DQ assessment framework

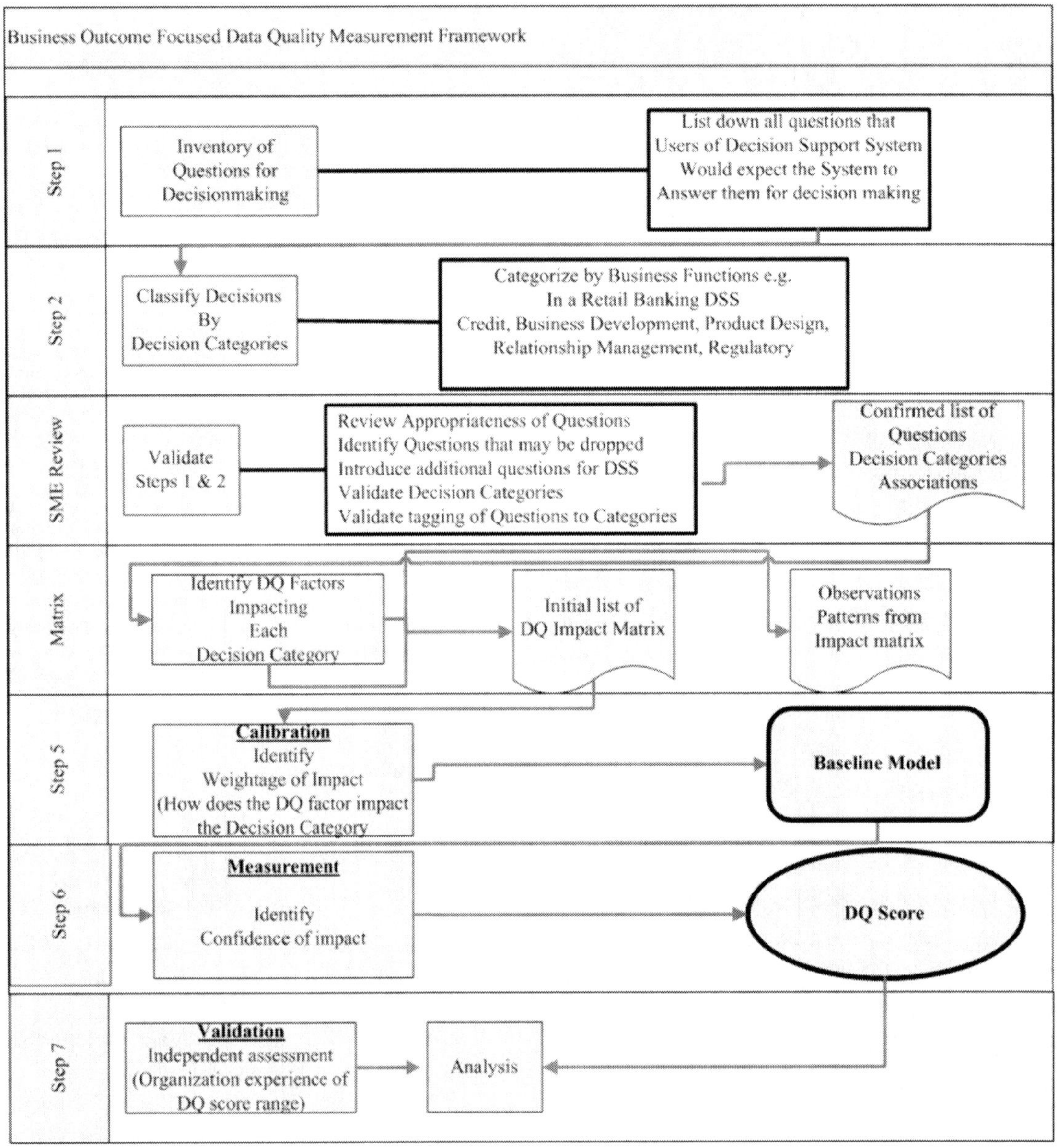

with arriving at the master list of potential questions for which answers are expected from the underlying BI;

Step 2: Group these decisions logically into sets of "decision categories". This concept of decision category is the central theme of the framework, values for which needs to be derived based on the functional context of the BI for which DQ is being measured. This logical grouping is based on business context and "related issues" are to be grouped into "decision categories". This grouping is an essential aspect of this framework, as the process of logical grouping provides the context sensitive measurement of DQ. As discussed in the previous section a major gap that exists in the current literature pertains to lack of context for use;

Step 3: Validate the list of questions and decision categories with subject matter experts from the selected business function. This step involves proofing the base identified so far, by seeking expert inputs from industry specialists in the selected function for which the framework is proposed to be implemented. The objective is to validate the completeness of the questions and more importantly validate correctness of their logical grouping into decision categories;

Step 4: Build the decision category-DQ dimensions matrix to evaluate the applicability or otherwise of each DQ dimension to selected decision category and vice versa. Creating this matrix is again significant as it adds further context to DQ measurement. In addition to the context (of decision categories) introduced in the previous step, this matrix provides further context to follow different set of DQ dimensions for different decision categories, based on their specific applicability;

Step 5: Calibrate the above association by industry experts by capturing value for "weightage". The objective of this step is to get the model calibrated with appropriate weightage assignments for selected decision category-DQ dimension combination. This calibrated weightage factor serves as the baseline for subsequent steps;

Step 6: Measure DQ for each decision category, using the baseline model and capturing the confidence of the users in the quality of data, capturing value for confidence level component within the boundary of above calibration.

At this stage, 2 sets of variables are introduced i.e. weight and confidence level. Weight represents how strongly a specific DQ dimension influences a decision category of interest, and confidence level represents confidence of BI users in quality of data existing in "their" organization for each DQ dimension. Appropriate scale for capturing values for these 2 variables may be used, based on the choice of the measuring organization:

Step 7: Validate the scores. In this step, the DQ score computed through the previous steps is subjected to independent validation. A different set of users are asked to provide their overall assessment of the DQ as it exists in BI under study. This independent measure is based on the quality of business outcomes they have experienced from decisions arrived using the DSS under study. The objective of this independent assessment is to compare the DQ scores computed by the framework with these objective assessments and carry out appropriate statistical tests of validity. The responses from this second group of users serve as the gold standard, and outputs produced by the framework are compared to the gold standard to determine the validity of the framework.

Recommended Framework: Summary View

The composite DQ score computed by the framework may be expressed through the following equation:

$$\text{DQ Score}(d) = \frac{\sum_{i \epsilon DQ}^{n} w(i)\, c(i)\, a(i,d)}{\sum_{i \epsilon DQ}^{n} a(i,d)}$$

where:

d = Decision Category (i.e. Credit, Tactical, etc.)

DQ = DQ Criteria

w(i) = Weight (and hence impact) of DQ factor i on decision category d.

c(i) = Confidence in the quality of DQ factor i

$a(i,d)$ = Whether DQ factor i applies to decision category d – 0 or1

such that:

$$\sum_{i\epsilon DQ}^{n} a\left(i,d\right) <> 0$$

Measuring DQ through a composite score can be tricky, since such a measure is expected to meet both precision and practicality expectations. These 2 are conflicting goals and achieving a balance remains a significant aspect of the framework. A DQ score should reflect reality as precisely as possible; yet, the assessment method adopted for such a measure should be as practical as possible. Any assessment method should be understood by the user and should be easy to adapt. Despite the sizeable body of literature available on DQ, relatively few researchers have tackled the difficult task of quantifying some of the conceptual definitions DQ. In fact, a general criticism within the DQ research field is that most approaches lack methods or even suggestions on how to assess quality scores, Naumann and Rolker, 2000.

The DQ score computed by the framework recommended in this Chapter represents an objective view of the quality of data that exists in BI System under study, for each of the decision categories and thus serves as the basis to link DQ to the quality of decisions derived from BI. As explained in this section, this work introduces a framework that is comprehensive, based on existing DQ assessment methodology, context sensitive and addresses the gaps in current literature listed in the previous section. This approach also addresses the key concern raised by Kaiser, 2010 i.e.; *What is still lacking is an approach towards a unified measure of DQ based on metrics for different dimensions.*

Results and Analysis from Research Work on the Framework

Sundararaman (2011) carried out an empirical study in retail banking to experiment the recommended framework. The said empirical study was carried out in 3 stages to capture data from different target subjects. The overall approach of the study was to involve the actual business users in DQ measurement.

Stage 1 of the study was focused on engaging industry subject experts (retail banking) to calibrate the DW measurement framework. At the end of this stage the DQ scoring model was baselined with appropriate weightage factors assigned for each decision category that served as the basis for rest of the study. Inputs captured from experts in this stage served as value for the variable related to context of the DQ factor for the selected decision category i.e. a(i,d) and weightage variable for each DQ for each Decision category - $w(i)$

Stage 2 of the study involved capturing confidence of actual users of DSS in DQ, which when applied to the DQ scoring model calibrated in the previous stage generated a set of DQ scores. Inputs captured from the users in this stage served as value for the variable related to confidence of the users i.e. c(i).

In Stage 3, another team of users were involved for providing independent assessment of DQ based on their experience in using DSS. The objective of this step is to validate the DQ score calculated by the model in stage 2, with the feedback from users within the organization.

To validate the model outcomes different users of DSS were approached independently to obtain their assessment levels of DQ which served as the gold standard. Almost half of the results show that DQ scores measured by the framework match with the assessment level expressed by the data users (45%); this metric was higher at 49%, considering the instances where the result from the framework and assessment level expressed by users varied marginally +/- 2%. Outputs produced by the framework were compared to the above gold standard and to determine the validity of the framework Pearson's chi-squared test was performed. Chi-square test conducted on the entire set of DQ scores generated from the model using the framework introduced in this research yielded a p-value of 0.0000000001.

This result is statistically significant to support the applicability of the framework for measurement of DQ for BI. Open research challenges from published literature have been addressed through the current research work. For example, Keeton et. al., 2010 had outlined a research challenge related to DQ metrics when they state that the first research challenge is in providing light-weight, scalable mechanisms for determining DQ metrics, without which users of Systems cannot make decisions with high confidence.

FUTURE RESEARCH DIRECTIONS

Emphasis on Normative Requirements

Future research in the study of DQ measurement for BI needs to be in the direction of consolidating the current theoretical advances and focus on implementation aspects with specific reference to meeting the normative requirements of DQ introduced in the earlier section. The following sections discuss importance of some of these requirements and suggested directions for future research.

Focus on Implementation

Interpretability, one of the normative requirements, emphasizes that value of the DQ metrics have to be comprehensible. In a recently published work Ge et. al., 2011 have dealt with the difficulties associated with measuring DQ. Through their work, while they acknowledge that research provides several approaches to measure DQ and many case studies constantly illustrate the difficulties in assessing DQ, they reveal that even though a number of DQ measurement frameworks have been proposed, in practice, organizations are still facing difficulties when implementing these assessment frameworks.

Adaptivity, one of the normative requirements, emphasizes that DQ is to be quantified in a goal-oriented way and that DQ metrics need to be adaptable to the context of a particular application. In the specific context of DQ for BI, this may be interpreted as the need for DQ to be measured in the context of decision tasks and quality of business outcomes. The field of BI is witnessing several technology advances such as use of data mining techniques or predictive analytics models or visualization techniques for BI. A noticeable development in this regard is that such applications which were previously limited to highly trained specialists are now made accessible to a wide range of users expanding the user base of BI. DQ of any data mining models should be carefully measured and any findings should either be cleaned or used as an indicator for the confidence level of the resulting data mining model (Stang et. al.).

CONCLUSION

The importance of DQ for better decision making and thus for better business outcomes can never be over emphasized. Corporate success hinges on the quality of its executive decisions, which in turn depends, to a large extent, on the quality of data in their BI Systems. In this larger context of executive corporate decision making, BI refers to a larger landscape of corporate Business Intelligence function and culture, often comprising a collection of decision support applications, be it DW or EDW or DSS or EIS or any other form. Understandably, lack of DQ or low levels of DQ in the decision making process leads to poor-quality decisions adversely impacting company's future. A recently published book (English, 2011) quantifies the cost of poor DQ for organizations to be in the range of 20-35% of operating revenue.

There has been a growing interest among researchers and industry practitioners in DQ, DQ assessment and improvement. Research interest in DQ remains an enduring subject, which is reiterated even in very recent literature. However, several basic problems related to DQ measurement, more specifically, in the case of specialized systems such as BI still remain largely open. This state has attracted attention both from the Industry and academics either in parallel tracks or through joint initiatives. For example, Massachusetts Institute of Technology (MIT) has instituted Total Data Quality Management (TDQM) research Program which is grown from industry needs for high DQ. The objective of this program is to establish a solid theoretical foundation and devise practical methods for business and industry to improve DQ. The research scope of this program covers 3 areas i.e. 1) definition of DQ that addresses issues of data quality definition, measurement, and derivations; 2) Analysis of DQ Impact on Business that addresses the value chain relationship between DQ and business outcome and 3) improvement of DQ that addresses various methods for improving DQ.

To conclude, the topic of DQ measurement for BI has been extensively researched which has contributed to multiple frameworks and methodologies. The need of the hour is not necessarily to explore newer methodologies or framework, but, to focus on adoption, tailoring and implementation of these methodologies and frameworks, so that real industry experiences can be captured for further making advances in this topic of research.

In summary, the problem is of having more than adequate theories (in the form methodologies and frameworks), but, limited real life experiences to validate these theories. Therefore, the focus needs to shift from discovery to implementation, towards which the following guidelines may serve as a reference checklist:

1. There is a strong need for DQ measurement for BI to be context specific and any framework for DQ measurement needs to be able to meet this requirement;
2. DQ factors that are of special consideration for BI needs to be carefully identified and adopted in the measurement process;
3. The key characteristics of any framework for measurement of DQ in BI are practicality in implementation and easy in adoption;
4. Involvement of users in the measurement of DQ is extremely critical and DQ measurement frameworks should address this special requirement, as part of the framework design itself;
5. Independent validation mechanisms need to be planned as part of the measurement framework;
6. Keep the DQ measurement process simple to comprehend and implement, yet, effective in the results.

REFERENCES

Alkharboush, N., & Li, Y. (2010). A decision rule method for data quality assessment. In *Proceedings of the 15th International Conference on Information Quality*. IEEE.

Batini, C., & Scannapieco, M. (2006). *Data quality: Concepts, methodologies and techniques.* Berlin: Springer.

Cong, G., Fan, W., Geerts, F., Jia, X., & Ma, S. (2007). Improving data quality: Consistency and accuracy. In *Proceedings of the 33rd International Conference on Very Large Databases*, (pp. 315-326). IEEE.

English, L. (1999). *Improving data warehouse and business information quality*. Hoboken, NJ: Wiley & Sons.

English, L. (2011). *Information quality applied: Best practices for improving business information processes and systems*. Hoboken, NJ: Wiley Publishing.

Even, A., & Kaiser, M. (2009). A framework for economics-driven assessment of data quality decisions. In *Proceedings of the 14th International Conference on Information Quality*. IEEE.

Fehrenbacher, D., & Helfert, M. (2012). Contextual factors influencing perceived importance and trade-offs of information quality. *Communications of the Association for Information Systems, 30*, 111–126.

Ge, M., Helfert, M., & Jannach, D. (2011). Information quality assessment: Validating measurement dimensions and processes. In *Proceedings of the 19th European Conference on Information Systems*. IEEE.

Ge, M., Helfert, M., & Jannach, D. (2011). Information quality assessment: Validating measurement dimensions and processes. In *Proceedings of the 19th European Conference on Information Systems*. IEEE.

Gibson, N. (2010). *Improving information products for system 2 design support*. (Ph. D. Thesis). University of Arkansas, Little Rock, AR.

Gustafsson, P., Lindström, Å., Jägerlind, C., & Tsoi, J. (2006). A framework for assessing data quality – From a business perspective. *Software Engineering Research and Practice*, 1009-1015.

Heinrich, B., Kaiser, M., & Kier, M. (2009). A procedure to develop metrics for currency and its application in CRM. *ACM Journal of Data and Information Quality, 1*, 1–28. doi:10.1145/1515693.1515697

Heinrich, B., Kaiser, M., & Klier, M. (2007). How to measure data quality? A metrics based approach. In *Proceedings of 28th International Conference on Information Systems*. IEEE.

Heinrich, B., Kaiser, M., & Klier, M. (2008). Does the EU insurance mediation directive help to improve data quality? A metric-based analysis. In *Proceedings of the 16th European Conference on Information Systems (ECIS)*. ECIS.

Heinrich, B., & Klier, M. (2009). A novel data quality metric for timeliness considering supplemental data. In *Proceedings of the 17th European Conference on Information Systems (ECIS)*, (pp. 2701-2713). ECIS.

Helfert, M., & Foley, O. (2009). *A context aware information quality framework*. Paper presented at Fourth International Conference on Cooperation and Promotion of Information Resources in Science and Technology. Beijing, China.

Helfert, M., Foley, O., Ge, M., & Cappiello, C. (2009). Limitations of weighted sum measures for information quality. In *Proceedings of Americas Conference on Information Systems*. AMCIS.

Junho, S. (2013). Roadmap for e-commerce standardization in Korea. *International Journal of IT Standards and Standardization Research.*

Kaiser, M. (2010). A conceptional approach to unify completeness, consistency, and accuracy as quality dimensions of data values. In *Proceedings of European and Mediterranean Conference on Information Systems*. IEEE.

Keeton, K., Mehra, P., & Wilkes, J. (2010). Do you know your IQ? A research agenda for information quality in systems. *SIGMETRICS Performance Evaluation Review*, *37*(3), 26–31. doi:10.1145/1710115.1710121

Knight, S. (2011). The combined conceptual life-cycle model of information quality: Part 1, an investigative framework. *International Journal of Information Quality*, *2*, 205–230. doi:10.1504/IJIQ.2011.040669

Naumann, F., & Rolker, C. (2000). Assessment methods for information quality criteria. In *Proceedings of the 14th International Conference on Information Quality* (pp. 148-162). IEEE.

Nelson, R., Todd, P. A., & Wixom, B. H. (2005). Antecedents of information and system quality: An empirical examination within the context of data warehousing. *Journal of Management Information Systems*, *21*, 199–235.

Pipino, L., Lee, Y., & Wang, R. Y. (2002). Data quality assessment. *Communications of the ACM*, *45*(4), 211–218. doi:10.1145/505248.506010

Popovič, A., Coelho, P. S., & Jaklič, J. (2009). The impact of business intelligence system maturity on information quality. *Information Research, 14*(4).

Prat, N., & Madnick, S. (2008). Measuring data believability: A provenance approach. In *Proceedings of the 41st Hawaii International Conference on System Sciences*. IEEE.

Shankaranarayanan, G. (2005). Towards implementing total data quality management in a datawarehouse. *Journal of Information Technology Management*, *16*, 21–30.

Shankaranarayanan, G., & Cai, Y. (2006). Supporting data quality management in decision-making. *Decision Support Systems*, *42*, 302–317. doi:10.1016/j.dss.2004.12.006

Stang, J., Hartvigsen, T., & Reitan, J. (2010). The effect of data quality on data mining – Improving prediction accuracy by generic data cleansing. In *Proceedings of the 2010 International Conference on Information Quality*. IEEE.

Sundararaman, A. (2012). *Information quality strategy - An empirical investigation of the relationship between information quality improvements and organizational outcomes*. (Unpublished doctoral dissertation). Birla Institute of Technology and Science, India.

Sundararaman, A. (n.d.). A framework for linking data quality to business objectives in decision support systems. In *Proceedings of 3rd International Conference on Trendz in Information Sciences and Computing (TISC)* (pp. 177-181). TISC.

Turban, E., Sharda, R., & Delen, D. (2011). *Decision support and business intelligence*. Upper Saddle River, NJ: Pearson Education.

Woodall, P., & Parlikad, A. (2010). A hybrid approach to assessing data quality. In *Proceedings of the 15th International Conference on Information Quality*. IEEE.

Zhao, F. (Ed.). (2006). *Maximize business profits through e-partnerships*. Hershey, PA: IGI Global.

ADDITIONAL READING

AlMabhouh, A., & Ahmad, A. (2010), Identifying quality factors within data warehouse, *Second International Conference on Computer Research and Development*, pp.65-72.

Ballou, D., & Tayi, G. (1999). Enhancing data quality in datawarehouse environments. *Communications of the ACM*, *42*(Issue 1), 73–78. doi:10.1145/291469.291471

Batini, C., Barone, D., Mastrella, M., Maurino, A., & Ruffini, C. (2007), A Framework and a Methodology for Data Quality Assessment and Monitoring, *proceedings of the 12th International Conference on Information Quality*, pp. 333-346.

Batini, C., Cappiello, C., Francalanci, C., & Maurino, A. (2009). Methodologies for Data Quality Assessment and Improvement. *ACM Computing Surveys*, *41*(3), 16. doi:10.1145/1541880.1541883

Bogza, R. M. (2008). Business intelligence as a competitive differentiator, IEEE International Conference on Automation, Quality and Testing. *Robotics*, *1*, 146–151.

Daniel, F., Casati, F., Palpanas, T., & Chayka, O. (2008). Managing Data Quality in Business Intelligence Applications, *Program Committee Workshop on Management of Uncertain Data,* pp. 133.

Even, A., & Shankaranarayanan, G. (2005). Value-Driven Data Quality Assessment, Research Paper - IQ Concepts, Tools, Metrics, Measures, Models, and Methodologies.

Fehrenbacher, D., & Helfert, M. (2008), An empirical research on the evaluation of data quality dimensions, *Proceedings of the 13th International Conference on Information Quality*.

Helfert,M & Herrman, C. (2005). Introducing data quality management in data warehousing. *Information Quality,* Advances in Management Information Systems, 135-152.

Idris, N., & Ahmad, K. (2011). Managing Data Source quality for data warehouse in manufacturing services, *International Conference on Electrical Engineering and Informatics*, pp. 1-6.

Lima, L. F. R. Maçada, Antonio Carlos Gastaud & Vargas, Lilia Maria. (2006), Research into Information Quality – A study of the state-of-the art IQ and its consolidation, *Proceedings of the International Conference on Information Quality*.

Lin, G., Jing, G., & Fang-fang, D. (2011). Evaluation method of enterprise information quality based on QFD, *International Conference on Consumer Electronics*, pp. 325-328.

Lönnqvista, A., & Pirttimäkib, V. (2006). The Measurement of Business Intelligence. *Information Systems Management*, *23*, 32–40. doi:10.1201/1078.10580530/45769.23.1.20061201/91770.4

Madnick, S., Wang, R. Y., & Zhu, H. (2009). Overview and Framework for Data and Information Quality Research. *ACM Journal of Data and Information Quality*, *2*, 1–22. doi:10.1145/1805286.1805287

Manfred, A. J. Christoph.Q & Matthias. J. (1998). Design and analysis of quality information for data warehouses. Lecture notes in Computer Science, Vol. 1507, pp. 349-362.

Matthias, J. Manfred. A.J., Christoph, Q., & Panos. V. (1999). Architecture and quality in data warehouses: An extended repository approach, Information Systems, *10th International Conference on Advanced Information Systems Engineering*, Vol. 24, Issue 3, pp. 229–253.

Maydanchick, A. (2007). *Data Quality Assessment*. Technics Publications.

McGilvray, D. (2010). *Executing Data Quality projects – Ten steps to quality data and trusted information*. Morgan Kaufmann Publishers.

Pipino, L. L., Wang, R. Y., Kopsco, D., & Rybolt, W. (2005). *Developing measurement scales for data-quality dimensions* (pp. 37–51). Information Quality.

Portela, F. Vilas, Marta-boas & Filipe, M. (2010). Improvements in data quality for decision support in Intensive Care, *3rd International ICST Conference on Electronic Healthcare for the 21st century*.

Rudra, A., & Yeo, E. (1999). Key Issues in Achieving Data Quality and Consistency in Data Warehousing among Large Organisations in Australia, *32nd Hawaii International Conference on System Sciences*.

Shankaranarayanan, G. (2005). Towards implementing total data quality management in a datawarehouse. *Journal of Information Technology Management*, *XVI*, 21–30.

Shankaranarayanan, G. Zhu,B., & Cai,Y. (2008), Decision support with data quality metadata, *proceedings of the International Conference on Information Quality*.

Shankaranarayanan,G & Bin, Zhu. (2012), Data Quality Metadata and Decision Making, *45th Hawaii International Conference on System Sciences*, pp.1434-1443.

Sintchenko, V., Magrabi, F., & Tipper, S. (2007). Are we measuring the right end-points? Variables that affect the impact of computerised decision support on patient outcomes: A systematic review. *Medical Informatics and the Internet in Medicine*, 225–240. PMID:17701828

Stvilia, B., Gasser, L., Michael, B. T., & Linda, C. (2007). A framework for Information Quality Assessment. *Journal of the American Society for Information Science and Technology*, *58*(12), 1720–1733. doi:10.1002/asi.20652

KEY TERMS AND DEFINITIONS

DQ Dimension: An attribute or factor of the data that serves as a perspective for study of DQ. E.g. correctness or timeliness or accuracy.

DQ Assessment Framework: A structured approach, derived from methodology, comprising multiple steps, for assessment of DQ.

Decision Category: Logical classification or grouping of business decisions to derive context based on subject of discussion.

Weightage: A mechanism to capture relative importance in the process of objective assessment

DQ Score: A comprehensive measure of DQ that can be used to quantify the level of DQ that exists in the System under assessment.

Data Warehouse (DW): A data store or repository created by integrating data from disparate sources, used for reporting and data analysis.

Decision Support Systems (DSS): An unified system that supports decision making process in an organization at different levels and in multiple business functions such as tactical or strategic or planning.

Executive Information System (EIS): A specialized form of DSS to support decision making process of executive / senior management teams in an organization.

Chapter 13
Data Profiling and Data Quality Metric Measurement as a Proactive Input into the Operation of Business Intelligence Systems

Scott Delaney
Hydro Tasmania, Australia

ABSTRACT

Business intelligence systems have reached business critical status within many companies. It is not uncommon for such systems to be central to the decision-making effectiveness of these enterprises. However, the processes used to load data into these systems often do not exhibit a level of robustness in line with their criticality to the organisation. The processes of loading business intelligence systems with data are subject to compromised execution, delays, or failures as a result of changes in the source system data. These ETL processes are not designed to recognise nor deal with such shifts in data shape. This chapter proposes the use of data profiling techniques as a means of early discovery of issues and changes within the source system data and examines how this knowledge can be applied to guard against reductions in the decision making capability and effectiveness of an organisation caused by interruptions to business intelligence system availability or compromised data quality. It does so by examining issues such as where profiling can be best be applied to get appropriate benefit and value, the techniques of establishing profiling, and the types of actions that may be taken once the results of profiling are available. The chapter describes components able to be drawn together to provide a system of control that can be applied around a business intelligence system to enhance the quality of organisational decision making through monitoring the characteristics of arriving data and taking action when values are materially different than those expected.

DOI: 10.4018/978-1-4666-4892-0.ch013

INTRODUCTION

Business intelligence and decision support systems are becoming increasingly important in the operation of the modern day corporation with many achieving business or mission critical status (Thierauf, 2001). However, despite their criticality, many of these systems often have fragility in the extract transform and load (ETL) processes that ingest data into data warehouses and similar repositories (Kimball & Ross, 2010). When such processes encounter problems the decision making ability of an organisation is compromised to some degree, either through reduced speed / agility, quality or some combination of the two. It is not uncommon for such circumstances to trigger expensive investigations to uncover the root cause of the problem before designing and implementing a means of rectification. Such circumstances often arise as the result of shifts in the characteristics of the data being loaded in to the business intelligence system.

This paper demonstrates the business case for, and value of, a non-traditional use for data profiling as a solution to this problem. Specifically, an application of these techniques which is able to assist in the early detection of issues within source data with the potential to cause problems when entering the ETL process, thereby protecting against unplanned downtime. In so doing they contribute to the improvement of the overall decision making agility of the enterprise by removing impediments to an organisation's decision making ability, as well as delivering operational cost savings and avoidance.

Techniques allowing practitioners to initiate and carry out such an undertaking in their own organisations will be introduced within the paper. Whilst it is specifically aimed at introducing business intelligence practitioners to methods which they could apply it will also help data and information governance practitioners understand how they can leverage their knowledge to benefit the discipline of business intelligence.

MAIN FOCUS OF THE CHAPTER

Problem Statement

Business intelligence and decision support systems often have fragility in the extract transform and load (ETL) processes that are used to bring data into the data repositories underpinning business intelligence systems. When such processes encounter problems the decision making ability of an organisation is compromised to some degree, either through reduced speed / agility, quality or some combination of the two. It is not uncommon for such circumstances to trigger expensive investigations to uncover the root cause of the problem before designing and implementing a means of rectification. In essence these are reactive data profiling, discovery and data quality rule establishment undertakings. Often such circumstances arise as the result of subtle (or not so subtle) shifts in the profile of the data arriving at the warehouse, but they can also occur as a result of incomplete or immature understanding of the data or the business rules at the time of the design and original implementation of the ETL processes.

A Victim of Our Own Prudence

It can be the very measures put in place to protect the integrity of the business intelligence system, and the data repository below it, that cause the financial (and other) impacts to the business that are described in this chapter. Data warehouses are often protected by their designers and builders by introducing checks and validations at either or both of the database tier or ETL layer. The system analysis and requirements gathering exercises which occurred during the project to bring the business intelligence system in to being will have provided the designers with much information about the data within the source systems which will supply the future data warehouse. It is considered good practice (Kimball, et al, 2008) to ensure that rules and checks provide coverage to ensure that the business intelligence repository has a defense against "bad" or unexpected data entering it. This is all well and good so long as the data arriving is of static form and all cases and variants within the data were uncovered during the analysis phase. Any shift in the data arriving from the source systems then has the potential to fail these rules and be prevented from entering the warehouse.

Two broad classes of issues can occur when the data ingested in to a decision support system differs in some way from that catered for during the design, build and implementation of that system. The first is the more obvious to those using the system and, although more disruptive, can at least be recognised and efforts put in place to attempt to address it. This class of errors manifest as the data arriving at the business intelligence data repository being rejected, either in the form of individual or sets of rows being unable to be loaded, or as entire load processes terminating and coming to a hard stop.

These data load failures will occur due to one of a number of reasons:

- Fields (columns) which had always contained a value in the source system (and hence had been designed as mandatory in the business intelligence system's data tier) begin arriving with no value;
- The field length or data type of a column coming from the source system is inconsistent with that expected in the business intelligence system;
- A field value arriving from the source system does not fall within the domain of the constraints for the corresponding field in the business intelligence system;
- The number of rows expected to arrive from the source system within a given time window varies significantly from that currently arriving; and
- Sequencing mechanisms in the source system either stop working or behave in such a way as to render the data load inoperable or compromised (for example time stamped objects which must be processed in temporal order begin to arrive out of sequence).

Whatever the cause, the result is either a reduced set of data from which to make decisions or a stalled process which renders the business intelligence system unable to be used for a range of data inside a given domain (for example a load failure in source data for a postal sorting facility for a matter of hours can, and does, render schedulers effectively blind when planning routes and adjusting casual staff levels for the following day, which can result in missed delivery KPIs entailing financial penalties and some degree of brand damage (and potentially customer churn) as well as the potential for increased staffing costs due to unplanned overtime).

Each incident also requires a response and with this response comes a cost. Often this cost hits the (often stretched) operational budgets of both the IT department and the business users of the business intelligence system. Direct costs are incurred in the investigation and the root cause analysis, as well as costs required in later attempting to reload data. In extreme cases there may also be the need to make programmatic changes to the ETL process and undertake testing processes downstream of that.

The second class of errors is more insidious as it may often go unnoticed. As such there is no obvious interruption to the operation of the business intelligence system. Analytics and other operations continue despite the problems. However as issues exist in the source data, those same issues now exist within the data warehouse. This situation has the potential to compromise the analytic and reporting output delivered by the business intelligence system and impair the quality of decisions based upon those reports. When this happens the effectiveness of the decision making ability of the organisation is reduced, but this may not be seen or realised by those within the organisation. Often such soft issues are not uncovered until some future time and it is not uncommon for them not to be uncovered at all (Darmont & Boussaid, 2006). In these scenarios events such as loss of market share may occur, which otherwise may have been avoided if the decision making process was operating unfettered. Eventually there may be a trigger for some audit or retrospective investigation which, although uncovering the issue and its root cause, offer few levers to allow the organisation to recover prior positions or losses sustained.

Magnified by Emerging Trends

With the emergence of big data the risk of ETL fragility manifesting in such a way as to negatively impact business decision making is likely to increase. Firstly, several of the characteristics of big data, namely volume and velocity, add complexity for ETL process and effectively shrink the window of opportunity within which any problems that occur can be rectified.

Further compounding the demands placed upon IT departments will be pressure from business stakeholders to allow them to realize the benefits that the hype around big data has promised. With significant investments in gathering and storing high volumes of data in near real time there is highly likely to be pressure to reduce the time to value for big data initiatives. This will result in a further shift away from the more traditional batch processing ETL process which ran overnight or in off peak times throughout the day. These will be the ETL jobs of your grandfather when compared with the ETL and other data movement processes supporting business intelligence and analytics solutions leveraging big data. The new generation of processes will be built to run in as close to real time as possible and may have little, if any, available float time to reprocess failed data loads let alone allocate time to investigation and rectification of problems.

Improved Business Intelligence through Information Quality Governance

Business intelligence systems can deliver tremendous insight to a business entity but left unfettered there is potential for an organisation to be subjected to significant issues either from loss or restriction of system availability or from loss of accuracy stemming from unrecognised subtle changes in source data semantics. Without a degree of governance an organisation is effectively taking a leap of faith, placing a bet that what they experience and know now will continue to hold into the future. Some monitoring, feedback and action is required if an organisation wants to avoid situations analogous to an airplane or auto pilot edging ever closer to the ground without the pilots noticing. A system of control in which standards, norms and tolerable ranges are understood and used as a yardstick to measure the data from the source systems feeding a business intelligence system is a powerful tool in guarding against such scenarios. If these standards can be established and understood then informed choices can be made and, more importantly, actions taken at effective and appropriate times in order that the control loop can be closed in such a way as to protect the organisation from undesirable impacts upon the business intelligence systems manifesting as detriments to the quality of the organisation's decision making ability.

Data Profiling as a Solution

Whilst the use of information governance, specifically data profiling and data quality metric definition and measurement has more established and accepted uses in scenarios such as data migration and data quality exercises, there is also a place for it in support of enabling robust ETL processes.

Used here it can provide the lynchpin of a system of control. The act of profiling helps develop an understanding of the standards and the basis of what is acceptable. These newly understood standards can be expressed as data quality metrics with further data profiling supplying the inputs to governance in the form of identifying what variances are material or important enough to warrant action or intervention.

Injected ahead of the ETL process (i.e. in the chain before the data is ingested to the warehouse) data quality metric monitoring can be used to find and act on problems before they halt the ETL process or otherwise undermine decision making ability.

Once problems are uncovered some combination of the appropriate resources can be marshaled to correct the problem:

- Data stewards to correct the problem data at the source system (quickly if possible) perhaps allowing recovery with the same reporting cycle;
- Technologists to restrict or otherwise filter out problem data until such time as a data resolution can be reached, enabling continuation of the reporting cycle with the bulk of the information available;
- Developers learn from the discovery and take action to rectify, extend or otherwise modify the ETL process either to recognise and handle the specific case or, preferably, to extrapolate it to a larger pattern capable of handling an emergent new class of data or business rules;
- (By exception) business subject matter experts to assist in assessing the material impact of issues uncovered as required.

Executed well, this approach will ensure fewer interruptions to business intelligence system availability and therefore provide faster decision making and higher confidence in the base data from which the decisions are being made. Self monitoring and self aware ETL processes enabled by embedded data quality metric monitoring can also result in a lowered need for support, bringing with it the opportunity for operation cost saving.

What to Profile

Early profiling steps should not be concerned with uncovering subtle data quality problems. Such problems do have the potential to cause some reduction in decision quality but they rarely will cause system downtime (an event which effectively renders a much wider reaching impost on decision making ability). Instead, the first steps into profiling should look for quick and easy wins, the proverbial low hanging fruit. Such profiling should examine the obvious, the things that would cause records to be rejected from being loaded into the business intelligence data repository or, in sufficient number, cause a hard stop of the ETL process. The situations to check for can be distilled into a number of rule classes:

- **(System) Mandatory field checks:** Fields which are required by the specific configuration of the business intelligence system and must contain a value for a piece of data to be successfully loaded into the business intelligence system;
- **Data types and field lengths:** The size (or number of characters) in a field and, where the data repository for the business intelligence system uses strongly typed data, the specific data type used. In order for a piece of data to be loaded in to the business intelligence system no field can exceed its defined field length, nor vary from the expected field type;
- **Cross reference checks:** Integrity validation against master data held elsewhere in the system. Orphaned child data (i.e. that data which does not have a corresponding master data entry) cannot be loaded into the business intelligence system;

- **Constraint checks:** Validation against a defined and constrained list of values (other than that held as master data elsewhere in the business intelligence system). In order for a piece of data to be loaded in to the business intelligence area it cannot fail any constraint checks;
- **Expected row numbers:** In certain scenarios data may have a defined shape which allows the approximate (or at times exact) number or rows to be loaded to the business intelligence system in any given load window to be known. By way of an example of this class consider a case where machinery logs a single reading every five minutes, resulting in an expected 288 rows arriving at the business intelligence system via an overnight ETL process;
- **(Business Scenario) Mandatory field checks:** Fields which are not enforced by the specific configuration of the business intelligence system but which are required for successful operation of reporting or analytics from that system. Data failing these rules can still be successfully loaded in to the business intelligence system (i.e. it will not cause a hard stop or otherwise destabilise the ETL process) but will have an impact on the decision making ability of those working from the business intelligence system in this area; and
- **Duplicate checks:** Records which appear more than once in the source system(s). Duplicate data may or may not be successfully loaded in to the business intelligence system. This class requires case by case investigation to understand both the business context and the manner in which the ETL process treats duplicate data. For example, an ETL process implemented with SQL constructs such as DISTINCT or GROUP BY will most likely not encounter problems when processing duplicate data but those attempting to work with the reports and analytics over the business intelligence system may well then be working with flawed data. Hence profiling with this class of rules provides the potential to prevent information workers basing decisions upon flawed data all the while unaware that any problem exists.

When to Profile

In order to allow maximum benefit to be derived from this technique, profiling must be conducted against the source data and occur as early as possible in the pipeline. The closer to the execution time of the ETL process that the data profiling occurs then the more limited the window for taking remedial actions and hence the fewer such options available for viable use.

The Bigger Question – Where's the Value?

Effort must be applied to determine the key areas of the business intelligence solution to profile. This should be an exercise in estimating where the best value can be derived. Adding profiling across the entire business intelligence solution is highly unlikely to be cost effective and in fact may be counterproductive, particularly in scenarios where the available data load window is already highly occupied. A key aspect in order to be successful in this style of endeavour is to first determine the most appropriate areas to apply profiling to strengthen the data ingestion process. While there is no one size fits all template or formula that can be leveraged to make these choices there are a number of questions that can be asked which will guide the choices and highlight a number of candidate areas.

First considerations should centre on areas with historical instability in the ETL process; the areas which have regularly failed in the past. There are several sources of information that may be leveraged to determine where candidates with this characteristic lie. At a low level, system logs often provide the information about where failures occur, but these are likely voluminous and may well mask patterns in the sheer volume of information and white noise.

A better first port of call may well be the help desk or trouble ticket system of the support organisation for the business intelligence system. If the system in question has the capability to capture enough detail about where failures occur (and has been used in a consistent fashion) then it may well be possible to quickly identify a few key suspect domains and specific ETL processes to investigate further. Failing the availability of suitable reports then consider interviewing key support first and second level help desk operators and support analysts. They may have a sense of where they have spent their time (and where problems have been harder to fix).

Informally surveying the end user audience (report consumers and information workers) often also provides a useful starting point. In fact there may already be candidate areas that are often talked about in derogatory fashion, as most organisations have their share of these, which require almost no investigation work to uncover. However information gathered from this source should be recognised and acknowledged for its unproven lineage. Initially it is best treated as organisational myth, an item that may be problematic, but with a level of impact that has built its own momentum from a ground swell of shared and unaddressed frustration or from the squeaky wheel impact of a particularly vocal user or group. Caution should be exercised to ensure that a specific seemingly high profile incident does not spiral into an inappropriate application of funds which serve no purpose other than to threaten the believability of the value proposition for data profiling inline to the ETL process. Verify this myth by cross-referencing it against the more factual information from the help desk system analysis and the lower level system logs. This process can be used to suggest a candidate pool of the order to five to ten areas to take forward in to the next area of the evaluation process.

Having determined areas with a history of some degree of instability, effort should now be applied to understand the impact of that instability. This impact may have a number of dimensions:

- The cost of root cause analysis to uncover the nature of the problem;
- The cost of the fix to rectify the issue once it is understood; and
- The aggregate cost of the combination of the two above items for reoccurring problems.

Reports from the help desk system may be able to provide quantitative information around these items. Other potential sources for this information are time sheeting systems and project control systems. Again, do not discount the information that may be gained from undertaking discussions with, or interviewing, key people in these areas, such as support or contract managers. They may well have a sense of the quantum of the hours expended or fees charged or track such costs in shadow IT systems such as purpose built spreadsheets.

These costs, while important, will often not be where the majority of cost occurs. The business may well incur greater cost due to one or more of the following scenarios:

- The cost to the business of downtime for the business intelligence solution or the cost of delay to the availability of reports (in environments where high currency information and analysis provides competitive advantage);
- The cost to the business of sub-optimal decisions made in the past due to incomplete or inaccurate data due to ETL instability; and
- The cost to the business due to activities to defuse or otherwise deal with fallout from the occurrences of the above item.

By way of using an example to illustrate the final two points and aid understanding, healthcare organisations reliant upon activity based costing methods for their funding can incur extra cost or forgo the opportunity to collect the full range amount of funding to which they are entitled when problems occur with data loads into their business intelligence system (Kaplan & Porter, 2011). When data is late arriving or incompletely loaded due to errors or issues encountered during ETL runs, then key indicators such as the number of procedures carried out or the average time and length of stay per procedure can be misstated having direct impact on the amount of funding provided. Further discrepancies in current reporting against past reporting of these indicators require investigation and explanation both inside and outside of audit scenarios. Such investigations can consume several staff on effectively a full tine basis and are costs that could be largely avoided if the underlying data quality and timeliness issues in the business intelligence system could be avoided.

Unfortunately, these items are far harder to accurately ascertain quantitative data for. Where such information is readily available it should be leveraged, but excessive time spent in attempting to gather or verify exact costs will most likely provide diminishing returns. Instead use whatever estimates are available and couple them with indicators such as the seniority (within the business) of the stakeholder whom the events impacted to further narrow the candidate selection.

This (small) number of key high impact areas can now be moved through the process of designing and implementing the profiling and supporting processes which will provide greater resilience in their ETL processes.

Establishing Data Profiling

A number of commercially available data profiling tools exist which can be used to achieve and enable the steps and outcomes described below. The example screenshots provided herein have been taken from the SAP product Business Objects Information Steward.

The process of establishing a data profiling component to protect an ETL process can be broken down in to a number of steps that build upon each other and hence should be executed in order.

The profiling rules which will be introduced will to some degree mirror the checking and validation logic that have been implemented in the business intelligence system or the ETL process that feeds it. Hence an appropriate and useful starting point is to obtain an understanding of the rules already applied to the data sets of interest within the business intelligence system. These rules will come from a number of areas and all must be examined to avoid leaving unmonitored areas that may continue to provide unexpected failures in the ETL process. The areas to be examined include the rules applied at the database tier of the data warehouse. These will manifest as mandatory fields (those with NOT NULL constraints), strongly typed data (including items such as size and precision of numeric data and character length of string data elements), data constrained by referential integrity (via foreign key relationships) or data limited by constraints. A useful tool for capturing and documenting the rules uncovered is a transformation mapping spreadsheet (an example of which is provided later in this piece). This artifact bears much in common with mapping spreadsheets used by many business intelligence practitioners when designing and building ETL processes and broadly is broken up in to three vertical areas:

- A right hand section describing the target fields and their characteristics (data type, null ability, size, etc.) in the data tier of the business intelligence system;
- A left hand section describing the fields in the source system which will populate the target fields; and

- A section in the middle mapping the source fields to the target fields and describing any logic that is applied in the transformation process.

This first investigative step provides the information with which to complete the target section of the spreadsheet.

Armed with this information now analyse the existing ETL lineage to determine firstly the source of those fields (identified during the above step) with rules applied to them and secondly any additional rules which are imposed within the ETL process itself. Several tools are at hand to assist with the performing of these tasks. System documentation may have a good degree of this information at hand, but it must be assessed to determine how much faith can be placed upon it. Questions should be asked of its accuracy and contemporariness. Documentation which shows a history of many updates post the go-live date of the project that installed the system and / or incudes updates in the recent past is more likely accurately reflect the as built state of the ETL process than documentation that remains at version 1.0 as it was when the project team handed the system over to the support organisation. Tools able to infer lineage, such as SAP's Business Objects Information Steward product can also be utilized. Where gaps in the information still exist then some benefit may be available from interviewing the programming staff that built and delivered the solution (if available). The final, and definitive, answer will come from ETL process code investigation. However this is, in most circumstances, also the most costly approach. This information allows the transformation mapping spreadsheet started in the previous step to be completed by adding the source details and the transformation logic (Figure 1).

Once completed, the transformation mapping spreadsheet becomes the design basis from which to build the data quality profiling rules that will be measured. These rules are built not against the data warehouse (or other repository) for the business intelligence system, but rather against the source data to allow some degree of early detection. In practice these rules should be executed on a schedule designed with consideration of the frequency with which particular sets of data are ingested into the business intelligence solution and how fast the data arrives or is created at the source. A one-size fits all approach is not the optimal approach with regard to this schedule.

Figure 1. An example transformation mapping spreadsheet showing key aspects

Legacy Object: Cost Element

Field Name	Table Name	Field Length	Description (Status: not used, move/transfer, translation etc.)	System Required	Enrichment Rule	Look Up Required	Text Description	Field Name	SAP_Table	SAP_Technical_Field_name	Field Length
Key Fields for Create				E1BP1022_KEY-Key Fields for Create							
Company (faco)	F1201	5	Company number (FACO) used in lookup table to obtain SAP company number. Lookup Table E1_SAP' columns J and K. For E1 transaction only use company numbers 00005 and 01900	*		+	Company Code(COMPANYCODE)	COMPANYCODE	ANLA	BUKRS	4
ParentNumber (faaaid)	F1201	8		*			Main Asset Number(ASSET)	ASSET	ANLA	ANLN1	12
AssetNumber		2	Derived. AssetNumber minus ParentNumber				***Asset Sub Number***	Asset Sub Number	ANLA	ANLN2	4
Reference asset for creating				E1BP1022_REFERENCE-Reference asset for creating							
See above							Main Asset Number(ASSET)	ASSET	ANLA	ANLN1	12
See above				*		+	Company Code(COMPANYCODE)	COMPANYCODE	ANLA	BUKRS	4
See above				*			Main Asset Number(ASSET)	ASSET	ANLA	ANLN1	12
Logical field group 001 - General data				E1BP1022_FEGLG001-Logical field group 001 - General data							
See above				*			Main Asset Number(ASSET)	ASSET	ANLA	ANLN1	12
Asset Cost Account - Subsidiary (FAASUB)	F1201	8	Use FAASUB code in lookup tabe (tab Lookup Table E1_SAP) Column P to get SAP asset class (Column Q)	*		+	Asset class(ASSETCLASS)	ASSETCLASS	ANLA	ANLKL	8
	F1201	50	Derived from concatenating description fields : description1 (fadl01) + description2 (fadl02) less the last ten characters	*			Asset Description(DESCRIPT)	DESCRIPT	ANLA	TXT50	50
	F1201	40	Last 10 chars of Description2 (fald02) and all of Description 3 (fadl03)				Asset Description(DESCRIPT2)	DESCRIPT2	ANLA	TXA50	50
faasid							Serial number(SERIAL_NO)	SERIAL_NO	ANLA	SERNR	18
apid			Currently not used				Inventors number(INVENT_NO)	INVENT_NO	ANLA	INVNR	25

Even if all data is loaded to the same schedule, for example in batch overnight at 4am, then there is still benefit in profiling different areas of that data in line with its rate of creation, so more active data is profiled more frequently. The aim here is to uncover potential issues as early as possible to allow corrective or preventative action to be put into play with as much chance as possible to avoid issues manifesting during the run time of the ETL process.

Figure 2 shows a single profiling rule from the set that is required to be implemented based upon the documentation in the transformation mapping spreadsheets. This rule is designed to ensure that the records arriving are not orphaned, a situation that would arise in this case if transactions from the source system for a newly established subsidiary company arrived ahead of the master data for the new entity, and which would likely cause either a rejection of the orphaned records or a hard stop of a complete section of the ETL process.

A section of an ETL process with anything but the simplest degree of complexity will require a number of profiling rules in order to provide a sufficient level of coverage of the items which could impact the ETL process during its run time. The monitoring of a significant number of rules is challenging and becomes even more so when a number of areas of the ETL process (or processes) are subject to profiling activity. This problem of information overload can be solved with the use of scorecards. A number of profiling tools offer this type of construct that effectively rolls up the individual rules and displays a summarized representation of the profiling results on a data set by data set basis. Visualisation techniques used include numeric scores, histogram style displays to indicate the progress toward perfection and colour coding to indicate areas of concern or problem. The example shown below makes use of all three techniques and provides a rolled up view of all of the profiling rules listed in the transformation mapping spreadsheet introduced in earlier examples. In this particular case a data quality score of 9.72 (from a maximum score of 10) is indicated. This points to some level of deviation from the expected characteristics in the data within the source system that is in scope for the next ETL run. The high level graphical breakdown in Figure 3 suggests that while the data

Figure 2. Profiling rule: Company code distribution

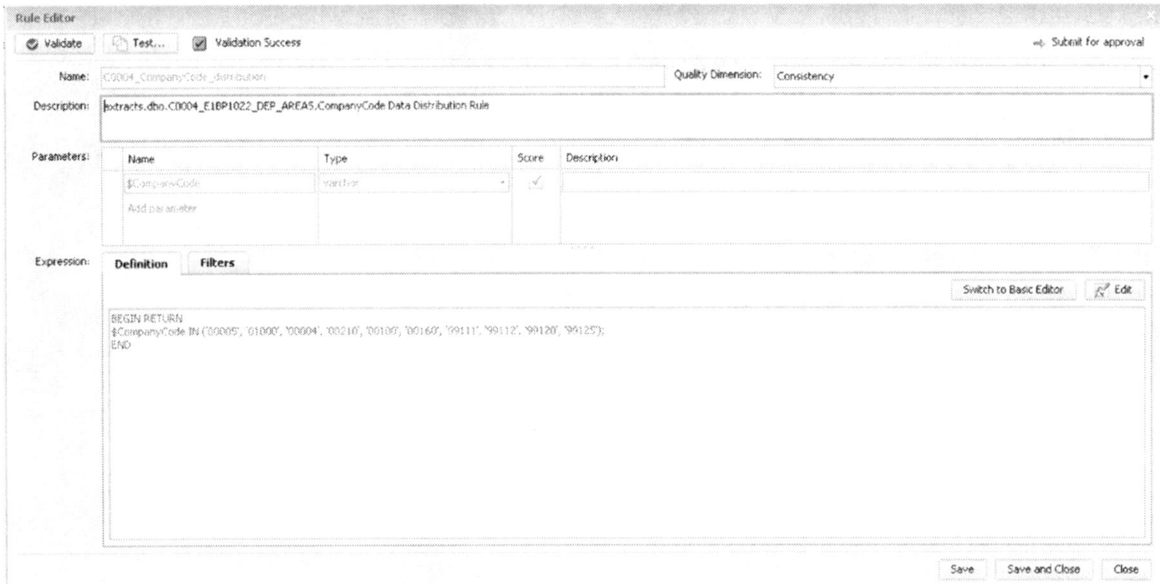

Figure 3. Data profiling scorecard showing summarised results

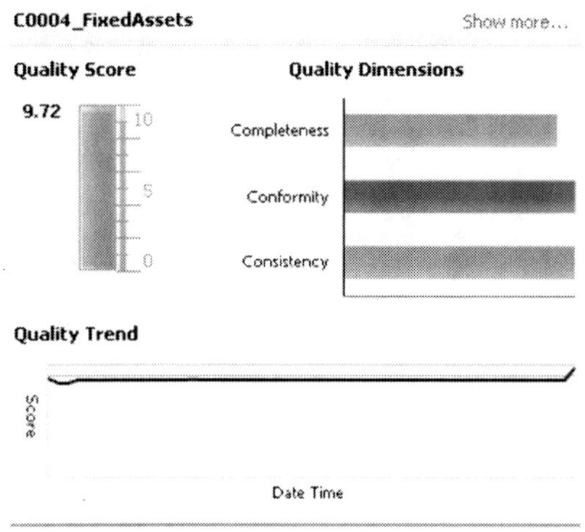

generally conforms with expectations that the completeness and consistency dimensions have some problems, indicating that there is some degree of missing data (compared to what was expected) and that some referential integrity or domain constraint issues also exist.

Once all identified data profiling rules have been implemented then building a scorecard based upon these rules provides a reasonably cost effective means to get a rudimentary feedback loop underway. This becomes the dashboard for measuring data readiness (to be loaded into the business intelligence system) and is the early warning mechanism to sense when problems will occur without the need for operational staff to be constantly down in the detail of the particular rules and their results.

With this tool in place it is now possible to predict with greater certainty when data issues will cause material failures in the ETL processes which deliver data into the business intelligence system. Forewarned is forearmed. Knowing ahead of time that a failure will occur allows a number of potential corrective, preventative or protective actions to be taken.

Acting Upon the Warning Signs: Using Profiling Results to Prevent Sub-Optimal ETL Runs

Knowing the state of cleanliness of data shortly to arrive at the business intelligence system is useful in and of itself in that it can instill a sense of confidence during normal operations when all systems and data are behaving as expected. However in and of itself this value is unlikely to justify the investment in establishing and operating the profiling alongside the ETL process and hence it is unlikely that a business case attempting to secure funding for such an initiative would be successful. In order to be able to demonstrate significant value from this type of project the profiling results must provide actionable insights, that is findings that can be acted upon to prevent, lessen the impact of, or at least understand and plan for that impact ahead of the time that the problems that would occur during the execution of the process. Armed with this information ahead of time it is often possible to prevent the costs of down time (both in investigative and remedial actions and deferral of reporting and analytic availability) due to a failed ETL process. In order to gain the information required to formulate responsive actions a more granular understanding of the profiling rule violations is needed. This can be found be drilling down and examining the results of individual rules as shown in Figure 4 which illustrates that one of the problems is occurring with information pertaining to company code details, as well as identifying where in the source systems (the table) that problem data is located.

This is useful information it is not yet truly actionable in that it is not yet possible to say what the impact of the problem will be nor take any action to rectify problem data at the source or quarantine the failing rows ahead of the next ETL run. However, drilling down further on a spe-

Figure 4. Lower level investigation of rules with failures

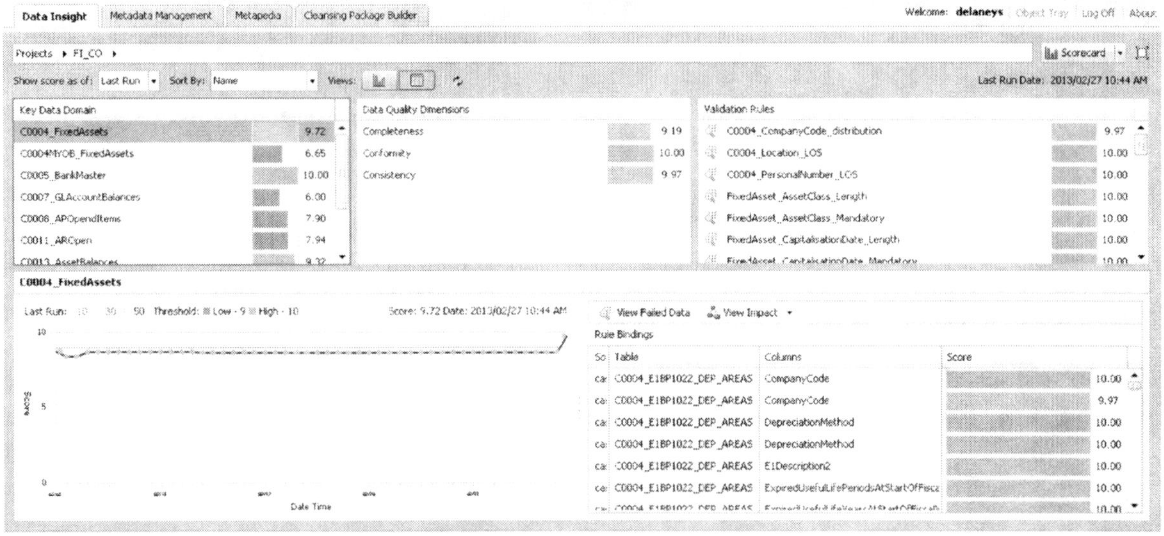

cific source and profiling rule combination can provide the missing information. Figure 5 highlights that the company code information coming from the first of the sources has 129 records which fail the company code distribution rule shown earlier. At this point it is possible to begin assessing the likely impact of this impending problem data. Whilst 129 records not being able to be brought in to the business intelligence system at the next load may seem to be of material impact other factors should be considered. In relative terms is this a significant number? Given that the load will bring in almost 50,000 records from this one source and over 78,000 records from other sources, the loss of 129 records may not be considered problematic by the business users of the

Figure 5. Rule result summary: Showing numbers of failures

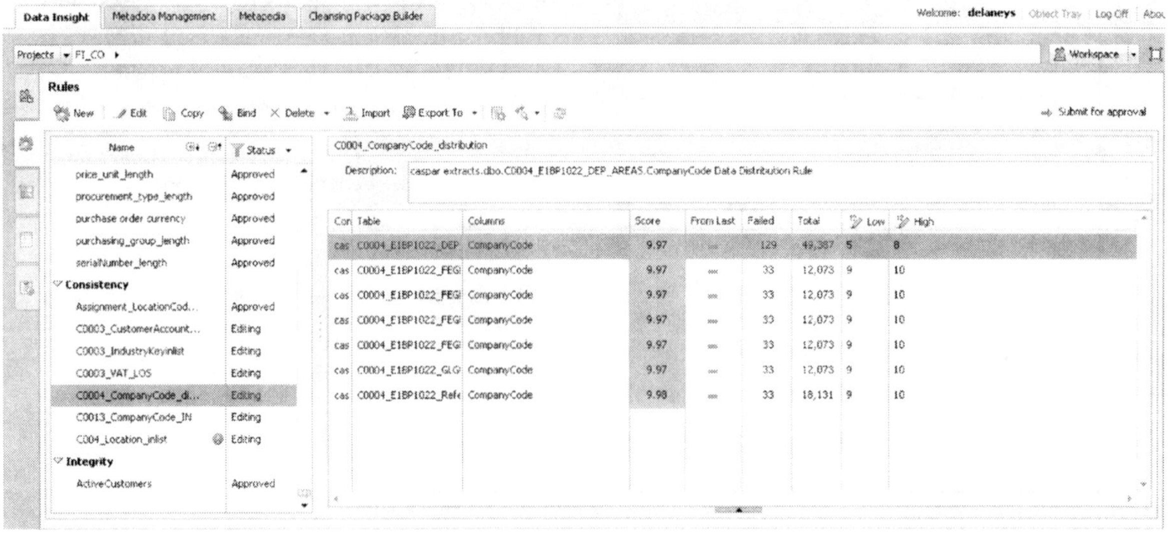

business intelligence system. Such considerations sit in a grey area that may well require business input to determine the anticipated impact. Other checks can be more defined. Error tolerance settings for the area of the ETL process in question can be checked to determine if the number of failing rows (as an absolute value and / or relative percentage) would cause a failure of a component of the ETL process, hence preventing a much larger volume of data from entering the business intelligence system.

There will be cases where the full impact of identified impending load failures can only be assessed if the rows that will fail can be identified and the values in the various fields presented for analysis. Most commercially available data profiling systems provide drill down between summarized rule failure information and the failing rows themselves. The information in Figure 6 when read in conjunction with the rule itself, quickly shows that data for company code 00006 is arriving when no such company code value is expected. Put in to a business context, this could represent a case where master data for a new subsidiary company either had not yet been set up in the provisioning source system or had yet to be loaded in to the business intelligence system.

Prevention is Better than Cure: Taking Action to Avoid ETL Failures

Data profiling ahead of ETL process runs provides visibility of problems that will cause material impact before they occur. To extract maximum value from the process, steps must be taken to deal with those problems. A number of approaches may be taken, with different situations being best dealt with using different responses. The guiding principle in using the profiling information at hand to craft a response is that prevention is better than cure. The financial risk or other impact will most likely be less if the problem is avoided rather than allowed to happen before a response and rectification (however speedy) is undertaken. The approaches presented below are listed in descending order of effectiveness in avoiding unwanted cost or risk arising from issues encountered when loading data in to the business intelligence system:

Figure 6. Failed data report

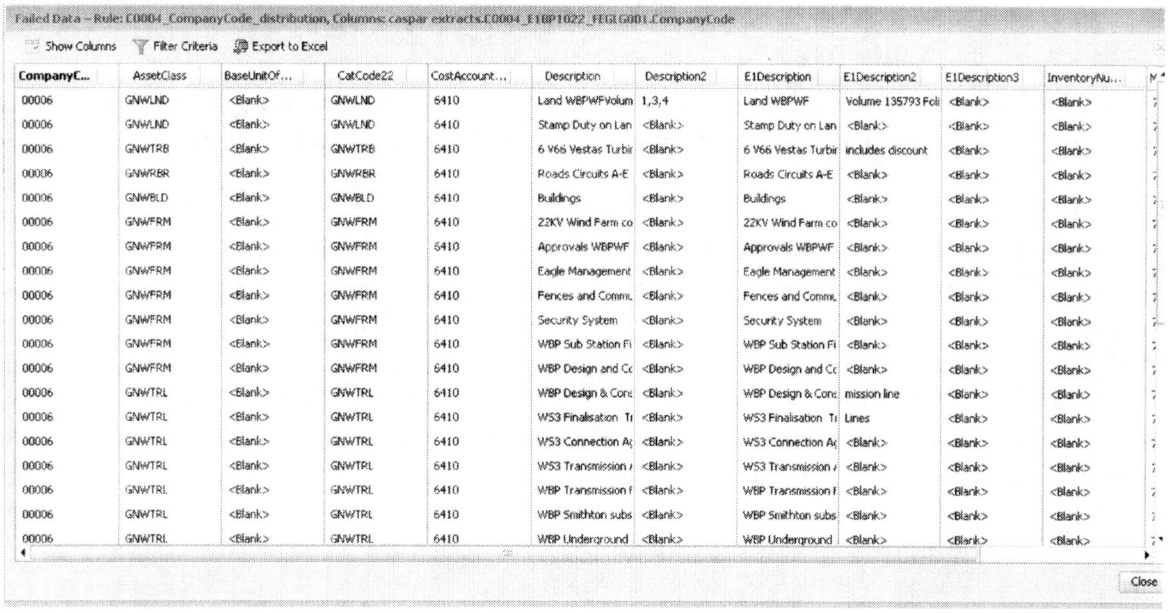
Failed Data – Rule: C0004_CompanyCode_distribution, Columns: caspar extracts.C0004_E1BP1022_FEGLG001.CompanyCode

Show Columns Filter Criteria Export to Excel

CompanyC...	AssetClass	BaseUnitOf...	CatCode22	CostAccount...	Description	Description2	E1Description	E1Description2	E1Description3	InventoryNu...
00006	GNWLND	<Blank>	GNWLND	6410	Land WBPWFVolum	1,3,4	Land WBPWF	Volume 135793 Foli	<Blank>	<Blank>
00006	GNWLND	<Blank>	GNWLND	6410	Stamp Duty on Lan	<Blank>	Stamp Duty on Lan	<Blank>	<Blank>	<Blank>
00006	GNWTRB	<Blank>	GNWTRB	6410	6 V66 Vestas Turbir	<Blank>	6 V66 Vestas Turbir	includes discount	<Blank>	<Blank>
00006	GNWRBR	<Blank>	GNWRBR	6410	Roads Circuits A-E	<Blank>	Roads Circuits A-E	<Blank>	<Blank>	<Blank>
00006	GNWBLD	<Blank>	GNWBLD	6410	Buildings	<Blank>	Buildings	<Blank>	<Blank>	<Blank>
00006	GNWFRM	<Blank>	GNWFRM	6410	22KV Wind Farm co	<Blank>	22KV Wind Farm co	<Blank>	<Blank>	<Blank>
00006	GNWFRM	<Blank>	GNWFRM	6410	Approvals WBPWF	<Blank>	Approvals WBPWF	<Blank>	<Blank>	<Blank>
00006	GNWFRM	<Blank>	GNWFRM	6410	Eagle Management	<Blank>	Eagle Management	<Blank>	<Blank>	<Blank>
00006	GNWFRM	<Blank>	GNWFRM	6410	Fences and Commu	<Blank>	Fences and Commu	<Blank>	<Blank>	<Blank>
00006	GNWFRM	<Blank>	GNWFRM	6410	Security System	<Blank>	Security System	<Blank>	<Blank>	<Blank>
00006	GNWFRM	<Blank>	GNWFRM	6410	WBP Sub Station Fi	<Blank>	WBP Sub Station Fi	<Blank>	<Blank>	<Blank>
00006	GNWFRM	<Blank>	GNWFRM	6410	WBP Design and Cc	<Blank>	WBP Design and Cc	<Blank>	<Blank>	<Blank>
00006	GNWTRL	<Blank>	GNWTRL	6410	WBP Design & Cons	<Blank>	WBP Design & Cons	mission line	<Blank>	<Blank>
00006	GNWTRL	<Blank>	GNWTRL	6410	WS3 Finalisation Tı	<Blank>	WS3 Finalisation Tı	Lines	<Blank>	<Blank>
00006	GNWTRL	<Blank>	GNWTRL	6410	WS3 Connection Aç	<Blank>	WS3 Connection Aç	<Blank>	<Blank>	<Blank>
00006	GNWTRL	<Blank>	GNWTRL	6410	WS3 Transmission /	<Blank>	WS3 Transmission /	<Blank>	<Blank>	<Blank>
00006	GNWTRL	<Blank>	GNWTRL	6410	WBP Transmission I	<Blank>	WBP Transmission I	<Blank>	<Blank>	<Blank>
00006	GNWTRL	<Blank>	GNWTRL	6410	WBP Smithton subs	<Blank>	WBP Smithton subs	<Blank>	<Blank>	<Blank>
00006	GNWTRL	<Blank>	GNWTRL	6410	WBP Underground	<Blank>	WBP Underground	<Blank>	<Blank>	<Blank>

Close

- Fix the data quality issues in the source system before the execution of the next ETL run. This could take the form of altering or enhancing the failing rows or ensuring that missing master data is entered;
- Quarantine the failing rows so that they are not loaded when the ETL process next executes. This can be a viable option when the frequency of ETL loads is too high or the next load is too close to allow source data fixes to occur before the next run. This action should be followed by a fix to the issues when practical;
- Delay the next execution of the ETL process to allow source data fixes to be made. This is a viable option when a significant number of upcoming failures are detected in data in scope for the next load or when a smaller set of failing data is deemed to be critical to the analysis functions to be conducted in the business intelligence system; and
- Isolate the failing records so that they are never allowed to enter the business intelligence system. This is a potentially dangerous option and usually only a viable option if the rows failing are not expected to be significant in reporting and analytics.

In assessing all of above options the potential to make changes to the ETL process itself to cater for the data scenarios manifesting should be considered. Whilst not advisable to deal with a single occurrence of profiling rule failures, a longitudinal point of view should be adopted to avoid situations when work around or reactionary action is repeatedly and frequently being taken to deal with the same patterns.

The adoption of this approach has impact on the way in which Business Intelligence Competency Centres or similar departments are staffed. In order to optimize costs, consideration should be given to reduce the need for someone with the ability to perform break and fix investigation and work at an ETL programming level, and replace it with personnel capable of monitoring approaching data flows and their profiling results as well as coordinating efforts to remove or otherwise deal with problematic data. Such a person is likely someone able to talk to the business more than a pure technologist; this is a role part business analyst, part consultant, part planner and scheduler.

Data Quality, But not for Data Quality's Sake Alone

The introduction of data profiling alongside ETL processes can bring significant and noticeable benefits and hence can quickly garner favour with key stakeholders within the enterprise. However, caution must be exercised to rein in too enthusiastic use of these techniques. Embedded inline with the ETL process is not the appropriate place to attempt to undertake a pure data quality exercise. Trying to achieve too much is likely to make the process too heavy which may result in one or more of a number of unwanted events. The processing time for the ETL process may exceed the available processing window, and the number of moving parts is increased, heightening the chance that something may go wrong, which may in essence actually trigger the very event that the approach is trying to guard against.

Perhaps the best approach here is not to act as a blocker to the new found urge to embrace data quality but to make use of the data profiling tools in their more traditional use case, thereby allowing the profiling to still occur without jeopardising the efforts to improve the stability of the business intelligence system. Given the time, pure data quality initiatives may actually pay dividends back to robustness of the business intelligence platform and the overall decision making quality and capability of the business as the quality of data arriving at the warehouse is higher, both from a structural and a semantic point of view.

A Changed Approach to ETL Design

The use of profiling as a tool to add robustness to the ETL process has the potential to change the way in which ETL processes are designed. The design process should be approached with the expectation that data shape is likely to change over time, either due to longer term trends or short term anomalies, and the ETL process should be built with the flexibility to cater for that and provide mechanisms for dealing with such changes. Rather than hard coding and embedding validation logic within the ETL process components, such rules may be better held separately, perhaps in a configuration area of sorts able to be accessed by operational rather than project or programming staff. Such a framework would allow adjustments and additions to these validations based on the ongoing profiling of data. Additionally, mechanisms that allow rule tolerances to be adjusted (if appropriate) based on earlier profiling of the source system data in scope for the next load to the business intelligence system. Catering for this approach when new ETL processes are first designed and built will be a far more cost effective approach than attempting to retrofit it to a process when later searching for a solution to frequent issues with the execution of a particular ETL process.

FUTURE RESEARCH DIRECTIONS

Emerging forces, specifically the velocity and volume dimensions of big data and the increasing speed of uptake of analytics as a more common place business tool, are bringing more focus to the time to value proposition and will mean that business intelligence systems will have more drivers than ever to bring in increasing volumes of data and / or move to near real time systems. The result of this will be pressure on available load windows. It is likely that in increasing numbers of business intelligence systems there will be little if any time to perform analysis and remediating actions with the available ETL load windows.

Discussions within this paper have focused on scenarios in which human action, analysis and intervention is still required. If the level of human involvement required can be reduced then further cost reduction opportunities may well become available. Additionally such advancements would result in a widening of the classes of business intelligence systems and ETL processes that inline data profiling could be applied to.

Research and fieldwork to date undertaken in developing the techniques described in this paper has identified a number of candidate areas and approaches worthy of further investigation. These are:

- Amassing a learning area of profiling results to identify when particular patterns of data issues become commonplace. This could provide the basis by which systems could be developed to allow an ETL process to act on past profile results to substitute replacement values (or fill in blank values, truncate certain fields, etc.) based on the way in which operators dealt with past occurrences of such problems;
- Allow of matching of data in (profiling) failed data reports to the source data sets during ETL process execution to allow the automatic exclusion of rows which would fail to load to the business intelligence system. This approach has the potential to allow profiling techniques to be employed on ETL processes that are near real time, rather than just systems with less frequent batch loads.

Research directed at identifying viable approaches to these areas will lay the groundwork for a future in which best in class business intelligence systems will make use of data quality metrics to keep watch over the ingestion data flows, automatically adjusting and filtering to avoid, or reduce, the impact of shifts in data quality or data shape and notifying data stewards or others to take action only when required. Further advances will also see such systems able to sense subtle changes in the data profile and suggest areas where changes should be built within the ETL process to smoothly handle the changing inputs.

Successful implementations of such functionality will require robust mechanisms to be able to evaluate and understand what it is acceptable for any given set of data to look like and when such data is sufficiently different from what is standard and expected to take automated action or raise exceptions requiring intervention. Appropriate and judicious application of stochastic methods may well be key to enabling future endeavours in finding effective levels of profiling and automated feedback checks and actions with sufficient control and risk mitigation whilst still allowing activities to continue in organisations operating in high volume, real time environments with strong reliance on business intelligence systems.

CONCLUSION

The fragility of the extract transform and load routines that ingest data in to business intelligence systems can be a bane to both those charged with keeping such systems operating smoothly and those who depend upon the reporting and analytic capability provided by such systems. This paper introduces a potential solution to this fragility and the flow on impacts it can have to an organisation's decision making ability and effectiveness. It has shown how the discipline of data profiling can be borrowed from the worlds of data quality and information governance to take a pivotal role in a system of control designed to protect business intelligence systems from detrimental events caused by unrecognised shifts in data characteristics or semantics. Applied ahead of, or inline, with the ETL process it can provide an early warning mechanism capable of signaling when changes within source system data would cause execution problems or failures with an ETL process. Appropriately targeted application of data profiling has the capability to provide information that enables those supporting business intelligence systems to assess the impact of transient or trending changes to the data shortly to be delivered to the business intelligence system. Armed with impact analysis and other insights from the profiling process allows action to be taken to avoid business intelligence system downtime and lessen the impact of problematic data on the quality of data in the business intelligence system. Such techniques can provide value and benefit to organisations choosing to employee them now, however further research will be required to extend them, particularly in the areas of automatic use of profiling results, to allow the application of profiling techniques across a wider range of business intelligence systems and to deal with the anticipated extra demands that the emerging trends of big data and business analytics will place upon business intelligence platforms.

REFERENCES

Darmont, J., & Boussaid, O. (2006). *Processing and managing complex data for decision support*. Hersey, PA: Idea Group Publishing. doi:10.4018/978-1-59140-655-6

Kaplan, R. S., & Porter, M. E. (2011). The big idea: How to solve the cost crisis in health care. *Harvard Business Review*, *89*(9), 47–64.

Kimball, R., & Ross, M. (2010). *The Kimball group reader: Relentlessly practical tools for data warehousing and business intelligence*. Indianapolis, IN: Wiley Publishing Inc.

Kimball, R., Ross, M., Thornthwaite, W., Mundy, J., & Becker, B. (2008). *The data warehouse lifecycle toolkit* (2nd ed.). Indianapolis, IN: Wiley Publishing Inc.

Thierauf, R. J. (2001). *Effective business intelligence systems*. Westport, CT: Quorum Books.

ADDITIONAL READING

Aspin, A. (2012). *SQL Server 2012 Data Integration Recipes Solutions For Integration Services and Other ETL Tools*. New York, NY: Apress. doi:10.1007/978-1-4302-4792-0

Castellanos, M., Dayal, U., & Miller, R. J. (Eds.). (2010). *Enabling Real-Time Business Intelligence*. Berlin, Heidelberg: Springer-Verlag. doi:10.1007/978-3-642-14559-9

Darmont, J., & Boussaid, O. (2006). *Processing and Managing Complex Data for Decision Support*. Hersey, PA: Idea Group Publishing. doi:10.4018/978-1-59140-655-6

Door, B., & Herbert, P. (2005, April). *Data Profiling: Designing the Blueprint for Improved Data Quality*. Paper presented at SAS User Group International 30, Philadelphia, PA.

Fisher, C. et al. (2011). *Introduction to Information Quality*. Bloomington, In AuthorHouse.

Kimball, R., & Ross, M. (2010). *The Kimball Group Reader: Practical Tools for Data Warehousing and Business Intelligence*. Indianapolis: In Wiley Publishing Inc.

Kimball, R., Ross, M., Thornthwaite, W., Mundy, J., & Becker, B. (2008). *The Data Warehouse Lifecycle Toolkit* (2nd ed.). Indianapolis: In Wiley Publishing Inc.

Madsen, L. B. (2012). *Healthcare Business Intelligence A Guide to Empowering Successful Data Reporting and Analytics*. Hoboken, NJ: John Wiley and Sons Inc.

McGilvray, D. (2008). *Executing Data Quality Projects Ten Steps to Quality Data and Trusted Information*. Burlington, MA: Morgan Kaufmann Publishers.

Redman, T. C. (2001). *Data Quality The Field Guide*. Woburn, MA: Butterworth-Heinemann.

Solomon, M. D. (2005). Ensuring a successful data warehouse initiative. *Information Systems Management*, *22*(1), 22–36. doi:10.1201/1078/44912.22.1.20051201/85736.4

Trillium Software. (2007). *Solving the Source Data Problem With Automated Data Profiling* [White Paper]. Retrieved from http://static.progressivemediagroup.com/Uploads/Whitepaper/31/34fcaf18-a5de-44f5-9ddb-d8493dcaf056.pdf

Vucevic, D., & Yaddow, W. (2012). *Testing the Data Warehouse Practicum Assuring Data Content, Data Structures and Quality*. USA: Trafford Publishing.

Welsh, J. (2010). Incorporating data profiling in the ETL process. In J. Bleiel (Ed.), *SQL Server MVP Deep Dives* (pp. 718–737). Greenwich, CT: Manning Publications.

KEY TERMS AND DEFINITIONS

Big Data: A general term used to describe the emerging trend of rising data volumes. Big data is often also characterised by a much faster rate of data creation than has previously occurred.

Business Intelligence Competency Centre (BICC): An organizational team charged with responsible for the operation and advancement of business intelligence systems within an organization.

Business Intelligence System: A computerized system which takes data from one or more source systems and assembles it such a way that it may be effectively utilised for decision support via reporting and analytics processes.

Data Profiling: A process in which a set of data is examined (often with computerized tools) to ascertain information about its content both in a general and a specific sense.

Data Quality Metric: A specific item to be measured during a data profiling exercise. For example, the compliance of the data value held in a particular field against the domain of expected and allowable values for that field.

Data Steward: A person (commonly from outside the IT function) charged with day to day responsibility for ensuring the data quality of a given domain of data.

Extract, Transform and Load Process - ETL Process: A computerized process, often programmatic or leveraging database technology to extract data from a source system and transform it into a suitable form for loading into a target system. ETL processes are commonly used to bring data into a business intelligence system.

Chapter 14
Agile Information Management Governance:
Can You Scale it to the Enterprise?

Conrad Bates
C3 Business Solutions, Australia

ABSTRACT

Research has shown that IT project failure rates increase in line with project size, and by the time you reach projects over $10M, the failure rate hits 100% (The Standish Group International, Inc., 1999). Hughes and Stodder (2012) go on to show that at an average cost of $12.8M, large data warehousing projects were failing 65% of the time for internally built apps and 86% of the time for purchased packages. The outtake here is that small projects are by far more successful. "We have long been convinced that shorter time frames, with delivery of software components early and often, increase the success rate" (The Standish Group International, Inc., 1999, p. 3). How can this be achieved on large projects? It is possible to be successful at the enterprise level, but it requires a fresh approach to project execution, an ability to deliver projects in small, incremental chunks while maintaining business involvement and support, and setting clear, achievable objectives throughout the program.

DOI: 10.4018/978-1-4666-4892-0.ch014

INTRODUCTION

While the agile approach has been around for many years - indeed, 2011 was the ten year anniversary of the agile manifesto (http://agilemanifesto.org/) - the adaptation to a data-driven application is relatively recent. Rather than the traditional use case or general systems integration, agile data warehousing became topical in August 2008 when Ralph Hughes, inventor of the concept, published his first book, *"Agile Data Warehousing: Delivering World-Class Business Intelligence Systems Using Scrum and XP"*.

Whatever term you use - information management (IM), data warehousing (DW) or business intelligence (BI) - an agile approach is able to successfully connect the business and the outcomes sought, to the development teams doing the actual work. It's about synthesising the 'contract' which details the business requirements between the two areas.

The importance of this 'contract' is heightened in IM, DW and BI as it's all about the data, not the technology being used or the process being created. The aim is to uncover those truly valuable nuggets of information hidden in masses of data within an organisation. Even when you successfully combine the right technical tools and experience with business knowledge and desire, you still need a bit of luck to uncover data gold. No surprise that IM is a field littered with implementation failures, budget overruns and timeline blowouts.

I believe an agile approach to IM is more successful because it forces the business and IT to connect regularly throughout the program – something many enterprises pay lip service to, but rarely achieve.

An agile IM approach is about making the complex, simple; stripping back to bare minimum with a singular goal in mind. The goal is what's important not the documentation and bureaucracy. Agile IM by its pure nature is a highly adaptive approach; it's light on process and heavy on outcome.

If you try to overlay heavy bureaucracy, common in enterprise size organisations, you confuse the project and the business outcomes you seek. Overlay that with the myriad of individuals who have competing agendas and potentially divisional or departmental conflicts of interest, and you have exponentially complicated your project and your outcomes. The fundamental problem is that when an enterprise wants to scale, it imposes more process and governance on the activity which results in non-agile activity such as service level agreements between organisational business units.

Everything gets heavier, more complex and goes against the core philosophy of the agile manifesto thereby removing its agility. Enterprises need to scale without the bureaucratic weight of process and governance.

Don't get me wrong, process and governance are critical in an agile IM methodology; but they don't rule the program; they are elements within the program.

Agile is simple in its construct and definitely achievable at enterprise level but it is by no means easy to implement and the larger the organisation, the harder it is to 'go agile'. Ultimately, if the CEO (private sector) or the Secretary (public sector) wants to constantly deliver value to their customers/citizens, eliminate wasted effort and significantly increase accountability, they need to adopt an agile approach to IM and be able to scale it accordingly.

In this chapter, we will take you through how an agile information management delivery approach can be used to successfully deliver projects within the enterprise.

OVERVIEW: AGILE INFORMATION MANAGEMENT

Why Agile?

The answer is simple. Because waterfall was failing. Based on research conducted by DM Review Magazine in October 2004, data warehousing projects were taking an average of 17 months to deliver (too long) and costing on average $12.8M (too much). And, on top of that, they were failing 65% of the time for internally built apps and 86% of the time for purchased packages (Hughes & Stodder, 2012).

Ralph Hughes, from Ceregenics (www.ceregenics.com), in conjunction The Data Warehousing Institute (www.tdwi.org) undertook some additional research with just under 300 organisations worldwide in May-June 2012 called *Adoption of Agile Methods among Business Intelligence and Data Warehousing Teams* (Hughes & Stodder, 2012), which highlighted that 82% of respondents see better success with an agile approach. Most successful were those using the Scrum agile method, with 87% seeing success rates improve.

It was also interesting that Hughes' and Stodder's (2012) research showed that experience had a significant impact on success. Those who had done just one pilot project were failing 50% of the time, whereas, success rates climbed steadily from there with respondents who'd done in excess of 14 projects. When agile projects do fail, the main criticisms from respondents were around governance difficulties and architectural issues.

Agile's Impact on KPIs

In terms of agile's impact on key performance indicators, Hughes' and Stodders' (2012) respondents said that they achieved 80% better productivity, 81% better client satisfaction, 60% better quality output, but only 30% saw lower costs. When investigating the cost issue, there was no correlation between cost blowouts and experience, industry, tools or method. However, it appeared that big companies struggled more to contain cost blowouts with 57% of respondents (those with more than 100,000 employees) saying that costs were higher.

Addressing Cost Blowouts at Enterprise Level

We believe that the cost blowouts experienced by enterprise organisations are largely due to the issues identified in the research where projects fail, i.e. governance and architecture. An agile IM approach can definitely be scaled, and we'll show you how later in this chapter, but essentially, you need to create an environment where governance is tangible and well supported by agile tools and workflow. You can do this by using automated agile tools and workflow to produce governance reports regularly and maintain open communications with the governance stakeholder group. By aggregating the story boarding process right up to program level and enabling burndown charts by pre-defined dimensions such as business outcome, architecture component, sprint team or individual developer, you will have detailed visibility from individual resource level right through to whole-of-program level. You'll be able to run QA (quality assurance) across your program by any dimension you require. See more later in this chapter under: "What Does Agile Look Like?"

Architecture must also be more adaptable; to make this work, you'll need to look at new approaches that can scale. You have to be able to protect your architecture from the flow-on effects of a small change in requirements, leading to a change in data models which results in significant changes to the ETL (extract transform load) layer that is timely and expensive.

The aim is to design for now using flexible principles that enable you to adapt your architecture as your business requirements change over time. Hyper modelling solutions, which aren't yet popular in Australia, but showing promising results in Europe and the States, are a potential solution. Hyper Normalisation and Hyper Generalisation are two such techniques that will enable you to design your architecture to work today and to adapt to your future state. The general principal is to future proof your data model and insulate against changes that will be timely and costly to implement.

What does Agile IM Look Like?

An agile approach to information management overlays the agile manifesto (below) onto a data-driven project. There are a number of methods in common use including Scrum, Lean or Kanban, Scrumban, FDD and xUP. Most common is Scrum, which we will focus on in this chapter.

Agile IM's single-most important goal is to constantly deliver value to the customer by removing wasted effort; that is, eliminating anything that does not deliver value in the short term. According to Ralph Hughes, from Ceregenics, known as the inventor of Agile Data Warehousing, the agile IM concept is simple, but it isn't easy.

The Agile Manifesto (2001) stated:

We are uncovering better ways of developing software by doing it and helping others do it. Through this work we have come to value, individuals and interactions over processes and tools, working software over comprehensive documentation, customer collaboration over contract negotiation, and responding to change over following a plan. That is, while there is value in the items on the right, we value the items on the left more. (www.agilemanifesto.org, 2001, p. Manifesto for Agile Software Development).

The aim is to maximise the work not done and deliver incremental value to the business along the way.

The Agile IM Process

An agile IM approach brings the business close to the development team with a Product Owner (the Business Partner) defining what is required. The Product Owner defines a 'user story'; the who, what, and why. These user stories are combined to form the project backlog. The Project backlog is prioritised based on value and dependencies and fed into an iterative development cycle called a flywheel (Hughes, 2008, 2013). The flywheel 'spins' once during each sprint. Out of the sprint comes the release pool which is the code that is released into production.

The Hughes Flywheel (2008) Scrum Sprint Concept

The Hughes flywheel (2008) based on Schwaber and Sutherland's SCRUM Sprint (2013) is made up of five key elements:

1. Story conference;
2. Task plans;
3. Develop;
4. Sprint demo;
5. Retrospective.

For each agile team, the Hughes flywheel (2008) spins once during a sprint and is separated as per the diagram in Figure 1.

Agile Levels of Business Requirements

- **EPIC:** Huge requests;
- **Theme:** Between EPICs and user stories. EPICs can be broken down into themes and then the themes are further broken down into stories;
- **Story:** This is what the business owner needs in a self-contained, stand-alone story. There should be no interdependence

Figure 1. The Hughes Flywheel (2008) outlines the activity undertaken by an agile development team during one iteration sprint. The Hughes Flywheel (2008) spins once, through steps one to five.

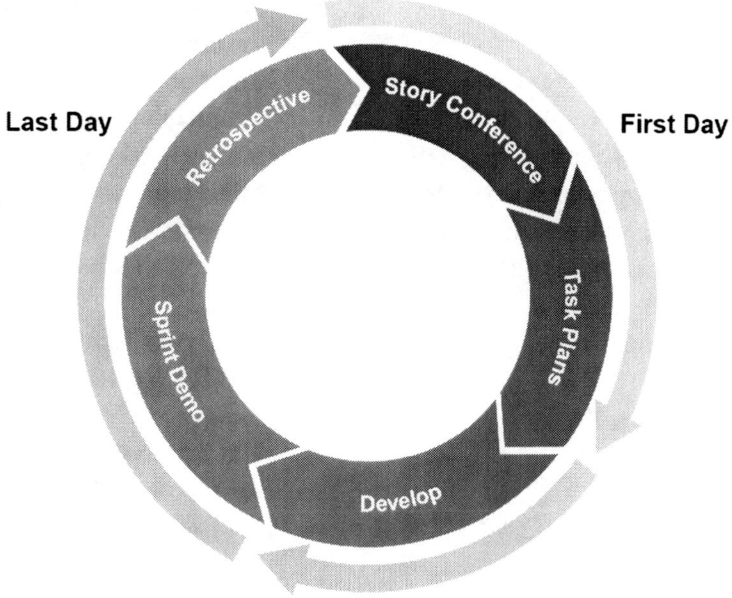

with other user stories and these can be adjusted until they are part of an iteration. The user story must deliver value back to the business owner and the development team must be able to estimate the size of a user story. Test development based on the user story must be possible;

- **Developer Stories:** This is further decomposition of the user story for data integration activity.

Agile IM Estimating

Estimating accurately is critical to the agile IM approach. The idea is to use a familiar reference structure such as types of cats, dogs, cars etc to determine the amount of work involved in each element of the sprint:

- Cards have story points on them;
- Use the Fibonacci sequence only;
- Use reference stories from a past sprint.

For each new story:

- Everyone picks a card;
- The team shows them simultaneously;
- Then discuss the outliers; and
- Revotes until a consensus is reached.

Most estimates should take between three and five minutes. Good estimating is what will provide you with accurate plans and will answer the big questions of how much will it cost and when will it be delivered. Ideally, you'd take a day to story board the entire project backlog by release after estimation has stabilised and you're accurately estimating each sprint. Basically you should:

- Bracket all user stories by team velocity;
- Add release boundaries;
- Establish project level of effort estimation by multiplying head count by number of iterations; and

- Rework the estimation after each story conference.

Agile IM Tracking

The scrum task board is a lightweight, division of work which identifies extra effort required, and is fully transparent. Each scrum task board details all activity from EPIC, through theme to user story and then onto individual task – it is clear what is being done, what is coming up, what is in development and what is awaiting business approval.

What Agile IM Looks Like in the Project Room

Based on Ralph Hughes' teachings (2008, 2013), Agile IM consists of a number of specific features in the project room:

- **Co-located teammates:** The business and development team work in the same room ideally;
- **Time-boxed development:** The development team is given one to three weeks to deliver their sprint (depending on the environment they are working within);
- **Self-organised teams:** Teams are responsible for organising themselves. The theory behind this is simple – they know what will work best;
- **Just-in-time requirements:** Team are able to figure out details as they go through their sprint;
- **Sized-based estimation:** Estimating by comparison first (then hours) which gives you a clearly relative level of complexity on different tasks;
- **Test-led development:** Teams use a tough definition of "done" which involves defining how you test the outcome and writing that test before you build the code. This is a very clear definition of done and you continue to develop until you pass the test;
- **Automated testing:** On a daily cycle to ensure any errors are caught early in the iteration;
- **Scrum master management:** Turns task boards into burndown charts, providing detailed views of the program across business outcomes, teams, EPICs and stories (see Figure 14 for burndown chart examples).

Where Does Speed Come From with Agile IM?

An agile IM approach will help you avoid big mistakes that cost time and money. It does this in a number of ways according to Hughes (2008, 2013):

- Coding starts early with a good feedback loop that involves the business;
- Self–organised teams know how to get the best result through the effective use of team skills;
- Visibility of the outcomes from the data allowing for a real conversation with the business around data quality and meeting business requirements;
- Pays off tech debt early and resolves outstanding data quality issues efficiently.

In addition to saving time and money, agile IM gets its speed from:

- 80/20 specifications;
- Test-driven development;
- Business owner staying available and involved;
- More accurate estimation;
- Automated testing catches coding errors;
- The client de-scoping unnecessary work by determining where the effort to produce an outcome outweighs the return you may get.

SCALING AGILE IM TO THE ENTERPRISE

Unification with Agile IM

Whatever term you use - information management (IM), data warehousing (DW) or business intelligence (BI) - an agile approach is able to successfully connect the business and the outcomes sought, to the development teams doing the actual work. It's about synthesising the 'contract' which details the business requirements between the two areas. This approach:

- Connects the business and its outcomes to the development teams doing the actual work;
- Promotes collaboration and enables motivated, self-organising teams to form; everyone is focused on the business outcomes they're trying to achieve;
- Is new as it's a data-driven agile approach and differs from general systems 'use case' scenario development; and
- Gives you tighter governance over your data and your project, and better productivity from your development teams.

The Big Issue: "The Contract"

In large organisations, constructs such as the Business Requirements Document or BRD becomes the "Contract" between the business and IT. The pure function of its creation actually insulates the business from IT and in my experience, the BRD process results in escalating distrust between the two. I have seen BRDs as long as 700+ pages – tomes that are virtually impossible to achieve. Essentially, this type of BRD sets the IT team up for failure, not success. The BRD starts out as requirements but is then transformed into the all-powerful funding mechanism enabling the business to hide behind the process. The aim is to create accountability and maintain control; in reality, no one is held to account and control is lost to all. The BRD aims to avoid misunderstood requirements and attempts to detail every, single element of the program – this is virtually impossible because as the IT team plows through their hundreds of pages of requirements, the business is constantly changing and therefore so do the program's requirements.

And, more often than not, BRD's miss fundamental elements. Imagine trying to design an entire city with no information about location, size, type of use. That is what IM projects often call for – an impossible task, no matter how talented and committed your team is. Critical to scaling with an agile IM approach is fundamentally changing this 'trust' – and I use that term loosely! – relationship.

Achieving Cultural Change

You'll need a strategy to manage the enormous change in stakeholder expectations. Agile IM is a completely new way to interact and manage data-driven projects. You need to get stakeholders comfortable with the way long term projections are done; they need to get comfortable with the fact that points along the journey are just as important, if not more so, than the journey itself.

In simple terms, your organisations must shift variability from time to scope; the concept of diminishing value determines project priorities; what will return the most value to the business is done first.

IT'S ALL ABOUT THE DATA

The importance of this 'contract' is heightened in IM, DW and BI as it's all about the data, not the technology being used or the process being created. The aim is to uncover those truly valuable nuggets of information hidden in masses of data within an organisation. Even when you successfully combine the right technical tools and experience with business knowledge and desire, you still need a bit of luck to uncover data gold. No surprise that IM is a field littered with implementation failures, budget overruns and timeline blowouts.

I believe an agile approach to IM is more successful because it forces the business and IT to connect regularly throughout the program – something many enterprises pay lip service to, but rarely achieve. An agile IM approach is about making the complex, simple; stripping back to bare minimum with a singular goal in mind.

The goal is what's important not the documentation and bureaucracy. Issues commonly experienced at the enterprise level and how best to address these with an agile IM approach include:

- **Offshore development & operations:**
    - One team or separate teams with separate backlogs;
    - Work one iteration directly before moving to remote model; or get model working onshore before segmenting;
    - Use workflow or virtual card wall tools to mitigate any cultural or language barriers;
    - Organise teams to work independently onshore and offshore (i.e. hyper normalisation);
- **Historically delivery results are poor:**
    - The right product (business) owner is key in an agile environment;
    - The business owner must own the process and take responsibility for aligning requirements with outcomes;
    - There needs to be flexibility in procurement processes; if you're outsourcing, you need to be able to move rapidly and not get bogged down in red tape;
    - **Agile on a:**
        - Purchased data model is inflexible and most often, won't allow for hyper normalisation or hyper generalisation;
        - Package solution means you are likely to spend more time customising the solution than you do solving business problems and delivering outcomes.

BUT HOW DO YOU SCALE?

Research (Hughes & Stodder, 2012) shows that the size of an organisation has the biggest impact on cost blowouts and when you ask something to scale, the response in the enterprise is typically "governance". The problem is that some approaches work at a certain level but are difficult to move up to the next level. For example, I find that an outstanding Project Manager often struggles with the leap to Program Manager. The same applies to Team Leads transitioning to Project Manager. A Project Manager can juggle more priorities than a Team Lead but a Program Manager must be able to juggle exponentially more priorities.

A Program Manager role is an order of magnitude more difficult that a Project Manager role. There is just more to do, more stakeholder management and more activity streams. A Project Manager must be able to make the transition from 'diving into the detail' to using leadership techniques and mature processes to resolve the issues.

Additionally, a Program Manager is highly skilled at compartmentalising issues; the aim is that one program issue does not impact another. In old software engineering vernacular, this is referred to as "tightly organised but loosely coupled". If you think about a stereo, it is a tape deck, a CD player, an AMP and speakers – all completely discrete functions, highly designed themselves (i.e. tightly organised) but linked together (i.e. loosely coupled).

Scaling the agile construct and extending it to enterprise level is all about moving from a project management approach to a program management approach. To do this, you take Hughes (2008) agile scrum flywheel construct (detailed earlier in this chapter) and add leadership. In true agile style, you build a program level, scalable, agile approach rather than a project level approach. Think of it as a meta agile solution.

There are two intersecting iterative processes: the horizontal process which is program management level and the vertical process which is project level agile sprints, where Hughes flywheels spins for one or many parallel streams or teams (see Figure 2). It's the orchestration of these two constantly revolving, intersecting, iterative processes that enables scale – it's program management but not as we know it:

1. The agile program engages the enterprise stakeholders and defines the vision (and mission);
2. The program then coverts the Vision into the Strategy using the strategy map. This is the conversion of the Vision into the goals and measures; the goals and measures into strategy and tactics; and the definition of principles & rationale, policies and the constraints guide for the strategy and tactics;
3. The Planning function adopts the goals, strategy, tactics, and principles, and balances the timeframes of:
    a. The optimal efficient to build order; and
    b. The business priorities;
4. The release teams then assess, plan, generate backlog and write program level storyboard activities to feed into the sprint teams;
5. The sprint teams iterate solution design (sprints), build and test the code;
6. The program and architecture functions conduct design reviews and coordinate across release teams, with potential realignment and potentially raise program level technical debt;
7. Periodic delivery release by teams, and/or across multiple teams, are scheduled;
8. Product releases are reviewed by the business (generally at the EPIC or theme level);
9. Consolidated program level technical debt issues are raised and potentially refactored into the strategy for subsequent planning purposes.

Figure 2. C3's Agile program management methodology involves two intersecting iterative processes. The horizontal, program management process sets the vision and governs the program, and the vertical, Hughes (2008) flywheel process is used by each agile development team to complete each work sprint.

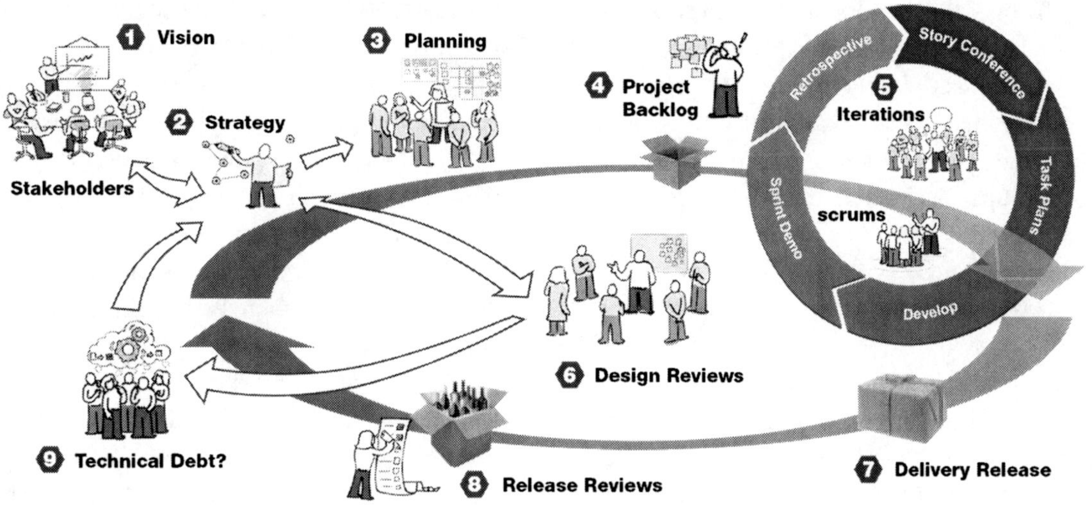

To Scale, Program Governance is Critical

In his books, Ralph Hughes (2008, 2013) outlines a set of tools that aid agile development, in particular, story boards and burn down charts, that can be implemented manually. The reality of large scale organisations is that manual processes will not work due to geographic and other cultural constraints. You need a solution that facilitates and automates the orchestration of the two constantly revolving, intersecting, iterative processes to enable a successful outcome. Agile shows that the traditional communication approaches do not work (such as email and text documents). Yes, we're all addicted to email and text documents but imagine for a minute, an entire program that does not use Microsoft Word.

What is required is a solution that:

- Workflows requirements (user stories);
- Aggregates them to themes and epics;
- Facilitates the steering group engagement and reporting;
- Provides program and project (or sprint) level timeline forecasting but allows the functional decomposition of the story into development activities;
- Allocates ownership of activities to individuals;
- Allows the developers to continually update their activities and pass it on;
- Allows activity aggregation to provide instantaneous status across all sprints and the program as a whole;
- Groups specific outcomes into releases;
- Reports on quality assurance across the releases; and
- Orchestrates the releases to production.

The result is a highly ordered yet loosely coupled, self-organising program of agile activity that can scale to the enterprise. It's a process: phased planning, followed by communication and management of the planned requirements, then delivery is scheduled and delivered with reduced risk and a higher level of quality assurance.

We are all Business Intelligence professionals…just imagine a data-driven program management dashboard of outcomes, developer and team productivity as well as benefits to the business… it's a BI dashboard for BI programs.

While this cannot be accomplished in the one tool, it is possible to achieve with a set of complementary tools that work well together and achieve all of the outcomes described above.

And Automated Quality Assurance is Mandatory

To make agile work, a flurry of development needs even tighter quality assurance control. Mandatory is:

- An automated test solution;
- A regression test to make sure old code is not broken prior to releasing developed code;
- Consistent delivery of product releases that needs to be managed to products; and
- Automated migration of coded objects is a necessity.

Agile IM; Where Information Governance and Business Intelligence Intersect

Agile IM is both a delivery method and a fundamental change in the way an organisation governs their IM solution development. The method embeds data quality and governance issues into the development cycle, as you iterate using real data, and thereby increases information quality along the way.

Traditional information management project and program delivery methods focus on the solution without considering the data. In fact, only test data is used. Agile IM delivery on the other hand, implants real data into the method throughout the entire program which incrementally improves the quality of your data as you develop.

ENTERPRISE AGILE IM: A CASE STUDY

Now that you know what to do, we'd like to show you how it can be achieved. The following case study has been sanitised to protect the client's identity but reflects a business unit that manages a multi-billion dollar budget each year and has been using an agile IM approach to develop the latest phase of a large-scale, multi-year data warehousing project. The project is considered industry best practise in its field and currently enables the department to accurately allocate their multi-billion budget each year.

We were engaged by the client to implement a planned, phased replacement of the legacy reporting applications into a single data warehouse solution. The vision is to deliver a holistic view of the client's management information over time, whilst delivering incremental business benefit along the way. Our approach has resulted in a data warehouse and reporting solution that is used across Australia by both internal and external users.

The solution assists the client manage their billions of dollars in annual budget spend by providing accurate, timely and consistent data for more informed decision making. It provides the client with intelligence on its individual clients around the country, through their use of service provider services.

Some key metrics follow:

- System Users: 150;
- Source Systems: 25+;
- Data Updates: 20% daily, 50% weekly and 30% quarterly;
- Data volume: 1.5TB;
- Team size: 30+ FTEs.

The C3 Agile IM Program Methodology

Using the C3 agile IM methodology outlined earlier in this chapter, we have been able to scale to the enterprise.

Step 1: Planning: Setting the Vision

The steering committee agrees on high level priorities for the solution components (known in agile terms as the EPIC Business Outcome) and themes (based on rough backlog story point aggregation estimates) to be built. Individual themes are assigned to sprint teams and delivered over the X sprint cycles (in this case, three weeks each) and packaged into releases (see Figure 3).

Planning Commitment

A town plan is a pictorial representation of delivery releases and scope over an extended time period. In Figure 4, the town plan is separated by release, aggregating EPICs over time.

Step 2: Forecasting

Medium range forecasting is reported using high level estimates based on the individual sprint team's velocities. For example, at this rate (our velocity), we expect delivery of the XX EPIC at YY (time) by sprint (see Figure 5).

Step 3: Project Backlog

Sprint Teams work with business-based product owners to breakdown themes into a number of user stories. Each sprint cycle, a sprint team defines the developer stories required to deliver the user story. Developer stories are tracked by time spent and completion is estimated based on each assigned owner (see Figure 6).

Figure 3. EPIC activities managed by sprint teams

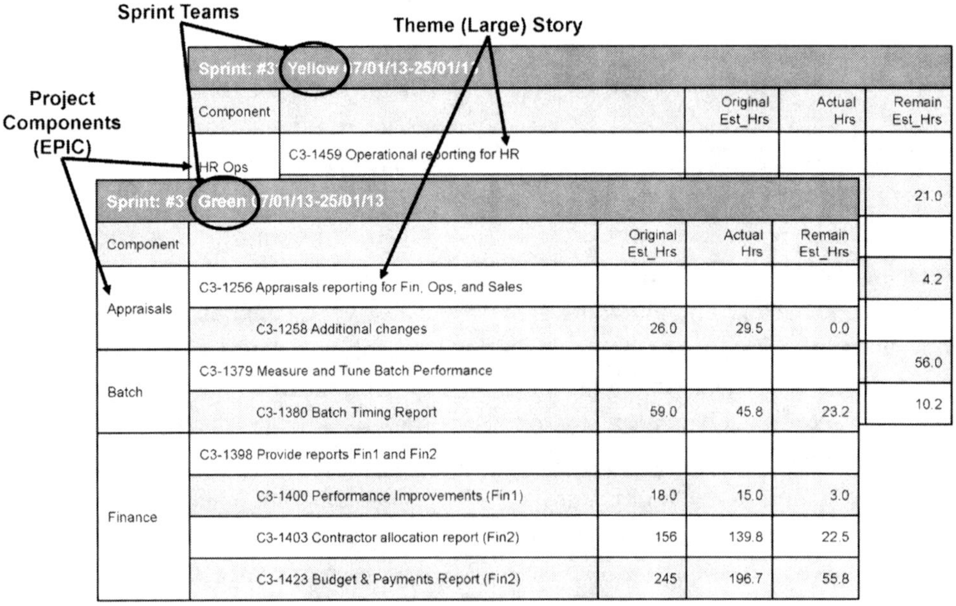

Figure 4. Pictorial order of how to populate the target data model over a long time period (in this case 15 months broken down into 3 months segments). Those in squares represent an EPIC. Grey shading is completed. This clearly shows what is happening when.

Step 4: Pipeline

Delivery pipeline maps deliverables to roles and sprints within sprint cycles from initial business engagement to production release (see Figure 7).

Step 5: Retrospective

Continuous improvement is built into the method – constantly looking at estimate variants that need to be improved. Sprint Teams analyse accuracy

Figure 5. Short term forecast by sprint (top row of numbers is the sprint). This ties a sprint to a date to when an epic is going to be completed. An agile project's representation of a GANTT chart for interfacing to an enterprise PMO based on assumptions around velocity.

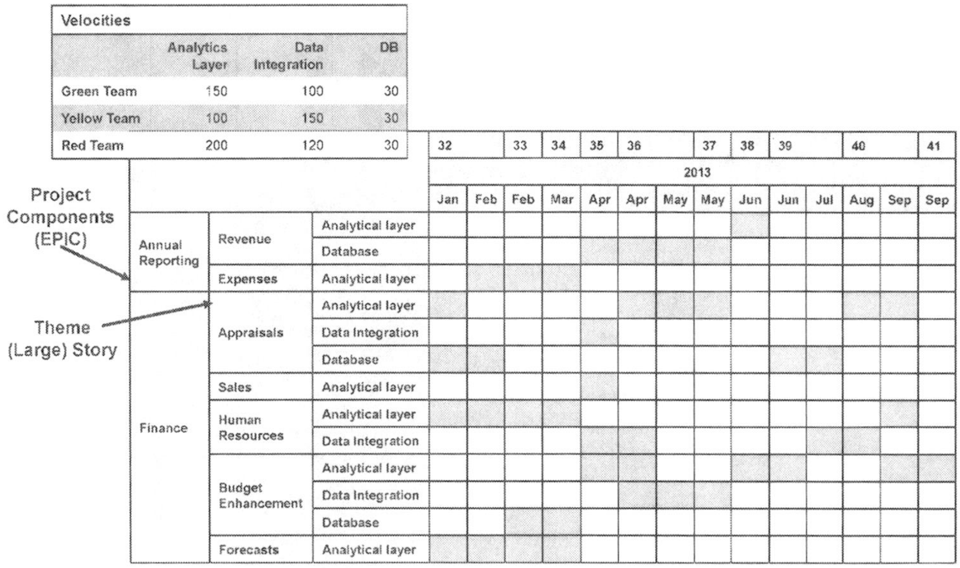

Figure 6. Developer activities relating to user stories, themes, and EPICs. Each development activity creates code objects.

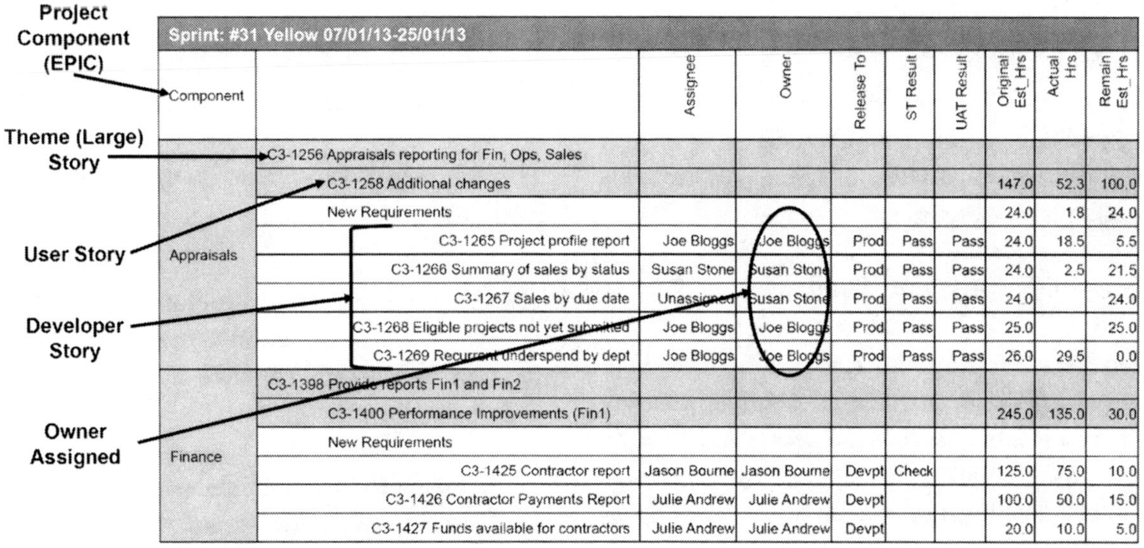

Figure 7. Pipeline of activity between sprint releases to allow the upfront analysis to pipeline development activity between sprint teams

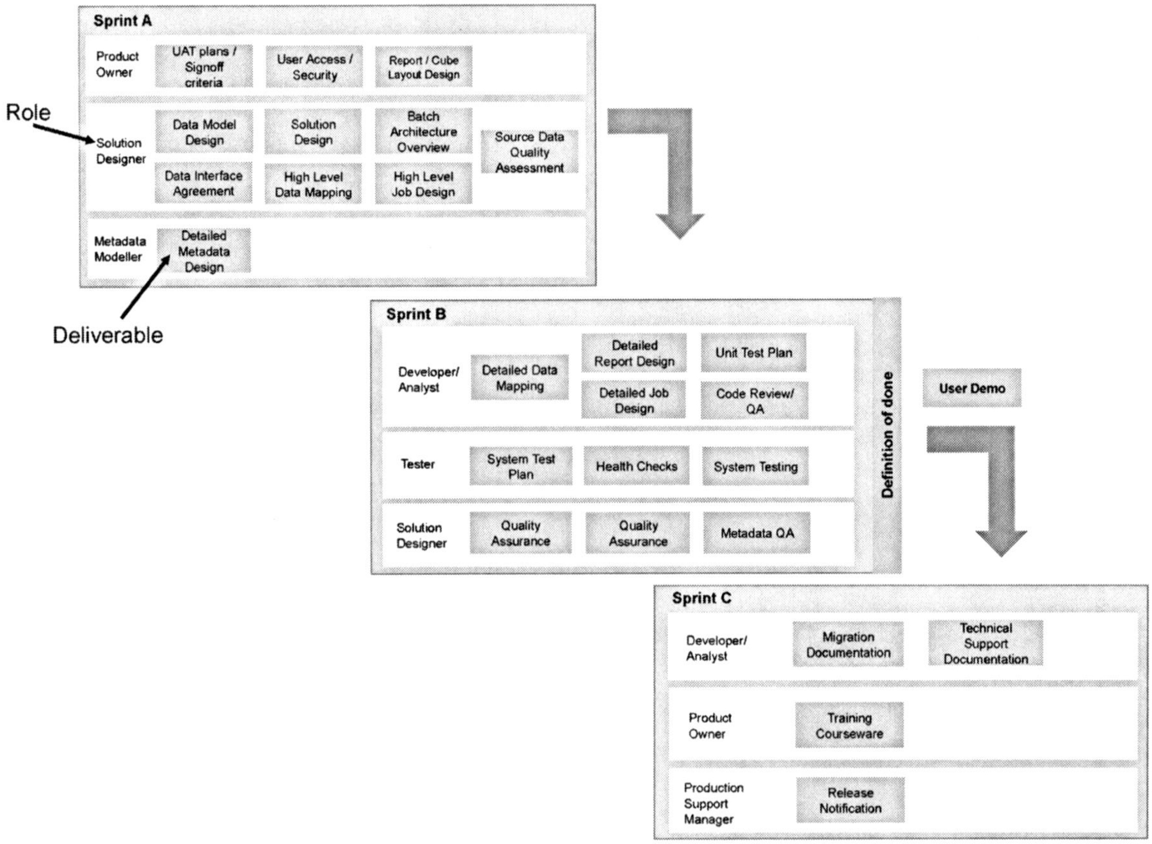

of estimation to improve over each sprint. Design patterns are updated thus increasing the efficiency and estimation accuracy of future, similar story backlogs (see Figure 8).

Step 6: Regression Testing

Regression testing runs across all database environments and provides an ongoing measure of data integrity within the data warehouse. In this case, the testing is grouped by key source systems to allow targeted analysis of data issues (see Figure 9).

Step 7: Development Workflow

Development Workflow: Component Summary

Developers interact with developer stories within the workflow tracking tool (see Figure 10).

The key details captured against developer stories are:

- Estimated time required to complete a task;
- Current workflow status;
- Assignee for current task.

Figure 8. Estimation accuracy report showing the largest variance to improve for next time

SPRINT VERSION: Sprint: #31 Yellow 07/01/13-25/01/13

Key	Description	Classification	Owner	Estimate todo at start	Estimate still todo at end	Actual Effort	Actual / Initial Estimate	Work Log Details: User	Comment	Time Spent	Remaining Estimate
C3-1256	Appraisals	Database	Susan Stone	15	2	31.8	244%	Joe Bloggs	Debugged	6.3	18.7
								Susan Stone	Update script	1.5	26
								Joe Bloggs	Will req thorough testing	4	7
								Susan Stone	Three new keys supplied	20	45
C3-1258	Annual Reporting	Analytical Layer	Jason Bourne	80	0	92.5	115%	Jason Bourne	Batch design & documentation	65	1
								Jason Bourne	Tested in UAT	23	38
								Julie Andrew	Scheduled script-run	4	15
								Jason Bourne	Job not completing	0.5	0.5

Figure 9. QA (quality assurance) report that shows coded object pass rates by source system

Result Count		Pass	Tolerated Pass	Fail	Pass Rate
Finance	Accounts Payable	142			100.00%
	Accounts Receivable	111	7		100.00%
	Cash Receipting	57			100.00%
	Fixed Assets	54			100.00%
	Quality Management	150		2	98.70%
	General Ledger	81			100.00%
	Travel	83			100.00%
Human Resources	Payroll	64			100.00%
	Headcount	128			100.00%
	Time recording	109			100.00%
	Forecast	33	2		100.00%
Marketing	Expenses	145			100.00%
	Success KPIs	79			100.00%
	Budget	57			100.00%
Sales	Budget	134			100.00%
	Targets	55		15	72.72%
Inventory	Product lines	97			100.00%
	Category	58			100.00%
	Depreciation	58			100.00%

Figure 10. Status of individual user story

Key	Components	Summary	Status	PR	Release To	Assignee	Owner	Issue Sub Type	Classification	Remaining Estimate
C3-1256	Appraisals	Appraisals Reporting	Open	⬆		Joe Bloggs	Susan Stone	New Requirement	Database	30 minutes
C3-1258	Annual Reporting	Project Reporting	In Development	⬆	Development	Susan Stone	Susan Stone	New Requirement	Analytical Layer	1 hr 30 minutes
C3-1456	Batch Reporting	Batch Timing	In Development	⬆		Susan Stone	Julie Andrew	New Requirement	Data Integration	0 minutes
C3-1398	Sales	Summary of sales	In Development	⬆		Jason Bourne	Jason Bourne	New Requirement	Data Integration	1 day, 5 hours
C3-1427	Finance	Recurrent Underspend	Open	⬆		Joe Bloggs	Joe Bloggs	New Requirement	Analytical Layer	2 days, 6 hours
C3-1269	HR	Contractor Report	Open	⬆		Julie Andrew	Julie Andrew	New Requirement	Database	7 hours

Development Workflow: Workflow

Developers and Testers on each sprint team move developer stories through the workflow tool from an initial OPEN state through to migration to acceptance. Final migration to Production is performed by team scrum master (see Figure 11).

Development Workflow: Storyboard

From the detailed workflow, a virtual story board view is used by developers and team scrum masters to track story progress and dependencies (see Figure 12).

Development Workflow: Individual Team

Defining all of the detail including requirement, test case, activity by individual object – shows level of detail drilled down (see Figure 13).

Step 8: Team Tracking

Team Delivery Reporting – a BI solution for reporting:

- Burn down Overall;
- Burn down by Business Outcome;
- Burn down by Developer;
- Burn down by Architecture (ETL, DB, BI etc);
- Requirements released; QA Reports etc.;
- Transparency of Delivery.

These charts provide a real-time understanding of the program's delivery output over a time-boxed sprint period. They are used by many parties within the program including program and project sponsors, team leaders, developers, project managers and business owners. A specific action is taken with the engagement of any new stakeholders to ensure the interpretation of these charts is clearly understood.

Step 9: Releases

Releases are tagged across the sprint teams and migrated to production at a set release schedule (aligned to 3 week sprints). Candidate user stories are flagged early and organised into releases which are then grouped and migrated through the change environments to production. The workflow tool maps user stories to production release allowing for requirements traceability and includes business approval for each release (see Figure 15).

Step 10: Status

Half page summary status by team (see Figure 16).

Figure 11. Workflow defined for the stories to production

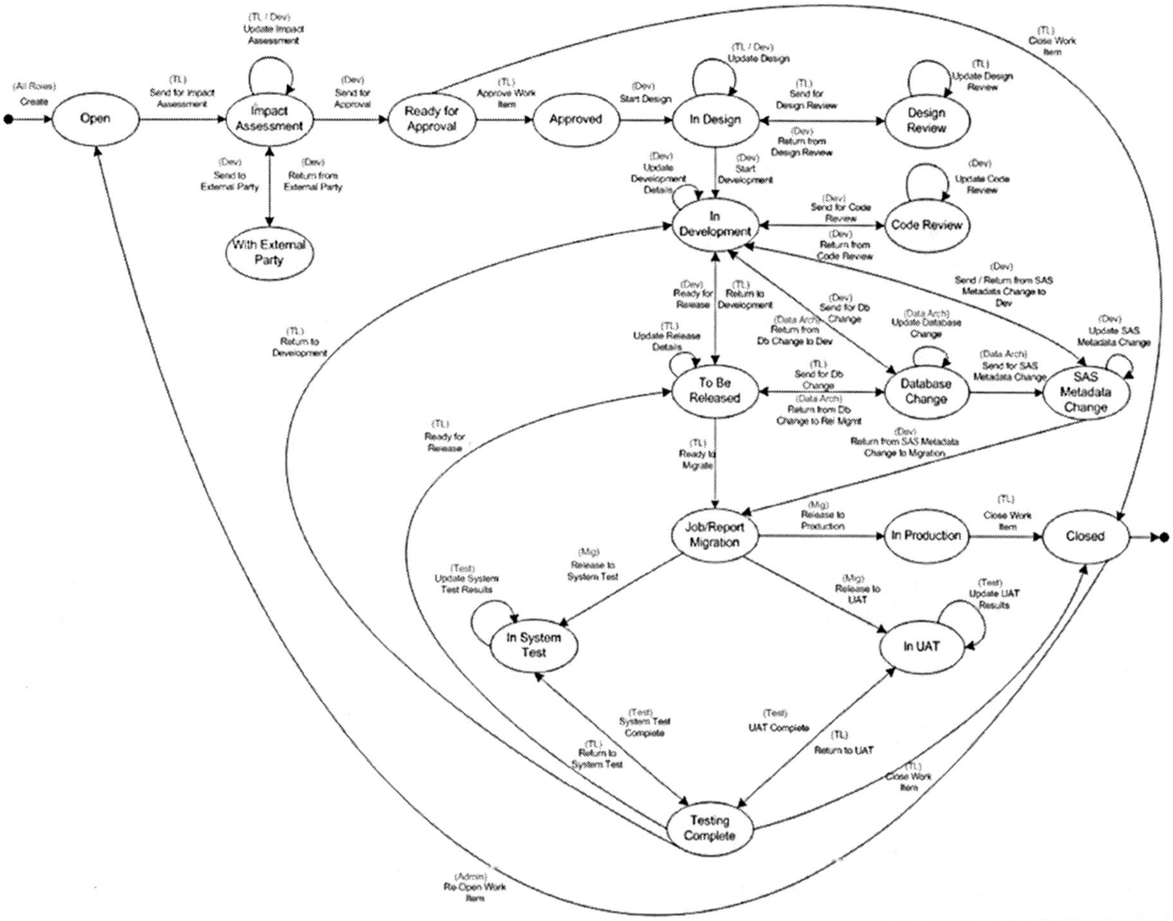

Step 11: Program Governance

The entire program is governed using burndown charts from individual sprints right up to program level (see Figure 14 for examples):

- **Sprint Burndowns:** Each sprint produces its own burndown chart per agile team;
- **Release Burndowns:** Each team's sprint burndowns are then mapped to a release burndown chart;
- **Program Burndowns:** Release burndowns are mapped up to a program burndown chart.

At every level of the program, from individual developer through to aggregated business outcomes, the business is able to see progress.

Step 12: Steering Committee Reporting

Observing value from projects or what project sponsors will report to the Steering Committee (see Figure 17).

SETUP IS KEY TO AGILE ADOPTION SUCCESS

When asked where a program failed, many program managers will tell you that it was "at the

Figure 12. Virtual storyboard used by all program participants

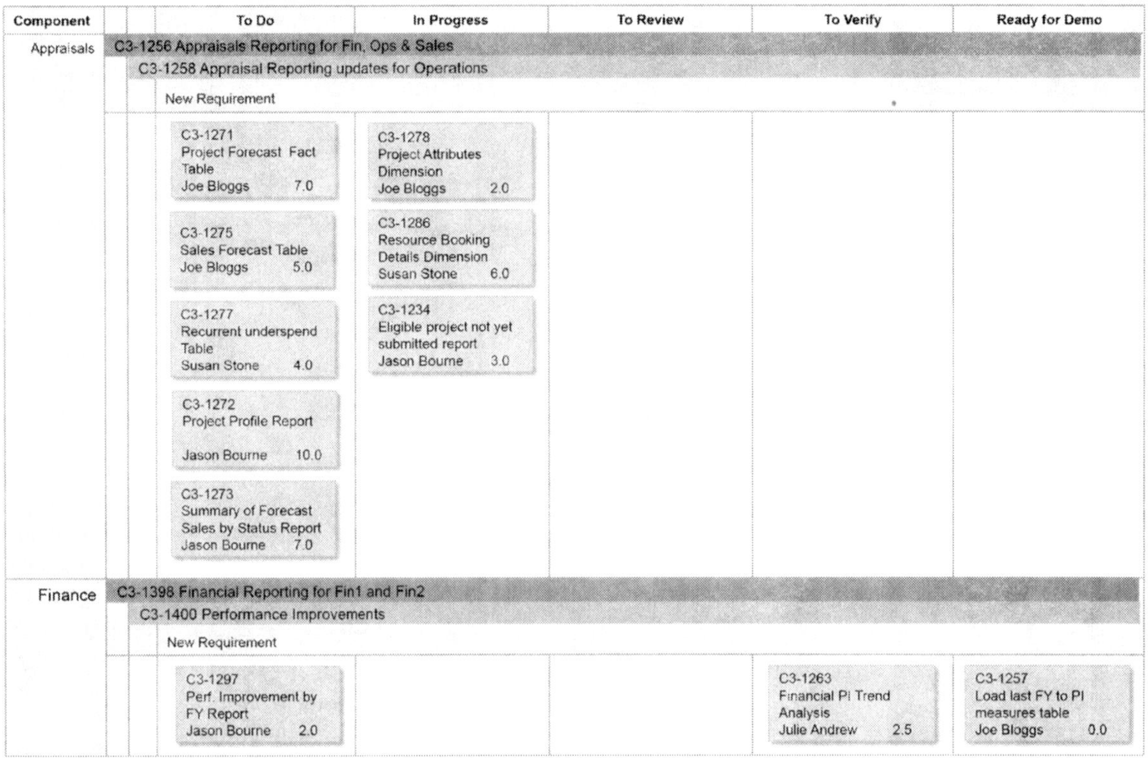

start". Invariably, I am asked, "we like the idea of agile, and we can see the benefits, but how do I get started?". My answer is always the same, agile is simple, but it isn't easy; you can't just 'go agile' overnight. It is a significant shift in culture and requires buy-in at all levels of your organisation, from the steering committee or business owners down to the individual developers writing the code.

When I hear that 50% of pilot projects fail (Hughes & Stodder, 2012), my view is that these organisations haven't set their programs up correctly in the first place. The main reason for this is that they treat it like an IT project, they forget about the enormous cultural shift required to support agile information management. This is highlighted even more at enterprise level. In addition to the complete vocabulary change, the cultural change is underestimated every time. Based on current, real-world experience, I advocate a staged approach to achieving a best practise agile IM approach. By narrowing down our stages to three key steps, we've be able to achieve success at enterprise level:

Step 1: Planning;
Step 2: Enablement;
Step 3: Execution.

In this chapter, we focus on Steps 1 and 2.

Step 1: Planning

Program Management

- **High Level Planning:** Briefings to team and stakeholders on objectives, approach, deliverables and schedules;
- **Deployment Scheduling:** Prioritise and sequence town plan based on business value and stakeholder input, within ar-

Figure 13. Workflow management example

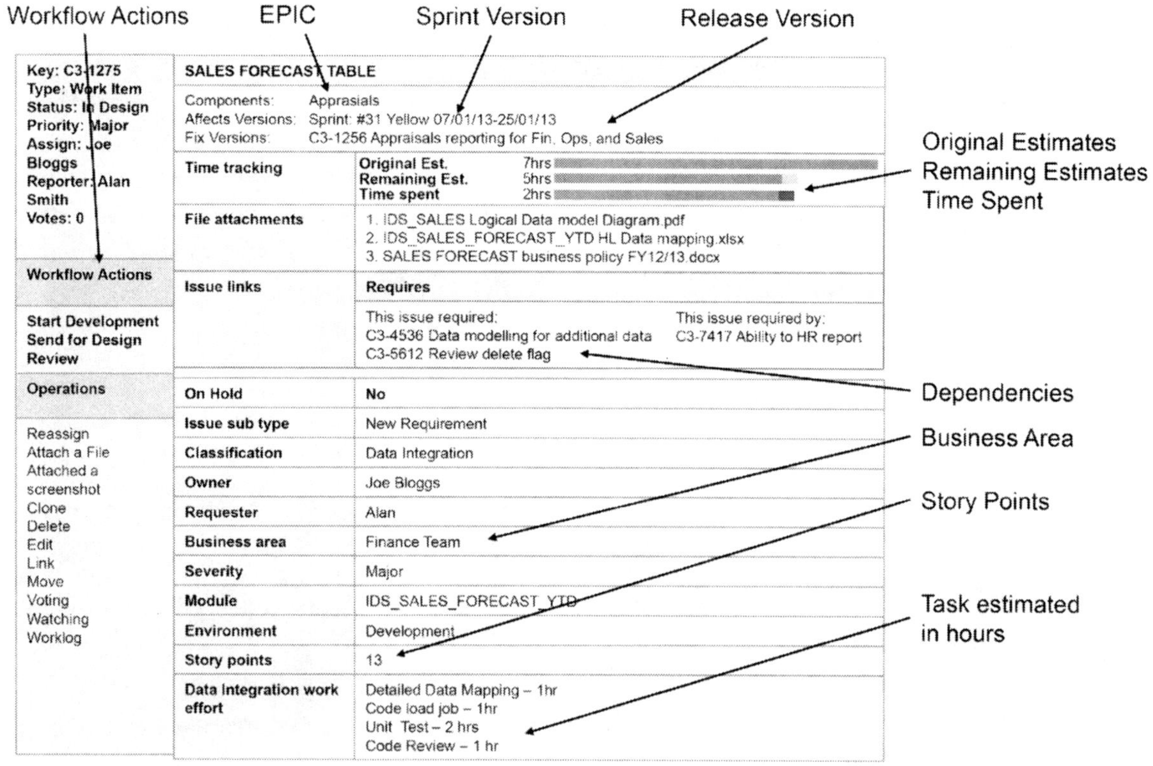

chitectural constraints and initial sizing estimates;

- **Milestone Definition:** Collation from streams and presentation of client-specific program roadmap and schedule from enablement onward.

Architecture

- **Solution Architecture:** Definition of architectural tiers and layers for consistent processing of data including tool and infrastructure foundation;
- **Solution Infrastructure:** Define and secure hardware platform and promotion environments for project delivery;
- **Source System Interface Agreements:** Agreements with upstream source systems and data providers to provision data for reporting, including composition, location, frequency and format;
- **Town plan (CDM):** High-level abstraction and components in normalised and denormalised layers, including enough detail to prioritise projects and keep separation between project teams;
- **Agile Method Toolset selection:** Evaluation and selection of workflow and engineering tools (requirements, testing, configuration) to insert into client's architecture specifically to enable agile teams.

Business Engagement

- **Exec briefings and overviews:** Engagement on intent and governance of agile portfolio with financial (e.g. CFO), delivery (e.g. sponsoring BU execs), and governing (e.g.

Figure 14. Shows the way burndown charts can be individualised to the project. Here, from left to right, the charts are divided by business delivery output (left) which shows a standard agile team delivery view of agreed scope within a sprint period. The program provides additional insight into the breakdown of the scope showing details around externally blocked requirements and issues arising from user acceptance testing. By business outcome (middle) showing a burndown view of each high level business requirement that is included in a sprint period. This is used primarily to provide detailed insight into an individual business area's implementation and to provide context around the many potentially competing priorities within the sprint. And, by developer resource (right) which shows a burndown view of each individual development resource within a program team. This view is used primarily to understand if an individual's contribution to overall team output maybe affecting the required outcome.

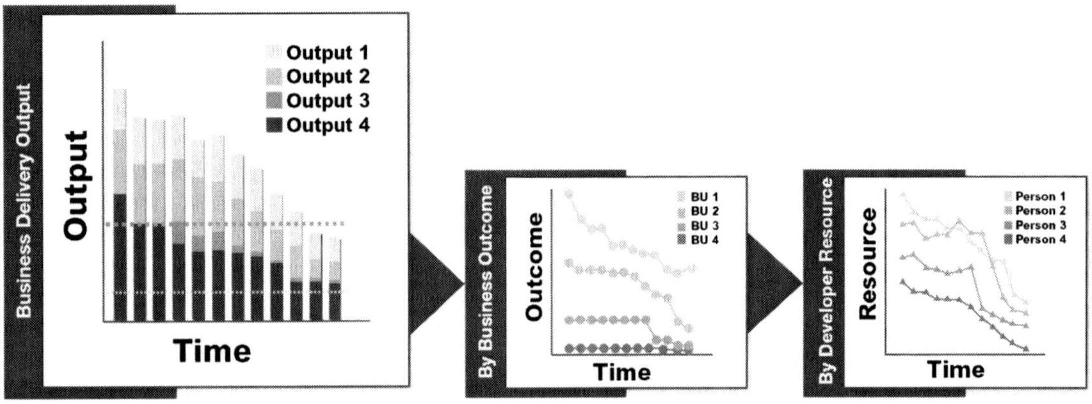

Figure 15. Delivery release report, coded objects associated with a release to an environment

Released – Package #478 - scheduled for release 25/01/2013

Component	Sprint	Key	Summary	Assignee	Status	Release To	ST Result	Unit Results	DB Change	Dependencies
Appraisals	Sprint: #31 Yellow 07/01/13-25/01/13	C3-1278	Project Attributes Dimension	Joe Bloggs	In Prod	Production	Pass	Pass	Yes	None
Appraisals	Sprint: #31 Yellow 07/01/13-25/01/13	C3-1286	Resource Booking Details Dimension	Susan Stone	In Prod	Production	Pass	Pass		None
Appraisals	Sprint: #31 Green 07/01/13-25/01/13	C3-1234	Eligible project not yet submitted report	Julie Andrew	In Prod	Production	Pass	Pass		None

Unreleased – Package #479 - scheduled for release 08/02/2013

Component	Sprint Version	Key	Summary	Assignee	Status	Release To	ST Result	Unit Results	DB Change	Dependencies
Appraisals	Sprint: #31 Yellow 07/01/13-25/01/13	C3-1271	Project Forecast Fact Table	Joe Bloggs	To be released	Production	Pass	Pass		
Appraisals	Sprint: #31 Yellow 07/01/13-25/01/13	C3-1275	Sales Forecast Table	Joe Bloggs	To be released	Production	Pass	Pass	Yes	
Appraisals	Sprint: #31 Yellow 07/01/13-25/01/13	C3-1277	Recurrent underspend Table	Susan Stone	To be released	Production	Pass	Pass		

Unreleased – Candidates

Component	Sprint Version	Key	Summary	Assignee	Status	Release To	ST Result	Unit Result	DB Change	Dependencies
Finance	Sprint: #32 Green 26/01/13-15/02/13	C3-1297	Perf. Improvement by FY Report	Jason Bourne	In UAT	Acceptance	Pass	Pass		C3-1257
Finance	Sprint: #32 Green 26/01/13-15/02/13	C3-1263	Financial PI Trend Analysis	Julie Andrew	To be released	Acceptance		Pass		

Figure 16. Program level status report

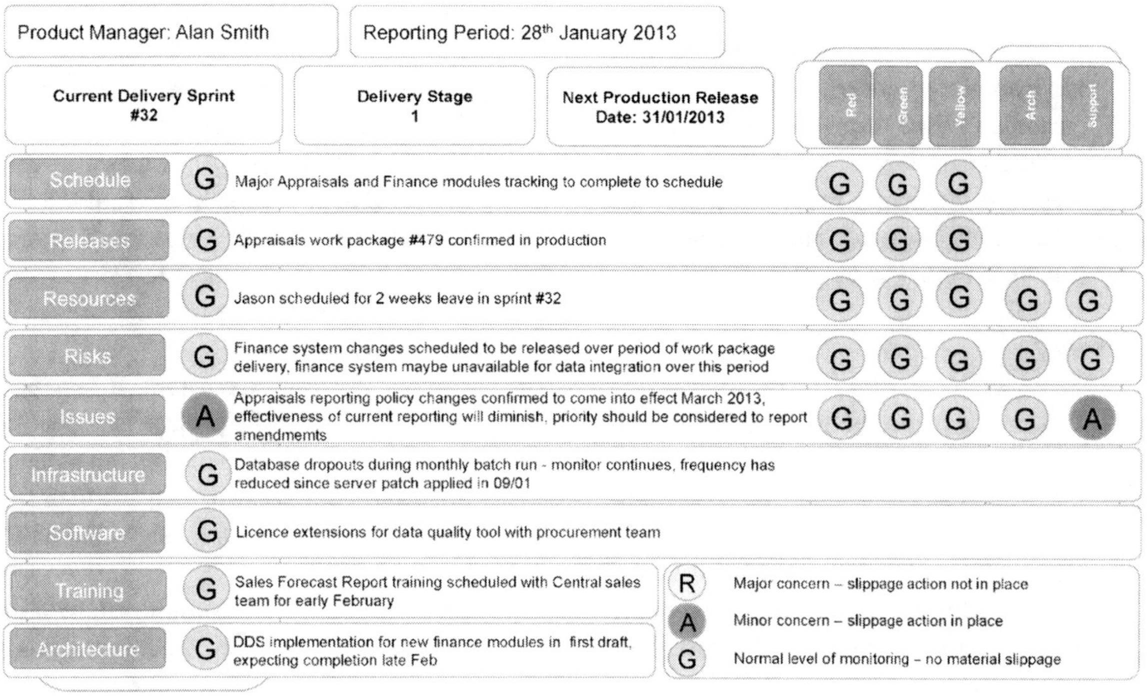

Figure 17. Steering committee reporting

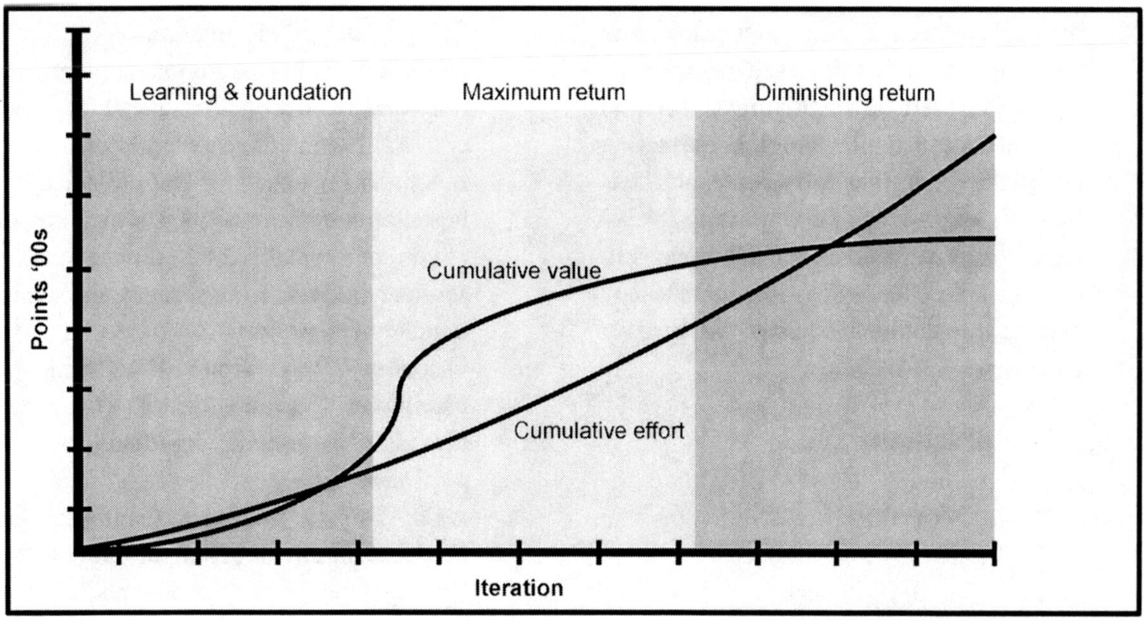

Enterprise IT and Architecture) including control and engagement points;

- **Confirm Governance Model:** Define meeting cycles, and governance artefacts (e.g. customer board terms of reference), including members;
- **Vision to Strategy:** Presentation of agile method objectives and approach, including timelines for key stakeholders.

Delivery

- **Customise Agile IM method for the client:** Understand the client's baseline delivery method and identify key constraints which must be worked around and key changes for agile method adoption to find a workable starting point. Must understand e.g. how software can be tested and released regularly given other potentially non-agile projects and programs, including change-control sign-offs. How can support requests for reporting in PROD be directed to the correct project team and business reps? How much consistency do we demand between agile project teams, and how much do we let them self-organise?
- **Agile IM method deployment:** Method documentation (agile iteration estimation and planning, testing and release, artefacts by role) and briefings and practice for selected team members. Establish agile skill competencies including: scrum masters and agile solution designers for support and knowledge exchange.

Step 2: Enablement

Program Management

- **High Level Program Planning Communication and Endorsement:** Call out iterations and deliverable points;
- **Subject Area (CDM) Benefits Statements:** Breaking down the enterprise into key subject area domains, identify core information models and standards;
- **Iteration and Release Planning Detail:** Creation of each project's terms of reference and demarcation of areas of the town plan and road-map in scope for the project. At this point the business rep, scrum master and solution designer for the project can be mobilised;
- **Sprint Backlog Creation:** Initial backlog ensures that the project has identified work and can be productive immediately. Also provides context and specifics from the business around how the value will be realised;
- **Management Tool Configuration:** Install and configure selected workflow management tool including reporting of project team productivity and progress against technical delivery and business value.

Architecture

- **Town Plan (LDM) and Linkages:** Details on the town plans incorporate project directions and some modelling ahead for project context. The intent is not to perform design functions on behalf of the project but to maintain a contextual view which can aid uptake of normalised and dimensional assets and assist with consistency and separation between projects;
- **Ongoing Modelling Pipelining & Planning:** Continuation of Town Plan providing data model coordination across portfolio;
- **Agile Toolset Setup & Configuration:** Implementation and configuration of engineering tools (e.g. requirements, configuration, quality assurance, release) where changes required for agile processes;

- **Agile Toolset, Usage Management & Championing:** Ongoing adoption and value from engineering tools, including skills transfer, best practices, and customisation to reduce agile cycle time and overheads.

Business Engagement

- **Team Method Training:** Train team members for pilot project;
- **Product Owner Training:** Train product owner for pilot project;
- **Define and Implement Governance Tools:** Governance reporting on progress and business value delivered, both in terms of Earned Value and benefits indicators. Also highlights visibility of backlog priorities and estimated timeframes supporting business planning and prioritisation. Enables decisions about points of diminishing return where new sponsors and business represent the highest and best use of available capacity;
- **Define Operating Model:** Processes, management structures, and enabling tools for a BI capability support function, underpinned by the agile BI project portfolio. To be agreed by management as the model for documentation implementation including key decisions around trade-offs between personalised service, business involvement, and product/service standardisation. Should include defined services, and critical few measures of service – e.g. service availability, service request ageing, town-plan coverage;
- **Define Operating Processes:** Provide process and role documentation to ensure that participants (e.g. Developers, managers, testers, analysts, business people, infrastructure support people) all know how to efficiently engage and deliver to expectations;
- **Implement Factory Structure:** Skills inventory of candidate staff for new structure, search for and appoint additional/replacement staff, training in vision and mission, processes and tools. Seed registers (e.g. report product register, user group register) and knowledge repositories.

Delivery Enablement

- **Trial Project:** The trial project is designed to initiate client resources in the localised agile method and surface issues which pure desk-based design will miss. By focusing a balanced team on a real problem, and enhancing the team to include agile-experienced resources and a coach or observer, the method will emerge significantly more usable and helpful to the client's teams. Expectations should be set that productivity will be reduced for the iterations during the pilot, and some of the team's time will be dedicated to incorporating the new tools into their work routines;
- Across Steps one and two runs continuous team training, education and coaching to help embed an agile approach into the business.

THE 'AGILE IM' CHECKLIST

Agile IM Adoption: Core Components for Success

We have identified a list of core components that will enable successful agile IM adoption within the enterprise:

- A desire to do things differently and recognising that a change is required; to make the outcome the value, not the process;

- The right problem must have a moderate amount of unknowns as a fully known problem does not need collaboration! And you need a team to collaborate on making unknowns known in a timely manner;
- A Product Owner:
  - Business committed to suppling the resource and time allocated;
  - Business employs the product owner to provide authority to define story and accept outcome;
  - IT can provide a proxy product owner; business has to invest in bringing that person up to speed and will have a second round of acceptance;
- Recognition of a change in governance which is actually increased visibility;
- Change the estimation approach and use story points and constant re-estimation;
- Change requirements management approach and recognise that it's data driven; you must think user stories rather than detailed BRD documentation;
- Ability to get program office concessions and recognise the change in scheduling approach;
- Ability to implement a team focused on a joint outcome that is independent of organisation structure or operating model. You must also empower that team to be responsible for the outcome;
- Tools to support the agile process including requirements management, testing and migration;
- Ability to implement quality assurance and interface it with testing and enable environment migration;
- Ability to implement timely service transition and interface with that team for governance of migration processes. The project team writes migration / backout scripts.

CONCLUSION

Data-driven agile delivery can be scaled to the enterprise and if enabled and executed correctly, it will reap all the benefits you seek. However, as simple as the concept of agile information management is, it's not easy. You need to ensure your enablement process is robust and that your program is set up to successfully achieve the outcomes you require. It won't happen overnight and it will take time, effort and commitment from the business.

Program governance can be as detailed as individual developer performance or as high level as whole-of-program by business outcome. It's about implementing the right processes and structures to get this right. Use the tools and approaches that have been developed to enhance data-driven agile delivery and make your governance process tangible. Your approach to architecture must also shift; it's about flexibility, catering for a future that you just can't know yet. This can be achieved, but again, it's a different approach and will require some significant investment in business change management.

The bottom line? A strong management structure, with flexible architecture, a tightly enabled program implemented alongside a comprehensive business change management strategy will provide you with successful agile information management program delivery.

Well governed.

REFERENCES

Beck, K., Beedle, M., van Bennekum, A., Cockburn, A., Cunningham, W., Fowler, M., et al. (2001). *Manifesto for agile software development.* Retrieved from www.agilemanifesto.org

Hughes, R. (2008). Agile data warehousing: Delivering world-class business intelligence systems using scrum and XP. Bloomington, IN: iUniverse.

Hughes, R., & Stodder, D. (2012). *DM review survey of readership, October 2004, quoted in accelerating BI/DW value with agile methods, an inside look at trends and best practices.* Boston: TDWI World Conference Research.

Schwaber, K., & Sutherland, J. (n.d.). *The scrum guide.* Retrieved from https://www.scrum.org/Portals/0/Documents/Scrum%20Guides/2013/Scrum-Guide.pdf#zoom=100

Standish Group International, Inc. (1999). *CHAOS: A recipe for success.* Author.

ADDITIONAL READING

Hughes, R. (2013). *Agile Data Warehousing Project Management: Business Intelligence Systems Using Scrum.* Massachusetts: Elisevier Inc.

Hughes, R., & Stodder, D. (2012, September). *Accelerating BI/DW Value with Agile Methods, An Inside Look at Trends and Best Practices.* TDWI 2012 Boston World Conference Thursday Keynote Presentation, Boston MA. http://www.youtube.com/watch?v=SYyUR2RtzOs

Schwaber, K., & Sutherland, J. *The Scrum Guide,* https://www.scrum.org/Portals/0/Documents/Scrum%20Guides/2013/Scrum-Guide.pdf#zoom=100, July 2013 (pp7)

KEY TERMS AND DEFINITIONS

Agile IM: Data-driven agile delivery methodology.

Agile Manifesto: The alternative process to SDLC (software development lifecycle) or waterfall software development methodologies as written in February 2001 by a group of independent-minded software development practitioners.

Architecture: Information system infrastructure, the target conceptual framework or reference model for information system infrastructure and the specific applications and tools that the information system supports.

Burndown: The reporting mechanism embedded into Agile development split by pre-defined dimensions such as business outcome, architecture component, sprint team or individual developer, providing detailed visibility of the activity of individual developer resources right through to the entire program's output.

Developer Stories: Further decomposition of a User Story for data integration activity.

Enablement: The phase between planning and execution that is focused on 'enabling' the organisation to adopt and adapt to agile information management delivery techniques.

EPIC: The 'agile' term used for the major requests from the business. EPICs are then broken down into 'working' parts to enable the team to deliver on the EPIC requirement.

Hughes Flywheel: At the heart of agile scrum methodology on data-driven projects, the Hughes flywheel (2008) represents the steps that the agile team undertakes during one delivery sprint.

Iteration: See Sprint – predetermined time period for achieving specific tasks.

Product Owner: The Business representative working with the agile development team.

Product Release: The code that is released to production at the end of each sprint.

Scrum Task Board: The scrum task board is a lightweight, division of work which identifies extra effort required, and is fully transparent. Each scrum task board details all the activity required for the project making it clear what is being done, what is coming up, what is in development and what is awaiting business approval.

Sprint: Is the pre-determined time period that an agile development team takes on a specific set of tasks. Most common are two and three week sprints.

User Story: A self-contained, stand-alone story that articulates what the Product Owner needs. There is no interdependence with other user stories and these can be adjusted until they are part of an iteration (sprint). The user story must deliver value back to the business owner and the development team must be able to estimate the size of a user story. Test development based on the user story must be possible.

Theme: Is the breakdown of EPICs into areas of work that can then be broken down further into user and developer stories.

Velocity: Is the speed at which the agile development team works and is based on the agile estimating conducted at the start of every sprint.

Chapter 15
Challenges of Structure and Organization in Medium-Sized Content

Madhavi M. Chakrabarty
Verizon Wireless, USA

ABSTRACT

Organizational knowledge management resources are a combination of articles, guidelines, and process documents. The content in these resources typically ranges from about a few words to a few hundred words. These pieces of content are called medium-sized content. While most organizations do not pose a limit on how long or short each content piece should be, most content sizes default to this limit due to various reasons. Assigning a metadata and taxonomy to the medium-sized content pieces are challenging because of a limited number of repetition of keywords, the limited size of the content, and the existence of other content without which this content is not conceptually complete. This results in challenges for knowledge managers in organizing and structuring this content as well as making it intelligent enough for search engines and business intelligence tools. This chapter presents an approach to creating metadata for these content pieces by proposing a three structure metadata consisting of a static part, a dynamic part, and a conceptual part that links to other pieces of related information.

DOI: 10.4018/978-1-4666-4892-0.ch015

INTRODUCTION

Organizational knowledge resources are used by employees to improve their explicit knowledge (Alavi & Leidner, 2001). These resources help the employees to perform their job responsibilities efficiently. Organizations have dedicated individuals and teams that develop these knowledge resources. Most of the knowledge resources within an organization are in the form of articles, how-tos, learning assessments, Frequently Asked Questions (FAQs) and data sets (Alavi, Timothy R. Kayworth, & Leidner, 2005-6). While the exact guidelines used to create and develop these articles vary from organization to organization, the main goal in creating them is to be able to convey the right message to the right user base at the right time of need (Grant, 1996). As is the case with most organizational content, the content sizes are neither too lengthy like scholarly articles and book chapters, nor too small like short Message Services (SMS) and chat session conversations (Burbidge, 2003-12-03), twitter feeds (Johnson, 2009) and ticker notifications. All the content that fits this profile are referred to as medium sized content.

In order to create an effective knowledge management system, it is necessary to structure and organize the different pieces of content such that user can find the right information at the right time (Becerra-Fernandez, Gonzalez, & Sabherwal, 2004). In most large organizations, content gets created by content authors and stored in a content management system. The content resides in a conceptual structure so that it is easy for the knowledge managers to fetch and display the information in different knowledge management systems that are used in the organization (McInerney & Day, 2007). To make the content smart and easily readable by the different systems, search engines and other meta-analytics tools, the content is marked up and tagged with suitable keywords and metadata. The metadata of the content is a description of the data as well as the rules that will be used to display the data. The knowledge management systems use this metadata to decide if the particular content should be visible to a given user base and the location in the navigation where it resides. Most content management systems have a provision to assign keywords and metadata to a piece of content and it is the responsibility of the content author to make sure that the right metadata is applied to the right pieces of content.

As is the case in most organizational knowledge management systems, the content (like articles, technical documents, how-tos and FAQs) are created as a medium sized content (Karner & Droschl, 2002). This is a deliberate decision by most content authors since the article size is just sufficient to hold the user's attention span and deliver the appropriate information to him or her. From a cognitive point of view, users may deter reading a larger piece of content in their busy work schedule where they may not have a single slot of time available for them to read the entire content in one session. From a user experience point of view, many user experience experts recommend the use of medium sized content as the size is most suitable for display in web-based and mobile devices. The screens on desktops, laptops, smart phones and tablets can effectively be used to display the medium sized articles without having the user to scroll up and down the screen (Karner & Droschl, 2002). Even if the user chooses to print the articles out, they can be fit in a one or two page format that is cognitively easier for the user to process.

In addition to the most common model of knowledge management systems where content authors are responsible for creating content and adhering to guidelines, more and more of the content generated is derived from the users themselves. Capturing and integrating user generated content is becoming a very prominent aspect of the knowledge in knowledge management systems. Outside the bounds of the organization, the statistics favor the importance of user generated content. As per Wikipedia, the average number of words in a Wikipedia article varies between 300 and 400 words (Wikipedia, 2013). Studies suggest that more than 50% of electronic content has been generated in the last two years (Zikopoulos, Deutsch, Deroos, Corrigan, Parasuraman, and Giles, 2013). Most of these content are in form of blogs, iscussions, forum posts, review posts and online content all of which are medium sized. Therefore, user generated content has become a part of every knowledge repository system.

However, given the prominence and significance of medium sized content, and the need of organizations to continue creating medium sized content for all their organizational knowledge management needs, there are certain challenges that are posed by the size of the content in creating effective metadata for describing the content.

The existing methodology for defining metadata and keywords is not very efficient for medium sized content for a number of reasons. Guidelines to define metadata and keywords state that only if a term is repeated a certain number of times in the content, that it can qualify as a keyword (Jacob, 2003). The same holds true for metadata as well. Unless the piece of content clearly specifies the characteristics of the content, or is descriptive enough for the content author to create and assign the metadata, it may be very challenging for them to add all the appropriate metadata to the content. Even if an automatic text analyzer is used for keyword and metadata extraction, the length of the content can become a limiting factor on how successful the analyzer is. Manual intervention becomes a rule rather than an exception. Enforcing content authors to strict guidelines for enforcing structure and wording in the content may help to a certain extent, but requiring the authors to focus more on how the text is analyzed rather than focusing on the content, readability and quality of the content could negatively impact the information quality and subsequently the experience of the users. Strict guidelines requiring every concept in the article to be repeated a significant number of times to justify its qualification for a metadata becomes a limitation given the size of the articles. The choice of words and phrases in the articles are strictly dictated by the organizational vocabulary and terminology (Dephi Group, 2004), thereby limiting the use of synonyms in the metadata. Also, since the size of the articles is limited, it often takes multiple articles to tell a complete story or present a complete concept to the users. Therefore, it becomes imperative to provide a cue to the user that there are other supporting documents that need to be accessed in addition to the document they are viewing to comprehend the concept completely. Apart from these challenges, depending on the type of content, not all articles will have a valid value for every piece of metadata that the system requires the authors to create. Most often than not, only certain values of the metadata structure hold true for a given content piece. But depending on how the content management system is designed, and to what extent content authors manually assign the metadata, there is a chance that many metadata values are either defaulted to a common value or the content authors fill them up with a value that does not compromise the integrity of any other content piece. In some instances, content authors put in more effort in developing and managing the metadata then they do on the actual content (Duval, 2004). It also results in a metadata structure that is very sparse, and most of the times incomplete.

With the fast changing landscapes of businesses, their priorities and models, knowledge management systems are always in a catch-up mode. As businesses change and the user bases are impacted by the change, their need in terms of reference and learning content also changes. New roles may get added, the responsibilities and job profiles of existing users may change and new content types may get added to the systems as a result of a new line of business that the organization takes up. There is a need for knowledge managers to continuously make sure that all the users have access to the right knowledge at the right time. In order to account for the continuously changing business landscape, it becomes necessary for the metadata assigned to the content to reflect the changes in the organization. This results in additional challenges and work load when the metadata assignment is already lagging behind the content and there is no mechanism to extend the metadata in the existing systems.

To address the concerns related to the metadata assignment in medium sized content in the knowledge management resources in an organization; this chapter proposes the creation of a metadata that can exist independent of the content management system. The next section presents the background on the need of a content management systems and a sustainable metadata management system. The following section on issues, challenges and current problems examines the issues and challenges with current metadata structures. The section on solutions and recommendations will provide the recommendations and approach for rethinking the way metadata is currently presented. The recommended approach to creating a metadata includes a 3 part metadata structure that exists for every pieces of content. The metadata structure being proposed includes (i) a static part that contains information regarding the content and exists for all content in the content management system, (ii) a dynamic part that is specific for a given content type and does not exist for all content in the content management system and (iii) a conceptual part that logically connects a content with other content that is related and will add to the user's explicit knowledge if read in tandem. A sample content piece is examined and the new approach is explained in context of the sample content. A few possible next steps are mentioned in the future recommendations section followed by the conclusion for the chapter.

BACKGROUND

Information creation and maintenance is an important way for organizations to build and upkeep their organizational knowledge (Becerra-Fernandez et al., 2004). Organizations use this knowledge to keep employees updated with day to day operational knowledge. It also helps to adapt to the changing consumer needs, technology ecosystem and other organizational dynamics so that the organization and its employees continue to be productive in the future (Dianne, 2005). Organizational knowledge, hence, includes both operational knowledge for the present and knowledge related to the business acumen and competitive advantage that prepares its workforce for the future.

Medium Sized Content

At an organizational level, most of the knowledge created and maintained is in the form of articles that are medium-sized. The term medium-sized includes news articles, training modules and knowledge base articles that are in the range of a few words to a few hundred words, and can typically be fit into a single page view. The significance of size becomes evident when it is compared to small sized content like text messages or SMS (where the maximum character length is limited to 160 characters), twitter posts (where the maximum character length is limited to 140 characters). Small sized content can be content that ranges in size from one to approximately 20 words (assuming the average word size to be eight characters). Large-sized content can be loosely defined as content that runs into multiples pages like journal papers, research articles and industry white papers.

Medium-sized content pieces hold a significant amount of interest in the business and corporate world for multiple reasons. The length of medium sized contents are best suited to the attention span of casual readers as well as people who are glancing over the article to probe and search for an answer to complete their business transaction (Vandenbosch & Huff, 1997). The size is also most suited to impart a new or updated knowledge piece to the employees of an organization announcing a change or improvement in a process. For example, consider the example of a customer service representative in an organization's contact center who receives a call from a customer regarding a transaction they are seeing on their account. While the customer service representative may be well versed with most of the offerings of the organization and will be able to answer the customer's question from his or her tacit knowledge, there may a scenario where the representative has to look up a special code or explanation from the knowledge resources to give a specific code or information, the representative will be able to glance over a document to find the relevant piece of information to relay back to the customer. Similarly, if a user in the organization needs to complete a required training on a newly released product, he or she can retrieve the document while performing some other task and occasionally keep browsing at the content to understand the specific information that impacts their role and responsibilities. The employee should be able to go back and forth in the document to browse the most important piece of content so that it becomes a part of his or her tacit knowledge. Even at the time when many organizations have adapted social media and collaborative technologies as a part of their organization's knowledge management plan, the primary source of content produced continues to be in the medium-sized category (Pipek, Wulf, & Johri, 2011). And complementary information sources like blogs, discussion forums and other social media channels used to share information fall under the category of medium sized content.

Another factor that has confirmed the continuing interest in medium sized content for organizations is the changing landscape of the organizations. With more and more organizations going mobile, employees are using mobile devices on the job as well as using their mobile devices outside their job hours. E-readers available on these devices are designed to best display medium sized content pieces (Eaton, 2011). Therefore, in order to serve the mobile population of its users, content authors are recreating their writing guidelines to focus on content presentation that is best suited for handheld devices and mobile devices.

Organization Content Management

Most of the knowledge resources used in organizations are created in a content management system (Dalkir, 2005). Typically the content is created by content authors who are work with subject matter experts to ensure that the content follows the guidelines prescribed at an organizational level and is written in an unambiguous language recommended by the organization. The content is stored in a content management system and is viewable in a knowledge management system (Keyes, May 22, 2006). The content is structured and organized based on a taxonomy and metadata created by the knowledge managers who understand the business as well as the requirement of the users of the knowledge management system. The metadata defined for a content can be used to decide if the content is visible or not to a certain group of users, and if it is visible, where in the system navigation it is placed (Oberbeck, 2004). Having a robust metadata also helps to improves the performance of search engines (Robertson, 2006). Since most search engines rely on keywords, appearance of search terms in the content and other data about the content being searched; having a robust metadata can significantly enhance the performance of the search engines. As the organization grows and evolves, the metadata and taxonomy used by the systems may require to be updated (Manning, Raghavan, & Schütze, 2008). Knowledge managers are also the experts who review the content management system and the knowledge management system and are responsible for periodically updating the systems with the changes in the organization.

Most content management systems provide a feature for maintaining the metadata for the content. The systems let the users specify any metadata when the content is created. Metadata is stored in the system as a key-value pair where the "key" is the specific attribute of interest in the knowledge management system and the "value" is the specific category that the content gets classified into for the given "key". For example, for content on shipping policy, there may be a separate policy on shipping domestically vs. shipping internationally; and the international policies and charges could again vary based on the destination country. Also, depending on the organization's operations and warehouse locations across the globe, the value of "domestic" could reflect the warehouse location from where the shipping and handling charges can be minimized. So a key could be defined as "destination country" and a value could either be "domestic" or "international" or could be the name of the country to make the system more intelligent. On the consumption end of the knowledge management system, when a user is inquiring about the shipping and handling policies of a package to Argentina, the knowledge management system is already aware of the location of the user. Therefore based on the location of the warehouse that serves Argentina, the right shipping policy can be retrieved for the user the user.

Using the content management system for creating and maintaining the metadata makes the metadata too integrated in the content management system. Unless the content management system has been configured in a way to handle later upgrades to the metadata, any update to the metadata requires the entire content in the system to be revamped with the new metadata (Curtis, Foster, & Stentiford, 1999). There may also be restrictions on new additions and upgrades on metadata. Some knowledge managers have taken an approach to separate the metadata manager away from the content management system (An Informatica White Paper, 2013; Swoyer, 2010), which is effective in managing the metadata independently of the content itself. There are several pros and cons of separating the metadata from the content management system but if implemented and maintained correctly can help to resolve many of the existing metadata management issues.

While planning and designing the metadata is a challenging and never ending task for most knowledge managers, the challenges and issues become more confounded when the metadata being designed is for content that is medium sized. This challenge is discussed in details in the next section.

Impact on Information Quality and Business Intelligence

The previous sections have explained the issue faced by knowledge managers in managing the metadata in the knowledge management systems and the specific issue of medium sized content in managing the metadata effectively. These challenges are real problems faced by many organizations for several reasons. While adding metadata and managing the content is only one aspect of the issue, in order to make the content useful to all the users, there is a need to ensure that the metadata being applied is serving the needs of the business. Adding metadata to content makes the content rich and intelligent. Robust search engines, answering engines and other information retrieval processes depend on the metadata of the content to retrieve the right information at the right time.

Information quality is a relative term that translates differently for different people (English, 1999). Therefore based on how well the piece of information answers the question, the quality of information is rated. In order for the content to be rated high, it is necessary to assign the appropriate metadata to it. Business Intelligence (BI) systems and teams retrieve information based on business rules. In order to answer the questions asked by business owners of the business systems, the content has to be tagged using the same taxonomy that was used to create the rules in the BI system. Based on different business owners and teams, the expectations from a system are very disparate. Governance teams in conjunction with knowledge managers are responsible for maintaining the metadata and content taxonomy. These teams are also responsible for evolving the metadata and taxonomy as the organization grows, changes and evolves.

MAIN FOCUS OF THE CHAPTER

Challenges of Medium Sized Content and Metadata Management

For knowledge managers in an organization, creating a better and more effective knowledge management system is a never ending task (Sharmin, Bailey, Coats, & Hamilton., 2009). They try to address issues with reference and learning content in how they are created, managed and governed. The main objective of the knowledge managers is to ensure easy, fast and accurate delivery of relevant information to the users of their systems. The objectives are mostly driven from user feedback. The number one feedback from users of most knowledge management system is an inefficient search engine (Several Presentations, October 17-19, 2012).Many organizations have reported that in going back to the users, the top feedback received was the need for a "Google" search engine (Several Presentations, October 17-19, 2012). While a search engine like Google may work very efficiently in a chaotic web environment, it is not the best solution for a more structured source of content like an organization's knowledge management system (Kleinberg, 1999; Song, Luo, Wen, Yu, & Hon, 2007). To address the concerns of its user based, many companies have taken some far reaching steps like overhauling the business process to replacing the content management system to recreating the content itself. While some of the overhaul measures may make sense in many organizations, it is usually a very huge initiative with not as high return on investment. A knowledge management system in most organizations is not a revenue generating proposition. In addition, businesses change so rapidly that it is neither cost effective nor practical to overhaul the content management system or knowledge management system every few years. The structure and organization of the content in the knowledge management system is defined by the metadata of the content. Many of the issues regarding improving organization of content, improving access to content and improving accuracy of content accessed can be solved just by improving the metadata that is used to define the content. Adding appropriate, relevant and a robust metadata make the content more intelligent and the knowledge management system more efficient. Therefore, the focus on this chapter is to try and solve for an effective knowledge management system by rethinking the metadata approach that exists for the content.

Though medium-sized content is best suited for organizational learning and reference resources as mentioned in the background section, they have certain limitations when it comes to metadata assignment and management. Owing to the size limitations, many of these content pieces are chunks of a larger piece of information that presents a bigger concept, process or workflow for the organization. They are either pieces of content taken from a larger piece of information that presented the bigger concept or they are created as separate entities of information which when joined together convey a larger message. But the content pieces are dependent on other pieces of contents for completeness. It is a challenge to assign metadata for these content pieces for multiple reasons. When metadata management is manual, it is prone to more error as the content authors may not realize the significance of a piece of content in respect to a larger concept. Maintaining the knowledge management system requires maintaining multiple resources to author multiple documents with different metadata. Even if metadata assignment is done automatically using an automatic business intelligence (BI) tool, metadata extractors are not able to extract meaningful keywords or metadata from these content pieces because picking word repetitions and associations are a challenge when they are rare or sparse in nature(Plaisant, Marchionini, Bruns, Komlodi, & Campbell, 1997). The metadata has many empty dimensions that make knowledge organization and usage a challenge.

In many organizational knowledge management systems, the metadata for a piece of content does not help in connecting multiple pieces of content so that a complete story can be presented to the user. The content and its assigned metadata could lead to inefficiency and inaccuracies when users are trying to retrieve information from the user. Users typically look up for content in response to an issue they have come across in their work or because they were seeking an answer to a query. In referring to the knowledge management system at their moment of information need, they may end up referring to one particular content piece that they think are providing them the answer while they may be missing out other key pieces of content that are critical in providing a complete answer to the query. But since the complete picture can be presented by grouping several pieces of contents together, the user may never even access all the key parts when working under strict time constrains. Similarly, users may also miss out key aspects of a certain piece of content while making business recommendations to clients. Some knowledge managers may work around this issue by repeating certain key points, context and pretext to every piece of content so that users are not mis-informed but this approach also leads to an additional overhead of keeping all the related pieces of content in sync and up-to-date with every change happening in the organization (Gold, Malhotra, & Segars, 2001).

The issue of incomplete metadata also has an impact on the search engines used in the knowledge management systems (Curtis et al., 1999; Swoyer, 2010). Inefficient mechanism of metadata assignment makes the search engine inefficient as well. Since the metadata structure in medium sized content is sparse, the results in a search engine that is processing several empty key-value pairs before it can index the content. Results also fail to show up when the term used to search does not align with the organization's vocabulary. Moreover, taxonomy in the organization is ever changing with every business decision that makes it a large effort in re-indexing the content for the search engine. Metadata can help with taxonomy changes by creating appropriate keys and assigning the right metadata to the keys so that the right content shows up in response to a search query. The next section presents a new approach to creating metadata for knowledge resources that addresses the issues related to medium sized content in particular but could also help in resolving the other challenges resulting from ever changing reference and learning content in an organization.

An Approach to Creating Metadata for Medium Sized Content

The solution being proposed here is a metadata manager that can be created independent of the content management system being used. It can be a tool developed internally or an extension of a standalone database structure. It can be created and maintained independently from the content in a logical manner even though physically it can be in the same content management system. Keeping the metadata manager separate is beneficial because changes to the content management system do not need recreation of the metadata structure and the metadata manager can be improved independent of the content management system. Also, business intelligence tools can be used for the metadata manager for analysis and creation of better automated rules that can help knowledge management lead the business instead of the other way around. However, this discussion is out of scope for the current chapter.

The proposed metadata solution is created as a three part structure for each piece of content.

The three parts are the static part, the dynamic part and the conceptual part. The first part, called the static part is a key-value pair for the attribute and the metadata value. This is similar to the metadata implementations that is prevalent in existing knowledge management systems and has been used by many knowledge managers. The second part is called the dynamic part. It is also a key value pair but the keys in the dynamic part are created dynamically based on specific values of the "value" in the static part of the metadata structure. The keys in the dynamic part can also be based on a specific requirement of the knowledge management system. While the final implementation detail is at the discretion of the knowledge manager, this part of the metadata can either be implemented as a key-value pair or as a list of keywords that are qualified with the attribute names. The third part of the metadata structure is an identifier for other pieces of content that are related to this content item conceptually. The implementation of the conceptual part can be as straight forward as having the identifiers of the related pieces of content or keywords. The conceptual part of the metadata structure can be generated automatically using a rule based engine that can read and process the metadata structure of all content in the content management system. It can also be manually created and updated by the content authors to connect different pieces of content that are related conceptually. From an implementation point of view, the metadata manager results in maintaining a database of metadata that can, in theory, be expanded exponentially.

The benefits from this approach are manifold. Different knowledge management systems and tools that are directed towards different audiences can be developed as a service from the same repository. Based on the static, dynamic part of the metadata and the conceptual linked contents, the different tools can be designed to display the information that the audience needs based on their moment of need. The same piece of content can appear in multiple locations in the navigation by displaying them with other pieces of content based on metadata like audience, location, task (and others) while preserving the core of the content. It would potentially lead to saving content creation time, as authors would need to create and update content in only one place. If a metadata is impacted by a business change, the changed metadata can trigger a notification to notify the knowledge managers of any other pieces of content that may be impacted by the same change. Therefore, it also addresses the issue with different pieces of content going out of sync when only certain pieces of content need to get updated.

To better illustrate the approach for the metadata structure, an example is presented in the next section.

Illustration of the Suggested Approach with an Example

In order to illustrate the three part metadata structure, this section presents a hypothetical example. Consider a piece of content that is a user review of a book on Amazon.com (Nadler, 2013). The review is for a novel *Wise Men* written by Stuart Nadler. The book is Amazon's Best Book of the Month February 2013. The 352 page book is published by Reagan Arthur Books (February 5, 2013). It has an average Customer Review of 4.4 out of 5 stars. There were 16 customer reviews as of Feb 25th 2013. The book also ranks as Amazon Best Sellers Rank: #486 in Books.

Here is a review of the book by Sara Nelson of Amazon.com. *Wise Men begins with an irresistible description of the narrator's father--an arrogant, preening, but still somehow lovable ambulance-chasing lawyer who becomes superrich and famous by prosecuting the airlines--and goes on to create a perfect picture of mid-20th-century America: a country naïve, ambitious, and possessed of a racism and anti-Semitism both genteel and pervasive. With stunning understanding--especially for a young author born well after the time his book describes--Nadler has written a story about fathers and sons, about love and longing and loss; a book that is funny and sad and local and global. Think Harper Lee crossed with Philip Roth: This is a truly Great American Novel.*

This piece of content was selected for a number of reasons. To articulate the metadata process in a conceptual way, it was necessary to pick a piece of content that was publicly available, and did not come from the same domain as the domain of this chapter, i.e., knowledge management. Having a publicly available piece of metadata makes it easy to access for all readers. Also, the language of the content piece is less likely to include terminologies and words that are domain specific. Hence any compounding factor related to the language, ambiguity and terminology are removed. Having a piece of content from a public site like Amazon.com makes it convenient for a metadata discussion without going into absolute details of the correctness of the content or the metadata. Having a content piece from the same domain may end up in a controversy on the choice of metadata versus the methodology and process which is the focus in this chapter. Then, many organizations are currently using user generated data to complement their internal knowledge resources. These user generated content are either being used verbatim to reduce false positive returns by the internal search engines or are used part of a forum or discussion panel for users to be able to follow a thread of similar user feedbacks improving their overall knowledge of a product, service or business process being used by the organization. This defense will justify the use of this piece of content as an example in this chapter.

Defining the metadata for this piece of content is done in the three parts as discussed. The three parts are the static metadata part, dynamic metadata part and conceptual linkage part. For the static part, metadata is chosen from the keywords and key concepts presented in the content. In the example being considered, the content type is a review. The object which can be a product or a service is being reviewed. Therefore, the value for the key "Review Object" is a "book". The reviewer/author of the review could be an organization that provides reviews as a service, a consumer who has used the product or service or a subject matter expert. In this case, the value for "Reviewer Type" is a "Person". Similarly, there may be other key-value pairs associated with the piece of review content. Table 1 below illustrates three other metadata values for rating, review type and review size. Please note that the key value pair is for illustration purposes only. The actual keys and possible values for the keys are decided by the organization based on the user base accessing the content and the context in which the content is being used.

The next part for defining the metadata is the dynamic part. The dynamic part of the metadata is dependent on the specifics of the content. These metadata values also appear as key-value pair, but the keys are not fixed. The keys are a function of the values that appear in the static metadata part, but there may be others that are enforced by the knowledge managers or subject matter experts depending on the ultimate use for this piece of content. For illustrative purposes, referring to the example of the book review, a possible aspect of interest could be the author of the book being reviewed, the type of book and when it was published. These metadata are of interest only because the review object is a book. If there was a need to define a special key-value pair to further clas-

Table 1. Metadata values for static part of example content (book)

Static Metadata for a Book Review	
Key	**Value**
Review Object	Book
Reviewer Type	Person
Rating	5
Review type	Positive
Review size	121

sify the content based on who the reviewer is, how the reviewer is rated or what is the affiliation of the reviewer, the values for these fields could be added to the dynamic part. They would not be justified for all types of reviews and would not be valid if the product being reviewed was a television, or a can of beans. Table 2 below shows some of the dynamic metadata values that hold for this piece of content.

If the review was for a different product, say a Samsung television set, the keys in Table 2 would not add any value. In that case, the static metadata would still have the same keys as book review but the values would be different. As shown in Table 3, the values would refer to the specifics of the television.

The dynamic part of the metadata as shown in Table 2 is no longer applicable to a television review. Therefore, the dynamic metadata table for a television review is created as shown below. The keys in the dynamic metadata are a function of the values in the static metadata part. Table 4 shows the dynamic metadata for a television review.

The third part of the metadata is the conceptual part that connects the current piece of content to other pieces of content. This is done to increase the richness of this piece of information. Since the example content is a review on a book, possible concepts that it can be connected to are similar genres of books, anthropological articles on life in 20th century America, and a couple of other authors that appear in the text of the review that the reviewer thinks were similar to the book's author. Table 5 illustrates a few values for the conceptual metadata part. Again, the values presented are for illustration purposes only and will depend on the possible use cases for the content itself.

Table 2. Metadata values for dynamic part of example content (book)

Dynamic Metadata for a Book Review	
Key	**Value**
Author	Stuart Nadler
Genre	Novel
Publication Date	February 5, 2013
Pages	352
Reviewer Profile	Amazon.com reviewer

Table 3. Metadata values for static part of example content (television)

Static Metadata for a Book Review	
Key	**Value**
Review Object	Television
Reviewer Type	Person
Rating	4
Review type	Positive
Review size	450

Table 4. Metadata values for dynamic part of example content (television)

Dynamic Metadata for a Television Review	
Key	**Value**
Manufacturer	Samsung
Retailer	Best Buy
Model	XYZ 1010
Screen size	42"
Reviewer Profile	Tech Blog Author

Table 5. Metadata values for the conceptual part of example content (book)

Conceptual
Similar Genre of books
Life in 20th century America
Harper Lee
Philip Roth

Metadata is presented as a key-value pair for the static and dynamic part of the metadata definition but not for the conceptual part.

FUTURE RESEARCH DIRECTIONS

The above sections present an approach to define metadata for content that overcomes the challenges presented by medium sized content. Future work in this area could be in evaluation and validation of the different implementation techniques for this approach.

The process of generating metadata has been automated in many organization using text analytics tools. In the approach here a suggestion has been made to create and update the conceptual part of the metadata using an automated system. But other options of automating the metadata generation have not been investigated. As has been mentioned in this chapter, there are scenarios in organizations where the metadata system is so robust that the content authors spend more time to create the metadata as compared to the creating the content itself. While metadata adds intelligence to the content, adding a very large number of metadata increases the content creation time. Automating any part of the process will be a boon to the content authors.

Another future research direction could focus on a process or approach to feed, seed and weed the metadata for a piece of content. This chapter focused on how easy it would be to extend the metadata when created using the approach mentioned here. But making the process easy may result in an unchecked growth of metadata. Also, as the business changes and some of the existing metadata ceases to become irrelevant, the metadata manager may become filled with information that is no longer required. Therefore a future research direction could focus on keeping the metadata clutter free and an effective way to include that in the process of content life cycle.

A last approach may include extending the concepts of the lessons learnt from this approach to system beyond knowledge management systems. It may also include content that are not medium sized in nature. Extending the metadata approach to user generated content could result in integrating Subject Matter Expert content with user generated content that could drive the business intelligence tools to a new level.

CONCLUSION

This chapter provides an approach to define metadata for organizational knowledge resources. Most organizational knowledge management resources are medium sized content. While medium sized content have many benefits for providing information to the users in an organization, there are several challenges that they pose in management of an effective knowledge system. The goal of all knowledge management system is to provide effective knowledge resources to the user at the time of need. However, structuring and organizing the medium sized content is challenging. Knowledge resources are referred to by users to supplement their tacit knowledge in answering a business query or to complete a business transaction. Therefore, when users access the content, they try to scan through the document and look for key pieces of information that helps them to interpret the content in the shortest possible time. Medium sized content is most suitable for the amount of time and attention that the users have to find an answer.

Given the significance of medium sized content, it is necessary for knowledge management systems to be designed such that only the relevant content is presented to the users. To be able to organize and structure the knowledge management systems, metadata plays a very important part. However, the current implementations of metadata are not created to in a way to increase the efficiency of the knowledge management systems, the search engines or any other state-of-the-art business intelligence tools available to the knowledge managers. This chapter presents an approach to create a metadata structure that can be created and maintained independently of the knowledge management system and the content management system. The approach proposes a three part metadata structure that can be used to identify each content piece. The first part is a static part that can be used to identify the overall characteristics of the content, its type, accessibility, permission and restrictions. The second part is a dynamic part that defines the content in light of its primary characteristics, based on the type of the content, and any special parameters that it may need to address. The third part that is called the conceptual part is used to connect it to other pieces of information that adds value and a context to the content. It also identifies other pieces of content that would add value to this content and help to improve the overall explicit knowledge of the user.

The approach does not dictate any implementation strategy for the metadata structure which can be defined and maintained by the knowledge managers as suited for their organizational learning needs.

REFERENCES

Alavi, M., Kayworth, & Leidner, D. E. (2005). An empirical examination of the influence of organizational culture on knowledge management practices. *Journal of Management Information Systems*, *22*(3), 191–224. doi:10.2753/MIS0742-1222220307

Alavi, M., & Leidner, D. E. (2001). Review: Knowledge management and knowledge management systems: Conceptual foundations and research issues. *Management Information Systems Quarterly*, *25*(1), 107–136. doi:10.2307/3250961

Becerra-Fernandez, I., Gonzalez, A., & Sabherwal, R. (2004). *Knowledge management: Challenges, solutions and technologies*. Upper Saddle River, NJ: Pearson Prentice Hall.

Burbidge, R. (2003). *3GPP: Specification detail 3GPP TS 03.40, Technical realization of the short message service*. SMS.

Curtis, K., Foster, P. W., & Stentiford, F. (1999). *Metadata - The key to content management services*. Washington, DC: IEEE.

Dalkir, K. (2005). *Knowledge management in theory and practice*. New York: Routledge.

Dephi Group. (2004). *Information intelligence: Content classification and the enterprise taxonomy practice*. Author.

Dianne, J. H., Croasdell, D. (2005). Inquiring organizations: An organizational form perspective. In Inquiring Organizations: Moving from Knowledge Management to Wisdom (pp. 1-21). Academic Press.

Duval, E. (2004). Making metadata go away: Hiding everything but the benefits. In Learning Objects Metadata (LOM). IEEE Learning Technology Standards Committee(LTSC).

Eaton, M. L. (2011, February 24). Medium length content, a perfect fit for e-readers. *March Communications.*

English, L. P. (1999). *Improving data warehouse and business information quality, methods for reducing costs and increasing profits*. New York: Wiley Computer Publishing.

Gold, A. H., Malhotra, A., & Segars, A. H. (2001). Knowledge management: An organizational capabilities perspective. *Journal of Management Information Systems*, *18*(1), 185.

Grant, R. M. (1996). Prospering in dynamically-competetive environments: Organizationa capability as knowledge integration. *Organization Science, 7*(4), 375–387. doi:10.1287/orsc.7.4.375

Informatica. (2013). Manage your metadata to better manage your business (White Paper). Author.

Jacob, E. K. (2003). Ontologies and the semantic web. *Bulletin of the American Society for Information Science and Technology.*

Johnson, S. (2009, June 5). How Twitter will change the way we live. *Time Magazine.*

Karner, H., & Droschl, G. (2002). Usage-centered interface design for knowledge management software. *Journal of Universal Computer Science, 8*(6).

Keyes, J. (2006). *Knowledge management, business intelligence, and content management: The IT practitioner's guide*. Boston: Auerbach Publications. doi:10.1201/9781420013863

Kleinberg, J. M. (1999). Authoritative sources in a hyperlinked environment. *Journal of the ACM, 46*(5), 604–632. doi:10.1145/324133.324140

Manning, C. D., Raghavan, P., & Schütze, H. (2008). *Introduction to information retrieval*. Cambridge, UK: Cambridge University Press. doi:10.1017/CBO9780511809071

McInerney, C. R., & Day, R. E. (2007). *Rethinking knowledge management: From knowledge artifacts to knowledge processes*. Berlin: Springer. doi:10.1007/3-540-71011-6

Nadler, S. (2013). *Wise men*. Reagan Arthur Books.

Oberbeck, H. (2004). *Learning with hypermedia: The impact of content design and learner characteristics on navigation and the knowledge acquisition process*. Braunschweig: Technischen Universität Carolo-Wilhelmina zu.

Pipek, V., Wulf, V., & Johri, A. (2011). Bridging artifacts and actors: Expertise sharing in organizational ecosystems. *Computer Supported Cooperative Work.*

Plaisant, C., Marchionini, G., Bruns, T., Komlodi, A., & Campbell, L. (1997). *Bringing treasures to the surface: Iterative design for the library of congress national digital library program.* Paper presented at the CHI 97 Electronic Publications: Design Briefings. New York, NY.

Robertson, J. (2006). *Good search is knowledge management.* Retrieved from www.steptwo.com.au

Sharmin, M., Bailey, B. P., Coats, C., & Hamilton, K. (2009). *Understanding knowledge management practives for early design activity and its implication for reuse.* Paper presented at the CHI 2009. Boston, MA.

Song, R., Luo, Z., Wen, J.-R., Yu, Y., & Hon, H.-W. (2007). *Identifying ambiguous queries in web search.* Paper presented at the 16th International Conference on World Wide Web. New York, NY.

Swoyer, S. (2010). *Metadata management: An imperative for your enterprise.* TDWI Onsite Education.

Vandenbosch, B., & Huff, S. (1997, March). Searching and scanning: How executives obtain information from executive information systems. *Management Information Systems Quarterly*, 81–105. doi:10.2307/249743

Wikipedia: The Free Encyclopedia. (2013, June 5). Retrieved August 10, 2004, from http://www.wikipedia.org

Zikopoulos, P., Deutsch, T., Deroos, D., Corrigan, D., Parasuraman, K., & Giles, J. (2013). *Harness the power of big data*. New York: The McGrawHill Companies.

ADDITIONAL READING

Becerra-Fernandez, I., Gonzalez, A., & Sabherwal, R. (2004). *Knowledge Management: Challenges, Solutions and Technologies*. New Jersey: Pearson Prentice Hall.

Blankson, S. (June 30, 2008). *Search Engine Optimization (SEO) How to Optimize Your Website for Internet Search Engines (Google, Yahoo!, MSN Live, AOL, Ask, AltaVista, FAST, GigaBlast, Snap, LookSmart and more)*, Blankson Enterprises Limited.

Bruijn, F. d., & Dekkers, H. L. (2010). Ambiguity in Natural Language Software Requirements: A Case Study. Requirements Engineering: Foundation for Software Quality Lecture Notes in Computer Science, 6182, 233-247.

Charan, R. (Feb 2001). *What the CEO wants you to Know*: Crown Business.

Collins, H. (2012). Tacit and Explicit Knowledge (Reprint Ed. (December 11, 2012) ed.), University Of Chicago Press. Dublin Core® Metadata Initiative.DCMI Specifications, from dublincore.org/specifications/

Fleischner, M. M. H. (February 13, 2011). SEO Made Simple: Strategies For Dominating The World's Largest Search EngineCreateSpace (Second Ed. ed.), Independent Publishing Platform, 2 Exp Upd Ed.

García, Á., & Medinilla, N. (2007, November 5-9, 2007). *The Ambiguity Criterion in Software Design*. Paper presented at the Conference'07, Atlanta, Georgia, US.

Hedden, H. (May 3, 2010). *The Accidental Taxonomist*: Information Today, Inc. Information Today.*Publication in the information industry*, from http://www.infotoday.com/IT/default.asp

International Standards Organization (ISO). (2011a). *Information and documentation -- Thesauri and interoperability with other vocabularies -- Part 1: Thesauri for information retrieval, ISO 25964-1*.

International Standards Organization (ISO). (2011b). ISO 25964-2: Information and documentation -- Thesauri and interoperability with other vocabularies -- Part 2: Interoperability with other vocabularies.

KMWorld. *KM World Magazine*. Knowledge Management Practitioners.*Resources and publications*, from http://www.kmci.org/

Lamb, P. (2007). *Organising Knowledge: Taxonomies, Knowledge and Organisational Effectiveness (Chandos Knowledge Management)*. Neal-Schuman Publishers.

Manning, C. D., Raghavan, P., & Schütze, H. (2008). *Introduction to Information Retrieval*: Cambridge University Press. NISO.*Understanding Metadata*, from www.niso.org/standards/resources/UnderstandingMetadata.pdf

Pirolli, P., & Card, S. K. (1995). *Information foraging in information access environments*. Paper presented at the Proceedings of the conference on Human Factors in Computing - CHI'95, Denver, CO.

Rowley, J., & Hartley, R. (2008). *Organizing Knowledge: An Introduction to Managing Access to Information* (4th ed.). Ashgate.

Snowden, D. J. (1996). Story telling: an old skill in a new context. *Business Information Review*, *16*(4), 30–37.

Strigl, D., & Swiatek, F. (March 9, 2011). Managers, Can You Hear Me Now?: Hard-Hitting Lessons on How to Get Real Results (1 Ed. ed.), McGraw-Hill.

Thietart, R.-A., & Wauchope, S. (2001). *Linking concepts and Data from Doing Management Research*: Sage Research methods.

Tozer, G. V. (1999). *Metadata management for information control and business success*. Artech House.

Vandenbosch, B., & Huff, S. (1997). Searching and Scanning: How Executives Obtain Information from Executive Information Systems. *Management Information Systems Quarterly*, (March): 81–105. doi:10.2307/249743

Weiser, M. (1991, September). The Computer for the Twenty-First Century. *Scientific American*, 94–100. doi:10.1038/scientificamerican0991-94 PMID:1675486

White, M. (2012). Enterprise Search: O'Reilly Media, Reissue Ed.

Woods, W. (1995). *Finding Information on the Web: A Knowledge Representation Approach.* Paper presented at the Fourth International World Wide Web Conference, Boston, MA.

KEY TERMS AND DEFINITIONS

Content Author: The individuals or teams in an organization that is responsible for creating and managing the content in the content management system. These individuals are responsible for making sure that the content is follows the organizational guidelines, are complete and accurate and have been qualified by the organization's legal department for publishing in the content management system.

Key-Value Pair: Metadata for a piece of content is a value assigned for a particular characteristic in the content. The characteristic of the content is predefined as a key and the value for that particular characteristic for that piece of content is stored as a value of the key. For example, "content state" could be a key and "active", "achieved" could be a value.

Knowledge Managers: Knowledge managers are individuals or teams in an organization whose primary job responsibility is to provide the best in class knowledge management system to its user base.

Large-Sized Content: For this purpose of this book chapter, large sized content is loosely defined as content that runs into multiple pages like journal papers, research articles and industry white papers.

Medium Sized Content: The term medium-sized includes any articles or written material that are in the range of a few words to a few hundred words, and can typically be fit into a single page view.

Metadata: Metadata can be defined as the description of a piece of content. It can provide information about the content as to when it was created, if it is still valid, who is the intended audience and such details.

Organizational Knowledge Management: Organizational Knowledge Management refers to the organizational process through which organizations and corporate offices create, update and maintain their business processes, procedures, workflows and other documents that guide their employees through their job responsibilities.

Organizational Taxonomy: Taxonomy is an ordered classification of all the terms, systems and processes used within an organization. It helps to resolve any ambiguity that may arise in using plain English during business transactions.

Reference Content: Reference content is the information that an organization maintains regarding itself, its business processes, policies and procedures. The reference content is available the employees of the organization for the purpose of customer support and conducting other business transactions.

Small Sized Content: For the purpose of this chapter, small-sized content are content that ranges from one to about 20 words like text messages (maximum character length of 150 characters), twitter posts (maximum character length of 140 characters) etc.

Chapter 16
A Case Study to Improve Data Vendor Selection

Rick McGraw
Black Oak Partners, LLC, USA

ABSTRACT

All financial services companies use external sources of consumer income data to assess credit risk, develop risk mitigation strategies, and create pre-approved marketing offers. International credit card issuers spend more than a billion dollars in marketing and invest hundreds of millions in product development based on data from third party vendors. The accuracy of income data is the foundation for their business decisions. The purpose of this engagement was to evaluate the accuracy of third party data providers by measuring the data across six dimensions – Accuracy, Relevancy, Completeness, Coverage, Effectiveness, and Cost. The data provided by the three vendors for this project was incorrect by more than 20% on 75% of the records. The goal of the project was to demonstrate the ability to improve the accuracy of multi-source income data used in credit card marketing applications.

THE CHALLENGE

- Data has become a commodity – broad availability, similar characteristics;
- Generally, commodities carry metrics-based standard grades to gauge suitability, but today, data does not;
- Without an established baseline and score, it is impossible to calculate the quality, and therefore, the unique value and contribution of a specific data source.

The inability to resolve data conflict leads to less effective models and sub-optimal decisions.

BACKGROUND

Black Oak analyzed three data vendors under three different operating scenarios and measured several performance metrics for each. The analysis quantified the value each data source provided to any user-defined, decision-making process.

DOI: 10.4018/978-1-4666-4892-0.ch016

We will refer to the data sources used in the analysis as 'Source A,' 'Source B' and 'Source C'. Each vendor was presented with the same set of records for income append. The results were compared to a known truth file created by Black Oak and its' client. The vendor results were compared to the truth file to determine accuracy. A tolerance range was allowed at 10% and 20% to the vendors (see Relevancy). Vendor records that were within the tolerance interval of the true result were considered accurate.

The operating scenarios were Mortgage Applications, Credit Card Applications and Employee Records. The Employee Records were used as a control on the measurements since the income for the client's employees was known. This data was used to control for potential variances present in the Mortgage and Credit Card Applications.

PERFORMANCE MEASURES

Performance measures were computed for each vendor under each operating scenario. The performance measures computed were the six dimensions of Accuracy, Relevancy, Completeness, Coverage, Effectiveness and Cost. The sections below detail the performance measures and data analyzed.

Completeness

Completeness measures the number of records appended by a vendor that have income information For this particular test, only one element was provided by the vendor–income, so completeness percentages were very high. However, in most cases, vendors are asked to provide multiple elements and they can be measured per element or at a higher composite level.

Coverage

Coverage measures the number of records with income information appended by a vendor to the total number of records requested. This is a direct measure of the utility of the vendor data. A vendor with low coverage may be very good data, but with very few records.

Accuracy

Accuracy measures how close the reported income is relative to the true value.

Two of the data vendors provided an income range rather than a specific value for income. Records are considered accurate if the true value is within the income band provided by the vendor.

One vendor did not provide an income band, but instead provided a specific value. For this vendor, each income was matched to an equivalent band from the other vendors and the result is treated as if the vendor had reported the band.

Relevancy

Accuracy measured the vendor performance against the bands set up by the vendor. Because the vendor sets up the bands, there is a subjective component to accuracy. For example, if one vendor reports many small bands while a second vendor reports fewer larger bands, the second vendor may be measured as more accurate. This is a misleading result because the first vendor reports more precise results and this precision is typically desired.

Relevancy removes the vendor component and measures performance against a tolerance range for truth. For vendors reporting income bands, the result is considered relevant if the midpoint of the band is within the tolerance level of the true value.

Relevancy is computed for tolerance at 10% and 20%. For example, a vendor reporting an income that is 15% higher than the true value is considered accurate at 20% tolerance, but inaccurate at 10% tolerance.

Effectiveness

Effectiveness is a variant of both Relevancy and Accuracy. Relevancy and Accuracy measure the performance of the vendor in relation to the total number of records appended by the vendor. Instead of measuring relative to the number of records appended, Effectiveness measures relative to the total number of records requested.

Essentially, Effectiveness is Accuracy (or Relevancy) multiplied by the coverage.

Cost

Cost is measured as the cost of using a vendor in a particular scenario. Cost information is expressed in relevant terms (cost index), thus the results are presented for comparisons only and do not represent actual results. The cost index used:

- Source "A": 1.50
- Source "B": 1.00
- Source "C": 1.25

ORIGINAL DATA STRUCTURE

The data analyzed covered income-specific information from multiple vendors. The reporting areas were mortgage, credit card and employee information.

Reporting Files

The vendor data was comprised of three separate files containing mortgage, credit card and employee information. Each file was comprised of a series of rows, where each row is an entity for the data (information related to an individual). Each row has a unique ID identifying the row. However, it is important to note that the individual IDs reported in each of these files *do not* correlate to the same IDs across the three files. Even though two different files may contain the same ID, this ID does not represent the same entity (individual). Thus, each file had to be examined by itself without using data from related files.

Mortgage Reporting

The mortgage-reporting file consisted of a true income amount, which was compared with the reported amounts from each of the vendors that supplied income data for mortgage loans. The loans that were deemed accurate in this file were all loans categorized as CONF, FHA or VA, since the income reported on these was verified for accuracy. The mortgage-reporting file consisted of only CONF, FHA and VA loans with 26,477 records.

Credit Card Reporting

The credit card reporting file consisted of an income amount, which was compared with the reported amounts from each of the vendors that supplied income data for credit card applicants. As this file contained applicants self-reporting their income, this data was expected to be less accurate. The credit card reporting file consisted of 146,157 records.

Employee Reporting

The employee-reporting file consisted of a true income amount, which was compared with the reported amounts from each of the vendors that supplied income data for the employees' reported income. This file was deemed accurate in its reporting of income due to the client's knowledge of employee salaries. The employee-reporting file consisted of 44,711 records.

VENDORS

Each of these files contained individual income data provided by the vendors as described below.

'Source A'

The information provided by 'Source A' was presented in an exact dollar amount. This posed the challenge of comparing against a truth source while allowing for an acceptable range within the specified amount in order to be considered allowably accurate.

'Source B'

The information provided by 'Source B' was presented in dollar ranges. These bands allow for an accurate range specification of an individual's income when compared to a truth source but does not present as much precision of the actual income as an exact dollar amount. The range specification does allow for easier comparison to a truth source dollar amount in allowing an acceptable range to be considered allowably accurate. 'Source B' provided ranges spanning between $0 - $250,000+ with an average span of $5,000 for each range.

'Source C'

The information provided by 'Source C' was presented in dollar ranges similar to 'Source B'. 'Source C' provided ranges spanning between $0 - $2 million+; however, the span of each range is wider than that of 'Source B,' with an average $10,000 for each range.

SINGLE VENDOR ANALYSIS

In this section, each vendor was analyzed separately for each operational scenario. The performance measures for each vendor were computed and presented as a series of tables. A summary of these results is provided in Tables 1-3.

Analysis: Data Accuracy

A data accuracy analysis was conducted on each of the different vendors to determine the accuracy of each record reported with respect to income when compared to the truth source. The following subsection details the findings by Black Oak's analysis for each vendor across the three different reporting areas.

Table 1. Summary results for metrics applied to reference mortgage records

	Completeness	Coverage	Accuracy	Relevancy 10%	Relevancy 20%	Effectiveness 10%	Effectiveness 20%	Cost
'Source A'	100.00	100.00	10.27	16.84	28.16	16.84	28.16	1.50
'Source B'	100.00	79.09	14.14	20.19	30.92	15.97	24.45	1.00
'Source C'	100.00	96.32	9.16	14.87	24.76	14.33	23.85	1.25

Table 2. Summary results for metrics applied to reference credit card records

	Completeness	Coverage	Accuracy	Relevancy 10%	Relevancy 20%	Effectiveness 10%	Effectiveness 20%	Cost
'Source A'	100.00	100.00	9.33	15.62	25.46	15.62	25.46	1.50
'Source B'	87.34	99.97	11.70	16.75	24.10	16.75	24.09	1.00
'Source C'	100.00	94.55	8.43	14.10	22.30	13.33	21.08	1.25

Table 3. Summary results for metrics applied to reference employee records

	Completeness	Coverage	Accuracy	Relevancy 10%	Relevancy 20%	Effectiveness 10%	Effectiveness 20%	Cost
'Source A'	100.00	100.00	7.22	9.02	12.74	9.02	12.74	1.50
'Source B'	73.81	96.71	5.12	7.45	11.61	7.21	11.23	1.00
'Source C'	100.00	89.75	10.65	13.29	18.52	11.93	16.62	1.25

Data Accuracy Findings

Table 4 delineates data accuracy on household income for the 'Source A', 'Source B' and 'Source C' vendors.

The findings for 'Source A' were expected to be extremely low considering that 'Source A' is the only vendor of the three that reported an exact dollar amount, meaning that if the truth source did not have the exact same amount (down to a single penny) the record would be considered inaccurate for 'Source A,' whereas 'Source B' and 'Source C' reported ranges for the household incomes. To normalize 'Source A''s data with 'Source B' and 'Source C,' 'Source A' was processed to map the incomes reported to the ranges specified for 'Source C.'

'Source B' reported household income based on dollar ranges that averaged a $5,000 spread for each range, resulting in a narrow allowance in comparison to the truth source.

'Source C' reported household income based on dollar ranges that averaged a $10,000 spread for each range, giving a little wider allowance in comparison to the truth source, as well as allowing for higher ranges of income ($2 million).

Table 4. Summary comparison between each source and the reference files

Vendor	Description	Mortgage Reporting	Credit Card Reporting	Employee Reporting
'Source A'	Records Reported	26,477	146,157	44,711
	Data Accuracy	10.27%	9.33%	7.22%
'Source B'	Records Reported	20,940	146,118	43,239
	Data Accuracy	14.14%	11.7%	5.12%
'Source C'	Records Reported	25,502	138,189	40,127
	Data Accuracy	9.16%	8.43%	10.65%

Analysis: Relevancy

A relevancy analysis was conducted on each of the different vendors to determine if, given a specified percentage range of allowance, how many more records from each vendor could be considered "accurate" within that specified range. This analysis was conducted *only* on the records reported back as inaccurate from the previous data accuracy analysis. Each vendor was analyzed on how many more records would be considered "accurate" if a variance of 10% was concluded to be relevant, as well as if a variance of 20% was concluded to be relevant. The following subsection details Black Oak's findings for each vendor across the three different reporting areas.

Relevancy Findings

Table 5 delineates relevancy on household income for the 'Source A,' 'Source B' and 'Source C' vendors. The percentage results are the ratio of the number of records that were considered within the specified variance over the number of total inaccurate records reported from the data accuracy analysis.

Analysis: Over and Under Reporting

An additional analysis was conducted in light of the relevancy findings. The over and under-reporting analysis was conducted against all of the records

Table 5. Summary comparison between each source and the reference files

Vendor	Description	Mortgage Reporting	Credit Card Reporting	Employee Reporting
'Source A'	Total Records Reported	26,477	146,157	44,711
	Inaccurate Records	23,758	132,517	41,482
	10% Variance from Truth	16.84%	15.62%	9.02%
	20% Variance from Truth	28.16%	25.46%	12.74%
'Source B'	Total Records Reported	20,940	146,118	43,239
	Inaccurate Records	17,979	129,023	41,024
	10% Variance from Truth	20.19%	16.75%	7.45%
	20% Variance from Truth	30.92%	24.10%	11.61%
'Source C'	Total Records Reported	25,502	138,189	40,127
	Inaccurate Records	23,167	126,541	35,853
	10% Variance from Truth	14.87%	14.10%	13.29%
	20% Variance from Truth	24.76%	22.30%	18.52%

that were considered inaccurate from each vendor in the data accuracy analysis.

The over and under-analysis on this data was conducted the same as the relevancy analysis. For all records that were deemed "accurate" when given a 10% and 20% variance from the truth source, the over and under-reporting analysis determined the percentage of those records that were over-reported by the vendor (meaning the vendor reported higher than the truth source) and those records that were under-reported by the vendor (meaning the vendor reported lower than the truth source).

Not only was this analysis conducted against the records that fell within the 10% and 20% variances, but was also conducted on the records that did not fall within the 10% and 20% variances from the truth source. The following subsections detail the findings for each vendor across the three different reporting areas.

'Source A'

Table 6 delineates over and under-reporting on household income for the 'Source A' vendor. These percentages are the inaccurate records determined in the data accuracy and relevancy analyses.

'Source B'

Table 7 details the over and under reporting on household income for the 'Source B' vendor. These percentages are with respect to the inaccurate records determined in the data accuracy and relevancy analyses.

Table 6. Summary comparison of under/over reporting bias for Source A

Vendor	Description	Mortgage Reporting	Credit Card Reporting	Employee Reporting
'Source A'	Total Records Reported	26,477	146,157	44,711
	Inaccurate Records Total	23,758	132,517	41,482
	Inaccurate Records Over-Reported	55.37%	60.91%	88.17%
	Inaccurate Records Under-Reported	44.63%	39.09%	11.83%
	Records within 10% Variance from Truth	1,740	9,184	804
	10% Variance Records Over-Reported	46.09%	19.00%	55.85%
	10% Variance Records Under-Reported	53.91%	81.00%	44.15%
	Records within 20% Variance from Truth	4,737	23,576	2,466
	20% Variance Records Over-Reported	47.35%	34.14%	57.91%
	20% Variance Records Under-Reported	52.65%	65.86%	42.09%

Table 7. Summary comparison of under/over reporting bias for Source B

Vendor	Description	Mortgage Reporting	Credit Card Reporting	Employee Reporting
'Source B'	Total Records Reported	20,940	146,118	43,239
	Inaccurate Records Total	17,979	110,522	29,701
	Inaccurate Records Over-Reported	45.05%	47.61%	83.33%
	Inaccurate Records Under-Reported	54.95%	52.39%	16.67%
	Records within 10% Variance from Truth	1,267	7,381	1,008
	10% Variance Records Over-Reported	41.67%	13.85%	52.88%
	10% Variance Records Under-Reported	58.33%	86.15%	47.12%
	Records within 20% Variance from Truth	3,513	18,120	2,805
	20% Variance Records Over-Reported	40.34%	28.84%	53.51%
	20% Variance Records Under-Reported	59.66%	71.16%	46.49%

Table 8. Summary comparison of under/over reporting bias for Source C

Vendor	Description	Mortgage Reporting	Credit Card Reporting	Employee Reporting
'Source C'	Total Records Reported	25,502	138,189	40,127
	Inaccurate Records Total	23,167	126,541	35,853
	Inaccurate Records Over-Reported	54.08%	50.31%	86.54%
	Inaccurate Records Under-Reported	45.92%	49.69%	13.46%
	Records within 10% Variance from Truth	1,458	7,838	1,058
	10% Variance Records Over-Reported	48.08%	16.10%	49.43%
	10% Variance Records Under-Reported	51.92%	83.90%	50.57%
	Records within 20% Variance from Truth	3,979	19,169	3,159
	20% Variance Records Over-Reported	47.00%	30.65%	54.13%
	20% Variance Records Under-Reported	53.00%	69.35%	45.87%

'Source C'

Table 8 details the findings on over and under-reporting on household income for the 'Source C' vendor. These percentages are with respect to the inaccurate records determined in the data accuracy and relevancy analyses.

Analysis: Data Completeness

A data completeness analysis was conducted on each of the different vendors to determine if the data reported by the vendors was complete. A record reported by a vendor is considered complete if *all* the fields are populated with data for that record. The following subsection details the findings by Black Oak's analysis for each vendor across the three different reporting areas.

Data Completeness Findings

Table 9 delineates data completeness for the 'Source A,' 'Source B' and 'Source C' vendors. As specified at the beginning of this section, a record is only considered complete if *all* fields are populated with data.

'Source A' maintains 100% data completeness due to only reporting a single field to the total dataset.

'Source B' contributes five fields to the total dataset and several of the fields are similar in

Table 9. Summary results for record completeness

Vendor	Description	Mortgage Reporting	Credit Card Reporting	Employee Reporting
'Source A'	Records Reported	26,477	146,157	44,711
	Data Completeness	100%	100%	100%
'Source B'	Records Reported	20,940	146,118	43,239
	Data Completeness	0%	87.34%	73.81%
'Source C'	Records Reported	25,502	138,189	40,127
	Data Completeness	100%	100%	100%

nature thus, they may not require that *all* fields be populated.

'Source C' contributes two fields to the total dataset, giving a smaller scope of potential fields to be incomplete, hence allowing 'Source C' to maintain 100% data completeness.

Analysis: Data Coverage

A data Coverage analysis was conducted on each of the different vendors to determine how much of the total records for each reporting area is covered by that vendor. The following subsection details the findings for each vendor across the three different reporting areas.

Data Coverage Findings

Table 10 shows findings concerning data coverage for the 'Source A,' 'Source B' and 'Source C' vendors.

Table 10. Summary results for source coverage

Vendor	Description	Mortgage Reporting	Credit Card Reporting	Employee Reporting
Total Records		26,477	146,157	44,711
'Source A'	Data Coverage	100%	100%	100%
'Source B'	Data Coverage	79.09%	87.32%	71.38%
'Source C'	Data Coverage	96.32%	94.55%	89.75%

MULTI-VENDOR ANALYSIS

We presented each data source with a number of records for appending. We asked the vendor to append income information for each record requested. Coverage measures the number of records appended by a vendor relative to the number of records requested. Coverage is a global metric that scales with the number of records requested. If a data source has 80% coverage with one set of requests, we expect to receive similar results when another data request is made with different records.

Accuracy is a logical metric. Accuracy measures the number of correct records within a data source relative to the number of records in that data source. This value is independent on the records requested. The accuracy value is computed using only information from the vendor itself. This does not depend in any way on the records we request.

Effectiveness is the result of multiplying the coverage with the accuracy. The result is a measure of accuracy relative to the records requested. This accuracy measurement is global in nature. The effectiveness is measured against the records requested and we can expect that this value will scale as the number of requested records scales (see Table 11).

These metrics were computed for the Mortgage, Cards and Employee data at both 10% and 20% for each. The results are shown in Table 12 for each possible combination of the three data sources. There are 15 different possible combinations of data sources when we account for the permutations of ordering the sources.

Combining data sources together can decrease accuracy. For example, 'Source B' has an accuracy of 20.2% for the Mortgage 10% category. However, when we combine 'Source B' with 'Source C,' the accuracy of the combination *decreases* to 18.8%. Furthermore, if we add 'Source A' to this, the accuracy of this combination of all three decreases again to 18.7%.

Table 11. Accuracy for each data source combination for Mortgage, Cards and Employee data

	Mortgage 10%	Mortgage 20%	Cards 10%	Cards 20%	Employee 10%	Employee 20%
	Accuracy	Accuracy	Accuracy	Accuracy	Accuracy	Accuracy
'Source A' (3)	0.168	0.282	0.156	0.255	0.090	0.127
'Source B' (I)	0.202	0.309	0.168	0.241	0.075	0.116
'Source C' (G)	0.149	0.248	0.141	0.223	0.133	0.185
3+I	0.168	0.282	0.156	0.255	0.090	0.127
3+G	0.168	0.282	0.156	0.255	0.090	0.127
I+3	0.196	0.303	0.167	0.241	0.072	0.114
I+G	0.188	0.291	0.168	0.241	0.075	0.116
G+3	0.148	0.247	0.141	0.222	0.127	0.178
G+I	0.149	0.248	0.138	0.218	0.126	0.176
3+I+G	0.168	0.282	0.156	0.255	0.028	0.039
3+G+I	0.168	0.282	0.156	0.255	0.028	0.039
I+3+G	0.196	0.303	0.167	0.241	0.022	0.035
I+G+3	0.187	0.290	0.167	0.241	0.022	0.035
G+3+I	0.148	0.247	0.141	0.222	0.039	0.055
G+I+3	0.149	0.248	0.138	0.218	0.037	0.053

Table 12. Coverage for the fifteen possible data combinations

	Mortgage	Cards	Employee
	Coverage	Coverage	Coverage
'Source A' (3)	1.000	1.000	1.000
'Source B' (I)	0.791	1.000	0.967
'Source C' (G)	0.963	0.945	0.897
3+I	1.000	1.000	1.000
3+G	1.000	1.000	1.000
I+3	1.000	1.000	1.000
I+G	0.984	1.000	0.967
G+3	1.000	1.000	1.000
G+I	0.984	1.000	0.967
3+I+G	1.000	1.000	1.000
3+G+I	1.000	1.000	1.000
I+3+G	1.000	1.000	1.000
I+G+3	1.000	1.000	1.000
G+3+I	1.000	1.000	1.000
G+I+3	1.000	1.000	1.000

The coverage for these data sources is provided in Table 12. 'Source A' has 100% coverage by itself. Any combination containing 'Source A' also has 100% coverage.

Comparing Table 11 and Table 12, there is a tradeoff between accuracy and coverage. 'Source B' generally has the highest accuracy, but it has the lowest coverage for Mortgage. The information from this data source is better, but it does not provide information for all of the cases of interest. Alternatively, 'Source A' has a lower accuracy, but coverage of 100%. The information is less accurate, but 'Source A' provides information in every case.

To balance this tradeoff, we examine the Effectiveness dimension, the values of which are shown in Table 13. The effectiveness only increases as data sources are added together in combination. This demonstrates the useful accuracy results

Table 13. Effectiveness for each of the fifteen possible data source combinations

	Mortgage 10%	Mortgage 20%	Cards 10%	Cards 20%	Employee 10%	Employee 20%
	Effectiveness	Effectiveness	Effectiveness	Effectiveness	Effectiveness	Effectiveness
'Source A' (3)	0.168	0.282	0.156	0.255	0.090	0.127
'Source B' (I)	0.160	0.245	0.167	0.241	0.072	0.112
'Source C' (G)	0.143	0.238	0.133	0.211	0.119	0.166
3+I	0.168	0.282	0.156	0.255	0.090	0.127
3+G	0.168	0.282	0.156	0.255	0.090	0.127
I+3	0.196	0.303	0.167	0.241	0.072	0.114
I+G	0.185	0.286	0.167	0.241	0.072	0.112
G+3	0.148	0.247	0.141	0.222	0.127	0.178
G+I	0.147	0.244	0.138	0.218	0.122	0.170
3+I+G	0.168	0.282	0.156	0.255	0.090	0.127
3+G+I	0.168	0.282	0.156	0.255	0.090	0.127
I+3+G	0.196	0.303	0.167	0.241	0.072	0.114
I+G+3	0.187	0.290	0.167	0.241	0.072	0.114
G+3+I	0.148	0.247	0.141	0.222	0.127	0.178
G+I+3	0.149	0.248	0.138	0.218	0.122	0.172

against the requested rows and is expected to remain constant if more rows (or different rows) are requested.

Finally, the cost of the data source combinations is shown in Table 14. The cost is computed per hit on a relative basis using per hit cost as: 'Source A' – 1.50, 'Source B' – 1.00, 'Source C' – 1.25. The cost is computed by multiplying the cost per hit of the data 'Source B' against the total number of unique hits from that data source, adding these together for each data source in the combination and then dividing the result by the total number of unique hits in the combined data source.

The Cost Effectiveness metrics may be plotted together to find the operating space for each category. Based on this, the Pareto frontier (Given a set of choices and a way of valuing them, the Pareto frontier is the set of choices that are most efficient.) may be identified which lists the rational choices for data set combinations. One such plot and frontier may be created for each category.

Table 14. Cost per unique hit for each of the fifteen possible data source combinations

	Cost per Unique Hit
'Source A' (3)	1.500
'Source B' (I)	1.000
'Source C' (G)	1.250
3+I	2.291
3+G	2.704
I+3	2.291
I+G	2.027
G+3	2.704
G+I	2.027
3+I+G	3.495
3+G+I	3.495
I+3+G	3.495
I+G+3	3.495
G+3+I	3.495
G+I+3	3.495

Mortgage 10%

Figure 1 shows the fifteen data source combinations for the Mortgage 10% data. The green points indicate the Pareto frontier. The ideal data source combination is one of these points. The frontier points and their tradeoffs are shown in Table 15.

Moving between the points on the frontier increases the cost but also increases the effectiveness. No three-source combination is on the frontier. Always a two-source combination performs as well or better than every possible three-source combination.

Mortgage 20%

Figure 2 shows the fifteen data source combinations for the Mortgage 20% data. The green points indicate the Pareto frontier. The ideal data source combination is one of these points. The frontier points and their tradeoffs are shown in Table 16.

Moving between the points on the frontier increases the cost but also increases the effectiveness. No three-source combination is on the frontier. Always a two- source combination per-

Table 15. Pareto frontier for the Mortgage 10% data. The cost and effectiveness increase are shows relative to the point above in the table.

Data Source Combination	Cost per Hit	Effectiveness	Cost Increase (%)	Effectiveness Increase (%)
'Source B' (1)	1.00	.160	-	-
'Source A' (3)	1.50	.168	50	5.4
'Source B'+'Source C'	2.03	.185	35	9.8
'Source B'+'Source A'	2.29	.196	13	5.8

Table 16. Pareto frontier for the Mortgage 20% data. The cost and effectiveness increase are shows relative to the point above in the table.

Data Source Combination	Cost per Hit	Effectiveness	Cost Increase (%)	Effectiveness Increase (%)
'Source B' (1)	1.00	.245	-	-
'Source A' (3)	1.50	.282	50	15.2
'Source B'+'Source C'	2.03	.286	35	1.6
'Source B'+'Source A'	2.29	.303	13	6.1

Figure 1. Effectiveness versus cost per hit for the Mortgage 10% data set. Each possible data source combination is shown and the Pareto frontier is indicated with green markers.

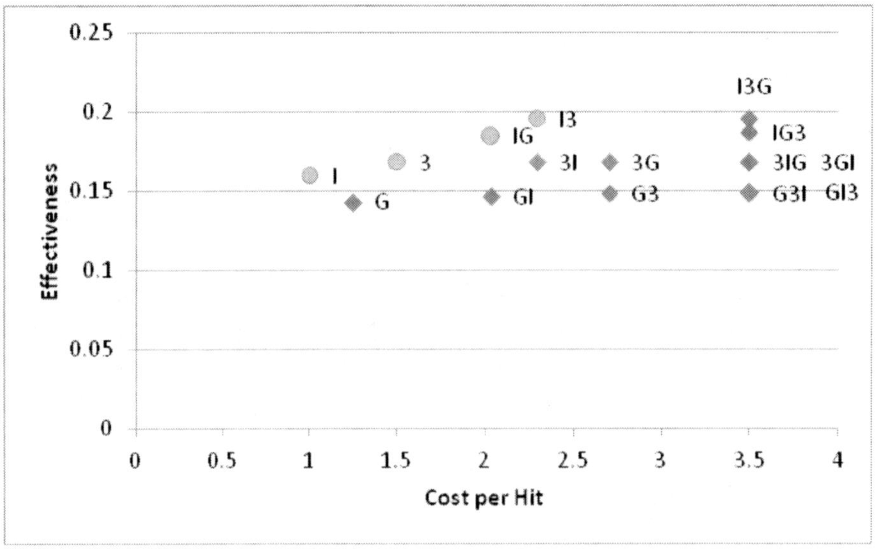

Figure 2. Effectiveness versus cost per hit for the Mortgage 20% data set. Each possible data source combination is shown and the Pareto frontier is indicated with green markers.

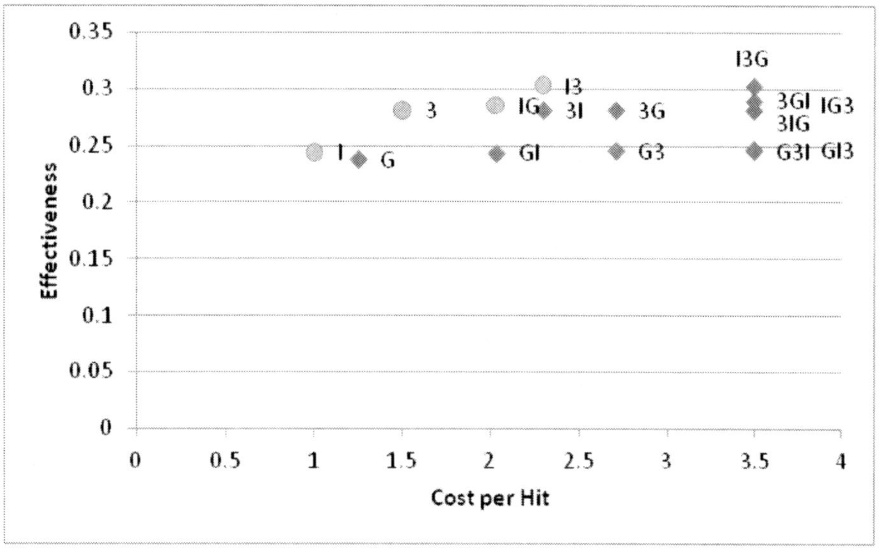

forms as well or better than every possible three-source combination.

Cards 10%

Figure 3 shows the fifteen data source combinations for the Cards 10% data. The green points indicate the Pareto frontier. The ideal data source combination is one of these points. The frontier points and their tradeoffs are shown in Table 17.

'Source B' dominates the frontier. Combining other data sources together never improves the effectiveness of the 'Source B' data source.

Cards 20%

Figure 4 shows the fifteen data source combinations for the Cards 20% data. The green points indicate the Pareto frontier. The ideal data source combination is one of these points. The frontier points and their tradeoffs are shown in Table 18.

'Source B and Source A' dominate the frontier. No combination of data sources outperforms these two.

Employee 10%

Figure 5 shows the fifteen data source combinations for the Employee 10% data. The green points indicate the Pareto frontier. The ideal data source combination is one of these points. The frontier points and their tradeoffs are shown in Table 19.

Moving between the points on the frontier increases the cost but also increases the effectiveness. No three-source combination is on the frontier. There is always a two- source combina-

Table 17. Pareto frontier for the Cards 10% data

Data Source Combination	Cost per Hit	Accuracy	Cost Increase (%)	Accuracy Increase (%)
'Source B' (1)	1.00	.167	-	-

Table 18. Pareto frontier for the Cards 20% data

Data Source Combination	Cost per Hit	Accuracy	Cost Increase (%)	Accuracy Increase (%)
'Source B' (1)	1.00	.241	-	-
'Source A' (3)	1.50	.255	50	5.7

Figure 3. Effectiveness vs. cost per hit for the Cards 10% data set. Each possible data source combination is shown and the Pareto frontier is indicated with green markers.

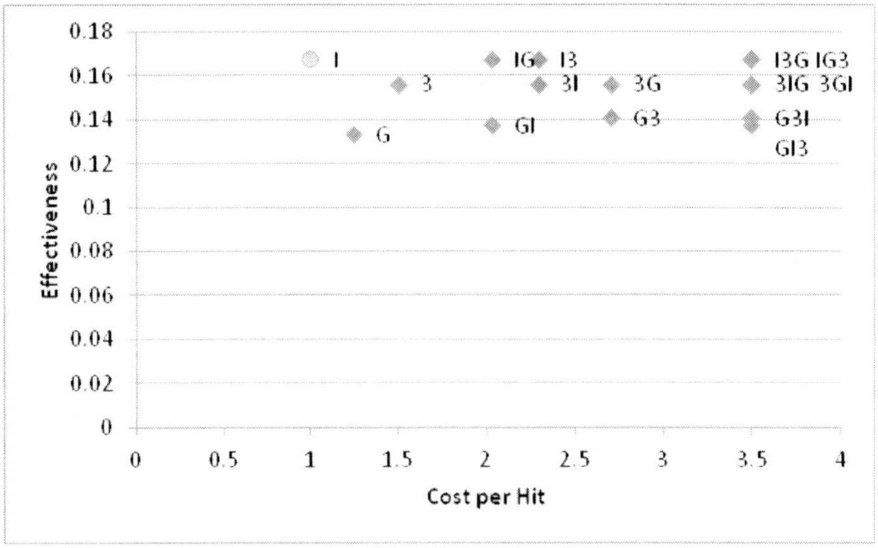

Figure 4. Effectiveness versus cost per hit for the Cards 20% data set. Each possible data source combination is shown and the Pareto frontier is indicated with green markers.

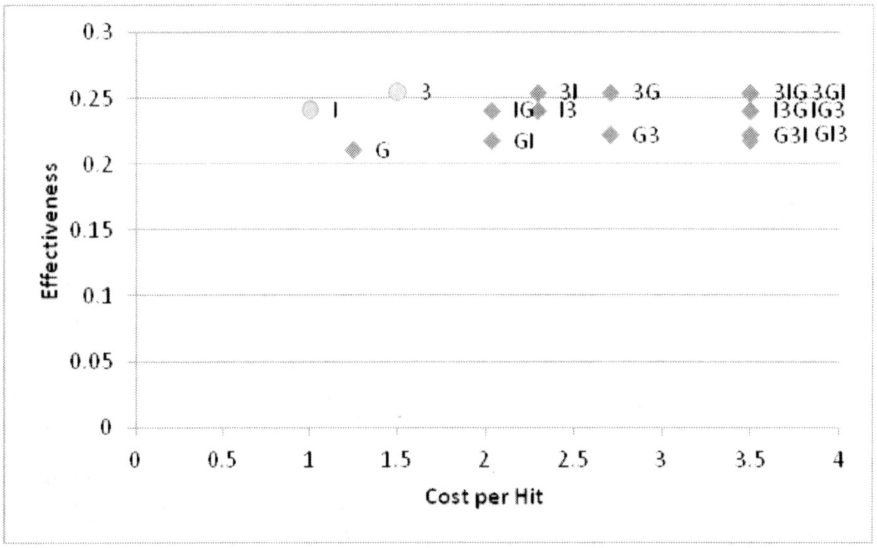

tion that performs as well or better than every possible three-source combination.

Employee 20%

Figure 6 shows the fifteen data source combinations for the Employee 20% data. The green points indicate the Pareto frontier. The ideal data source combination is one of these points. The frontier points and their tradeoffs are shown in Table 20.

Moving between the points on the frontier increases the cost but also increases the effectiveness. No three-source combination is on the frontier. Always a two-source combination per-

Figure 5. Effectiveness versus cost per hit for the Employee 10% data set. Each possible data source combination is shown and the Pareto frontier is indicated with green markers.

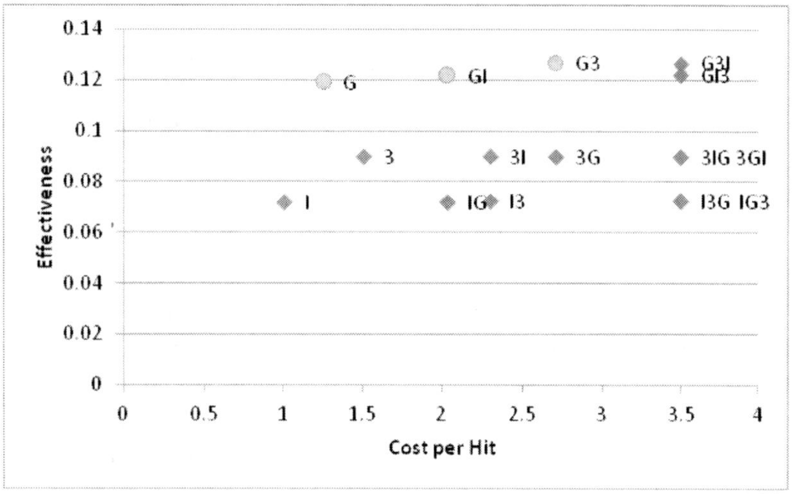

Figure 6. Effectiveness versus cost per hit for the Employee 20% data set. Each possible data source combination is shown and the Pareto frontier is indicated with green markers.

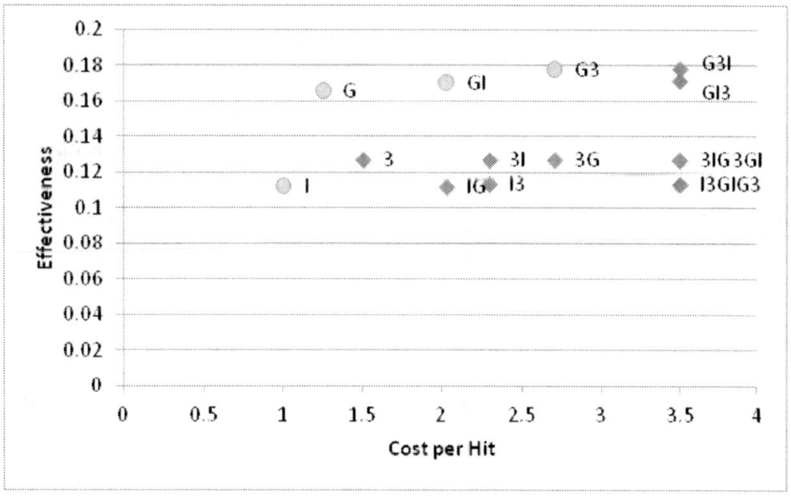

Table 19. Pareto frontier for the Employee 10% data

Data Source Combination	Cost per Hit	Accuracy	Cost Increase (%)	Accuracy Increase (%)
'Source C' (G)	1.25	.119	-	-
'Source C'+'Source B'	2.03	.122	62	2.2
'Source C'+'Source A'	2.70	.127	33	3.9

Table 20. Pareto frontier for the Employee 20% data

Data Source Combination	Cost per Hit	Accuracy	Cost Increase (%)	Accuracy Increase (%)
'Source B' (I)	1.00	.112	-	-
'Source C' (G)	1.25	.166	25	48
'Source C'+'Source B'	2.03	.170	62	2.5
'Source C'+'Source A'	2.70	.178	33	4.5

forms as well or better than every possible three-source combination.

SUMMARY OF FINDINGS

- Accuracy is a measure of how close the vendor-reported income is to true value. *Less than 15% of vendor records for income were accurate*;
- Relevancy measures the degree of accuracy. By including records that are accurate within 20% - tolerance, the number of accurate records increased by 6% - 9% for a *maximum adjusted accuracy score of 24%*;
- Since overall accuracy scores decline when all vendors are used, *combining more than two sources increases costs with no additional benefit.*

KEY TERMS AND DEFINITIONS

Accuracy: Accuracy is a logical metric. Accuracy measures the number of correct records within a data source relative to the number of records in that data source. This value is independent on the records requested.

Coverage: Coverage measures the number of records with income information appended by a vendor to the total number of records requested. This is a direct measure of the utility of the vendor data. A vendor with low coverage may be very good data, but with very few records.

Cost: Cost is measured as the cost of using a vendor in a particular scenario. Cost information is expressed in relevant terms (cost index), thus the results are presented for comparisons only and do not represent actual results.

Completeness: Completeness measures the number of records appended by a vendor that have income information.

Relevancy: Relevancy measured the vendor performance against the bands set up by the vendor.

Effectiveness: Effectiveness is a variant of both Relevancy and Accuracy. Relevancy and Accuracy measure the performance of the vendor in relation to the total number of records appended by the vendor. Instead of measuring relative to the number of records appended, Effectiveness measures relative to the total number of records requested.

Chapter 17
Strategies for Large-Scale Entity Resolution Based on Inverted Index Data Partitioning

Yinle Zhou
IBM Corporation, USA

John R. Talburt
University of Arkansas – Little Rock, USA

ABSTRACT

Inverted indexing is a commonly used technique for improving the performance of entity resolution algorithms by reducing the number of pair-wise comparisons necessary to arrive at acceptable results. This chapter describes how inverted indexing can also be used as a data partitioning strategy to perform entity resolution on large datasets in a distributed processing environment. This chapter discusses the importance of index-to-rule alignment, pre-resolution index closure, post-resolution link closure, and workflows for record-based identity capture and update, and attribute-based identity capture and update in a distributed processing environment.

BACKGROUND

Entity Resolution

Entity resolution (ER) is the process of determining whether two references to real-world objects in an information system are referring to the same object, or to different objects (Talburt, 2011). ER has long been recognized as a key data cleaning process for removing duplicate records in database systems (Naumann & Herschel, 2010), and in entity-based data integration as a way to aggregate information about the same entity across different information sources.

DOI: 10.4018/978-1-4666-4892-0.ch017

In these types of applications, the entire ER process comprises executing a set of matching rules that link together those records determined to be equivalent (duplicate), selecting one best example, called a survivor record, from each cluster of equivalent records, discarding the duplicate records, then passing the surviving records to the next process. In this role of addressing the data quality problem of redundant and duplicate data and as a precursor to data integration, ER is fundamentally in a data cleansing tool (Herzog et al, 2007). However, ER is increasingly being used in a broader context for two important reasons.

The first is that as information quality has matured and follows more of a product management focus organizations are giving more attention to problem of not only achieving high-levels of information quality, but also sustaining information quality over time (Wang, 1998). This is evidenced by several important developments of recent years including the recognition of Sustaining Information Quality as one of the six domains in the framework of information quality developed by the International Association for Information and Data Quality (Yonke et al, 2012) as the basis for the Information Quality Certified Professional (IQCP) credential, the recent approval of the ISO 8000-110:2009 standard for master data quality, and the growing interest by organizations in adopting and investing in master data management (MDM).

Master data in an organization are the data items that reference the entities that are the organization's critical, non-fungible assets, such as customers, employees, products, and equipment. MDM comprises the policies, procedures, and infrastructure needed to accurately capture, integrate, and manage master data (Loshin 2008). MDM is essentially an effort to maintain the constraint of entity identity integrity over master data.

Entity identity integrity is one of the basic tenets of data quality that applies to the representation of a given domain of real-world entities in an information system (Maydanchik, 2007). Entity identity integrity has also been described as proper representation (Huang et al, 1999). Entity identity integrity requires that:

- Each real-world entity in the domain has one and only one representation in the information system;
- Distinct real-world entities have distinct representations in the information system.

Entity Identity Information Management

Entity Identity Information Management (EIIM) is the collection and management of identity information with the goal of sustaining entity identity integrity over time (Zhou & Talburt, 2011). It is an iterative process that combines ER and data structures representing entity identity into specific operational configurations (EIIM configurations) that when executed in concert, work to maintain the entity identity integrity of master data over time.

One of the primary motivations for introducing the EIIM model is to broaden the thinking and research about ER in two ways. The first is to bring more focus on the problem of identity management by describing different strategies and data structures for capturing and managing identity information and some of the trade-offs among these strategies. The second motivation is to place more emphasis on the temporal aspects of ER and to recognize that identity information has a life cycle that can be managed over time through the use of EIIM Configurations.

A distinguishing feature of the EIIM model is the entity identity structure (EIS), a data structure that represents the identity of a specific entity and that persists from process to process. In the model presented here, the EIS is an explicitly defined structure that exists and is maintained independently of the records being processed by the system. Although all ER systems address the issue of identity representation in some way, it is often done implicitly rather than being an explicit component of the system. Figure 1 shows the persistent (output) form of an EIS as implemented in the open source ER system called OYSTER (Zhou et al, 2010). During processing, OYSTER EIS exist as in-memory Java objects. At the end of processing, the EIS are output as XML documents that reflect the hierarchical structure of the memory objects. The XML format also serves to serialize the EIS objects so that they can be re-loaded into memory at the start of a later ER process.

In the XML document shown in Figure 1, the <Identity> element encloses a single EIS assigned the identifier value of "X9KTZ5GOQ5RVHOWV". This particular identity comprises the identity information captured from two records resolved during the same process (Run001) on March 29, 2012. This can be seen from the <References> element that encloses two <Reference> elements. Each <Reference> element reflects the identity information captured from a single source record processed during the run. The <Value> element contains a compressed version of the identity attributes and their values in a pipe-delimited (|) string where each attribute-value pair is a single character tag representing the attribute separated from the attribute value by the caret (^) character. The tags used in the compression are related to the actual identity attribute labels in the <Metadata> section of the document. For example in

Figure 1. Example of an EIS in XML format created by the OYSTER ER system

```xml
<root>
   <Metadata>
      <Modifications>
       <Modification ID="1" OysterVersion="3.2" Date="2012-03-29 04.51.07" RunScript="Run001" />
      </Modifications>
      <Attributes>
       <Attribute Name="@RefID" Tag="A"/>
       <Attribute Name="Phone" Tag="B"/>
       <Attribute Name="FirstName" Tag="C"/>
       <Attribute Name="StrNbr" Tag="D"/>
       <Attribute Name="LastName" Tag="E"/>
       <Attribute Name="SSN" Tag="F"/>
     </Attributes>
</Metadata>
<Identities>
    <Identity Identifier="X9KTZ5GOQ5RVHOWV" CDate="2012-03-29">
  <References>
    <Reference>
        <Value>A^ListA.A953698|C^ANTONIOV|D^247H|E^CARDONA|F^196369947</Value>
        <Traces>
            <Trace OID="X9KTZ5GOQ5RVHOWV" RunID="1" Rule="[@]"/>
        </Traces>
   </Reference>
   <Reference>
        <Value>A^ListA.A989582|C^ANTONIOV|D^5221|E^CARDONA|F^196369974</Value>
        <Traces>
            <Trace OID="X9KTZ5GOQ5RVHOWV" RunID="1" Rule="[2]"/>
        </Traces>
  </Reference>
</References>
   </Identity>
...
  </Identities>
</root>
```

the first <Reference>, the values were captured from the record labeled "A953698" in the source labeled "ListA" and that the value of the LastName attribute in this record was "CARDONA" as indicated by the tag "E".

While basic record linking processes can consistently identify references to the same entity for a given dataset, the goal of EIIM is to consistently label references to the same entity with the same identifier across different datasets processed at different times. Through the management of persistent EIS, EIIM provides the added functionality for an ER system to create and assign persistent entity identifiers, i.e. entity identifiers that do not change from process to process. Thus EIIM contributes a technological underpinning to MDM which also encompasses many non-technical issues related to master data policy and governance. EIIM can also be thought of as forming a nexus between ER and MDM by adding an explicit longitudinal dimension to the management of identity information.

Although there has been a great deal of identity management research, it has primarily focused on two issues related to information technology (IT) security. The first is the problem of issuing system users with credentials and unique identifiers during an initial identity registration phase. The second is the problem of authenticating users and controlling their access to services and resources based on their identifiers and credentials during the service operation phase (Josang & Pope, 2005). EIIM focuses on the problem storing and managing identity information at the data structure level.

Identity management has wide application in areas such as healthcare, financial services, government, national security, energy, and consumer services (Center for Identity, 2011). EIIM can also play an important role here by providing the functionality necessary for the management of authentication, authorization, roles, and privileges and permissions activities. EIIM-based research could promote additional insights into optimal techniques for the management of identity information and into ways to support more stable and persistent entity identifiers across multiple identity management applications.

PROBLEMS WITH LARGE-SCALE ER

The ER process has two major components: resolution (reference comparison) and integration (reference linking) (Zhou & Talburt, 2011) and both present problems in scaling to large datasets, especially in a distributed processing environment. Most ER systems follow the Fellegi-Sunter Model for record linking (Fellegi & Sunter, 1969) in which pairs of references (records) are judged to be "link", "non-link", or "possible link" pairs depending upon which pairs of identity attribute values agree and disagree. A particular specification detailing which attributes must agree or disagree and to what level they must agree or disagree is called an *identity rule*. For example in comparing two student enrollment records an identity rule might require that the student's first name values agree to the level of a common Soundex code, the last name values agree as identical string values after conversion to all uppercase letters, and the date-of-birth values represent the same calendar date after conversion to a standard date format. In the same way, other rules may take into account agreements on other attributes such as street address or parent's name. Rules of this style are called *Boolean rules* or *deterministic rules* and are the basis for the discussions in the sections that follow.

Other ER system employ a single rule that compares the values of all of the identity attributes. In this type of rule, the comparison of the values for each attribute contributes a integer value called an attribute weight. The overall comparison score for the rule is the total of all the individual attribute weights. If the total score of the comparison exceeds a pre-defined threshold score, then the two references are linked. In the simplest case, each attribute has two weights, an agreement weight that applies when the attribute values agree at a specified level, and a disagreement weight that applies otherwise. In more sophisticated systems there may be multiple agreement weights that depend on the actual values of the agreement. For example if the student enrollment system were to follow this scheme, common first name values that are shared by many different students in the target population would be assigned a smaller agreement weight than if the agreement is on first name values that are only used by a few students in the school system. The values for agreement and disagreement weights of an attribute are computed from estimates of the probability that values of attribute agree on references to the same entity versus the probability the values agree on references to different entities (Herzog et al, 2007).

The comparison component of the ER process uses an ER algorithm to systematically select and compare pairs of records. In the worst case, ER algorithms require O (N^2) comparisons where N is the number of references to be resolved. This is exacerbated by the fact that some ER processes do not strictly follow the Fellegi-Sunter Model of record-to-record comparisons. In the broader context of EIIM, identity information does not comprise the information from a single reference (record), but is the aggregation of the information from several references in the form of an entity identity structure (EIS) such as the one shown in Figure 1.

For these kinds of systems, there is a design choice as to how two EIS are to be compared using an identity rule. For example, an EIS representing the identity of a student may contain different first name values and different last name values that are all valid for the student due to legal adoption, the use of nicknames, or changes in name preference. If a rule specifies the comparison of a first name and a last name, it raises the issue as to which values should be used in the comparison.

Consider a simple example of two EIS labeled X and Y. Suppose that X has information from two references R1=(F1, L1) and R2=(F2, L2) where F and L represent first and last name values. Similarly suppose that Y has information from two references R3=(F3, L3) and R4=(F4, L4). Finally suppose that there is an identity rule that requires and exact match on first name values and an exact match on last name values. In this example, both X and Y have the capability of provide two first name values and two last name values. The algorithm used by an ER system to provision attributes values from an EIS to an identity rule is called its *EIS projection function*. The two most common designs for projection functions are attribute-based projection and record-based projection. In attribute based projection, the value provided by an EIS for an attribute in the identity rule can come from any reference in the EIS that has a value for the attribute. The selection of the value for one attribute is independent of the choice of the value for any of the other attributes being compared by the identity rule. So in the example of comparing the EIS X and Y, attribute-based projection would create 16 comparison scenarios, four pairs of first name combinations and four pairs of last name combinations.

On the other hand, record-based projection has the constraint that all of the values provided to an identity rule must come from the same reference in the EIS. This constraint creates a dependency among the attributes projected onto the identity rule. In the case of X and Y, the use of record-based projection would only create 4 comparison scenarios because the choice of a first name value fixes the choice of the last name value, e.g. the choice F1 to F3 for first name values would fix the choice for last name values as L1 to L3.

The importance of the projection scheme is that it has an impact on the ER resolution algorithm. ER processes that use attribute-based projection require a stronger algorithm (more comparisons in the worst case) than ER processes that use record-based projection. In the case of record-based projection, the worst case number of comparison required to resolve N references is (Zhou & Talburt, 2011):

$$\frac{N \cdot (N-1)}{2}$$

Whereas for attribute-based projection, the worst case comparisons is given by (Zhou & Talburt, 2011):

$$(N-1)^2$$

In either case, the number of comparisons needed assure that an ER process finds every possible match is an $O(N^2)$ problem. Therefore for practical considerations, most ER processes are willing to sacrifice some completeness in order to achieve a reduction in the total number of comparisons. The consequence of this reduction is that some potential matches will be missed by the process, and that some references that should be brought together in the same EIS are left unlinked, thus creating false negative resolution errors.

The most common approach to reduction is to index the references in such a way that when an input reference is processed, the system can use the index to easily retrieve a relatively small set of previously processed references that are the most likely candidates to match the input reference. The underlying principle of this technique is that references that generate the same index value are the references most likely to match when compared by one the identity rules. Many approaches to indexing have been developed including blocking, sorted neighborhoods, Q-gram indexing, suffix-array indexing, canopy clustering, and mapping-based indexing (Christen, 2012; Kolb et al, 2012). While some ER systems have a fixed indexing scheme, others allows the user to configure the indexing scheme at run-time, i.e. user-defined indexing.

The remainder of this chapter focuses strategies and techniques for large-scale integration in the specific context of ER systems that have two characteristics. First is that they implement user-defined inverted indexing where each reference can potentially generate more than one index value. The second is that they use Boolean identity rules.

BOOLEAN RULES

In rule-based ER systems (Christen, 2012), pairs of references are resolved by the identity rules into matches and non-matches, and in some cases, possible matches needing clerical review (Naumann & Herschel, 2010). Boolean rules are rules that give a true (match) or false (no match) decision on the similarity values of the comparison vectors generated in the comparison step (Whang & Garcia-Molina, 2012).

In Zhou et al (2012) a Boolean Matching Rule is defined as collection of one or more Rule Terms connected with AND logic between the terms, i.e. all rule terms must be true in order for the rule itself to be true. In addition, an ER system may use more than one rule, and when it does, the design asserts OR logic between rules, i.e. the final resolution decision between two references is true if and only if at least one rule is true.

Each Rule Term represents a logical proposition that two attribute values are similar (true) or not similar (false) as defined by a specific similarity function and threshold. A Boolean matching rule may have several terms, but must have at least one term. An example of a rule term would be that the first names on two student records must be at least 0.80 (80%) similar as measured by the Levenshtein normalized edit distance (Levenshtein, 1966; Christen, 2006).

Ideally, each rule in a set of rules should be of high precision and high recall (Han & Kamber, 2006). A high precision means that a rule that resolves reference pairs into a certain identity cluster should mostly cover pairs that do belong to this cluster but not pairs that belong into another cluster. A high recall means that the result of a rule covers a large portion of all candidate reference pairs. The overall system accuracy and recall are affected by the indexing as well. More discussion on this topic will be covered in later sections.

There are two basic approaches to generate the rules, either develop a rule set manually or learn a set of rules from training data (Christen, 2012). This paper focuses on manually selecting attributes to form Boolean matching rules and selecting appropriate indexing.

USER-DEFINED INVERTED INDEX

Match Key

The aim of indexing is to reduce the reference pairs to be compared, often called candidate pairs. User-defined inverted index gives the user a way to design match keys and store the match keys and reference ID in an inverted index data structure (Zobel & Moffat, 2006) which can help quickly locate all previously processed references that share the same match key. This method is also called Standard Blocking (Christen, 2006). A match key is a string of characters generated by applying algorithms (hash functions) to selected attribute values in a reference and concatenating the results in fixed order.

Hash functions to encode attribute values before they are used as matching key values are commonly used in the indexing step (Christen, 2006). The function could be phonetic encoding functions, such as Soundex (Holmes & McCabe, 2002), NYSIIS (Borgman & Siegfried, 1992), Double-Metaphone (Philips, 2000), or string manipulation functions such as uppercasing or substring extraction. The purpose of hashing the attribute values is to get references that potentially match to produce the same match key even though the original attribute values may vary because of phonetic or edit distance misspelling, e.g. the Soundex codes for "SMITH" and "SMYTHE" are same.

In most cases, not all of the identity attributes are used to generate a particular match key. For example, if a reference has five attributes A, B, C, D, and E, an index value could be generated by three hash algorithms, one acting on the value of attribute A, another on the value of attribute B, and another on the value of attribute D. To arrive at the final match key value, the three hashed values of the attributes are concatenated in a fixed order to create a single value.

Take as an example a student enrollment record where the attributes of first name and last name are selected to create index keys. The hash algorithm LeftSubstring(1) is chosen for hashing first name value and LeftSubsting(5) is chosen for hashing last name value. If first name value is "PHILIP", then after applying the hash algorithm, the hash output is "P". Similarly, if the last name value is "DOBSON", the hash value is "DOBSO", and the final match key value is "P"+"DOBSO"="PDOBSO".

Alignment of Match Key Index with the Match Rules

Match key generators work independently of the match rules. For systems that support user-defined indexing, it is the user's responsibility to assure that the match rules and match key generators work together. The match rules only compare an input reference to other references previously generated the same match key as the input reference. Even though an input reference matches a previously processed reference, that match will only be discovered by the system if the matching reference is returned by the index, i.e. the matching reference must generate same match key and the input reference.

The primary goal of rule-to-index alignment is that if two references match each other by the rules, then the two references generate the same match key by at least one of the match key generators. A secondary goal is to minimize the number of references that generate the same match key, yet do not match by the rules. The misalignment occurs when some references that match each other do not generate the same match key.

Using the same student enrollment record example, suppose that there is single match rule that requires the last names to be the same (exact match), but allows the first name values to be nicknames for each other, e.g. allow "JAMES" and "JIM" to be a match. Further suppose that the hash generator for the first name is LeftSubstring(1) and for the last name is LeftSubstring(5). Then the enrollment records "JAMES SMITH" and "JIM SMITH" would match by the rule and also generate the same match key "JSMITH". However, the enrollment records "ROBERT CAMP" and "BOB CAMP" would match, but their match keys "RCAMP" and "BCAMP" are not the same. The last example shows that the rules and the index generators are not in alignment.

Index Measurements

There are three primary measurements used to evaluate index performance. These measurements are recall, precision, and reduction ratio (Christen & Goiser, 2007).

Index Recall

Index recall is the percentage of all matching pairs of references that also generate the same match key. An alternate definition of rule-to-index alignment is the requirement that the index must have a recall of 100%.

Index Precision

Index precision is the percentage of all pairs generating the same match key that also match by the rules. The precision represents the "efficiency" of the index in that higher precision means fewer pairs of references that generate the same index value fail to match. Lower precision can mean longer processing time for large datasets.

Index Reduction Ratio

The reduction ratio calculates how many candidate reference pairs are generated by an index compared to all possible reference pairs, i.e. the full naïve or "brute force" pair-wise comparison of all pairs. For a set of N references the number of distinct pairs is given by $C(N, 2) = N(N+1)/2$. The actual reduction ratio can be difficult to calculate precisely because the number of possible reference comparisons will vary at each step of the ER algorithm.

Reduction is an important consideration in rule alignment. Even though the rules are in alignment with the indices (100% recall), if the precision is less than 100%, then the reduction ratio will be lower as well. For large numbers of references, a low reduction ratio may result in a run time that is unacceptable, e.g. days or weeks rather than hours or minutes.

Index Strategies and Analysis

Index Fewer Attributes Strategy

It is not necessary to index every attribute used in a rule. For example, the misalignment described earlier for the student enrollment records can be repaired by changing the index definition to drop the hash generator LeftSubstring(1) for the first name and only use the hash generator LeftSubstring(5) on the last name. This simple index is now in alignment with the rule, which means 100% recall. However, the disadvantage of this change is that the number of candidate pairs is likely to increase and the precision of the index will decrease. This is because the new index definition only constrains the last name value. All enrollment records that agree on the first 5 characters of the last name will create the same index value regardless of the first name value. Removing attributes from index tends to increase recall while lowering precision.

Multiple Indices Strategy

ER processes that support the use of multiple indices can use an additional strategy for increasing reduction while maintaining rule-to-index alignment. When multiple indices are used, each match rule will compare all candidate reference pairs returned by all indices. Multiple indices are useful when different rules have terms that compare different sets of identity attributes. This allows multiple indices to be combined to achieve 100% recall.

As an example, consider the case where there are two rules for matching student enrollment records:

- **Rule 1:**
  - First Name match by Soundex;
  - Last Name match is Exact;
  - Date-of-Birth is Exact;
- **Rule 2:**
  - First Name match on first letter (initial);
  - Last Name match is Exact;
  - School Identifier is Exact.

A naïve approach would be to have one index by Last Name such as:

Index 1: LeftSubstring (12) of Last Name

Index 1 would assure alignment since both rules require an exact match on Last Name. However, Index 1 would not have high precision since many different students may share common last names. Precision can be increased by observing that in both rules, the First Name values must agree on the first letter since the Soundex hash algorithm always keeps the first letter of the name. Thus replacing Index 1 with Index 2 defined below would still be in alignment with the rules while providing higher precision and reduction ratio:

Index 2: Leftsubstring(1) of First Name + Leftsubstring(12) of Last Name

A more efficient approach is to create two indices where each aligned with one of the matching rules. For example:

Index 3: Soundex Code of First Name + Leftsubstring(12) of Last Name + Leftsubstring(10) of Date-of-Birth;
Index 4: Leftsubstring(1) of First Name + Leftsubstring(12) of Last Name + Leftsubstring(6) of School Identifier.

The multiple index approach should provide the highest precision and reduction because it more tightly constrains the possible candidates. Even though both indices will contribute candidate pairs, the overall number candidate pairs will be smaller because each index is more precise.

Analysis and Validation

For large datasets where time-to-process performance is critical, some analysis and experimentation can be helpful. An important first step in any data process is to profile the data. Column profiling will indicate which attributes have high uniqueness and completeness, two characteristics desirable in an identity attribute. The matching rules are designed first, then the index rules.

When the references are in, or can be loaded to, a database, then SQL queries that emulate index generation can be used assess the expected numbers of candidate pairs that a proposed index will produce. In particular, group-by queries that count and rank occurrences of particular value combinations can help validate proposed index designs.

ER systems that support user-defined indices often provide index statistics such has a list of the most frequently generated index keys and the average number of references per index key. Generating these statistics may require special settings such as turning on debug mode or creating special log files. These statistics allow the user to experiment with index designs using small datasets.

The ability to turn indexing on and off is also a very useful feature for validating rule-to-index alignment. For a given set of rules, if the indices are in proper alignment, then the resolution results from running with indexing and the results of running without indexing should be identical. If they are not, then the rules and indices are misaligned. Again, this is only practical with small datasets since runs without indexing have no reduction and will have dramatically increased run-times.

INVERTED INDEXING AS A DATA PARTITIONING STRATEGY

Inverted indexing or blocking is one of the primary strategies for addressing the problem of large-scale ER (Bianco et al, 2011; Kirsten et al, 2010; Yancey, 2007). However, these approaches do not address ER issues raised by the use multiple indices and transitive closure, identity update and persistent identity identifiers, and attribute-based resolution discussed here.

Suppose that for a given set of identity rules there is a single, properly aligned index generator. Alignment of the index generator with the identity rules implies that all pairs of references that match by one of the identity rules must generate the same index value. Therefore from an entity resolution standpoint, each index value segment, i.e. all references generating the same index value will be independent of every other index value segment. By the assumption of alignment, references from different index value segments should never match. Consequently in the case of single index generator, the complete resolution of a dataset can be accomplished in two steps as shown in Figure 2.

The first step is the generation of the index values. Because the value produced by an index generator only depends upon the values of the identity attributes in a single reference, there is no dependency between references. Thus the first data distribution (D1) is an arbitrary distribution of the input references (A) into equal size and disjoint blocks of references that are processed independently by the index generator processes.

After each block of references has been processed by an index generator, the next step is to merge the references (B) and perform a second

Figure 2. Distributed workflow based on single index generator

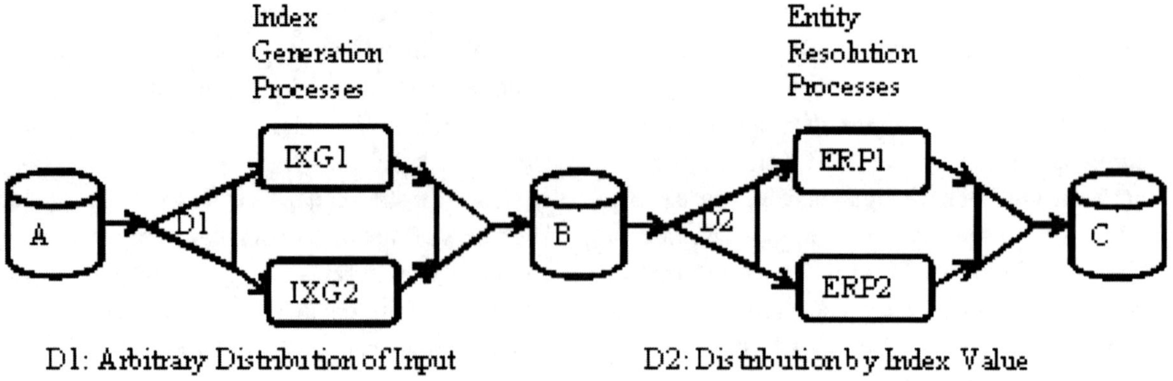

distribution D2. The distribution D2 assigns data to the processes based on common index value, i.e. all references generating the same index value are assigned to the same process. As noted earlier, the references within each of these index value segments can be resolved by independent ER processes without the concern that references in one segment might match a reference in another segment being resolved in a different ER process.

In the case of a single index, both distributions D1 and D2 actually create true partitions of the datasets A and B, respectively, i.e. the distributed segments are non-overlapping. D1 partitions A by simply counting off equal size blocks of references. D2 partitions B because with a single index generator, each reference can only be in one index value segment, thus the index value segments cannot overlap.

The distribution D2 assigns each index value segment to one of the ER Processes for resolution. Assuming that each ER process produces consistent ER results, i.e. is sequence neutral, then the clusters of linked references output from each ER process will always comprise a partition the input references. Because the segmentation S2 partitions B into index value segments, and each ER process partitions the index value segment into cluster of linked references, the end result C is also a partition of A, the original set of input references. Moreover, the final partition C of A into clusters of linked references will always be a refinement (sub-partition) of the partition B into index value segments.

The Transitive Closure Problem

The problem with the process described in the Figure 2 is that in most large-scale entity resolution applications, a single index generator is not practical. Data quality problems such as typographical errors in attribute values, missing values, and inconsistent representation of the values will require the use of more than one index generator in order to obtain good resolution results with a reasonable amount of reduction.

When each input reference can potentially create a different index value for each index generator, the processing scheme outlined in Figure 2 will not always lead to the correct resolution of A. The reason is the requirement for transitive closure of an ER process. Transitive closure states that if a reference R1 is linked to a reference R2, and reference R2 is linked to a reference R3, then reference R1 must be linked to reference R3. This requirement also implies that matching is not always the same as linking, i.e. if two references match by an identity rule, then they should be linked, but because of transitive closure, not all linked references match. In the example given where R1 matches R2 and R2 matches R3, it does not necessarily follow that R1 matches R3 because matching itself is not transitive. For example consider a matching rule that requires two strings to differ by at most one character. Then it would be true that "ABC" matches "ADC", and that "ADC" matches "ADE", but "ABC" does not match "ADE".

To see how having multiple index generators disrupts the process described in Figure 2, suppose there are three distinct references R1, R2, and R3 such that R1 and R2 both generate an index value I1, and R2 and R3 both generate a different index value I2. Furthermore, suppose that R1 does not generate index value I2, and that R3 does not generate has index I1. If S(I1) represents the index value segment for I1, i.e. the set of references generating I1, then S(I1) = {R1, R2}. On the other hand, S(I2) = {R2, R3}, thus S(I1) and S(I2) have a non-empty intersection containing R2. In the case of multiple index generators, the distribution D2 shown in Figure 2 may not generate a true partition of B because some distinct index segments may overlap.

Now suppose that S(I1) is acted upon by ERP1 (ER Process P1) and that ERP1 links R1 and R2. Similarly, suppose that S(I2) is acted upon by ERP2 (ER Process P2) and that ERP2 links R2 and R3. By transitive closure, the cluster of references linked to R2 by P1 should be merged with the cluster of references linked to R2 by P2. Clusters of linked references produced by a consistent ER process cannot overlap, they must be identical or disjoint. In other words, R1, R2, and R3 must all belong to the same cluster of linked references. The problem is that different processes are working on different segments of the data. Even though each separate resolution process properly resolves the references in the segments that are given to it as input, the overall process may not resolve the entire set of input references (A) correctly because references that should be linked are in different segments acted upon by different processes.

The approach to solving the multiple-index problem depends upon whether the ER processes are using record-based resolution or attribute-based resolution as defined earlier. The situation for record-based resolution is simpler and has two solutions, either the transitive closure of the index values prior to distribution to the ER processes or the transitive closure of the link identifiers after the ER processes are complete.

Post-Resolution Closure for Multiple-Index, Record-Based Resolution

The post-resolution transitive closure workflow begins the same as the process outlined in Figure 2 for a single index workflow. The difference is that the use of multiple indices may cause the result C to contain clusters of overlapping references as described above. One solution to this problem is to add a post resolution process as shown in Figure 3.

For record-based resolution, arriving at the transitive closure among the clusters of linked references is only a matter of performing a set union operation to join the overlapping clusters. Since each cluster is defined by a single link identifier, when the union operation is performed only one of the link identifiers is selected to replace all other identifiers for the references in the merged cluster.

These concepts can be explained with a simple example where:

A = {R1, R2, R3, R4, R5, R6, R7, R8, R9, R10}

A is a set of 10 references input to a distributed ER process. Assume that for a given set of identity

Figure 3. Distributed workflow with post-resolution transitive link closure

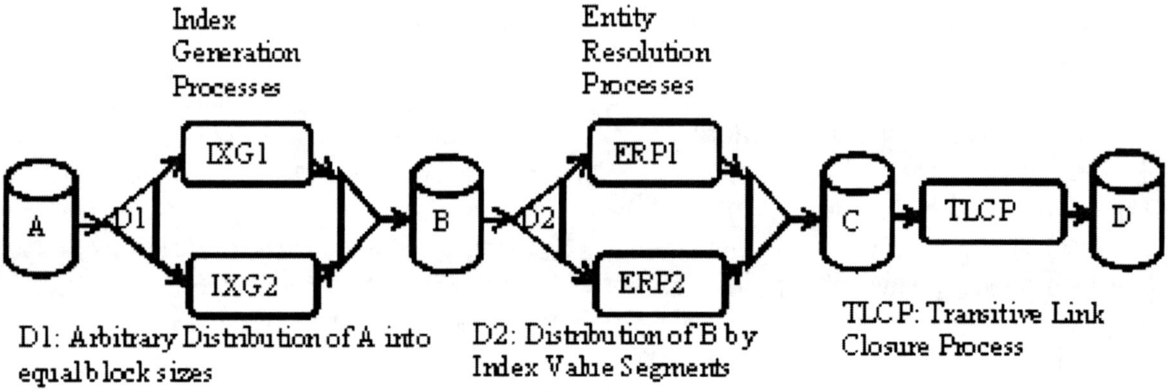

rules the references in A should link together into 5 clusters given here as:

Cluster1 = {R1}

Cluster2 = {R4, R5}

Cluster3 = {R2, R3, R7, R8}

Cluster4 = {R6}

Cluster5 = {R9, R10}

Further assume that the identity rules are properly aligned with two or more index generators so that any given reference can be indexed by more than one value. Table 1 shows how the 10 references generate 7 different index values I1, I2, I3, I4, I5, I6, and I7.

Each column of Table 1 corresponds to an index value segment, i.e. a set of references that generating the same index value. The "X" in the cell of the table indicates that the reference labeling that row generates the index value labeling the column. For example, reference R4 generates two index values, I1 and I2. The index segments from Table 1 are:

Table 1. References by index value

Ref	I1	I2	I3	I4	I5	I6	I7
R1	X						
R2			X				
R3				X			
R4	X	X					
R5		X					
R6						X	X
R7					X		
R8			X	X	X		
R9						X	X
R10						X	

S(I1) = {R1, R4}

S(I2) = {R4, R5}

S(I3) = {R2, R8}

S(I4) = {R3, R8}

S(I5) = {R7, R8}

S(I6) = {R6, R9, R10}

S(I7) = {R6, R9}

Now assume that instead of two processes as shown in Figure 3 there are actually three ER processes, ERP1, ERP2, and ERP3, all using the same set of identity rules. Furthermore, assume that D2 distributes the 7 index value segments as follows:

S(I1) ∪ S(I3) ∪ S(I5)
= {R1, R2, R4, R7, R8} → ERP1

S(I2) ∪ S(I6) = {R4, R5, R6, R9, R10} → ERP2

S(I4) ∪ S(I7) = {R3, R6, R8, R9} → ERP3

Each ER process will assign a link identifier to each reference that it processes to indicate the decisions of the identity rules. References assigned the same link identifier are deemed to represent the same entity according to the identity rules. Table 2 shows the link values assigned by the three ER processes.

In Table 2, ERP1 has assigned 3 link identifiers, L1 to R1, L2 to R2, R7, and R8, and L3 to R4. ERP2 has also assigned 3 link identifiers, L4 to R4 and R5, L5 to R6, and L6 to R9 and R10. ERP3 has assigned L7 to R3 and R8, L8 to R6, and L9 to R9. In all there are 9 distinct link identifiers L1 through L9. Even though each ER

Table 2. Link values assigned

Ref	ERP1	ERP2	ERP3
R1	L1		
R2	L2		
R3			L7
R4	L3	L4	
R5		L4	
R6		L5	L8
R7	L2		
R8	L2		L7
R9		L6	L9
R10		L6	

process correctly linked the references it was given as input, the combined results do not reflect the correct linking of the original set A of 10 references which should comprise only the five non-overlapping clusters listed earlier.

However, the correct result can be obtained taking the clusters produced by the ER processes and successively forming the union of those clusters that overlap. This process is called the union closure by link identifiers since each cluster corresponds to a distinct link identifier. For example, Table 2 shows that ERP1 produced the L2 cluster of {R2, R7, R8} and ERP3 produced the L7 cluster of {R3, R8}. Because they both contain R8 these cluster overlap. In the union closure process these two clusters are replaced by their union, the cluster {R2, R3, R7, R8}.

Following this same process, the nine clusters created by the three ER processes will collapse into only five union clusters that correspond to the correct resolution of A:

L1 = {R1}

L2 ∪ L7 = {R2, R3, R7, R8}

L3 ∪ L4 = {R4, R5}

L5 ∪ L8 = {R6}

L6 ∪ L9 = {R9, R10}

The union closure can also be viewed as a graph problem by thinking of each reference as a node in a graph G. Two nodes are connected by an edge in G if and only if they share the same link identifier. For example, because ERP2 links R9 and R10, there is an edge between nodes R9 and R10 in the graph G. In a graph representation of A, the transitive closure corresponds to the connected components of G. A connected component of a graph is a maximal set of nodes for which there is a path of edges between any two nodes.

The connected components of a graph can be found in linear time using a simple breadth-first or depth-first tree search. To apply this to the example given here, suppose that there are three lookup tables and that each has an argument and a corresponding lookup value. In the first table LinksByRef, each reference in A can be used as a lookup argument to return the list of links that were assigned to the reference by all of the ER processes, e.g. LinksByRefs.lookUp(R4) would return the list {L3, L4}. In the second table RefsByLink each link value can be used as a lookup argument to return the list of all references were assigned that link, e.g. RefsbyLink.lookUp(L4) would return the list {R4, R5}. The third table CompList is the output from Algorithm 1. The arguments for CompList are all of the references in A and the value returned is an integer from 1 to N that represents the number (label) of the component to which the reference belongs. Initially all of the values in CompList are set to 0.

The application of this algorithm to the graph represented by Table 2 gives the following result that corresponds to both the union closure and the correct linked clusters of A:

Component1 = {R1}

Component2 = {R2, R3, R7, R8}

Component3 = {R4, R5}

Algorithm 1. Connected Component Algorithm

```
0→CurrNbr
While (CompList.getNextArgument() → Ref)
{
    If (CompList.getValue(Ref) is equal to 0)
    {
        Increment(CurrNbr)
        LinksByRef.getValue(Ref) → ListOfLinks
        Call RecursiveProcess(ListOfLinks)
    }
}
RecursiveProcess(ListOfLinks)
{
    While(ListOfLinks.getNextItem() → WorkLink)
    {
        RefsByLink.getValue(Link) → ListOfRefs
        While(ListOfRefs.getNextItem() → WorkRef)
        {
                If(CompList.getValue(WorkRef) is equal to 0)
                {
                        CompList.setValue(WorkRef, CurrNbr)
                        LinksByRef.getValue(WorkRef) → WorkList
                        Call RecursiveProcess(WorkList)
                }
        }
    }
    Return
}
```

Component4 = {R6}

Component5 = {R9, R10}

Pre-Resolution Closure for Multiple-Index, Record-Based Matching

In some sense, the index values generated by a reference represent pre-links. In the case of record based matching, two references can only be linked together if there is a sequence of references starting with the first and ending with the second where each intermediate pair of references match each other, and therefore under the assumption of index alignment, they must share a common index value. Hence it follows that if the connected component algorithm is applied to the reference-index pairs, the resulting index value connected components will be supersets of the final resolution clusters. More importantly this means that each index value connected component can be processed independently, i.e. all of the references that will be linked together by the ER process will all be in the same index value connected component. Consequently when the ER process inputs are index value connected components, the post resolution closure is no longer required. The workflow for the pre-resolution index closure is show in Figure 4.

The pre-resolution index closure proceeds in the same way as the post-resolution link closure except that instead of starting with outputs from the ER processes as shown in Table 2, the pre-resolution closure operates on the outputs from the index generation processes. Following the algorithm, the seven index value segments of Table 1 yield three connected components:

I1∪ I2 = {R1, R4, R5}

I3 ∪ I4 ∪ I5 = {R2, R3, R7, R8}

I6 ∪ I7 = {R6, R9, R10}

It is important to remember the even though two references share a common index value, they will not always match. Nevertheless, each index connected component can be resolved independently of every other cluster so that the final resolution of the original set of references is simply the set of clusters found by processing each index connected component.

If each one of these index connected components is distributed to one of three ER processes, the final linking results will again be five clusters that agree with the earlier post-resolution link closure and also agree with the correct clustering of the original set of references A:

I1∪I2={R1,R4,R5}→ERP1→{{R1},{R4,R5}}

I3∪I4∪I5={R2,R3,R7,R8}→{{R2,R3,R7,R8}}

I6 ∪ I7 = {R6, R9, R10} → {{R6}, {R9, R10}}

The Identity Update Problem

EIIM is an extension of ER that includes the management of the entity identity information life cycle through a series of EIIM Configurations. Each configuration addresses a particular life cycle management task for identity information. A commonly used model for the information life cycle is the six-phase POSMAD model (McGilvray, 2008). POSMAD is an acronym that stands for life cycle phases of Plan, Obtain, Store and Share, Maintain, Apply, and Dispose.

The previous sections have only touched on two of the life cycle phases for identity information, the Store and Share and the Obtain Phases. The EIS structures and IKB are foundational to the EIIM approach to the Store and Share Phase for identity information whereas the identity capture configuration addresses the Obtain Phase. Identity capture is the configuration that initially builds

Figure 4. Distributed workflow with pre-resolution transitive index value closure

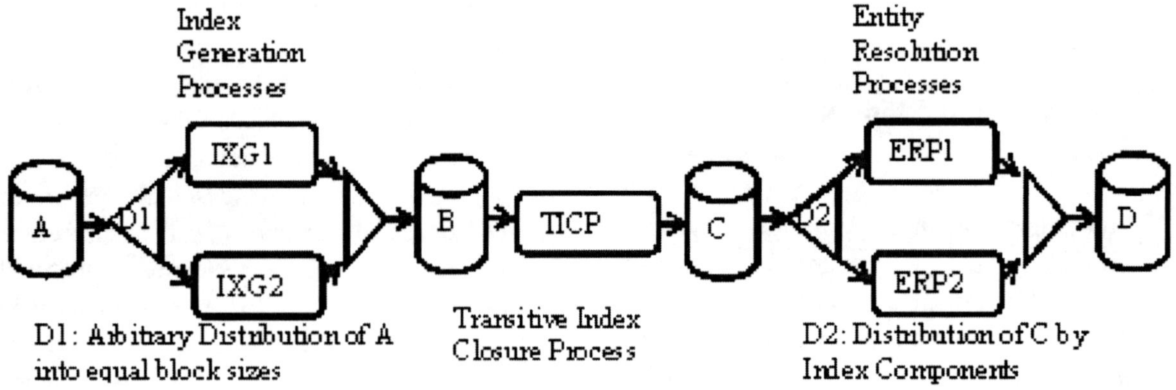

a set of entity identity structures (EIS) based on an initial set of references represented by A in Figures 3 and 4. The output D of these identity capture configurations comprises a collection of EIS where each EIS represents a separate identity that has been assigned a unique identifier.

Another important EIIM configuration is the update configuration that addresses the Maintain Phase of the life cycle. The identity update configuration of EIIM applies when new entity references are received that potentially related to an existing EIS. In the update configuration, the system uses the identity rules to decide if each new reference is referring to an entity identity already represented in the IKB by an existing EIS, or if it is referring to some new entity not yet represented in the system. In the former case, the system should integrate the new reference into the EIS representing the identity. In the latter case, the system must create an EIS and add it to the IKB to represent the new identity. There are two inputs to the update process, the existing EIS that were created in a previous process, and the new references.

Figure 5 shows the general approach to the update configuration for a distributed processing environment that is basically the identity capture workflow of Figure 4 with an added input D, the set of prior EIS to be updated. The output E is a new set of EIS that represent the integration of the new references in A with prior EIS in D.

One problem in adapting the identity capture workflow of Figure 4 to identity update is that identity capture workflow was based on the assumption that all of the inputs are single references, each with a unique reference identifier, but in Figure 5 only the inputs from A are single references, the inputs from D are EIS. One way that the workflow in Figure 5 makes sense if either each EIS in D can be decomposed into the set of references that originally created it, or if the aggregate set of references used to create the EIS in D has been save or archived in some way. In either case, by discarding the prior EIS of D and going back to the original references, it means that the workflow in Figure 5 is essentially a re-capture of the prior references combined with the new references.

Even if the original references comprising D are available, there are still two problems with the re-capture approach. The first issue concerns the evolution of identity rules. Over time, the identity rules may be modified to improve the entity identity integrity of EIS or to accommodate changes in the reference data. Therefore, the identity rules used to create or update the prior EIS in D may be different from the identity rules currently in effect. A simple re-capture process will apply the current identity rules to the prior references as well as the new references. In other words, the identities represented by the prior EIS from D are essentially discarded, and the identities

Figure 5. The basic workflow for the update configuration

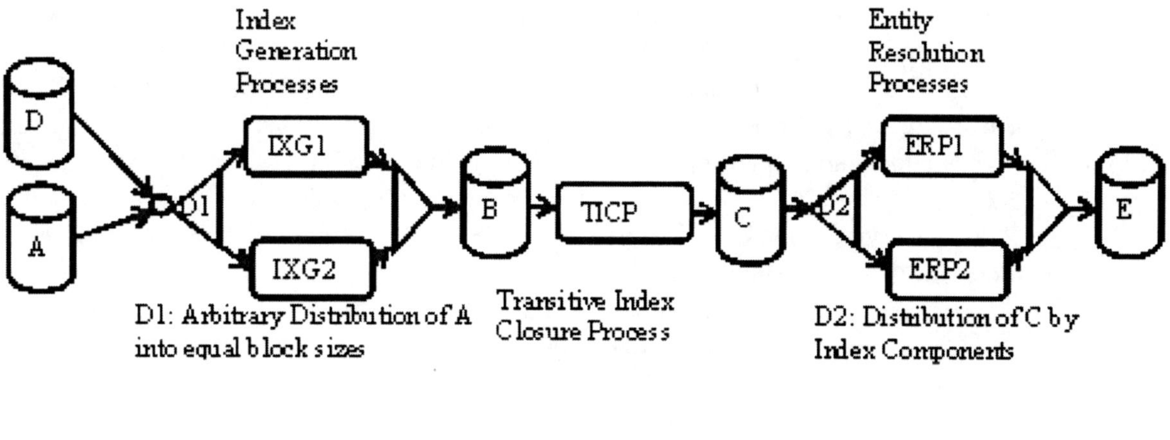

represented by the EIS in E are based entirely on the current rules. This issue may or may not be a problem, but it is an artifact of the re-capture approach that should be noted. The second problem with using a re-capture approach relates to the issue of persistent identifiers for the identities represent in the system.

Persistent Entity Identifiers

An important goal of EIIM is to create and maintain persistent entity identifiers for each identity under management, i.e. each EIS retains the same identifier from process to process. This is not the case for basic ER systems that do not create and maintain EIS. In these systems the link identifier assigned to a cluster of references at the end of the process is transient because it is not part of a persistent identity structure. The entity identifiers assigned by these systems are only intended to represent the linking (identity) decisions for that particular process acting on that particular input. Typically these system select one survivor record from each link cluster to go forward into further processing steps. After the survivor record has been selected, the link identifier is no longer needed.

If the only objective were to build the identities represented by combining the references from D with the references in A, then a re-capture approach to the workflow shown in Figure 5 would be sufficient. The problem is that even though the new EIS in E would be correct in the sense that they bring together all of the references that represent the same identity in the combined inputs, an EIS in D and an EIS in E representing the same entity may be assigned different identifiers. In other words from an EIIM perspective, it would have the undesirable side-effect that the identifiers for same entity identity could change after each update process.

In order to show a different approach to how the process shown in Figure 5 can address the two issues of persistent identifiers and retention of prior EIS, it is necessary to add more detail concerning the actual structure of the datasets at different points in the dataflow. The first is that the inputs coming from both A and D can be considered to have the bipartite structure of <Identifier, ContentString>. For each reference coming from A, the Identifier value of this structure would simply be a unique record identifier of the reference in the dataset A, and the ContentString value would be a single character string that serializes the content of the reference. The ConentString might be an XML document, a comma separated value (CSV) string, or any other text-based format. For the EIS coming from D, the Identifier would be the entity identifier of the EIS, and the ContentString would be the serialized content of the EIS such as the XML example shown in Figure 1.

The combined inputs from both A and D would then be distributed to the index generation processes. An important aspect of this new approach is that each index generation process (IXG) must now have the capability of generating index values for both types of inputs, both single references and EIS. In other words, an IXG process would have to be able to generate the index values from the serialized reference content, and also have the ability to generate the index values from the serialized EIS content.

By requiring this functionality in the IXG process, it is no longer necessary to assume that each EIS can be decomposed into its constituent references or that archives of the original references must be recovered in order to create the input for the IGX process. The capability to generate index values directly from the EIS content is particularly important in the next section that describes an identity update process for attribute-based ER processes. In the new approach described here, the prior EIS remain intact as they move forward through the workflow, which also addresses the problem of rule evolution.

The combined outputs from the IXG, represented by B in Figure 5, would have a tripartite structure of <Identifier, Index, ContentString> where the Index value is a value produced by one of the index hash generators in IXG. Because there could be many different index hash generators in each IXG and because there could be many references in each EIS, one input to an IXG could produce many outputs.

As a practical consideration, the ContentString only needs to be populated in one of the outputs from a given input. Repeating the ContentString for each output is redundant and could be costly in terms of storage and data transfer efficiency. The ContentString value of a prior EIS can be quite large in comparison to the ContentString value of a new reference from A.

The transitive index closure process operating on the records in B is the same as previously described. However in the index closure process, only the Identifier and Index data items are used in this process. The connected components generated by the index closure process may contain only references from prior EIS, only input references, or a combination of both. These combinations reflect the different situations that can occur in an EIS update process. For example:

- If the component contains only references from a single prior EIS, it means that there are no new references in A that share an index value with the references in the prior EIS, thus the prior EIS will not be modified by the update process, and it will also retain its original identifier;
- If the component contains references from one prior EIS together with references from A, then there is the potential that the prior EIS will be updated. It is only a potential update because sharing an index only means a match is possible, but not guaranteed. Whether a match actually occurs will not be known until the references and EIS go into the next step (the ER process) where they are tested according to the identity rules. The input references that don't match the prior EIS, will form one or more new EIS in the output E;
- If the component contains only input references from A, then the references will form one or more new EIS in the resolution process that follows and will not update any prior EIS;
- It is also possible that a component could include references along with more than one EIS. This would mean that there is the potential that some combination of the prior EIS may be merged into a single EIS should they match with the same reference in the resolution process that follows, i.e. undergo transitive closure.

In the next step of the process in Figure 5, the connected components are distributed to the individual ER processes by D2. If a component contains references from prior EIS, the ER process must first reconstruct the prior EIS from the serialized information in the ContentString. In this way, the integrity of the prior EIS from D is preserved as is its identifier. Next the individual ER process (ERPx) runs a normal update process using the reconstructed EIS and any input references from A in the component given to it as input.

The last step is to collect all of the EIS generated from the individual ER processes into a single identity knowledgebase E. Because the overall process is based on pre-resolution index closure, no post-resolution reconciliation in necessary, i.e. the EIS coming from the individual ER processes are all disjoint, and the update process is complete.

Identity Capture and Update for Attribute-Based Resolution

Everything described to this point has assumed that the overall and individual ER processes are using record-based resolution. In the case the attribute-based resolution, the purely sequential workflows given so far will not always work correctly. The reason is that in attribute-based resolution, the matching process is not just between two references, it is between references and EIS.

In particular, if a reference is integrated into an EIS, this may cause the updated EIS to match other references that it did not match prior to the update. This creates a problem for both the pre- and post-resolution closure methods. For example in the pre-resolution index closure workflows shown in Figures 4 and 5, the index values are generated from the input references and prior EIS before starting the ER process. This is not a problem in record-based resolution because the connected components are sufficient to contain all of the possible matches among the input references and prior EIS in the component.

However in the case of attribute-based resolution, if a reference updates (i.e. merged into) an EIS during the resolution process, the updated EIS can potentially generate new index values that would not have been generated by the EIS before the update. These new, post-resolution index values may connect this EIS with other input references or EIS that were not included in the component during the transitive closure step that took place before the EIS was updated.

One solution for the attribute-based resolution problem is to simply iterate the pre-resolution update workflow given in Figure 5. This workflow already assumes that EIS from previous processes are (or can be) included as part of the input. If any prior EIS are included in the input, then index values are generated for these EIS by the IXG processes before starting the transitive index closure step. Figure 6 shows how the workflow from Figure 5 can be adapted to attribute-based resolution.

In the case of attribute-based resolution, the first step is the same as for record-based resolution. The set of references (A) and any prior EIS (D) are the inputs that produce the new set of EIS in E. The workflow in Figure 6 also assumes that both the IXG and ER processes are properly configured for attribute-based resolution. During the first step, if any EIS have been created, updated, or merged with other EIS, then E, the output from Step 1, is used as the input for a second process in Step 2.

Figure 6. Attribute-based resolution workflow for identity update

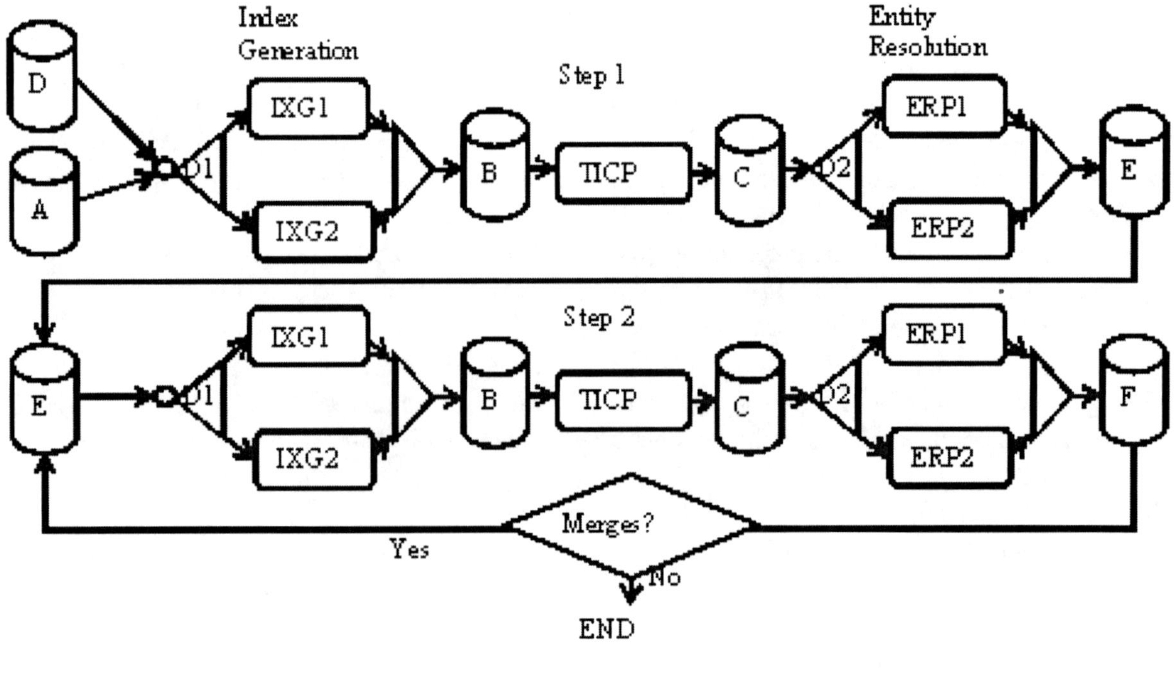

In Step 2, all of index values are generated for the EIS in E followed by the transitive closure and the resolution process output to F. If during the Step 2 process some of the EIS in E are merged, then F must now become the input to Step 2, and Step 2 is repeated until there are no merges. The same process shown in Figure 6 also works for attribute-based identity capture. The only difference is that the input to Step 1 is only the set of reference A and there is no set D of prior EIS. Again, Step 2 must be repeated until there are no merges of EIS from E, i.e. E and F are the same.

CONCLUSION

ER and EIIM are practical in a distributed computing environment by partitioning the data based on inverted index values. The keys to success are starting with properly rule-to-index alignment and understanding whether the processes are based on record-based or attribute-based resolution. In the case of simple record linking (identity capture) either pre-resolution transitive closure of index values or post-resolution transitive closure of link values is sufficient. However for the EIIM update configuration, pre-resolution transitive closure is more practical.

Although the principals are outlined in the workflows, lots of details must be addressed in actually adapting an existing ER system to a distributed environment. The workflows presented here assume that the index generation logic used in the ER process can be duplicated in a separated index generation process. For systems where the index generation logic is embedded in the ER logic, this may be difficult to achieve. The workflow for the update configuration presented here also assumes that the prior EIS are carried along in the process as a serialized string object. For some systems this may not be practical and references to individual EIS or an external repository of EIS may be a better solution. However, approaches that require all distributed processes to access a common location violates the spirit of many distributed environments such as Hadoop that are most efficient where communication between storage blocks or between storage blocks and external storage impair efficiency.

FUTURE RESEARCH DIRECTIONS

The next steps of this research are to implement the identity capture and update workflows in a distributed environment. The initial candidate for the ER process for the research is OYSTER, an open source entity resolution system that supports EIIM and also supports both record-based and attributed-based resolution (Talburt & Zhou, 2013). Work is currently underway to create these workflows using OYSTER as the ER process and Hadoop Map/Reduce as the distributed processing environment which has been used by the Saarland University research group (Dittrich et al, 2012).

REFERENCES

Bianco, G. D., Galante, R., & Heuser, C. A. (2011). A fast approach for parallel deduplication on multicore processors. In *Proceedings of SAC'11*. TaiChung, Taiwan: SAC.

Borgman, C., & Siegfried, S. (1992). Getty's synonameTM and its cousins: A survey of applications of personal name-matching algorithms. *Journal of the American Society for Information Science American Society for Information Science*, *43*(7), 459–476. doi:10.1002/(SICI)1097-4571(199208)43:7<459::AID-ASI1>3.0.CO;2-D

Center for Identity. (2011). *The center for identity risk assessment model (CIRAM)*. Retrieved from http://identity.utexas.edu/research/model

Christen, P. (2006). A comparison of personal name matching: Techniques and practical issues. In *Proceedings of Sixth IEEE International Conference on Data Mining-Workshops* (pp. 290-294). IEEE.

Christen, P. (2012). *Data matching: Concepts and techniques for record linkage, entity resolution, and duplicate detection*. Berlin: Springer.

Christen, P., & Goiser, K. (2007). Quality and complexity measures for data linkage and deduplication. In F. Guillet, & H. Hamilton (Eds.), *Quality measures in data mining, studies in computational intelligence* (Vol. 43, pp. 127–151). Berlin: Springer. doi:10.1007/978-3-540-44918-8_6

Dittrich, J., Quiane-Ruiz, J. A., Richter, S., Schuh, S., Jinal, A., & Schad, J. (2012). Only aggressive elephants are fast elephants. *PVLDB*, *5*(11), 1591–1602.

Fellegi, I., & Sunter, A. (1969). A theory for record linkage. *Journal of the American Statistical Association*, *64*(328). doi:10.1080/01621459.1969.10501049 PMID:12332319

Han, J., & Kamber, M. (2006). *Data mining: Concepts and techniques* (2nd ed.). San Francisco, CA: Morgan Kaufmann.

Herzog, T. N., Scheuren, F. J., & Winkler, W. E. (2007). *Data quality and record linkage techniques*. New York: Springer.

Holmes, D., & McCabe, C. (2002). Improving precision and recall for Soundex retrieval. In *Proceedings of the IEEE International Conference on Information Technology-Coding and Computing*. Las Vegas, NV: IEEE.

Huang, K., Lee, Y. W., & Wang, R. Y. (1999). *Quality information and knowledge management*. Upper Saddle River, NJ: Prentice Hall.

Josang, A., & Pope, S. (2005). User centric identity management. In *Proceedings of AusCERT Conference*. AusCERT.

Kirsten, T., Kolb, L., Hartung, M., Gross, A., Kopche, H., & Rahm, E. (2010). Data partitioning for parallel entity matching. *Proceedings of the VLDB Endowment*, *3*(2).

Kolb, L., Thor, A., & Rahm, E. (2012). Multi-pass sorted neighborhood blocking with MapReduce. *Computer Science Research and Development*, *27*(1).

Levenshtein, V. (1966). Binary codes capable of correcting deletions, insertions and reversals. *Soviet Physics, Doklady*, *10*(8), 707–710.

Loshin, D. (2008). *Master data management*. Knowledge Integrity, Inc.

Maydanchik, A. (2007). *Data quality assessment*. Technics Publications.

McGilvray, D. (2008). *Executing data quality projects: Ten steps to quality data and trusted information*. San Francisco, CA: Morgan Kaufmann.

Naumann, F., & Herschel, M. (2010). An introduction to duplicate detection. In *Synthesis Lectures on Data Management*. New York: Morgan and Claypool Publishers.

Philips, L. (2000). The double-metaphone search algorithm. *C/C++ User's Journal, 18*(6).

Talburt, J., & Zhou, Y. (2013). A practical guide to entity resolution with OYSTER. In S. Sadiq (Ed.), *Handbook on research and practice in data quality*. Berlin: Springer. doi:10.1007/978-3-642-36257-6_11

Talburt, J. R. (2011). *Entity resolution and information quality*. San Francisco, CA: Morgan Kaufmann.

Wang, R. Y. (1998). A product perspective on total data quality management. *Communications of the ACM*, *41*(2), 58–65. doi:10.1145/269012.269022

Whang, S., & Garcia-Molina, H. (2012). Entity resolution with evolving rules. *Proceedings of the VLDB Endowment*, *3*(1-2), 1326–1337.

Yancey, W. (2007). *BigMatch: A program extracting possible matches from a large file*. Washington, DC: Statistical Research Division, U.S. Census Bureau.

Yonke, C. L., Walenta, C., & Talburt, J. R. (2012). *Industry report: The job of the information/data quality professional*. Retrieved from http://iaidq.org/publications/yonke-2011-02.shtml

Zhou, Y., Talburt, J., Su, Y., & Yin, L. (2010). OYSTER: A tool for entity resolution in health information exchange. In *Proceedings of the 5th International Conference on the Cooperation and Promotion of Information Resources in Science and Technology* (pp. 356-362). IEEE.

Zhou, Y., Talburt, J. R., Kobayashi, F., & Nelson, E. (2012). Implementing Boolean matching rules in an entity resolution system using XML scripts. In H. Arabnia, L. Deligiannidis, & R. Hashemi (Eds.), *2012 International Conference on Information and Knowledge Engineering*. Las Vegas, NV: CSREA Press.

Zhou, Z., & Talburt, J. R. (2011). Entity identity information management. In *Proceedings of 16th International Conference on Information Quality* (pp. 327-34). Adelaide, Australia: Electronic Media.

Zobel, J., & Moffat, A. (2006). Inverted files for text search engines. *ACM Computing Surveys*, *38*(2), 6. doi:10.1145/1132956.1132959

KEY TERMS AND DEFINITIONS

Entity Resolution (ER): The process of determining whether two references to real-world objects in an information system are referring to the same object, or to different objects.

Entity Identity Information Management (EIIM): The collection and management of identity information with the goal of sustaining entity identity integrity over time.

Match Key: A string of characters generated by applying algorithms (hash functions) to selected attribute values in a reference and concatenating the results in a fixed order.

Inverted Index: A data structure that associates each match key with all of the references that generate that key.

Distributed Processing: A method for reducing the run-time of a process by using more than one processor to share the computational workload.

Data Partitioning: A strategy for distributed processing in which the input data is divided into segments that are worked on by different processors.

Transitive Closure: The partitioning of a set of records into maximal subsets that share an undirected, pair-wise relationship such as matching.

Chapter 18
A Dual-Database Trusted Broker System for Resolving, Protecting, and Utilizing Multi-Sourced Data

Neal Gibson
Arkansas Research Center, USA

Greg Holland
Arkansas Research Center, USA

ABSTRACT

A longitudinal database structure, which allows for the joining of data between disparate systems and government agencies, is outlined. While this approach is specific to government agencies, many of the ideas implemented are from the commercial world and have relevance to problems associated with data integration in all domains. The goal of the system is to allow for the sharing of data between agencies while upholding the strictest interpretations of rules and regulations protecting individual privacy and confidentiality. The ability to link records over time is central to such a system, so a knowledge-based approach to entity resolution is outlined along with how this system that integrates longitudinal data from multiple sources can still protect individual privacy and confidentiality. Central to this protection is that personally identifiable information should not be proliferated on multiple systems. The system, TrustEd, is a hybrid model that provides the simplicity of a centralized model with the privacy protection of a federated model.

DOI: 10.4018/978-1-4666-4892-0.ch018

INTRODUCTION

The majority of state governments are for the first time creating interagency data systems that link data from disparate agencies together. The purpose of these systems is to measure the outcomes of publically funded programs, for example, how college graduates are faring in the workforce. The creation of such systems raises a number of concerns about privacy and confidentiality, and there are numerous regulations regarding how each agency's data must be handled. Such integrated systems also represent a number of technical hurdles as well, especially in terms of matching records to individuals over a long time span.

The architecture of one such system, TrustEd, is described in detail. Its design addresses both privacy and technical issues. While this solution is specific to a single state, the issues involved and solutions developed have significance for any organization that must integrate data from multiple disparate systems. A great deal of the research for this system revolved around identity management. The two main issues are how to get the best possible match rates and how to manage changes once a bad match is discovered. At the center of the design is the protection of individual privacy and confidentiality, achieved through a dual-database design which keeps personally identifiable information (PII) and the data for research in separate systems.

BACKGROUND

There has been a push in recent years for government agencies to share data, especially at the federal level. The impetus for this was 9/11. Subsequent hearings showed that a number of agencies were aware of and even actively monitoring some of the hijackers involved, but that the full scope of the danger remained somewhat hidden by the fact that data were not being shared between agencies (National Commission on Terrorist Attacks Upon the United States [9/11 Commission], 2004, p. 79). The response was to create an "Information Sharing Environment," to facilitate the exchange and integration of data on matters dealing with national security (http://www.ise.gov/). The federal government has also encouraged state agencies to share data, by awarding funds through competitive grants for states to create longitudinal data systems through which such programs as Early Learning, K12 Education, Higher Education, and Workforce can be integrated into what are known as state P20W systems. The U.S. Department of Education and the U.S. Department of Workforce have provided significant grant monies to encourage states to integrate data from early childhood, elementary and secondary education, higher education, and workforce.

Two general models are being used by states to create these longitudinal systems that can track individuals from early learning programs, on to school and college, and their outcomes in the workforce (Garcia & L'Orange, 2012, p. 13). A centralized model is the simplest, where data is brought together in a central data warehouse. For the purposes of privacy, PII can be stripped from the data and a unique identifier used to link data together. A federated model allows agencies to retain the data within their institutions, and a system is put in place to allow for the querying of data across disparate systems.

Issues and Problems: Privacy

Initiatives which link data from multiple agencies give rise to questions regarding privacy. While the term "privacy" is often used as a general term to cover a host of topics, it is important to differentiate between privacy and confidentiality. The difference between the two, as Kenneth Prewitt, former Director of the U.S. Census Bureau, states is between *"don't ask"* and *"don't tell"* (Prewitt, 2011, p. 42). Data breaches, such as the theft of a laptop from the Bureau of Veterans affairs which contained the names, dates of birth, and Social

Security Numbers (SSN) for 26.5 million veterans in 2006 represent confidentiality problems. The veterans entrusted the bureau not to disclose information about them that could be used to steal their identity. There were not questions as to whether or not the Bureau needed these data to serve veterans' needs. This breach does drive home the point that that such sensitive data should be secured through basic techniques such as encryption.

In contrast, the issue of privacy, "*don't ask*," is central to discussions concerning the joining of data between different agencies. While a citizen may not have an issue with giving an agency their personal information in order to receive services, such transactions usually do not include warnings that such data may be shared with other agencies. In fact, few citizens are aware that data they submit to one agency might be shared with another. This represents a clear privacy issue. As a veteran, I allowed an institution to collect data about myself in order to receive services. I did not authorize that institution to share my data with other institutions which may also have information about me. In private life, we are often given a choice as to whether or not data about ourselves can be shared with others, but such choices are not always available in dealing with government agencies.

A system entrusted with any private data should protect both confidentiality and privacy. In terms of confidentiality, the best protection would be to store no PII information in the system. The laptop containing the PII of 26.5 million veterans probably didn't need SSNs or even names. A unique identifier in place of all the PII would still allow for research while making the consequences of these data possibly being exposed much less severe. If data is to be integrated from multiple agencies, then such a system should not proliferate the existence of PII on yet more systems.

To protect privacy, a system that integrates data from multiple agencies should not allow for the joining of data between agencies unless a specific research topic or reporting request needs answered. In other words, to protect the privacy of individuals who have data in multiple agencies, the system should not allow for someone to play "Go Fish." The right to individual privacy trumps any need say a researcher might have to "explore" the data. The system's architecture should reflect that these data from disparate agencies should remain separate but allowed to be joined together for approved specific purposes.

Whichever model is chosen for the development of the system, data governance plays a key role. Agencies are often not allowed to share data with each other directly, so a third party of some kind is most often needed, to serve as the trusted broker for data integration. It is the trusted broker's responsibility to ensure both privacy and confidentiality and that all regulations concerning these data are being followed. Ownership of the data still resides with the data provider. The trusted broker serves to extend the capacity for what can be done with such data.

Issues and Problems: Identity Management

Obviously it is personally identifiable information which allows data to be matched between agencies. At the heart of such matching is the SSN, which in most states will allows, for example, a link between data about higher education and workforce. Depending upon the data source, the accuracy of SSN numbers varies wildly. Too much reliance upon SSN as part of a matching system is fraught with problems, not only in the possibility of confidentiality breaches. While match rates may seem suitable for research purposes, it should be a common goal to have match rates as high as reasonably possible. This problem requires using some kind of process to analyze a combination of entity attributes to determine matches between records. This is especially important in longitudinal data systems, as many individualws may change their name over time.

Traditional matching processes are often "merge/purge" affairs, where two sets of data are brought together and the data merged on records where attribute values match and all others discarded (Herzog, Scheuren and Winkler, 2007). This is not the best approach for historical data because of the name problems cited above. A more comprehensive approach would be to use a knowledgebase to maintain all representations of an entity, so when a record is processed that contains a new last name for an individual, the system can make note of that and be prepared for when another record has the new last name.

This knowledgebase approach lends itself to the creation of what is referred to in the medical field as an Enterprise Master Patient Index (EMPI), the creation of a single ID for an individual that is used across an organization ("Enterprise Master Patient Index," n.d.). At the state level, it would be relatively easy to create a new unique ID for an individual which was not an SSN, which they could use to access services and which could be used to bring data together for research. However, proliferation of such an ID would only be trading in one confidentiality problem for another. If this new unique ID is ever compromised, whoever has access to that ID would possibly also have access to lots of information about an individual.

This master index of individuals, all known representations of an entity, is crucial for the creation of a longitudinal data system that will hold data from multiple agencies. However, there is no need for a new ID to be given to citizens and agencies. This ID can be used solely in the multi-agency longitudinal data system to link agency data together. Unfortunately, if there is a single ID across all agencies we create an opportunity for Go Fish. To respect individual privacy by maintaining these data in disparate systems requires a unique architecture.

A similar problem was faced by Acxiom, a marketing services provider headquartered in Little Rock, Arkansas, which has annual revenues exceeding $1 billion. Acxiom maintains multiple databases of consumer information, which it can combine with a client's customer data to provide marketing insight and other uses. If Acxiom were to use a single ID to manage both its internal processes and to provide to clients for customer integration, that client could possibly combine their data from Acxiom with data from a different client from Acxiom but which uses this same single ID. Such collaboration would represent lost business opportunities for Acxiom.

Issues and Problems: Entity Matching Rules

The goal of identity resolution is to replicate and automate processes and algorithms for determining identity. At each step in the process of developing and applying business rules for consolidation of entities and identity resolution, it should be asked, "Would a knowledgeable data manager, domain expert, or reasonable third-party conclude that two entities are actually the same individual?" If so, those entities should be combined in the knowledgebase. Would the same party conclude that a match had been found between an input record and a record in the knowledgebase? If so, the matching identifier from the knowledgebase should be applied to the input record. How would this example person reach their conclusion? Those decision-making steps should be clearly-defined, replicated and automated. Exact matching is the traditional plan, but inexact or "fuzzy" matching must also be included in a complete identity resolution system. No single query or function is likely to emulate the full decision-making process, so a series of steps with if-then-else logic will be required.

When a record containing PII is provided to the knowledgebase, there are three potential outcomes of identity resolution. The first (and preferred) outcome is "single match", where the identification system finds one-and-only-one identity from the knowledgebase to assign. The two other outcomes are "no match" (zero matches) and "ambiguous match" (two or more potential matches). Both of these other outcomes impact the ability of the trusted broker system to provide identifiers on 100% of data. An early decision for identity resolution systems is the determination of whether each record must receive an identifier during the process, and the overall system will be reliant upon whichever decision is made.

In the case of a "no match", one identity resolution approach is to generate an identifier using some combination of attribute values available, which may be the PII values or even a hash of an arbitrary record number. These types of dynamically-assigned identifiers can be problematic both immediately and long-term. Immediate problems occur when the same individual is recorded twice within the data source being processed. The two identifiers assigned dynamically may not match, resulting in two apparent individuals where only one exists. The long-term problem occurs when dynamically-assigned identifiers are stored and attempted to match against future processed data. If the dynamic assigning of identifiers utilizes either a different method or different attribute values, it is unlikely that the individual will maintain a consistent identifier in longitudinal systems.

The problem of "ambiguous matching" occurs when more than one entity from the knowledgebase is a potential match for an individual. These types of ambiguous matches occur primarily as a result of incomplete PII. For example, twins will share a date of birth and surname. Often, twins' first names are very similar, either rhyming or sharing an initial. In the event that a match is needed for only the first initial with the last name and date of birth, there may be two individuals in the knowledgebase who are potential matches. Additionally, common last names may share a date of birth and first initial for individuals who are not related. One approach to the problem of ambiguous matches is simply to select one from the available matching entities, either selecting the first entity found, selecting randomly, or establishing some sort of priority or scoring algorithm. While these methods may have benefits, including higher overall match rates, it is very likely that error will be introduced.

Another approach to both the "no match" scenario and the "ambiguous matching" scenario is to return no identifier from the trusted broker system. While these records would still be included in an agency's database for the purposes of aggregate statistics, joining between records without an identifier might be excluded. However, it is often more advantageous to allow a field to have null values than to imply certainty where it is not justified.

Issues and Problems: Splits and Consolidations

The ability to merge data sets is central to the creation of a longitudinal data system. All organizations that keep records on individuals have some level of problems with identity management. A person may use different first names depending on the situation, and life changes may prompt the changing of the last name. As mentioned previously, the SSN can be an unreliable identifier because of simple data entry problems. Once an SSN number is mistakenly entered into a system for a person, that wrong SSN will most likely never been updated, and all of an individual's records in that system over time will all have that wrong SSN. Such a problem with an SSN will not necessarily be apparent because it could still uniquely identify the individual from within that system. However, when there is an attempt to link such a record with data from another agency where the SSN is correct, the records will not be linkable.

Over time, information used to identify an individual may change. However, if the system used for linking data together can gain knowledge about an individual over time, these changes can be incorporated into the criteria used for identification and records can be matched regardless of whatever particular identity information is being used at the time. Such knowledge works both backwards and forward in time.

Since the system is always expanding its knowledge of individuals, new "truths" about individuals will be discovered over time. For example, you might incorporate a new record which tells you that William Ray and Billy Ray are actually two different individuals, even though you had previously brought those two individuals together as the same person. You might also discover a new record that links Elizabeth Smith and Beth Jones together as the same person, even though up to that time the system had kept them as separate individuals. As such, the system needs some way to manage identities, to handle changes that arise when new records either consolidate together what were once believed to be two different individuals into a single entity or split apart records that were originally believed to belong to the same individual.

The building blocks of an identity manager are entities, all representations of an individual brought together based on whatever rules were implemented. If a new identity record comes in and the system cannot find a match with any existing records, the system will generate a new entity ID for this record. When the system does find a match for a new record, the entity ID generated from previous records is appended to the new record. There is no need to keep multiple records of the same entity information for an individual, so only new representations of any attributes are saved. For example, when a new record indicates that Katherine Smith also goes by "Kate," you only need to append that new first name field for Katherine's knowledgebase entity ID.

Solutions and Recommendations: Format Preserving Encryption

Knowledgebase IDs are only used internally to the system and never exposed. A system for assigning agency specific IDs is needed to append to the research data in order that it can be linked. A simple way to do this would be through some form of a hash specific to each agency. However, research into this method revealed U.S. Patent number 6523041, which outlines a similar process Acxiom uses to assign customer "tokens," essentially a reversible encryption of the knowledgebase ID specific to each customer, in order that an Acxiom customer would be unable to share their data with another Acxiom customer (U.S. Patent No.6523041, 2003). While the topic of software patents is somewhat controversial, it is best to avoid potential problems. A simple lookup table, which can be stored in a system and used to create a crosswalk as needed to link data between different agencies, will achieve the same effect.

Each identity is determined by the knowledgebase identification manager (KIM), while the identifiers to be utilized are determined by the trusted-broker identifier manager (TIM). The trusted-broker identifier manager utilizes format-preserving encryption, a method to transform a character string of length n into an encrypted character string, also length n. Traditional hashing methods often result in a character string which is a different length than the original input, and may need to be truncated to achieve consistent lengths. Truncation of encrypted strings may result in inadvertent duplication of identifiers. Format preserving encryption allows identifiers from various agencies to maintain a single format, providing a consistent data definition and structure across various agency databases, without introducing possible duplication.

Again, the goal of this system is to allow for the joining of data between disparate government agencies, but to do so only temporarily as needed for specific reporting or research needs. The databases which contain the research data with agency specific IDs have no way to join different agencies' data together, so there are no opportunities for Go Fish. While the data is deidentified, there is no PII data contained within the research databases, this does not mean that an individual cannot be identified from the data. If I am at a school with only one Asian student and I see anonymized data for my school that includes records for a single Asian student, I know to which student those records belong.

The eventual end state for this system would be an automated process whereby agencies would maintain their own research databases, submitting files to be processed by TrustEd via an SOA model, and receiving back records where the PII has been stripped and replaced with an agency-specific ID. The agencies involved in the sharing agreement would maintain these research databases but expose them for queries from TrustEd. The system could also suppress information such as the example above, where the data is deidentified but where the individual is statistically knowable.

Solutions and Recommendations: TrustEd

TrustEd (see Figure 1) uses a dual database architecture to provide for the integration of data among multiple agencies. The PII, name, date of birth, SSN, etc., are kept separate from data that is used for research. Research data from each agency is maintained in a federated model, with each agency having its own separate database and an agency specific ID for their records. Again, no PII data is contained with the agency's research database. An agency specific ID, used only for the purposes of this P20W system, is generated as part of the process by which data is submitted to the system.

TrustEd is composed of three loosely coupled systems, a Knowledgebase Identity Manger (KIM), a TrustEd Identifier Manager (TIM), and the research databases. When data is submitted to TrustEd, it is first loaded to TIM. TIM splits the source data into PII data and research data and appends to both a source ID and record ID. The PII data is sent to KIM, for entity resolution, and the research data is sent to the agency's research database. Once KIM has determined matches for the records, it assigns a KIM ID and sends this back with the source ID and record ID to TIM. TIM can then take this KIM ID and generate an agency specific ID using format preserving encryption, which it then can append to the research data.

Figure 1. Workflow for TrustEd

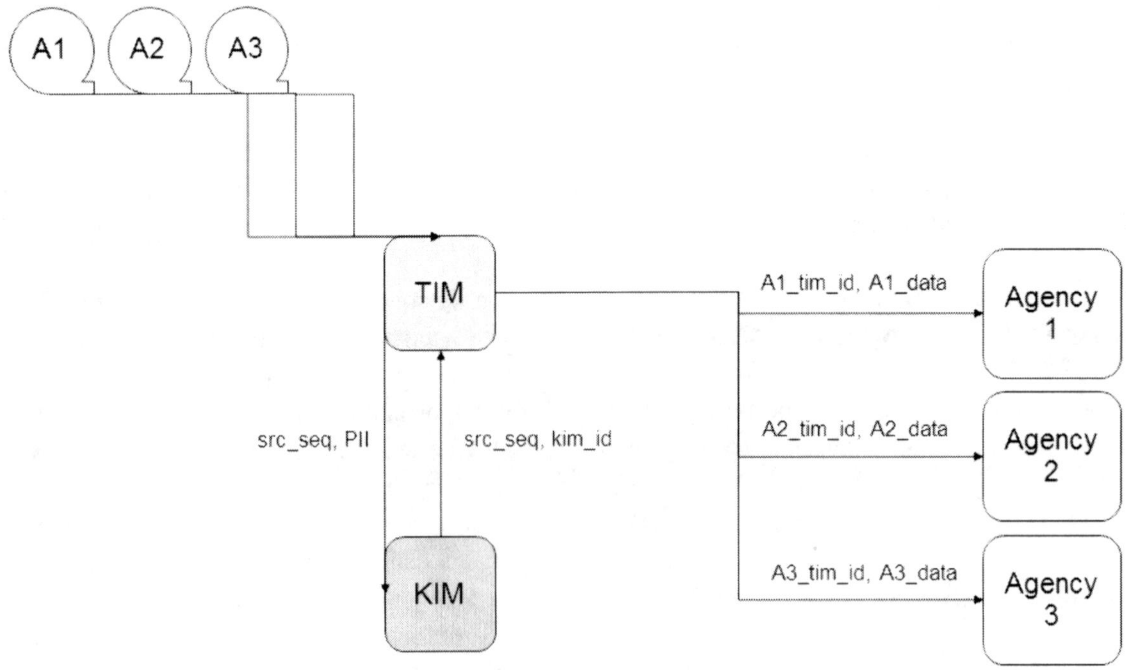

The PII data, without any context for such agency specific things as grades or wages, is maintained in one system, while the data of research interest remains deidentified in a separate system.

Because the agency research data exists in separate databases without a common ID, the linking of data between two different agencies purposely requires an extra step. By design, the architecture of the system requires a specific crosswalk of IDs to be generated by TIM for the purposes of joining data between two agencies, and the crosswalk is destroyed once the result set is generated. This extra step is a design element to prohibit Go Fish.

Output from TrustEd can take multiple forms, depending upon need and what is allowed by regulation. Consider a report on how recent college graduates are faring in the workplace. Data from higher education is combined with data from workforce. TrustEd could provide these data at the individual student level and with a higher education ID, it could return individual student level data with a new ID specific to this research request, it could provide individual student level data without any PII or ID and in a random order, or it could provide the results as aggregates.

What should be clear from this simple description that for TrustEd, TIM is the trusted broker. TIM does not contain either PII or research data. It instead facilitates the assignment and encryption of identifiers, which allows for the separation of PII and deidentified research data. It also allows for the joining of disparate data between different agencies, while at the same time prohibiting research queries which do not have a specific approved purpose and authorization.

Solutions and Recommendations: Splits and Consolidations

In the event that two entities in KIM are later determined to be the same entity, the consolidation of those two entities to a single identifier could be reported to TrustEd users through a simple notification of TIM ID update. That is to say, TrustEd users could be informed that all instances of TIM ID 2 should be updated to TIM ID 1. In simple terms, this consolidation represents a case of "all B are also A, therefore, replace B with A". The problem of entity consolidations is significantly easier to solve than the problem of entity splitting.

In the event that one entity in KIM is later determined to be two different entities, the only way to propagate the resulting entity splitting information to TrustEd users is to utilize the log of source and sequence for input records to TIM. Having a record of which KIM Record Sequence ID was matched during the KIM processing of the Agency Source would allow reporting of the correct KIM Entity ID to be updated in TrustEd users' data. In simple terms, this split represents a case of "some A are actually B, therefore, replace some A with B". It is not possible to know which of the split entities belongs to B and which belongs to A without also knowing the original KIM Record Sequence ID. Each KIM Entity ID is shared by one or more KIM Record Sequence IDs. When an entity split occurs, some KIM Record Sequence IDs will not change, and some KIM Record Sequence IDs will change to a new (second) KIM Entity ID.

The TIM logs allow TrustEd to know which KIM Record Sequence ID within the knowledgebase matched to the original source file record. After the entity splitting process, some KIM Entity IDs have been updated to the new (second) entity ID, and those KIM Record Sequence IDs point to the new KIM entity ID. Records which originally pointed to the affected KIM Record Sequence IDs in the TIM logs can be targeted for update in the TrustEd users' data, without ambiguity.

FUTURE RESEARCH DIRECTIONS

The current state of the system, disparate research databases, each with an agency specific ID to prevent the unauthorized joining of data, is a simplified model of what a dynamic trusted broker system implementation might look like in the near future. The current TrustEd model does reflect the federated nature of the agencies involved, and ownership of the data provided remains with the agency. However, since the data is now being held by a third party, TrustEd, an agency does not have complete control of what may be happening with their data offsite. If instead the agency could retain physical control of the data they allow to become part of this interagency system, then they have complete control and ownership. However, such a system is much more complicated on a technical level.

TrustEd could be reconfigured to offer integration through a Service Oriented Architecture (SOA) model. True SOA implementation would require an enterprise architecture. This is somewhat unrealistic at this time for most states and even many large-scale enterprises. In fact, the data warehousing domain is ripe with the number of large-scale implementations which have failed spectacularly (Gootman, 2008, p. 1). TrustEd's current implementation is something of a preliminary step toward the development of a full SOA implementation. In fact, a great deal of the work needed for the creation of an enterprise architecture is contained within the steps needed for TrustEd, to get agreements in place and the data conformed to a consistent and standardized form.

The two competing data models in the domain of interagency data sharing, centralized and federated, both have advantages. A centralized model, housing data from multiple agencies in a deidentified state in a central repository, is much simpler to implement. However, since the data from different agencies are all in a single system with a common unique identifier, the architecture lends itself to the unauthorized joining of data instead of requiring a predefined research request. This invites the opportunity to Go Fish. In contrast, a federated model allows agencies to retain both virtual and physical ownership of the data by allowing an external entity to perform the linking. This is a much more complicated model, requiring a great deal of enterprise architecture to implement in a successful manner.

TrustEd is a hybrid of both, or perhaps better understood as a preliminary step on the journey toward a fully automated, comprehensive, SOA approach to a federated longitudinal data system which fully supports agency autonomy as well as individual privacy and confidentiality. The basis for an enterprise architecture is the initial work needed to implement the current model of TrustEd, data sharing agreements, extracts and transformations to present the data in a standardized form, and actual use of the data. It is recognized that iterative development, driven by actual use of the system, offers the best development path for such large scale systems ("Best practice: Develop iteratively," 2011).

The creation of state interagency data systems is relatively new, their creation spurred on by recent federal grants. At the same time, there is a shifting regulatory framework in which these systems will operate. For example, the U.S. Department of Education has recently revised rules regarding FERPA ("Revised FERPA Regulations," 2011). One of the primary changes was to redefine what could be identified as an "Authorized Representative" for the purposes of handling education data. This was to provide flexibility for states trying to create interagency data systems that included education data but which existed outside the existing formal K12 and post-secondary framework. Under the revised regulations, a state can now designate a third party, such as the state's technology authority, as an authorized representative to have education data ("Safeguarding Student Privacy," 2011, p. 7).

The other major change brought by the revised regulations was to allow for student data to "flow backward." Under previous FERPA regulations, a student's data "followed the child." As a student moved from elementary to secondary and on to college, each new institution the student enrolled at could see that student's historical records, but the previous institutions were not allowed to receive feedback on how that student did once they left their school. New regulations allow for such feedback, so early learning programs can understand how well prepared their students were for kindergarten, for a high school to know how well their former students were doing in college, and for colleges to know how their students are doing in the workplace.

In this changing regulatory framework, agility should be a key design feature. New purposes for the use of these data will be proposed as the use of interagency data becomes more standard, and the system will need to be able to respond. There will also likely be requests for other agencies' data to be integrated, and the system will need to be flexible in order to incorporate data that, for example, might not have an SSN. New regulations address data going back to previous institutions at the individual level, which means the system will also need some way to transform what was previously deidentified research data into merged records that include name and other PII. It would be difficult to design a system that plans to become active in say two years, when the regulatory framework in which this system will operate is likely to change during that time.

CONCLUSION

The design and implementation of TrustEd addresses both the privacy and technical issues. Identity management is achieved through entity matching rules, facilitating appropriate splits and consolidations. Privacy and confidentiality are protected using format preserving encryption and separated agency identifiers. The dual database architecture ensures separation of PII and deidentified agency data, and the trusted broker allows approved research to be conducted via temporary identifier crosswalks. The TrustEd solution has met all of the existing goals for the state's multi-agency longitudinal data system. While this solution is specific to a single state, the issues involved and solutions developed have significance for any organization that must integrate data from multiple disparate systems.

REFERENCES

Best Practice: Develop Iteratively. (2011). Retrieved from http://www.upedu.org/references/bestprac/im_bp1.htm

Enterprise Master Patient Index. (n.d.). Retrieved from http://en.wikipedia.org/wiki/Enterprise_master_patient_index

Garcia, T. I., & L'Orange, H. P. (2012). *The state of postsecondary data systems*. Retrieved from http://www.sheeo.org/sites/default/files/publications/20130107%20StrongFoundationsUpdate_FinalcNoAppendices.pdf

Gootman, E. (2008, October 23). As schools face cuts, delays on data system bring more frustration. *The New York Times*, pp. 1-2. Retrieved from http://www.nytimes.com

Herzog, T., Scheuren, F., & Winkler, W. E. (2007). *Data quality and record linkage techniques*. Oxford, UK: Oxford University Press.

Morgan, C., Talley, T., Talburt, J., Bussell, C., Kooshesh, A., Anderson, W., et al. (2003). *U.S. patent no. 6523041*. Washington, DC: U.S. Patent and Trademark Office.

National Commission on Terrorist Attacks upon the United States. (2004). *The 9/11 commission report*. Retrieved from http://www.9-11commission.gov/report/911Report.pdf

Prewitt, K. (2011). Why it matters to distinguish between privacy & confidentiality. *Journal of Privacy and Confidentiality*, *3*(2), 41–47.

Revised FERPA Regulations: An Overview for SEAs and LEAs. (2011). Retrieved from http://www2.ed.gov/policy/gen/guid/fpco/pdf/sea-lea_overview.pdf

U.S. Department of Education Safeguarding Student Privacy. (2011). Retrieved from http://www2.ed.gov/policy/gen/guid/fpco/ferpa/safeguarding-student-privacy.pdf

KEY TERMS AND DEFINITIONS

Consolidation: The act of joining two or more identity records when two individuals are determined to be the same individual.

Entity: Any real-world person, thing, or organization which needs to be individually identified within a data set.

Format Preserving Encryption (FPE): An algorithm which obscures the original values in a data set by providing unique value substitution in the same format as the original value.

Match Rule: An algorithm which determines if two separate identities should be joined within a data set due to the similarity of data values observed.

Personally-Identifiable Information (PII): Any data value or set of values which are unique to an individual making the real-world identification of the individual within a data set possible.

Split: The act of separating previously-joined identity records when two individuals are determined to exist independently.

Trusted Broker: A third-party system which allows for the integration from disparate systems for which direct sharing is prohibited.

TrustEd: The name given to the trusted broker system described in this chapter.

Chapter 19
Business Intelligence Architecture in Support of Data Quality

Tom Breur
XLNT Consulting, The Netherlands

ABSTRACT

Business Intelligence (BI) projects that involve substantial data integration have often proven failure-prone and difficult to plan. Data quality issues trigger rework, which makes it difficult to accurately schedule deliverables. Two things can bring improvement. Firstly, one should deliver information products in the smallest possible chunks, but without adding prohibitive overhead for breaking up the work in tiny increments. This will increase the frequency and improve timeliness of feedback on suitability of information products and hence make planning and progress more predictable. Secondly, BI teams need to provide better stewardship when they facilitate discussions between departments whose data cannot easily be integrated. Many so-called data quality errors do not stem from inaccurate source data, but rather from incorrect interpretation of data. This is mostly caused by different interpretation of essentially the same underlying source system facts across departments with misaligned performance objectives. Such problems require prudent stakeholder management and informed negotiations to resolve such differences. In this chapter, the authors suggest an innovation to data warehouse architecture to help accomplish these objectives.

DOI: 10.4018/978-1-4666-4892-0.ch019

INTRODUCTION

Companies launch business intelligence projects in pursuit of their broader information governance objectives. To leverage data assets, often some centralized business intelligence competence center (BICC) is appointed, with broad oversight of diverse groups of information consumers. For reasons of consistency and efficiency, often a centralized repository integrated data gets implemented, a data warehouse. To mitigate confusion and drive unified strategy, BICC's will aspire a "single version of the truth" to ensure all departments sing of the same hymn sheet.

Data governance programs invariably (also) want to ensure high data quality. BI projects are sometimes fraught with data quality issues. This could typically be for one of three reasons:

- The content of source system data that was supplied to the date warehouse was inadequate;
- The source system data were accurate, but the data warehouse transformations turned out to be erroneous;
- The content of source data was accurate, and data warehouse transformations were *technically* correct. However, the content of the report did not meet expectations, and further work in exploring requirements and specifying data interpretation should lead to an improved report.

The source of 'errors' in reporting can typically not immediately be known. This needs to be discovered through interaction with end-users of BI reports. This poses considerable risk to progress of data warehouse projects. To mitigate the risks associated with these various sources of data quality issues we propose choosing a hyper normalized data warehouse architecture that will better support resolving of data quality issues associated with such projects.

Business intelligence (BI) projects are risky. According to analyst firms like for instance Gartner, or the Standish Group reports, these projects have petrifying failure rates. In large part, these risks are caused by data quality problems that complicate data integration. When data from disparate business silos are confronted for the first time in the data warehouse, this often surfaces heretofore-unknown data quality issues.

BI teams merely 'hold' corporate data (as in: provide stewardship), they do not 'own' them. However, under organizational pressure to complete a project, they feel sometimes 'forced' into a role of pseudo ownership of data (and accompanying data quality errors) while they struggle to integrate fundamentally misaligned source data in the data warehouse.

This problem can either be mitigated, or exacerbated, depending on the architecture chosen for the data warehouse. An optimal architecture for data warehousing should allow interpretation of data to be left to their owners. This is *not* a responsibility of the BI team. They can facilitate discussions about its content, and shed light on source system characteristics, but the BI team should never be tasked to 'own' (as in: commit to long-term choices) interpretation of data quality problems. Interpretation of data, and decisions on how to deal with data quality errors, should be the realm of (senior) management in charge of the incumbent business silos that control source systems.

To (better) deal with quality issues that arise in the course of data integration, in this chapter I will suggest using an architecture that provides auditable and (easily) traceable data transformations. During project development, data modeling choices need to be changeable (at reasonable cost). Currently, the dominant data warehouse design paradigm (Kimball bus architecture) falls short on providing these features.

Data warehouse requirements, often carry considerable ambiguity. To cope with this ambiguity in requirements and resulting changes in the data integration engineering, I recommend a relatively new hyper normalized data warehouse architecture that enables both incremental development, as well as data model reengineering at limited cost.

BACKGROUND

In this chapter I will explain why hyper normalized hub-and-spoke architectures provide better support for data governance and data quality management, and are also better suited to more agile development of BI solutions. We know from experience that BI requirements are often ambiguous, and therefore amenable to change. That's why you need a modeling paradigm that is resilient to change, and that safeguards against a loss of historical information when changes to the data model need to be made over the course of a complex data integration project.

The raison d'être for an enterprise data warehouse (EDW) is to provide integrated historical data, and to be able to do so for a (relatively) long period of time. As such, an EDW is bound to outlive ever changing operational systems, and ever changing reporting needs. In order to be able to do so, the structure of the data warehouse itself needs to be resilient so that it can gracefully absorb these changes that are entirely expected over the course of its lifetime.

In the 90s an 'ideological war' raged between Bill Inmon and Ralph Kimball, two eminent thought leaders from the early years of data warehousing. It is safe to conclude that Kimball emerged as the 'winner' of this debate. Nowadays, the majority of data warehouse architectures are based on Kimball's proposed "bus architecture", a two-tiered data warehouse architecture.

In this chapter I will recommend a revival of three-tiered data warehouse architectures, also called hub-and-spoke topologies. But contrary to Bill Inmon's (initial) suggestion, I recommend *against* using third normal form as the modeling paradigm for the data warehouse. Instead, I suggest using a hyper normalized data-modeling paradigm for the central hub that was specifically designed for data warehousing. For reasons of maintainability and data governance I recommend implementing business rules only *downstream* from the data warehouse (between data warehouse and data marts).

A two-tiered data warehouse architecture transforms source data in one fell swoop straight into data marts that are directly available to end-users. In a three-tiered architecture, an intermediate layer (the "hub" in a hub-and-spoke topology) is built that is (usually) *not* directly accessible to end-users. From there, data marts are sourced. Controversy between these two schools of thought ("Inmon" versus "Kimball") has been whether this intermediate layer is desirable or unnecessary overhead.

I will demonstrate (using artificially simplified modeling challenges to demonstrate the principle) why third normal form modeling in a data warehouse, does *not* handle change very well. This has to do, among others, with the way Inmon (initially) suggested the time dimension should be modeled into the data warehouse, namely by appending a time stamp to the primary key in a third normal form (3NF) model. This causes serious maintenance problems, as practitioners who tried to implement this approach have discovered. Also, changes in the data model can ripple through existing table structures, and cause considerable maintenance overhead (see Figure 1-2).

In this chapter, I will also explain why Kimball's approach to data warehousing (a two-tiered topology, or so-called bus architecture) has important drawbacks, and is intrinsically non-agile. The *primary* reason for this is that the smallest increment of delivery is a star (dimensional data mart), which is considered too big for frequent and early delivery of value to end-users, as specified by agile principles (Agile Manifesto, 2001). On top of that, the bus architecture forces developers to commit too early which attributes to include, and how to conform dimensions. This

Figure 1. Simplified data model for a business selling products to customers

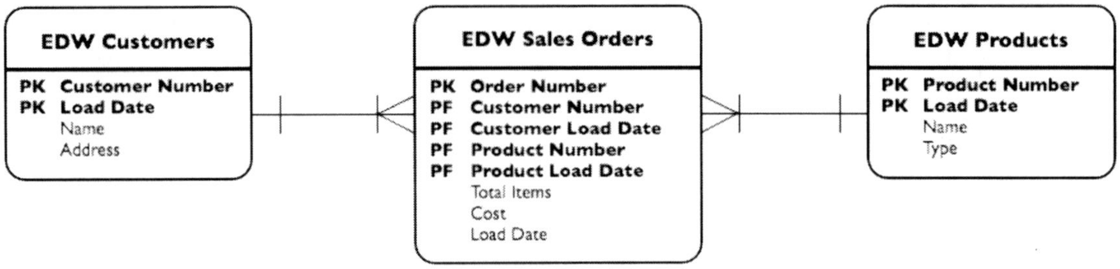

Figure 2. New supplier table

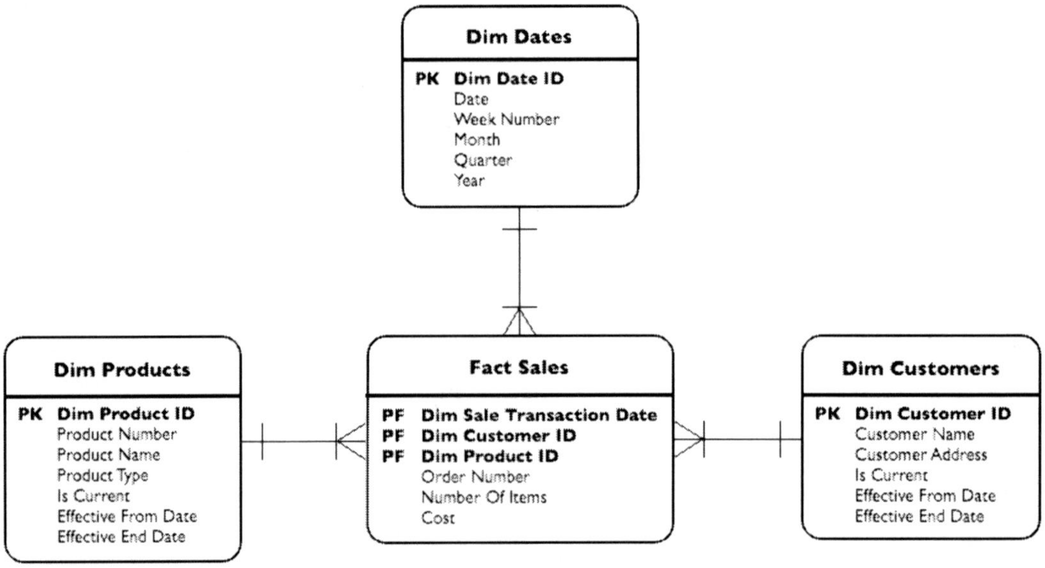

defies the principle of delaying decisions to the last responsible moment (Poppendieck & Poppendieck, 2003).

Nowadays, a number of hyper normalized modeling approaches are available that were specifically designed for data warehousing. Examples are Anchor Modeling, Focal Point Modeling, 2G Modeling, or Data Vault. What these approaches have in common, is that core business entities like "Customer", "Sale", "Shipment", etc., are broken out in multiple tables (hence "hyper normalization"). Connecting these associated tables around some natural business key has been labeled Ensemble Modeling (Hultgren, 2012). The manner and degree to which tables are broken out differs between these approaches, but always enables the data warehouse to cope more gracefully with change.

A thriving community of BI experts have emerged that embrace an approach to data warehousing that is often based on some version of the Data Vault modeling paradigm as first described and advocated by Dan Linstedt (Linstedt, 2011). However, the approach I recommend is in no way tied, nor limited to Data Vault modeling. Instead, I suggest using 'a' hyper normalized paradigm that has been specifically designed for data warehousing.

Because of high standardization and self-similarity within the model (Scholten, 2010), Data Vault modeling is particularly well suited for support by automation tools (Bilali, 2013). This has played a decisive role in its adoption. A number of Open Source and commercially sold tools are available for this, and application of such tools has been shown to dramatically expedite development. Model (meta data) driven design shortens development cycle times and also improves code reusability and maintainability.

One of the alternative approaches to Data Vault modeling for three-tiered architectures for data warehousing is Anchor Modeling, as described by Lars Rönnbäck (Rönnbäck, 2012). A suite of code generation tools are also available for Anchor Modeling. Other structured approaches to hyper normalization for data warehousing are likely to emerge in the future in this young and burgeoning field.

It should be noted here that some Industry Logical Models (ILM's) apply forms of hyper normalization, too. Because these ILM's are commercially sold, their structure unfortunately (mostly) isn't part of the public domain, and for reasons of intellectual property therefore cannot be included in academic publications.

Data integration projects face both technical as well as semantic challenges. The technical challenge is finding suitable business keys to match records belonging together. The semantic challenge is interpreting source facts in line with the meaning business stakeholders associated with them. Bridging the semantic gap from (technical) representation of atomic details into a form that represents the business view on reality is (by far) the most challenging task. BI experts refer to this as the "Big T" (short for transformation).

From a project (risk) management perspective, the most daunting challenge is to clarify detailed specifications of *how* this "Big T" transformation should be done. A three-tiered architecture provides the following benefits for this:

- You break up structural transformation for purposes of efficient storage of history (source to data warehouse) separate from the "Big T" (data warehouse to data marts) so that you 'divide and conquer' the workload. This enables you to efficiently advance development in the smallest possible steps;
- You disentangle historizing detailed storage from aggregation and transformation, which allows you to refer data elements directly back to source files as provided to the data warehouse (traceability);
- You disentangle confounding of *interpretation* by this two-step approach because disputes about accuracy of corporate reporting can be viewed in light of raw data elements provided at a specific point in time by an indentified system, compared to report numbers *after* semantic transformation ("Big T") has taken place. This way you can answer whether the 'bad data' in corporate reports were caused by inaccurate data elements that went *into* the data warehouse, or inappropriate transformations that result in erroneous representation going *out* of the BI system.

THREE-TIERED DATA WAREHOUSE ARCHITECTURE

The Impact of Requirements Changes on Redesign

There are a few reasons why hyper normalized approaches to data modeling for the central hub in a three-tiered data warehouse architecture have proven superior. First of all, in agile fashion, BI developers want to embrace change. Experience has shown that a hyper normalized data modeling paradigm can deal better with changing requirements. I will illustrate this with an example.

The fundamental reason why hyper normalized data models absorb change more gracefully is that core business concepts (so-called business keys) are stored separately from their (historical) descriptive attributes, and separate from interconnected relationships (Hultgren, 2012). The effect this has is that model changes stay (and always will remain) *local* so that later updates don't ripple through the model via parent-child key relations.

In the following example, I will demonstrate how this "insulation" from change works. It becomes manifest in the minimal impact when expanding Figure 6 to Figure 7.

Figure 1 shows a (simplified) data model for a business selling products to customers, firstly modeled in 3NF (Inmon approach to data warehousing):

Now let's suggest a 'late' requirement arrives to also report these sales by supplier. This causes a new "Supplier" table to be added (see Figure 2), but also note how this triggers an update to the keys in the Product and Sales table.

Because in 3NF business keys and relations are stored *together* in one table, changes therefore ripple through the model when parent-child relations propagate updates. This makes it difficult and expensive to contain the risks of (unforeseen) changes in requirements when these impact the structure of the data model. This can easily happen if the scope of requirements change.

3NF modeling is also undesirable for another reason. It makes it hard to determine data model boundaries. That is why it doesn't support incremental development very well, which agile developers value. They want to be able to start very small and efficiently grow in tiny increments, without adding significant overhead because of these 'little baby expansions'.

Because 3NF modeling doesn't facilitate incremental development very well, scoping out small iterations is difficult *and* adds overhead. Data warehouse projects that attempt to 'boil the ocean' take too long to deliver value, and fail to reassure stakeholders about progress because they cannot demonstrate tangible results early on. Big releases also bombard developers with change requests during the testing phase. This is less than prudent given known project risks in BI.

The previous reengineering problem would look slightly different in a dimensional model (see Figure 3) (Kimball approach to data warehousing).

If the supplier data have a one-to-one relation to products (each product is procured from only one supplier), they could get added to this data model by 'simply' appending suppliers to the product dimension. This results in the diagram shown in Figure 4.

This would constitute only a small change to the data warehouse. All this requires is that the ETL for the product dimension needs to be updated, and (besides possible impact on downstream reporting) the data warehouse could continue to run very much just like before. When business stakeholders assure this one-to-one relation between product and supplier always holds, many BI teams would happily implement this solution.

Drawbacks of Implementing Business Rules in the Data Warehouse

The design in Figure 4 works fine if, and only if the one-to-one relation between product and supplier is maintained for *all* products. This might well be a viable solution in an operational system, because in most operational systems there is not too much concern for historical changes. You are typically concerned with ensuring the right supplier gets marked for each product, and the fact that a product might have been procured from different suppliers over time is (usually) less of a concern (for operational purposes).

But there is another, more subtle problem with the solution in Figure 4, one that is of major concern from a data governance perspective. The relation between product and supplier is now 'hard wired' into the structure of the data warehouse. What this effectively does is that it *enforces* a structure on

Figure 3. Dimensional model

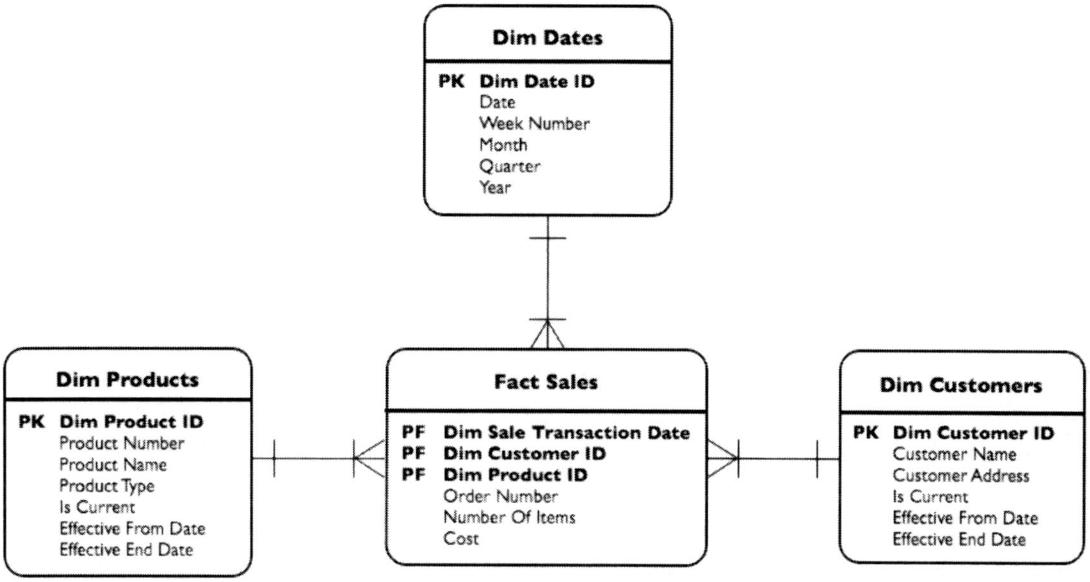

Figure 4. Updated dimensional model

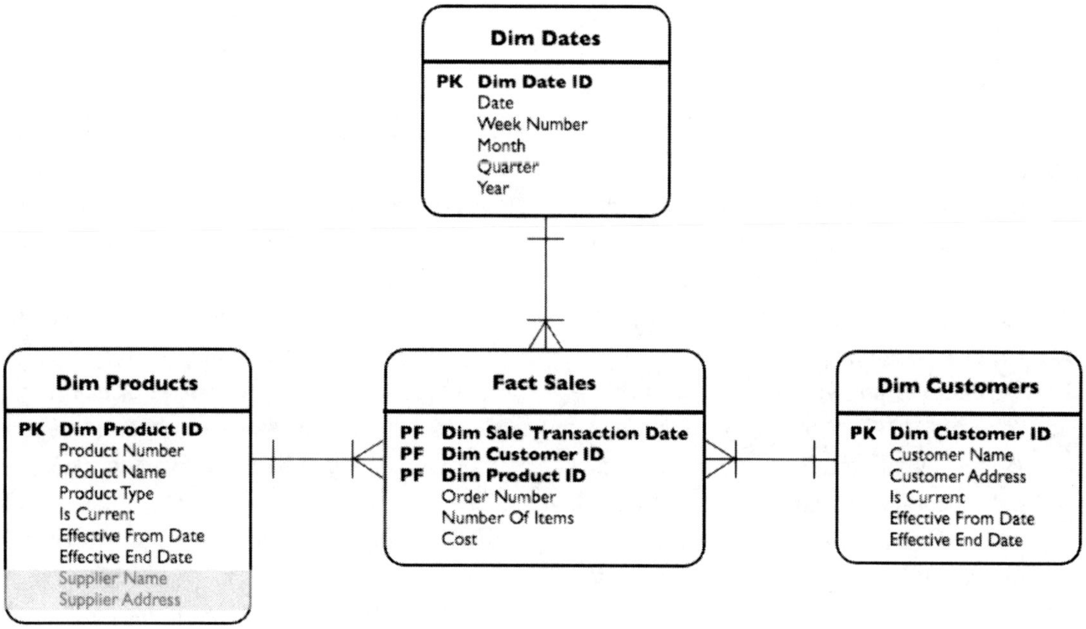

data arriving into the data warehouse. But this is not the role of the BI team, to enforce what is or is not allowed to happen in source systems.

BI professionals should report what has happened, not impose rules on what is 'allowed' to happen in real life. The former is the role of BI professionals; the latter is the responsibility of business management. In fact, it is important that a BI team retains the capability to report on what *has* happened (including exceptions), even though such events *should* not happen. The BI team should always strive to remain data agnostic, or else they would risk loosing their independence.

When business rules are imposed on data arriving into the data warehouse, the affected data are not loaded into the data warehouse, but instead are dropped in exception reports during loading of the data warehouse. Auditability in the data warehouse is lost, and the independence of the BI team is compromised. There are also other concerns with implementing business rules upstream from the data warehouse that I will address in the section "Consequences of business rules upstream from a data warehouse."

The Impact of Requirements Changes on Redesign (Continued)

When products can be procured from several suppliers, *and* the business would like to make comparisons across suppliers, then the solution in Figure 4 does not work. What is needed in a dimensional model is adding a supplier dimension. Note that in this scenario, the impact would be considerable. Updating the "Product" table here, *also* affects the grain in the central fact table. Before this change there was only one record per product in the "Sales" fact table. After adding the "Supplier" dimension, there will be separate records for every supplier (see Figure 5).

This problem is known, and has been documented (Mundy, 2012). It results in redoing the initial load of the data warehouse. For large data volumes, this becomes a (very) resource intensive task. Because data volumes grow over time, the cost of redoing this initial load also grows over time.

Another reason why redoing the initial load is so daunting, is because changes in the structure of the source files, or, changes in the way their content should be interpreted, require going through multiple versions of extract, transform, load (ETL) packages as used over time. For sequential sets of source input files, sequential versions of ETL need to be called, in accordance with corresponding periods of history. This becomes a serious maintenance challenge, in particular as more time goes by.

End-users don't always have their requirements clear at the outset of a project. Agile methods suggest we should make it as easy (and inexpensive) as possible for end-users to *change* their requirements. We want to *embrace* change, rather than resist it. Underlying business needs often only emerge in the course of *using* BI solutions, which makes it fundamentally impossible to provide stable requirements upfront. In this context, Corr (Corr & Stagnito, 2011) speaks of BI requirements being *accretive*, gradually building up over time like layers of sediment. BI architecture should support this design agility goal, and should not make it prohibitively expensive for end-users to change their mind later on.

The Case for a Three-Tiered Data Warehouse Architecture

For the reasons I explained above, late changes to a data model that was designed using the Kimball bus architecture tend to be cumbersome and expensive. They require keeping a full history of all loaded tables in a persistent staging area, all versions of ETL ever used, and careful engineering while redoing the initial load.

One of the Lean software engineering principles is delaying decisions until the last responsible moment (Poppendieck & Poppendieck, 2003). This principle is used in conjunction with concurrent development to enhance agility. Decisions that haven't been made, yet, never need to be reverted, and therefore carry zero reengineering cost.

A fundamental problem with two-tiered architectures is that (all) dimensions need to be conformed *before* you can make data available to end-users. You need to decide which attributes to include upfront, because adding attributes afterwards requires that you either:

Figure 5. Added "Supplier" dimension

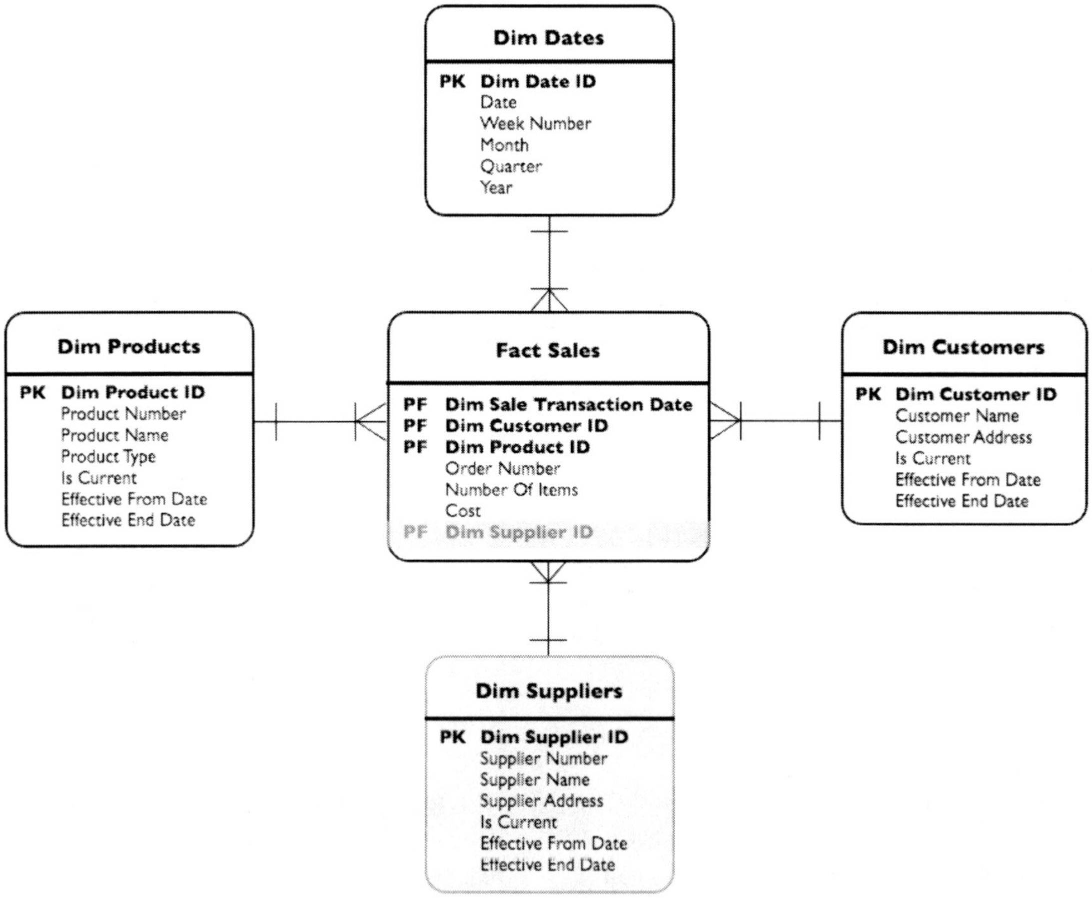

Figure 6. Initial example with only "Customers" and "Products" but (first) without "Supplier"

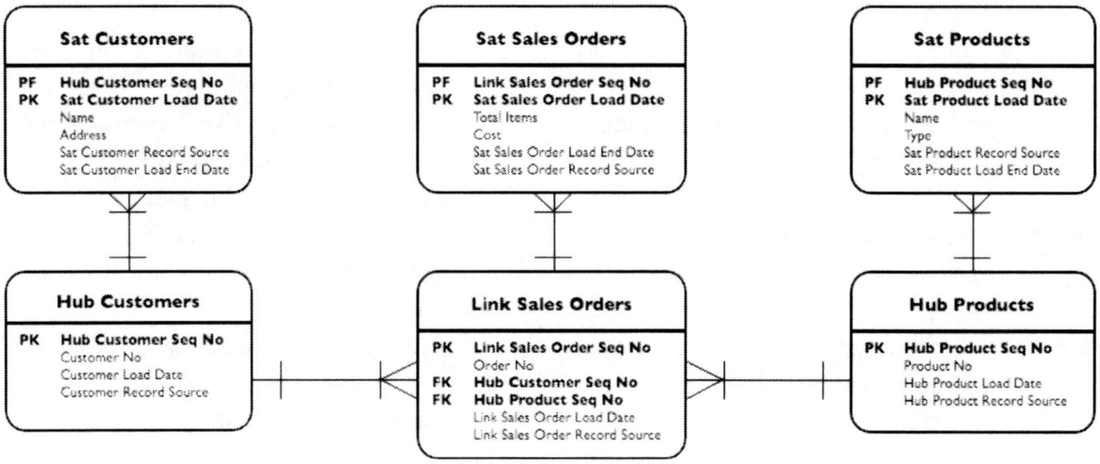

Figure 7. Hyper normalized model when a new business requirement surfaces

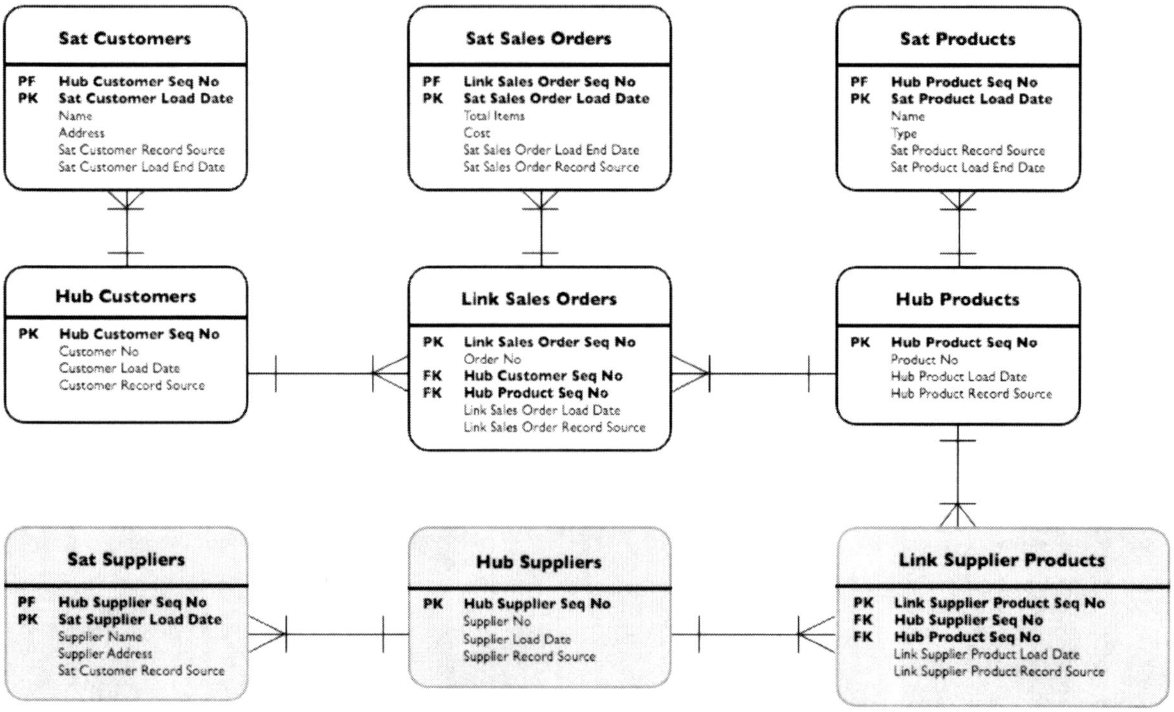

- Set this value to missing for the time slice prior to including it in the data warehouse. This is a misrepresentation when in actual fact its value is known;
- Set this attribute to the *current* value (treat it as a Type I Slowly Changing Dimension, SCD), which most likely is wrong because if this value never changed there would probably be no reason to include it;
- Redo the initial load, this time including the new attribute.

None of these options look pretty, and they were all caused by a late arriving requirement for this new attribute. If you want to avoid this risk, you will need to decide *early* which attributes to include. By the same token, you will need to decide *early* how to conform dimensions in a two-tiered architecture.

I recommend three-tiered hyper normalized data warehouse architectures for the following reasons:

- Such architectures facilitate incremental delivery in (very) small steps, without adding excessive overhead;
- Such architectures enable concurrent development, and allow developers to delay (risky) decisions like how to conform dimensions, and which attributes to include, to the last responsible moment;
- Design commitments can be reverted, even late in the development process, at limited cost;
- Reengineering in the data model is guaranteed to remain localized, thus containing the cost of late changes;

- A three-tiered architecture (with business rules enforced *downstream* from the data warehouse) provides superior support to data quality enforcement and data governance.

This last "business rules downstream" argument merits some elaboration. Business rules are *always* needed to transform data in source systems into some representation that is meaningful to end-users. The source system will often be a 3NF structure, the target will usually be a dimensional structure as this facilitates access for end-users. The problem with implementing business rules *upstream* from the data warehouse is manifold: maintainability, requirements gathering, but the issue we are most concerned about with regards to data governance is (immediate) traceability and auditability.

For reasons of data governance, it is vitally important that for all data elements in the data warehouse, a record source and date/time stamp of arrival be appended. This will provide reference to a specific source file that was provided by a particular system with an immediately available date and time when these data were received by the data warehouse team.

This poses somewhat of a conundrum: traceability is a requirement that is imposed by the data warehouse team. It is not (usually) an *explicit* requirement from the business sponsors of a data warehouse project. This need ("requirement") follows from an *implicit* business requirement that all data in the data warehouse be trusted (reliable). This accountability of each and every data element will eventually cause successful data warehouses to become a system of record for the state of affairs throughout the business, because most source systems only keep a partial (and non-auditable) trace of history. When designed in the way I suggest, the data warehouse will contain the entire corporation's history for all data included.

The immediately available data lineage of each and every data element to identified systems, and specifically marked source files as supplied on a given date and time, allows the BI team to take their steward role very serious, yet at the same time avoid becoming (being seen as) 'owners' of corporate data.

Consequences of Business Rules Upstream from a Data Warehouse

When testing data quality in the warehouse and in data marts, there is a confounding between accuracy of source data provided, and the impact of business rules when transforming data for 'consumption' by end-users to its desired shape and form. This has a negative impact on data governance, which is why I recommend embedding business rules exclusively *downstream* of the data warehouse to facilitate data quality work, and hence better support data governance.

Immediate backward data lineage from the output of business intelligence reports back to data files as provided by source system owners enables a BI team to stay "semantics agnostic" with regards to data interpretation as required for integration in the data warehouse. Such an architecture allows the team to focus on and limit themselves to their data stewardship role. When someone expresses his doubts about the accuracy of a corporate report, it is highly beneficial and enlightening to immediately be able to relate that report to sources files as provided by an identified supplying system on a particular date and time.

Because of elaborate sequential transformations in the ETL layer, which passes form source systems straight into data marts, Kimball style architectures *include* interpretation as part of data storage. There is no evident lineage from a report to a 'raw' number that was received from some source because of the business rules embedded in ETL. In a bus architecture, business rules need to be implemented *upstream* from the data warehouse.

A disadvantage of Bill Inmon's original data warehouse architecture (although it uses three layers), is that business rules are embedded upstream *as well as* downstream from the data warehouse. In this architecture, the transformation goes through two stages, a "semantic" one from source to data warehouse hub, and a "selection/aggregation" transformation from the data warehouse to data mart. This (severely) hampers auditability and traceability of data because the upstream business rules have impacted what data made it to the hub (and how).

In my proposed architecture, there should always be direct and straightforward traceability of data to their sources. The type of hyper normalized data model I recommend provides only structural change to the data to efficiently store a historized version of the data. The content is not semantically transformed or modified on the way from the source system to the data warehouse hub. *No* business rules are embedded upstream from the data warehouse. So all data are loaded, all the time. The good, the bad, and the ugly. Data are integrated around business keys that are already commonly used throughout the business to refer to relevant corporate entities (e.g.: "Product", "Sale", "Shipment", etc.).

Origins of Data Quality Problems and Business Alignment

A fundamental reason why three-tiered architectures like I propose provide better support for data quality objectives, has to do with the overarching corporate objective to support consistent, company wide decision-making. BI should strictly limit itself to fulfilling a stewardship role. To make a "single version of the truth" possible, BI teams need to conform dimensions. This holds regardless of whether they use a two-tiered *or* three-tiered architecture for data warehousing. Conforming dimensions is one of the areas where many purported 'data quality' problems arise.

Data quality problems stem largely from one of two sources: either inaccurate data entry, or semantically incorrect *interpretation* of data that are essentially correct from a technical point of view for a particular source system. I argue the latter category constitutes the majority of purported 'data quality' errors, that are in reality semantic interpretation errors.

The single most important driver for these data interpretation discrepancies is misaligned conforming of dimensions. How to conform dimensions is *largely* a political corporate discussion. It hinges on two (or worse: even more) departments agreeing to a shared 'view' on the facts as they have been surfaced from source systems by the BI team.

Note that *not* conforming dimensions doesn't provide a solution, either. In that case, two seemingly similar constructs, e.g.: "Customer" as defined by Marketing, versus "Customer" as identified by Finance will each have their own dimension. However, because of (slight) differences in definition, (typically small) differences in counts will result when you query the same facts using these two different "Customer" dimensions. Antithetical to our desired "single version of the truth."

The way that dimensions should be conformed can rarely be decided at the outset of a data warehouse project. If conforming dimensions were easy, then you wouldn't have a challenge to integrate data. This is for the exact same reasons as why there is no single version of the truth, either. Converging on a *shared* interpretation of a dimension *prior* to building a data mart (with these conformed dimensions) is hard, because when no data are available to end-users, they cannot carry an *informed* discussion on the impacts of settling on various options for how to define this dimension (e.g.: "Customer").

This challenge surfaces a fundamental flaw in the bus (two-tiered) architecture: the BI team needs to facilitate a discussion between two or more stakeholders of the data, on *how* exactly to conform dimensions, i.e., how to define the meaningful entities as described in dimensions for an enterprise wide data warehouse. Precisely because there *is* no commonly agreed upon enterprise wide definition of these entities, data integration is such hard work. For the same reason, master data management (MDM) projects struggle to come to completion. The BI team should *facilitate* these discussions, but carefully avoid not to (prematurely) take ownership of the eventual decision.

However, in the early stages of a data warehouse project (when using a bus architecture), none of the business end-users have access to data because the BI team hasn't finished building their solution, yet. Therefore, end-users cannot run reports using one or the other definition for a dimension to see what impact these choices will have on the numbers as they appear in corporate reporting.

Because data aren't available to end-users, yet, the BI team falls short in facilitating an informed discussion between stakeholders throughout the business. If they chose a two-tiered architecture, they 'have' to (prematurely) take ownership themselves for how they choose to conform dimensions. Either they build and deploy a pilot solution, or they take hypothetical guesses on what the quantitative impact will be of one choice over another. Both of these outcomes are both highly undesirable, and largely the result of being 'forced' into early design decisions because of the nature of data propagation in a two-tiered data warehouse architecture.

This ownership for *how* to conform dimensions, gets the BI team caught smack in the middle of corporate cross-fire: no matter how you define an entity in a conformed dimension, 'the numbers' (relative to management performance objectives) will *always* come out better for one manager (or department) than for another. Hopefully you were either very smart or lucky, and happened to choose a definition that favors the more influential stakeholder. But if you consistently need luck to stay out of trouble, it becomes only a matter of time before 'Murphy' strikes.

What tends to happen in most data warehouse projects using the 'traditional' Kimball (bus) architecture, is that the BI team commits to a certain view on how to conform dimensions, but this commitment needs to be made too early. There appears no way out of this conundrum without making 'a' decision. The BI team otherwise cannot proceed with development of their data mart.

Making changes to a Kimball data warehouse becomes prohibitively more expensive as time goes by because the volume keeps growing every day. Furthermore, complexity keeps growing as changes to source file structures (e.g.: additional attributes added) necessitate updating ETL code. Therefore, the BI team finds itself 'locked into' a design, and looses flexibility. This situation becomes even more problematic when data quality issues don't surface until much later.

The dynamic at play here is that delays in releasing data for corporate 'consumption' (or acceptance testing) delays feedback on the appropriateness of the delivered solution. This feedback from end-users is essential to keep development on track. By making increments of delivery as small as possible (design agility), you effectively shorten these feedback cycles. This ensures timely changes, and minimizes the amount of rework in case a transformation *does* need to be corrected. Resolving issues quickly and progressing piecemeal is significantly more efficient.

Note that in a three-tiered architecture you might *still* need to rebuild a data mart using new (adjusted) transformation rules and/or using a new definition for our conformed dimension. However, you do *not* need to redo the initial load because all of those data are (still) available in the central hub.

Note that for these same reasons, many BI teams resort to virtual data marts. Deploying data marts as Views avoids physically copying data, which makes the release of alternative renditions of these data marts so much quicker and more agile. All that is involved is changing a few lines of code and releasing this update.

This approach using virtual data marts usually does not work for two-tiered architectures. Besides performance challenges when you relay data directly from source systems straight into a data mart, most source systems don't keep a comprehensive history of values required for time variant reporting.

Conforming dimensions is *largely* a political corporate discussion. These discussions become 'risky' when (individual) performance objectives of incumbent managers are at stake. He who finds himself with a less favorable number in corporate reports (relative to his individual target) will quite 'naturally' resist this new view on how to conform the dimension.

We, as BI professionals, don't own the data. We merely hold them for the business. As stewards it is our responsibility to surface discrepancies in definitions, and quantify where and how the business is loosing money as a result of this confusion (i.e.: these data quality issues). When an acquisition department has captured details for customers that Marketing doesn't 'recognize' (because they use a slightly different definition of "Customer"), those prospects are effectively lost for further cross- and up-sell opportunities. Acquisition efforts and money are wasted. Those cracks in the corporate value chain are invariably quite interesting to senior management, in particular when you are able to quantify the magnitude of these losses.

Data quality problems don't often originate from truly 'technical' causes. I argue that mostly, purported data quality problems are fundamentally the result of poor (internal) alignment of corporate objectives. These misaligned objectives place corporate stakeholders at odds because for some of them, changing the definition for a business entity (e.g.: "Customer", "Sale", "Shipment", etc.) causes their performance to look worse (at least for some).

But sometimes, data quality problems *are* the result of sloppy data entry. Still, this can usually be traced back to a misalignment of corporate objectives. The classic, albeit hackneyed example is rewarding people for speed of data entry, rather than for its accuracy. The back office manager (problem owner) is expected to process as much work as possible, with the least amount of resources. He is rewarded for speed. Downstream information users (problem holders) bear the brunt of hasty work, and failure to install ("time consuming") inspect-and-adapt cycles to prevent data entry errors. They need accuracy. This, again, points to misaligned performance objectives for the problem owner (back office manager) who is expected to work 'efficiently' (i.e.: minimize resource usage), and downstream information consumers (problem holders) who require accurate data to be able to do their job properly.

The grand perspective on this dynamic goes further. The majority of data quality issues point to cracks in the corporate value chain. In this chapter I argue that information loss (either 'errors' or inappropriate reporting) is mostly caused by a failure to conform dimensions (politically: align corporate objectives). In that way, BI team members take on the burden of misalignment between cross-departmental objectives when they feel 'forced' to choose sides in a corporate discussion on how to interpret facts in the source systems. This is unnecessary if that results from their choice of warehouse architecture, i.e., the Kimball bus architecture. It doesn't have to be that way.

How to Avoid These Problems?

If you store all the (source) facts in your data warehouse, you can keep them available in more or less original state. By this I mean *efficiently* with regards to historizing data (capturing all changes in source data, with minimal redundancy) and also *flexible* with regards to anticipated changes and inherent ambiguity of requirements. The data warehouse hub should contain at the most only basic (non-semantic) transformations so that all data elements remain traceable to the supplying source system and specific file provided. Data remain auditable when no business rules have been applied. Then there is a way out of this conundrum. This requires you move away from 20th century data warehouse architectures that have required BI practitioners to conform dimensions (too) *early* in the project.

The practice of combining data integration and transformation in one fell swoop (e.g.: a two-tiered architecture) puts ETL developers at a disadvantage, because requirements are often ambiguous (when end-users cannot 'see' the proposed solution, yet), and amenable to change. If the cost of change over time then further becomes prohibitive (because redoing the initial load becomes ever more cumbersome), you take irresponsible risks by committing too early which attributes to include and how to conform dimensions. Instead, you would like to achieve the opposite; you want to mitigate those risks. We want to keep the costs of change low to enable business stakeholders to change their mind at limited cost, throughout the course of data warehouse development.

Delaying Decisions to the Last Responsible Moment

In agile software development practices we like the idea of "deciding at the last responsible moment", in conjunction with concurrent development practices (Poppendieck & Poppendieck, 2003). That way, we can show end-users bits of functionality (very) early on. This gives us credit with our sponsors, and business stakeholders will gain confidence in our progress. But at least as important: the sooner reliable feedback about data accuracy is passed back to the development team, the more efficient and effective they will be able to make necessary (small) changes and continue with their work.

Imagine you could run your BI projects like this. You inform all departments involved what the consequences are (counts, frequencies, amounts, etc.) of choosing various definitions to conform data across systems and departments. That way, you empower all stakeholders to have an informed discussion about what 'view' on the facts would best support *their* particular (end-to-end) value stream.

All business stakeholders have good reasons to cling to their departmental specific view on the source system facts. When you apply this approach to managing BI project risk, stakeholders are well-placed to explain why the numbers for (global) corporate reporting don't exactly line up with the numbers for any specific department. This doesn't necessarily point to any (technical) data quality errors, there may well be *business process specific* reasons for these discrepancies. Not only can these reasons be alluded to, by utilizing a three-tiered architecture in the way I have outlined (with business rules embedded *downstream* from the data warehouse), you can *also* report on the magnitude of the differences and shed light on the business case for continuing department-specific interpretation of source system facts.

Conversely, one can also imagine that when you attempt to conform dimensions *before* 'the business' has agreed on common dimensions, this leads to dispute that can only be solved elegantly by providing counts under different scenarios, using (slightly) different definitions for the conformed dimensions. Uninformed arguments over 'the right' way to conform dimensions can have a detrimental effect on the progress of a data warehouse project. Potentially, the BI team might bear the brunt of their frustration when business stakeholders are confronted with 'erroneous' reports.

When BI teams inadvertently become 'owners' of corporate data and their interpretation, this creates a problem in business alignment. Every time you become problem holder (the person experiencing pain) without adequate resources to solve the problem at its root (the problem owner), you risk getting caught in the (corporate) line of fire. Fundamentally, this problem was caused because the BI team chose to decide how to align data from different data providers (business silos), without access to the resources to resolve the underlying discrepancies. BI teams can prevent this straddle by moving from a two-tiered architecture to a three-tiered architecture with traceable and auditable data contents in the central hub.

A Hyper Normalized Three-Tiered Architecture

As I have outlined before, to make a data model resilient to change, you need to break out business keys in separate tables from the relations, and separate from descriptive attributes (and history). I will now show how such an approach might look if you apply Data Vault modeling. To begin with, I show the same initial example again with only "Customers" and "Products", but (first) without "Supplier" (see Figure 6).

The first thing that is apparent from Figure 6 is that you now need more tables to describe the (exact) same data structure we saw in Figure 1 (3NF model) and Figure 3 (dimensional model). In this particular example, the business event "Sale" has been modeled as a (many-to-many) relation ("Link") between "Customer" and "Product", with descriptive attributes for "Customer", "Sale Order" and "Product" represented in their respective tables "Sat Customers", "Sat Sale Orders", and "Sat Products."

What is also apparent is that query paths through this model will contain more joins, and therefore will have slower response times. To some extent this degradation in performance will be attenuated by query optimizers (available in almost all relational database management systems) that execute selective joins. If a join that is *logically* present in a query path does not affect the selected set, it will be dropped from the *executed* query, hence improving (optimizing) performance.

Now let us see what happens in this hyper normalized model when a new business requirement surfaces to include "Supplier" data into the model (see Figure 7).

A few conclusions become apparent when you compare Figure 7 to Figure 6:

- The existing data structure ("Hub Product") was not affected in any way by appending the "Supplier" data;
- The many-to-many relationship between "Hub Products" and "Hub Suppliers" does not enforce any business rule on the relationship between these two entities.

Because the "Link Supplier Products" represents a many-to-many relation between "Products" and "Suppliers", both a one-to-one, and one-to-many relation can be captured in this data model. Bear in mind that even *if* the business reassures us that there is a one-to-one relationship (similar to Figure 4) between "Product" and "Supplier" (every product is only procured from one supplier), there is still no enforcement of this business rule in the data model. If such a relationship were to hold, this will become apparent in the data. The data model does not enforce this business rule on incoming data. So when this relationship changes over time, and the business starts to procure products from multiple suppliers, this has zero impact on the data model (it requires no change).

What is not (immediately) apparent from Figure 6 and Figure 7 is that when later additional (descriptive) attributes need to be included in the data model, this can be done in one of two ways:

- Attributes can be appended to an existing Sat table;
- An additional Sat table can be modeled to form a one-to-many relationship with the corresponding Hub or Link table.

The former would require some reengineering of the existing Sat ETL code, and the history of this new attribute would be missing for dates prior to being added to the Sat (or could be set to the current value). Including history in the existing Sat table would require the same type of complex reengineering we saw in a dimensional model when attributes are added to the data model later on. The latter (adding a new, additional Sat) can be done with *no* reengineering, and (all) the history that is still available for this attribute can be easily loaded for this attribute, using the default ETL loading procedure for this table structure.

This design flexibility in case a need arises to add new descriptive attributes to the data model gives data warehouse architects elegant options to quickly (and inexpensively) respond to changing requirements.

FUTURE RESEARCH DIRECTIONS

Data warehousing is (still) a fairly young discipline. Design patterns for how to effectively build maintainable solutions are only beginning to see the light. The inherent self-similarity in hyper normalized data models lends itself particularly well to automation. It has proven possible to generate code, which has several advantages. Generating code can be done by using templates, or by using data warehouse automation tools. This has advantages both in terms of development speed and maintainability of code.

There is impressive anecdotal evidence for efficiency improvement as a result of using data warehouse automation tools. An improvement factor of 5-10 times has been reported. It would be good if these claims, and the preconditions required to achieve such benefits could be substantiated in carefully controlled scientific experiments.

Ensemble modeling is a new data modeling paradigm particularly well suited for data warehousing that has evolved into a number of 'flavors' like Data Vault, Focal Point Modeling, or Anchor Modeling, for instance. As of yet, we lack sound empirical evidence on how they compare when it comes to handling changing requirements. These approaches have slightly different requirement gathering methods, which might have an effect on the 'likelihood' that late changes might trigger updates to the data model. Some approaches are more restrictive in terms of prerequisite information analysis, and will therefore mean that developers will spend more time in this initial requirements gathering phase. Is that time well spent? Or should progress rather be pursued by commencing sooner on the basis of lightweight requirements? The jury is still out, and scientific research could shed light on these questions.

All of these approaches employ some form of hyper normalization. Therefore, you may expect to find more tables (it is estimated a factor 2-3, and more for Anchor Modeling) to model the same business process. These additional tables and joins are largely mitigated by the intrinsic self-similarity in these data models. There are only a (very) limited number of loading and querying patterns, which is why templates or automation can easily support these approaches. This is where spectacular efficiency gains originate. Again, how different modeling approaches compare in that respect remains to be explored. How performance is affected in practice is relevant, but again, no empirically sound research seems available to date.

CONCLUSION

Data warehousing is a relatively new and dynamic field. Ralph Kimball initially emerged as the 'winner' from the "big debate" in the 90s over proposed data warehouse architecture. The two-tiered approach to architecture that he proposed has almost become the industry standard. Most data warehouses nowadays are built using the approach he laid out in his "Toolkit" book series.

Although I acknowledge and support that dimensional modeling will usually be the preferred way to present data to end-users, I have put my case forward in this chapter why three-tiered data warehouse architectures are superior in support of data quality and data governance.

Besides recommending a three-tiered architecture, I also suggest you avoid implementing business rules upstream from the data warehouse. This hampers auditability and traceability of data, which is clearly needed to support data stewardship when questions arise over the correctness of reporting.

There are two essential reasons for my endorsement of three-tiered architectures. Firstly, the three-tiered architecture enables incremental agile development in tiny steps without adding prohibitive overhead. What this accomplishes is that feedback loops to indicate accuracy and usefulness of delivery are dramatically shortened. This helps to keep risky BI projects on track, or when timelines are in jeopardy, at least you are notified early. Secondly, the three-tiered architecture with business rules downstream provides superior support to data stewardship work in BI teams.

The confounding between accuracy of input data (as provided by source systems) and appropriateness of transformations ("Big T" ETL) can be resolved by providing auditable traceability to data elements in the data warehouse hub. These data are marked with their supplying source system and date/time of origin. When the accuracy of reports gets questioned by business stakeholders, you can immediately refer to the data that went into the data warehouse, and compare that with what had been expected. If the input data were correct, you may then compare transformations imposed on source data to resolve ambiguity in requirements or detect errors in transformation logic.

Hyper normalized data models cope (much) better with change. Over the lifetime of a data warehouse change is to be expected. Systems change, data structures change, so your choice of data model should cater to that. My simplified example has demonstrated superior resilience to change. Those effects become (much) bigger in real life applications.

In the architecture I propose, an integral traceable history of all source data elements is persistently captured in a central data warehouse hub. Downstream data marts may contain physical extracts, or, can be delivered virtually (as Views). The advantage of virtual data marts is that updates to its transformation logic can be deployed (much) more rapidly. This enables (quickly) running reports using different definitions of conformed dimensions to assess what the impact will be, and how they compare.

Business intelligence professionals have been pursuing a so-called "single version of the truth." This requires conforming dimensions. In order to arrive at corporate-wide agreement on how to conform a dimension, you need to persuade *some* stakeholders to adjust the way they have been defining business constructs (e.g.): "Customer", "Sale", "Shipment", etc. The most elegant way to get there is through a democratic process where all parties have information about the implications and consequences of making such changes. Having auditable and traceable data readily available in your data warehouse provides an excellent starting point for facilitating such discussions *before* you make irreversible design commitments.

REFERENCES

Beck, K., et al. (2001). *Agile manifesto*. Retrieved 20 December 2012 from http://www.agilemanifesto.org

Bilali, L. (2013). *Data warehouse generation algorithm explained*. Retrieved 17 February 2013 from http://www.datawarehouseautomation.org

Corr, L., & Stagnito, J. (2011). *Agile data warehouse design: Collaborative dimensional modeling, from whiteboard to star schema*. Leeds, UK: DecisionOne Press.

Hultgren, H. P. (2012). *Modeling the agile data warehouse with data vault*. Denver, CO: New Hamilton Press.

Linstedt, D. (2011). *Super charge your data warehouse: Invaluable data modeling rules to implement your data vault*. Albany, NY: CreateSpace Independent Publishing Platform.

Mundy, J. (2012). *Design tip #149 facing the re-keying crisis*. Retrieved February 22, 2013 from http://www.kimballgroup.com/2012/10/02/design-tip-149-facing-the-re-keying-crisis/

Poppendieck, M., & Poppendieck, T. (2003). *Lean software development: An agile toolkit*. Boston, MA: Addison-Wesley.

Rönnbäck. (2012). Retrieved 20 December 2012 from http://www.anchormodeling.com

Scholten, H. (2010). *Musings on the data vault*. Retrieved 20 December 2012 from http://www.bi-team.com

KEY TERMS AND DEFINITIONS

Anchor Modeling: A 6th normal form data modeling paradigm, specifically geared to enterprise data warehousing.

Conformed Dimension: where two or more data marts share a logical (may also be physical) representation of a core business entity ("dimension"), to align reporting across business processes and data marts.

Data Mart: A business process oriented subset of data, specifically geared to end-user access.

Data Vault: A hyper normalized data modeling paradigm, specifically geared to enterprise data warehousing.

Topology: Data warehouse architecture, notably a layout of data logistics as it flows through various stages in the data warehousing process.

Traceability: The ability to relate a data element through backward data lineage to its supplying source system.

Chapter 20
The Value of Data Quality

Robert Hillard
Deloitte, Australia

ABSTRACT

Almost everyone acknowledges the importance to business of data quality, however most organisations treat it as a technology issue. Increasingly, organisations are moving from cost recovery models to ones where they reward behaviours that develop their data as an asset. At their core, these models recognise that businesses live in an information economy that needs to be reflected at the micro level within the enterprise with individuals being rewarded as "information traders." Introducing a trading approach to information changes, the mindset of the originators and managers of information who become motivated to maximise the value of the content they are responsible for. Just like any other resource, poor quality directly impacts its value. The approach also creates the opportunity to move the focus of data governance away from what is often perceived to be compliance activities to helping to establish pricing and the market as a whole.

INTRODUCTION

Data quality is a concept that makes sense, everyone wants the data they use to be right or at least no-one will make the case for it to be wrong. However, achieving high quality data seems to be an elusive goal. Most executives complain of being forced to make decisions with incomplete data and spending excessive time arguing about the accuracy of the information that is presented to them.

Information is still largely treated as the responsibility of the information technology department, largely because the word "information" is included in the description and the job title of the chief information officer. However, the IT department is asked to take a largely tools-based approach to managing this most valuable of enterprise assets.

DOI: 10.4018/978-1-4666-4892-0.ch020

Any mechanised approach to data quality is naturally limited in its reach given the value that the people who work with the subject matter every day can add. No matter how many value ranges are placed on a given data field there is no replacing the "sniff test" that an experienced stakeholder can apply. Similarly, people are constantly touching the source of data through conversations with customers, suppliers and regulators which provides the perfect opportunity to check validity.

For instance, many organisations believe that they have the definitive address templates for the country that they operate in. These often lock-in the alignment of locations with the relevant postal or zip code and allowable formatting of street and town or city. While IT have defined a technically correct approach to forcing data quality, often with behind the scenes corrections, the front-line staff are constantly frustrated by customers who do not accept these rigid rules. Every customer-facing team member will have a story of a customer who does not accept the technically correct name for their suburb or town and has a more prestigious or perhaps historically correct name that they refuse to move away from. The reality of dealing with people is that these differences driven by vanity must be allowed for and the definition of what is correct needs to be far more nuanced and needs the input of those who truly understand the stakeholders involved.

CHANGING BEHAVIOURS

Increasingly, business and government is realising that treating repositories of data as part of a computer system encourages all of the wrong behaviours when it comes to managing information. This situation is not helped by current accounting treatments which don't allow for information to be explicitly recorded on the balance sheet as a standalone item, but rather require it to be wrapped-up in the capitalisation of the system that created it as well as the goodwill of transactions that brought the system into the organisation.

The treatment of a database as a system first, and a resource second, allows stakeholders across the organisation to abdicate their involvement. This abdication quickly turns into hostility under the regime of cost recovery which most large information technology departments operate under.

Cost recovery is the process by which information technology pays for itself by assuming that work is either operational and funded as part of the base load of the department or it is project based in which case it must be clearly funded with a beginning, middle and end. Only activities that are funded under either of these two scenarios are undertaken.

The implication of the cost recovery model is that the information technology team take less and less interest in the prioritisation or decision making around what gets done. They have to make the assumption that the team with the most budget will also correspond to the greatest business value.

The problem is that projects are large and the political activities required getting them funded means that value and budget aren't always aligned. Even when they are, much that is valuable gets left behind. Data quality with it.

Confusing the situation more are the architectural requirements that are imposed by large information technology teams. The most common, relating to information, is the mandate that information is an enterprise resource and so reporting must be consolidated in the form of an enterprise data warehouse.

Consider the situation where the marketing team develop a useful campaign management tool. They decide that they would like to do some reporting from the database but are quickly told by the information technology team that they will need to submit a project request, together with a budget, to load their data into the enterprise data warehouse. Then, after spending a considerable amount of money for which they see no value, they will be allowed to submit another project request with budget to develop a business intelligence report against their own data.

No wonder they regard the information technology team as bureaucratic. While they might comply with these requirements, they do so reluctantly and certainly don't factor the downstream data warehouse into their daily planning which leads to constant tension between the teams with changes to the database causing load and consistency problems or worse not being noticed at all and leading to the content of the enterprise data warehouse being simply wrong.

INFORMATION TRADERS

The enterprise data warehouse bureaucracy can be turned on its head by moving to a model where the information platform and the databases that feed it are not treated as individual systems but rather as capabilities that support a group of "information traders."

An information trader is someone whose job it is to achieve the maximum possible value for data and information resources. They do this by buying information from creators inside and outside the enterprise and then on-selling it usually with some sort of added value.

For instance, in the example described earlier, rather than waiting for the marketing department to identify that they needed the help of information technology to do some reporting on the campaign data, the information trader would spot that there was a valuable dataset developing and seek to buy a feed. They would offer money upfront and ongoing to keep on providing the data. This is the exact opposite of the model where the enterprise data warehouse owner asks for money from marketing for the privilege of providing them back their own data.

The incentives are now around the right way. In fact, the information trader doesn't care if reports are developed directly against the marketing database by the local team, but the trader will try to offer a higher value service at a fee that encourages them to buy-back their own data with the addition of information from elsewhere (perhaps external demographics or internal product costing data).

Regardless of whether the original marketing team buy-back their own data in its enriched form, the trader is constantly looking for new uses and ways for the organisation to make money with this data feed. Acting as a true profit centre, the trader might even seek external buyers of the data depending on its nature, regulatory and privacy implications.

The organisation that embraces this type of role is well on its way to meeting the objectives of being an "analytical competitor" as defined by Tom Davenport (2007) in "Competing on Analytics": "[Analytical competitors] are also integrating their systems more thoroughly and sharing data with their suppliers."

With this model in place, the data quality value chain is much more aligned to the incentive value chain. In this example, the data quality value chain requires the marketing team to ensure that the data they provide is fit for all purposes that the enterprise data warehouse might apply it to. If they operate on the most common current incentive model they have had to pay for the privilege and resent the information technology team for making them do so. There is little incentive for them to go over and above and notify anyone of issues that could affect the wider organisation.

In the trading model, the marketing team are paid to provide the data based on a contract which includes its level of quality and a commitment that it is fit for a range of purposes.

ESTABLISHING AN INFORMATION MARKET

Although many organisations and people talk of information having value, and even though increasingly this value is represented within products and services such as digital advertising, usage statistics and loyalty schemes, framing a market is not an easy task. It is made particularly difficult by the fact that a price needs to be put onto something that has traditionally been free, or at least a byproduct of other investments. In most organisations, value has been placed on business processes rather than the resulting information.

Robert M. Losee (1997) has published one of the most succinct definitions of information to argue that information and processes are inextricably linked: "Information is produced by all processes and it is the values of characteristics in the processes' output that are information". A properly framed market will take the pressure off the development of good processes, by putting a value on the commodity that can actually realise the greatest return for business in the twenty first century: information.

A good starting point is to look at information resources in total. For instance, the author has previously suggested using the total market capitalisation of companies as one method (Hillard *et al.*, 2006). In this approach, all physical and liquid assets are totalled-up and deducted from the market value of the business. What's left can be argued to be at least represented by information. For instance, the relationship with customers (goodwill) is best described through the information held about the customer.

Financial institutions can find that about 80 percent of their value is tied-up in the information they hold about customers and the market. Even mining companies find that their real value is in the information they hold about their current prospective projects in the form of geophysical and management data.

Middle managers typically find it difficult to move to paying for information in its granular form. At the start, it is worth setting the expectation of the market by showing the aggregate value using techniques like this one and then attributing it across the organisation's datasets by use of a simple division. The approach is not intended to set a price, but rather establish an expectation of the future price.

Having set the expectations, the pressure can be reduced by using a central allocation and planning scheme. This needs to be run by the data governance function which can can use this to give itself a real reason to exist. The savings that the market approach will achieve through avoided data quality interventions will justify these activities on their own, however the benefits are far greater with the opportunity to motivate whole products and lines of business.

In undertaking this transition, some organisations are focusing on the so-called "cottage industry" of data or business intelligence reporting that occurs throughout almost every large organisation. Identifying the scale of activity being undertaking by enthusiastic amateurs or external contractors hired directly into business and system teams. This is real expenditure which can be redirected to achieve much more when applied in a coordinated way. Showing middle managers that this money will be made freed-up and applied into data quality, consolidation and reporting often helps them to understand why the transition to a market-based approach will ultimately benefit them as well as the enterprise as a whole.

THE FIRST TRANSACTIONS

To achieve the behaviour change, the market has to be initiated. Because people are not familiar with the real value of the information, start with relative priorities. A simple survey of dataset priorities will ensure that projects making the most commonly needed data is given the highest priority.

The survey approach can be as simple or sophisticated as the needs or the organisation warrant. Either way, the intention is that this model should only be used for a short period until market participants get used to the idea of paying for information. Inevitably, the early days of the market will see a close alignment between price and cost (equating largely to the labour of sourcing and manipulating the data). Over time, though, markets start to incorporate scarcity, impact and quality in the value they assign to datasets. Inevitably information traders start to consider external buyers and then sellers of information, overcoming initial regulatory hurdles with appropriate data governance.

The data governance forum, committee or similar group should act like a market regulator. In the first few months this will consider the relative priorities of data covering customers, products, staff, finance and other subject areas with the data governance group allocating scarce investment funds based on relative priorities decided independently through the forum.

Quickly, the data governance group will bring together buyers and sellers. First within the enterprise and ultimately outside as well. With buyers and sellers matched, prices for data can be created.

For instance, one scenario might have bankers with high value customers offering up valuable information about their clients to their fellow bankers in exchange for a share of the profits. In a another scenario, an information trader who manages a data warehouse might buy campaign information from marketing, customer profiles from risk and product configuration details from the individual lines of business. This information trader might then combine the information to support targeted sales campaigns.

Importantly, buying and selling is an operational not capital cost so it represents ongoing transactions. That means that payment is dependent upon service and quality.

SERVICE LEVELS

The buying and selling of information is dependent on a contract. The data governance forum should develop standard agreements with a particular focus on linking ongoing payment to the quality of the information provided. With organisations spending tens or hundreds of millions of dollars a year on managing, manipulating and reporting information these payments will rapidly become material for many parts of the organisation and a focus on data quality will result in some lines of business making handsome profits which they can plow back into front line activities or use to bolster their profit contributions.

As the number of agreements increase, there will be pressure on the data governance group to make it easier to transact. This will initially be in terms of the form of agreements and helping to strike manageable bargains. Over time, though, the focus will move to providing brokering technology to make it easier to source, manipulate, track and deliver data between seller and buyer.

The introduction of technology is analogous to the move by stock exchanges from trading floors to electronic transactions. Much of the common infrastructure required is described in the architecture promoted by MIKE2.0, the widely accepted open approach to information management (www.openmethodology.org).

While many businesses already have much of this brokering capability in place, it is generally focused on the technical elements of sourcing, manipulating and delivering information. This is the equivalent of a stock exchange settling a share transaction without providing a mechanism for the exchange of any funds! In other words, it is just half of the story.

Most data quality and governance teams know how important good metadata is, yet few organisations manage to achieve more than the most superficial coverage and struggle to keep any metadata repository current. People just don't seem to be motivated even though they are the first to complain when they are searching for information to meet their urgent needs.

A metadata repository is really an asset register, tracking the information assets held and should include their value. With the price and cost now included, the metadata has a compelling and immediate reason to exist and to be maintained by all parties.

OBJECTIONS TO A MARKET-BASED APPROACH

Despite apparent consensus on the importance of data quality, many people don't initially feel comfortable with measuring the value of data or the financial impact of data quality on their business. This objection is well covered by Douglas Hubbard (2007) in "How to Measure Anything: Finding the Value of Intangibles in Business". Hubbard argues that "if you are betting a lot of money on the outcome of a variable that has a lot of uncertainty, then even a marginal reduction in your uncertainty has a computable monetary value".

Further discussion with these stakeholders typically breaks the objectors into two camps. The first group object because they don't believe that information can be valued. The second group are worried that that the value won't be universally accepted. While the first group is usually easily convinced by arguments such as those by Hubbard, the second group however are effectively raising the issue of "the greater fool", the idea that an investor in an intangible asset, like information, is relying on being able to on-sell it in the future to a "greater fool".

The "greater fool" concern is only solved by creating a robust and enduring information economy across the enterprise. Something that information providers such are Reuters have been able to do effectively for many years but is only now gaining popularity within the enterprise.

INFORMATION-DRIVEN BUSINESS

The author coined the term "Information-Driven Business" (Hillard, 2010) to describe the enterprise that successfully re-engineers itself around the data that it has at its disposal. The information-driven business does not regard data quality as optional, but nor does it pursue it for its own sake. Each dataset has value and the importance of the quality of that data is directly proportional to the contribution that it can make to the running of the organisation.

Data that relates to interesting, but low value, activities has less value, and hence its quality is less important. For instance, the staff might have assembled a football tipping database which clearly falls into this category. Traditional approaches to data quality scorecards can catch this data and assign equivalent importance simply because it relates to the topic of personnel and contains information that is categorised as personal. A market-based approach turns this on its head and assigns a more appropriate priority against the quality of this information.

Similarly, analytical techniques are finding that apparently trivial data can have an enormous impact on value-deriving activities of the business. For instance, risk departments are often concerned about borrowers who are up-to-date with their payments, but who have a wide variance in their payment dates, as they can often pose a higher risk than those who are late but consistently pay on the same date. The former indicating a cash flow problem while the latter suggests a misalignment between receivables and the required payment date.

In this example, traditional techniques of data quality might only measure days early/late as being of equivalent importance as dozens of other attributes of each facility. The market-based approach would recognise the greater interest in this attribute and because there would be a greater financial value assigned to the data, the information traders of the organisation would be motivated to ensure that the content is correct.

CONCLUSION

In fact many organisations already trade in information. Anyone who has ever bought a marketing list or packaged-up expert advice to a client has probably assigned a value to the information involved. That value drops when the quality of the information is suspect. The more customer contact details that are wrong in the marketing the less that anyone will be willing to pay. Similarly, clients don't want expert advice that references tables or statistics that turn out to be suspect.

Turning this case-by-case approach to valuing data into an institutionalised approach to managing information is the most sustainable approach to solving the perennial data quality dilemma. With data quality aligned to the financial success of the enterprise the whole team are naturally motivated to keep it at the top of their agenda.

REFERENCES

Davenport & Harris. (2007). *Competing on analytics: The new science of winning*. Cambridge, MA: Harvard Business School Publishing Corporation.

Hillard & Na. (2006). *Economic value of data for financial services organisations, the local and global in knowledge management*. Paper presented at the Australian Conference for Knowledge Management and Intelligent Decision Support. Canberra, Australia.

Hillard. (2010). *Information-driven business*. Hoboken, NJ: John Wiley & Sons.

Hubbard. (2007). *How to measure anything: Finding the value of intangibles in business*. Hoboken, NJ: John Wiley & Sons.

Losee. (1997). A discipline independent definition of information. *Journal of the American Society of Information Science, 48*(3), 254-269.

KEY TERMS AND DEFINITIONS

Cost Recovery: The process by which information technology pays for itself by assuming that work is either operational and funded as part of the base load of the department or it is project based.

Data Governance: The oversight of the information asset by a leadership group.

Information Market: The buying and selling of information as a resource with value like any physical asset.

Information Trader: Someone whose job it is to achieve the maximum possible value for data and information resources through buying information from creators inside and outside the enterprise and then on-selling it usually with some sort of added value.

Information-Driven Business: The enterprise that successfully re-engineers itself around the data that it has at its disposal.

Chapter 21
Data Protection and BI:
A Quality Perspective

Daragh O Brien
Castlebridge Associates, Ireland

ABSTRACT

Data Protection (DP) and Privacy are increasingly important quality characteristics of Information, particularly in the context of Business Intelligence and Big Data. This relationship between Data Protection and Information Quality (IQ) is often poorly understood, and DP itself is often misunderstood as being an issue of security control rather than information governance. This chapter examines the relationship between DP, IQ, and Data Governance (DG). It provides an overview of how techniques and practices from IQ and DG can ensure that BI projects are grounded on appropriate privacy controls that ensure that the right information is being used in the right way by the right people to answer the right questions.

INTRODUCTION

We live in an information-rich age. Social networks, electronic point of sale systems, ecommerce sites, mobile phones with GPS, cellular communications networks, and an increasingly dizzying array of technologies provide the ability, in theory at least, for organizations to obtain data for a variety of analytics purposes. Entire industries have grown up around the tracking of how we use the Internet for example. Multi-billion dollar IPOs have been launched on the promise of dollars from data provided by people using 'free' services like Facebook.

However, consumers and citizens are increasingly aware of and resistant to the idea that their data is being logged, tracked, and analyzed in this way. In a recent EURO Barometer survey

DOI: 10.4018/978-1-4666-4892-0.ch021

(European Commission, 2011) 54% of EU citizens were concerned about their behavior being recorded via payment cards, with relatively high levels of concern recorded regarding behavior tracking via mobile phone and mobile internet (49% and 40% respectively). 70% of Europeans were concerned that organizations would use data that they held about individuals for purposes ***other*** than that for which it was collected. These findings are echoed in similar research in Canada. In a study conducted for the Office of the Privacy Commissioner of Canada 65% of Canadians felt that "*protecting the personal information of Canadians will be one of the most important issues facing the country in the next ten years*", with 55% expressing concerns about data privacy on social networking sites (Office of the Privacy Commissioner of Canada, 2011).

With such concern being shown in Europe and Canada, two jurisdictions with relatively mature Data Protection laws, it is unsurprising that in 2012 the FTC in the United States published its report on *Protecting Consumer Privacy in an Era of Rapid Change* (Federal Trade Commission, 2012) that set out a number of clear Data Protection/Privacy principles that organizations in the US that are proposed to supplement the existing statutory privacy regulations in sector-specific legislation such as HIPAA (Health Insurance Portability and Accountability Act), the Graham-Leech-Bliley Act, and the HITECH Act (Health Information Technology for Economic and Clinical Health Act). This, coupled with the FTC's increased enforcement actions on data protection issues in 2011 and 2012, and the release in February 2012 of the Obama Administration's "Consumer Privacy Bill of Rights" (The White House, 2012), represents a clear message to US organisations that respect for Data Protection and Privacy is essential in the digital economy.

However, recent developments such as the disclosure of the nature and extent of data processing by US Intelligence services has been hailed by FTC Commissioner Julie Brill (Brill, 2013) as a spark for what she terms "a necessary and overdue debate". In particular she highlights how the disclosures mean that:

Americans are now more aware than ever of how much their personal data is free-floating in cyberspace, ripe for any data miner – government or otherwise – to collect, use, package, and sell.

This renewed awareness on the part of Americans should not be equated with an absence of consumer demand however. Consistently studies have highlighted consumer concern about and resistance to the excessive capture of, sharing of, and analysis of personal information. For example a 2012 study (Hoofnagle, Urban, & Li, 2012) found that 81% of respondents to their survey objected to the transfer of telephone number data to retailers where they used mobile payment services (e.g. Near Field Communication). The same percentage of respondents objected to the transfer of their home address to the retailer. A report from the Pew Research Center found that 68% of respondents were "not okay" with targeted advertising as they did not like having their online behaviour tracked and analysed. Interestingly, 55% of 18-24 year olds shared this view despite the 'conventional wisdom' that that demographic is less concerned with their privacy (Purcell, Brenner, & Rainie, 2012).

The Spread of Legislation and Regulation

Globally there are approximately 90 countries with specific data protection laws on their statute books (Banisar, 2012), with others in development. This does not count countries with sector-specific legislation such as the United States. In general, the majority of these laws are based on the EU's Directive 95/46/EC (European Commission, 1995) or the OECD Guidelines on the Protection of Privacy and Transborder Flows of Personal Data (OECD, 1981).

There is a growing consensus on fundamental information processing principles that should be applied, and we are in the midst of a period of unprecedented activity in the development of data protection regulation globally which is already having a profound impact on the way in which global businesses are required to approach the collection and management of personal information.

Cultural and trade considerations are a key driver but the struggle to keep pace with emerging technology and online business methods is also a significant factor. The proposal for a new EU data protection regulation, (discussed later) is likely to effect a fundamental change in approach to the existing EU framework. However, of equal significance is the toughening of requirements in countries such as Korea, Hong Kong and Singapore, and the emergence of laws in countries which previously had no data protection law in place, including a large number of countries in Asia, Latin America, and the Middle East.

It is unfortunately outside the scope of this Chapter to consider every granular aspect of the evolution of Privacy and Data Protection laws globally but a number of factors are worth noting:

1. Many of the new laws or newly strengthened laws can be mapped to the principles and structures of EU legislation. A key root cause for this is almost inevitably the need for countries that have significant presence of outsource service providers operating in their economies to demonstrate 'adequacy' under EU Data Protection regulations and ideally attain 'Safe Country' status which simplifies the operation of data processing in those countries;
2. Sanctions are increasingly stringent in these jursidictions. For example Hong Kong's Data Protection Ordinance carries a penalty of up to HK$50,000 or 2 years in prison for failure to comply with an enforcement order. As is common in Data Protection regulation, electronic marketing carries higher penalties (up to 5 years in prison) (DLA Piper, 2013).

The discussion of the privacy implications of intelligence services data gathering and data mining practices leveraging the data assets of free on-line services has re-ignited the debate about the fundamental principles and purposes of Data Privacy/Data Protection laws in Europe, which will have implications for the final content of this legislation given the fresh memories in many parts of Europe and elsewhere of the negative impacts of governments gathering and analysing data about their citizens.

What is Data Protection?

In this chapter I discuss "Data Protection" from the EU context. This is somewhat broader than simply keeping data safe or ensuring your organization has appropriate backup strategies and systems in place. It encompasses fundamental concepts of privacy as a human right and how that right should be balanced against competing rights and goals in a society. Indeed a fundamental right to personal data privacy is recognized in the EU and a right to privacy has been recognized in the United Nations Declaration of Human Rights and the European Convention on Human Rights. Similarly the right to Privacy has been recognized in the US as far back as Louis Brandeis' famous definition of it in 1890 as "the right to be left alone" (Brandeis & Warren, 1890). However, in all cases, the right to privacy is never absolute.

It is outside the scope of this chapter to give a full history of data protection. However it is important to recognize that this right has evolved in response to evolutions in technology for capturing and processing information about people (Brandeis' article was prompted by developments photography) and a reaction to the abuse and misuse of personal data by governments and others to the detriment of entire sections of society (the processing of personal data by Nazi and Communist regimes in Europe being the most pertinent examples). The concerns of citizens in Europe, Canada, and elsewhere referenced earlier in this chapter highlight that today, just as in the 1890s, the development of technological means to process information about individuals is still a concern.

The development of these privacy rights is a clear indication that society, in general, views unwarranted intrusion into the "right to be left alone" to be a non-quality outcome of technological innovation. The interference in that right must be balanced by a some duties and obligations on the part of the entity engaging in the processing to ensure that it is done under appropriate controls, and with the appropriate level of transparency, such that the right to privacy is balanced against other rights such as the right to free speech and the legitimate rights of an organization to generate revenues and deliver services.

Data Protection laws are the response of the legislature in society to address a power imbalance in the relationship between the entity who wishes to process data about individuals and the individual themselves. Yes, privacy may be invaded, but only within the context of a set of defined checks and balances and a governing framework of principles that allow a balance to be struck-quite often placing a burden or limitation on the organization with regard to what it seeks to do and how it seeks to do it. The findings in 2011 against Facebook by the FTC (Federal Trade Commission, 2011) centered on the transparency of their terms and conditions and practices which resulted in the terms and conditions which governed the processing of personal data being changed in a way which was unfair to the consumer.

Likewise, the findings le against Google's amendments to its Terms and Conditions and Privacy policies of the EU's Article 29 Working Group, led by the French Data Protection Authority CNIL, also raised concerns regarding of transparency of "the deal", the potential current and future uses for data, and the ability of the individual to exercise their right to "opt-out" and be left alone from any such analysis of their joined up profile, and how long data about individuals would be retained by Google (CNIL, 2012). At the time of writing, EU Data Protection Regulators have indicated they will commence enforcement proceedings against Google on this if changes are not made (Arthur, 2013).

In this context, Data Protection laws and regulations can best be described as *the definition of expectation by society of how organizations who are processing data about individuals can ensure an appropriate balance is struck between the right to privacy of the individual and the objectives and goals of the organization*. The legislative or policy recommendations that are set out by the law makers or Regulatory bodies represent a statement of duties and standards of care that should be met and principles that should be followed. Failing to comply with these principles and standards means that the organization has failed to meet the expectation of society. This non-quality outcome can lead to financial or other criminal sanctions, risk of litigation, and inevitable brand damage to the organization due to negative publicity.

The laws are enacted to provide protection from the consumer. In doing so, two customers are created for any organization to serve: the individual whose data is being processed and the Regulator who seeks to enforce the laws. Therefore Business Intelligence and Information Quality practitioners are advised to consider Data Protection rules not in the context of barriers that are erected by bureaucrats to *prevent* a thing from being done, but rather as a set of guiding statements about *how* information about people should be processed so as to meet one of society's explicit quality expectations for data, which in turn should inform decisions and choices around the management of quality and the operation of Governance and controls.

The Impacts of Getting it Wrong – Penalties

One area of complaint from Privacy activists about many Data Protection/Privacy laws is that the penalties levied by Regulators are often weak in comparision to the financial benefits to organisations from unlawful activities. The penalties currently vary from jurisdiction to jurisdiction but usually include both a criminal sanction and the right of affected individuals to take civil actions to recover for any loss or damage incurred. Even within the EU the penalties currently vary widely, ranging from fines of €3000 per offence to €500,000 fines per offence or even incarceration.

Examples of recent penalties levied include:

- A fine of stg£50,000 levied against a UK insurer for failing to correct incorrectly matched records in a pension fund which had resulted in payments made by Party A being credited against Party B's account. This was (Information Commissioners Office (UK), 2012);
- Google were fined €100,000 by CNIL for collecting data on Wi-Fi networks detected by Street View camera cars, data which included passwords and other sensitive data (CNIL, 2011);
- Google were fined over US$7 million by the FTC for Street View violations (Streifield, 2013);
- Stg£250,000 penalty levied by ICO against Sony Computer Entertainment Europe Ltd arising from a massive data security breach in 2011 which resulted in data of millions of Sony Entertainment Network and Playstation Network customers being stolen[1] (Information Commissioners Office, 2013).

Most jurisdictions also give Data Protection Regulators the power to require that data being processed unlawfully be deleted and the processing activity stopped. This can have a potentially significant impact on organisations. Also fines and penalties are often levied in multiple jurisdictions for the same data processing activitity. Google's Street View breaches, for example, resulted in penalties in the US, France, and Germany and faces fines in the UK if data is not deleted appropriately.

Of course, the penalties and sanctions are just part of the bottom line impact that arises where a breach of Data Protection rules occurs. The other impacts would include:

- Cost of conducting investigations (internal and external costs);
- Cost of providing credit checking services to customers;
- Brand damage and associated costs;
- Legal fees arising from defending a prosecution;
- Increased insurance costs;
- Potential personal liability on the part of Directors or Officers of an organisation.

It is also important to bear in mind that, where a Data Protection breach arises, it may give rise to potentially long term impacts on the career prospects of those involved, particularly in the Financial Services sector, where involvement or implication in a Data Protection breach could give rise to difficulties on the part of individuals meeting 'fitness and probity' tests which are imposed for senior managers and Directors in Financial Services organisations under a variety of international statutory controls. This is a significant cost of 'non-quality' in the management of Personal Data Protection obligations.

If 'quality of information' is defined from the perspective of the customer then it is clear: striking an appropriate balance between the individual's personal data privacy and the objectives of the organisation processing that information will be a key strategic challenge for organistations. A commonly used metaphor is that data is the 'new oil'. In that context, data privacy rules and legislation perhaps can be described as the new environmental regulation. In that context, Data Privacy Regulators and the laws they enforce should be seen as equivalent to environmental safety laws.

DATA PROTECTION – UNDERSTANDING PRINCIPLES

We now turn to consider what is meant by "Data Protection", the types of data that fall under the scope of Data Protection legislation, some core fundamental principles of Data Protection. We will then explore the relationship between Data Protection and Information/Data Quality.

What are Personal Data and Sensitive Personal Data?

Of course, not all data falls within the scope of Data Protection legislation. Instinctively we would all recognize name, address, email address, telephone numbers, and other contact information as "personal" data. However the definition of what is "personal data" is actually much broader, particularly in the context of EU Data Protection laws. As Article 2 of Directive 95/46/EC defines "*Personal Data*" as:

...any information relating to an identified or identifiable natural person ("data subject"); an identifiable person is one who can be identified, directly or indirectly, in particular by reference to an identification number or to one or more factors specific to his physical, physiological, mental, economic, cultural or social identity.

The key test is whether it is possible to identify an individual from this data or other data that might be likely to come in to the possession of the organization directing the processing (referred to in EU law and the OECD Guidelines on the Protection of Privacy as a "Data Controller"). This definition of "Personal Data" is consistent with the OECD definition and definitions found in the Data Protection legislation of non-EU jurisdictions (e.g. Canada, South Africa, Argentina etc).

Examples of information which can be "personal data" in this context include:

- Biometric data;
- Images (still and video);
- Audio recordings;
- IP addresses (in some jurisdictions but not in others).

If an individual is in a sufficiently small population size even anonymised data may be sufficiently unique to single them out for identification indirectly. This can pose risks in the context of "big data" were re-identification of anonymised data can occur when multiple data sets are combined.

Sensitive Personal Data is defined in EU Law as data which relates to ethnicity, religious or philosophical beliefs, trade union membership, physical or mental health or sexual life, allegations of criminal offences, or criminal proceedings to which the Data Subject is party and any sentencing information associated to those proceedings. Similar concepts are found in a variety of Data Protection legislations, for example the South African Protection of Personal Information Bill (Bhagattjee, 2012). Data relating to children can often be classified as 'sensitive' or 'special' data in Data Protection laws as well (e.g. COPPA in the United States).

In general, "Sensitive" personal data is subjected to a much stricter set of controls in Data Protection laws than "normal" personal data. This stricter set of controls usually includes a requirement for explicit informed consent, more restrictions on purposes for use of the data, and restrictions on disclosure of the data.

It is extremely important that an organisation understand the nature of the data it is processing in the conduct of a Business Analytics or Business intelligence activity. The context of data, the combination of data, and the content of data are all important to the correct classification of data.

A simple scenario is this: You are processing two data files of person names and addresses and marital status (married/cohabiting/single). This is personal data in each file. Your data load processes derive a gender for each of the names on each file. You then perform a matching process on the basis of the addresses and identify a number of Male/Female married or co-habiting couples, a number of Male/Male married or co-habiting couples and a number of Female/Female married or cohabiting couples. As a result of the processing that has taken place to identify people at the same address who might be part of a household, you have potentially derived sensitive personal data about the individuals involved and as such the level of care and consideration that must be taken with regards to that data has changed.

Personal Financial Data is another category of personal data which is also subject to varying degrees of statutory or regulatory protection in various jurisdictions, as well as industry standards based protections such as PCI. In general terms Personal Financial data is defined as an account number plus other data which might allow the name or other personal data of the account holder to be derived. Note that this is different to the idea of personal data about the individual and their financial status which can fall under the heading of Personal data if it constitutes a statement about the person (e.g. their creditworthiness) and would fall under the protection of general Data Protection principles which we will discuss shortly but which would include a requirement for accuracy and "up-to-date-ness".

Why Does it Matter?

In order to effectively manage the risks associated with the processing of data of any kind it is important to correctly identify the types of data that you are processing. If your business intelligence initiative is looking solely at non-personal information then Privacy laws and regulations are not going to be much of a concern. If the scope of your analysis includes sensitive personal data then you need to be conscious of the higher standard of care that would apply to that data.

Anonymisation is often touted as a panacea to privacy issues. However in the age of "Big Data" it is increasingly clear that anonymisation is not the panacea we might assume it to be given the ease with which depersonalised data can be analysed to identify an individual. A 2008 study (Narayaan & Shmatikov, 2008) on the anonymity of data showed that 80% of *Netflix* users could be identified uniquely based solely on when and how they rated movies they had rented from the service.

The UK's Information Commissioner's Office issued a guidance note on anonymisation in 2012 (Information Commissioner's Office, 2012) which reflects, insofar as is possible, the concern of re-identification of anonymised data. They advise that the kinds of good practice that apply to the sharing of non-anonymised data are still relevant to anonymised data sets – in other words that anonymisation should be seen as a layer of defence rather than a solution in and of itself.

They suggest that the appropriate test to apply to assessing the suitability of your anonymisation approach would be the "motivated intruder test", in which organisations would need to consider the level of difficulty posed to a motivated person who was to try and re-identify your data based on reasonable competence of the intruder and their ability to access libraries, the Internet, or similar public resources. No specialist technical skills should be assumed on the part of this intruder other than reasonable competence in investigation skills. Likewise it is not necessary that the "motivated intruder" have used any illegal means to perform their re-identification in order for your anonymisation to be viewed as an ineffective protection.

For example, if the data you are processing relates to the patterns of diagnosis, treatment and prognosis of an illness that is rare in a population, and your data could allow analysis by a geographic area which might result in a single patient in a single hospital in a particular geographic area being identified, then even in its anonymised state this data would likely constitute Sensitive Personal Data and would require appropriate safeguards be put in place to limit its use and disclosure.

So, it matters that you can correctly identify the kinds of data you are working with in a BI context so you can best determine the kinds of controls and governance mechanisms you might need to have put in place to ensure that data that identifies your customers, clients, or employees is not put at risk of unauthorised disclosure or use. That risk assessment needs to consider whether anonymisation of data would, on its own, provide sufficient protections or whether you would need to apply the principles of 'defence in depth' and layer governance and other controls around your data to ensure the quality outcome of privacy protection is met.

Core Principles from EU and Elsewhere

In our discussion above of why it is important to understand the kinds of data you are working with and the limitations of anonymisation as a tool to depersonalize data we touched on one of the more commonly recognized principles of Data Protection: the need to keep personal data safe and secure. Indeed it is a shortcoming of most media coverage of Data Protection issues that the concepts of Data Protection and Privacy are often conflated with that of Information Security. As with many things, the reality is slightly different and significantly more complex.

It is important to manage expectations of what is possible in a single book chapter. The intent of this review is simply to present the broad scope and outline of core principles that exist in the EU and elsewhere and show the commonality that exists. The specifics of national enforcement regimes or the underlying cultural reasons for differences in approach to and philosophy of privacy and privacy enforcement between jurisdictions is a topic worthy of its own library, let alone a book or a contributed chapter. The focus of discussion will be mainly on principles, with reference to legislative trends or looming changes where appropriate.

The OECD Guidelines on the Protection of Privacy and Transborder Flows of Personal Data (OECD, 1981) set out eight core principles for the processing of personal data in a manner that respects the Right to Privacy. These are considered to be a set of minimum standards that are often referred to as Fair Information Processing Standards. The Data Protection legislative frameworks of EU Member States and other countries can be mapped to these guidelines.

The European Union's current Data Protection regime is based on a set of eight core principles set out in Directive 95/46/EC which map to the OECD principles outlined in Table 1. While the overall Data Protection regime in Europe is being overhauled, there is a strong emphasis on retaining and building on these principles so it is important to understand them and their practical implications. Furthermore, an analysis of Data Privacy laws from other jurisdictions such as Norway, South Africa, New Zealand, Canada, Chile, or Argentina reveals a similar close mapping to the core OECD principles, with local variations largely arising in the areas of emphasis and priority and penalties for breach.

This 'local variation' that can exist throws up another factor that needs to be considered when looking at Data Privacy issues that arise in data analytics and business intelligence: The Human Factor. Much of the local variation that exists in data privacy laws is reflective of cultural differences in different cultures or socio-geographic regions. For example, in Norway the Government publishes details of each citizen's tax returns every year. The cultural driver at play is the Viking culture of everyone being seen to contribute to society in proportion with their means. Likewise, while the EU Data Protection Directive was

Table 1. OECD fair information processing principles

OECD Fair Information Processing Principle	Description of Principle
1. The Collection Limitation Principle:	There should be limits to the collection of personal data and any such data should be obtained by lawful and fair means and, where appropriate, with the knowledge or consent of the data subject
2. The Data Quality Principle:	Personal data should be relevant to the purposes for which they are to be used, and, to the extent necessary for those purposes, should be accurate, complete and kept up-to-date
3. The Purpose Specification Principle:	The purposes for which personal data are collected should be specified not later than at the time of data collection and the subsequent use limited to the fulfillment of those purposes or such others as are not incompatible with those purposes and as are specified on each occasion of change of purpose.
4. The Use Limitation Principle:	Personal data should not be disclosed, made available or otherwise used for purposes other than those specified in accordance with [The Purpose Specification] except: a) with the consent of the data subject; or b) by the authority of law
5. The Security Safeguards Principle:	Personal data should be protected by reasonable security safeguards against such risks as loss or unauthorized access, destruction, use, modification or disclosure of data.
6. The Openness Principle	There should be a general policy of openness about developments, practices and policies with respect to personal data. Means should be readily available of establishing the existence and nature of personal data, and the main purposes of their use, as well as the identity and usual residence of the data controller.
7. The Individual Participation Principle	An individual should have the right: a) to obtain from a data controller, or otherwise, confirmation of whether or not the data controller has data relating to him; b) to have communicated to him, data relating to him within a reasonable time; at a charge, if any, that is not excessive; in a reasonable manner; and in a form that is readily intelligible to him; c) to be given reasons if a request made under subparagraphs(a) and (b) is denied, and to be able to challenge such denial; and to challenge data relating to him and, if the challenge is successful to have the data erased, rectified, completed or amended.
8. The Accountability Principle	A data controller should be accountable for complying with measures which give effect to the principles stated above.

drafted to protect primarily the living, Italian law provides for Data Protection and privacy rights for the deceased as well (PriviReal.org).

The basic implications for Business Intelligence professionals seeking to ensure they are processing personal data in a quality manner (i.e. consistent with the expectations of the customer and of society) are manifold and it is important that BI professionals do not ignore the potential impacts of legislation, regulatory requirements, and cultural issues in their design of analysis or the formulation of hypotheses for testing. It is an unfortunate truism of Data Protection that just because you can ask and answer a particular question does not mean that you should. In that context it is worth noting that some technology organizations in Norway have questioned Norway's practice of publishing tax payer information in light of the disproportionate ease of access to that data in the Internet Age and the implications for privacy that that practice raises (EPTA, 2010).

Beyond Just Principles

In addition to the core principles illustrated below, many jurisdictions extend specific restrictions on the processing of personal data for electronic marketing, the processing of biometric data, and the processing of location based data. In many cases these regulations impose specific requirements for explicit informed consent for the processing of that data. Other laws define restrictions on the retention of and access to data retained by telecommunications service providers.

Examples of these kinds of laws would include the EU's Electronic Data Privacy Directive (European Commission, 2002) which requires (among other things):

- Explicit opt-in Consent be obtained for cookies which are not essential to the operation of a website, in particular third party tracking cookies;
- Explicit opt-in consent is required for marketing by electronic means (e.g. SMS, email, fixed line phone, mobile phone etc.).

Furthermore, the application of the principles often requires an insight into a range of ancillary legislation or international treaties, particularly where such legislation is being relied upon as the basis for lawful processing of personal data.

Therefore it is important to look beyond the core Data Protection legislation and principles that are in force in a given jurisdiction. While principles are a valuable guideline for day to day practice, it is important to invest in appropriate legal and regulatory advice on relevant and applicable legislation that might affect any proposed processing of personal data. For that reason the concept of Privacy by Design and the tools of Privacy and Data Protection Impact Assessments, which will be discussed later in this chapter, are increasingly important.

Linking EU Principles to OECD Guidelines

Table 1 above summarizes the core OECD principles Personal Data Processing. Table 2 summarizes the core EU Principles as set out in current EU legislation. Table 3 above illustrates how the EU Principles map to OECD principles.

In addition, organizations in the EU are answerable to both national regulators (criminal sanction) and owe a statutory Duty of Care (civil liability) with regard to their compliance with the core Data Protection principles and related controls on Electronic Marketing and customer tracking in the on-line environment.

Different Perspectives on Data Protection – Individuals, Organizations and Regulators

The three key players in any Data Protection/Privacy regime are the Individuals about whom data is recorded or processed, the Organizations who are developing products or services to obtain or process information, or are making strategic decisions based on that information, and the Regulators, whose role should be seen striving to strike a balance between the rights of the individual to their privacy and the rights of organizations to achieve their legitimate goals.

Individuals

In line with the general principles outlined above individuals are entitled to expect that the minimum amount information necessary will be processed for the specified purposes they gave it and it will be kept safe and secure. This is a simple trust relationship and the importance to consumers of this trust relationship is borne out repeatedly in surveys and research. In my company's Data Protection consulting and advisory work we recognize this as the 'surprised customer test' – is the customer surprised by what is being done with their data?

Regulators

Regulators have the unenviable task of seeking to ensure balance is maintained between compet-

Table 2. EU data protection principles (based on Directive 95/46/EC)

European Data Protection Principle	Description of Principle
1. Personal Data must be obtained fairly and lawfully 2. Personal data must be processed for a specified and lawful purpose 3. Personal data cannot be processed for any other purpose that is incompatible with the specified purposes	These principles are essentially a transparency requirement which require the Data Controller (the entity that is directing the processing of the personal data) to be able to show: • How they have obtained the information • How they have communicated what the information would be used for • How they have obtained consent for that processing or, if not relying on consent, to be able to show which of the other specific grounds for processing personal data they are relying on (e.g. required to conclude a contract, required by law) Finally, the principles act together to impose a "Purpose limitation" on the processing of data. Once you have it you cannot use it for *any* purpose. It must be compatible with the original purpose. The example I give in training is that it would not be compatible for me to use class registers to sell timeshare to students who register for a class with me.
4. Personal data must be kept safe and secure	This is what is commonly understood by people as "Data Protection". What is required is that "appropriate" security measures be taken to prevent unauthorized access to, alteration of, or deletion of the data.
5. Personal data must be kept accurate and up to date, relative to the purpose for which it was obtained.	In the context of the purpose and process for which the data was obtained, it must be kept accurate and up to date.
6. Personal data must be adequate, relevant, and not excessive in the context of the purpose for which it was obtained.	In the context of the purpose for which it was obtained, the data must be adequate (i.e. enough to achieve the goal), relevant (used in the achieving of the goal), and not excessive (data minimization – only what is needed to achieve the goal).
7. Personal data must not be retained for longer than is necessary for the purpose for which it was obtained.	Data should be kept only for as long as it is needed for a specified purpose or for a related legal requirement. The key factor is to identify why you have data and minimize it over its life cycle (delete data, aggregate data etc.)
8. Data Subjects have Rights of Access/Rectification/ Erasure/Blocking	Whatever data you have about individuals they are entitled to a copy of, entitled to correct, and can ask to have it erased or blocked from future use for a particular purpose.

ing rights. This can be particularly problematic where organizations fail to embrace the Openness principles in Data Protection law and fail to implement appropriate systems and controls to ensure data is being obtained and processed fairly with a focus on relevance and quality but are potentially providing a service that is of value to consumers or society. A prior assessment of the impact on privacy, and the designing in of appropriate controls, by organizations is one way this challenge can be addressed.

Organizations

Organizations either direct the nature and objectives of data processing activities or directly carry out that processing themselves. In heavily outsourcer-reliant or 'cloud-friendly' organizations for example much of the actual processing may be carried out by third parties on behalf of the organization. In order to ensure that Data Protection risks are appropriately identified and mitigated organizations must have regard of the fundamental principles of Fair Information processing and put in place appropriate structures, governance, controls, and metrics.

In this context Business Intelligence practitioners are in a challenging position. Business Intelligence teams exist to provide new insights and drive innovation from the organization's data. However they are entirely reliant on that data having been obtained and processed for that purpose

Table 3. Mapping EU principles to OECD principles

EU Principle	Related OECD Principle
1. Personal Data must be obtained fairly and lawfully	Collection Limitation Principle; Openness Principle
2. Personal data must be processed for a specified and lawful purpose	Purpose Specification Principle; Openness Principle
3. Personal data cannot be processed for any other purpose that is incompatible with the specified purposes	Use Limitation Principle
4. Personal data must be kept safe and secure	Security Safeguards
5. Personal data must be kept accurate and up to date, relative to the purpose for which it was obtained.	The Data Quality Principle;
6. Personal data must be adequate, relevant, and not excessive in the context of the purpose for which it was obtained.	The Data Quality Principle;
7. Personal data must not be retained for longer than is necessary for the purpose for which it was obtained.	The Purpose Principle; The Data Quality Principle
8. Data Subjects have Rights of Access/Rectification/Erasure/ Blocking	The Individual Participation Principle
9. Criminal Sanctions and Civil Liability	The Accountability Principle

and they are reliant on the data being of sufficient quality to support that purpose. Furthermore, if the processing is illegal it is often the Business Intelligence team who are held to account in the organization for the wasted effort and investment in developing the analysis.

By pushing back to the organization that trusted BI insights can only be built on trusted data that is of an appropriate level of quality and which can actually be lawfully used for this purpose, BI teams can help minimize those risks to the organization. By applying Privacy by Design and Privacy Impact Assessment techniques to the design of BI activities the BI professional can better work around potential barriers rather than run head long into them.

An Overview of the EU Data Protection Regulation (as Currently Proposed)

At the time of writing the final text of the EU's new Data Protection Regulation is being finalized. While some specific details are to be worked out, the broad brush strokes of the Regulation have been well publicized. In the context of this chapter we will look at some of these broad topics as they would relate to the use of and analysis of Personal Data for BI.

One of the key themes of the revised Regulation is a key shift towards internal control and Data Governance, with a strong emphasis on documentation of internal processes and internal controls. This is similar to what is required under Sarbanes-Oxley and other similar legislation.

Data Protection by Design and by Default

The Regulation proposes that organizations will be required to design systems and processes with a focus on identifying and mitigating privacy and Data Protection compliance risks at the design stage and as a priority requirement.

This philosophy of 'privacy by design' is seen by many in the Data Protection/Privacy domain as being new and ground breaking. However from the perspective of Quality Management principles applied to Information and Data, the clear parallel with fundamental quality planning principles as set out by Deming, Juran, Shingo and others which have been adapted and applied in the sphere of Information Quality Management.

In this 'Privacy by Design' mindset, privacy principles and Data Protection legislation are viewed as statements of requirements[2] which need to be considered in the design of the system, process, or business model. The challenge for Business Intelligence and Analytics professionals is to push this requirement back up stream to the points of capture and collection of data such that the data being analyzed is a trustworthy source for the insights being sought.

Related to the concept of Data Protection by Design is the tool and practice of Data Protection Impact Assessment. This is a structured process whereby the proposed processing is 'impact assessed' against the requirements, business needs, and statements of quality standards as set out in legislation (a Data Protection Impact Assessment, aka DPIA) and the perception of the customer (a Privacy Impact Assessment, aka PIA). The Regulation recommends the inclusion of customers in the conduct of any such assessment to ensure that the 'Voice of the Customer' is heard in the impact assessment process.

It is outside the scope of this chapter to provide a detailed insight into the methodologies for PIA and DPIA. An excellent resource is Wright and De Hert's *Privacy Impact Assessment* (Wright & De Hert, 2012). Suffice it to say that the purpose, principles, and practices of a DPIA or PIA overlap significantly with the Business Impact Analysis/Cost and Risk of Non-Quality process steps outlined in a number of Information Quality methodologies such as Danette McGilvray's 'Ten Steps' method (McGilvray, 2008) or Larry P English's TIQM methodology (English, 2009).

Extra Territorial Effect

Another significant change in the draft Regulation is the introduction of a degree of extra-territorial effect which would require organizations based outside the European Union to comply with EU Data Protection laws. This requirement is contained in Article 1(2) of the draft Regulation which states that:

- This Regulation applies to the processing of personal data of data subjects residing in the Union by a controller not established in the Union, where the processing activities are related to:
  - The offering of goods or services to such data subjects in the Union; or
  - The monitoring of their behavior.

So, if an organization is engaged in selling goods or services to individuals in the EU or are engaged in any form of behavioral monitoring, tracking or profiling of individuals residing within the EU then the organization will have to comply with EU Data Protection rules under this new Regulation. Of course, if a company with a base of operations (a "main establishment") within the EU will need to comply with EU laws in any event.

This provision has been the subject of much lobbying by US companies but it is conceptually no different to the requirements that exist under the Sarbanes-Oxley Act for non-US based organizations who are financed through instruments filed with the SEC (e.g. bonds, share listings etc.). having to comply with certain sections of the Sarbanes-Oxley Act, in particular sections 302 and 404.

Consent and Purpose Limitation

The original draft Regulation moved towards a stricter emphasis on explicit informed consent for the processing of personal data of EU citizens. The EU Commission has been at pains to point out that there are a number of other grounds for lawful processing of personal data, as there is under the current legislation.

Proposed amendments voted on by members of the European Parliament have diluted this somewhat, to the dismay of privacy advocates world-wide (Reuters, 2013).

Risk Management and Internal Governance Focus

The draft EU Regulation creates a significant shift towards strong internal governance and evidence of the effective operation of internal controls. This includes the creation of a specific role for a Data Protection Officer who must be directly supported by the executive management of the organization and who must be properly trained and resourced to execute their role in overseeing and monitoring the execution and operation of Data Protection controls in the organization, including the execution of Privacy Impact Assessments and verifying that mitigating actions and detective and preventative controls are in place and operating effectively.

Details of this role are still being debated based on various potential thresholds, but it is clear that a Risk-based approach to Data Protection will require application of Data Governance principles with appropriate metrics to support the role of the Data Protection Officer.

Anonymous and Pseudonymous Data

While not mentioned in the original draft Regulation, amendments tabled by members of the European Parliament have introduced specific concepts of Anonymous and Pseudonymous data into the draft that is being debated at this time.

Anonymous Data is defined in the current draft Regulation as: "information that has never related to a data subject or has been collected, altered or otherwise processed so that it cannot be attributed to a data subject."

Pseudonymous Data is defined in the current draft Regulation as: "any personal data that has been collected, altered or otherwise processed so that it of itself cannot be attributed to a data subject without the use of additional data which is subject to separate and distinct technical and organizational controls to ensure such non attribution."

The challenges of preserving anonymity of anonymized data or pseudonymized data are well documented in the cases of Netflix, AOL and others (Anderson, 2009) . The draft Regulation places a very strong emphasis on the need for internal controls and security protections to prevent non-attribution. Given the role of human error and failures of control in data breaches at present this is a risk.

Data Profiling

The draft EU Data Protection Regulation introduces a number of restrictions on what is termed 'data profiling'. As recently as May 2013 this has been the subject of discussion with the publication of a formal advice from the Article 29 Working Group (the collegiate body of Data Protection Authorities in the EU) (Article 29 Working Group, 2013).

The advice note from the Article 29 Working Group focuses on four key points:

1. It provides a suggested definition for Profiling that relates to the automated processing of information about people across a range of characteristics for analysis and prediction of behaviors;
2. They recommend that the Regulation considers the requirement around ensuring data had been correctly obtained, such as providing information about the nature of profiling being performed and any logic involved in automatic processing;
3. Individual data subjects should have the right to access, modify, or delete profile information linked to them;

4. Individuals should be entitled to challenge or have a human review of any measure or decision taken on the basis of profiled data.

This raises interesting challenges for Business Intelligence regarding the transparency of processing (e.g. how do you publish the algorithms if pursuing an 'agile BI' model?), the governance of access to and modification of profile data, and the potential need to have human review of the effects of decisions taken based on profile data (which could affect the design of future profiles).

Each of these recommendations can be mapped back to one or more of the fundamental principles for Data Protection, which suggests the Regulatory focus is one that sees BI as yet another evolution in the processing of personal data which must be grounded in these principles.

Impact

The breadth of detailed changes in the EU Data Protection Regulation is substantial. As of the end of June 2013 approximately 4000 amendments have been tabled. It is beyond the scope of this chapter, and perhaps premature, to engage in a detailed analysis of the impact of the EU's Data Protection Regulation on Business Analytics and Business Intelligence practices.

However, beyond the headline grabbing issues of consent and the proposed changes to fines (with maximum fines of up to 2% of global turnover for offences) there is a significant shift towards a model of privacy protection that aligns with Data Governance and Information Quality best practices. In particular the evolution of a risk-based model will lend itself to the use of BI tools and capabilities, coupled with Information Quality practices to ensure measurable and actionable controls are in place to ensure data is being appropriately governed to meet the requirements of the legislation.

Clearly the more trustworthy the data is that forms the basis of your profile data in terms of its quality and the transparency applied to its gathering, the lower risk of Regulatory penalties or operational issues arising from challenges to an organization's profiling activities.

Organizations that engage with the new Regulation from a position and perspective of Quality Management and Governance of Information will likely be better positioned to take advantage of the opportunities for brand differentiation that the Regulation presents. By aligning the requirements of the Regulation with their Governance and Information Quality initiatives organizations will also be better able to realize economies of scale and operational efficiencies by managing these requirements holistically.

DP, DG, IQ AND BI – A THREE LEGGED STOOL

The metaphor of the three legged stool is appropriate to any discussion of Data Protection, Information/Data Governance, and Information/Data Quality in the context of Business Intelligence. BI is the seat of the stool, on which the organization may place its strategic decisions. That seat is supported by the three legs of Data Protection compliance, Data Governance, and Information Quality:

- **Data Protection:** If you cannot legally use the data for this purpose you risk your ability to have and use the data and risk Regulatory penalties;
- **Data Governance:** If you do not have appropriate management structures in place to properly manage the information assets underpinning your BI endeavors and appropriately manage and mitigate risks, such as Data Protection compliance risks

around the obtaining, use of, and sharing of data, the seat of your BI strategy is undermined;
- **Information Quality:** If the information you have obtained is out of data, incomplete, or simply not fit for the purposes of your BI function your BI strategy is also undermined.

The interplay and interdependence between these three 'legs' ultimately provides the strength and stability for the seat of your BI strategy and execution. The link between Data Protection and Data Quality has been recognized as far as the OECD Guidelines in 1981 the fundamental principles of Data Protection have been discussed with reference to "Data Quality". The role of Data Governance in executing Data Protection programs is also recognized in standards such as BS10012:2009 (British Standards Institute, 2009), which stresses the need for a formal management system for managing personal information in organizations, and in concepts such as Privacy Impact Assessments.

We have already discussed the concept of law and regulation providing a means to give effect to the 'Voice of the Customer', particularly given the strong pro-privacy findings in studies in the EU, Canada, and the US. However it is important to remember that organizations do not need (and indeed perhaps should not) wait for legislation or industry standards to hear the voice of their customers.

The response of internet browser developers to the concerns of their customers about on-line privacy and cookies an example of this: despite there being a stop-start development of a Do Not Track (DNT) standard, many browser developers have already implemented DNT features in their browsers to help protect their user's on-line privacy. Privacy has effectively become a competitive issue for them. The latest is Mozilla Firefox who announced a new Cookie-handling policy for Firefox. This will have potentially significant impacts on the on-line advertising industry (Bott, 2013).

Data Protection and Information Quality Characteristics

One of the key ways in which Data Protection and Information Quality dovetail is in the area of the measurable characteristics/dimensions of Information Quality, examples of which can be found in books by any number of information and data quality thought leaders.

This dovetailing operates at two levels:

- **Above the line:** Specific quality characteristics of information which are explicitly referenced in the Data Protection principles (whether OECD guidelines or EU law);
- **Below the line:** Quality characteristics of information which need to be considered to support Data Protection compliance goals and requirements but which are not immediately obvious from the principles or legislation. Often these metrics support governance functions related to Data Protection Compliance.

For the purposes of this chapter we will refer to the data quality dimensions defined by Danette McGilvray in her 2008 book (McGilvray, 2008). However equivalent mappings can be done to the methodologies of David Loshin (Loshin, 2001) others. Readers are directed to Chapters 5 and 9 of Loshin's work.

Above the Line Metrics

From these Above-the-Line metrics it is possible to develop a basic "Data Protection scorecard" which can allow the organization to more proactively measure the cost and risk of non-quality (i.e. not compliant) data protection practices (see Table 4).

Table 4. Above the line information quality for data protection

Data Protection Principle	Information Quality Characteristics	Derived Business Rule to Test
Keep safe and Secure	• Data Specifications	• Is there a Data Protection Policy? • Is there an Information Security Policy?
Keep Accurate, Up-to-date	• Accuracy • Timeliness/Availability • Data Decay	• How correct is data vs Reality • Is the data available for use when needed? • How fast does the data become out of date?
Adequate, Relevant, Not Excessive	• Perception, Relevance, Trust • Duplication • Data Specifications • Data Coverage	• How much data is not being used? • Do stakeholders 'trust' the data • What is the level of unwanted duplication of data? • How well is the data model documented? Is there too much data? • Are all the things that need to be known known
Retained for no longer than necessary	• Timeliness/Availability • Data Integrity Fundamentals	• How old is data? • Has data over X age been archived/deleted • What is average age of data? • What is oldest record?

Below the Line Metrics

Of course, the "Above the line" measures only tell half the story. Below-the line metrics would include:

- The quality of your data models (Data Specifications, Data Integrity Fundamentals):
  - Are you recording data that is not being accessed or used?
  - Have you designed your data model to allow you to flexibly add new means of contacting customer (e.g. Skype, WhatsApp) or new purposes for contacting them? (Data Specification of data model);
- How well you replicate key customer facts across different data sets (Consistency and Synchronization):
  - If you are using multiple mailing list platforms, are the contact preferences for customers correctly reflected across all of them or might you send marketing emails in error?
- Transactability:
  - Is it possible for knowledge workers to use information to execute plans and projects with the desired outcome (no Data Protection breaches, customer satisfied and not freaked out by 'Big Brother')?

The Importance of Metrics in the Risk-Based Compliance World

Historically Data Protection has been a largely reactive pursuit, with organizations responding to complaints and issues as they arise. The new EU Data Protection Regulation shifts the focus more towards Data Governance and Information Quality principles. Likewise the emergence of standards like BS10012:2009 (British Standards Institute, 2009) brings in the disciplines of Data Governance. Central to any successful Data Governance or Information Quality program is the need to be able to measure the improvement of 'critical to quality' metrics. Data Protection is no different.

By identifying metrics that are 'critical to Data Protection' and having a process and procedure to measure them and track trends, leading organizations can apply the discipline and rigor of Information Quality to Data Protection compliance.

ASSEMBLING THE STOOL FOR YOUR BI INITIATIVE

Returning to the image of the three-legged stool we find ourselves in a position where a Business Intelligence practitioner can begin to ask key questions in the organization to assess just how stable the platform on which the BI initiatives of the organization is, notwithstanding the usual role of the BI team as an 'end-of-food-chain' consumer of data gathered through other processes.

Table 5 below sets out a basic checklist for verifying whether the overall Data Protection System in the organization (people, processes, technology etc.) provides the appropriate basis for trusted BI processing, by ensuring attention is paid to the three legs of the stool supporting BI.

Ultimately it is not for the Business Intelligence function to necessarily answer these questions. However it is prudent to ask them.

Opportunities and Solutions

Of course, the shift towards a risk-based view of Data Protection and the Quality systems per-

Table 5. Sample questions to be asked by BI teams

'Stool Leg'	Example Questions for BI Teams	Impact/Implication
Data Protection Compliance	1. Are we processing data relating to EU citizens in this data set? 2. Was our Business Intelligence / Profiling purpose communicated to customers when they gave their data? 3. Is the data accurate enough for our purposes? 4. Is data complete or up-to-date enough for our purposes? 5. Have we verified that our processing activity (including code) is not contrary to company policies/ procedures or national/international data protection laws?	• If yes, EU Data Protection rules may apply • If no, then it processing may breach EU and other Data Protection regulations • If data is not accurate/complete/timely enough it will give invalid BI results – what is 'risk appetite' for error? • Have you tested your code to make sure data is not be processed incorrectly? Have you tested assumptions for legal/compliance validity?
Data Governance	1. What standards are being applied to Data Protection Governance (e.g. BS10012:2009)? 2. Where can BI go to seek clarification on processing plans? 3. Have we conducted a Privacy Impact Assessment? 4. Are the processing rules and algorithms being used documented?	• The organization needs to have a structure where people can raise questions re: Data Protection compliance. • Adopting a standards-based model supports appropriate formal structures. • Assessing risks as part of governance improves compliance • Documentation is an important component of compliance and auditability of data.
Information Quality	1. Do we have metrics for how old the data is? 2. Do we have metrics for how incomplete the data is? 3. How are 'null' values to be interpreted? 4. Do we have records of customer consent to profiling of data (particularly where explicit consent is required by law)? 5. Do we have metrics for accuracy of our data? 6. What actions are taken to correct defective data?	• Age of source data affects the validity of results in BI models. • If data is complete and accurate the results of analysis will be more trusted. • If data is of poor quality BI outputs will be second guessed. • If no auditable records for consent (e.g. opt-in flags with date stamps) it can be difficult to support Data Protection audits with evidence. • If data is interpreted incorrectly when developing BI analytics, BI results will not be trusted in the organization.

spective that comes through the application of Information Quality techniques to the management and measurement of Data Protection compliance creates opportunities for BI professionals.

Drives a Focus to Data, Process, and Metadata

Bluntly it will be difficult if not impossible to comply with future Data Privacy and Data Protection laws without a focus on the data, the processes that create, manage, and dispose of it, the processes that govern it, and the metadata that describes it.

Meta data such as the classification of types of data, the classification of sensitivity of data in a particular context, and the roles and responsibilities and decision rights that surround the data will be increasingly important to audit and control functions. The emphasis on Privacy by Design and Privacy Impact Assessments will drive organizations to be more process focused with regard to personal information. The need to control anonymous and pseudonymous data more effectively and securely (so it stays anonymised and pseudonymized) will drive a focus on process control and governance.

What is Measured Gets Done

Organizations that deploy information quality metrics to measure Critical-to-Data-Protection information characteristics will be better positioned to prevent breaches of the Data Protection principles. Whether it is having a structured metric system for data model design that ensures that models are not built that cannot be flexible for future needs without requiring excessive amounts of data to be captured or having a tracking metric of data accuracy or how recently customer data has been verified (on average), any metric will trigger a change in behavior as what is measured gets done in most organizations.

BI Professionals are in a key position in organizations to lead or at least be key enablers of this kind of measurement. They have the tools, the discipline, and the access to data sets to conduct basic measurements. They understand (or should understand) how to present the information in a way that can support and drive action on the part of business stakeholders.

The Data Protection Officer Role

In the context of an organization model that is moving to increasingly formalized governance and control of Data Protection, BI professionals could occupy a key position in the organization to step into the Data Protection Officer role envisaged by the EU Data Protection Regulation (subject to them developing expert knowledge of Data Protection laws and practices).

BI Practitioners often sit between the Business and IT sides of the organization with an insight into the questions that drive the business and an overview of the IT systems that feed the answers to those questions. They usually have a strong logical perspective and should be competent at defining and analyzing business rules and the logic of how to implement a requirement.

Much of the discussion of the Data Protection Officer role presumes it to be a role for the Legal or Regulatory teams in an organization. It may well be, however, that it is easier to teach an Information Quality focused Business Intelligence professional the principles, practices, and legislation related to Data Protection than it would be for a lawyer to develop an appropriate understanding of Data Profiling techniques and tools.

FUTURE RESEARCH DIRECTIONS

While historically both academia and industry have addressed the questions of data protection and information quality as separate topics, perhaps it is time to adopt a quality management principle and break down barriers between these silos. By considering Data Protection compliance as a

"Quality System for Information" a number of potential avenues for future research may become open for exploration.

For example, does the impact of training in data quality methods and principles (Levis, 2011) transfer over into data protection compliance, and if not does that indicate a flaw in the way in which data protection compliance training has historically been undertaken? Does the application of quality metrics to data protection obligations through an information life cycle (e.g. relevance and completeness of data models as quality characteristics in data modeling) influence the overall awareness of and application of data protection principles and practices in the organization culture? Finally, one may seek to determine if "Privacy by Design" principles might help refine the quality and focus of "Big Data" analytics by requiring increased rigor in the Design of Experiments and basic hypothesis formulation given that "just because you can doesn't mean you should."

The question of maturity of information quality practice and its correlation with data protection compliance and business intelligence practices is also a topic which may interest future research across Computer Science faculties, Business schools, and Law schools.

CONCLUSION

Data Protection and Data Privacy is the elephant in the room when it comes to Business Intelligence and analytics in this age of "Big Data". With the prospect of increasingly severe penalties and a growing consensus on core principles (if not necessarily standard practices) organizations face an increasing challenge to derive value from data in a manner that results in quality outcomes for the organization, its customers, and society as a whole. When faced with the array of potential data sources that are available to them today, BI practitioners understandably feel like children in a candy store. However, just because you can doesn't mean you should.

By approaching Data Protection as a Quality System applied to Information and by applying proven Information Quality principles and practices and implementing good Data Governance structures and behaviors organizations will be better placed to manage the privacy and compliance risks inherent in any consolidation and analysis of personal data. As 'end-of-food-chain' stakeholders, BI practitioners are well placed to push for this rigor in their organizations so that they can be sure they are building their analytic models on high quality trustworthy data that has been obtained for the purposes of *that* analysis.

Only then will the organization be able to fully trust the answers and trust that asking the questions won't have triggered a regulatory breach that will prove expensive in terms of both regulatory penalties and brand damage. This should be a key definition for "fit for purpose" in an analytics driven organization.

Viewing Data Protection as purely a response to a legislative/Regulatory driver misses the point. Just as web-browser developers have begun to listen to the "Voice of the Customer" and offer improved cookie handling features, organizations world-wide need to pay attention to the growing concerns about the safe and protected processing of personal information. The statistics are consistent across the EU, Canada, Europe, and beyond: People expect organizations to process their personal data with respect and on trust. Breaching that trust would be a singularly significant incident of poor quality information with potentially terminal results for an organization.

Just as automobile makers had to learn to build quality in BI, Big Data, and Data Analytics need to build quality and protections in to satisfy the increasingly nervous Voice of the Customer.

REFERENCES

AFP Newswire/ Yahoo News. (2013, February 18). *Europe to move against Google over privacy laws.* Retrieved February 25, 2013, from http://sg.news.yahoo.com/eu-act-against-google-over-privacy-french-agency-005337585.html

Anderson, N. (2009, September 8). *Anonymized data really isn't—And here's why not.* Retrieved from http://arstechnica.com/tech-policy/2009/09/your-secrets-live-online-in-databases-of-ruin/

Arthur, C. (2013, July 5). European watchdogs order Google to rewrite privacy policy or face legal action. *The Guardian*. Retrieved 07 05, 2013, from http://www.guardian.co.uk/technology/2013/jul/05/google-privacy-policy-legal-action

Article 29 Data Protection Working Group. (2007). *Opinion 04/2007 on the concept of personal data.* Brussels: Article 29 Working Group.

Article 29 Working Group. (2013, May 13). *Advice paper on essential elements of a definition and a provision on profiling within the EU general data protection regulation.* Retrieved from http://ec.europa.eu/justice/data-protection/article-29/documentation/other-document/files/2013/20130513_advice-paper-on-profiling_en.pdf

Banisar, D. (2012, October 19). *National comprehensive data protection/privacy laws and bills 2012 map.* Retrieved January 15, 2013, from http://ssrn.com/abstract=1951416

Bhagattjee, P. (2012, June 1). *Data protection: South Africa.* Retrieved January 15, 2013, from http://ipandit.practicallaw.com/5-503-0787# Bott, E. (2013, February 25). *Firefox raises the online privacy bar with new cookie policy.* Retrieved February 25, 2013, from http://www.zdnet.com/firefox-raises-the-online-privacy-bar-with-new-cookie-policy-7000011740/

Brandeis, L., & Warren, S. (1890). The right to privacy. *Harvard Law Review*, 193.

British Standards Institute. (2009, May). *BS10012:2009*. BSI.

CNIL. (2011, March 21). *Google street view: CNIL pronounces a fine of 100,000 Euros.* Retrieved February 25, 2013, from http://www.cnil.fr/english/news-and-events/news/article/google-street-view-cnil-pronounces-a-fine-of-100000-euros/

CNIL. (2012, October 16). *Google's new privacy policy: Incomplete information and uncontrolled combination of data across services.* Retrieved January 15, 2013, from www.cnil.fr/english: http://www.cnil.fr/english/news-and-events/news/article/googles-new-privacy-policy-incomplete-information-and-uncontrolled-combination-of-data-across-ser/

English, L. P. (2009). *Information quality applied.* Indianapolis, IN: Wiley.

EPTA. (2010). *Policy brief on the publication of the Norwegian income tax settlements.* Retrieved February 15, 2013, from http://eptanetwork.org/projects.php?pid=670

European Commission. (1995). *Directive 95/46/EC of the European parliament and of the council of 24 October 1995 on the protection of individuals with regard to the processing of personal data and on the free movement of such data.* Retrieved January 15, 2013, from http://eur-lex.europa.eu/LexUriServ/LexUriServ.do?uri=CELEX:31995L0046:en:HTML European Commission. (2002, July 12). *Directive 2002/58/EC.* Retrieved February 13, 2013, from http://eur-lex.europa.eu/LexUriServ/LexUriServ.do?uri=CELEX:32002L0058:EN:HTML European Commission. (2011). *Eurobarometer 359: Attitudes on data protection and electronic identity in the European Union.* Brussels: European Commission.

Federal Trade Commission. (2011, November 29). *Facebook settles FTC charges that it deceived consumers by failing to keep privacy promises.* Retrieved January 15, 2013, from www.ftc.gov: http://www.ftc.gov/opa/2011/11/privacysettlement.shtm

Federal Trade Commission. (2012). *Protecting consumer privacy in an era of rapid change.* Washington, DC: FTC.

Hoofnagle, C. J., Urban, J. M., & Li, S. (2012). *Mobile payments: Consumer benefits and new privacy concerns.* Berkeley, CA: Berkley Center for Law and Technology. doi:10.2139/ssrn.2045580

Information Commissioner's Office. (2012). *Anonymisation: Managing data protection risk code of practice.* ICO.

Information Commissioners Office. (2013, January 24). *Sony fined £250,000 after millions of UK gamers' details compromised.* Retrieved February 25, 2013, from http://www.ico.gov.uk/news/latest_news/2013/ico-news-release-2013.aspx

Information Commissioners Office (UK). (2012). *Prudential fined £50,000 for customer account confusion.* Retrieved 02 25, 2013, from http://www.ico.gov.uk/news/latest_news/2012/prudential-fined-50000-for-customer-account-confusion-06112012.aspx

Levis, M. (2011, January 17). *Information quality training requirements analysis guideline demonstrated in a healthcare context.* (PhD Thesis). Dublin City University, Dublin, Ireland. Retrieved January 15, 2013, from doras.dcu.ie: http://doras.dcu.ie/16068/

Loshin, D. (2001). *Enterprise knowledge management: The data quality approach.* San Francisco: Morgan Kaufmann.

McGilvray, D. (2008). *Executing data quality projects: Ten steps to quality data and trusted information.* Burlington, MA: Morgan Kaufmann.

Narayaan, A., & Shmatikov, V. (2008). Robust de-anonymization of large sparse data sets. In *Proceedings of IEEE Symposium on Security and Privacy* (pp. 111-121). IEEE.

O'Brien, K. J. (2013, January 25). *Silicon valley companies lobbying against Europe's privacy proposals.* Retrieved February 20, 2013, from http://www.nytimes.com/2013/01/26/technology/eu-privacy-proposal-lays-bare-differences-with-us.html

OECD. (1981). *Guidelines on the protection of privacy and transborder flows of personal data.* Retrieved January 15, 2013, from http://www.oecd.org/internet/interneteconomy/oecdguidelinesontheprotectionofprivacyandtransborderflowsofpersonaldata.htm

Office of the Privacy Commissioner of Canada. (2011). *2011 Canadians and privacy survey.* Ottawa, Canada: Office of the Privacy Commissioner of Canada.

Piper, D. L. A. (2013, March). *Data protection laws of the world.* Retrieved from http://www.dlapiper.com/files/Uploads/Documents/Data_Protection_Laws_of_the_World_2013.pdf

PriviReal.org. (n.d.). *Italy - Data protection.* Retrieved February 15, 2013, from http://www.privireal.org/content/dp/italy.php

Purcell, K., Brenner, J., & Rainie, L. (2012). *Search engine use 2012.* Washington, DC: Pew Research Center.

Reuters. (2013, February 20). *EU lawmakers vote against mandatory data protection fines*. Retrieved February 25, 2013, from http://www.reuters.com/article/2013/02/20/eu-dataprotection-idUSL6N0BKF4X20130220

Streifield, D. (2013, March 12). *Google concedes that drive-by prying violated privacy.* Retrieved from http://www.nytimes.com/2013/03/13/technology/google-pays-fine-over-street-view-privacy-breach.html

The White House. (2012, February 23). *We can't wait: Obama administration unveils blueprint for a privacy bill of rights to protect consumers online.* Retrieved January 15, 2013, from http://www.whitehouse.gov/the-press-office/2012/02/23/we-can-t-wait-obama-administration-unveils-blueprint-privacy-bill-rights

Wright, D., & De Hert, P. (2012). *Privacy impact assessment*. New York: Springer. doi:10.1007/978-94-007-2543-0

ADDITIONAL READING

O Brien, D. (2011). *The Data Governance & Strategy Toolkit*, Ark Group

Soares, S. (2012). *Big Data Governance*. MC Press.

KEY TERMS AND DEFINITIONS

Anonymized/Anonymous Data: Anonymous data is data that is in such a format that it is impossible to establish the identity of any individuals whose details are contained in a database.

Consent: "Consent" is one of the grounds on which data can legally be processed under EU Data Protection law and other Data Protection regimes. However, to be effective the consent must be validly given and should be freely given, specific to the processing that will take place, and must be "informed". The requirement for "informed consent" means that appropriate language must be used to ensure that the Data Subject can understand what they are consenting to and the implications of granting such consent. This information must be made obvious to the individual for consent to be valid. In the context of this Chapter, the issue of ensuring valid consent for BI analytics is a significant challenge that must be considered and addressed if no other legal basis can be identified for the analytics processing.

Data Protection: Data Protection is the term used to describe the system of legislative and Regulatory requirements, business practices and controls, and technical solutions and tools that applied to the collection of, processing of, and securing of data relating to identifiable individuals such that the Privacy rights of the individual are appropriately balanced against other rights and duties in society and the legitimate activities of organizations engaged in the processing of personal data. Data Protection principles apply to both electronic and hard-copy records. The term "Data Protection" is often used to describe technical solutions for the protection of electronic data through the administration of backup processes to ensure that tasks run on schedule, and that data is securely backed up and recoverable. This represents a sub-set of the wider scope of tasks, activities, and disciplines that an organization should consider when addressing Data Protection obligations for Privacy.

Data Protection Impact Assessment/Privacy Impact Assessment: A systematic process for evaluating the potential impact of risks where processing operations are likely to present specific risks to the rights and freedoms of data subjects by virtue of their nature, their scope or their purposes. While often used synonymously, the focus of a Data Protection Impact Assessment (DPIA) is subtly different to that of a Privacy Impact

Assessment (PIA). A DPIA primarily focuses on the assessment of risks to compliance with Data Protection legislation. A PIA has a broader scope, considering the wider issues of Privacy risks beyond basic legislative compliance.

Data Subject: An individual who can be identified, either directly or indirectly, from data which is in the possession of an organization, or which is likely to come into their possession, in particular by reference to an identification number or to one or more factors specific to his physical, physiological, mental, economic, cultural or social identity. In the context of this Chapter, the concept of an identifiable person, even indirectly so, raises challenges for organizations conducting analysis on, for example, multiple anonymized data sets.

Personal Data: Personal Data is defined as any information which relates to an identified or identifiable individual. Usually this definition applies only to living individuals, but some jurisdictions (e.g. Italy) extend formal Data Protection protections to the deceased. Data relating to legal persons (e.g. corporations) is not considered Personal Data.

Processing: In the context of Data Protection legislation, the concept of processing is broadly defined and encompasses activities such as: Holding or Handling, Obtaining or Organizing, Altering or Aligning, Recording or Retrieving, Disclosing or Destroying, Storing or Sharing. In the context of BI and 'Big Data' it is important that organizations consider what processing activities they are undertaking and are able to identify an appropriate legal basis for that processing.

Pseudonymous / Pseudonymized Data: Personal data processed in such a way that the data cannot be attributed to a specific individual, without the use of additional information, provided the additional information is kept separately.

Purpose Limitation / Purpose Specification: In all Data Protection legislative frameworks or policy frameworks, organizations who obtain personal data from a data subject may do so for one or more specific, lawful and clearly stated purposes. It is, in general, unlawful to collect information about people routinely and indiscriminately – an organization must have a sound, clear and legitimate purpose for collecting personal data. The term "Purpose Specification" describes the principle that an organization must outline clearly their purposes for processing of personal data prior to the commencement of that processing. The term "Purpose Limitation" describes the principle that organizations may not engage in processing of data that is not compatible with the originally specified purposes. In practice this requires organizations to engage in dialogue with their Data Subjects to alert them to any planned changes to the specified purposes for processing. In the context of this chapter it is important that the implications of new processing purposes being 'spun up' in an organization without appropriate governance and controls and the Data Protection compliance risks that this raises be recognized.

Sensitive Personal Data: Sensitive personal data refers to that category of data about an individual that, because information about these matters could be used in a discriminatory way, and is likely to be of a private nature, it needs to be treated with greater care than other personal data. Within the European Union the following categories of personal data are classified as Sensitive Personal data: Data consisting of information relating to the racial or ethnic origin of the data subject, their political opinions, their religious beliefs or other beliefs of a similar nature, whether they are a member of a trade union, their physical or mental health or condition, their sexual life, the commission or alleged commission by the individual of any offence, or any proceedings for any offence committed or alleged to have been committed by that person, the disposal of such proceedings or the sentence of any court in such proceedings. Other jurisdictions may apply other categories, highlighting the importance of organizations ensuring that there is appropriate governance in place for the identification of and processing of sensitive personal data.

ENDNOTES

1 At the time of writing this penalty is under appeal by Sony in the UK.

2 This is alluded to earlier in this Chapter where we describe laws and regulations as statements of society's requirements for conduct.

Compilation of References

Aalders, H. (1999). The registration of QUALITY in a GIS. In *Proceedings from the International Symposium on Spatial Data Quality* (pp. 23-32). IEEE.

Aalders, H., & Morrison, J. (1998). Spatial data quality for GIS. In *Geographic information research: Trans-Atlantic perspectives* (pp. 463–475). London: Taylor & Francis.

Abate, M. L., Diegert, K. V., & Allen, H. W. (1998). A hierarchical approach to improving data quality. *Data Quality*, *4*(1), 10.

Aboelmaged, M. G. (2010). Six sigma quality: A structured review and implications for future research. *International Journal of Quality & Reliability Management*, *27*(3), 268–317. doi:10.1108/02656711011023294

AFP Newswire/ Yahoo News. (2013, February 18). *Europe to move against Google over privacy laws*. Retrieved February 25, 2013, from http://sg.news.yahoo.com/eu-act-against-google-over-privacy-french-agency-005337585.html

Agarwal, R., & Karahanna, E. (2000). Time flies when you're having fun: Cognitive absorption and beliefs about information technology usage. *Management Information Systems Quarterly*, *24*(1), 665–694. doi:10.2307/3250951

Agency for Healthcare Research and Qulaity. (2012). *Patient centered medical home*. Retrieved 1/16/2013, from http://pcmh.ahrq.gov/portal/server.pt/community/pcmh__home/1483/PCMH_Defining%20the%20PCMH_v2

Ajzen, I. (2001). Nature and operation of attitudes. *Annual Review of Psychology*, *52*, 27–58. doi:10.1146/annurev.psych.52.1.27 PMID:11148298

Ajzen, I., & Madden, T. J. (1986). Prediction of goal-directed behavior: Attitudes, intentions, and perceived behavioral control. *Journal of Experimental Social Psychology*, *22*(5), 453–474. doi:10.1016/0022-1031(86)90045-4

Akerlof, G. A. (1970). The market for lemons: Quality uncertainty and the market mechanism. *The Quarterly Journal of Economics*, *84*(3), 488–500. doi:10.2307/1879431

Alavi, M., Kayworth, & Leidner, D. E. (2005). An empirical examination of the influence of organizational culture on knowledge management practices. *Journal of Management Information Systems*, *22*(3), 191–224. doi:10.2753/MIS0742-1222220307

Alavi, M., & Leidner, D. E. (2001). Review: Knowledge management and knowledge management systems: Conceptual foundations and research issues. *Management Information Systems Quarterly*, *25*(1), 107–136. doi:10.2307/3250961

Albrecht, A., & Naumann, F. (2008). Managing ETL processes. In *Proceedings from the International Workshop on New Trends in Information Integration* (pp. 12 -15). IEEE.

Alexa. (2013). *The top 500 sites on the web*. Retrieved January 10, 2013, from http://www.alexa.com/topsites

Al-Hakim, L. (2007). *Information quality management: Theory and applications*. Hershey, PA: Idea Group Pub.

Alkharboush, N., & Li, Y. (2010). A decision rule method for data quality assessment. In *Proceedings of the 15th International Conference on Information Quality*. IEEE.

Alur, N., Takahashi, C., Toratani, S., & Vasconcelos, D. (2008). *IBM InfoSphere DataStage data flow and job design*. IBM Redbooks Publication.

Anderka, M., & Stein, B. (2012). *A breakdown of quality flaws in wikipedia*. Paper presented at the 2nd Joint WICOW/AIRWeb Workshop on Web Quality. Lyon, France.

Anderson, N. (2009, September 8). *Anonymized data really isn't—And here's why not*. Retrieved from http://arstechnica.com/tech-policy/2009/09/your-secrets-live-online-in-databases-of-ruin/

Ang, C.-L., Davies, M., & Finlay, P. N. (2001). An empirical model of IT usage in the Malaysian public sector. *The Journal of Strategic Information Systems, 10*(2), 159–174. doi:10.1016/S0963-8687(01)00047-6

Angeles. (2012). *How health reform's medicaid expansion will impact state budgets federal government will pick up nearly all costs, even as expansion provides coverage to millions of low-income uninsured Americans*. Retrieved March 5, 2013 http://www.cbpp.org/cms/index.cfm?fa=view&id=3801.

Ariyachandra, T., & Watson, H. (2005). Key factors in selecting a data warehouse architecture. *Business Intelligence Journal, 10*(2), 19–26.

Ariyachandra, T., & Watson, H. (2010). Key organizational factors in data warehouse architecture selection. *Decision Support Systems, 49*(2), 200–212. doi:10.1016/j.dss.2010.02.006

Arkansas Department of Education. (2009, May 28). Average Daily Membership. Little Rock, Arkansas, United States of America.

Arkansas Department of Education. (2011, August 01). Unpublished - Four Year Adjusted Cohort Graduation Rate FAQs. Little Rock, Arkansas, United States of America.

Arkansas Department of Education. (2012). *Annual Statistical Report*. Little Rock.

Arkansas Department of Education. (n.d.). *Statewide Information System Reports - Enrollment by Grade*. Retrieved March 3, 2012, from ADE Data Center: http://adedata.arkansas.gov/statewide/State/EnrollmentByGrade.aspx

Arkansas Legislature. (2005). *Chapter 86 General Provisions*. Retrieved July 24, 2012, from http://www.arkleg.state.ar.us/assembly/ArkansasCodeLargeFiles/Title%204%20Business%20and%20Commercial%20Law-Chapter%2086%20General%20Provisions.htm

Arthur, C. (2013, July 5). European watchdogs order Google to rewrite privacy policy or face legal action. *The Guardian*. Retrieved 07 05, 2013, from http://www.guardian.co.uk/technology/2013/jul/05/google-privacy-policy-legal-action

Article 29 Data Protection Working Group. (2007). *Opinion 04/2007 on the concept of personal data*. Brussels: Article 29 Working Group.

Article 29 Working Group. (2013, May 13). *Advice paper on essential elements of a definition and a provision on profiling within the EU general data protection regulation*. Retrieved from http://ec.europa.eu/justice/data-protection/article-29/documentation/other-document/files/2013/20130513_advice-paper-on-profiling_en.pdf

Arveson, P. (n.d.). *The Deming Cycle*. Retrieved January 3, 2012, from The Balanced Scorecard Institute: http://www.balancedscorecard.org/thedemingcycle/tabid/112/default.aspx

Associated Press. (2005, September 7). *Ex-student sentenced for computer hacking*. Retrieved July 4, 2011, from Security on MSNBC.COM: http://www.msnbc.msn.com/id/9239576/

Badard, T., & Dubé, E. (2009). Enabling geospatial business intelligence. *Technology Innovation Management Review*. Retrieved January 7, 2013, from http://timreview.ca/node/289

Bailey, J. E., & Pearson, S. W. (1983). Development of a tool for measuring and analyzing computer user satisfaction. *Management Science, 29*(5), 530–545. doi:10.1287/mnsc.29.5.530

Ballou, D. P., Chengalur-Smith, I. N., & Wang, R. Y. (2006). Sample-based quality estimation of query results in relational database environments. *IEEE Transactions on Knowledge and Data Engineering, 18*(5), 639–650. doi:10.1109/TKDE.2006.83

Banisar, D. (2012, October 19). *National comprehensive data protection/privacy laws and bills 2012 map*. Retrieved January 15, 2013, from http://ssrn.com/abstract=1951416

Barbosa, P., & O'Reilly, A. (2011). *Harvard trends: Tendências de gestão*. Porto, Portugal: Vida Económica.

Bardhan, I. R., & Thouin, M. F. (2012). Health information technology and its impact on the quality and cost of healthcare delivery. *Decision Support Systems, 55*(2),438-449. doi: http://dx.doi.org/10.1016/j.dss.2012.10.003

Bar-Haim, Y., Lamy, D., Pergamin, L., Bakermans-Kranenburg, M. J., & van IJzendoorn, M. H. (2007). Threat-related attentional bias in anxious and nonanxious individuals: A meta-analytic study. *Psychological Bulletin, 133*(1), 1–24. doi:10.1037/0033-2909.133.1.1 PMID:17201568

Basole, R., & Chao, R. (2004). *Location-based mobile decision support systems and their effect on user performance.* Paper presented at the Americas Conference on Information Systems (AMCIS) 2004. New York, NY.

Batini, C., & Scannapieca, M. (2006). *Data quality: Concepts, methodologies and techniques*. Berlin: Springer.

BBC. (1999). *Health hospital error blamed for smear scare.* Retrieved June 3, 2013, from http://news.bbc.co.uk/2/hi/health/394606.stm

Becerra-Fernandez, I., Gonzalez, A., & Sabherwal, R. (2004). *Knowledge management: Challenges, solutions and technologies*. Upper Saddle River, NJ: Pearson Prentice Hall.

Beck, K., Beedle, M., van Bennekum, A., Cockburn, A., Cunningham, W., Fowler, M., et al. (2001). *Manifesto for agile software development.* Retrieved from www.agilemanifesto.org

Beck, K., et al. (2001). *Agile manifesto.* Retrieved 20 December 2012 from http://www.agilemanifesto.org

Bédard, Y. (2005). Integrating GIS and OLAP: A new way to unlock geospatial data for decision-making. In *Proceedings from the Conference on Directions on Location Technology and Business Intelligence.* IEEE.

Bédard, Y., & Bernier, E. (2002). Supporting multiple representations with spatial databases view: Management and the concept of VUEL. In *Proceedings from the Joint Workshop on Multi-Scale Representations of Spatial Data*. IEEE.

Bédard, Y. (1999). Principles of spatial database analysis and design. In *Geographical information systems: Principles, techniques, application & management* (pp. 413–424). Hoboken, NJ: John Wiley & Sons.

Bédard, Y. (2008). Geomatics. In *Encyclopedia of geographical information science* (pp. 195–197). Thousand Oaks, CA: SAGE Publications.

Bedell, D. (2011, March). Business intelligence. *Global Finance,* 46-47.

Bell, D., & Grimson, J. (1992). *Distributed database systems*. Reading, MA: Addison Wesley.

Benbasat, I., Dexter, A. S., & Mantha, R. W. (1980). Impact of organizational maturity on information system skill needs. *Management Information Systems Quarterly, 4*(1), 21–34. doi:10.2307/248865

Berente, N., Vandenbosch, B., & Aubert, B. (2009). Information flows and business process integration. *Business Process Management Journal, 15*(1), 191–141. doi:10.1108/14637150910931505

Bergier, J. (1970). *A espionagem industrial.* Porto, Portugal: Editorial Inova.

Berkman, R. (2008). *The art of strategic listening: Finding market intelligence in blogs and social media.* Paramount Market Pub.

Berthon, P., Pitt, L., Plangger, K., & Shapiro, D. (2012). Marketing meets web 2.0, social media, and creative consumers: Implications for international marketing strategy. *Business Horizons*, (55): 261–271. doi:10.1016/j.bushor.2012.01.007

Besson, B., & Possin, J. (1996). *Do serviço de informação à inteligência económica: Detectar as ameaças e oportunidades da empresa.* Instituto Piaget.

Best Practice: Develop Iteratively. (2011). Retrieved from http://www.upedu.org/references/bestprac/im_bp1.htm

Best, D. (1996a). Business process and information management. In D. Best (Ed.), *The fourth resource: Information and its management.* Hampshire, UK: Aslib/Gower.

Best, D. (1996b). *The fourth resource: Information and its management.* Hampshire, UK: Aslib/Gower.

Beuren, I. M. (1998). *Gerenciamento da informação: Um recurso estratégico no processo de gestão empresarial.* São Paulo, Brazil: Atlas.

Bhagattjee, P. (2012, June 1). *Data protection: South Africa.* Retrieved January 15, 2013, from http://ipandit.practicallaw.com/5-503-0787# Bott, E. (2013, February 25). *Firefox raises the online privacy bar with new cookie policy.* Retrieved February 25, 2013, from http://www.zdnet.com/firefox-raises-the-online-privacy-bar-with-new-cookie-policy-7000011740/

Bhattacharya, S., & Basu, P. K. (1998). Mapping a research area at the micro level using co-word analysis. *Scientometrics, 43*(3), 359–372. doi:10.1007/BF02457404

Bianco, G. D., Galante, R., & Heuser, C. A. (2011). A fast approach for parallel deduplication on multicore processors. In *Proceedings of SAC'11*. TaiChung, Taiwan: SAC.

Bilali, L. (2013). *Data warehouse generation algorithm explained.* Retrieved 17 February 2013 from http://www.datawarehouseautomation.org

Bimonte, S., Wehrle, P., Tchounikine, A., & Miquel, M. (2006). GeWOlap: A web based spatial OLAP proposal. In *Proceedings from the 2nd International Workshop on Semantic-Based Geographical Information Systems* (pp. 1596–1605). IEEE.

Bing Maps. (2011). *Business intelligence.* Retrieved January 10, 2013, from http://www.microsoft.com/maps/solutions/business-solutions/business-intelligence.aspx

Bitterer, A., Schlegel, K., Hostmann, B., Gassman, B., Beyer, M. A., Herschel, G., & Andrews, W. (2007). *Hype cycle for business intelligence and performance management, 2007.* Stamford, CT: Gartner Research.

Blood, R. (2004). *O livro de bolso do weblogue: Conselhos práticos para criar e manter o seu blogue.* Porto, Portugal: Campo das Letras.

Bobrowski, M., Marre, M., & Yankelevich, D. (1999). A homogeneous framework to measure data quality. In *Proceedings of the 4th International Conference on Information Quality*, (pp. 115-124). IEEE.

Boin, A., & Hunter, G. (2005). Do spatial data consumers really understand data quality information? In *Proceedings from the 7th International Symposium on Spatial Accuracy Assessment in Natural Resources and Environmental Sciences* (pp. 215-224). IEEE.

Bonabeau, E. (2009). Decisions 2.0: The power of collective intelligence. *MIT Sloan Management Review, 50*(2), 45–52.

Borgatti, S. P. (2005). Centrality and network flow. *Social Networks, 27*(1), 55–71. doi:10.1016/j.socnet.2004.11.008

Borgman, C., & Siegfried, S. (1992). Getty's synonameTM and its cousins: A survey of applications of personal name-matching algorithms. *Journal of the American Society for Information Science American Society for Information Science, 43*(7), 459–476. doi:10.1002/(SICI)1097-4571(199208)43:7<459::AID-ASI1>3.0.CO;2-D

Boritz, J. E. (2005). IS practitioners' views on core concepts of information integrity. *International Journal of Accounting Information Systems, 6*, 20. doi:10.1016/j.accinf.2005.07.001

Bouzeghoub, M., & Lenzerini, M. (2001). Introduction to data extraction, cleaning, and reconciliation. *Information Systems, 26*(8), 535–536. doi:10.1016/S0306-4379(01)00038-2

Bramston, D. (2009). *Basics product design: Idea searching.* Lausanne: Ava Publishing.

Brandeis, L., & Warren, S. (1890). The right to privacy. *Harvard Law Review*, 193.

British Standards Institute. (2009, May). *BS10012:2009.* BSI.

Broaddus, M., & Park, E. (2012). *Number of uninsured fell in 2011, largely due to health reform and public programs.* Washington, DC: Dept of Health and Human Services.

Brohman, M. K., Parent, M., Pearce, M. R., & Wade, M. (2000). *The business intelligence value chain: Data-driven decision support in a data warehouse environment: An exploratory study.* Paper presented at the 33rd Hawaii International Conference on System Sciences. Hawaii, HI.

Brophy, P., & Coulling, K. (1996). *Quality management for information and library managers.* Guildford: Aslib/Gower.

Brown, E. (2012). Working the crowd: Social media marketing for business (2^a ed.). London: British Informatics Society.

Brown, J., & Duguid, P. (2000). *The social life of information*. Boston: Harvard Business School Press.

Brünger-Weilandt, S., Geiß, D., Herlan, G., & Stuike-Prill, R. (2011). Quality: Key factor for high value in professional patent, technical and scientific information. *World Patent Information*, *33*(3), 230–234. doi:10.1016/j.wpi.2011.04.007

Burbidge, R. (2003). *3GPP: Specification detail 3GPP TS 03.40, Technical realization of the short message service*. SMS.

Burgelman, R., Christensen, C., & Wheelwright, S. (2009). Strategic management of technology and innovation (5ª ed.). Singapore: McGraw-Hill.

Burk, C. Jr, & Horton, F. Jr. (1988). *InfoMap: A complete guide to discovering corporate information resources*. Hoboken, NJ: Prentice Hall.

Burnell, K., & Raghavendran, S. (2008). Spatial ETL tools: The bottom line of an enterprise GIS. In *Proceedings from the International Conference Map India*. IEEE.

Burns, M. (2005). Business intelligence survey. *CA Magazine*, *138*(5), 18.

Byrd, L. W., & Byrd, T. A. (2012). The impact of clinical information technology on information quality in US hospitals. *International Journal of Healthcare Technology and Management*, *13*(1), 71–87. doi:10.1504/IJHTM.2012.048948

Caballero, I., Verbo, E., Calero, C., & Piattini, M. (2007). A data quality measurement information model based on iso/iec 15939. In *Proceedings of the 12th International Conference on Information Quality* (pp. 393-408). IEEE.

Canhoto, A. (2013). *Social media as a source of competitive intelligence*. Retrieved 28-02-2013, from http://anacanhoto.com/2013/01/18/social-media-as-a-source-of-competitive-intelligence/

Carrera, F. (2012b). Marketing digital na versão 2.0: O que não pode ignorar (2ª ed.). Lisboa, Portugal: Sílabo.

Carrera, F. (2009). *Networking: Guia de sobrevivência profissional*. Lisboa, Portugal: Sílabo.

Carrera, F. (2012a). *Comunicar 2.0: A arte de bem comunicar no século XXI*. Lisboa, Portugal: Sílabo.

Castells, M. (2000). *The information age: The rise of the network society* (2nd ed.). London: Blackwell.

Castells, M. (2004). *A galáxia internet: Reflexões sobre internet, negócios e sociedade*. Lisboa, Portugal: Fundação Calouste Gulbenkian.

Cate, F. H. (2006). The Privacy and Security Policy Vacuum in Higher Education. *EDUCAUSE Review*, *41*(5), 18–29.

Center for Identity. (2011). *The center for identity risk assessment model (CIRAM)*. Retrieved from http://identity.utexas.edu/research/model

Chamoni, P., & Gluchowski, P. (2004). Integration trends in business intelligence systems - An empirical study based on the business intelligence maturity model. *Wirtschaftsinformatik*, *46*(2), 119–128. doi:10.1007/BF03250931

Chen, H., Chau, M., & Zeng, D. (2002). CI spider: A tool for competitive intelligence on the web. *Decision Support Systems*, (34): 1–17. doi:10.1016/S0167-9236(02)00002-7

Chen, H., Chiang, R. H. L., & Storey, V. C. (2012). Business intelligence and analytics: From big data to big impact. *Management Information Systems Quarterly*, *36*(4), 1165–1188.

Chen, W., Baldwin, J., Dunn, T., Grasselt, M., Hussain, S., & Mandelstein, D. et al. (n.d.). A practical guide to managing reference data with IBM InfoSphere master data management reference data management hub. *IBM Redbooks Publication*.

Chin, W. W., Marcolin, B. L., & Newsted, P. R. (2003). A partial least squares latent variable modeling approach for measuring interaction effects: Results from a Monte Carlo simulation study and an electronic-mail emotion/adoption study. *Information Systems Research*, *14*(2), 189–217. doi:10.1287/isre.14.2.189.16018

Chiou, J. S., Droge, C., & Hanvanich, S. (2002). Does customer knowledge affect how loyalty is formed? *Journal of Service Research*, *5*(2), 113–124. doi:10.1177/109467002237494

Choi, S. K., Lee, J. S., Kim, T. K., & Kim, W. H. (2005). *LG global standard six sigma training* (Vol. 1). LG Electronics.

Choo, C. W. (2003). *Gestão de informação para a organização inteligente: A arte de explorar o meio ambiente*. Lisboa, Portugal: Editorial Caminho.

Chrisman, N. (1983). The role of quality in the long term functioning of a geographical information system. In *Proceedings from the International Symposium on Automated Cartography* (pp. 79-87). IEEE.

Christen, P. (2006). A comparison of personal name matching: Techniques and practical issues. In *Proceedings of Sixth IEEE International Conference on Data Mining-Workshops* (pp. 290-294). IEEE.

Christen, P. (2008). Abstract Febrl – A Freely Available Record Linkage System with a Graphical User Interface. *Proceeding of the 14th ACM SIGKDD international conference on Knowledge discovery and data mining*, (pp. 1065-1068).

Christen, P. (2012). *Data matching: Concepts and techniques for record linkage, entity resolution, and duplicate detection*. Berlin: Springer.

Christen, P., & Goiser, K. (2007). Quality and complexity measures for data linkage and deduplication. In F. Guillet, & H. Hamilton (Eds.), *Quality measures in data mining, studies in computational intelligence* (Vol. 43, pp. 127–151). Berlin: Springer. doi:10.1007/978-3-540-44918-8_6

Christensen, C., Anthony, S., & Roth, E. (2004). *Seeing what's next: Using the theories of innovation to predict industry change*. Cambridge, MA: Harvard Business School Press.

Chuttur, M. Y. (2009). Overview of the technology acceptance model: Origins, developments and future directions, Indiana University, USA. *Sprouts: Working Papers on Information Systems, 9*(37).

Citroen, C. L. (2011). The role of information in strategic decision-making. *International Journal of Information Management, 31*(6), 493–501. doi:10.1016/j.ijinfomgt.2011.02.005

Claraview. (2005). *Business intelligence maturity model*. Retrieved January 20, 2007, from http://www.claraview.com

Classen, D. C., Resar, R., Griffin, F., Federico, F., Frankel, T., Kimmel, N., & James, B. C. (2011). Global trigger tool shows that adverse events in hospitals may be ten times greater than previously measured. *Health Affairs, 30*(4), 581–589. doi:10.1377/hlthaff.2011.0190 PMID:21471476

Clementini, E., & Di Felice, P. (1996). Model for representing topological relationships between complex geometric features in spatial databases. *Information Sciences: an International Journal, 80*(1-4), 121–136. doi:10.1016/0020-0255(95)00289-8

Cleveland, H. (1983). A informação como um recurso. *Diálogo,* (16), 7-11.

Cleveland, H. (1985). *The knowledge executive: Leadership in an information society*. New York: Dutton.

CNIL. (2011, March 21). *Google street view: CNIL pronounces a fine of 100,000 Euros*. Retrieved February 25, 2013, from http://www.cnil.fr/english/news-and-events/news/article/google-street-view-cnil-pronounces-a-fine-of-100000-euros/

CNIL. (2012, October 16). *Google's new privacy policy: Incomplete information and uncontrolled combination of data across services*. Retrieved January 15, 2013, from www.cnil.fr/english: http://www.cnil.fr/english/news-and-events/news/article/googles-new-privacy-policy-incomplete-information-and-uncontrolled-combination-of-data-across-ser/

Cohen, B. D., & Dean, T. J. (2005). Information asymmetry and investor valuation of IPOs: Top management team legitimacy as a capital market signal. *Strategic Management Journal, 26*(7), 683–690. doi:10.1002/smj.463

Cong, G., Fan, W., Geerts, F., Jia, X., & Ma, S. (2007). Improving data quality: Consistency and accuracy. In *Proceedings of the 33rd International Conference on Very Large Databases*, (pp. 315-326). IEEE.

Connelly, B. L., Certo, S. T., Ireland, R. D., & Reutzel, C. R. (2011). Signaling theory: A review and assessment. *Journal of Management, 37*(1), 39–67. doi:10.1177/0149206310388419

Cooke, A. (2001). A guide to finding quality information on the internet: Selection and evaluation strategies (2^a ed.). Cornwall, UK: Library Association Publishing.

Cooper, D. R., & Schindler, P. S. (2003). *Business research methods* (8th ed.). Boston: McGraw-Hill/Irwin.

Corr, L., & Stagnito, J. (2011). *Agile data warehouse design: Collaborative dimensional modeling, from whiteboard to star schema*. Leeds, UK: DecisionOne Press.

Cortada, J. (1996). *TQM for information systems management: Quality practices for continuous improvement*. Singapore: McGraw-Hill.

Costas, R., van Leeuwen, T. N., & Bordons, M. (2010). A bibliometric classificatory approach for the study and assessment of research performance at the individual level: The effects of age on productivity and impact. *Journal of the American Society for Information Science and Technology*, *61*(8), 1564–1581.

Crable, E., Brodzinski, J., & Frolick, M. (2008). The intelligent new business electronic application and automated underwriting solution at the western-southern life insurance company. *Information Systems Management*, *25*(2), 155–158. doi:10.1080/10580530801941231

Culnan, M. J. (1987). Mapping the intellectual structure of MIS, 1980-1985: A co-citation analysis. *Management Information Systems Quarterly*, *11*(3), 341–353. doi:10.2307/248680

Curtis, P. (2006). *Gleaning consumer intelligence from blogs and podcasts*. Retrieved 02-12-2012, from http://www.freepint.com/issues/040506.htm#tips

Curtis, K., Foster, P. W., & Stentiford, F. (1999). *Metadata - The key to content management services*. Washington, DC: IEEE.

Dafermos, M., & Rodnianski, I. (2005). A proof of Price's law for the collapse of a self-gravitating scalar field. *Inventiones Mathematicae*, *162*(2), 381–457. doi:10.1007/s00222-005-0450-3

Dalkir, K. (2005). *Knowledge management in theory and practice*. New York: Routledge.

Darmont, J., & Boussaid, O. (2006). *Processing and managing complex data for decision support*. Hersey, PA: Idea Group Publishing. doi:10.4018/978-1-59140-655-6

Dassonville, L. (1999). Quality management, data quality and users, metadata for geographical information. In *Proceedings from the International Symposium on Spatial Data Quality* (pp. 133-143). IEEE.

Davenport, T. (1997). *Information ecology: Mastering the information and knowledge environment*. New York: Oxford University Press.

Davenport, T. H. (2010). Business intelligence and organizational decisions. *International Journal of Business Intelligence Research*, *1*(1), 1–12. doi:10.4018/jbir.2010071701

Davenport, T. H., & Harris, J. G. (2007). *Competing on analytics: The new science of winning*. Cambridge, MA: Harvard Business School Press.

Davenport, T. H., Jarvenpaa, S. L., & Beers, M. C. (1996). Improving knowledge work processes. *Sloan Management Review*, *37*, 53–66.

Davenport, T., Marchand, D., & Dickson, T. (2004). *Dominando a gestão da informação*. Porto Alegre, Portugal: Bookmann.

Davis, F. D. (1989). Perceived usefulness, perceived ease of use, and user acceptance of information technology. *Management Information Systems Quarterly*, *13*(3), 319–331. doi:10.2307/249008

de Solla Price, D. J. (1986). *Little science, big science..., & beyond*. New York: Columbia Unviersity Press.

De Voe, L., & Neal, K. (2005). When business intelligence equals business value. *Business Intelligence Journal*, *10*(3), 57–63.

Dearlove, D. (1998). *Key management decisions: Tools and techniques of the executive decision-maker*. Wiltshire, UK: Financial Times/Pitman.

Delavar, M., & Devillers, R. (2010). Spatial data quality: From process to decisions. *Transaction in GIS*, *14*(4), 379–386. doi:10.1111/j.1467-9671.2010.01224.x

Delone, W. H., & McLean, E. R. (1992). Information systems success: The quest for the dependent variable. *Information Systems Research*, *3*(1), 60–95. doi:10.1287/isre.3.1.60

DeLone, W. H., & McLean, E. R. (2003). The DeLone and McLean model of information systems success: A ten-year update. *Journal of Management Information Systems, 19*(4), 9–30.

Dempsey, L., & Heery, R. (1998). Metadata: A current view of practice and issues. *The Journal of Documentation, 54*(2), 145–172. doi:10.1108/EUM0000000007164

Deng, Z., & Luo, L. (2007). An exploratory discuss of new ways for competitive intelligence on web 2.0. In Wang (Ed.), Integration and innovation orient to e-society (pp. 597-604). Boston: Springer.

Dephi Group. (2004). *Information intelligence: Content classification and the enterprise taxonomy practice.* Author.

Devillers, R., Gervais, M., Bédard, Y., & Jeansoulin, R. (2002). Spatial data quality: From metadata to quality indicators and contextual end-user manual. In *Proceedings from the OEEPE/ISPRS Joint Workshop on Spatial Data Quality Management* (pp. 45-55). IEEE.

Devillers, R., Bédard, Y., Fisher, P., Stein, A., Chrisman, N., & Shi, W. (2010). Thirty years of research on spatial data quality: Achievements, failures, and opportunities. *Transaction in GIS, 14*(4), 387–400. doi:10.1111/j.1467-9671.2010.01212.x

Devillers, R., Bédard, Y., Jeansoulin, R., & Moulin, B. (2007). Towards spatial data quality information analysis tools for experts assessing the fitness for use of spatial data. *International Journal of Geographical Information Science, 21*(3), 261–282. doi:10.1080/13658810600911879

Di Martino, S., Bimonte, S., Berttolotto, M., & Ferrucci, F. (2009). Integrating Google earth within OLAP tools for multidimensional exploration and analysis of spatial data. In *Proceedings from the International Conference on Enterprise Information Science* (pp. 940-951). IEEE.

Dianne, J. H. A. C. D. (2005). Inquiring organizations: An organizational form perspective. In Inquiring Organizations: Moving from Knowledge Management to Wisdom (pp. 1-21). Academic Press.

Dick, A. S., & Basu, K. (1994). Customer loyalty: Toward an integrated conceptual framework. *Academy of Marketing Science Journal, 22*(2), 99–113. doi:10.1177/0092070394222001

Dickins, J. (2013). Social media is an underused opportunity for luxury brands. *Digital Marketing Hub: The Guardian.* Retrieved 14-06-2013, from http://www.guardian.co.uk/media-network/media-network-blog/2013/jun/14/social-media-opportunity-luxury-brands

Dinter, B. (2012). *The maturing of a business intelligence maturity model.* Paper presented at the AMCIS 2012. Seattle, WA.

Dishaw, M. T., & Strong, D. M. (1999). Extending the technology acceptance model with task-technology fit constructs. *Information & Management, 36*(1), 9–21. doi:10.1016/S0378-7206(98)00101-3

Dittrich, J., Quiane-Ruiz, J. A., Richter, S., Schuh, S., Jinal, A., & Schad, J. (2012). Only aggressive elephants are fast elephants. *PVLDB, 5*(11), 1591–1602.

DNB ASA. (2012). *DNB ASA centralizes reference data management for more effective governance and reduced business risk.* Retrieved June 3, 2013, from http://www.ibm.com/common/ssi/cgi-bin/ssialias?subtype=AB&infotype=PM&appname=SWGE_IM_IP_USEN&htmlfid=IMC14762USEN&attachment=IMC14762USEN.PDF

Dodson, G., Arnott, D., & Pervan, G. (2008). *The use of business intelligence systems in Australia.* Paper presented at the ACIS 2008: 19th Australasian Conference on Information Systems. Christchurch, New Zealand.

Dondio, P., Barrett, S., Weber, S., & Seigneur, J. (2006). Extracting trust from domain analysis: A case study on the wikipedia project. In *Proceedings of the IEEE ATC 06*. IEEE.

Dorfman, R. (1979). A formula for the Gini coefficient. *The Review of Economics and Statistics, 61*(1), 146–149. doi:10.2307/1924845

Dreibelbis, A., Hechler, E., Milman, I., Oberhofer, M., Run, P. V., & Wolfson, D. (2008). *Enterprise master data management: An SOS approach to managing core information.* Boston, MA: Pearson PLC.

Druck, G., Miklau, G., & McCallum, A. (2008). *Learning to predict the quality of contributions to wikipedia.* Paper presented at the AAAI Workshop on Wikipedia and Artificial Intelligence. Chicago, IL.

Duval, E. (2004). Making metadata go away: Hiding everything but the benefits. In Learning Objects Metadata (LOM). IEEE Learning Technology Standards Committee(LTSC).

Eaton, M. L. (2011, February 24). Medium length content, a perfect fit for e-readers. *March Communications.*

Egghe, L. (1987). An exact calculation of Price's law for the law of Lotka. *Scientometrics*, *11*(1), 81–97. doi:10.1007/BF02016632

Eisenhardt, K. M. (1989). Building theories from case study research. *Academy of Management Review*, *14*(4), 532–550.

Elbashir, M. Z., Collier, P. A., & Davern, M. J. (2008). Measuring the effects of business intelligence systems: The relationship between business process and organizational performance. *International Journal of Accounting Information Systems*, *9*(3), 135–153. doi:10.1016/j.accinf.2008.03.001

Elwood, S. (2008). Grassroots groups as stakeholders in spatial data infrastructures: Challenges and opportunities local data development and sharing. *International Journal of Geographical Information Science*, *22*(2), 71–90. doi:10.1080/13658810701348971

English, L. (2011). *Information quality applied: Best practices for improving business information processes and systems.* Hoboken, NJ: Wiley Publishing.

English, L. P. (1999). *Improving data warehouse and business information quality, methods for reducing costs and increasing profits.* New York: Wiley Computer Publishing.

English, L. P. (2009). *Information quality applied.* Indianapolis, IN: Wiley.

Enterprise Master Patient Index. (n.d.). Retrieved from http://en.wikipedia.org/wiki/Enterprise_master_patient_index

Eppler, M. J., & Wittig, D. (2000). *Conceptualizing information quality: A review of information quality frameworks from the last ten years.* Paper presented at the Fifth Conference on Information Quality. St. Gallen, Switzerland.

Eppler, M. J. (2006). *Managing information quality: Increasing the value of information in knowledge-intensive products and processes* (2nd ed.). Berlin: Springer.

EPSG. (2013). *Spatial reference list.* Retrieved January 3, 2013, from http://spatialreference.org/ref/epsg/

EPTA. (2010). *Policy brief on the publication of the Norwegian income tax settlements.* Retrieved February 15, 2013, from http://eptanetwork.org/projects.php?pid=670

ESRI. (1998). *Shapefile technical description, an ESRI white paper.* Retrieved January 5, 2013, from http://www.esri.com/library/whitepapers/pdfs/shapefile.pdf

ESRI. (2012a). *ArcGIS for desktop extensions.* Retrieved January 5, 2013, from http://www.esri.com/software/arcgis/about/desktop-extensions

ESRI. (2012b). *Geodatabase: Overview.* Retrieved January 5, 2013, from http://www.esri.com/software/arcgis/geodatabase/index.html

ESRI. (2013a). *ArcGIS resource center: Data models.* Retrieved January 7, 2013, from http://resources.arcgis.com/content/data-models

ESRI. (2013b). *Data interoperability.* Retrieved January 7, 2013, from http://www.esri.com/software/arcgis/extensions/datainteroperability

ESRI. (2013c). *Geodatabase design steps.* Retrieved January 7, 2013, from http://webhelp.esri.com/arcgisdesktop/9.2/index.cfm?TopicName=Geodatabase_design_steps

European Commission. (1995). *Directive 95/46/EC of the European parliament and of the council of 24 October 1995 on the protection of individuals with regard to the processing of personal data and on the free movement of such data.* Retrieved January 15, 2013, from http://eur-lex.europa.eu/LexUriServ/LexUriServ.do?uri=CELEX:31995L0046:en:HTML

European Commission. (2002, July 12). *Directive 2002/58/EC.* Retrieved February 13, 2013, from http://eur-lex.europa.eu/LexUriServ/LexUriServ.do?uri=CELEX:32002L0058:EN:HTML European Commission. (2011). *Eurobarometer 359: Attitudes on data protection and electronic identity in the European Union.* Brussels: European Commission.

Even, A., & Kaiser, M. (2009). A framework for economics-driven assessment of data quality decisions. In *Proceedings of the 14th International Conference on Information Quality*. IEEE.

Even, A., Shankaranarayanan, G., & Watts, S. (2006). Enhancing decision making with process metadata: Theoretical framework, research tool, and exploratory examination. In *Proceedings of the 39th Hawaii International Conference on System Sciences* (HICSS-39). Kauai, HI: IEEE Press.

Federal Trade Commission. (2011, November 29). *Facebook settles FTC charges that it deceived consumers by failing to keep privacy promises*. Retrieved January 15, 2013, from www.ftc.gov: http://www.ftc.gov/opa/2011/11/privacysettlement.shtm

Federal Trade Commission. (2012). *Protecting consumer privacy in an era of rapid change*. Washington, DC: FTC.

Fehrenbacher, D., & Helfert, M. (2012). Contextual factors influencing perceived importance and trade-offs of information quality. *Communications of the Association for Information Systems*, *30*, 111–126.

Fellegi, I. P., & Sunter, A. B. (1969). A Theory for Record Linkage. *Journal of the American Statistical Association*, *64*(328), 1183–1210. doi:10.1080/01621459.1969.10501049

Fialka, J. (1997). *War by other means: Economic espionage in America*. Norton.

Fisher, C. W., Smith, I. C., & Ballou, D. P. (2003). The impact of experience and time on the use of data quality information in decision making. *Information Systems Research*, *14*(2), 170–188. doi:10.1287/isre.14.2.170.16017

Focalytic. (2013). Social media content analysis of the 2013 masters golf tournament. *Focal Point*. Retrieved 16-06-2013, from http://www.focalytic.com/Portals/182440/docs/themastersgolfebook.pdf

Forslund, H. (2007). Measuring information quality in the order fulfilment process. *International Journal of Quality & Reliability Management*, *24*(5), 515–524. doi:10.1108/02656710710748376

Foshay, N., Mukherjee, A., & Taylor, A. (2007). Does data warehouse end-user metadata add value? *Communications of the ACM*, *50*(11), 70–79. doi:10.1145/1297797.1297800

Freeman, L. C. (1977). A set of measures of centrality based on betweenness. *Sociometry*, *40*(1), 35–41. doi:10.2307/3033543

Freeman, L. C. (1979). Centrality in social networks conceptual clarification. *Social Networks*, *1*(3), 215–239. doi:10.1016/0378-8733(78)90021-7

Friedman, T. (2008). *Gartner study on data quality shows that IT still bears the burden*. Stamford, CT: Gartner Group.

Gabriel, R., Hoppe, T., & Pastwa, A. (2010). Classification of metadata categories in data warehousing - A generic approach. In *Proceedings of AMCIS 2010*. AMCIS.

Gangadharan, G. R., & Swami, S. N. (2004). Business intelligence systems: Design and implementation strategies. In V. Lužar-Stiffler (Ed.), *Proceedings of 26th International Conference on Information Technology Interfaces (ITI 2004)* (Vol. 1, pp. 139-144). Cavtat, Croatia: ITI.

Garber, R. (2001). Inteligência competitiva de mercado: Como capturar, armazenar, analisar informações de marketing e tomar decisões num mercado competitivo. São Paulo, Brazil: Madras.

Garcia, T. I., & L'Orange, H. P. (2012). *The state of postsecondary data systems*. Retrieved from http://www.sheeo.org/sites/default/files/publications/20130107%20StrongFoundationsUpdate_FinalcNoAppendices.pdf

Garvin, D. (1988). *Managing quality*. New York: Free Press.

Ge, M., & Helfert, M. (2007, November). A review of information quality research - Develop a research agenda. In *Proceedings of the 12th International Conference on Information Quality*. Cambridge, MA: MIT.

Ge, M., Helfert, M., & Jannach, D. (2011). Information quality assessment: Validating measurement dimensions and processes. In *Proceedings of the 19th European Conference on Information Systems*. IEEE.

Ge, M., & Helfert, M. (2007). *A theoretical model to explain effects of information quality awareness on decision making*. Funchal.

Ge, M., & Helfert, M. (2008). Effects of information quality on inventory management. *International Journal of Information Quality*, *2*(2), 15. doi:10.1504/IJIQ.2008.022962

Genuine, M. (2011). *Miller's genuine draft*. Retrieved April 20,2011, from http://millergd.blogspot.com/2011/04/interactive-chart-on-ryan-budget-vs.html

GeoMe. (2013). *Visual business intelligence maps*. Retrieved January 10, 2013, from http://www.geo.me/visualbusinessintelligence

Gervais, M., Bédard, Y., Levesque, M., Bernier, E., & Devillers, R. (2010). Data quality issues and geographic knowledge discovery. In *Geographic data mining and knowledge discovery* (pp. 99–116). New York: Taylor & Francis.

Giannangelo, K., & Fenton, S. (2008). EHR's effect on the revenue cycle management coding function. *Journal of Healthcare Information Management*, *22*(1), 26–29. PMID:19267004

Gibson, N. (2010). *Improving information products for system 2 design support*. (Ph. D. Thesis). University of Arkansas, Little Rock, AR.

Gibson, N., & Talburt, J. (2010). HIVE: Crowdsourcing Education Data. *Journal of Computing Sciences in Colleges*, *25*(5), 71–78.

Giles, J. (2005). Internet encyclopaedias go head to head. *Nature*, *438*(7070), 900–901. doi:10.1038/438900a PMID:16355180

Ginman, M. (1990). Quality information, and information for quality. In Wormell (Ed.), Information quality: Definitions and dimensions. London: Taylor Graham.

Gleick, J. (2011). *The information: A history, a theory, a flood*. St. Ives: 4th Estate.

Godeluck, S. (2000). *A explosão da economia na internet*. Lisboa: Livros do Brasil.

Godinez, M., Hechler, E., Koenig, K., & Lockwood, S. Oberhofer, & Michael, S. (2010). The art of enterprise information architecture: A systems-based approach for unlocking business insight. Boston, MA: Pearson PLC.

Goffin, K., & Koners, U. (2011). Tacit knowledge, lessons learnt, and new product development. *Journal of Product Innovation Management*, *28*, 300–318. doi:10.1111/j.1540-5885.2010.00798.x

Gold, A. H., Malhotra, A., & Segars, A. H. (2001). Knowledge management: An organizational capabilities perspective. *Journal of Management Information Systems*, *18*(1), 185.

Gomes, E., & Braga, F. (2001). *Inteligência competitiva: Como transformar informação em um negócio lucrativo*. Rio de Janeiro, Brazil: Campus.

Goodchild, M. (2010). Geographic information systems. In *Research methods in geography: A critical introduction* (pp. 376–391). Oxford, UK: Wiley-Blackwell.

Goodhue, D. L., & Thompson, R. L. (1995). Task-technology fit and individual performance. *Management Information Systems Quarterly*, *19*(2), 213–236. doi:10.2307/249689

Gootman, E. (2008, October 23). As schools face cuts, delays on data system bring more frustration. *The New York Times*, pp. 1-2. Retrieved from http://www.nytimes.com

Gorla, N., Somers, T. M., & Wong, B. (2010). Organizational impact of system quality, information quality, and service quality. *The Journal of Strategic Information Systems*, *19*(3), 207–228. doi:10.1016/j.jsis.2010.05.001

Graham, S., Coburn, D., & Oleson, C. (1996). *The foundations of wisdom: A study of the financial impact of data warehousing*. Toronto, Canada: International Data Corporation.

Grajek, S., & Pirani, J. A. (2012). Top-ten IT issues, 2012. *EDUCAUSE Review*, *47*(3), 36.

Granell, C., Gould, M., Manso, M., & Bernabé, M. (2009). Spatial data infrastructures. In *Handbook of research on geoinformatics* (pp. 36–41). Hershey, PA: IGI Global. doi:10.4018/978-1-59140-995-3.ch005

Grant, R. M. (1996). Prospering in dynamically-competetive environments: Organizationa capability as knowledge integration. *Organization Science*, *7*(4), 375–387. doi:10.1287/orsc.7.4.375

Grant, R. M. (2002). *Contemporary strategy analysis: Concepts, techniques, applications*. Oxford, UK: Wiley-Blackwell.

Gray, J. (2010). *Open geoprocessing standards and open geospatial data*. Retrieved February 4, 2013, from http://blog.okfn.org/2010/06/21/open-geoprocessing-standards-and-open-geospatial-data/

Greengard, S. (2011). Following the crowd. *Communications of the ACM*, *54*(2), 20–22. doi:10.1145/1897816.1897824

GSDI. (2012). *Global spatial data infrastructure*. Retrieved January 7, 2012, from http://www.gsdi.org/

Guisnel, J. (1997). *Espionagem na internet: As guerras no ciberespaço*. Lisboa: Difusão Cultural.

Gurbaxani, V., & Whang, S. (1991). The impact of information systems on organizations and markets. *Communications of the ACM*, *34*(1), 59–73. http://doi.acm.org/10.1145/99977.99990 doi:10.1145/99977.99990

Gustafsson, P., Lindström, Å., Jägerlind, C., & Tsoi, J. (2006). A framework for assessing data quality – From a business perspective. *Software Engineering Research and Practice*, 1009-1015.

Guynn, J. (2013). Facebook releases information on NSA requests for user data. *Los Angeles Times*. Retrieved 14-06-2013, from http://www.latimes.com/business/technology/la-fi-tn-facebook-releases-first-information-on-fisa-requests-20130614,0,3315731.story

Hackbarth, G., Grover, V., & Yi, M. Y. (2003). Computer playfulness and anxiety: Positive and negative mediators of the system experience effect on perceived ease of use. *Information & Management*, *40*(3), 221–232. doi:10.1016/S0378-7206(02)00006-X

Haider, A. (2011). *Information technologies implementation and organisational behavior: An asset management perspective*. Paper presented at the Technology Management in the Energy Smart World (PICMET). New York, NY.

Haley, B., & Watson, H. (1998). Managerial considerations. *Communications of the ACM*, *41*(9), 32–37. doi:10.1145/285070.285077

Hanauer, D. A., Zheng, K., Ramakrishnan, N., & Keller, B. J. (2011). Opportunities and challenges in association and episode discovery from electronic health records. *IEEE Intelligent Systems*, *26*(5), 83–87.

Han, J., & Kamber, M. (2006). *Data mining: Concepts and techniques* (2nd ed.). San Francisco, CA: Morgan Kaufmann.

Harmon, K. (2009). *Deaths from avoidable medical error more than double in past decade, investigation shows*. Scientific American Blog.

Hasan Dalip, D., André Gonçalves, M., Cristo, M., & Calado, P. (2009). *Automatic quality assessment of content created collaboratively by web communities: A case study of wikipedia*. Paper presented at the 9th ACM/IEEE-CS Joint Conference on Digital Libraries. Austin, TX.

Hashemi, R., Talburt, J. R., & Wang, R. (2006). Significance test for the talburt-wang similarity index. In J. R. Talburt, E. Pierce, N. Wu, & T. Campbell (Ed.), *9th International Conference on Information Quality* (pp. 125-132). Cambridge: MIT IQ Publishing.

Hawkins, D. T., Larson, S. E., & Caton, B. Q. (2003). Information science abstracts: Tracking the literature of information science: Part 2: A new taxonomy for information science. *Journal of the American Society for Information Science and Technology*, *54*(8), 771–781. doi:10.1002/asi.10275

Hawthorne, K., & Cromity, J. (2012, March/April). Social search for market intelligence. *Exploring Technology & Resources for Information Professionals*, 36-38.

Heinrich, B., & Klier, M. (2009). A novel data quality metric for timeliness considering supplemental data. In *Proceedings of the 17th European Conference on Information Systems (ECIS)*, (pp. 2701-2713). ECIS.

Heinrich, B., Kaiser, M., & Klier, M. (2007). How to measure data quality? A metrics based approach. In *Proceedings of 28th International Conference on Information Systems*. IEEE.

Heinrich, B., Kaiser, M., & Klier, M. (2008). Does the EU insurance mediation directive help to improve data quality? A metric-based analysis. In *Proceedings of the 16th European Conference on Information Systems (ECIS)*. ECIS.

Heinrich, B., Kaiser, M., & Kier, M. (2009). A procedure to develop metrics for currency and its application in CRM. *ACM Journal of Data and Information Quality*, *1*, 1–28. doi:10.1145/1515693.1515697

Hekmatpanah, M., Sadroddin, M., Shahbaz, S., Mokhtari, F., & Fadavinia, F. (2008). Six sigma process and its impact on the organisational productivity. *World Academy of Science. Engineering and Technology*, *43*, 365–369.

Helfert, M., & Foley, O. (2009). *A context aware information quality framework*. Paper presented at Fourth International Conference on Cooperation and Promotion of Information Resources in Science and Technology. Beijing, China.

Helfert, M., Foley, O., Ge, M., & Cappiello, C. (2009). Limitations of weighted sum measures for information quality. In *Proceedings of Americas Conference on Information Systems*. AMCIS.

He, Q. (1999). Knowledge discovery through co-word analysis. *Library Trends*, *48*(1), 133–159.

Herring, J. P. (2002). Tópicos fundamentais de inteligência: Processo para identificação e definição de necessidades de inteligência. In Prescott & Miller (Eds.), Inteligência competitiva na prática. Rio de Janeiro, Brazil: Campus.

Herring, J. P. (1992). The role of intelligence in formulating strategy. *The Journal of Business Strategy*, *13*(5), 54–60. doi:10.1108/eb039518 PMID:10121463

Herzog, T. N., Scheuren, F. J., & Winkler, W. E. (2007). *Data quality and record linkage techniques*. New York: Springer.

Higham, W. (2010). *The next big thing: Spotting and forecasting consumer trends for profit*. Bodmin: Kogan Page.

Hillard & Na. (2006). *Economic value of data for financial services organisations, the local and global in knowledge management*. Paper presented at the Australian Conference for Knowledge Management and Intelligent Decision Support. Canberra, Australia.

Hillard. (2010). *Information-driven business*. Hoboken, NJ: John Wiley & Sons.

Hinton, M. (2006). *Introducing information management: The business approach*. Burlington, UK: Elsevier Butterworth-Heinemann.

Hoffer, G. E., & Pratt, M. D. (1987). Used vehicles, lemons markets, and used car rules: Some empirical evidence. *Journal of Consumer Policy*, *10*(4), 409–414. doi:10.1007/BF00411482

Holland, G. (2010). *Knowledge-Driven Identity Resolution For Longitudional Education Data.*

Holland, G., & Talburt, J. R. (2010). q-Gram Tetrahedral Ratio (qTR) for Approximate Pattern Matching. *2010 Annual Acxiom Laboratory for Applied Research Conference*. Conway.

Holloman, C. (2012). *The social media MBA: Your competitive edge in social media strategy development and delivery*. Hoboken, NJ: John Wiley & Sons.

Holmes, D., & McCabe, C. (2002). Improving precision and recall for Soundex retrieval. In *Proceedings of the IEEE International Conference on Information Technology-Coding and Computing*. Las Vegas, NV: IEEE.

Hoofnagle, C. J., Urban, J. M., & Li, S. (2012). *Mobile payments: Consumer benefits and new privacy concerns*. Berkeley, CA: Berkley Center for Law and Technology. doi:10.2139/ssrn.2045580

Hortinha, J. (2002). *X-marketing*. Lisboa: Sílabo.

How are school districts in Arkansas funded ? (n.d.). Retrieved July 4, 2012, from Lamar Warriors: http://www.lamarwarriors.org/board/funding%20information/how_are_schools_funded.pdf

Hribar Rajterič, I. (2010). Overview of business intelligence maturity models. *Management*, *15*(1), 47–67.

Hsieh, C., Lin, B., & Manduca, B. (2007). Information technology and six sigma implementation. *Journal of Computer Information Systems*, *47*(4), 1.

Huang, K. T., Lee, J. Y., & Wang, R. Y. (1999). *Quality information and knowledge*. Upper Saddle River, NJ: Prentice Hall.

Huang, K., Lee, Y. W., & Wang, R. Y. (1999). *Quality information and knowledge management*. Upper Saddle River, NJ: Prentice Hall.

Huang, T. C., Liu, C., & Chang, D. (2012). An empirical investigation of factors influencing the adoption of data mining tools. *International Journal of Information Management*, *32*(3), 257–270. doi:10.1016/j.ijinfomgt.2011.11.006

Hubbard. (2007). *How to measure anything: Finding the value of intangibles in business*. Hoboken, NJ: John Wiley & Sons.

Huerta, E., & Ryan, T. (2003). *The credibility of online information*. (Doctoral dissertation). Claremont Graduate University.

Hughes, R. (2008). Agile data warehousing: Delivering world-class business intelligence systems using scrum and XP. Bloomington, IN: iUniverse.

Hughes, R., & Stodder, D. (2012). *DM review survey of readership, October 2004, quoted in accelerating BI/DW value with agile methods, an inside look at trends and best practices*. Boston: TDWI World Conference Research.

Hultgren, H. P. (2012). *Modeling the agile data warehouse with data vault*. Denver, CO: New Hamilton Press.

Human Inference. (2011). *DataCleaner*. Retrieved July 4, 2012, from DataCleaner: http://datacleaner.eobjects.org/

Huotari, M.-L., & Wilson, T. D. (2001). Determining organizational information needs: The critical success factors approach. *Information Research, 6*(3).

Hu, W., & Feng, J. (2005). Data and information quality: An information-theoretic perspective. *Computing and Information Systems, 9*(3), 32–47.

Igbaria, M. (1994). An examination of the factors contributing to microcomputer technology acceptance. *Accounting. Management and Information Technologies, 4*(4), 185–201. doi:10.1016/0959-8022(94)90023-X

IIMM. (2011). International infrastructure management manual (4th ed.). Wellington, NZ: National Asset Management Steering (NAMS) Group.

Imhoff, C. (2005). Streaming processes for front-line workers: Adding business intelligence for operations. *Operational Business Intelligence White Paper, Intelligent Solutions Inc*. Retrieved from http://www.tdwi.com

Indart, B. (2006). Operationalizing business intelligence – Turning insight into actions. *Business Intelligence Journal, 11*(2), 35.

Informatica. (2013). Manage your metadata to better manage your business (White Paper). Author.

Information Commissioners Office (UK). (2012). *Prudential fined £50,000 for customer account confusion*. Retrieved 02 25, 2013, from http://www.ico.gov.uk/news/latest_news/2012/prudential-fined-50000-for-customer-account-confusion-06112012.aspx

Information Commissioner's Office. (2012). *Anonymisation: Managing data protection risk code of practice*. ICO.

Information Commissioners Office. (2013, January 24). *Sony fined £250,000 after millions of UK gamers' details compromised*. Retrieved February 25, 2013, from http://www.ico.gov.uk/news/latest_news/2013/ico-news-release-2013.aspx

Information Quality. (2012, May 3). Retrieved May 12, 2012, from Wikipedia: http://en.wikipedia.org/wiki/Information_quality

Inmon, W. H. (1996). *Building the data warehouse*. New York: John Wiley & Sons Inc.

Inmon, W., Strauss, D., & Neushloss, G. (2008). A brief history of data warehousing and first-generation data warehouses. In *DW 2.0* (pp. 1–22). Burlington, UK: Morgan Kaufmann. doi:10.1016/B978-0-12-374319-0.00001-4

Institute of Education Sciences. (2011). *Public Elementary and Secondary School Student Enrollment and Staff Counts From the Common Core of Data: School Year 2009-10*. National Center of Education Statistics.

Institute of Education Sciences. (2011). *Statewide Longitudional Data Systems Grant Program*. Retrieved January 5, 2012, from National Center for Education Statistics: http://nces.ed.gov/programs/slds/stateinfo.asp

Integeo. (2013). *Integrated geographics for business and government*. Retrieved January 10, 2013, from http://www.integeo.com/

Intelli3. (2010). *Map4Decision*. Retrieved 2013, from http://www.intelli3.com/map4decision

Intergraph. (2013). *GeoMedia fusion*. Retrieved January 10, 2013, from http://www.intergraph.com/literature/geomedia_fusion.pdf

Isik, O., Jones, M. C., & Sidorova, A. (2011). Business intelligence (BI) success and the role of BI capabilities. *Intelligent Systems in Accounting. Financial Management, 18*(4), 161–176.

ISO 19113. (2002). *Geographic information – Quality principles*. International Standard Organization.

ISO 19114. (2003). *Geographic information – Quality evaluation procedures*. International Standard Organization.

ISO 19138. (2006). *Geographic information – Data quality measures*. International Standard Organization.

ISO 3166-1 Wiki Page. (n.d.). Retrieved Jan 27, 2013, http://en.wikipedia.org/wiki/ISO_3166-1

ISO 639 Web Page. (n.d.). Retrieved June 3, 2013. http://www.iso.org/iso/language_codes

Jacob, E. K. (2003). Ontologies and the semantic web. *Bulletin of the American Society for Information Science and Technology*.

Jagannatha, G. (2010, May). Data Privacy in Knowledge Discovery. 5-10.

Jakobsson, A., & Tsoulos, L. (2007). The role of quality spatial data infrastructure. In *Quality control handbook*. New York: McGraw-Hill.

Janert, P. K. (2011). *Data Analysts with Open Source Tools*. Sebastopol: O'Reilly Media, Inc.

Jarke, M., & Vassiliou, Y. (1997). Foundations of data warehouse quality - A review of the DWQ Project. In *Proceedings of the 2nd International Conference on Information Quality*. Cambridge, MA: MIT.

Jarke, M., Jeusfeld, M. A., Quix, C., & Vassiliadis, P. (1999). Architecture and quality in data warehouse: An extended repository approach. *Information Systems*, *24*(3), 229–253. doi:10.1016/S0306-4379(99)00017-4

Jaworski, B. J., & Kohli, A. K. (1993). Market orientation: Antecedents and consequences. *Journal of Marketing*, *57*(3), 53–70. doi:10.2307/1251854

Jhingran, A. D., Mattos, N., & Pirahesh, H. (2002). Information integration: A research agenda. *IBM Systems Journal*, *41*(4), 555–562. doi:10.1147/sj.414.0555

Johnson, A. (2005). Blogs, wikis & RSS: Colaborative social communities and the value of distributed CI. *Competitive Intelligence Magazine*. Retrieved 10-02-2013, from http://www.aurorawdc.com/blogswikisrss_scipcimag_20050102.pdf

Johnson, S. (2009, June 5). How Twitter will change the way we live. *Time Magazine*.

Josang, A., & Pope, S. (2005). User centric identity management. In *Proceedings of AusCERT Conference*. AusCERT.

Jourdan, Z., Rainer, R. K., & Marshall, T. E. (2008). Business intelligence: An analysis of the literature. *Information Systems Management*, *25*(2), 121–131. doi:10.1080/10580530801941512

Junho, S. (2013). Roadmap for e-commerce standardization in Korea. *International Journal of IT Standards and Standardization Research*.

Kahaner, L. (1997). *Competitive intelligence: How to gather, analyze, and use information to move your business to the top*. New York: Simon & Schuster.

Kahn, B. K., & Strong, D. M. (1998). Product and service performance model for information quality: An update. In *Proceedings of the 1998 Conference on Information Quality*. Cambridge, MA: MIT.

Kahn, B. K., Strong, D. M., & Wang, R. Y. (2002). Information quality benchmarks: Product and service performance. *Communications of the ACM*, *45*(4), 184–192. doi:10.1145/505248.506007

Kahneman, D., & Tversky, A. (1972). Subjective probability: A judgment of representativeness. *Cognitive Psychology*, *3*(3), 430–454. doi:10.1016/0010-0285(72)90016-3

Kaiser, M. (2010). A conceptional approach to unify completeness, consistency, and accuracy as quality dimensions of data values. In *Proceedings of European and Mediterranean Conference on Information Systems*. IEEE.

Kaplan, R. S., & Porter, M. E. (2011). The big idea: How to solve the cost crisis in health care. *Harvard Business Review*, *89*(9), 47–64.

Karner, H., & Droschl, G. (2002). Usage-centered interface design for knowledge management software. *Journal of Universal Computer Science*, *8*(6).

Kassel, A. (2008). *Social networking: A research tool*. Retrieved 15/12/2012, from http://web.fumsi.com/go/article/find/3196

Kawasaki, G. (2007). *Ten ways to use linkedin*. Retrieved 05-01-2007, from http://blog.guykawasaki.com

Keehan, S. P., Sisko, A. M., Truffer, C. J., Poisal, J. A., Cuckler, G. A., Madison, A. J., & Smith, S. D. (2011). National health spending projections through 2020: Economic recovery and reform drive faster spending growth. *Health Affairs*, *30*(8), 1594–1605. doi:10.1377/hlthaff.2011.0662 PMID:21798885

Keeton, K., Mehra, P., & Wilkes, J. (2010). Do you know your IQ? A research agenda for information quality in systems. *SIGMETRICS Performance Evaluation Review*, *37*(3), 26–31. doi:10.1145/1710115.1710121

Kerr, K. A., Norris, T., & Stockdale, R. (2008). The strategic management of data quality in healthcare. *Health Informatics Journal*, *14*(4), 259–266. doi:10.1177/1460458208096555 PMID:19008276

Keyes, J. (2006). *Knowledge management, business intelligence, and content management: The IT practitioner's guide*. Boston: Auerbach Publications. doi:10.1201/9781420013863

Kimball, R. (1996). *The data warehouse toolkit: Practical techniques for building dimensional data warehouses*. New York: John Wiley & Sons Inc.

Kimball, R., & Caserta, J. (2004). *The data warehouse ETL toolkit: Practical techniques for extracting, cleaning, conforming, and delivering data*. John Wiley & Sons.

Kimball, R., & Ross, M. (2002). *The data warehouse toolkit: The complete guide to dimensional modeling*. New York: Wiley.

Kimball, R., & Ross, M. (2010). *The Kimball group reader: Relentlessly practical tools for data warehousing and business intelligence*. Indianapolis, IN: Wiley Publishing Inc.

Kimball, R., Ross, M., Thornthwaite, W., Mundy, J., & Becker, B. (2008). *The data warehouse lifecycle toolkit* (2nd ed.). Indianapolis, IN: Wiley Publishing Inc.

Kirk, J. (1999). Information in organisations: directions for information management. *Information Research*, *4*(3).

Kiron, D., Shockley, R., Kruschwitz, N., Finch, G., & Haydock, M. (2012). Analytics: The widening divide. *MIT Sloan Management Review*, *53*(2), 1–22.

Kirsch, G., Brown, J., & Charley, F. (2006). Using patents in competitive intelligence. *Competitive Intelligence Magazine*, *9*(1), 17–21.

Kirsten, T., Kolb, L., Hartung, M., Gross, A., Kopche, H., & Rahm, E. (2010). Data partitioning for parallel entity matching. *Proceedings of the VLDB Endowment*, *3*(2).

Kittur, A., & Kraut, R. E. (2008). *Harnessing the wisdom of crowds in wikipedia: Quality through coordination*. Paper presented at the 2008 ACM Conference on Computer Supported Cooperative Work. San Diego, CA.

Klein, B. D. (2001). User perception of data quality: Internet and traditional text sources. *Journal of Computer Information Systems*, *41*(4), 9–15.

Klein, B. D. (2002). Internet data quality: Perceptions of graduate and undergraduate business student. *Journal of Business and Management*, *8*(4), 425–432.

Kleinberg, J. M. (1999). Authoritative sources in a hyperlinked environment. *Journal of the ACM*, *46*(5), 604–632. doi:10.1145/324133.324140

Knight, S. (2011). The combined conceptual life-cycle model of information quality: Part 1, an investigative framework. *International Journal of Information Quality*, *2*, 205–230. doi:10.1504/IJIQ.2011.040669

Koivumaki, T., Ristola, A., & Kesti, M. (2008). The effects of information quality of mobile information services on user satisfaction and service acceptance-empirical evidence from Finland. *Behaviour & Information Technology*, *27*(5), 375–385. doi:10.1080/01449290601177003

Kolb, L., Thor, A., & Rahm, E. (2012). Multi-pass sorted neighborhood blocking with MapReduce. *Computer Science Research and Development*, *27*(1).

Koronios, A., & Lin, S. (2007). Information quality in engineering asset management. In *Information quality management: Theory and applications*. Hershey, PA: Idea Group Pub.

Kotler, P., Armstrong, G., Saunders, J., & Wong, V. (1999). Principles of marketing (2ª ed.). Cambridge, UK: Prentice Hall.

Kotze, L. (2013). *Social media increasingly important in competitive intelligence*. Retrieved 08-03-2013, from http://www.ibis.co.za/Competitive-Intelligence-Blog/social-media-increasingly-important-in-competitive-intelligence.html

Kovai, A., & Bosilj-Vukšić, V. (2005). *Management poslovnih procesov: Prenova in informatizacija poslovanja s praktičnimi primeri*. Ljubljana: GV Založba.

Lahrmann, G., Marx, F., Winter, R., & Wortmann, F. (2011). *Business intelligence maturity: Development and evaluation of a theoretical model*. Paper presented at the 44th Hawaii International Conference on System Sciences (HICSS). Hawaii, HI.

Larrivée, S., Bédard, Y., Gervais, M., & Roy, T. (2011). New horizons for spatial data quality research. In *Proceedings from the 7th International Symposium on Spatial Data Quality*. IEEE.

Lattès, R. (1992). *O risco e a fortuna: A grande aventura da inovação*. Lisboa: Difusão Cultural.

Lawson, B. R., Baker, K. R., Powell, S. G., & Foster-Johnson, L. (2009). A comparison of spreadsheet users with different levels of experience. *Omega*, *37*(3), 579–590. doi:10.1016/j.omega.2007.12.004

Leape, L. L., Lawthers, A. G., Brennan, T. A., & Johnson, W. G. (1993). Preventing medical injury. *QRB. Quality Review Bulletin*, *19*(5), 144. PMID:8332330

Leem, C. S., Kim, B. W., Yu, E. J., & Paek, M. H. (2008). Information technology maturity stages and enterprise benchmarking: An empirical study. *Industrial Management & Data Systems*, *108*(9), 1200–1218. doi:10.1108/02635570810914892

Lee, S. H., & Haider, A. (2012). *Assessing information quality by six sigma method* (Vol. 7240, pp. 323–334). Berlin, Germany: Springer Berlin Heidelberg. doi:10.1007/978-3-642-29023-7_32

Lee, Y. W., Pierce, E., Talburt, J., & Wang, R. Y. (2007). A Curriculum for a Master of Science in Information Quality. *Journal of Information Systems Education*.

Lee, Y. W., Pipino, L. L., Funk, J. D., & Wang, R. Y. (2006). *Journey to data quality*. Cambridge, MA: The MIT Press.

Lee, Y. W., Pipino, L. L., Funk, J. D., & Wang, R. Y. (2006). *Journey to Data Quality*. Cambridge: The MIT Press.

Lee, Y. W., Strong, D. M., Kahn, B. K., & Wang, R. Y. (2002). AIMQ: A methodology for information quality assessment. *Information & Management*, *40*(2), 133–146. doi:10.1016/S0378-7206(02)00043-5

Leidner, D., & Kayworth, T. (2006). Review: A review of culture in information systems research: Toward a theory of information technology culture conflict. *Management Information Systems Quarterly*, *30*(2), 357–399.

Lenzerini, M. (2002). Data integration: A theoretical perspective. In L. Popa, S. Abiteboul, & P. G. Kolaitis (Eds.), *Proceedings of the 21st ACM SIGMOD-SIGACT-SIGART Symposium on Principles of Database Systems* (pp. 233-246). New York, NY: ACM.

Leonard, H. (2013). *Blogs outrank social networks in influence*. Retrieved 09-03-2013, from http://www.businessinsider.com/blog-influence-outranks-social-networks-2013-3

Lesca, H., & Lesca, E. (1995). *Gestion de l'information, qualité de l'information et performances de l'entreprise*. Paris: Litec.

Levenshtein, V. (1966). Binary codes capable of correcting deletions, insertions and reversals. *Soviet Physics, Doklady*, *10*(8), 707–710.

Levinson, D. R. (2010). *Adverse effects in hospitals: National incidence among medicare beneficiaries*. Washington, DC: Center on Budget and Policy Priorities.

Levis, M. (2011, January 17). *Information quality training requirements analysis guideline demonstrated in a healthcare context*. (PhD Thesis). Dublin City University, Dublin, Ireland. Retrieved January 15, 2013, from doras.dcu.ie: http://doras.dcu.ie/16068/

Li, L. (2010). A framework study of ETL processes optimization base on metadata repository. In *Proceedings from the International Conference on Computer Engineering and Technology* (pp. 125-129). IEEE.

Libert, B., & Spector, J. (2009). *Muitas cabeças pensam melhor: Como mobilizar o poder das multidões para o seu negócio*. Porto: Lua de Papel.

Lillrank, P. (2003). The quality of information. *International Journal of Quality & Reliability Management, 20*(6), 691–703. doi:10.1108/02656710310482131

Lin, M. O., & Hua, Z. (2008). A method for measuring data quality in data integration. In *Proceedings of International Seminar on Future Information Technology and Management Engineering*. FITME.

Linder, J. A., Ma, J., Bates, D. W., Middleton, B., & Stafford, R. S. (2007). Electronic health record use and the quality of ambulatory care in the United States. *Archives of Internal Medicine, 167*(13), 1400–1405. doi:10.1001/archinte.167.13.1400 PMID:17620534

Linderman, K., Schroeder, R. G., Zaheer, S., & Choo, A. S. (2003). Six sigma: A goal-theoretic perspective. *Journal of Operations Management, 21*(2), 193–203. doi:10.1016/S0272-6963(02)00087-6

Linstedt, D. (2011). *Super charge your data warehouse: Invaluable data modeling rules to implement your data vault*. Albany, NY: CreateSpace Independent Publishing Platform.

Lin, Y.-K., Brown, R. A., Yang, H. J., Li, S.-H., & Lu, H.-M. (2011). Data mining large-scale electronic health records for clinical support. *IEEE Intelligent Systems, 26*(5), 87–90.

Liu, J., & Ram, S. (2011). Who does what: Collaboration patterns in the wikipedia and their impact on article quality. *ACM Transactions on Manage. Information Systems, 2*(2), 1–23.

LOINC. (1999). *Logical observation identifiers names and codes (LOINC)*. Retrieved June 7, 2013, from http://loinc.org/faq/getting-started/loinc-and-other-standards/

Losee. (1997). A discipline independent definition of information. *Journal of the American Society of Information Science, 48*(3), 254-269.

Loshin, D. (2001). *Enterprise knowledge management: The data quality approach*. San Francisco: Morgan Kaufmann.

Loshin, D. (2008). *Master data management*. Knowledge Integrity, Inc.

Low, W., Lee, M., & Ling, T. (2001). A knowledge-based approach for duplicate elimination in data cleaning. *Information Systems, 26*(8), 585–606. doi:10.1016/S0306-4379(01)00041-2

Luenberger, D. G. (2006). *Information Science*. Princeton: Princeton University Press.

Madnick, S. E., Wang, Y. W., Lee, H., & Zhu, H. (2009). Overview and framework for data and information quality research. *Journal of Data and Information Quality, 1*(1), 1–22. doi:10.1145/1515693.1516680

Maguire, H. (2008). Extending the boundaries of IQ: Can collaboration with information management improve corporate governance? *International Journal of Information Quality, 2*(1), 23. doi:10.1504/IJIQ.2008.019561

Mäkelä, J. (2006). The impact of spatial data quality on company's decision making. *The International Archives of the Photogrammetry, Remote Sensing and Spatial Information Sciences, 34*.

Malinowski, E. (2012). Challenges for promoting decision-making processes based on spatial data analysis. In *Proceedings from the International Computer Symposium* (pp. 393-402). IEEE.

Malinowski, E., & Zimányi, E. (2009). *Advanced data warehouse design: From conventional to spatial and temporal applications*. Berlin: Springer.

Manning, C. D., Raghavan, P., & Schütze, H. (2008). *Introduction to information retrieval*. Cambridge, UK: Cambridge University Press. doi:10.1017/CBO9780511809071

Marchand, D. (1990). Managing information quality. In Wormell (Ed.), Information quality: Definitions and dimensions. London: Taylor Graham.

Marchand, D., & Horton, F. Jr. (1986). *Infotrends: Profiting from your information resources*. Hoboken, NJ: Wiley.

Marchand, M., & Raymond, L. (2008). Researching performance measurement systems: An information systems perspective. *International Journal of Operations & Production Management, 28*(7), 663–686. doi:10.1108/01443570810881802

Marjanovic, O. (2010). The importance of process thinking in business intelligence. *International Journal of Business Intelligence Research*, *1*(4), 29–46. doi:10.4018/jbir.2010100102

Martinet, B., & Marti, Y. (1995). *A inteligência económica: Os olhos e os ouvidos da empresa*. Instituto Piaget.

Mathew, G. (2012). *5 macro trends shaping next-generation BI and analytics*. Retrieved January 8, 2013, from http://tdwi.org/articles/2012/02/07/5-macro-trends-bi-analytics.aspx

Maydanchik, A. (2007). *Data quality assessment*. Technics Publications.

McAdam, R., & Bailie, B. (2002). Business performance measures and alignment impact on strategy. *International Journal of Operations & Production Management*, *22*(9), 972–996. doi:10.1108/01443570210440492

McGee, J. V., & Prusak, L. (1995). *Gerenciamento estratégico da informação: Aumente a competitividade e a eficiência de sua empresa utilizando a informação como uma ferramenta estratégica*. Rio de Janeiro, Brazil: Campus.

McGilvray, D. (2008). *Executing data quality projects: Ten steps to quality data and trusted information*. Burlington, MA: Morgan Kaufmann.

McInerney, C. R., & Day, R. E. (2007). *Rethinking knowledge management: From knowledge artifacts to knowledge processes*. Berlin: Springer. doi:10.1007/3-540-71011-6

McPherson, P. (1994). Accounting for the value of information. *Aslib Proceedings*, *46*(9), 203–215. doi:10.1108/eb051366

Meske, D. J. (2011, August). Data Loss: Protecting Personally Identifying Information (PII) at Public Higher . La Verne, California.

Miami University. (2005, September 15). *Privacy Help*. Retrieved July 4, 2011, from Miami University: http://www.miami.muohio.edu/documents_and_policies/privacyhelp.cfm

Miller, A. (2007). *Social tools for business use: Messages from a web 2.0 conference*. Retrieved 12-12-2012, from http://web.fumsi.com/go/article/find/3916

Miller, J., & Business Intelligence Braintrust. (2002). *O milênio da inteligência competitiva*. Porto Alegre. *The Bookman*.

Milovanovi. (2006). Knowledge sharing between users and information specialists: Role of trust. *Facta Universitatis, Series: Economics and Organization, 3*(1), 51-58.

MIT Information Quality Program. (2011). *MIT Information Quality Program*. Retrieved April 20, 2012, from MIT Information Quality: http://mitiq.mit.edu/

Mohr, J., Sengupta, S., & Slater, S. (2010). Marketing of high-technology products and innovations (3ª ed.). Upper Saddle River, NJ: Pearson.

Moore, G. C., & Benbasat, I. (1991). Development of an instrument to measure the perceptions of adopting an information technology innovation. *Information Systems Research*, *2*(3), 192–222. doi:10.1287/isre.2.3.192

Mordecai, V. (2013a). 4 things social media analysis can tell you about your business. *Focal Point: Focalytic*. Retrieved 23-05-2013, from http://www.focalytic.com/focal-point/bid/291330/4-Things-Social-Media-Analysis-Can-Tell-You-About-Your-Business

Mordecai, V. (2013b). What businesses can gain from a custom social media listening tool. *Focal Point: Focalytic*. Retrieved 20-05-2013, from http://www.focalytic.com/focal-point/bid/291331/What-Businesses-Can-Gain-from-a-Custom-Social-Media-Listening-Tool

Mordecai, V. (2013c). What is competitive intelligence? *Focal Point: Focalytic*. Retrieved 14-06-2013, from http://www.focalytic.com/focal-point/bid/297577/What-Is-Competitive-Intelligence

Morgan, C., Talley, T., Talburt, J., Bussell, C., Kooshesh, A., Anderson, W., et al. (2003). *U.S. patent no. 6523041*. Washington, DC: U.S. Patent and Trademark Office.

Morse, J. N. (2007). Beyond spreadsheets and silos: enriching financial planning using hyperion strategic finance. *Journal of Global Business Issues*, *1*(2), 115.

Moss, L. T., & Atre, S. (2003). *Business intelligence roadmap: The complete project lifecycle for decision-support applications*. Reading, MA: Addison-Wesley Professional.

Motro, A., & Rakov, I. (1996). Estimating the quality of data in relational databases. In *Proceedings of the 1st International Conference on Information Quality*. Retrieved from http://mitiq.mit.edu/ICIQ/Documents/IQ%20Conference%201996/Papers/EstimatingtheQualityofDatainRelationalDb.pdf

Mundy, J. (2012). *Design tip #149 facing the re-keying crisis*. Retrieved February 22, 2013 from http://www.kimballgroup.com/2012/10/02/design-tip-149-facing-the-re-keying-crisis/

Nadler, S. (2013). *Wise men*. Reagan Arthur Books.

Narayaan, A., & Shmatikov, V. (2008). Robust de-anonymization of large sparse data sets. In *Proceedings of IEEE Symposium on Security and Privacy* (pp. 111-121). IEEE.

Narayanan, R., Oberhofer, M., & Pandit, S. (2012). Metadata exploitation in large-scale data migration projects. In *Proceedings of AMCIS 2012*. AMCIS.

National Commission on Terrorist Attacks upon the United States. (2004). *The 9/11 commission report*. Retrieved from http://www.9-11commission.gov/report/911Report.pdf

Naumann, F., & Rolker, C. (2000). Assessment methods for information quality criteria. In *Proceedings of the 14th International Conference on Information Quality* (pp. 148-162). IEEE.

Naumann, F., & Herschel, M. (2010). An introduction to duplicate detection. In *Synthesis Lectures on Data Management*. New York: Morgan and Claypool Publishers.

Neely, M. P., & Cook, J. S. (2011). Fifteen years of data and information quality literature: Developing a research agenda for accounting. *Journal of Information Systems*, *25*(1), 79–108. doi:10.2308/jis.2011.25.1.79

Negroponte, N. (1995). *Being digital*. New York: Knopf.

Nelson, E. (2011). *Design and Construction of An Entity Resolution System that Supports Entity Identity Information Management and Asserted Resolution.*

Nelson, R. R., Todd, P. A., & Wixom, B. H. (2005). Antecedents of information and system quality: An empirical examination within the context of data warehousing. *Journal of Management Information Systems*, *21*(4), 199–235.

Newcombe, H. B. (1988). *Handbook of Record Linkage*. Oxford University Press.

Newcombe, H. B., & Kennedy, J. M. (1962). Record linkage: making maximum use of the discriminating power of identifying information. *Communications of the ACM*, *5*(11), 563–566. doi:10.1145/368996.369026

News, A. B. C. (2006). *Fast facts on the U.S. health care crisis*. Retrieved 01/15/2013, from http://abcnews.go.com/WNT/PrescriptionForChange/story?id=2563381

ObamaCare Facts. (2013). *ObamaCare facts: Dispelling the myths*. Retrieved 03/06/2013, from http://obamacarefacts.com/obamacare-facts.php

Oberbeck, H. (2004). *Learning with hypermedia: The impact of content design and learner characteristics on navigation and the knowledge acquisition process*. Braunschweig: Technischen Universität Carolo-Wilhelmina zu.

O'Brien, K. J. (2013, January 25). *Silicon valley companies lobbying against Europe's privacy proposals*. Retrieved February 20, 2013, from http://www.nytimes.com/2013/01/26/technology/eu-privacy-proposal-lays-bare-differences-with-us.html

Ocholla, D. N., Onyancha, O. B., & Britz, J. (2010). Can information ethics be conceptualized by using the core/periphery model? *Journal of Informetrics*, *4*(4), 492–502. doi:10.1016/j.joi.2010.05.001

OECD. (1981). *Guidelines on the protection of privacy and transborder flows of personal data*. Retrieved January 15, 2013, from http://www.oecd.org/internet/interneteconomy/oecdguidelinesontheprotectionofprivacyandtransborderflowsofpersonaldata.htm

Office of the Privacy Commissioner of Canada. (2011). *2011 Canadians and privacy survey*. Ottawa, Canada: Office of the Privacy Commissioner of Canada.

Ojala, M. (2012, July/August). Minding your own business: Social media invades business research. *Exploring Technology & Resources for Information Professionals*, 51-53.

Olinsky, A., & Schumacher, P. A. (2010). Data mining for health care professionals: MBA course projects resulting in hospital improvements. *International Journal of Business Intelligence Research*, *1*(2), 30–41. doi:10.4018/jbir.2010040104

Oliver, R. L. (1999). Whence customer loyalty? *Journal of Marketing, 63*, 3–44. doi:10.2307/1252099

Olsen, J. (2003). *Data quality: The accuracy dimension*. New York: Morgan Kaufmann Publishers.

OMB. (2010). Office of management and budget. *Circular No.A-2*. Retrieved January 4, 2013, from: http://www.whitehouse.gov/omb/circulars_a016_rev/

OMB. (2011). Retrieved June 10, 2011, from http://www.whitehouse.gov/omb/

Ong, C. S., & Lai, J. Y. (2007). Measuring user satisfaction with knowledge management systems: Scale development, purification, and initial test. *Computers in Human Behavior, 23*(3), 1329–1346. doi:10.1016/j.chb.2004.12.012

Oosterom, P., Quak, W., & Tijssen, T. (2005). About invalid, valid and clean polygons. In *Proceedings from the 11th International Symposium on Spatial Data Handling* (pp. 1-16). IEEE.

Oracle Corporation. (2011). *MySQL*. Retrieved July 4, 2012, from MySQL: http://www.mysql.com/

Oracle. (2011). Putting business intelligence on the map. *Oracle Magazine*. Retrieved January 12, 2013, from http://www.oracle.com/technetwork/issue-archive/2011/11-may/o31bi-354140.html

Orna, E. (1999). Practical information policies (2ª ed.). Cambridge, UK: Gower.

Orna, E. (1996). Valuing information: Problems and opportunities. In D. Best (Ed.), *The fourth resource: Information and its management*. Hampshire, UK: Aslib/Gower.

Otte, E., & Rousseau, R. (2002). Social network analysis: A powerful strategy, also for the information sciences. *Journal of Information Science, 28*(6), 441–453. doi:10.1177/016555150202800601

OYSTER Entity Resolution. (2012, June 13). Retrieved July 4, 2012, from SourceForge.NET: http://sourceforge.net/projects/oysterer/

Pandit, S., Oberhofer, M., & Milman, I. (2012). Ontology-guided reference data alignment in information integration projects. In *Proceedings of AMCIS 2012*. AMCIS.

Panko, R. R., & Aurigemma, S. (2010). Revising the Panko-Halverson taxonomy of spreadsheet errors. *Decision Support Systems, 49*(2), 235–244. doi:10.1016/j.dss.2010.02.009

Pentaho. (2013). *Pentaho Google maps dashboard*. Retrieved January 11, 2013, from http://community.pentaho.com/google_maps/

Penzias, A. (1989). *Ideas and information: Managing in a high-tech world*. New York: W. W. Norton.

Penzias, A. (1995). *Harmony: Business, technology & life after paperwork*. New York: Harper Collins.

Peppard, J., Ward, J., & Daniel, E. (2007). Managing the realization of business benefits from IT investments. *MIS Quarterly Executive, 6*(1), 1–11.

Peralta, V., Ruggia, R., Kedad, Z., & Bouzeghoub, M. (2004). A framework for data quality evaluation in a data integration system. In *Proceedings of the 19th Brazilian Symposium on Databases*. SBBD.

Petrini, M., & Pozzebon, M. (2009). Managing sustainability with the support of business intelligence: Integrating socio-environmental indicators and organisational context. *The Journal of Strategic Information Systems, 18*(4), 178–191. doi:10.1016/j.jsis.2009.06.001

Petter, S., DeLone, W. H., & McLean, E. R. (2008). Measuring information systems success: Models, dimensions, measures, and interrelationships. *European Journal of Information Systems, 17*(3), 236–263. doi:10.1057/ejis.2008.15

Petty, R. E., & Cacioppo, J. T. (1986). The elaboration likelihood model of persuasion. *Advances in Experimental Social Psychology, 19*, 123–205. doi:10.1016/S0065-2601(08)60214-2

Philips, L. (2000). The double-metaphone search algorithm. *C/C++ User's Journal, 18*(6).

Pighin, M., & Ieronutti, L. (2008). A methodology supporting the design and evaluating the final quality of data warehouses. *International Journal of Data Warehousing and Mining, 4*(3), 20. doi:10.4018/jdwm.2008070102

Pipek, V., Wulf, V., & Johri, A. (2011). Bridging artifacts and actors: Expertise sharing in organizational ecosystems. *Computer Supported Cooperative Work*.

Piper, D. L. A. (2013, March). *Data protection laws of the world.* Retrieved from http://www.dlapiper.com/files/Uploads/Documents/Data_Protection_Laws_of_the_World_2013.pdf

Pipino, L. L., Lee, Y. W., & Wang, R. Y. (2002). Data quality assessment. *Communications of the ACM, 45*(4), 211–218. doi:10.1145/505248.506010

Plaisant, C., Marchionini, G., Bruns, T., Komlodi, A., & Campbell, L. (1997). *Bringing treasures to the surface: Iterative design for the library of congress national digital library program.* Paper presented at the CHI 97 Electronic Publications: Design Briefings. New York, NY.

Polborn, M. K., Hoy, M., & Sadanand, A. (2006). Advantageous effects of regulatory adverse selection in the life insurance market. *The Economic Journal, 116*(508), 327–354. doi:10.1111/j.1468-0297.2006.01059.x

Popovi, A., Coelho, P. S., & Jaklič, J. (2009). The impact of business intelligence system maturity on information quality. *Information Research, 14*(4).

Popovi, A., & Habjan, A. (2012). Exploring the effects of information quality change in road transport operations. *Industrial Management & Data Systems, 112*(9), 1307–1325. doi:10.1108/02635571211278947

Popovi, A., Turk, T., & Jaklič, J. (2010). Conceptual model of business value of business intelligence systems. *Management, 15*(1), 5–30.

Popovič, A., Coelho, P. S., & Jaklič, J. (2009). The impact of business intelligence system maturity on information quality. *Information Research, 14*(4).

Popovic, A., Hackney, R., Coelho, S., & Jaklic, J. (2012). Towards business intelligence systems success: Effects of maturity and culture on analytical decision making. *Decision Support Systems, 54*(1), 729–739. doi:10.1016/j.dss.2012.08.017

Poppendieck, M., & Poppendieck, T. (2003). *Lean software development: An agile toolkit.* Boston, MA: Addison-Wesley.

Porter, M. (1980). *Competitive strategies: Techniques for analyzing industries and competitors.* New York: MacMillan.

Porter, M. E., & Millar, V. E. (1985). How information gives you competitive advantage. *Harvard Business Review, 63*(4), 149–160.

Pradinho, H., Alonso, J., Guerra, C., Pocas, I., Goncalves, J., & Marcos, B. (2011). *Report on pre-existing in situ and ancillary datasets for sites.* Retrieved January 15, 2013, from http://www.biosos.wur.nl/NR/rdonlyres/935FA85D-DC21-4FDC-ADE6-037FC172A312/156397/BIO_SOS_D41_Preexisting_data_sets.pdf

Prajogo, D. I., & McDermott, C. M. (2005). The relationship between total quality management practices and organizational culture. *International Journal of Operations & Production Management, 25*(11), 1101–1122. doi:10.1108/01443570510626916

Prat, N., & Madnick, S. (2008). Measuring data believability: A provenance approach. In *Proceedings of the 41st Hawaii International Conference on System Sciences.* IEEE.

Prescott, J. E., & Miller, S. H. (2002). *Inteligência competitiva na prática: Técnicas e práticas bem sucedidas para conquistar mercados.* Rio de Janeiro: Campus.

Prewitt, K. (2011). Why it matters to distinguish between privacy & confidentiality. *Journal of Privacy and Confidentiality, 3*(2), 41–47.

Prior, V. (2006). *Competitive intelligence: An introduction.* Retrieved 06-10-2008 from http://www.freepint.com/issues/050106.htm#feature

Prior, V. (2007). *DIY detection: Competitive intelligence for SMEs.* Retrieved from http://web.freepint.com/go/features/2483

PriviReal.org. (n.d.). *Italy - Data protection.* Retrieved February 15, 2013, from http://www.privireal.org/content/dp/italy.php

Purcell, K., Brenner, J., & Rainie, L. (2012). *Search engine use 2012.* Washington, DC: Pew Research Center.

Pushkarev, V., Neumann, H., Varol, C., & Talburt, J. (2010). An overview of open source data quality tools. *Information and Knowledge Engineering Conference.* Las Vegas.

Qualman, E. (2010). *Socialnomics: Como os media sociais estão a transformar o modo como vivemos e como fazemos negócios*. Lisboa: Presença.

Raghunathan, S. (1999). Impact of information quality and decision-maker quality on decision quality: A theoretical model and simulation analysis. *Decision Support Systems*, *26*(4), 275–286. doi:10.1016/S0167-9236(99)00060-3

Ramamurthy, K., Sen, A., & Sinha, A. P. (2008). An empirical investigation of the key determinants of data warehouse adoption. *Decision Support Systems*, *44*(4), 817–841. doi:10.1016/j.dss.2007.10.006

Ransbotham, S., & Kane, G. C. (2011). Membership turnover and collaboration success in online communities: Explaining rises and falls from grace in Wikipedia. *MIS Quarterly-Management Information Systems*, *35*(3), 613–627.

Ransbotham, S., Kane, G. C., & Lurie, N. H. (2012). Network characteristics and the value of collaborative user-generated content. *Marketing Science*, *31*(3), 387–405. doi:10.1287/mksc.1110.0684

Rasquilha, L. (2010). *Tendências e gestão da inovação: Como aplicar as tendências na estratégia de inovação empresarial*. Lousã: Verlag Dashöfer.

Rauscher, S., & Wheeler, J. R. (2008). Effective hospital revenue cycle management: Is there a trade-off between the amount of patient revenue and the speed of revenue collection? *Journal of Healthcare Management*, *53*(6), 392. PMID:19070334

Rauscher, S., & Wheeler, J. R. C. (2010). Hospital revenue cycle management and payer mix: Do Medicare and medicaid undermine hospitals' ability to generate and collect patient care revenue? *Editorial Board*, *37*(2), 90–104.

Redman, T. (1996). *Data quality for the information age*. Norwood, MA: Artech House.

Reidenber, J. R., & Debelak, J. (2009). *Children's Educational Records and Privacy*. Fordham Center on Law and Information Policy.

Reuters. (2013, February 20). *EU lawmakers vote against mandatory data protection fines*. Retrieved February 25, 2013, from http://www.reuters.com/article/2013/02/20/eu-dataprotection-idUSL6N0BKF4X20130220

Revelli, C. (2000). *Inteligência estratégica na Internet: Como desenvolver eficazmente actividades de monitorização e de pesquisa nas redes*. Instituto Piaget.

Revised FERPA Regulations: An Overview for SEAs and LEAs. (2011). Retrieved from http://www2.ed.gov/policy/gen/guid/fpco/pdf/sealea_overview.pdf

Ribault, J.-M., Martinet, B., & Lebidois, D. (1995). *A gestão das tecnologias*. Lisboa: D. Quixote.

Richard, P. J., Devinney, T. M., Yip, G. S., & Johnson, G. (2009). Measuring organizational performance: Towards methodological best practice. *Journal of Management*, *35*(3), 718–804. doi:10.1177/0149206308330560

Rigaux, P., Scholl, M., & Voisard, A. (2002). *Spatial databases with application to GIS*. New York: Morgan Kaufmann.

Ringle, C. M., Wende, S., & Will, A. (2007). *SmartPLS 2.0 M3*. Hamburg, Germany: University of Hamburg.

Robertson, J. (2006). *Good search is knowledge management*. Retrieved from www.steptwo.com.au

Romano, M. J., & Stafford, R. S. (2011). Electronic health records and clinical decision support systems: Impact on national ambulatory care quality. *Archives of Internal Medicine*, *171*(10), 897–903. doi:10.1001/archinternmed.2010.527 PMID:21263077

Romano, N. C., & Fjermestad, J. (2002). Electronic commerce customer relationship management: An assessment of research. *International Journal of Electronic Commerce*, *6*, 61–114.

Rönnbäck. (2012). Retrieved 20 December 2012 from http://www.anchormodeling.com

Rossin, D. F. (2007). An exploratory analysis of information quality in supply chains: Efficient and responsive models. *Journal of Global Business Issues*, *1*(2), 151–158.

Rueviius, J., & Gedminait, A. (2007). Business information quality and its assessment. *The Engineering Economist*, *52*(2), 18–25.

Russell, M. (2011). *Mining the social web: Analyzing data from Facebook, Twitter, LinkedIn, and other social media sites*. Sebastopol, CA: O'Reilly Media.

Rustmann, F., Jr. (2002). *CIA, Inc.: Espionage and the craft of business intelligence*. Dulles: Brassey's.

Saaty, T. L. (2008). Decision making with the analytic hierarchy process. *International Journal of Services Sciences*, *1*(1), 83–98. doi:10.1504/IJSSCI.2008.017590

Sabherwal, R., & Becerra-Fernandez, I. (2010). *Business intelligence: Practices, technologies, and management*. Hoboken, NJ: John Wiley & Sons Inc.

Safe Software. (2013). *About FME spatial data transformation platform*. Retrieved January 5, 2013, from http://www.safe.com/fme/fme-technology/

Sage, N. (2013). *How to create business value from social intelligence*. Retrieved 30-05-2013, from http://www.computerweekly.com/opinion/How-to-create-business-value-from-social-intelligence

Salaun, Y., & Flores, K. (2001). Information quality: Meeting the needs of the consumer. *International Journal of Information Management*, *21*(1), 21–37.

Sanderson, M., Ramage, S., & Van Linden, L. (2009). SDI communities: Data quality and knowledge sharing. In *Proceedings of the 11th International Conference for Spatial Data Infrastructure*. Retrieved January 7, 2013, from http://www.gsdi.org/gsdiconf/gsdi11/papers/pdf/283.pdf

Saunders, C. S., & Jones, J. W. (1992). Measuring performance of the information systems function. *Journal of Management Information Systems*, *8*(4), 63–82.

Schaffer, N. (2011). *Maximizing LinkedIn for sales and social media marketing: An unofficial, practical guide to selling & developing B2B business on LinkedIn*. CreateSpace Independent Publishing Platform.

Schiffman, L., & Kanuk, L. (2000). *Consumer behavior*. Upper Saddle River, NJ: Prentice Hall.

Scholten, H. (2010). *Musings on the data vault*. Retrieved 20 December 2012 from http://www.bi-team.com

Schoth, D. E., & Liossi, C. (2010). Attentional bias toward pictorial representations of pain in individuals with chronic headache. *The Clinical Journal of Pain*, *26*(3), 244. doi:10.1097/AJP.0b013e3181bed0f9 PMID:20173439

Schwaber, K., & Sutherland, J. (n.d.). *The scrum guide*. Retrieved from https://www.scrum.org/Portals/0/Documents/Scrum%20Guides/2013/Scrum-Guide.pdf#zoom=100

Scott, D. (2008). *As novas regras de marketing e relações públicas: Como usar os blogues, o podcasting, os media online e as notas informativas para chegar directamente aos consumidores*. Porto: Ideias de Ler.

Sen, A. (2004). Metadata management: Past, present and future. *Decision Support Systems*, *37*(1), 151–173. doi:10.1016/S0167-9236(02)00208-7

Sen, A., & Jacob, V. S. (1998). Industrial-strength data warehousing. *Communications of the ACM*, *41*(9), 28–31. doi:10.1145/285070.285076

Sen, A., Ramamurthy, K., & Sinha, A. P. (2012). A model of data warehousing process maturity. *IEEE Transactions on Software Engineering*, *38*(2), 336–353. doi:10.1109/TSE.2011.2

Sen, A., & Sinha, A. P. (2005). A comparison of data warehousing methodologies. *Communications of the ACM*, *48*(3), 79–84. doi:10.1145/1047671.1047673

Sen, A., & Sinha, A. P. (2007). Toward developing data warehousing process standards: An ontology-base. *IEEE Transactions on Systems, Man and Cybernetics. Part C, Applications and Reviews*, *37*(1), 17–31. doi:10.1109/TSMCC.2006.886966

Shankaranarayanan, G. (2005). Towards implementing total data quality management in a datawarehouse. *Journal of Information Technology Management*, *16*, 21–30.

Shankaranarayanan, G., & Cai, Y. (2006). Supporting data quality management in decision-making. *Decision Support Systems*, *42*, 302–317. doi:10.1016/j.dss.2004.12.006

Shankaranarayanan, G., & Even, A. (2004). Managing metadata in data warehouses: Pitfalls and possibilities. *Communications of the Association for Information Systems*, 14.

Shankaranarayanan, G., & Even, A. (2006). The metadata enigma. *Communications of the ACM*, *49*(2), 88–97. doi:10.1145/1113034.1113035

Shanks, G., & Darke, P. (1998). Understanding data quality in a data warehouse. *The Australian Computer Journal*, *30*(4), 122–128.

Shapiro, C., & Varian, H. (1999). *Information rules: A strategic guide to the network economy*. Boston: Harvard Business School Press.

Sharmin, M., Bailey, B. P., Coats, C., & Hamilton, K. (2009). *Understanding knowledge management practives for early design activity and its implication for reuse*. Paper presented at the CHI 2009. Boston, MA.

Shekhar, S., & Chawla, S. (2003). *Spatial databases: A tour*. Upper Saddle River, NJ: Prentice Hall.

Shi, Y. H., Yang, Z. K., Yang, H. H., & Liu, S. Y. (2012). *Study on the research hotspots of interactive whiteboards in education*. Paper presented at the 4th International Conference on Internet Multimedia Computing and Service. New York, NY.

Shin, A. (2003). An exploratory investigation of system success factors in data warehousing. *Journal of the Association for Information Systems*, *4*(1), 141–170.

Shortell, S. M. (2004). Increasing value: a research agenda for addressing the managerial and organizational challenges facing health care delivery in the United States. *Medical Care Research and Review*, *61*(3suppl), 12S–30S. doi:10.1177/1077558704266768 PMID:15375281

Sillup, G. P., Klimberg, R. K., & McSweeney, D. P. (2010). Data-driven decision making for new drugs: A collaborative learning experience. *International Journal of Business Intelligence Research*, *1*(2), 42–59. doi:10.4018/jbir.2010040105

Silvers, F. (2008). *Building and maintaining a data warehouse*. Boston: Auerbach. doi:10.1201/9781420064636

Simitsis, A., Vassiliadis, P., & Sellis, T. (2005). Optimizing ETL processes in data warehouses. In *Proceeding from the International Conference on Data Engineering* (pp.564-575). IEEE.

Simoes, D. (2010). *Conceptual framework for the construction and evaluation of data warehouses*. Paper presented at the Iberian Conference on Information Systems and Technologies. Santiago de Compostela, Spain.

Singh, S., Darwish, T. K., Costa, A. C., & Anderson, N. (2012). Measuring HRM and organisational performance: Concepts, issues, and framework. *Management Decision*, *50*(4), 651–667. doi:10.1108/00251741211220282

Sinkula, J. M. (1994). Market information processing and organizational learning. *Journal of Marketing*, *58*(1), 35–45. doi:10.2307/1252249

Smith, D., & Crossland, M. (2008). Realizing the value of business intelligence. In D. Avison, G. M. Kasper, B. Pernici, I. Ramos, & D. Roode (Eds.), *Advances in information systems research, education and practice* (Vol. 274, pp. 163–174). Berlin: Springer. doi:10.1007/978-0-387-09682-7-9_14

Smits, P., Düren, U., Østensen, O., Murre, L., Gould, M., & Sandgren, U. ... Konecny, M. (2002). INSPIRE: Infrastructure for spatial information in Europe, position paper. Brussels: European Commission, Joint Research Centre -Institute for Environment and Sustainability.

Song, R., Luo, Z., Wen, J.-R., Yu, Y., & Hon, H.-W. (2007). *Identifying ambiguous queries in web search*. Paper presented at the 16th International Conference on World Wide Web. New York, NY.

Souchon, A. L., & Diamantopoulos, A. (1996). A conceptual framework of export marketing information use: Key issues and research propositions. *Journal of International Marketing*, *4*(3), 49–71.

Spatialytics. (2013). *GeoKettle*. Retrieved January 5, 2013, from http://www.spatialytics/projects/geokettle

Spence, M. (1973). Job market signaling. *The Quarterly Journal of Economics*, *87*(3), 355–374. doi:10.2307/1882010

Spence, M. (2002). Signaling in retrospect and the informational structure of markets. *The American Economic Review*, 434–459. doi:10.1257/00028280260136200

Spoerri, A. (2007). What is popular on wikipedia and why. *First Monday*, *12*(4). doi:10.5210/fm.v12i4.1765

Standard University. (2011). *Stanford Entity Resolution Framework*. Retrieved March 6, 2012, from The Standard University InfoLab: http://infolab.stanford.edu/serf/

Standish Group International, Inc. (1999). *CHAOS: A recipe for success*. Author.

Stanford Entity Resolution Framework. (2010). Retrieved May 15, 2010, from http://infolab.stanford.edu/serf/

Stanford Trio Project. (2010). Retrieved May 15, 2010, from http://infolab.stanford.edu/Trio

Stang, J., Hartvigsen, T., & Reitan, J. (2010). The effect of data quality on data mining – Improving prediction accuracy by generic data cleansing. In *Proceedings of the 2010 International Conference on Information Quality*. IEEE.

Steckerl, S. (2007). *Survival guide: Online social networking*. Retrieved 12/12/2012, from http://web.fumsi.com/go/article/use/2346

Streifield, D. (2013, March 12). *Google concedes that drive-by prying violated privacy*. Retrieved from http://www.nytimes.com/2013/03/13/technology/google-pays-fine-over-street-view-privacy-breach.html

Strong, D. M., Lee, Y. W., & Wang, R. Y. (1997). Data quality in context. *Communications of the ACM*, *40*(5), 103–110. doi:10.1145/253769.253804

Stvilia, B., Gasser, L., Twidale, M. B., & Smith, L. C. (2007). A framework for information quality assessment. *Journal of the American Society for Information Science and Technology*, *58*(12), 1720–1733. doi:10.1002/asi.20652

Stvilia, B., Twidale, M. B., Smith, L. C., & Gasser, L. (2008). Information quality work organization in wikipedia. *Journal of the American Society for Information Science and Technology*, *59*(6), 983–1001. doi:10.1002/asi.20813

Suhr, C. (2004). A change of paradigms: looking back to the pioneer years of patent information management (1960-1990). *World Patent Information*, *26*(1), 41–43. doi:10.1016/j.wpi.2003.10.017

Summers, D. C. (2006). *Quality* (4th ed.). Upper Saddle River: Pearson Prentice Hall.

Sundararaman, A. (2012). *Information quality strategy - An empirical investigation of the relationship between information quality improvements and organizational outcomes*. (Unpublished doctoral dissertation). Birla Institute of Technology and Science, India.

Sundararaman, A. (n.d.). A framework for linking data quality to business objectives in decision support systems. In *Proceedings of 3rd International Conference on Trendz in Information Sciences and Computing (TISC)* (pp. 177-181). TISC.

Sunyaev, A., & Chornyi, D. (2012). Supporting chronic disease care quality: Design and implementation of a health service and its integration with electronic health records. *Journal of Data and Information Quality*, *3*(2). doi:10.1145/2184442.2184443

Surowiecki, J. (2007). *A sabedoria das multidões: Como a inteligência colectiva transforma a economia e a sociedade*. Porto: Lua de Papel.

Swoyer, S. (2010). *Metadata management: An imperative for your enterprise*. TDWI Onsite Education.

Taborda, J. P., & Ferreira, M. D. (2002). *Competitive intelligence: Conceitos, práticas e benefícios*. Pergaminho.

Talburt, J. R. (2011). *Entity Resolution and Information Quality*. Burlington: Morgan Kaufmann.

Talburt, J. R. (2011). *Entity resolution and information quality*. San Francisco, CA: Morgan Kaufmann.

Talburt, J., & Zhou, Y. (2013). A practical guide to entity resolution with OYSTER. In S. Sadiq (Ed.), *Handbook on research and practice in data quality*. Berlin: Springer. doi:10.1007/978-3-642-36257-6_11

Talhofer, V., & Hofmann, A. Hošková – Mayerová, S., & Kubícek, P. (2011). Spatial analyses and spatial data quality. In *Proceedings from the 14th Agile International Conference on Geographic Information Science*. IEEE.

Tannenbaum, A. (2002). *Metadata solutions: Using metamodels, repositories, XML, and enterprise portals to generate information on demand*. Boston: Addison-Wesley.

Tapscott, D., & Williams, A. (2008). *Wikinomics: A nova economia das multidões inteligentes*. Matosinhos: Quidnovi.

Tapscott, D. (1995). *The digital economy: Promise and peril in the age of networked intelligence*. New York: McGraw-Hill.

Tapscott, D. (1999). *Creating value in the network economy*. Boston: Harvard Business School Press.

Tapscott, D., Ticoll, D., & Lowy, A. (2000). *Digital capital: Harnessing the power of business webs*. Boston: Harvard Business School Press. doi:10.1145/341836.336231

Tayi, G. K., & Ballou, D. P. (1998). Examining data quality. *Communications of the ACM*, *41*(2), 54–57. doi:10.1145/269012.269021

TDWI. (2005). *2005 TDWI poster: Business intelligence maturity model*. Retrieved November 10, 2009, from http://tdwi.org/Publications/display.aspx?ID=7288

Tepping, B. J. (1968). A Model for Optimum Linkage of Records. *Journal of the American Statistical Association*, *63*(324), 1321–1332. doi:10.1080/01621459.1968.10480930

Tesch, D., Sobol, M. G., Klein, G., & Jiang, J. J. (2009). User and developer common knowledge: Effect on the success of information system development projects. *International Journal of Project Management*, *27*, 657–664. doi:10.1016/j.ijproman.2009.01.002

The Right of Privacy. (2004). Retrieved February 4, 2012, from Exploring Constitutional Conflicts: http://law2.umkc.edu/faculty/projects/ftrials/conlaw/rightofprivacy.html

The White House. (2012, February 23). *We can't wait: Obama administration unveils blueprint for a privacy bill of rights to protect consumers online*. Retrieved January 15, 2013, from http://www.whitehouse.gov/the-press-office/2012/02/23/we-can-t-wait-obama-administration-unveils-blueprint-privacy-bill-rights

Thierauf, R. J. (2001). *Effective business intelligence systems*. New York: Quorum Books.

Thomas, W., & Ralf, P. (2009). *Assessing the quality of wikipedia articles with lifecycle based metrics*. Paper presented at the 5th International Symposium on Wikis and Open Collaboration. Orlando, FL.

Trott, P. (2008). *Innovation management and new product development* (4ª ed.). Essex, UK: Prentice Hall | Financial Times.

Tsvetovat, M., & Kouznetsov, A. (2011). *Social network analysis for startups: Finding connections on the social web*. Sebastopol, CA: O'Reilly Media.

Turban, E., Sharda, R., Aronson, J. E., & King, D. (2008). *Business intelligence: A managerial approach*. Upper Saddle River, NJ: Prentice Hall.

Turban, E., Sharda, R., & Delen, D. (2011). *Decision support and business intelligence*. Upper Saddle River, NJ: Pearson Education.

Tversky, A., & Kahneman, D. (1973). Availability: A heuristic for judging frequency and probability. *Cognitive Psychology*, *5*(2), 207–232. doi:10.1016/0010-0285(73)90033-9

U.S. Department of Education Safeguarding Student Privacy. (2011). Retrieved from http://www2.ed.gov/policy/gen/guid/fpco/ferpa/safeguarding-student-privacy.pdf

U.S. Department of Education. (2004, February 10). *Executive Summary of the No Child Left Behind Act of 2001*. Retrieved July 4, 2011, from ED.gov: http://www2.ed.gov/nclb/overview/intro/execsumm.html

U.S. Department of Education. (2008). *High School Graduation Rate Non-Regulatory Guidance*.

U.S. Department of Education. (2008, October). *Elementary & Secondary Education: A Uniform, Comparable Graduation Rate*. Retrieved from ED.gov: http://www2.ed.gov/policy/elsec/reg/proposal/uniform-grad-rate.pdf

U.S. Department of Education. (2011, April 8). *Family Educational Rights and Privacy Act*. Retrieved January 17, 2012, from ED.gov: http://www2.ed.gov/policy/gen/guid/fpco/ferpa/index.html

U.S. Department of Health and Human Services. (2001). *Final rules for administrative simplification*. Retrieved 1/15/2013, from http://aspe.hhs.gov/admnsimp/final/PvcPre02.htm

UE. (2012). *Unidad ejecutora catastro, Costa Rica*. Retrieved January 12, 2013, from http://www.uecatastro.org/

University of Arkansas at Little Rock. (2011). *Center for Entity Resolution and Information Quality*. Retrieved November 14, 2011, from University of Arkansas at Little Rock: http://ualr.edu/eriq/

University of Hawaii. (2010, October 28). *Inadvertent data exposure by UH West O'ahu affects Mānoa students*. Retrieved July 4, 2011, from The University of Hawaii System: http://www.hawaii.edu/news/article.php?aId=3990

Vandenbosch, B., & Huff, S. (1997, March). Searching and scanning: How executives obtain information from executive information systems. *Management Information Systems Quarterly*, 81–105. doi:10.2307/249743

Vanden, J. M. (2008). Information quality and options. *Review of Financial Studies*, *21*(6), 2635–2676. doi:10.1093/rfs/hhl040

Vasseur, B., Devillers, R., & Jeansoulin, R. (2003). Ontological approach of the fitness of use of geospatial datasets. In *Proceedings from the 6th Agile Conference on Geographic Information Science* (pp. 498-504). IEEE.

Vercellis, C. (2009). *Business intelligence: Data mining and optimization for decision making*. Chichester, UK: John Wiley & Sons.

Veregin, H. (1999). Data quality parameters. In *Geographical information systems* (pp. 177–189). Hoboken, NJ: John Wiley & Sons.

Verizon. (2012). *2012 Data Breach Investigations Report*. Retrieved May 14, 2012, from Verizon Business: http://www.verizonbusiness.com/resources/reports/rp_data-breach-investigations-report-2012_en_xg.pdf

Vessey, I., Ramesh, V., & Glass, R. L. (2002). Research in information systems: An empirical study of diversity in the discipline and its journals. *Journal of Management Information Systems*, *19*(2), 129–174.

Vicini, J., & Stempel, J. (2012). *US top court upholds healthcare law in Obama triumph*. Retrieved from http://www.reuters.com/article/2012/06/28/usa-healthcare-court-idUSL2E8HS4WG20120628

Viégas, F., Wattenberg, M., & Mckeon, M. (2007). The hidden order of wikipedia. *Lecture Notes in Computer Science*, (4564): 445–454. doi:10.1007/978-3-540-73257-0_49

Vogel, D., Lee, F. S. L., & Limayem, M. (2003). Virtual community informatics: A review and research agenda. *Journal of Information Technology Theory and Application*, *5*(1), 47–61.

Wactler, H., Pavel, M., & Barkis, W. (2011). Can computer science save healthcare? *IEEE Intelligent Systems*, *26*(5), 79–83.

Wagner, G. (1990). The value and the quality of information: The need for a theoretical synthesis. In Wormell (Ed.), Information quality: Definitions and dimensions. London: Taylor Graham.

Wand, Y., & Wang, R. Y. (1996). Anchoring data quality dimensions in ontological foundations. *Communications of the ACM*, *39*(11), 86–95. doi:10.1145/240455.240479

Wang, R. Y., Lee, Y. W., Pipino, L. L., & Strong, D. M. (1998, July 15). *MIT Sloan Management Review*. Retrieved May 15, 2012, from Manage Your Information as a Product: http://sloanreview.mit.edu/the-magazine/1998-summer/3947/manage-your-information-as-a-product/

Wang, R. Y. (1998). A product perspective on total data quality management. *Communications of the ACM*, *41*(2), 58–65. doi:10.1145/269012.269022

Wang, R. Y., Kon, H. B., & Reddy, M. P. (1995). Toward data quality: An attribute-based approach. *Decision Support Systems*, (13): 349–372. doi:10.1016/0167-9236(93)E0050-N

Wang, R. Y., Lee, Y. W., Pipino, L. L., & Strong, D. M. (1998). Manage your information as a product. *Sloan Management Review*, *39*(4), 95–105.

Wang, R., & Strong, D. M. (1996). Beyond accuracy: What data quality means to data consumers. *Journal of Management Information Systems*, *12*(4), 5–33.

Wang, R., Ziad, M., & Lee, Y. (2002). Data quality. In *Spatial database systems: Design, implementation, and project management*. Berlin: Springer.

Ward, J., & Peppard, J. (2002). Strategic planning for information systems (3ª ed.). Chichester, UK: Wiley.

Wasserman, S., & Faust, K. (1994). *Social network analysis: Methods and applications*. Cambridge, UK: Cambridge University Press. doi:10.1017/CBO9780511815478

Watson, H. J., Fuller, C., & Ariyachandra, T. (2004). Data warehouse governance: Best practices at blue cross and blue shield of North Carolina. *Decision Support Systems*, *38*(3), 435–450. doi:10.1016/j.dss.2003.06.001

Watson, H. J., Goodhue, D. L., & Wixom, B. H. (2002). The benefits of data warehousing: Why some organizations realize exceptional payoffs. *Information & Management*, *39*, 491–502. doi:10.1016/S0378-7206(01)00120-3

Watson, H. J., Taylor, K. P., Higgins, G., Kadlec, C., & Meeks, M. (1999). Leaders assess the current state of the IS academic discipline. *Communications of the AIS*, *2*(2), 2–27.

Watson, H., & Haley, B. (1997). Data warehousing: A framework and survey of current practices. *Journal of Data Warehousing*, *2*(1), 10–17.

Watts, S., Shankaranarayanan, G., & Even, A. (2009). Data quality assessment in context: A cognitive perspective. *Decision Support Systems*, *48*(1), 202–211. doi:10.1016/j.dss.2009.07.012

Weber, K., Otto, B., & Österle, H. (2009). One size does not fit all---A contingency approach to data governance. *Journal of Data and Information Quality*, *1*(1), 4. doi:10.1145/1515693.1515696

WebiGeo. (2013). *WebiGeo location intelligence*. Retrieved January 13, 2013, from http://www.galigeo.com/en/page/geospatial-solutions/products/webigeo.html

Webster, F. (2000). *Theories of the information society*. Cornwall, UK: Routledge.

Weill, P., & Ross, J. W. (2004). *IT Governance*. Boston: Harvard Business School Publishing.

Weiss, A. (2008). *If they only knew: Finding competitive intelligence from the web sites of your competitors*. Retrieved 21/01/2013, from http://web.fumsi.com/go/article/find/3355

Wells, J. D., & Hess, T. J. (2002). Understanding decision-making in data warehousing and related decision support systems: An explanatory study of a customer relationship management application. *Information Resources Management Journal*, *15*(4), 16–32. doi:10.4018/irmj.2002100102

West, J., & Lakhani, K. R. (2008). Getting clear about communities in open innovation. *Industry and Innovation*, *15*(2), 223–231. doi:10.1080/13662710802033734

Whang, S., & Garcia-Molina, H. (2012). Entity resolution with evolving rules. *Proceedings of the VLDB Endowment*, *3*(1-2), 1326–1337.

Wickramasinghe, N., & Schaffer, J. L. (2006). Creating knowledge-driven healthcare processes with the intelligence continuum. *International Journal of Electronic Healthcare*, *2*(2), 164–174. PMID:18048242

Wikipedia. (2013). *List of wikipedias*. Retrieved January 10, 2013, from http://s23.org/wikistats/wikipedias_html.php

Wikipedia: The Free Encyclopedia. (2013, June 5). Retrieved August 10, 2004, from http://www.wikipedia.org

Williams, S., & Williams, N. (2007). *The profit impact of business intelligence*. San Francisco, CA: Morgan Kaufmann.

Wilson, T. (1985). Information management. *The Electronic Library*, *3*(1), 62–66. doi:10.1108/eb044644

Wilson, T. (1987). Information for business: The business of information. *Aslib Proceedings*, *39*, 275–279. doi:10.1108/eb051066

Winkler, I. (1997). *Corporate espionage: What it is, why it's happening in your company, what you must do about it. Rocklin*. Prima Publishing.

Wixom, B. H., & Watson, H. J. (2001). An empirical investigation of the factors affecting data warehousing success. *Management Information Systems Quarterly*, *25*(1), 17–41. doi:10.2307/3250957

Wixom, B. H., & Watson, H. J. (2010). The BI-based organisation. *International Journal of Business Intelligence Research*, *1*(1), 13–28. doi:10.4018/jbir.2010071702

Woodall, P., & Parlikad, A. (2010). A hybrid approach to assessing data quality. In *Proceedings of the 15th International Conference on Information Quality*. IEEE.

Worboys, M., & Duckham, M. (2004). *GIS: A computing perspective*. Boca Raton, FL: CRC Press.

Wormell, I. (1990). *Information quality: Definitions and dimensions*. London: Taylor Graham.

Wright, D., & De Hert, P. (2012). *Privacy impact assessment*. New York: Springer. doi:10.1007/978-94-007-2543-0

Wu, N., Pierce, E., Talburt, J., & Wang, R. (2006). An Information Theoretic Approach to Information Quality Metrics. *International Conference on Information Quality*, (pp. 13-25).

Wu, J. H., & Wang, Y. M. (2006). Measuring KMS success: A respecification of the DeLone and McLean's model. *Information & Management, 43*(6), 728–739. doi:10.1016/j.im.2006.05.002

Wu, S., Chaudhry, B., Wang, J., Maglione, M., Mojica, W., Roth, E., & Shekelle, P. G. (2006). Systematic review: Impact of health information technology on quality, efficiency, and costs of medical care. *Annals of Internal Medicine, 144*(10), 742–752. doi:10.7326/0003-4819-144-10-200605160-00125 PMID:16702590

Xia, J. (2012). Metrics to measure open geospatial data quality. *Issues in Science & Technology Librarianship, 68.*

Xu, F., Pandit, S., & Mandelstein, D. (2012). *Introduction to IBM InfoSphere master data management reference data management hub v10.* Retrieved Jan 27, 2013, from http://www.ibm.com/developerworks/data/library/techarticle/dm-1210mdmhubv10/index.html

Xu, X., Yuruk, N., Feng, Z., & Schweiger, T. (2007). SCAN: A Structural Clustering Algorithm for Networks. *The Thirteenth ACM SIGKDD International Conference on Knowledge Discovery and Data Mining.*

Yancey, W. (2007). *BigMatch: A program extracting possible matches from a large file.* Washington, DC: Statistical Research Division, U.S. Census Bureau.

Yeoh, W., & Koronios, A. (2010). Critical success factors for business intelligence systems. *Journal of Computer Information Systems, 50*(3), 23–32.

Yeung, A., & Hall, G. (2007). *Spatial database systems: Design, implementation, and project management.* Berlin: Springer. doi:10.1007/1-4020-5392-4

Yin, R. K. (2010). *Case study research: Design and methods* (4th ed.). London: Sage.

Yonke, C. L., Walenta, C., & Talburt, J. R. (2012). *Industry report: The job of the information/data quality professional.* Retrieved from http://iaidq.org/publications/yonke-2011-02.shtml

Zarrella, D. (2009). *The social media marketing book.* Sebastopol, CA: O'Reilly Media.

Zarrella, D. (2013). *The science of marketing: When to Tweet, what to post, how to blog, and other proven strategies.* Hoboken, NJ: John Wiley & Sons.

Zhao, F. (Ed.). (2006). *Maximize business profits through e-partnerships.* Hershey, PA: IGI Global.

Zhou, Y. (2012). *Modeling and Design of Entity Identity Information in Entity Resolution Systems.*

Zhou, Y., & Talburt, J. R. (2011). The Role of Asserted Resolution in Entity Identity Information Management. *The 2011 International Conference on Bioinformatics and Computational Biology.*

Zhou, Y., Talburt, J. R., Kobayashi, F., & Nelson, E. (2012). Implementing Boolean matching rules in an entity resolution system using XML scripts. In H. Arabnia, L. Deligiannidis, & R. Hashemi (Eds.), *2012 International Conference on Information and Knowledge Engineering.* Las Vegas, NV: CSREA Press.

Zhou, Y., Talburt, J., Su, Y., & Yin, L. (2010). OYSTER: A tool for entity resolution in health information exchange. In *Proceedings of the 5th International Conference on the Cooperation and Promotion of Information Resources in Science and Technology* (pp. 356-362). IEEE.

Zhou, Z., & Talburt, J. R. (2011). Entity identity information management. In *Proceedings of 16th International Conference on Information Quality* (pp. 327-34). Adelaide, Australia: Electronic Media.

Zikopoulos, P., Deutsch, T., Deroos, D., Corrigan, D., Parasuraman, K., & Giles, J. (2013). *Harness the power of big data.* New York: The McGrawHill Companies.

Zobel, J., & Moffat, A. (2006). Inverted files for text search engines. *ACM Computing Surveys, 38*(2), 6. doi:10.1145/1132956.1132959

About the Contributors

William Yeoh is a Lecturer in School of Information and Business Analytics at Deakin University. He received his PhD in Business Intelligence from the University of South Australia, and he has taught within Australia, Malaysia, and Hong Kong. He is a researcher in the areas of business intelligence and information quality. He has published numerous research papers in peer-reviewed journals and conference proceedings. He is a frequent invited speaker in practitioners' conferences. He has been providing consultancy services to a number of organisations including JobStreet.com. He was the Deputy Dean for Research and Development (R&D) in Faculty of Information and Communication Technology at University Tunku Abdul Rahman in Malaysia, and was also a Visiting Scholar at University of Arkansas in Little Rock.

John R. Talburt is Professor of Information Science at the University of Arkansas at Little Rock (UALR) where he is the Coordinator for the Information Quality Graduate Program and the Executive Director of the UALR Center for Advanced Research in Entity Resolution and Information Quality (ERIQ). He is also the Chief Scientist for Black Oak Partners, LLC, an information quality solutions company based in Little Rock, Arkansas. Prior to his appointment at UALR he was the leader for research and development and product innovation at Acxiom Corporation, a global leader in information management and customer data integration. Professor Talburt is an inventor for several patents related to customer data integration and the author of numerous articles on information quality and entity resolution, and is the author of Entity Resolution and Information Quality (Morgan Kaufmann, 2011). He also holds the IAIDQ Information Quality Certified Professional (IQCP).

Yinle Zhou is an IBM software architect and data scientist in the InfoSphere MDM development group in Austin, Texas, and also serves as an Affiliate Member of the Graduate Faculty at University of Arkansas at Little Rock (UALR). Dr. Zhou holds a PhD in Integrated Computing with Emphasis in Information Quality (IQ) from UALR where her doctoral research focused on modeling the management of entity identity information in entity resolution systems. She also holds a Master of Science in Information Quality from UALR, a Bachelor of Business Administration in Electronic Commerce from Nanjing University in China, and the Information Quality Certified Professional (IQCP) credential issued by the International Association for Information and Data Quality (IAIDQ). Her research and publications are in areas of information quality, identity management, entity and identity resolution, and social computing.

* * *

Ahmed AbuHalimeh's research interests are related to information quality, information visualization, human-computer applications/interaction, and medical and health data applications. His recent work is integrating information quality in visual analytics, which entails the integration of interactive visualization with analysis techniques to answer a growing range of questions in science, business, intelligence, and health. His research focus on subjective information quality dimensions, which are dimensions that typically require a user's opinion and do not have a clear mathematical technique for assessing their value. Dr. AbuHalimeh earned his PhD degree in Integrated Computing/ Information Quality from University of Arkansas at Little Rock in 2011.

Conrad Bates, currently a Managing Partner at C3 Business Solutions, has previously led the Public Sector BI Strategy practice for IBM and held consulting roles at PricewaterhouseCoopers and Teradata (NCR).He has over eighteen years of experience in Business Intelligence and Data Warehousing and has delivered large-scale public and private sector solutions in Australia, the US, New Zealand, Taiwan, the Netherlands and China.

Tom Breur has a background in Database Management and Market Research. In the past 10 years he has specialized in how companies can make better use of their data. He is an accomplished teacher at universities, MBA programs, and for the IQCP (Information Quality Certified Professional) and CBIP program (Certified Business Intelligence Professional). He is a regular keynoter at international conferences. At the moment he is a member of the editorial board of the *Journal of Targeting,* the *Journal of Financial Services Management*, and *Banking Review*. He is Chief Editor for the new *Palgrave Journal of Marketing Analytics*, and Director of Events for the International Association for Information and Data Quality.

Sehyris Campos is enrolled in a Computer Science master degree at the University of Costa Rica. She received her bachelor degree from University of Costa Rica (2012). She worked on projects related to automata and compilers, expert systems and conventional and spatial databases. BSc. Campos works developing applications for modern mobile operating systems, such as Android and iOS platforms.

Madhavi Chakrabarty is a User-Experience specialist at Verizon Wireless and an Adjunct Professor at Rutgers University, NJ. Her areas of expertise include information representation, cognitive processes in decision-making, visual problem solving, multi-modal communications, and cognitive design in human computer interaction. She received her Ph.D. in Information Systems from New Jersey Institute of Technology, Newark, NJ, and her Masters in Computer Applications from Indian Institute of Technology, New Delhi, India. Madhavi collaborates with different research and learning organizations in her research initiatives. She has presented and published in refereed peer reviewed journals and books. Before earning her Ph.D, Madhavi worked as a IT consultant with organizations like IBM, AstraZeneca, TMI, Nuance, Avaya, and Morotola. Madhavi also works with students in projects related to creative problem solving and improvisation in design. She currently serves as a Parent Coach for a group of elementary school students in "Odyssey of the Mind Experience."

Jack Cook, Ph.D., CFPIM, CSCP, CSQE is a professor, speaker, author, and consultant. He has been a professor for over thirty years, teaching operations and information systems at the Rochester Institute of Technology, Washington State University, and SUNY Geneseo. He currently teaches at SUNY Brockport. His areas of expertise include: supply chain management; lean thinking; information systems; operations management; and electronic commerce. Dr. Cook is a Certified Fellow in Production and Inventory Management (CFPIM), Certified Supply Chain Professional (CSCP), Certified Software Quality Engineer (CSQE), and a Master Lean Six Sigma Black Belt. He has conducted review courses for APICS, ISM and ASQ certifications, and has developed and delivered many seminars and on-site training programs. His education includes a Ph.D. in Business Administration, an MS in Computer Science, an MBA, MA in Mathematics, and a BS in Computer Science.

William "Cody" Decker is the Division Leader of Research and Technology at the Arkansas Department of Education (ADE) where he oversees the programming, data quality, data warehousing, systems, and technical support teams for the ADE. He holds a variety of certifications in the areas of systems engineering, networking and project management and is an active researcher in the field of information quality. The ADE has received three consecutive Statewide Longitudinal Data System (SLDS) grants from the U.S. Department of Education and has been nationally recognized as a leader in state-level information systems for education.

Scott Delaney is both a business intelligence and information governance practitioner. He has a consulting background of almost twenty years in various data centric information technology roles with a heavy focus on business intelligence. He currently works in the Utilities sector as the Manager of Business Intelligence and Data Integration for Australia's largest renewable energy provider where he has recently championed and introduced an enterprise-wide data governance program and is in the midst of establishing a new business intelligence platform and competency centre. Delaney holds a Masters Degree in Database Design and Management from Charles Sturt University.

Jia Tina Du is lecturer in the School of Information Technology and Mathematical Sciences at the University of South Australia, Australia. She is an associate member of Australian Library and Information Association (AALIA), member of American Society for Information Science and Technology (ASIST). She holds a PhD in Information Science from the Queensland University of Technology. She was 2010 Highly Commended Award Winner of Emerald/EFMD Outstanding Doctoral Research Awards in the Information Science Category. Her research interests are in interactive information retrieval, cognitive information retrieval, Web search research, and human information behavior.

Neil Foshay is a tenured faculty member in the Department of Information Systems in the Schwartz School of Business at St. Francis Xavier University. His research interests are in the areas of Business Intelligence (BI), metadata management, and user adoption of technology. Dr. Foshay teaches classes in Enterprise Systems, Database Management, Business Intelligence, Systems Analysis, and System Design. He has over 25 years of IT consulting experience including 17 years focused on business intelligence. He has provided strategic BI consulting services to organizations such as Apple, IBM, Honda, Caterpillar, and Walt Disney.

Neal Gibson is the director of the Arkansas Research Center (ARC). He has a PhD. in Applied Sciences and a master's in Information Quality from the University of Arkansas at Little Rock. He has a bachelor's and master's degree in History from the University of Arkansas at Fayetteville. Prior to the creation of ARC, he worked for the Arkansas Department of Education as a project manager and was a classroom teacher for 16 years. He is married with two children and enjoys fitness and farming.

Abrar Haider completed his doctoral thesis at the School of Computer and Information Science, University of South Australia. He also holds Bachelor of Science, Master of Computer Science, and Master of Business Administration degrees. His professional experience spans two decades, working in IT and education sector in Australia, Pakistan, North America, Middle East, South East Asia, and Far East. Dr. Haider has taught twenty-three information systems courses at undergraduate and postgraduate levels in Australia, Hong Kong, Malaysia, Singapore, and Pakistan.

Robert Hillard is Deloitte's Technology Agenda Managing Partner in Australia, with responsibility for shaping the firm's response to the huge changes to Australia's society and economy as a result of technology and digital disruption. With over 25 years in the profession, Robert is well known as an advisor and writer on these topics with a particular focus on information management including co-founding MIKE2.0 (a well-recognised standard approach to information and data management), his 2010 book *Information-Driven Business* and most recently his 2013 collaboration on Information Development using MIKE2.0 written with colleagues from the MIKE2.0 Governance Association. Robert sits on the Australian Information Industry Association board and national executive, the Swiss MIKE2.0 Governance Association board as well as various university and professional advisory groups.

Greg Holland is the Director of Research at the Arkansas Research Center. He received a Ph.D. in Applied Science and a Master's degree in Information Quality from the University of Arkansas at Little Rock. Prior to ARC, Greg worked for Acxiom Corporation as a data research analyst for ten years. Greg lives in central Arkansas and is married with one child. Greg enjoys time with family, Website administration, comic book collecting, and is an advisor for the Overstreet Comic Book Price Guide.

Linghe Huang is a doctoral student in the School of Information Management at Nanjing University, China. He obtained his master degree in Information Science in 2011 from Shandong University of Technology. His research interests include interdisciplinary studies in library and information science, and human information behavior.

Jurij Jaklič is a Professor of Information Management at the Faculty of Economics of the University of Ljubljana and visiting professor at the ISEGI-UNL. He holds a bachelor degree in applied mathematics from the University of Ljubljana, an MSc in Computer Science from Houston University (USA) and a PhD in Information Management from the Faculty of Economics of the University of Ljubljana. His current main research interests encompass the fiin C of information quality, business intelligence and business process management. He is the (co)author of around 100 papers and research reports; many of them have been published in international scientific journals such as *Decision Support System, Supply Chain Management, Information Research, and Simulation*. He is the Editor-in-Chief of the journal *Applied Informatics*. He has been involved in several research and consulting projects in the areas of business intelligence, business process renovation and IS strategic planning.

Sang Hyun Lee is a PhD candidate with the Department of Computer and Information Science, University of South Australia, Australia. He received a B.S. and M.S degrees in Computer Sciences and Engineering from Hanyang University, Korea. He has extensive experience in quality management area as a qualified Six Sigma black belt holder. His research interests include Six-Sigma implementation to Information Quality, assessment of Information Quality, and interrelationships of Information Quality Dimensions.

Fan Liu is a Ph.D candidate in the Department of Information Science at University of Arkansas at Little Rock. He received a B.Eng. degree in Information Science and Engineering in Southeast University, China, and an M.Eng degree in Computer Science in Nanyang Technological University, Singapore. His research interests are data mining, information quality, optimization methods, and simulation.

Hua Liu obtained his bachelor degree in Information Management and Information Systems in 2013 from Nanjing University, China, and he will pursue a master degree in Information System Management in Carnegie Mellon University. His research interests are in User-Generated Content (UGC).

Elzbieta Malinowski is a professor at the University of Costa Rica (Department of Computer Science and Informatics) and professional consultant in the area of conventional and spatial databases and warehouses. She received her master degrees from Saint Petersburg Electrotechnical University, Russia (1982), University of Florida, USA (1996), and Université Libre de Bruxelles (2003), and her Ph.D. degree from Université Libre de Bruxelles, Belgium (2006). Her research interests include conventional, spatial, and temporal databases, and data warehouses, data mining, OLAP and GIS systems. She is the author of numerous international publications, including the book *Advanced Data Warehouse Design: From Conventional to Spatial and Temporal Applications* (published by Springer in 2008). Dr. Malinowski is also a member of editorial boards for several international journals and conferences.

Sérgio Maravilhas has a PhD in Information and Communication in Digital Platforms (UA + UP), a Master in Information Management (FEUP and Sheffield University, UK), a Postgraduate Course in ICT (FEUP), a Specialization in Innovation and Technological Entrepreneurship (FEUP and North Carolina State University, USA), and a 5 years Degree in Philosophy, Educational Branch (FLUP). A Teacher and Trainer since 1998, passed by ESE - IPP as a Supervisor at the Internet @ School project between 2002 and 2005, and a university teacher since 2005 at UA (DEGEI), and since 2010 at ULP and IESFF in Masters and MBA levels. Teaches Marketing, Research Methods, Creative Processes in Innovation, Intellectual and Industrial Property, Technology Watch, Information Management, and Organizational Behaviour in universities and he's a trainer in ICT, Sales, Negotiation, and Neuro-Linguistic Programming (NLP). Publishes and attends conferences mainly in the subjects of patent information, innovation, Web 2.0, Web radio, and sustainability.

Rick McGraw is the Chairman of the Board and Chief Executive Officer Black Oak Partners, LLC. Rick's experience is in the technology and financial services industries. As a senior executive for Acxiom, an international data management company, he led the global financial services sales support organization, the healthcare industry practice, and the global government practice. His responsibilities included the development, acquisition, and divestiture of multiple businesses and product lines, including the leading international technology firm providing entity resolution and threat assessment software tools for homeland defense and national security. Rick has deep experience solving highly complex information collection and analysis challenges. Rick spent more than 20 years in commercial banking, including 13 years as president and CEO of Simmons First National Corporation's $2 billion mortgage banking company that became one the nation's largest issuer of GNMA securities. Rick also served as an advisory director for FNMA.

Ivan Milman is a Senior Technical Staff Member at IBM, working as a Security and Governance Architect for IBM Master Data Management (MDM) and InfoSphere product groups. Ivan co-authored the leading book on MDM: *Enterprise Master Data Management: An SOA Approach to Managing Core Information*. Ivan was on the original team that created the IBM InfoSphere Master Data Management Reference Data Management (RDM) product, and is currently working on integrating RDM with other IBM products.

Avinandan Mukherjee is Professor and Chairperson of the Marketing Department in the School of Business at Montclair State University, New Jersey, USA. He is the Editor-in-Chief of the *International Journal of Pharmaceutical and Healthcare Marketing*. Dr. Mukherjee is an expert on Digital Marketing, Services Marketing, and Healthcare Management. He has published more than 100 scholarly articles in academic journals, conference proceedings, edited books, and monographs. His research has been published in leading international journals like *Journal of Retailing, Journal of Business Research, Journal of the Operational Research Society, Communications of the ACM, Service Industries Journal, Journal of Services Marketing, Journal of Marketing Management, International Journal of Advertising, European Journal of Marketing*, etc.

Pamela Neely, CPA, is an assistant professor of Accounting at the College at Brockport, SUNY. She teaches accounting information systems and managerial accounting. Dr. Neely's publications have appeared in *The International Journal of Business Intelligence Research, Journal of Information Systems, Review of Business Information Systems, Journal of Informatics Education*, and *The Database for Advances in Information Systems*, among others. Her primary research area is in the area of Data and Information Quality (DIQ) and accounting information systems. She is also interested in the area of financial fraud and the impact of DIQ on the ability to detect fraud in a timelier manner. Dr. Neely earned a PhD in Information Systems from the University at Albany and an MS in Accounting from the University of Colorado, Boulder.

Martin Oberhofer is a certified Senior Architect and certified IBM Master Inventor with over 11 years of experience in the Information Management space. He specializes in master data management and information integration topics – specifically for customers running SAP applications. He co-authored 2 books on MDM and Enterprise Information Architecture, over 20 articles and is a co-inventor for over 50 patent applications.

Daragh O'Brien is Managing Director of Castlebridge Associates, a boutique Information Strategy and Governance consultancy based in Ireland. His clients include leading telecoms companies, not-for-profits, government, and financial services organisations. In addition to consulting services, Castlebridge Associates provides training and coaching services to help people in organisations think differently about information. Daragh serves as Privacy Advisor to DAMA International, is Chief Steward of the Data Governance Institute, and has previously served as a Director of the International Association for Information & Data Quality. In addition, he is an active contributing member of the Innovation Value Institute and is a Fellow of the Irish Computer Society. Daragh has contributed to the development of the Information Quality Certified Practioner qualification and was one of the first to qualify in the certification in 2011. He has lectured in Dublin City University's School of Computing on Legal Regulation of Information Systems and is a published author and regular blogger and presenter on Information Management issues.

Sushain Pandit is a lead engineer, hands-on software architect, and an IBM Master Inventor with a broad background in enterprise information and master data management. His recent work includes development, technical leadership and customer advocacy for IBM InfoSphere Master Data Management Reference Data Management (RDM) product. He has filed over 20 patent applications, co-authored several articles and published papers at conferences like Americas Conference on Information Systems, International Conference on Tools with Artificial Intelligence, etc. He holds a Master degree in Computer Science.

Aleš Popovič is an Assistant Professor of Information Management at the Faculty of Economics at the University of Ljubljana and visiting professor at ISEGI – University Nova in Lisbon. He holds BS, MSc, and Ph.D. degrees from the University of Ljubljana. His research focuses on business intelligence, information management, and business process management. He is the (co)author of numerous papers in international professional and scientific journals, such as *Decision Support Systems, International Journal of Information Management, Information Systems Management, Industrial Management and Data Systems*, and *Information Research*. He has collaborated in many applied projects in the areas of business process management and in the area of business intelligence.

Edmir Prado is an assistant professor at the University of São Paulo (Brazil) and has over twenty years of experience in Management and Information Systems. His research is focused on the topics of IT outsourcing, project management and process management. He holds a degree in Mechanical Engineering, an MBA and Ph.D. in Business Administration from the University of São Paulo.

Samuel Otero Schmidt is a student of M.Sc. in Management at University of Sao Paulo (USP), Brazil. He holds Bachelor's degree in Information System at USP. He worked as systems analyst and project manager in several companies located in Brazil. His research interests include Business Intelligence, Information Quality, IT Management, and Outsourcing.

Arun Sundararman, F.C.A., A.C.S., is an Industry practitioner and researcher in the field of Data Quality and Analytics. He carries over 20 years of experience in the IT Industry, specializing in DW/BI for over 12 years. In his current role at Accenture, India, as Lead – Healthcare Analytics he serves large International Healthcare clients in providing DW/BI and Analytics Solutions. Arun is currently pursuing his Ph.D. from BITS, Pilani in the area of Information Quality Strategy. His research work investigates relationship between Information Quality and Organizational Outcomes and introduces a framework for measuring DQ with special focus on DW/BI Systems. Arun has research publications to his credit in leading journals and forums. His research interests include data quality, business analytical, besides text mining.

Andrew Taylor holds degrees from Queen's University Belfast, including a PhD in Manufacturing Engineering and Management. Before taking up an academic career, he worked in aerospace, public utilities and government organisations, latterly advising firms on the implementation of new technologies and techniques for productivity improvement. He was awarded a Chair at Queen's University and then took up his professorial appointment in Operations and Information Systems at Bradford University School of Management in 1996. His research interests focus on business improvement techniques and technologies such as Performance Measurement, Lean Manufacturing, Total Quality Management, Business Intelligence, and Knowledge Management Systems.

M. Eduard Tudoreanu is Professor of Information Science and Technical Director of the Emerging Analytics Center at the University of Arkansas at Little Rock. Prof. Tudoreanu's research interests are related to the use of graphics to better understand data and the processes that affect data. His work encompasses areas in information visualization, human-computer interaction, information quality, and virtual reality. Prof. Tudoreanu earned his D.Sc. degree in Computer Science in 2002 from the Washington University in St. Louis. He has been the keynote speaker at ABSEL 2010, served as a panelist for the National Science Foundation, and received grants from the G. W. Donaghey Foundation, National Science Foundation, Air Force Research Laboratory, NASA, US Department of Education, and Acxiom Corporation.

Pei Wang is from Si Chuan province, China and is currently a master student of Information Quality in University of Arkansas at Little Rock (UALR). Pei received her Bachelor's degree in Information Engineering at Southwest University of Science and Technology in China, 2012. During her years of undergraduate study, Pei received an opportunity to study at UALR as an exchange student. She found a great interest in Information Quality during her experience in the exchange program, driving her to join the Information Quality program at UALR.

Ningning Wu is Professor of Information Science at the University of Arkansas at Little Rock, and the Coordinator for the Integrated Computing Doctoral Program of Donaghey College of Engineering and Information Technology. She received a B.S. and a M.S degree in Electrical Engineering from the University of Science and Technology of China and Ph.D. in Information Technology from George Mason University. Dr. Wu's research interests are data mining, network and information security, and information quality. She holds the IAIDQ Information Quality Certified Professional (IQCP) and the SANS GIAC Security Essentials Certified Professional.

Qinghua Zhu is professor in the School of Information Management at Nanjing University, China. He was a research student at Keio University, and a visiting scholar at Tsukuba University in Japan. He is a member of the executive council of the China Society for Scientific and Technical Information, a member of the American Society for Information Science and Technology (ASIST), and a member of the Association for Information Systems (AIS). His research interests are information resource management and human information behavior.

Index

Q

R

S

T

U

V

W

CPSIA information can be obtained at www.ICGtesting.com
Printed in the USA
BVOW04*1359280415
397654BV00007B/49/P

9 781466 648920